goldfish

by
BRIAN MICHAEL BENDIS

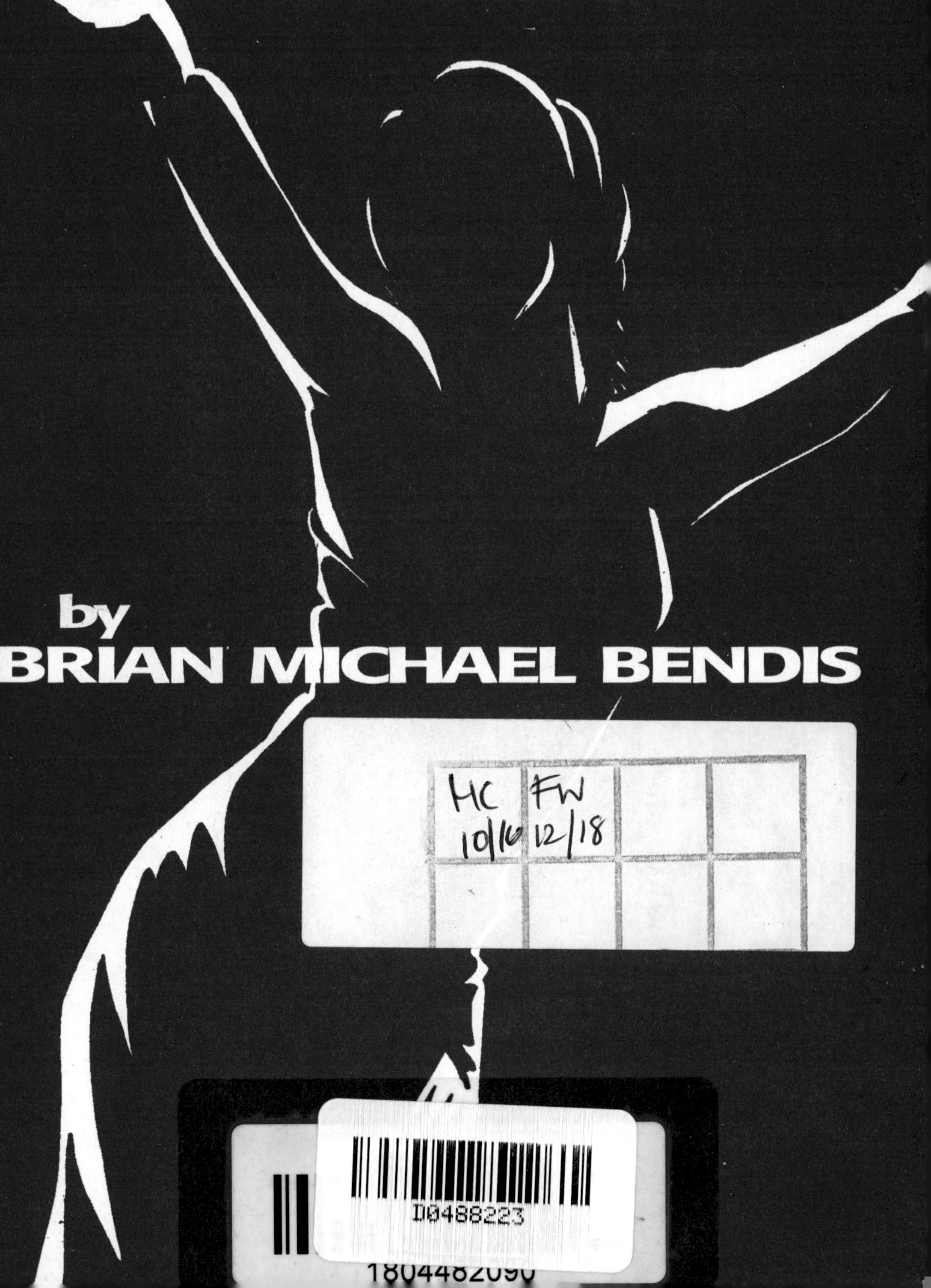

WHO'S GOT THE ACE?

My real exposure to David Gold, a.k.a GOLDFISH (I know, he hates that--s'why I threw it in) came about completely ass backwards and had a totally unexpected effect. Like a rube in one of the Fish's nocturnal stings, I couldn't predict what was coming at me and, by the time I did realize, it was too late.

I had seen the first several issues of this fledgling book as they came out through the determinedly independent efforts of Caliber Press. Caliber in the early 90's was home to a rash of impassioned and dedicated young comics creators. In the days when anything IMAGE was raking in obscene piles of dough, Caliber was, at tooth and nail, providing the vital ink and paper for the likes of David Mack, Vince Locke, Guy Davis and Brian Michael Bendis. What emerged was a handful of raw and unique visions-- the true protoplasm of comics that last, that sing, that rock the fucking house. And, gee, there was nary a scrap of spandex in sight.

I had read most of the offerings by the other members of this creative cadre (even worked with a couple of 'em), but the few issues of GOLDFISH that I had attempted left me confused and unconnected. It was only later, after consuming the entire novel you now hold in your hands (more on that later) that I realized this mistaken first impression was due to the unapologetic, labyrinthine and non-linear method of story-telling which the creator employed. Much like the scheme of a compli-cated con, GOLDFISH doesn't let you see around any blind corners, gives no hints of the heartache to come until--its too late. Those who can't keep up with the twisting pace of this tale are left like rummies in the dust, wondering what time the goddamn 7-11 opens in the morning.

But wait-a-minute...just what the hell was this guy doing, stretch-ing plot points out over several issues, giving pages and pages over to single conversations, demanding the reader decipher the story at more than just a glance? Is this guy fucking nuts?

A fine question, indeed.

When I agreed to do the intro for this volume, I received a battered (and delightfully cheap) version of the original Caliber edition to review. My wife and I were off to the beach to celebrate our tenth wedding anniversary and I stuck the book in our suitcase, never expecting to get very far into it that weekend. Well, like I said--I was conned. Nearly midnight, and I find myself just wrapping up the climax of a story I couldn't lay down. A sunny morning the next day, and I'm still considering the bone-crunchingly dark ending of one of the few true examples of Comics Noir.

Its a bleak and lonely world that Brian Bendis portrays. From the flinty, macadam tone of his artwork to the stumblebum, firecracker pace of his dialogue--Bendis understands that the soul of anything NOIR is to be found in the heart. His characters chase after money, respect and power but the thing they crave most of all is the one thing that always seems to elude them--love. From his mysteriously named femme fatale to his tragic, gay cop to the just-as-soon-remain-small-time title character, Bendis paints people as he sees them--flawed, vulnerable and sympathetic. Even the tough guys seem shocked by the violence that occasionally explodes herein. Nobody is immune to the pangs of belonging and acceptance. And death has a haunting, awful finality that goes far beyond the strum and drang of most "ordinary" comics.

A lot has been made of Brian's obvious cinematic influences--from his conversational quick-cuts to his use of real models to his wide-screen dramatic spreads. Still, this guy is producing comics and comics they remain. Somehow, it feels like this story would shoot past too quickly on screen. And one look at the manga-inspired climax should silence these battered film references for good. Bendis knows the difference betwixt the two mediums and, obviously, enjoys them both immensely. Still, the sheer inspiration and perspiration of Brian's growing body of work is a testimony to all the things that his peers had tried so hard to keep alive--an individual voice laid down in the unassuming and oh-so-affecting form of a comic book.

Is he fucking nuts? Maybe (gratefully) a bit...but Brian Michael Bendis has found the source of what he loves and discovered (again, gratefully) how to express it.

On some level, let's hope his characters never do.

MATT WAGNER

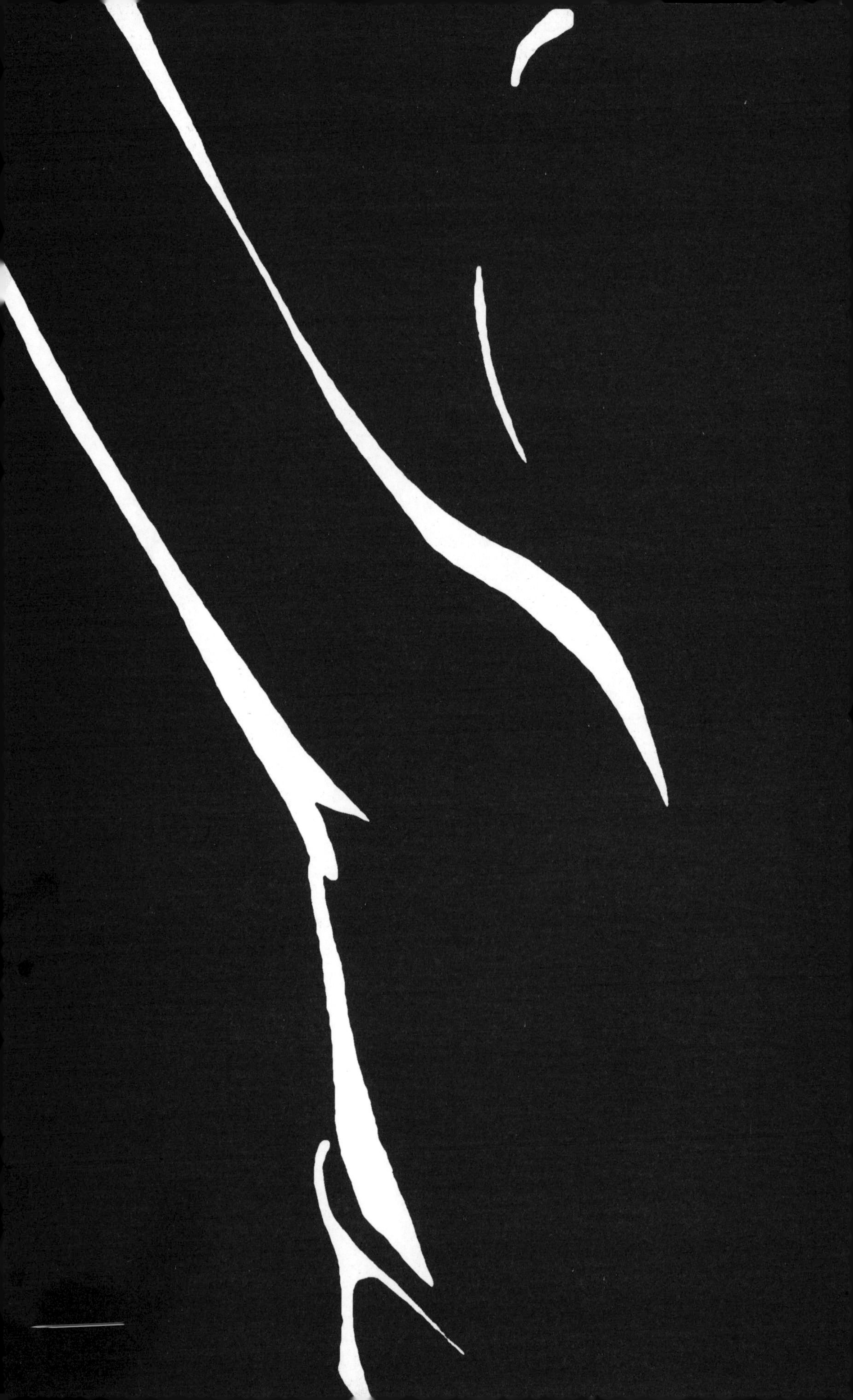

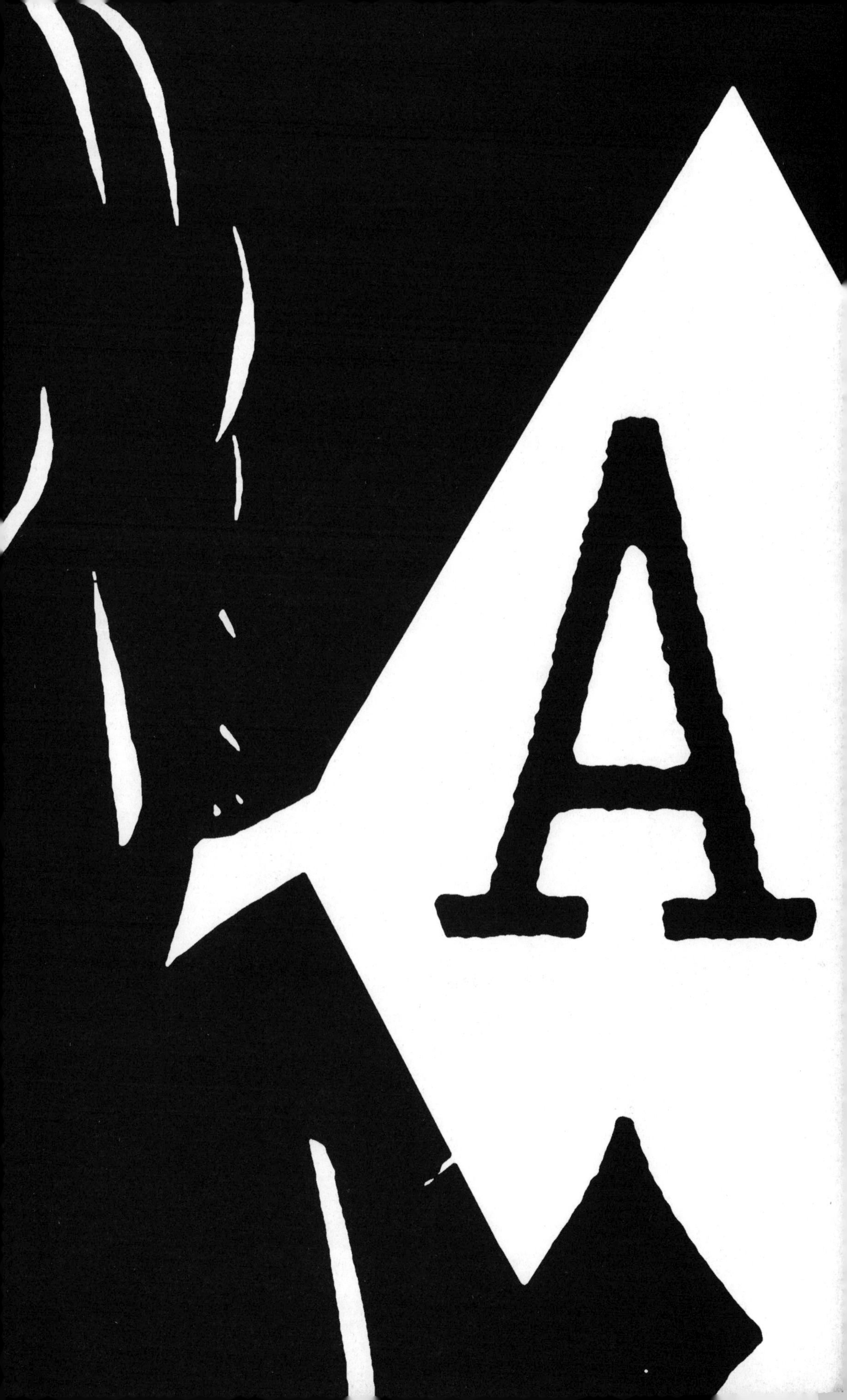
A

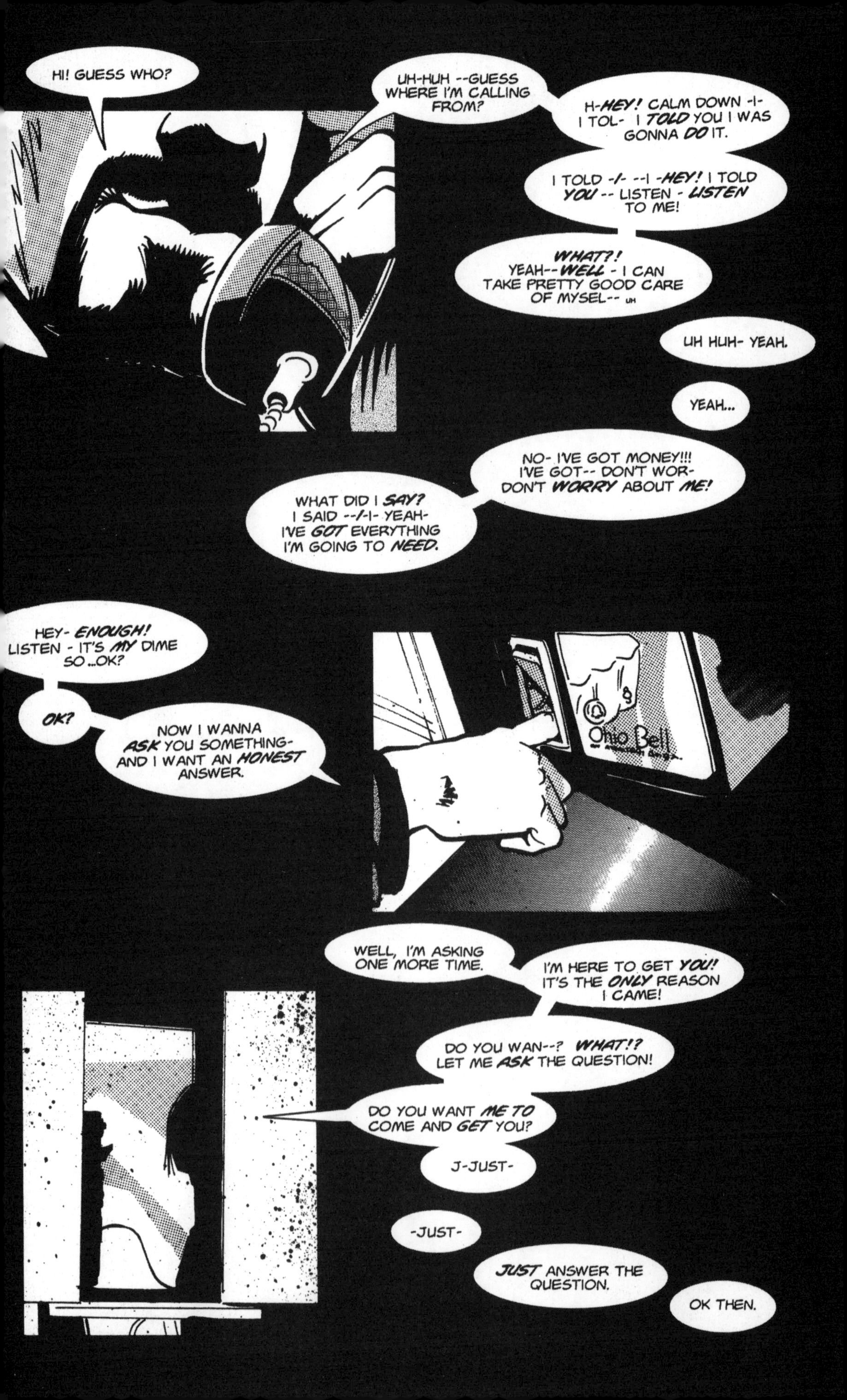
HI! GUESS WHO?
UH-HUH --GUESS WHERE I'M CALLING FROM?
H-HEY! CALM DOWN -I- I TOL- I TOLD YOU I WAS GONNA DO IT.
I TOLD -I- --I -HEY! I TOLD YOU -- LISTEN - LISTEN TO ME!
WHAT?! YEAH--WELL - I CAN TAKE PRETTY GOOD CARE OF MYSEL-- UH
UH HUH- YEAH.
YEAH...
NO- I'VE GOT MONEY!!! I'VE GOT-- DON'T WOR- DON'T WORRY ABOUT ME!
WHAT DID I SAY? I SAID --I-I- YEAH- I'VE GOT EVERYTHING I'M GOING TO NEED.
HEY- ENOUGH! LISTEN - IT'S MY DIME SO ...OK?
OK?
NOW I WANNA ASK YOU SOMETHING- AND I WANT AN HONEST ANSWER.
Ohio Bell
WELL, I'M ASKING ONE MORE TIME.
I'M HERE TO GET YOU! IT'S THE ONLY REASON I CAME!
DO YOU WAN--? WHAT!? LET ME ASK THE QUESTION!
DO YOU WANT ME TO COME AND GET YOU?
J-JUST-
-JUST-
JUST ANSWER THE QUESTION.
OK THEN.

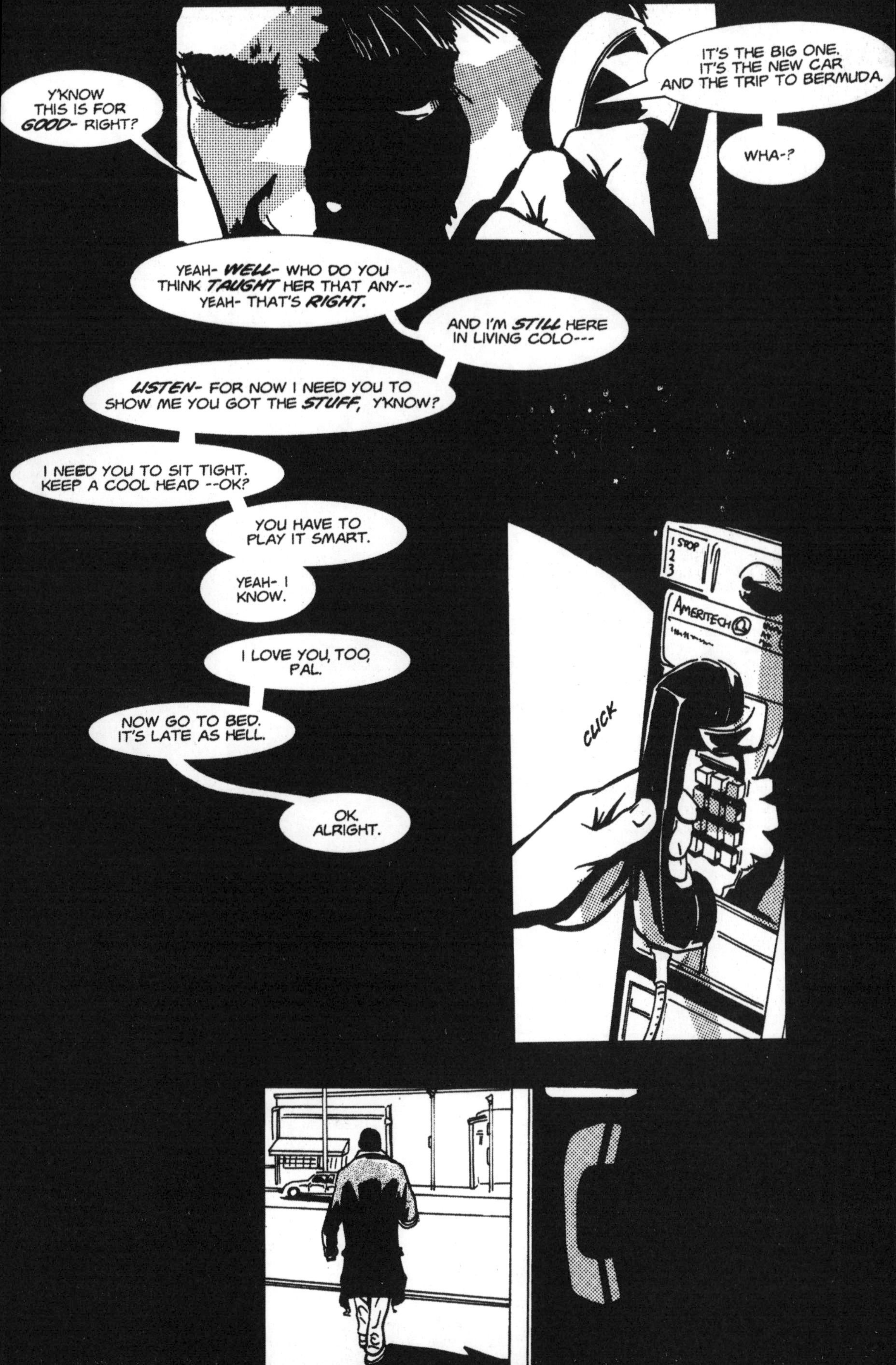

Y'KNOW THIS IS FOR GOOD- RIGHT?
IT'S THE BIG ONE. IT'S THE NEW CAR AND THE TRIP TO BERMUDA.
WHA-?
YEAH- WELL- WHO DO YOU THINK TAUGHT HER THAT ANY-- YEAH- THAT'S RIGHT.
AND I'M STILL HERE IN LIVING COLO---
LISTEN- FOR NOW I NEED YOU TO SHOW ME YOU GOT THE STUFF, Y'KNOW?
I NEED YOU TO SIT TIGHT. KEEP A COOL HEAD --OK?
YOU HAVE TO PLAY IT SMART.
YEAH- I KNOW.
I LOVE YOU, TOO, PAL.
NOW GO TO BED. IT'S LATE AS HELL.
OK. ALRIGHT.
1 STOP
2
3
AMERITECH
CLICK

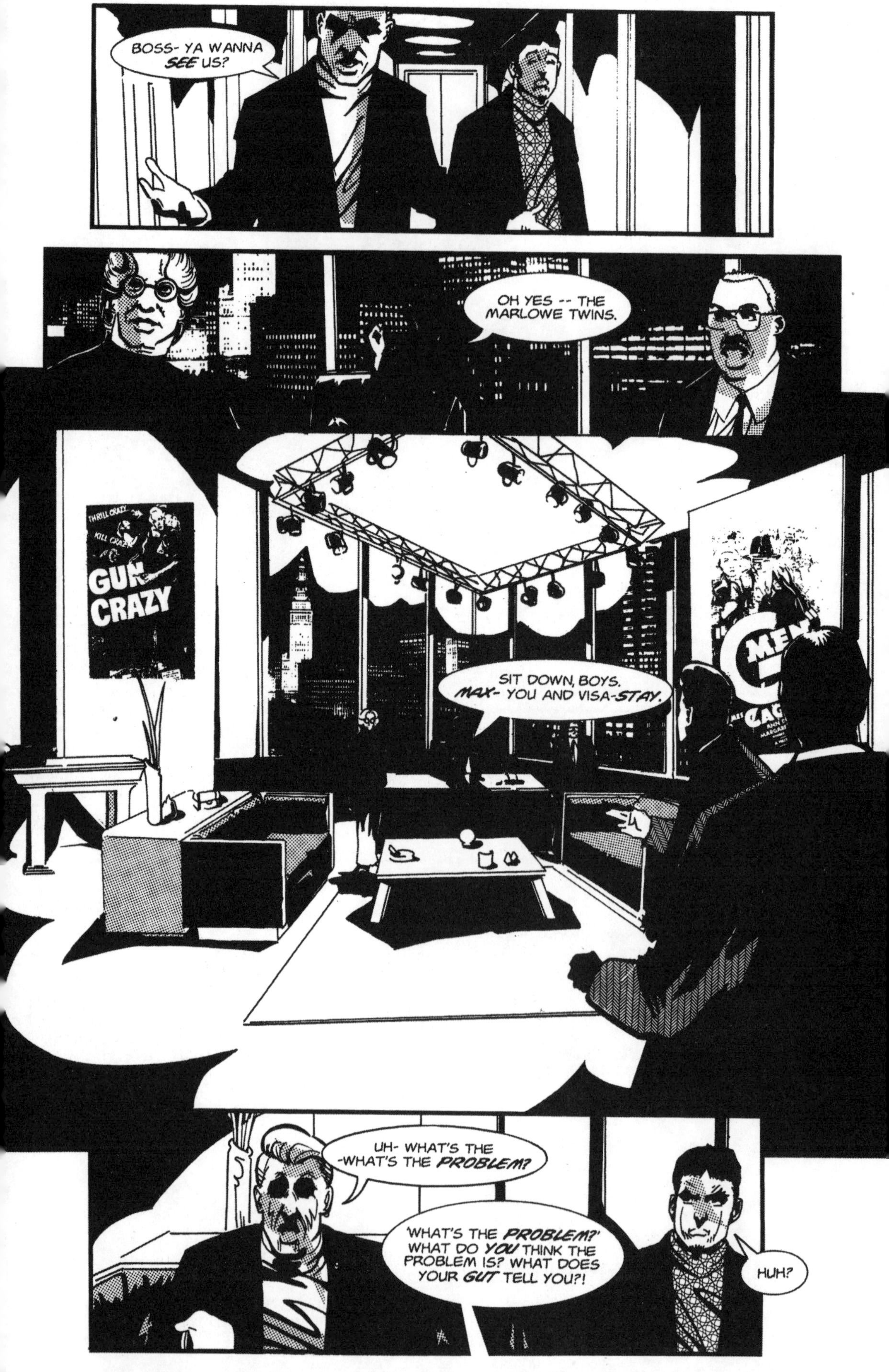
BOSS- YA WANNA SEE US?
OH YES -- THE MARLOWE TWINS.
THRILL CRAZY KILL CRAZY
GUN CRAZY
SIT DOWN, BOYS. MAX- YOU AND VISA-STAY.
UH- WHAT'S THE -WHAT'S THE PROBLEM?
'WHAT'S THE PROBLEM?' WHAT DO YOU THINK THE PROBLEM IS? WHAT DOES YOUR GUT TELL YOU?!
HUH?

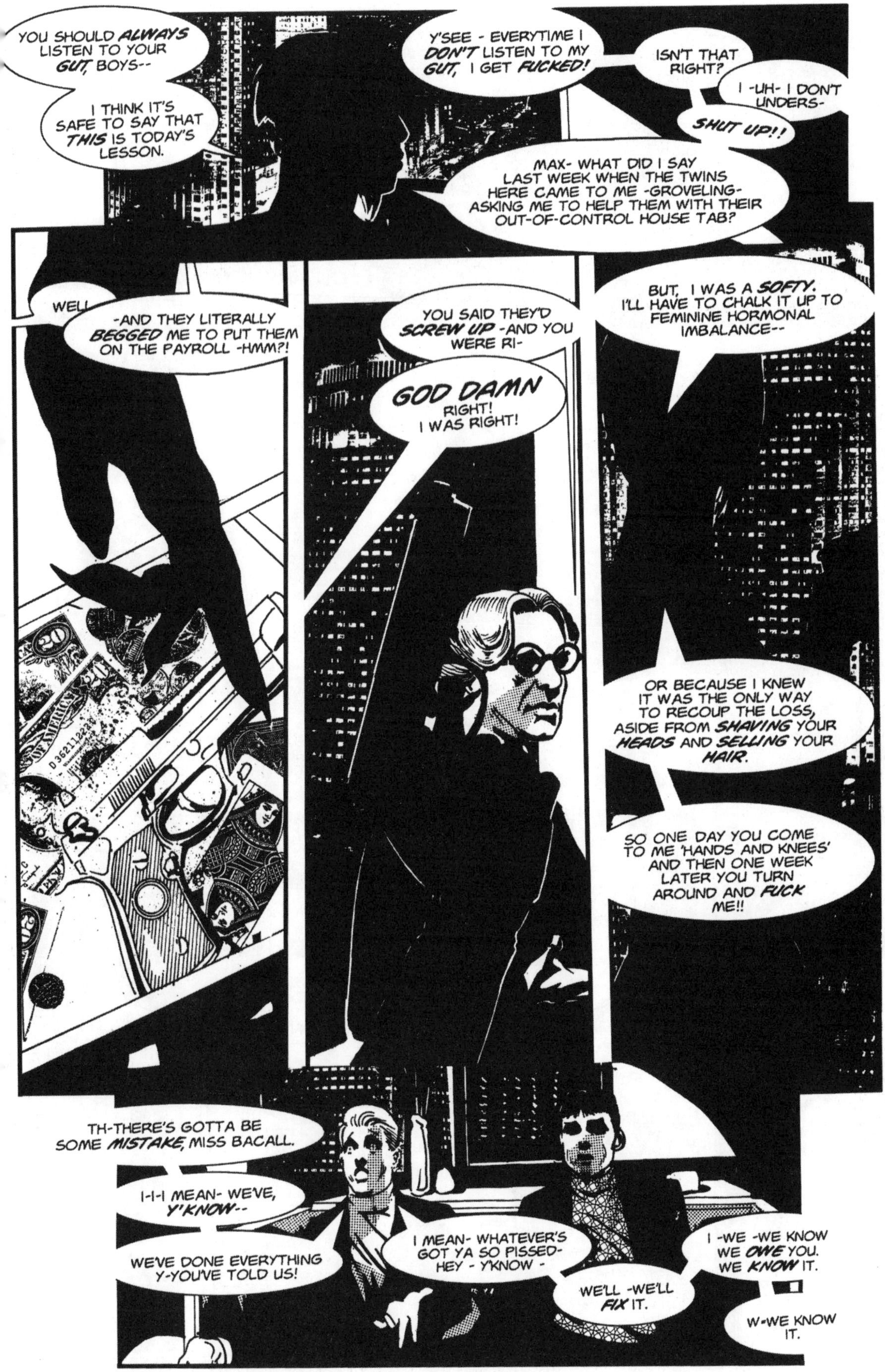
YOU SHOULD ALWAYS LISTEN TO YOUR GUT, BOYS--
I THINK IT'S SAFE TO SAY THAT THIS IS TODAY'S LESSON.
Y'SEE - EVERYTIME I DON'T LISTEN TO MY GUT, I GET FUCKED!
ISN'T THAT RIGHT?
I -UH- I DON'T UNDERS-
SHUT UP!!
MAX- WHAT DID I SAY LAST WEEK WHEN THE TWINS HERE CAME TO ME -GROVELING- ASKING ME TO HELP THEM WITH THEIR OUT-OF-CONTROL HOUSE TAB?
WELL
-AND THEY LITERALLY BEGGED ME TO PUT THEM ON THE PAYROLL -HMM?!
YOU SAID THEY'D SCREW UP -AND YOU WERE RI-
GOD DAMN RIGHT! I WAS RIGHT!
BUT, I WAS A SOFTY. I'LL HAVE TO CHALK IT UP TO FEMININE HORMONAL IMBALANCE--
OR BECAUSE I KNEW IT WAS THE ONLY WAY TO RECOUP THE LOSS, ASIDE FROM SHAVING YOUR HEADS AND SELLING YOUR HAIR.
SO ONE DAY YOU COME TO ME 'HANDS AND KNEES' AND THEN ONE WEEK LATER YOU TURN AROUND AND FUCK ME!!
TH-THERE'S GOTTA BE SOME MISTAKE, MISS BACALL.
I-I-I MEAN- WE'VE, Y'KNOW--
WE'VE DONE EVERYTHING Y-YOU'VE TOLD US!
I MEAN- WHATEVER'S GOT YA SO PISSED- HEY - Y'KNOW -
WE'LL -WE'LL FIX IT.
I -WE -WE KNOW WE OWE YOU. WE KNOW IT.
W-WE KNOW IT.

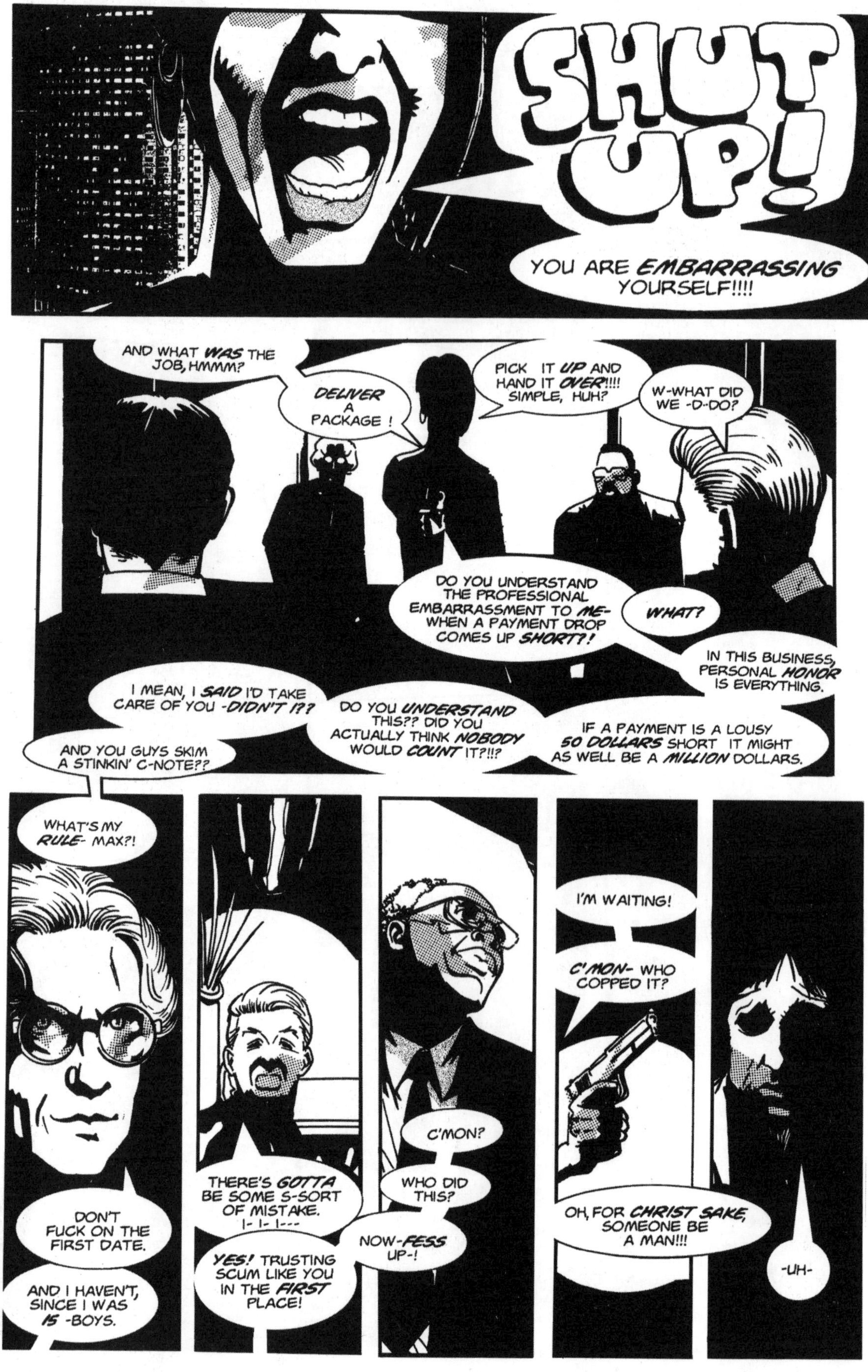
SHUT UP!
YOU ARE EMBARRASSING YOURSELF!!!!
AND WHAT WAS THE JOB, HMMM?
DELIVER A PACKAGE !
PICK IT UP AND HAND IT OVER!!!! SIMPLE, HUH?
W-WHAT DID WE -D-DO?
DO YOU UNDERSTAND THE PROFESSIONAL EMBARRASSMENT TO ME- WHEN A PAYMENT DROP COMES UP SHORT?!
WHAT?
IN THIS BUSINESS, PERSONAL HONOR IS EVERYTHING.
I MEAN, I SAID I'D TAKE CARE OF YOU -DIDN'T I??
DO YOU UNDERSTAND THIS?? DID YOU ACTUALLY THINK NOBODY WOULD COUNT IT?!!?
IF A PAYMENT IS A LOUSY 50 DOLLARS SHORT IT MIGHT AS WELL BE A MILLION DOLLARS.
AND YOU GUYS SKIM A STINKIN' C-NOTE??
WHAT'S MY RULE- MAX?!
DON'T FUCK ON THE FIRST DATE.
AND I HAVEN'T, SINCE I WAS 15 -BOYS.
THERE'S GOTTA BE SOME S-SORT OF MISTAKE. I- I- I---
YES! TRUSTING SCUM LIKE YOU IN THE FIRST PLACE!
C'MON?
WHO DID THIS?
NOW-FESS UP-!
I'M WAITING!
C'MON- WHO COPPED IT?
OH, FOR CHRIST SAKE, SOMEONE BE A MAN!!!
-UH-

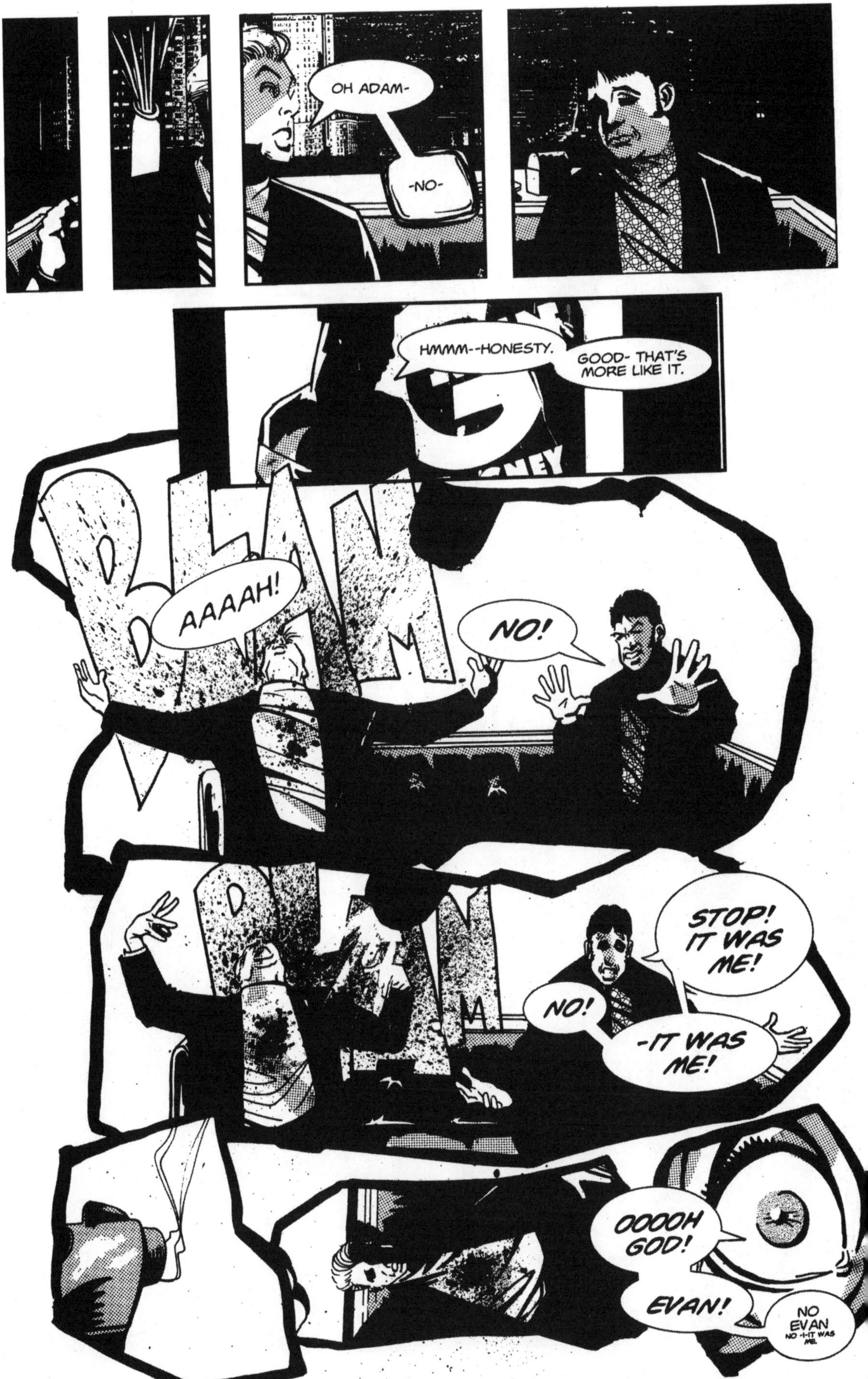
OH ADAM-
-NO-
HMMM--HONESTY.
GOOD- THAT'S MORE LIKE IT.
AAAAH!
NO!
STOP! IT WAS ME!
NO!
-IT WAS ME!
OOOOH GOD!
EVAN!
NO EVAN NO -I-IT WAS ME.

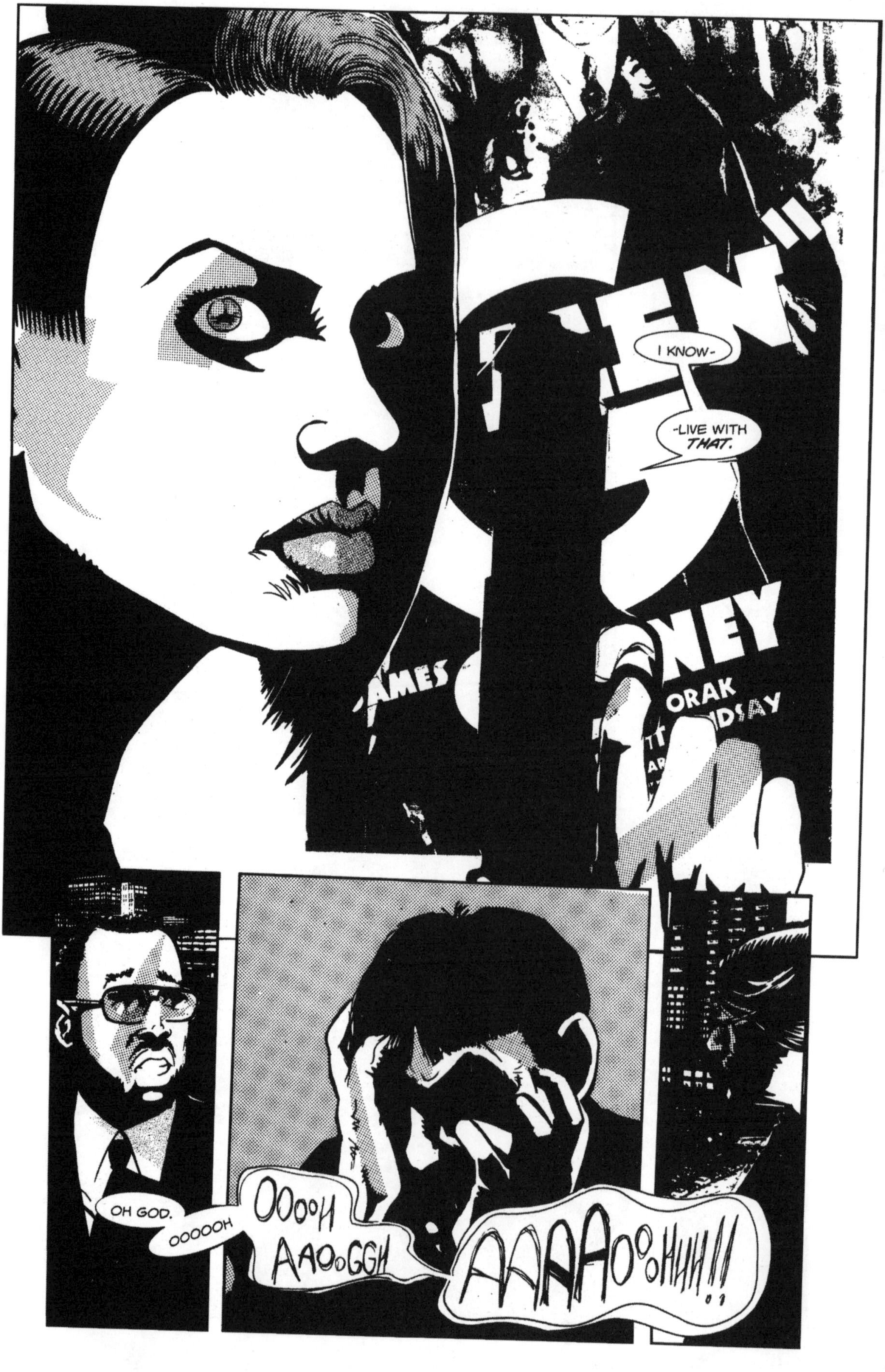

I KNOW-
-LIVE WITH THAT.
OH GOD.
OOOOOH
OOooH AAOoGGH
AAAAOooHHH!!

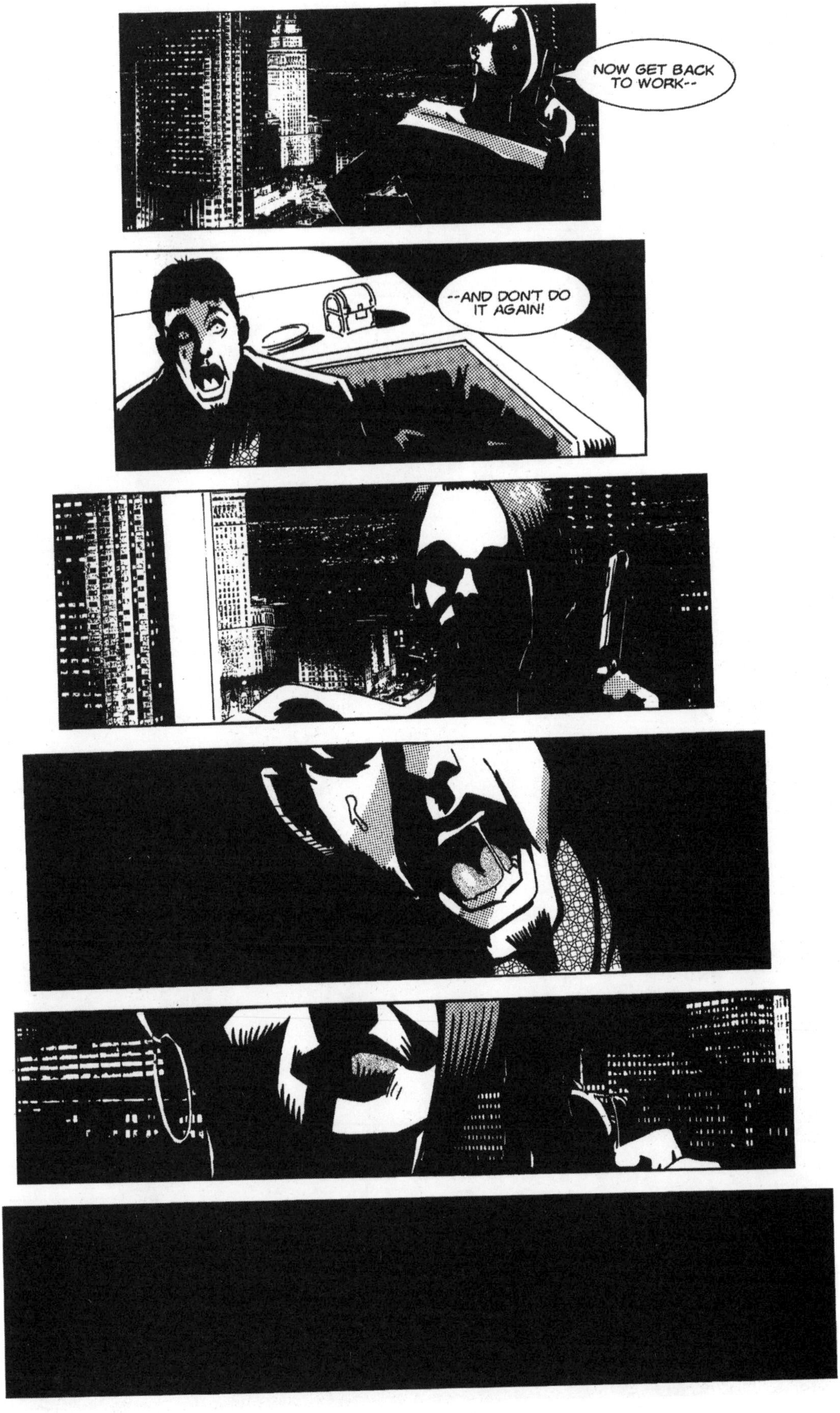
NOW GET BACK
TO WORK--
--AND DON'T DO
IT AGAIN!

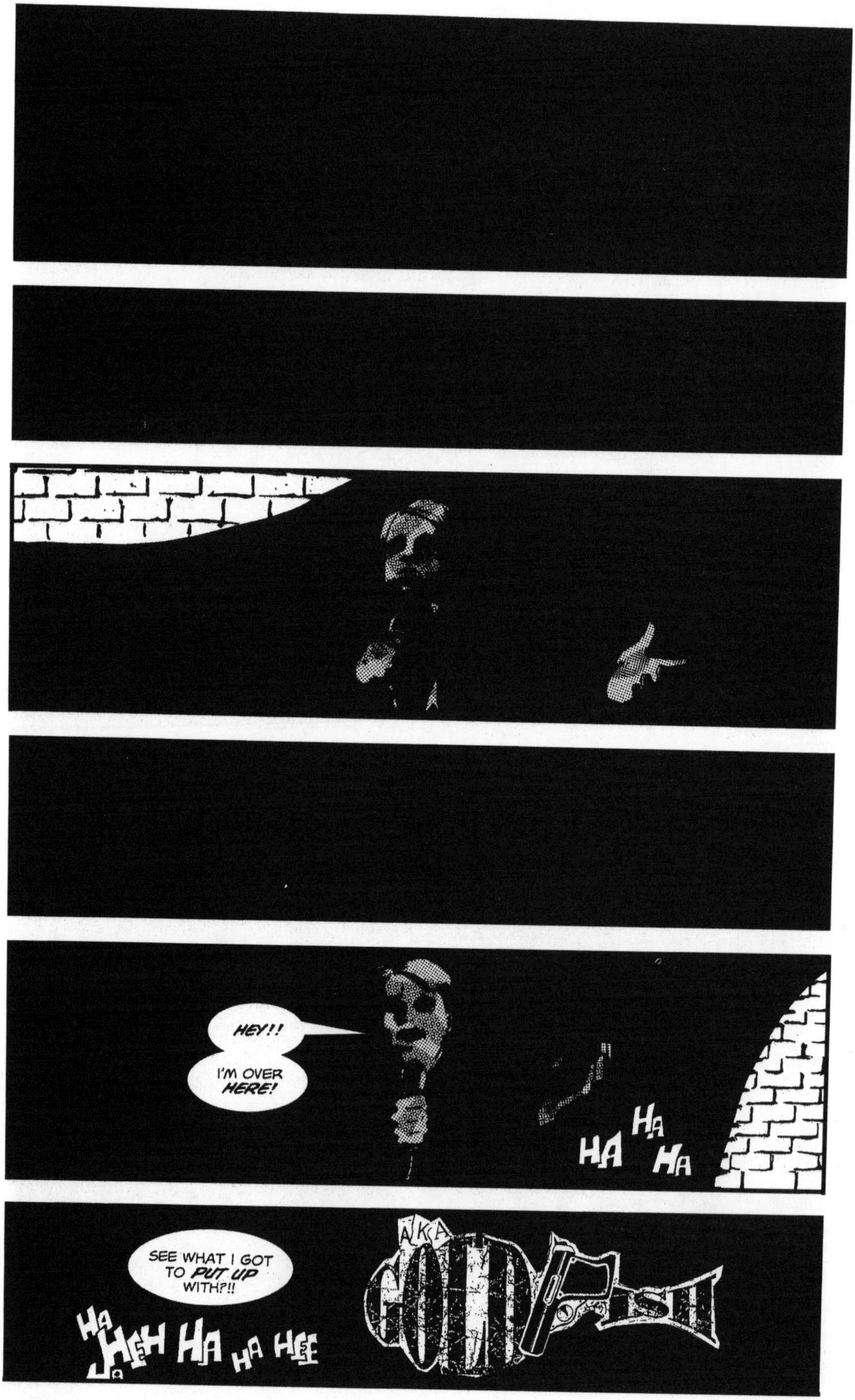
HEY!!
I'M OVER HERE!
HA HA HA
SEE WHAT I GOT TO PUT UP WITH?!!
HA HA HEH HA HA HEE
AKA
GOLDFISH

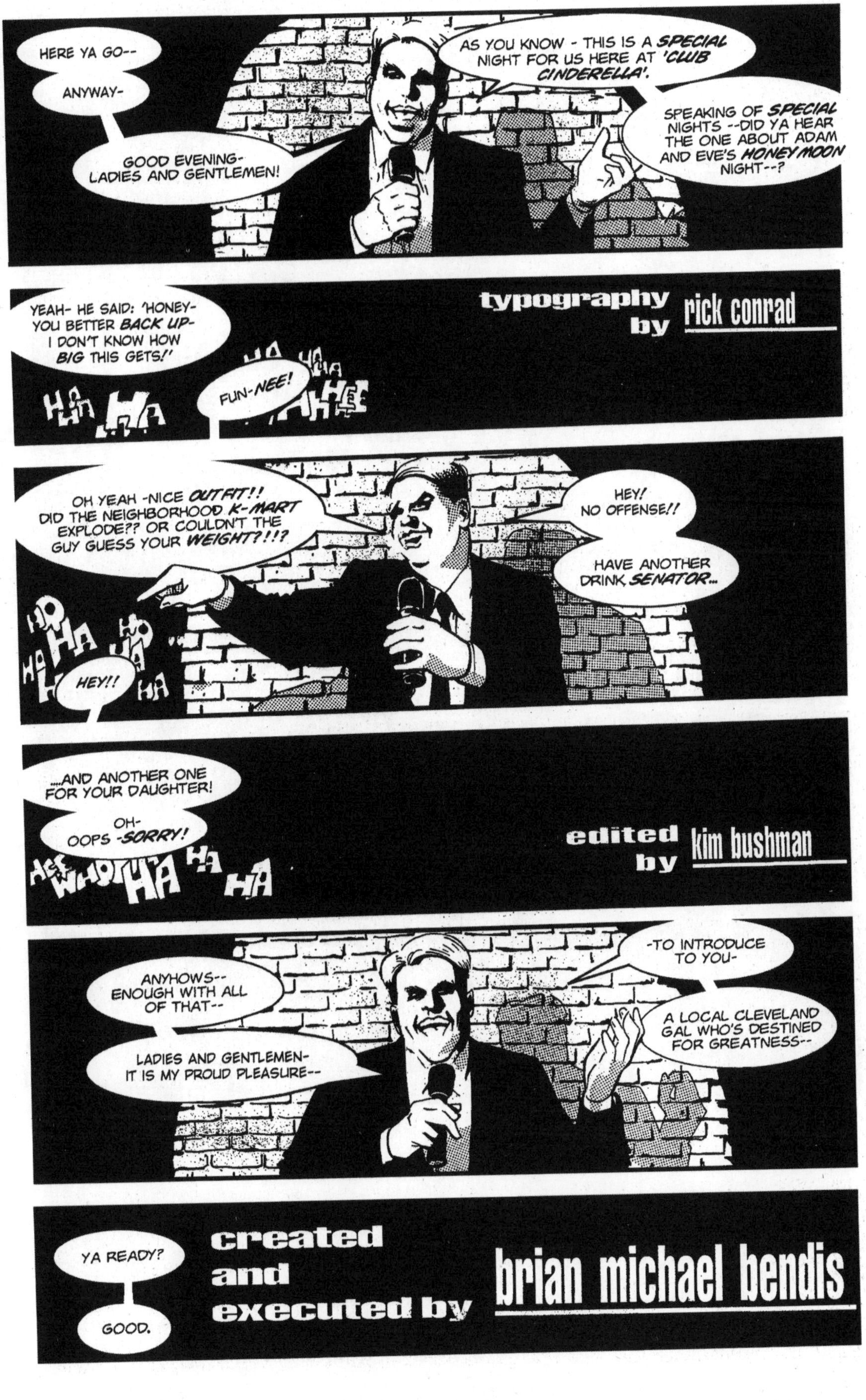
HERE YA GO--
ANYWAY-
GOOD EVENING-
LADIES AND GENTLEMEN!
AS YOU KNOW - THIS IS A SPECIAL NIGHT FOR US HERE AT 'CLUB CINDERELLA'.
SPEAKING OF SPECIAL NIGHTS --DID YA HEAR THE ONE ABOUT ADAM AND EVE'S HONEYMOON NIGHT--?
YEAH- HE SAID: 'HONEY- YOU BETTER BACK UP- I DON'T KNOW HOW BIG THIS GETS!'
typography by rick conrad
HA
FUN-NEE!
OH YEAH -NICE OUTFIT!! DID THE NEIGHBORHOOD K-MART EXPLODE?? OR COULDN'T THE GUY GUESS YOUR WEIGHT?!!?
HEY! NO OFFENSE!!
HAVE ANOTHER DRINK SENATOR...
HA
HEY!!
....AND ANOTHER ONE FOR YOUR DAUGHTER!
OH- OOPS -SORRY!
HA HA HA
edited by kim bushman
ANYHOWS-- ENOUGH WITH ALL OF THAT--
LADIES AND GENTLEMEN- IT IS MY PROUD PLEASURE--
-TO INTRODUCE TO YOU-
A LOCAL CLEVELAND GAL WHO'S DESTINED FOR GREATNESS--
YA READY?
GOOD.
created and executed by brian michael bendis

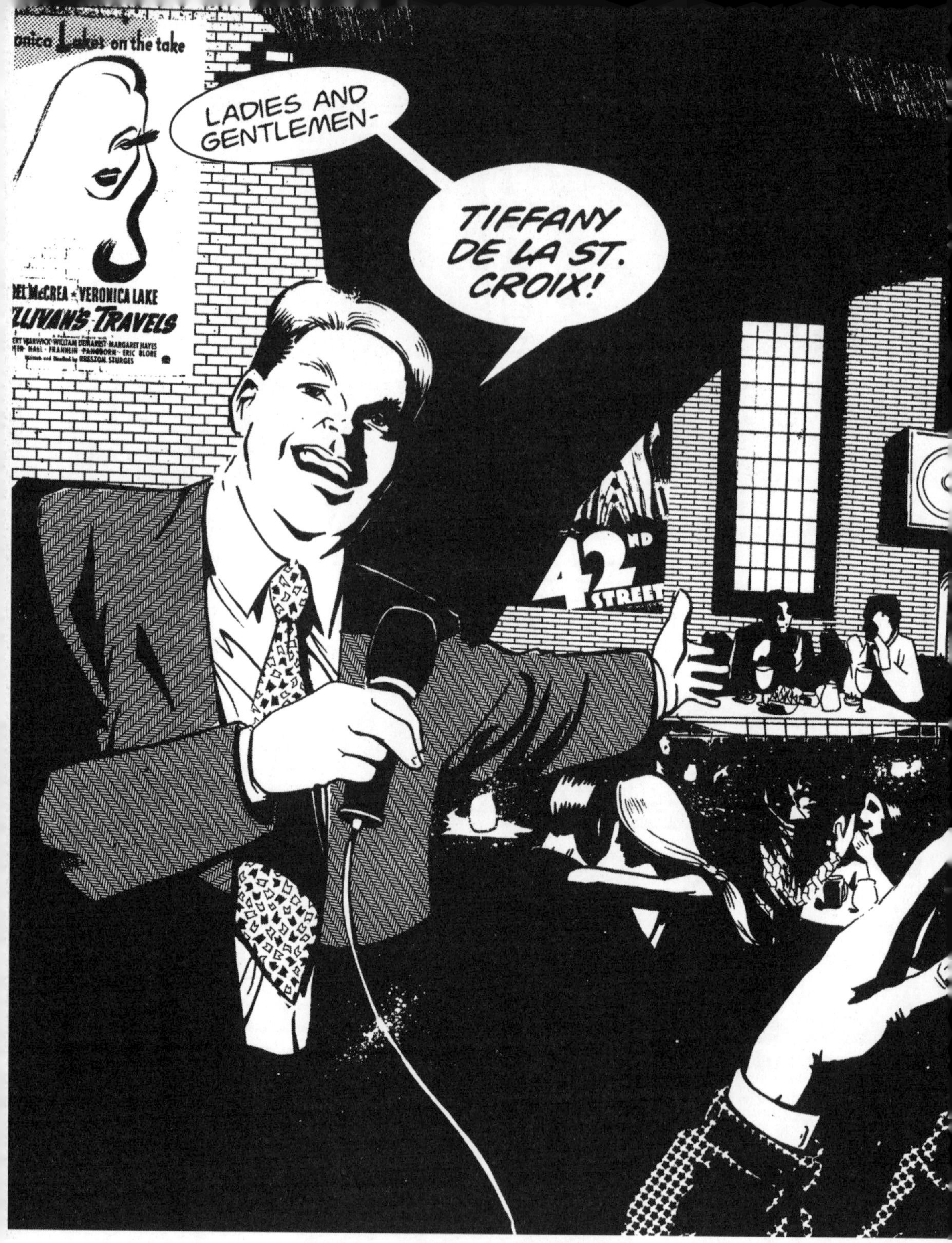
on the take
VERONICA LAKE
LADIES AND GENTLEMEN-
TIFFANY DE LA ST. CROIX!
42ND STREET

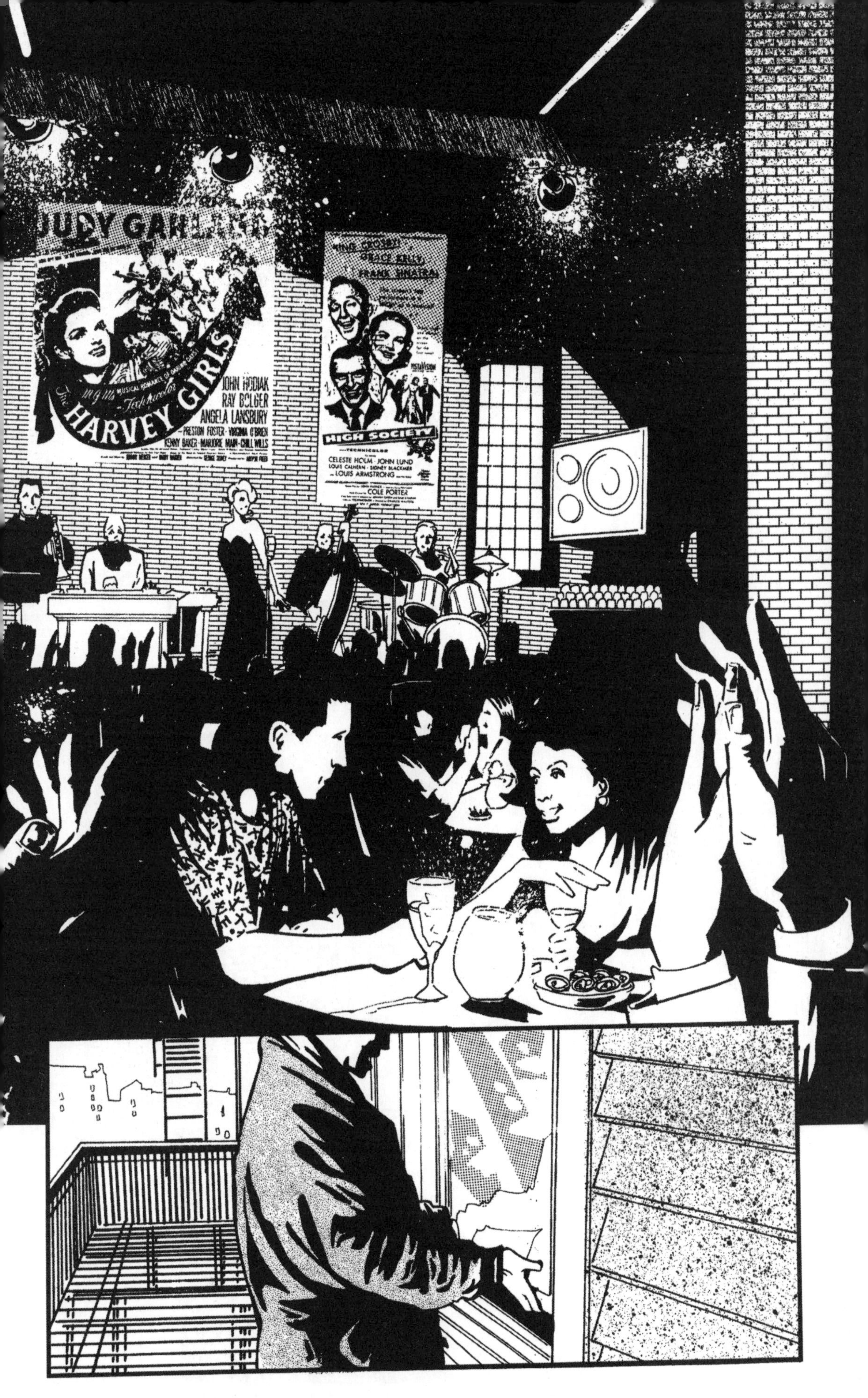
The HARVEY GIRLS
M-G-M's MUSICAL ROMANCE
Technicolor
JOHN HODIAK
RAY BOLGER
ANGELA LANSBURY
PRESTON FOSTER · VIRGINIA O'BRIEN
KENNY BAKER · MARJORIE MAIN · CHILL WILLS
VISTAVISION
HIGH SOCIETY
TECHNICOLOR
CELESTE HOLM · JOHN LUND
LOUIS CALHERN · SIDNEY BLACKMER
LOUIS ARMSTRONG
COLE PORTER

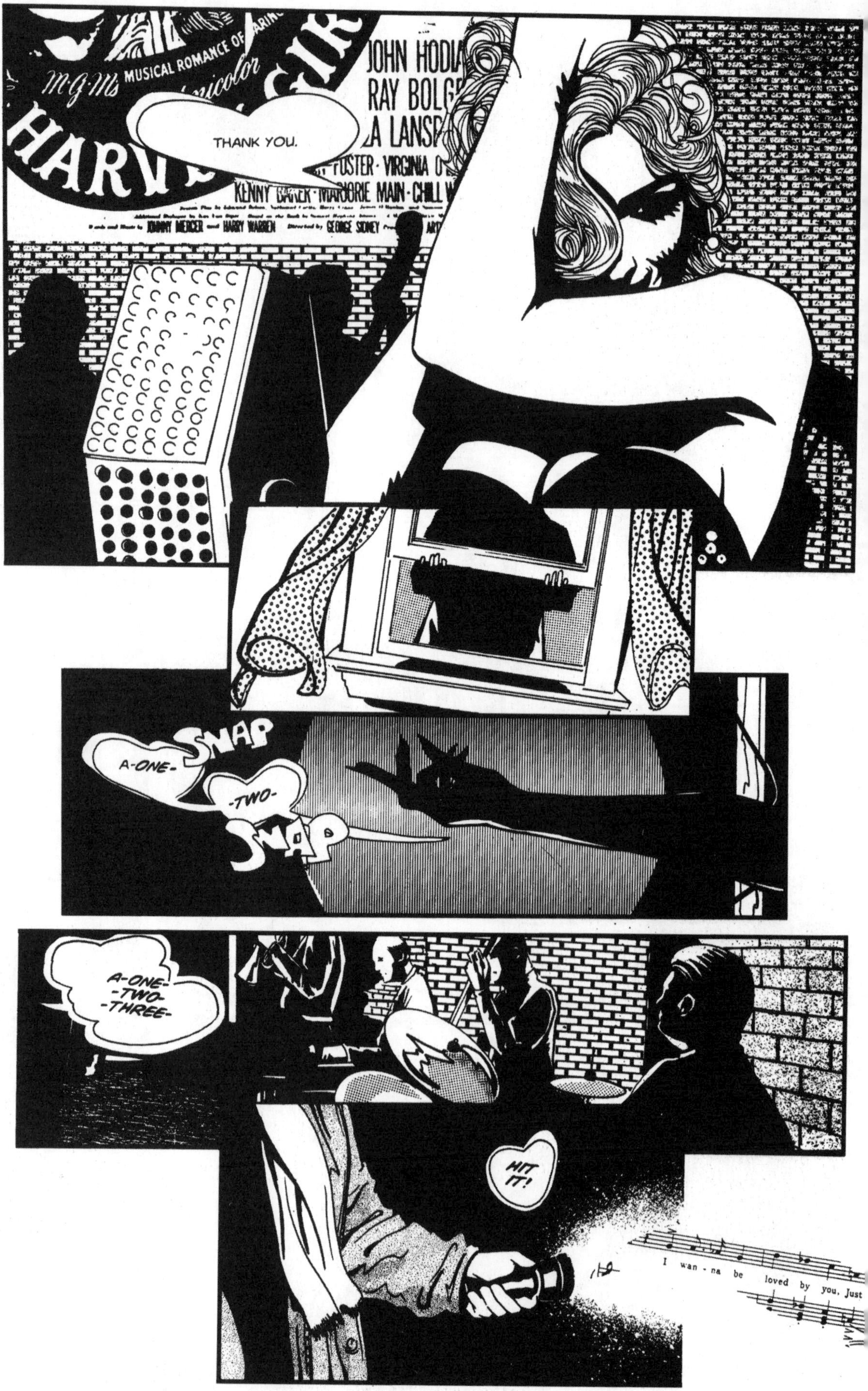

M-G-M's MUSICAL ROMANCE OF
JOHN HODIA
RAY BOLG
KENNY BAKER · MARJORIE MAIN · CHILL W
JOHNNY MERCER and HARRY WARREN
GEORGE SIDNEY
THANK YOU.
A-ONE-
SNAP
-TWO-
SNAP
A-ONE- -TWO- -THREE-
HIT IT!
I wan - na be loved by you, Just

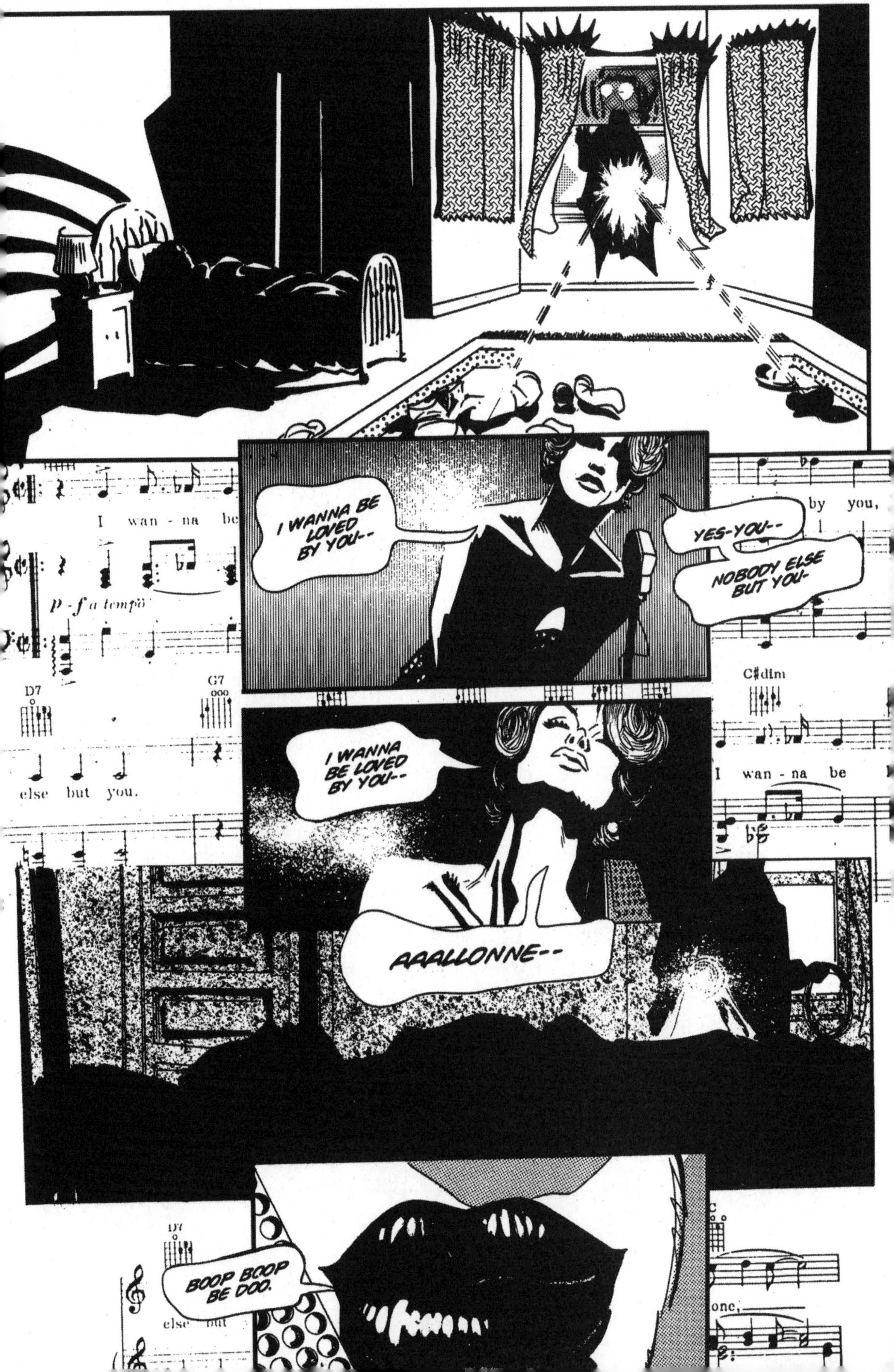
I wan - na be
by you,
I WANNA BE LOVED BY YOU--
YES-YOU--
NOBODY ELSE BUT YOU-
D7
G7
C#dim
else but you.
I wan - na be
I WANNA BE LOVED BY YOU--
AAALLONNE--
D7
C
BOOP BOOP BE DOO.
else but
one,

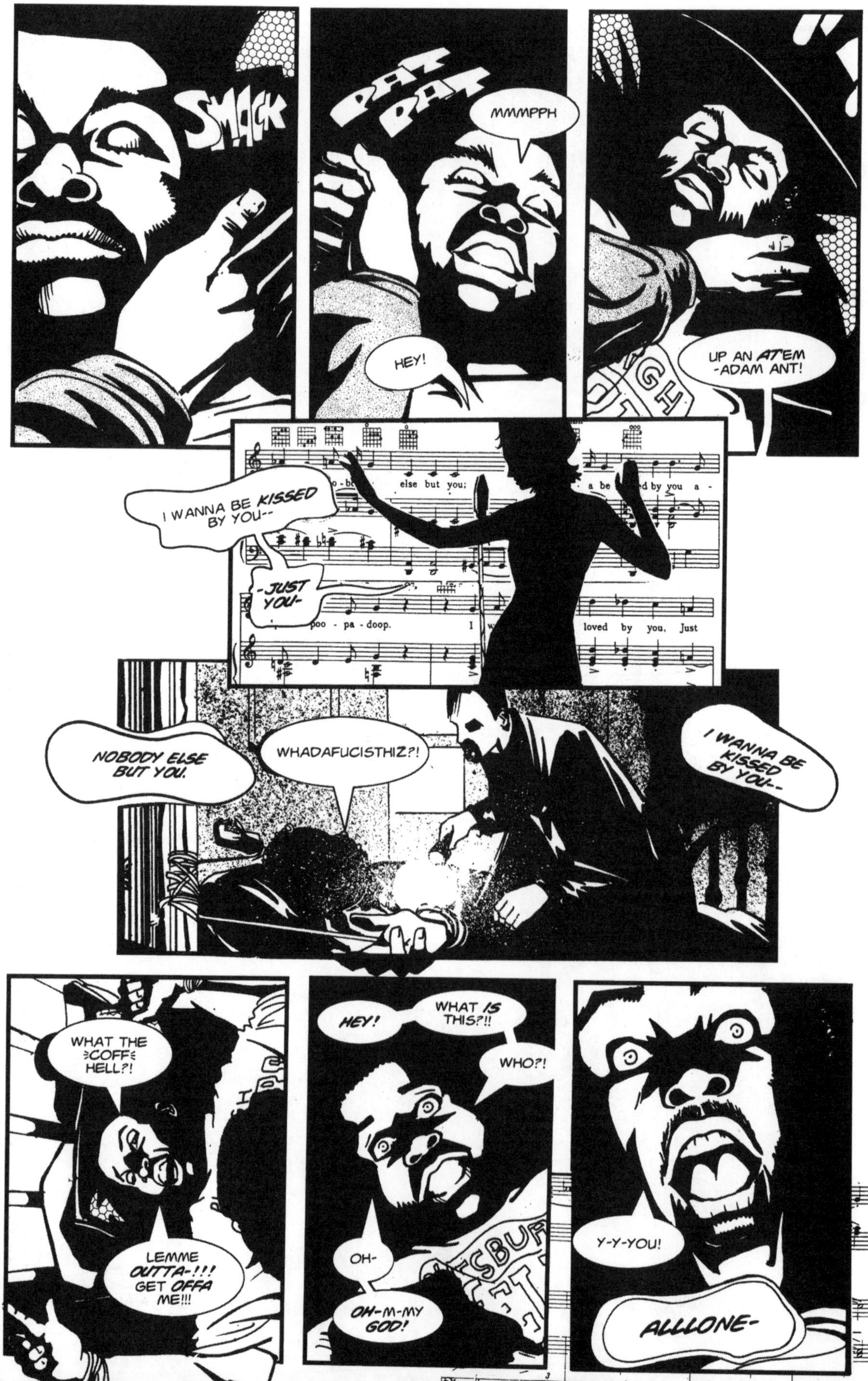
SMACK
PAT PAT
MMMPPH
HEY!
UP AN AT'EM
-ADAM ANT!
I WANNA BE KISSED BY YOU--
-JUST YOU-
else but you;
poo - pa - doop.
loved by you, Just
NOBODY ELSE BUT YOU.
WHADAFUCISTHIZ?!
I WANNA BE KISSED BY YOU--
WHAT THE COFF HELL?!
LEMME OUTTA-!!! GET OFFA ME!!!
HEY!
WHAT IS THIS?!!
WHO?!
OH-
OH-M-MY GOD!
Y-Y-YOU!
ALLONE-

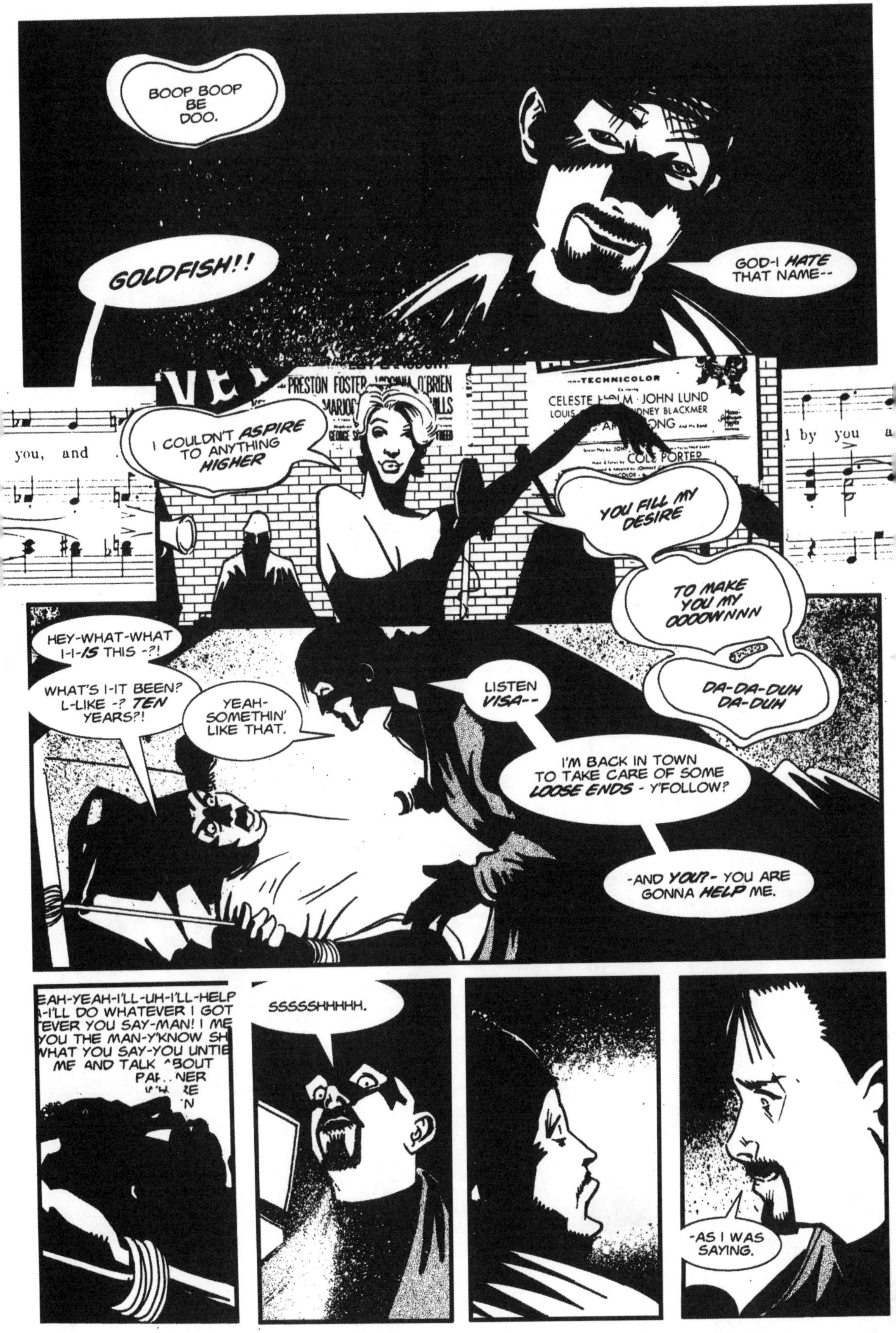
BOOP BOOP BE DOO.
GOLDFISH!!
GOD-I HATE THAT NAME--
PRESTON FOSTER
TECHNICOLOR
JOHN LUND
COLE PORTER
you, and
by you
I COULDN'T ASPIRE TO ANYTHING HIGHER
YOU FILL MY DESIRE
TO MAKE YOU MY OOOOWNNN
DA-DA-DUH DA-DUH
HEY-WHAT-WHAT I-I-IS THIS -?!
WHAT'S I-IT BEEN? L-LIKE -? TEN YEARS?!
YEAH-SOMETHIN' LIKE THAT.
LISTEN VISA--
I'M BACK IN TOWN TO TAKE CARE OF SOME LOOSE ENDS - Y'FOLLOW?
-AND YOU?- YOU ARE GONNA HELP ME.
EAH-YEAH-I'LL-UH-I'LL-HELP
A-I'LL DO WHATEVER I GOT
TEVER YOU SAY-MAN! I ME
YOU THE MAN-Y'KNOW SH
WHAT YOU SAY-YOU UNTIE
ME AND TALK
SSSSSHHHHH.
-AS I WAS SAYING.

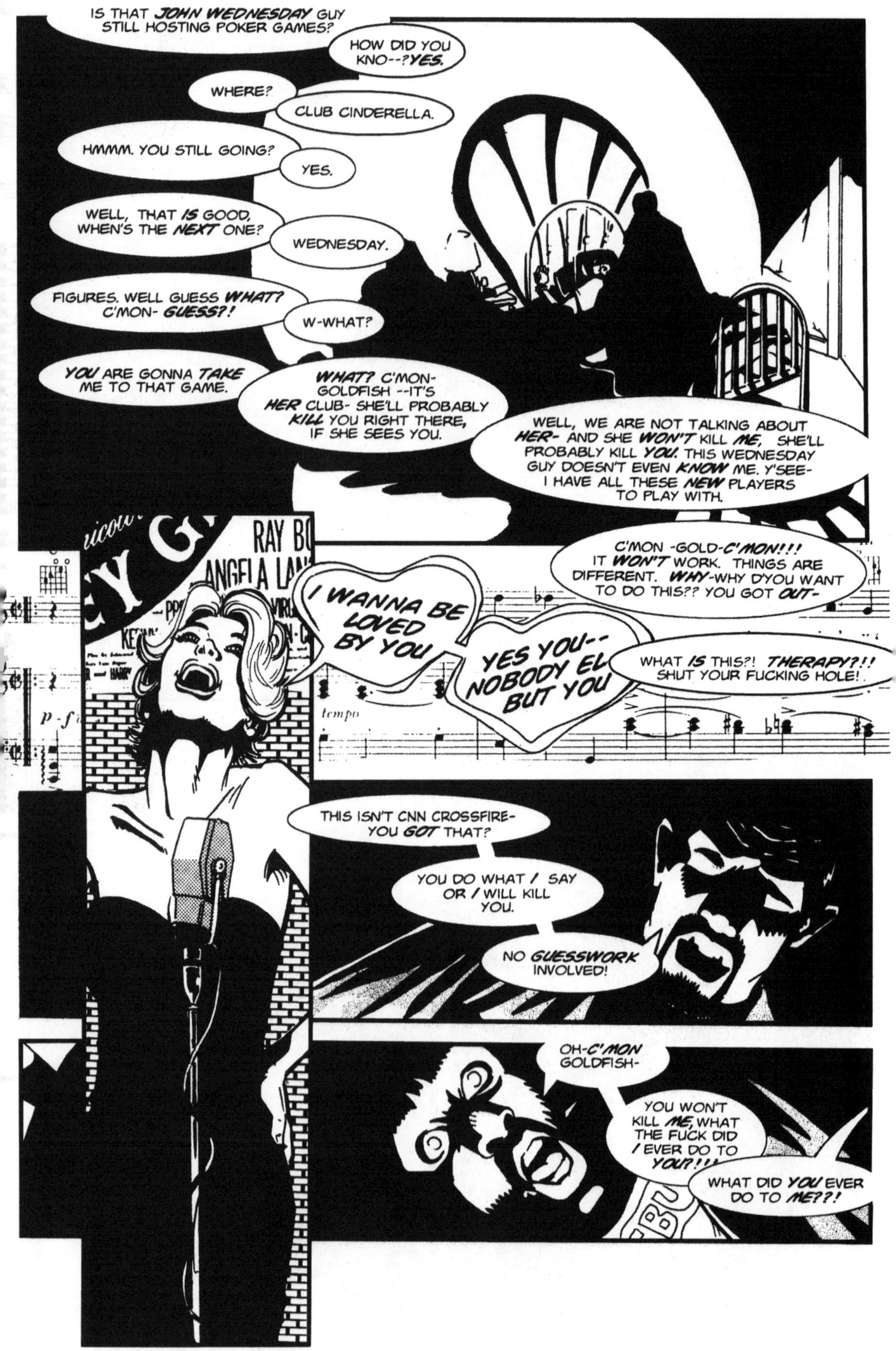
IS THAT JOHN WEDNESDAY GUY STILL HOSTING POKER GAMES?
HOW DID YOU KNO--?YES.
WHERE?
CLUB CINDERELLA.
HMMM. YOU STILL GOING?
YES.
WELL, THAT IS GOOD, WHEN'S THE NEXT ONE?
WEDNESDAY.
FIGURES. WELL GUESS WHAT? C'MON- GUESS?!
W-WHAT?
YOU ARE GONNA TAKE ME TO THAT GAME.
WHAT? C'MON- GOLDFISH --IT'S HER CLUB- SHE'LL PROBABLY KILL YOU RIGHT THERE, IF SHE SEES YOU.
WELL, WE ARE NOT TALKING ABOUT HER- AND SHE WON'T KILL ME, SHE'LL PROBABLY KILL YOU. THIS WEDNESDAY GUY DOESN'T EVEN KNOW ME. Y'SEE- I HAVE ALL THESE NEW PLAYERS TO PLAY WITH.
RAY BO
ANGELA LAN
C'MON -GOLD-C'MON!!! IT WON'T WORK. THINGS ARE DIFFERENT. WHY-WHY D'YOU WANT TO DO THIS?? YOU GOT OUT-
I WANNA BE LOVED BY YOU
YES YOU-- NOBODY EL BUT YOU
WHAT IS THIS?! THERAPY?!! SHUT YOUR FUCKING HOLE!
tempo
THIS ISN'T CNN CROSSFIRE- YOU GOT THAT?
YOU DO WHAT I SAY OR I WILL KILL YOU.
NO GUESSWORK INVOLVED!
OH-C'MON GOLDFISH-
YOU WON'T KILL ME, WHAT THE FUCK DID I EVER DO TO YOU?!!
WHAT DID YOU EVER DO TO ME??!

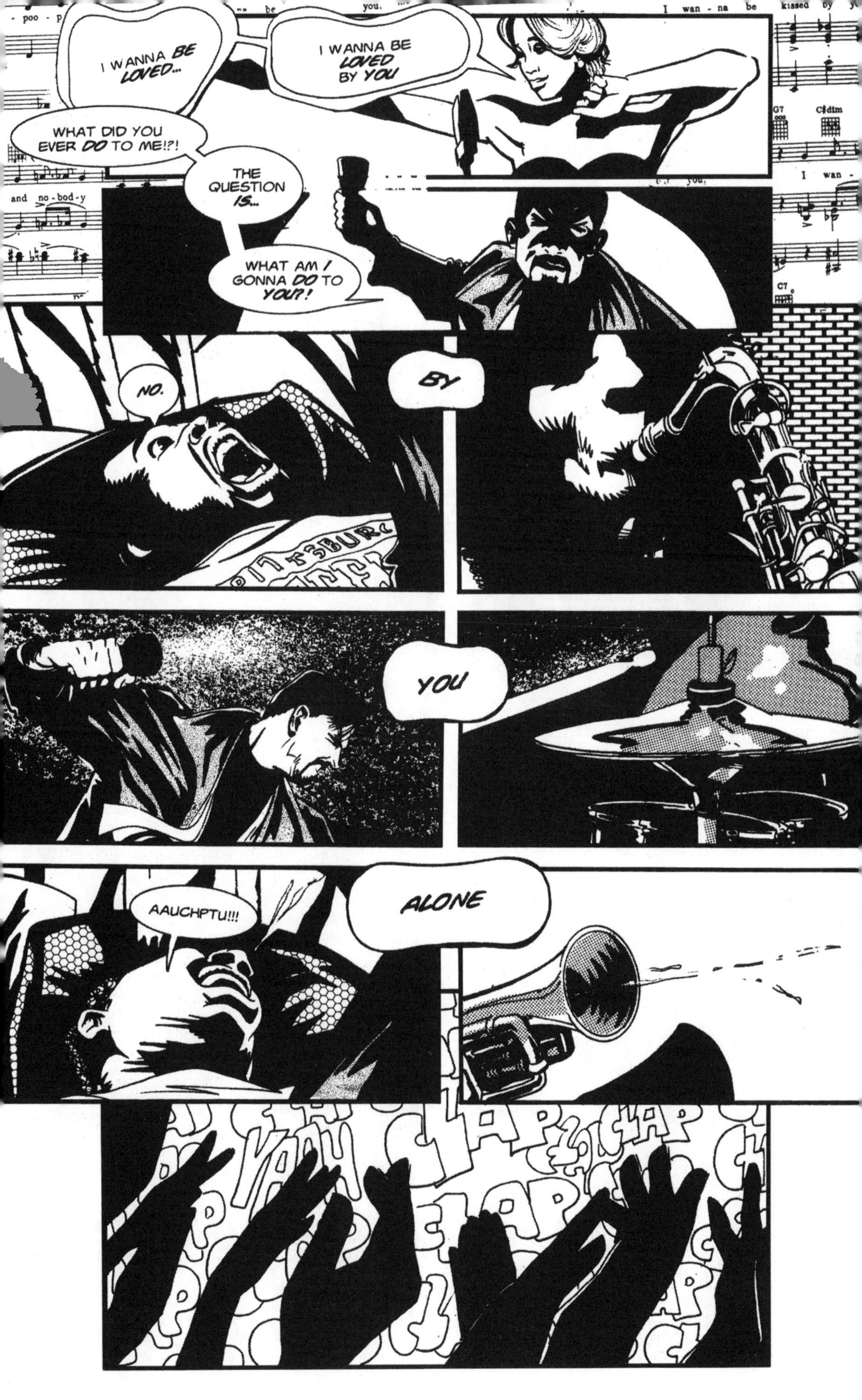
I WANNA BE LOVED...
I WANNA BE LOVED BY YOU
WHAT DID YOU EVER DO TO ME!?!
THE QUESTION IS...
WHAT AM I GONNA DO TO YOU?!
NO.
BY
YOU
AAUCHPTU!!!
ALONE

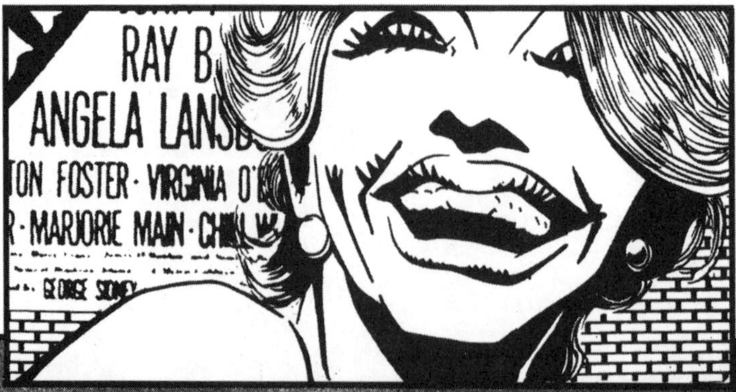
RAY B
ANGELA LANSB
TON FOSTER · VIRGINIA O'B
R · MARJORIE MAIN · CHILL W
GEORGE SIDNEY

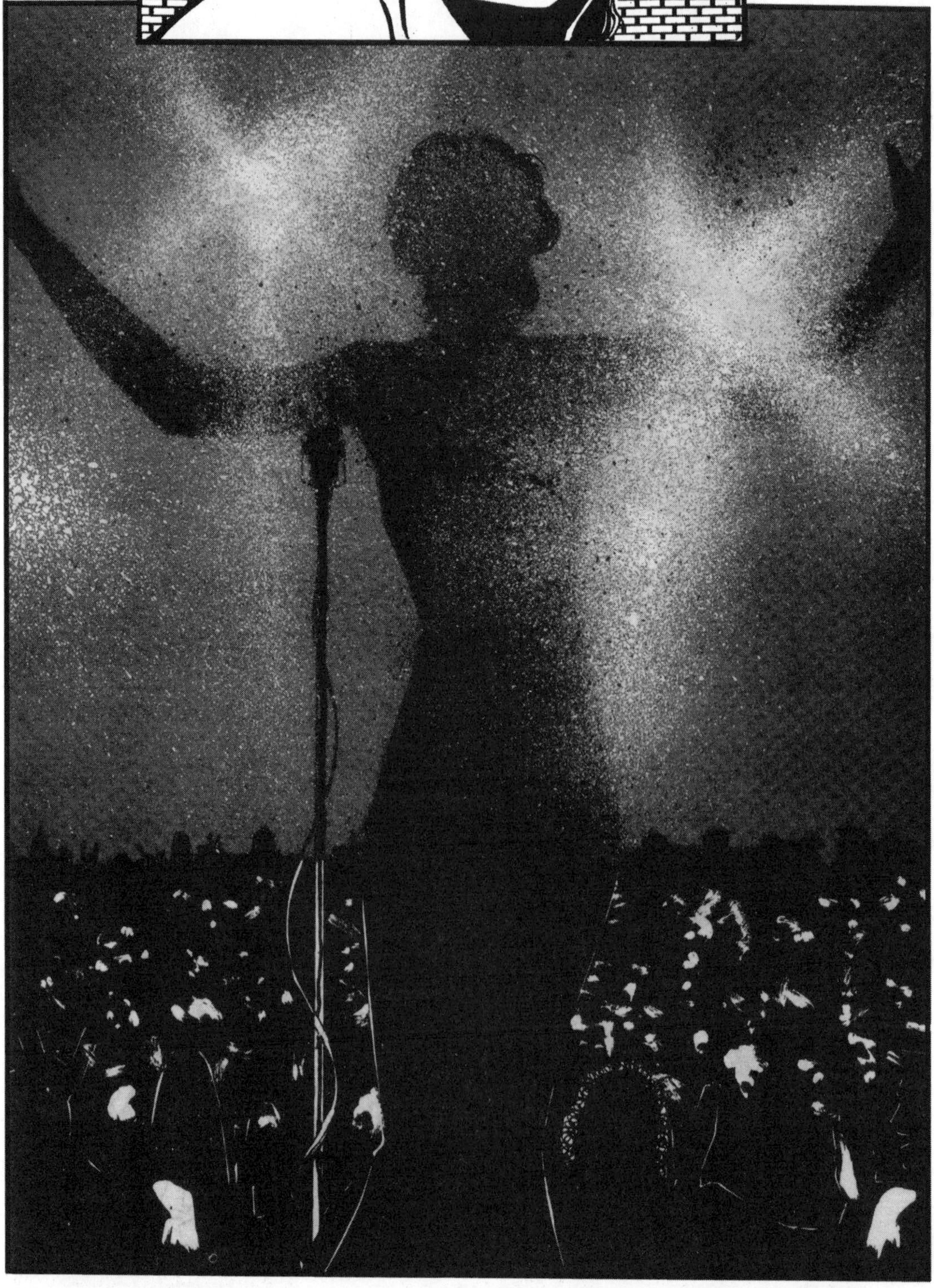

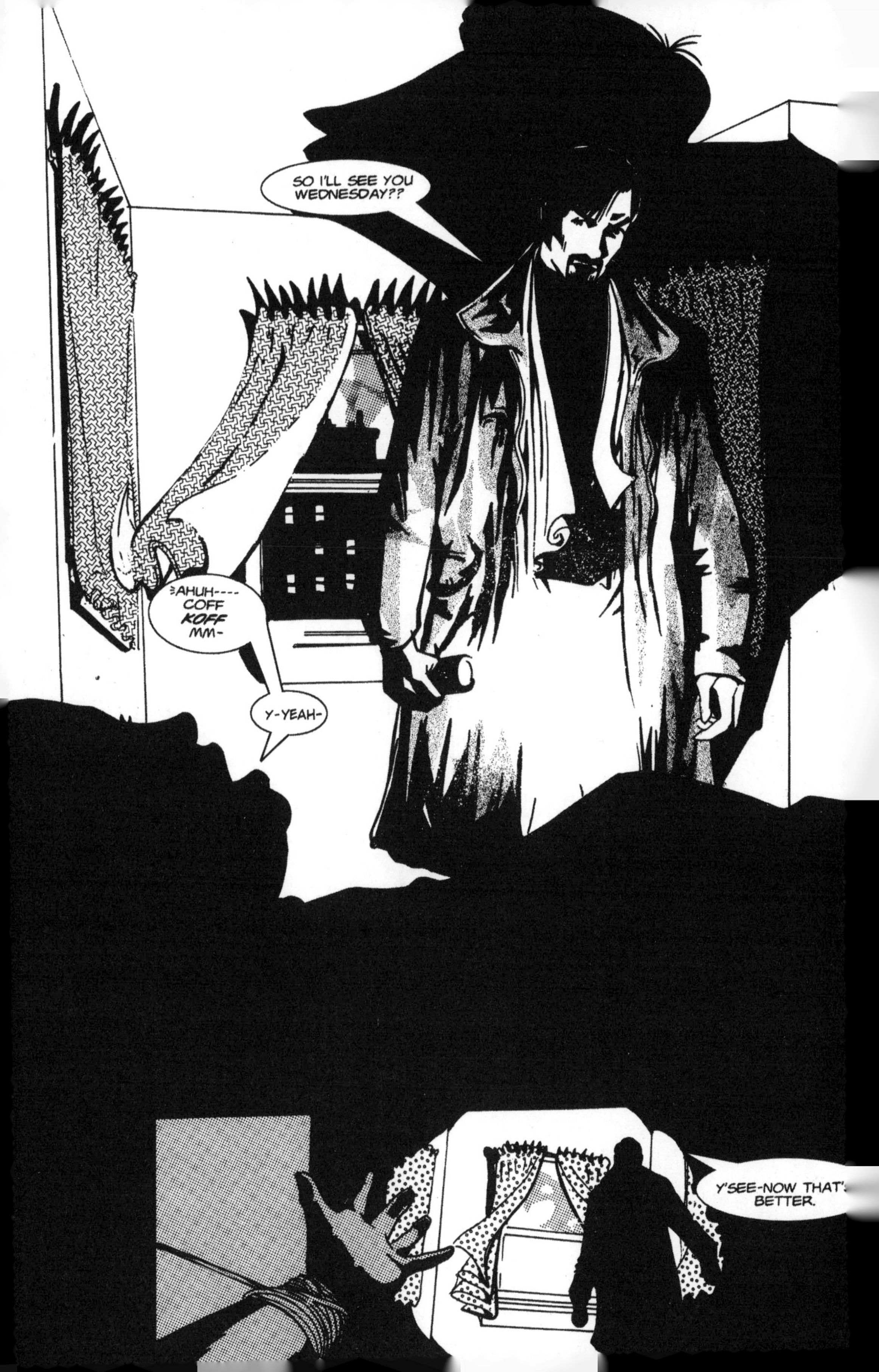

SO I'LL SEE YOU WEDNESDAY??
AHUH---- COFF KOFF MM-
Y-YEAH-
Y'SEE-NOW THAT'S BETTER.

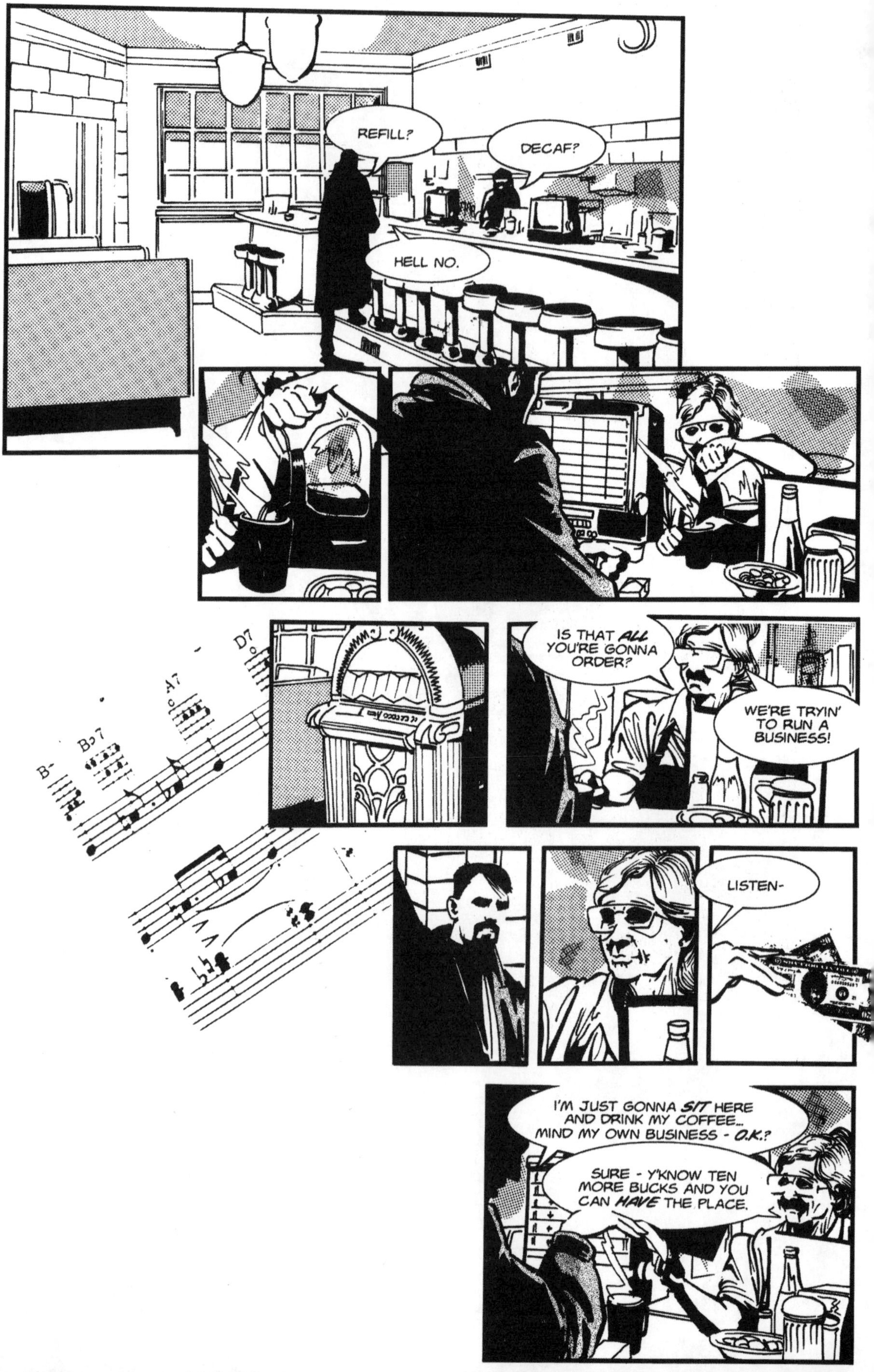

REFILL?
DECAF?
HELL NO.
B-
B♭7
A7
D7
IS THAT ALL YOU'RE GONNA ORDER?
WE'RE TRYIN' TO RUN A BUSINESS!
LISTEN-
I'M JUST GONNA SIT HERE AND DRINK MY COFFEE... MIND MY OWN BUSINESS - O.K.?
SURE - Y'KNOW TEN MORE BUCKS AND YOU CAN HAVE THE PLACE.

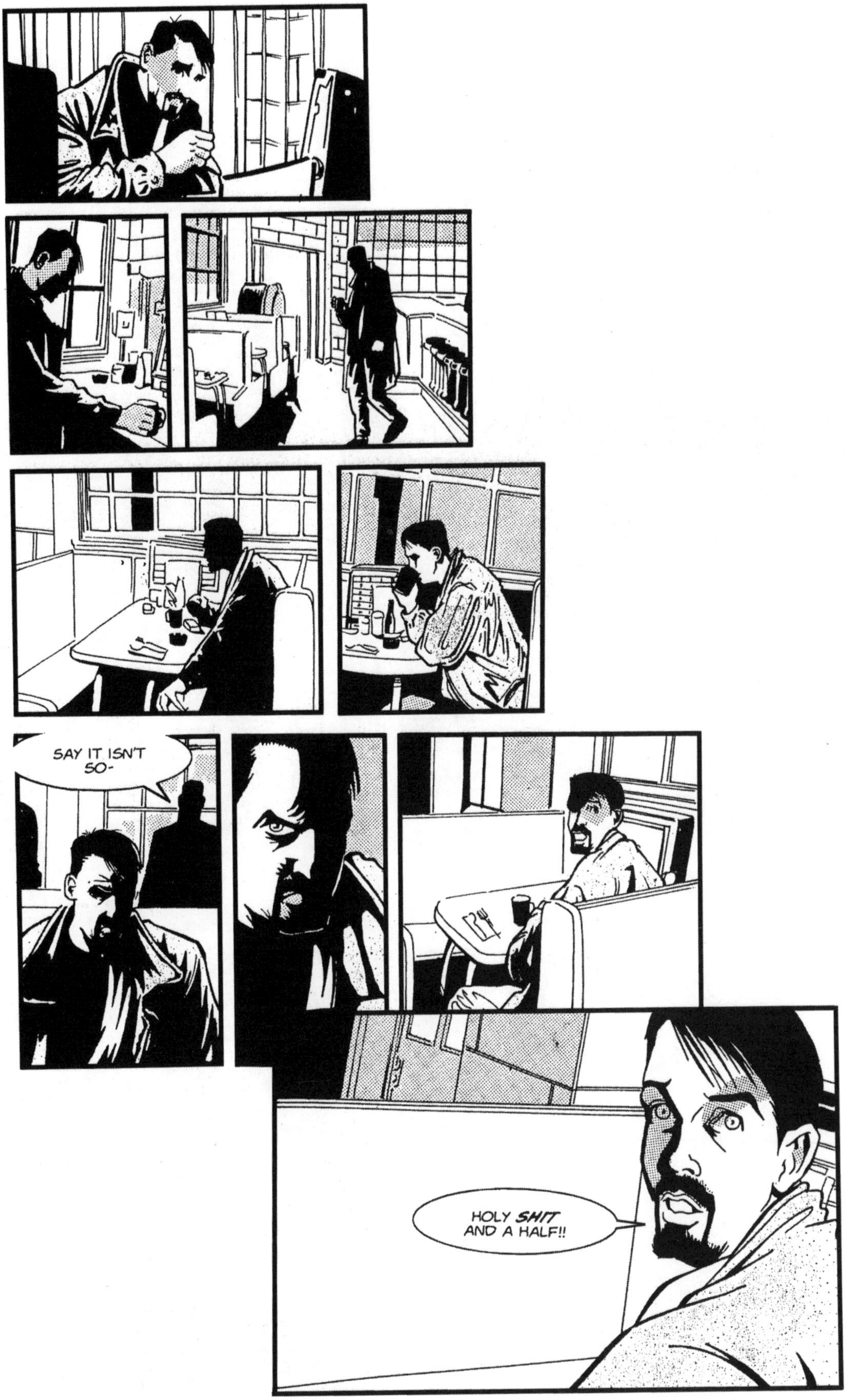
SAY IT ISN'T SO-
HOLY SHIT AND A HALF!!

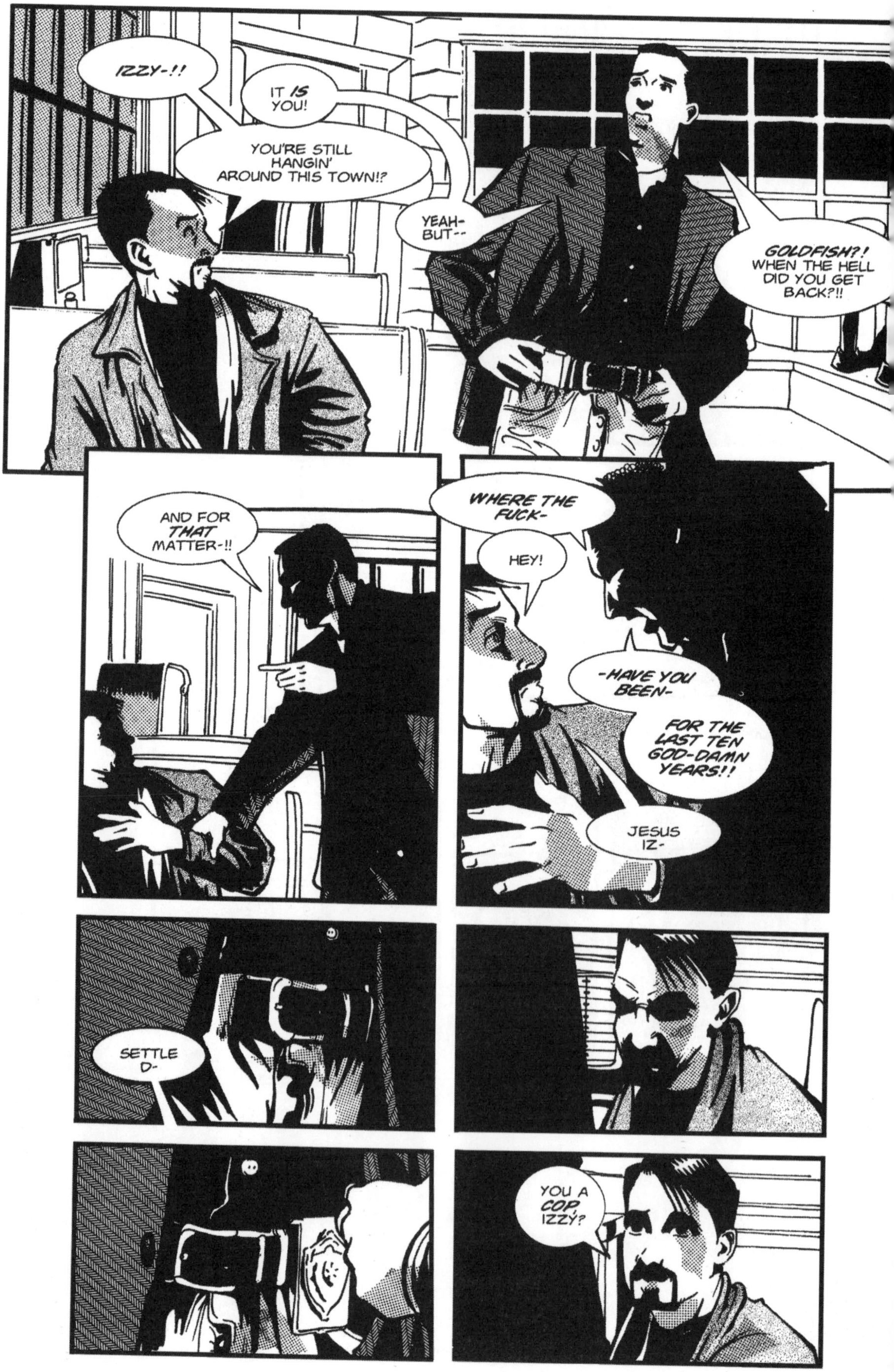
IZZY-!!
IT IS YOU!
YOU'RE STILL HANGIN' AROUND THIS TOWN!?
YEAH-BUT--
GOLDFISH?! WHEN THE HELL DID YOU GET BACK?!!
AND FOR THAT MATTER-!!
WHERE THE FUCK-
HEY!
-HAVE YOU BEEN-
FOR THE LAST TEN GOD-DAMN YEARS!!
JESUS IZ-
SETTLE D-
YOU A COP, IZZY?

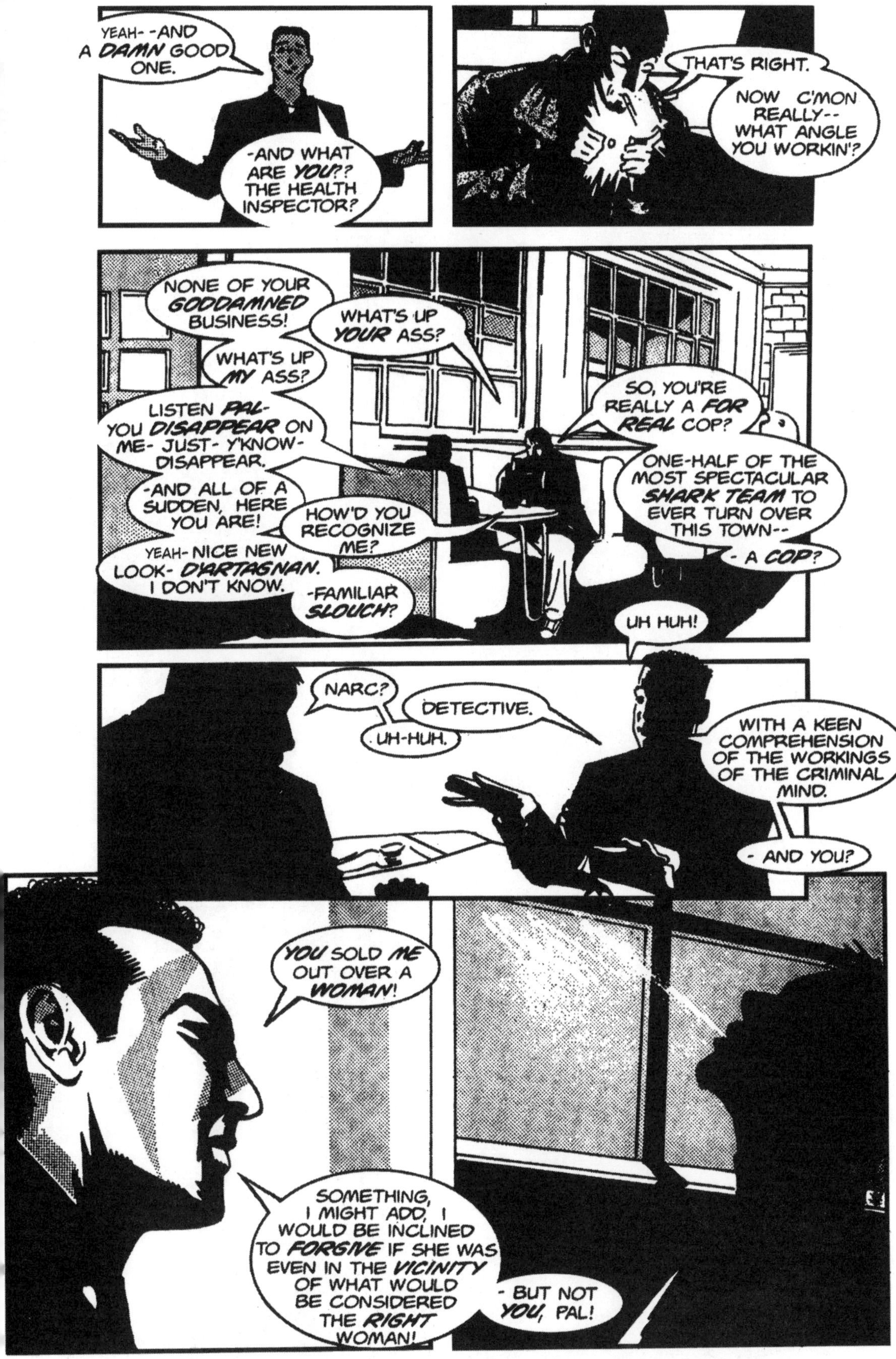
YEAH- -AND A DAMN GOOD ONE.
-AND WHAT ARE YOU?? THE HEALTH INSPECTOR?
THAT'S RIGHT.
NOW C'MON REALLY-- WHAT ANGLE YOU WORKIN'?
NONE OF YOUR GODDAMNED BUSINESS!
WHAT'S UP YOUR ASS?
WHAT'S UP MY ASS?
LISTEN PAL- YOU DISAPPEAR ON ME- JUST- Y'KNOW- DISAPPEAR.
-AND ALL OF A SUDDEN, HERE YOU ARE!
HOW'D YOU RECOGNIZE ME?
YEAH- NICE NEW LOOK- D'ARTAGNAN. I DON'T KNOW.
-FAMILIAR SLOUCH?
SO, YOU'RE REALLY A FOR REAL COP?
ONE-HALF OF THE MOST SPECTACULAR SHARK TEAM TO EVER TURN OVER THIS TOWN--
- A COP?
UH HUH!
NARC?
DETECTIVE.
UH-HUH.
WITH A KEEN COMPREHENSION OF THE WORKINGS OF THE CRIMINAL MIND.
- AND YOU?
YOU SOLD ME OUT OVER A WOMAN!
SOMETHING, I MIGHT ADD, I WOULD BE INCLINED TO FORGIVE IF SHE WAS EVEN IN THE VICINITY OF WHAT WOULD BE CONSIDERED THE RIGHT WOMAN!
- BUT NOT YOU, PAL!

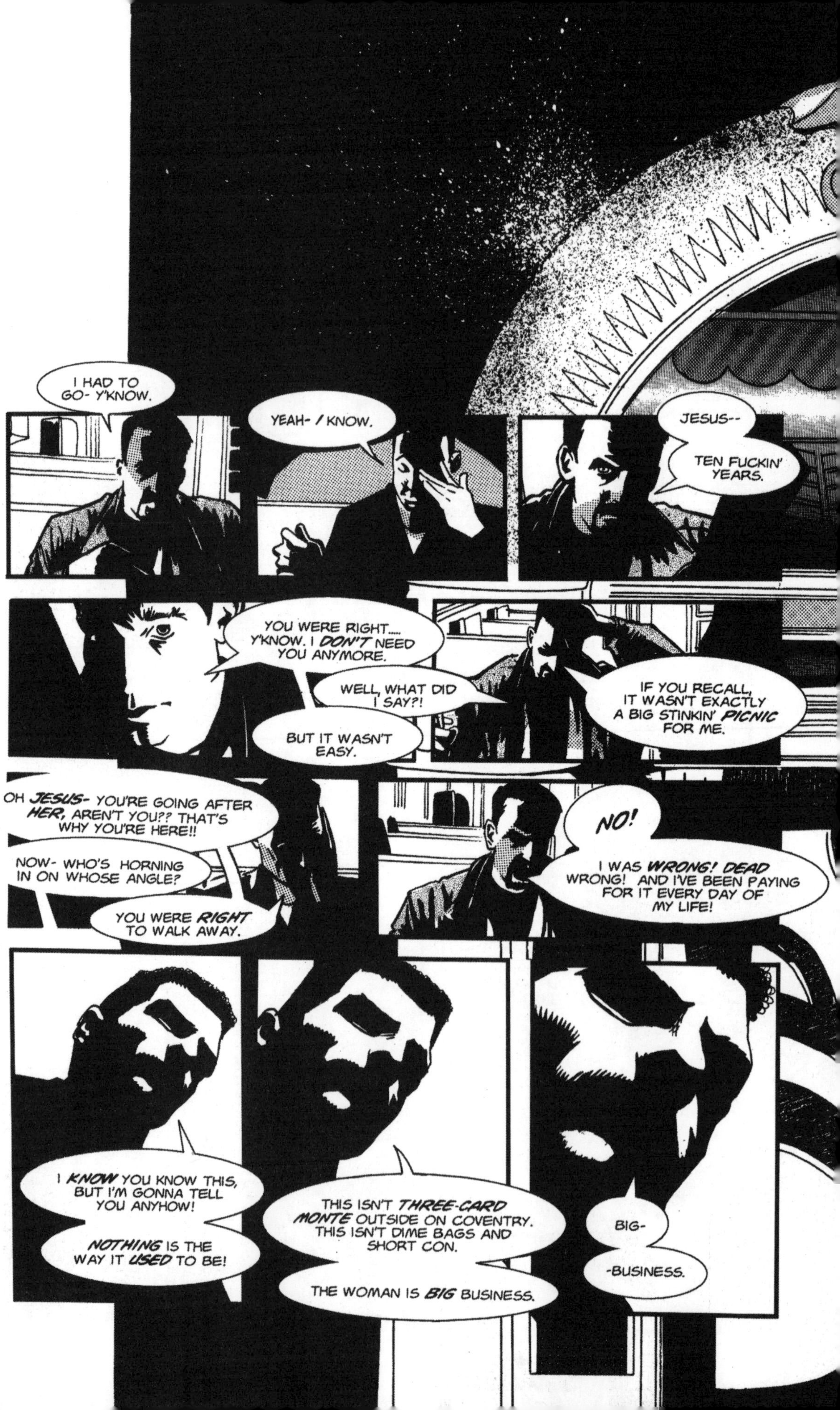
I HAD TO GO- Y'KNOW.
YEAH- I KNOW.
JESUS--
TEN FUCKIN' YEARS.
YOU WERE RIGHT..... Y'KNOW. I DON'T NEED YOU ANYMORE.
WELL, WHAT DID I SAY?!
BUT IT WASN'T EASY.
IF YOU RECALL, IT WASN'T EXACTLY A BIG STINKIN' PICNIC FOR ME.
OH JESUS- YOU'RE GOING AFTER HER, AREN'T YOU?? THAT'S WHY YOU'RE HERE!!
NOW- WHO'S HORNING IN ON WHOSE ANGLE?
YOU WERE RIGHT TO WALK AWAY.
NO!
I WAS WRONG! DEAD WRONG! AND I'VE BEEN PAYING FOR IT EVERY DAY OF MY LIFE!
I KNOW YOU KNOW THIS, BUT I'M GONNA TELL YOU ANYHOW!
NOTHING IS THE WAY IT USED TO BE!
THIS ISN'T THREE-CARD MONTE OUTSIDE ON COVENTRY. THIS ISN'T DIME BAGS AND SHORT CON.
THE WOMAN IS BIG BUSINESS.
BIG-
-BUSINESS.

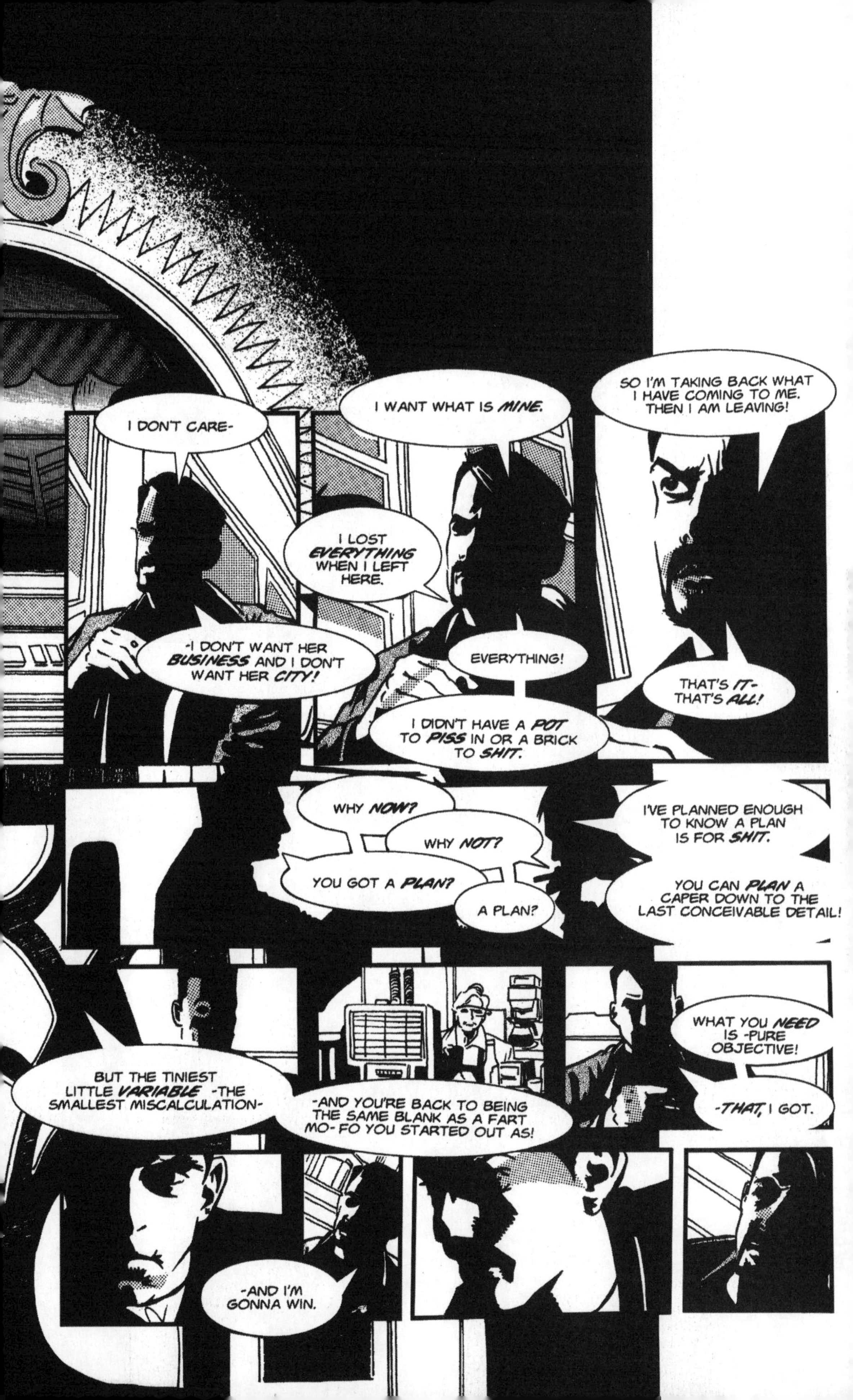
I DON'T CARE-
-I DON'T WANT HER BUSINESS AND I DON'T WANT HER CITY!
I WANT WHAT IS MINE.
I LOST EVERYTHING WHEN I LEFT HERE.
EVERYTHING!
I DIDN'T HAVE A POT TO PISS IN OR A BRICK TO SHIT.
SO I'M TAKING BACK WHAT I HAVE COMING TO ME. THEN I AM LEAVING!
THAT'S IT- THAT'S ALL!
WHY NOW?
WHY NOT?
YOU GOT A PLAN?
A PLAN?
I'VE PLANNED ENOUGH TO KNOW A PLAN IS FOR SHIT.
YOU CAN PLAN A CAPER DOWN TO THE LAST CONCEIVABLE DETAIL!
BUT THE TINIEST LITTLE VARIABLE -THE SMALLEST MISCALCULATION-
-AND YOU'RE BACK TO BEING THE SAME BLANK AS A FART MO- FO YOU STARTED OUT AS!
WHAT YOU NEED IS -PURE OBJECTIVE!
-THAT, I GOT.
-AND I'M GONNA WIN.

PAST IS PAST-
GO BACK TO WHOEVER YOU WERE. GO BACK TO WHAT-EVER YOU WERE DOING.
IF YOU CARE- I FORGIVE YOU.
AND I ACTUALLY WISH YOU WELL.
BUT I CAN'T HELP YOU.
YES- YOU CAN. BUT- I DON'T NEED HELP.
WELL- JUST PAY ATTENTION-
NOT EVERYTHING HERE IS BLACK & WHITE.
IT SURE FEELS BLACK & WHITE.

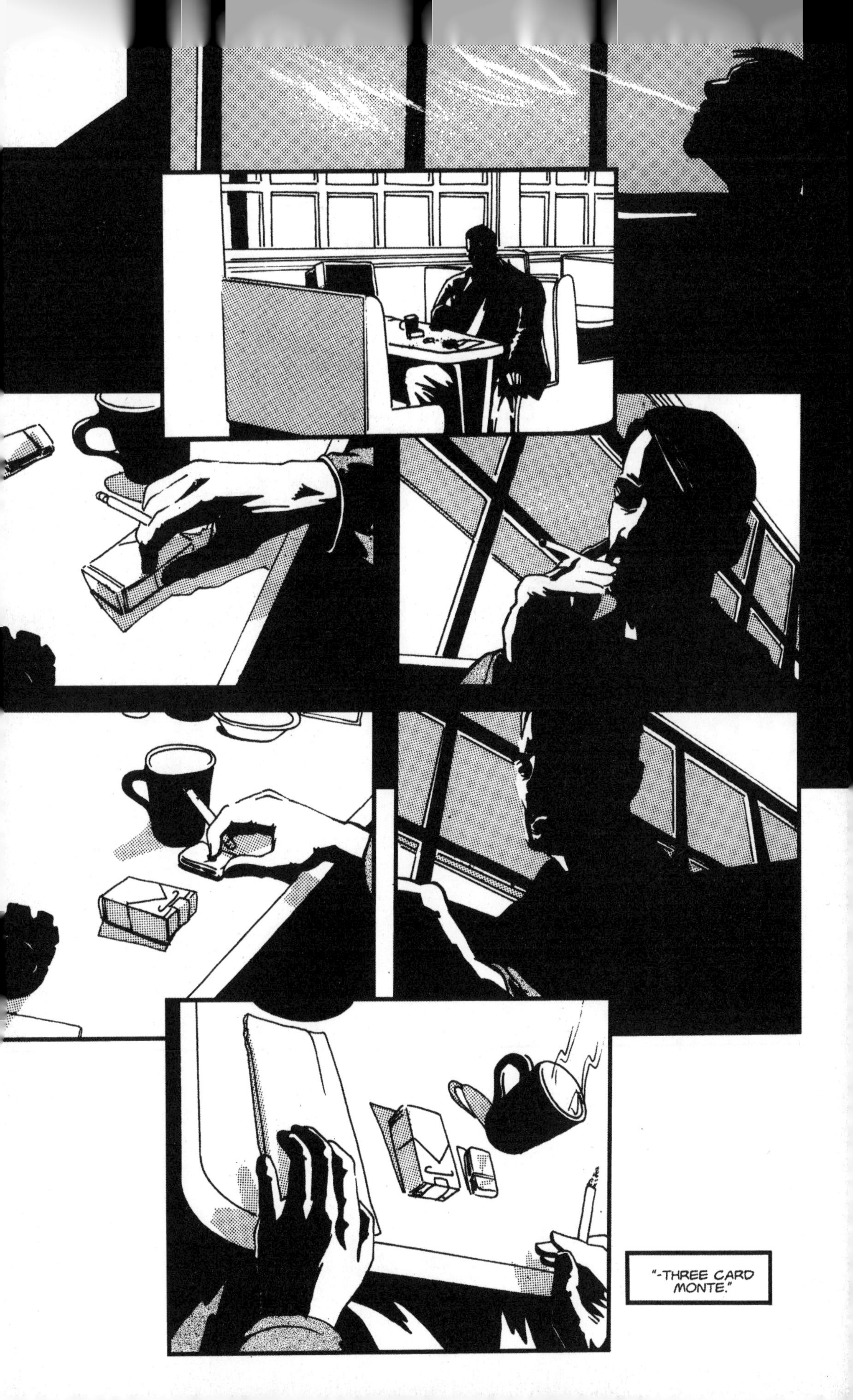
"-THREE CARD
MONTE."

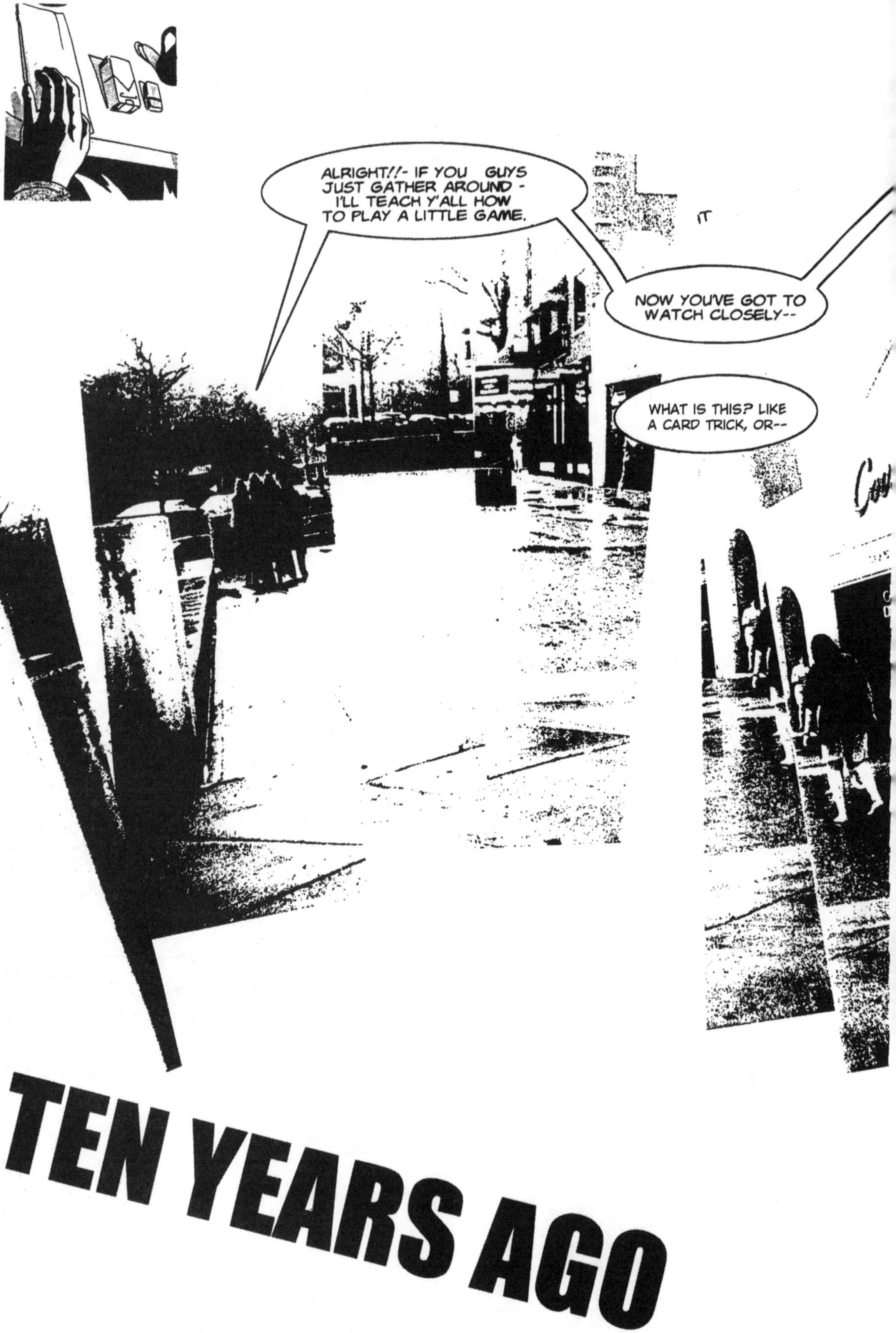
ALRIGHT!!- IF YOU GUYS JUST GATHER AROUND - I'LL TEACH Y'ALL HOW TO PLAY A LITTLE GAME.
NOW YOU'VE GOT TO WATCH CLOSELY--
WHAT IS THIS? LIKE A CARD TRICK, OR--
TEN YEARS AGO

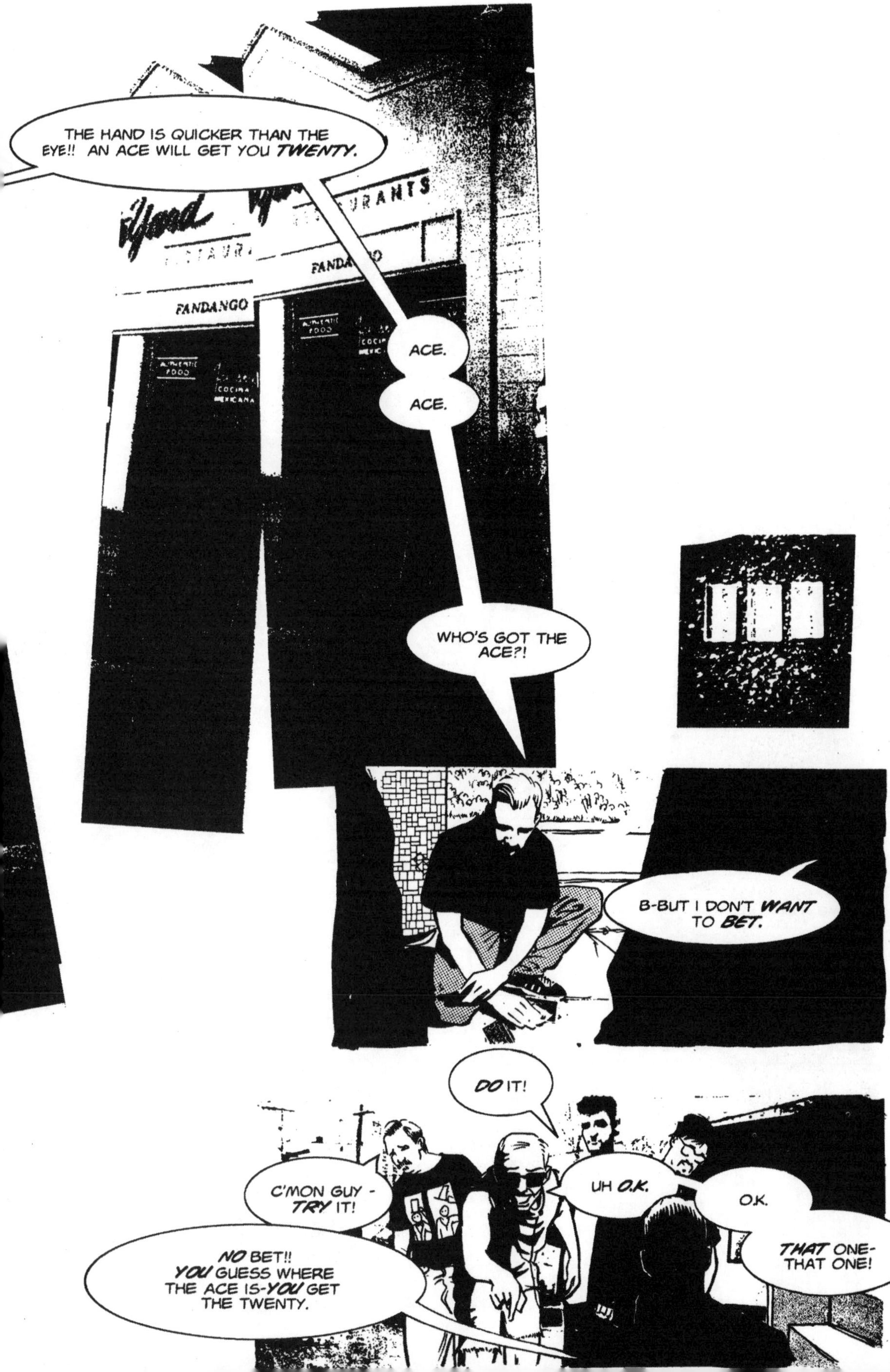
THE HAND IS QUICKER THAN THE EYE!! AN ACE WILL GET YOU *TWENTY.*
FANDANGO
ACE.
ACE.
WHO'S GOT THE ACE?!
B-BUT I DON'T *WANT* TO *BET.*
DO IT!
C'MON GUY - *TRY* IT!
UH *O.K.*
O.K.
NO BET!! *YOU* GUESS WHERE THE ACE IS-*YOU* GET THE TWENTY.
THAT ONE- THAT ONE!

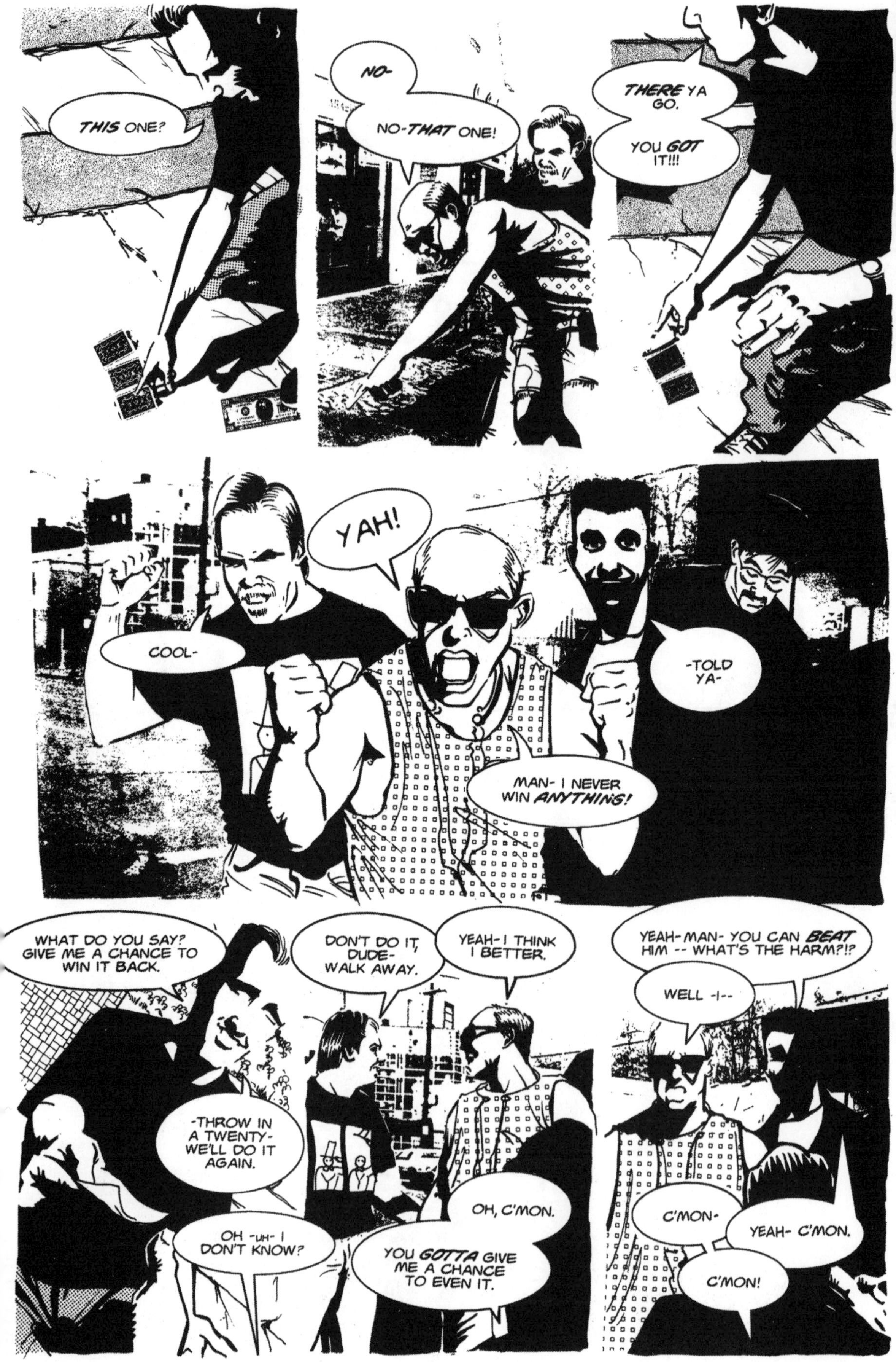
THIS ONE?
NO-
NO-THAT ONE!
THERE YA GO.
YOU GOT IT!!!
YAH!
COOL-
-TOLD YA-
MAN- I NEVER WIN ANYTHING!
WHAT DO YOU SAY? GIVE ME A CHANCE TO WIN IT BACK.
-THROW IN A TWENTY- WE'LL DO IT AGAIN.
OH -UH- I DON'T KNOW?
DON'T DO IT, DUDE- WALK AWAY.
YEAH- I THINK I BETTER.
OH, C'MON.
YOU GOTTA GIVE ME A CHANCE TO EVEN IT.
YEAH- MAN- YOU CAN BEAT HIM -- WHAT'S THE HARM?!?
WELL -I--
C'MON-
YEAH- C'MON.
C'MON!

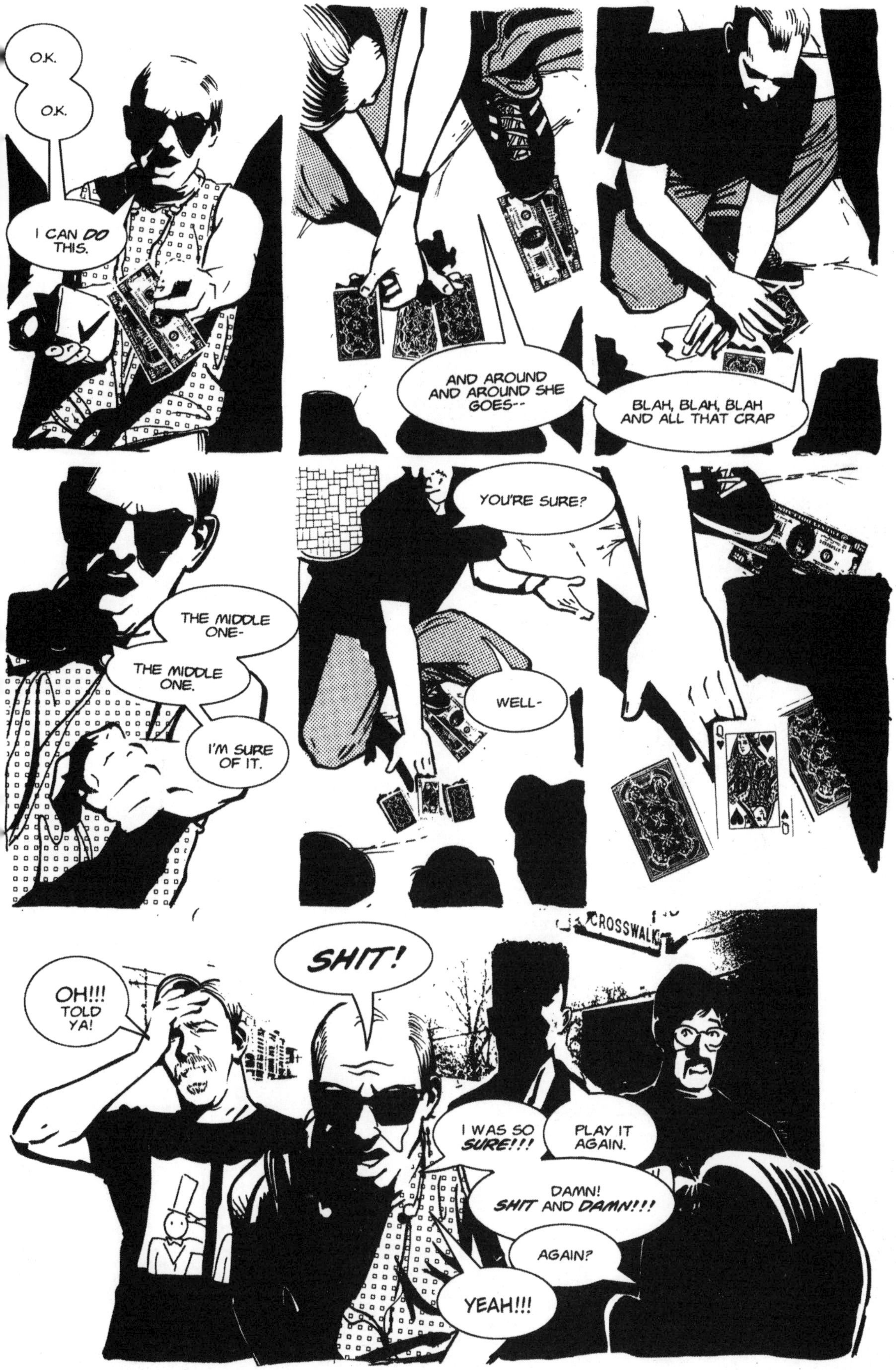
O.K.
O.K.
I CAN DO THIS.
AND AROUND AND AROUND SHE GOES--
BLAH, BLAH, BLAH AND ALL THAT CRAP
THE MIDDLE ONE-
THE MIDDLE ONE.
I'M SURE OF IT.
YOU'RE SURE?
WELL-
CROSSWALK
OH!!! TOLD YA!
SHIT!
I WAS SO SURE!!!
PLAY IT AGAIN.
DAMN! SHIT AND DAMN!!!
AGAIN?
YEAH!!!

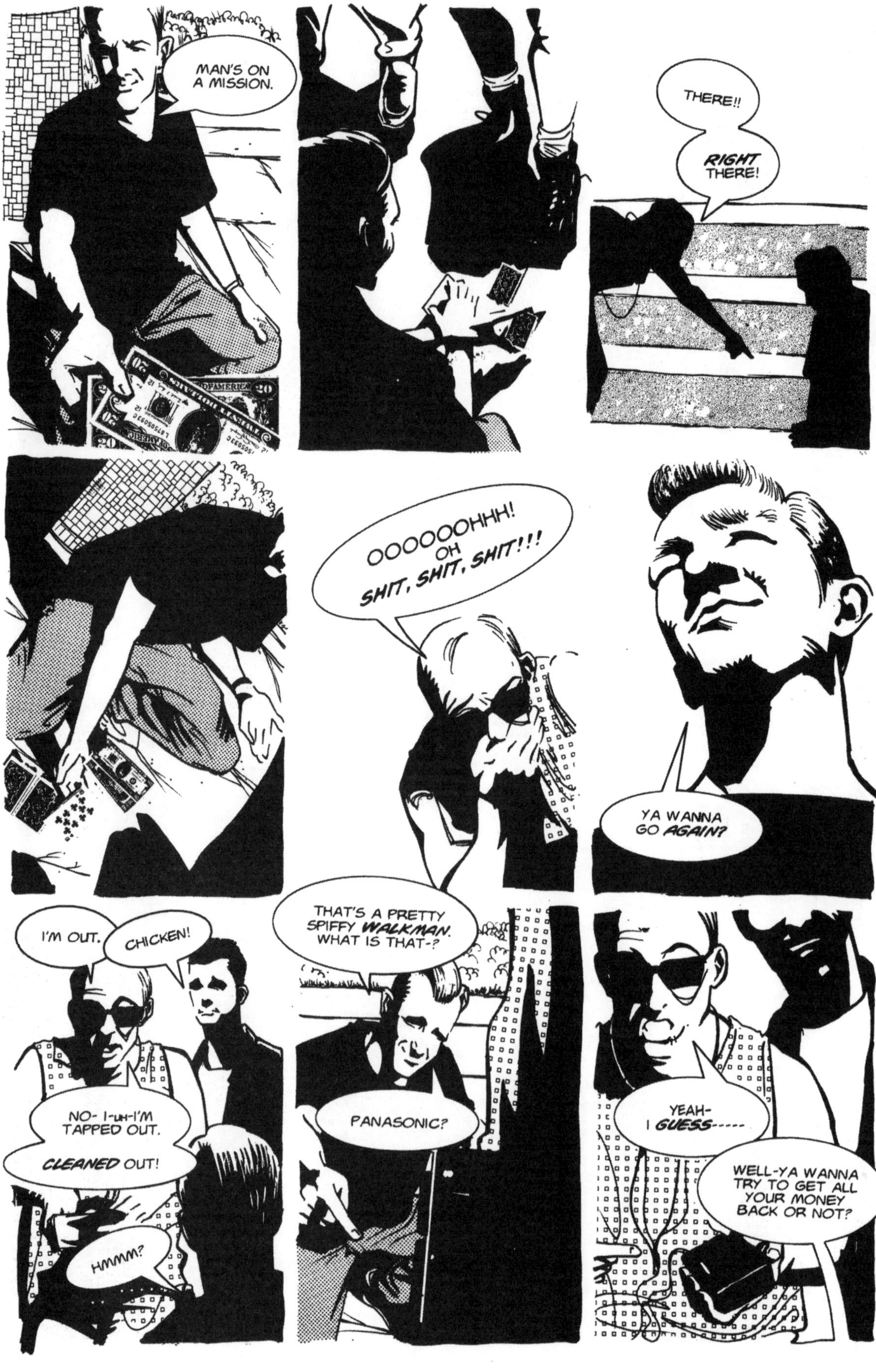
MAN'S ON A MISSION.
THERE!!
RIGHT THERE!
OOOOOOHHH! OH SHIT, SHIT, SHIT!!!
YA WANNA GO AGAIN?
I'M OUT.
CHICKEN!
NO- I-UH-I'M TAPPED OUT.
CLEANED OUT!
HMMM?
THAT'S A PRETTY SPIFFY WALKMAN. WHAT IS THAT-?
PANASONIC?
YEAH- I GUESS-----
WELL-YA WANNA TRY TO GET ALL YOUR MONEY BACK OR NOT?

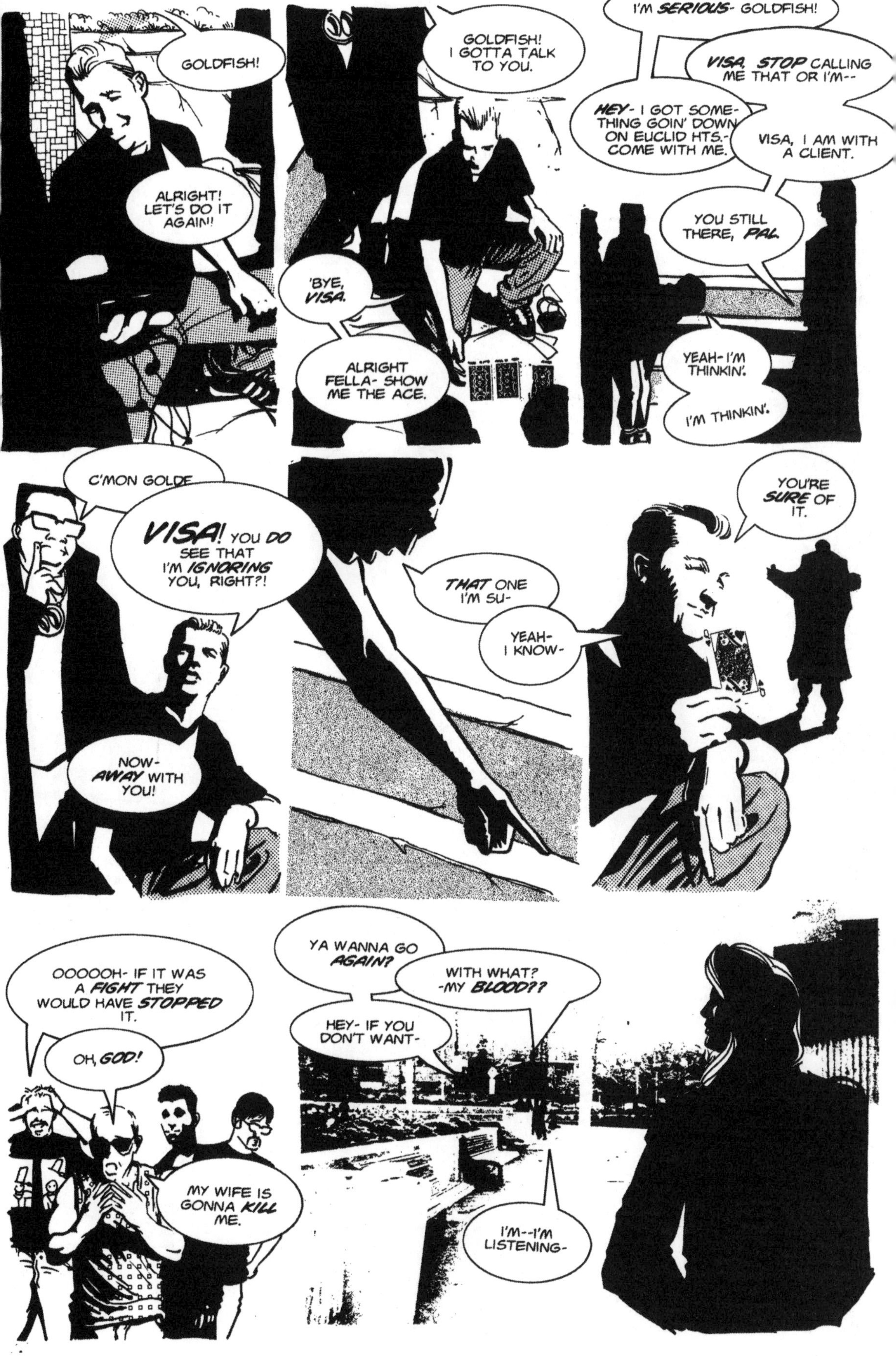
GOLDFISH!
ALRIGHT! LET'S DO IT AGAIN!
GOLDFISH! I GOTTA TALK TO YOU.
'BYE, VISA.
ALRIGHT FELLA- SHOW ME THE ACE.
I'M SERIOUS- GOLDFISH!
VISA, STOP CALLING ME THAT OR I'M--
HEY- I GOT SOMETHING GOIN' DOWN ON EUCLID HTS.- COME WITH ME.
VISA, I AM WITH A CLIENT.
YOU STILL THERE, PAL.
YEAH- I'M THINKIN'.
I'M THINKIN'.
C'MON GOLDE
VISA! YOU DO SEE THAT I'M IGNORING YOU, RIGHT?!
NOW- AWAY WITH YOU!
THAT ONE I'M SU-
YEAH- I KNOW-
YOU'RE SURE OF IT.
OOOOOH- IF IT WAS A FIGHT THEY WOULD HAVE STOPPED IT.
OH, GOD!
MY WIFE IS GONNA KILL ME.
YA WANNA GO AGAIN?
WITH WHAT? -MY BLOOD??
HEY- IF YOU DON'T WANT-
I'M--I'M LISTENING-

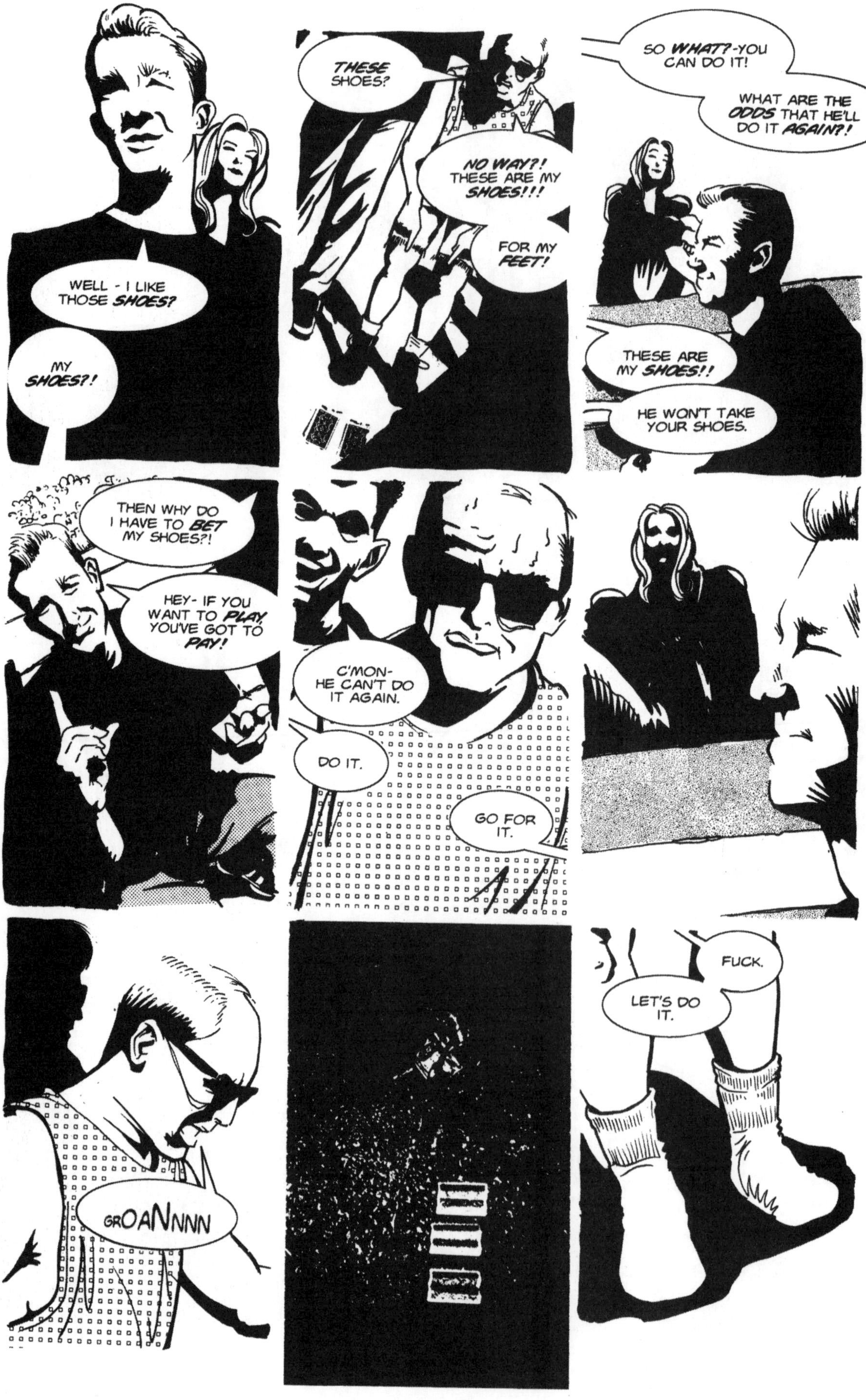
WELL - I LIKE THOSE SHOES?
MY SHOES?!
THESE SHOES?
NO WAY?! THESE ARE MY SHOES!!!
FOR MY FEET!
SO WHAT?-YOU CAN DO IT!
WHAT ARE THE ODDS THAT HE'LL DO IT AGAIN?!
THESE ARE MY SHOES!!
HE WON'T TAKE YOUR SHOES.
THEN WHY DO I HAVE TO BET MY SHOES?!
HEY- IF YOU WANT TO PLAY, YOU'VE GOT TO PAY!
C'MON- HE CAN'T DO IT AGAIN.
DO IT.
GO FOR IT.
GROANNNN
FUCK.
LET'S DO IT.

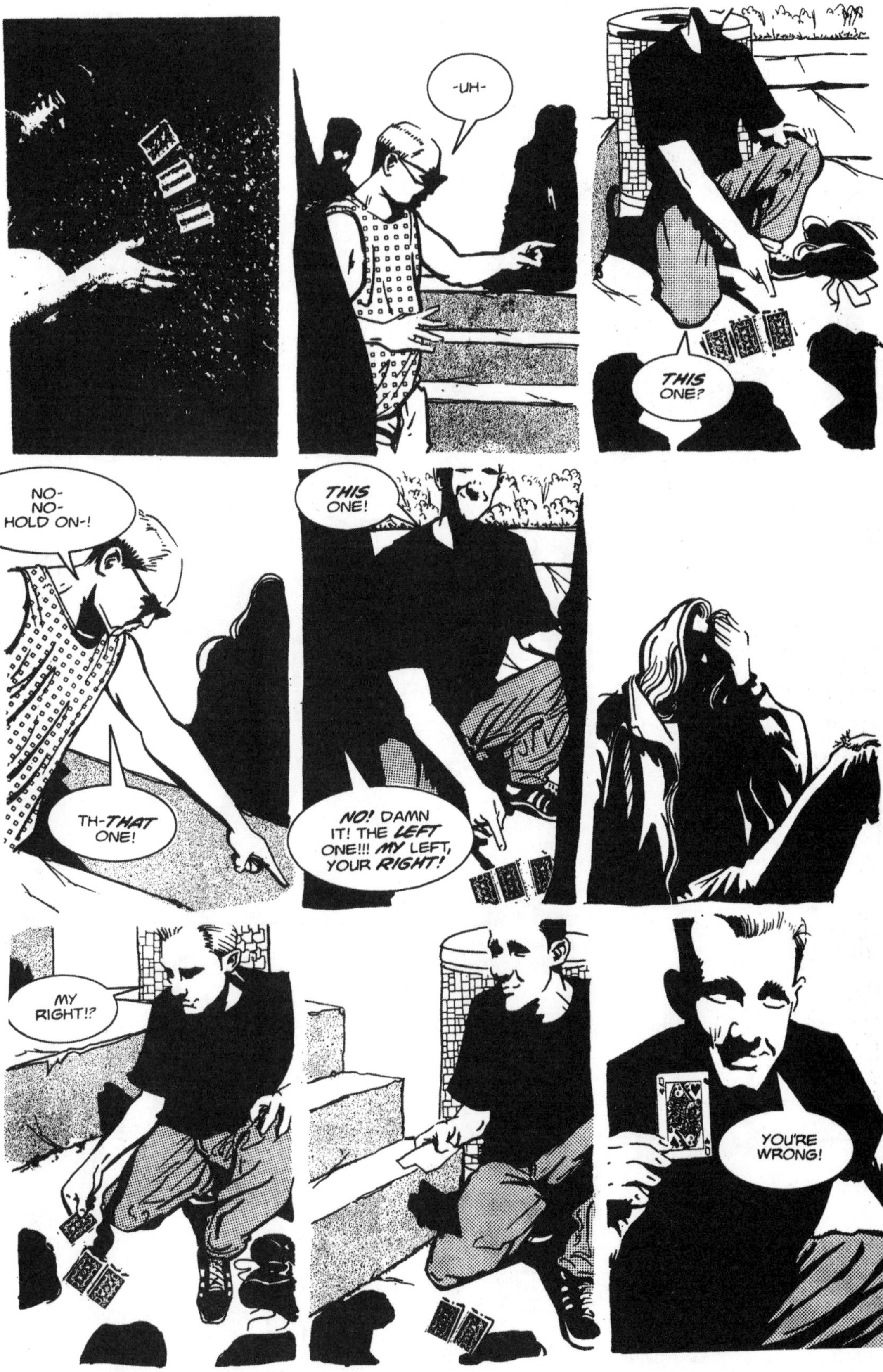
-UH-
THIS ONE?
NO- NO- HOLD ON-!
TH-THAT ONE!
THIS ONE!
NO! DAMN IT! THE LEFT ONE!!! MY LEFT, YOUR RIGHT!
MY RIGHT!?
YOU'RE WRONG!

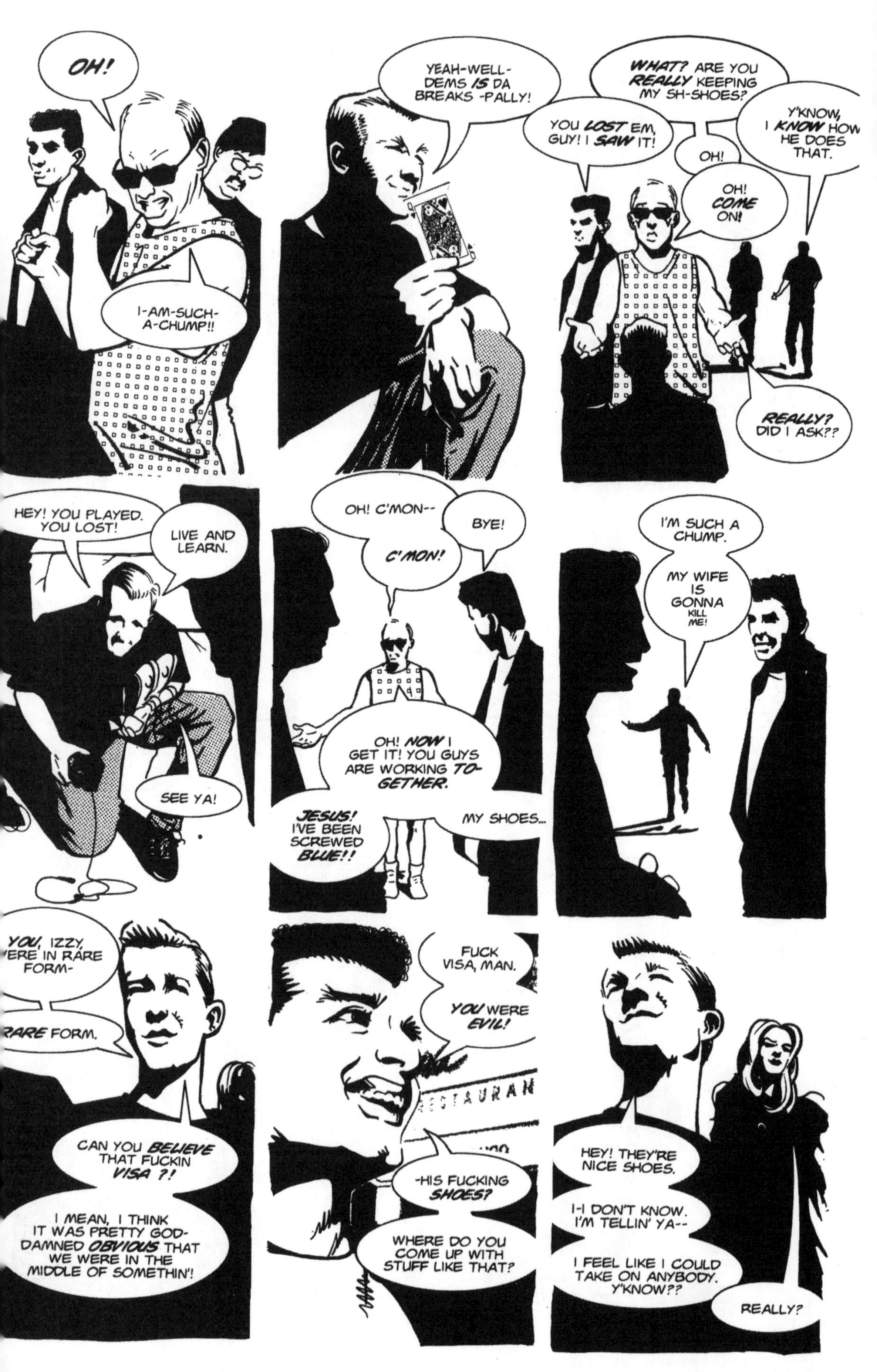

OH!
I-AM-SUCH-A-CHUMP!!
YEAH-WELL-DEMS IS DA BREAKS -PALLY!
WHAT? ARE YOU REALLY KEEPING MY SH-SHOES?
YOU LOST EM, GUY! I SAW IT!
OH!
Y'KNOW, I KNOW HOW HE DOES THAT.
OH! COME ON!
REALLY? DID I ASK??
HEY! YOU PLAYED. YOU LOST!
LIVE AND LEARN.
SEE YA!
OH! C'MON--
BYE!
C'MON!
OH! NOW I GET IT! YOU GUYS ARE WORKING TO-GETHER.
JESUS! I'VE BEEN SCREWED BLUE!!
MY SHOES...
I'M SUCH A CHUMP.
MY WIFE IS GONNA KILL ME!
YOU, IZZY, WERE IN RARE FORM-
RARE FORM.
CAN YOU BELIEVE THAT FUCKIN VISA ?!
I MEAN, I THINK IT WAS PRETTY GOD-DAMNED OBVIOUS THAT WE WERE IN THE MIDDLE OF SOMETHIN'!
FUCK VISA, MAN.
YOU WERE EVIL!
RESTAURAN
-HIS FUCKING SHOES?
WHERE DO YOU COME UP WITH STUFF LIKE THAT?
HEY! THEY'RE NICE SHOES.
I-I DON'T KNOW. I'M TELLIN' YA--
I FEEL LIKE I COULD TAKE ON ANYBODY. Y'KNOW??
REALLY?

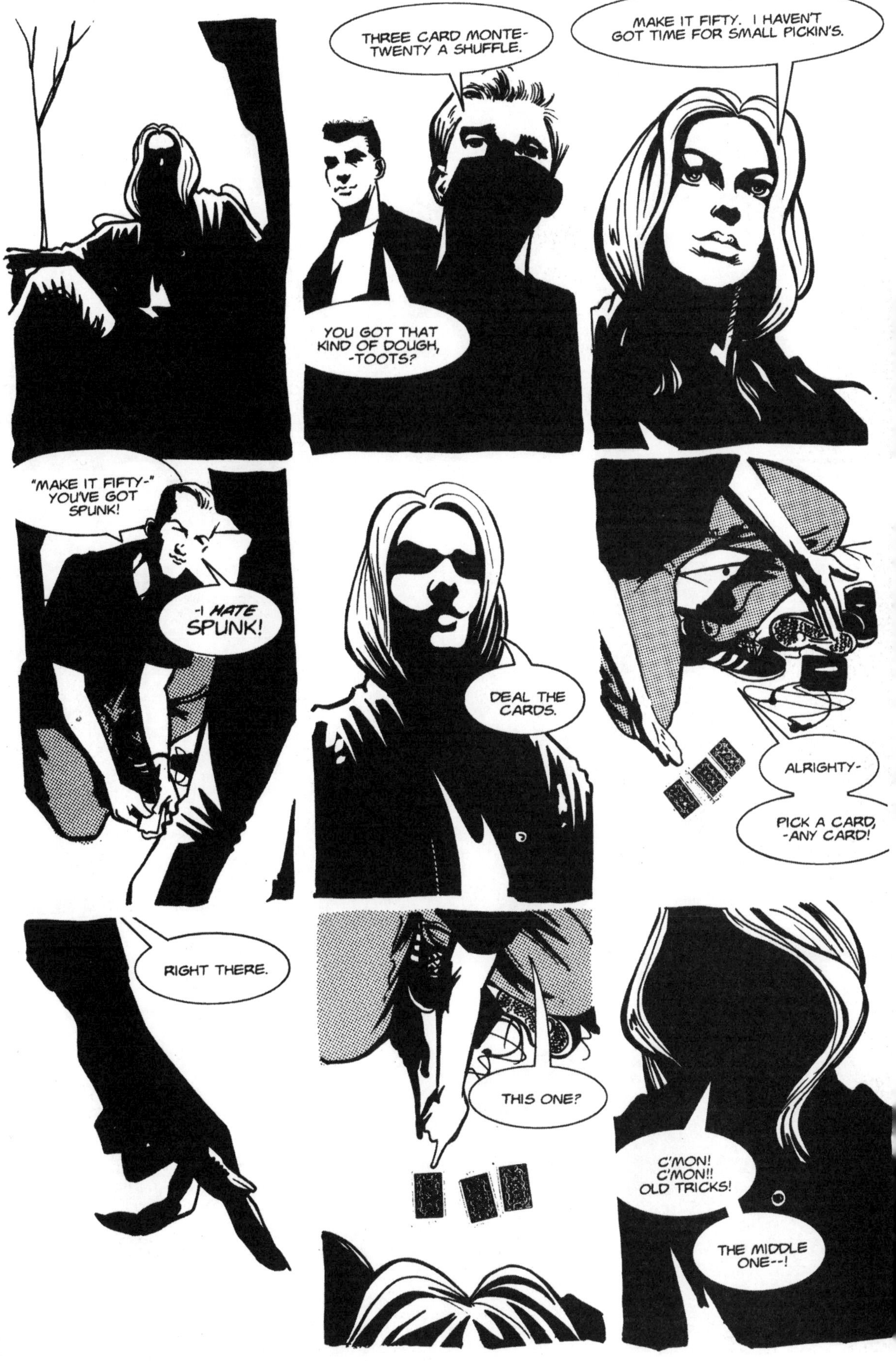
THREE CARD MONTE-
TWENTY A SHUFFLE.
YOU GOT THAT KIND OF DOUGH, -TOOTS?
MAKE IT FIFTY. I HAVEN'T GOT TIME FOR SMALL PICKIN'S.
"MAKE IT FIFTY-" YOU'VE GOT SPUNK!
-I HATE SPUNK!
DEAL THE CARDS.
ALRIGHTY-
PICK A CARD, -ANY CARD!
RIGHT THERE.
THIS ONE?
C'MON! C'MON!! OLD TRICKS!
THE MIDDLE ONE--!

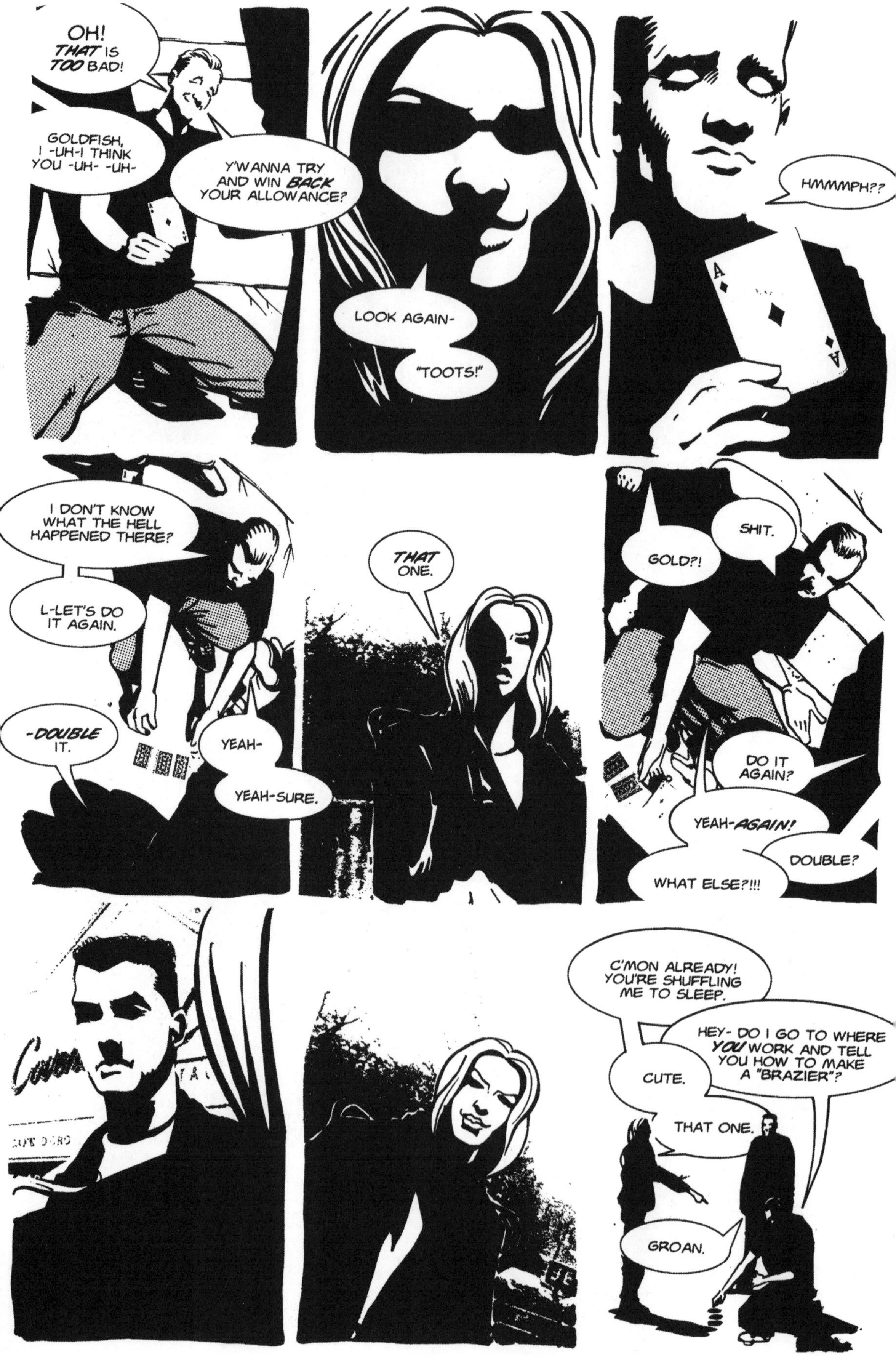
OH! THAT IS TOO BAD!
GOLDFISH, I -UH-I THINK YOU -UH- -UH-
Y'WANNA TRY AND WIN BACK YOUR ALLOWANCE?
LOOK AGAIN-
"TOOTS!"
HMMMPH??
I DON'T KNOW WHAT THE HELL HAPPENED THERE?
L-LET'S DO IT AGAIN.
-DOUBLE IT.
YEAH-
YEAH-SURE.
THAT ONE.
GOLD?!
SHIT.
DO IT AGAIN?
YEAH-AGAIN!
DOUBLE?
WHAT ELSE?!!!
C'MON ALREADY! YOU'RE SHUFFLING ME TO SLEEP.
HEY- DO I GO TO WHERE YOU WORK AND TELL YOU HOW TO MAKE A "BRAZIER"?
CUTE.
THAT ONE.
GROAN.

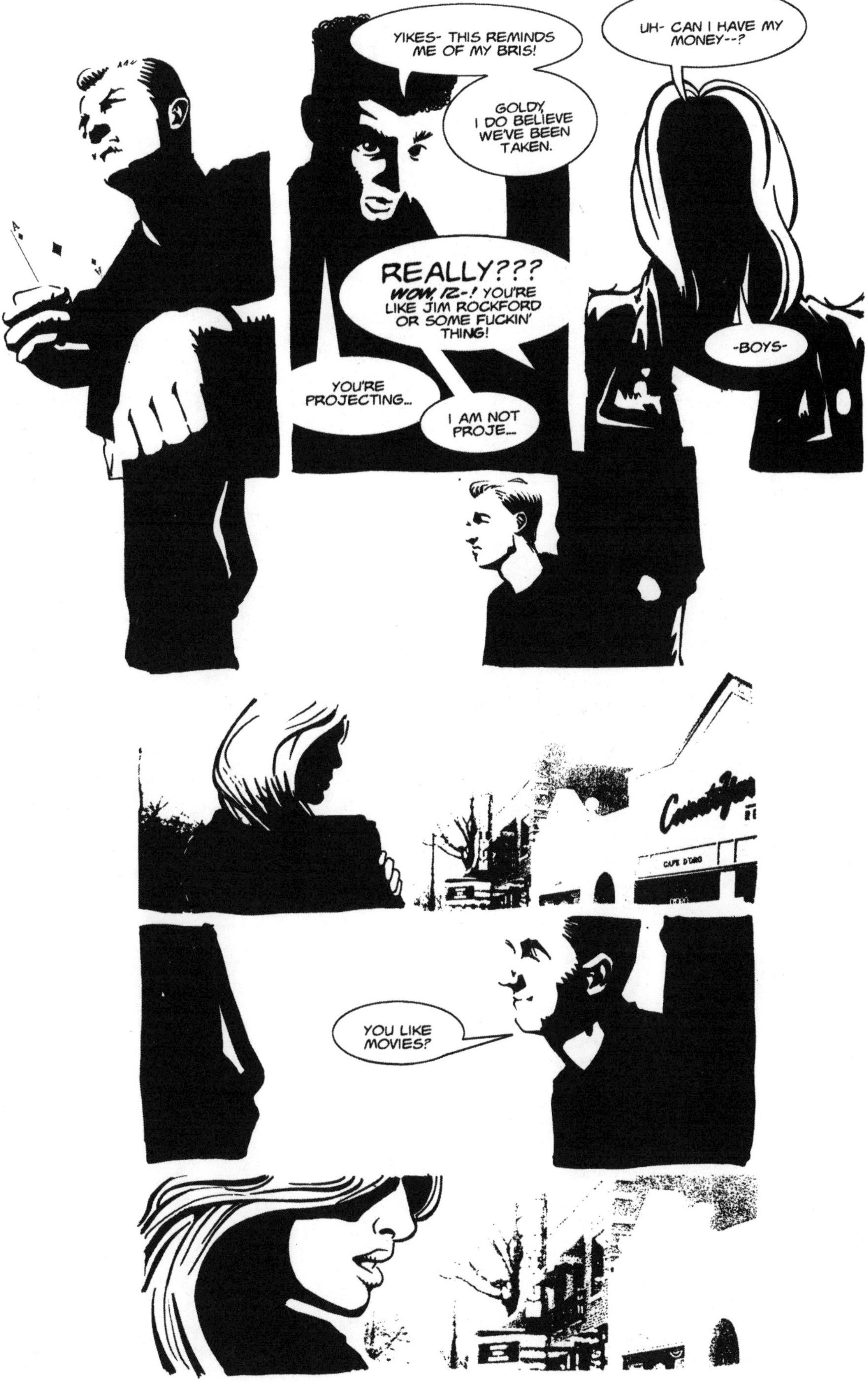
YIKES- THIS REMINDS ME OF MY BRIS!
GOLDY, I DO BELIEVE WE'VE BEEN TAKEN.
UH- CAN I HAVE MY MONEY--?
REALLY??? WOW, IZ-! YOU'RE LIKE JIM ROCKFORD OR SOME FUCKIN' THING!
-BOYS-
YOU'RE PROJECTING...
I AM NOT PROJE...
CAFE D'ORO
YOU LIKE MOVIES?

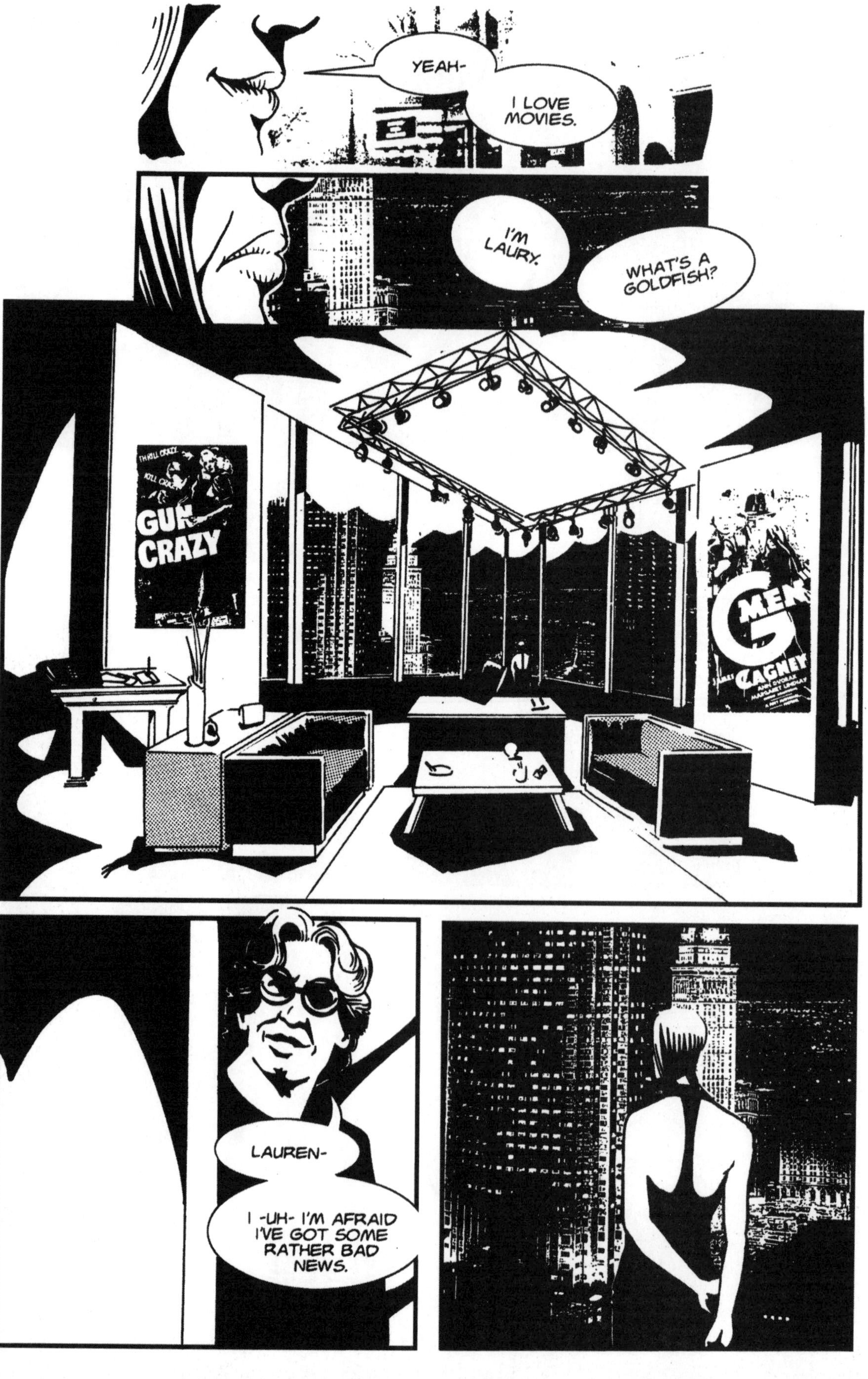
YEAH-
I LOVE MOVIES.
I'M LAURY.
WHAT'S A GOLDFISH?
GUN CRAZY
G MEN
CAGNEY
LAUREN-
I -UH- I'M AFRAID I'VE GOT SOME RATHER BAD NEWS.
...

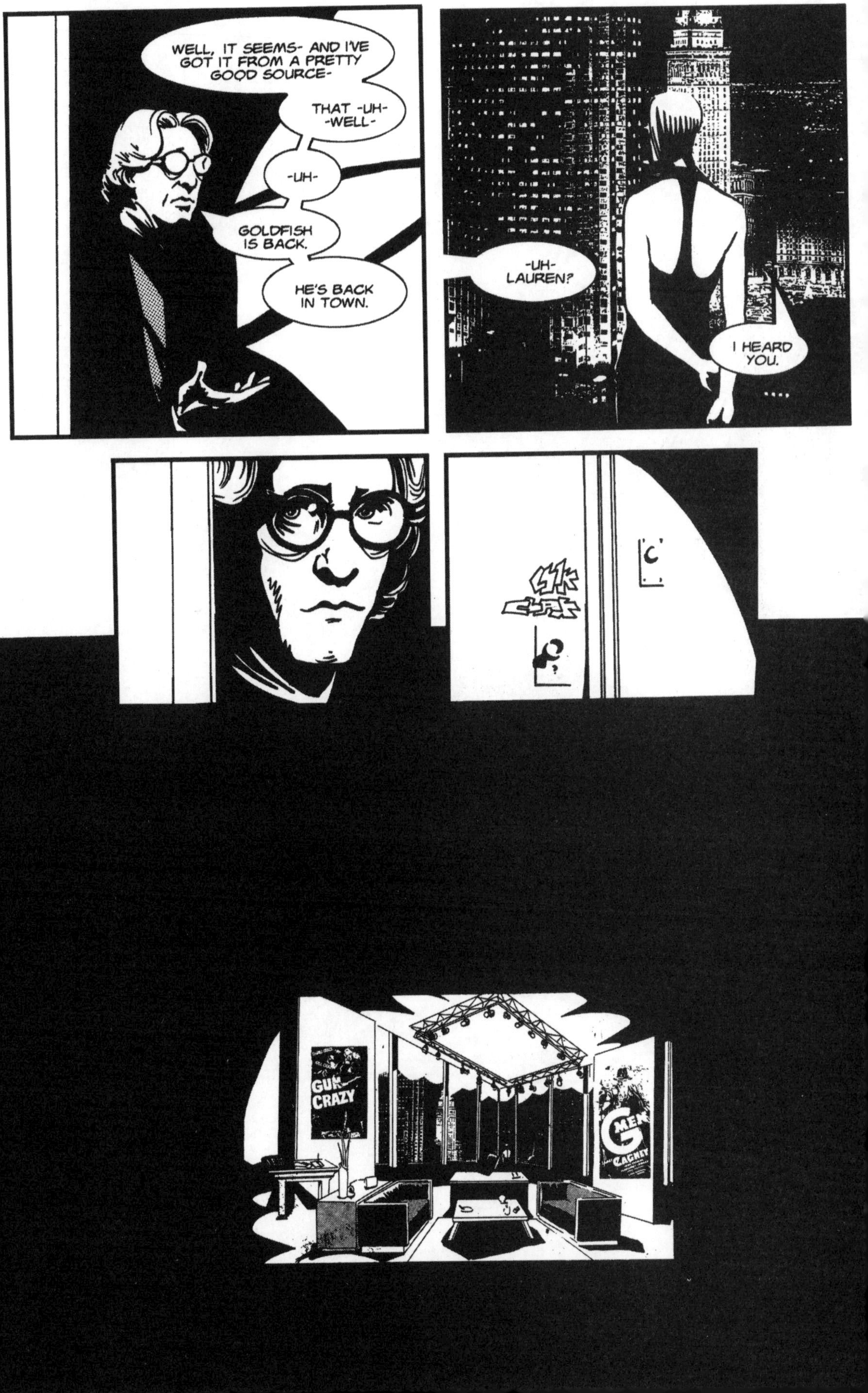

WELL, IT SEEMS- AND I'VE GOT IT FROM A PRETTY GOOD SOURCE-
THAT -UH- -WELL-
-UH-
GOLDFISH IS BACK.
HE'S BACK IN TOWN.
-UH- LAUREN?
I HEARD YOU.
GUN CRAZY
G MEN
CAGNEY

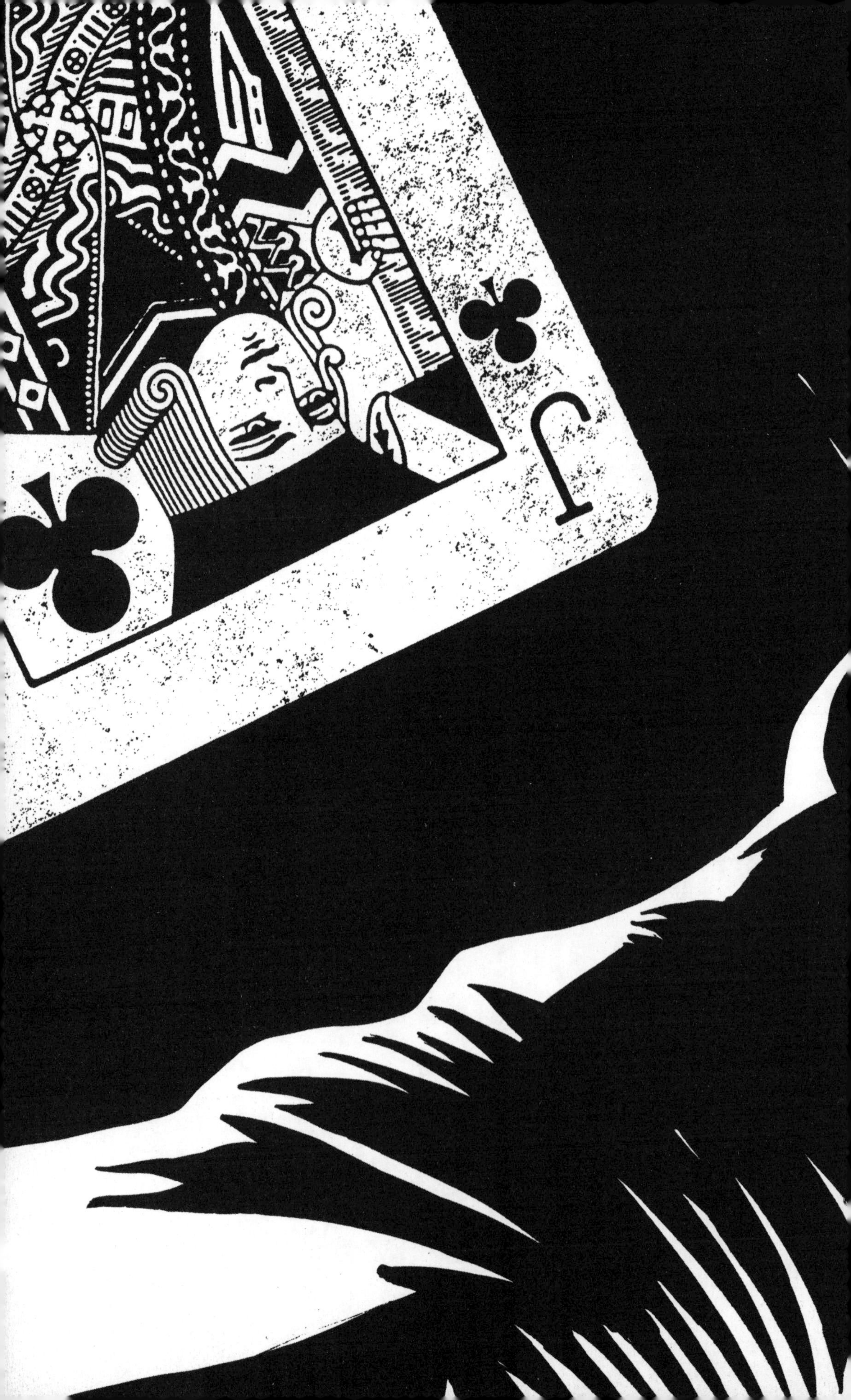

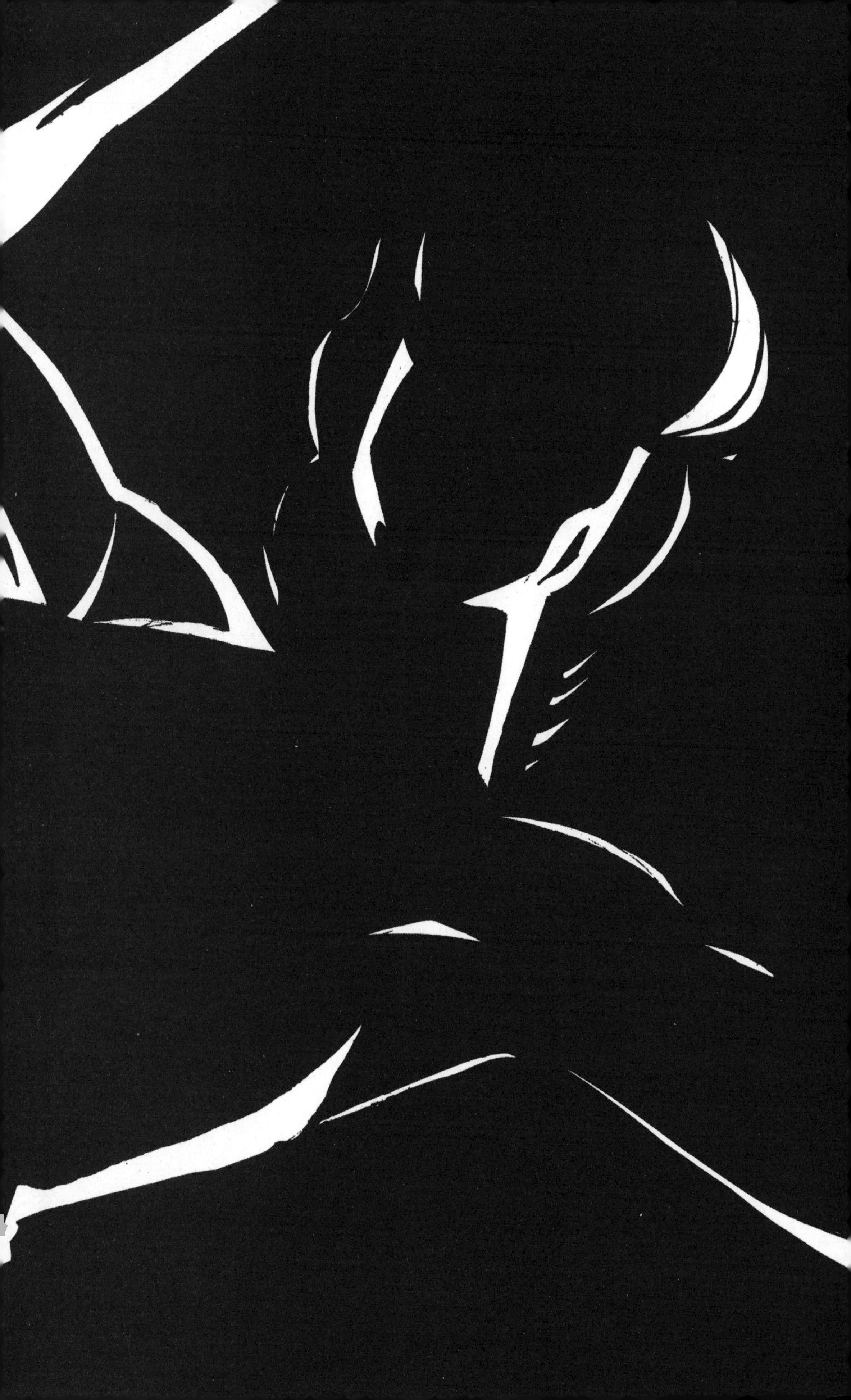

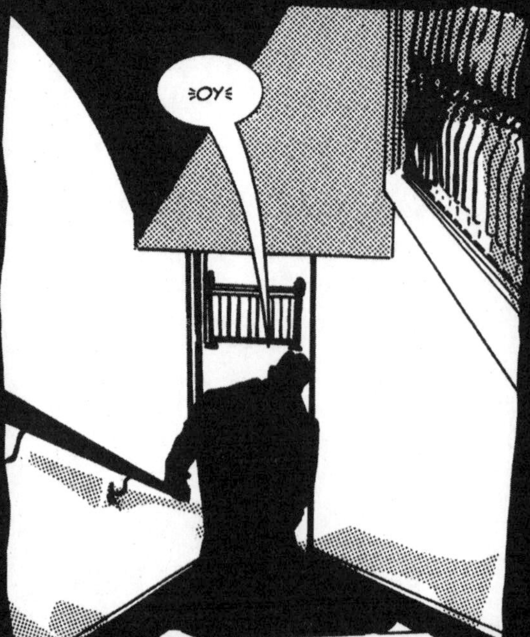
OY

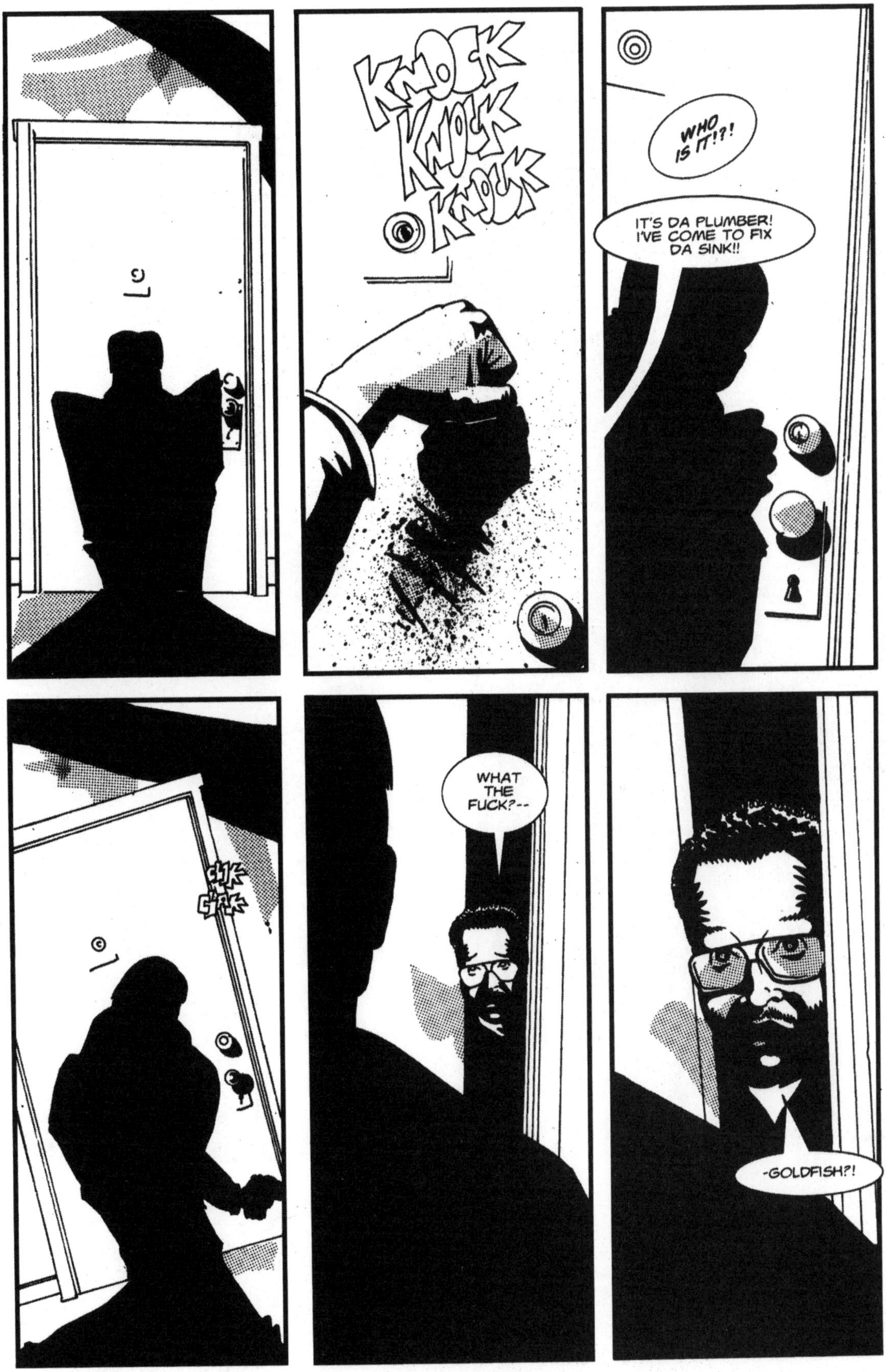
KNOCK
KNOCK
KNOCK
WHO IS IT!?!
IT'S DA PLUMBER! I'VE COME TO FIX DA SINK!!
CLIK
WHAT THE FUCK?--
-GOLDFISH?!

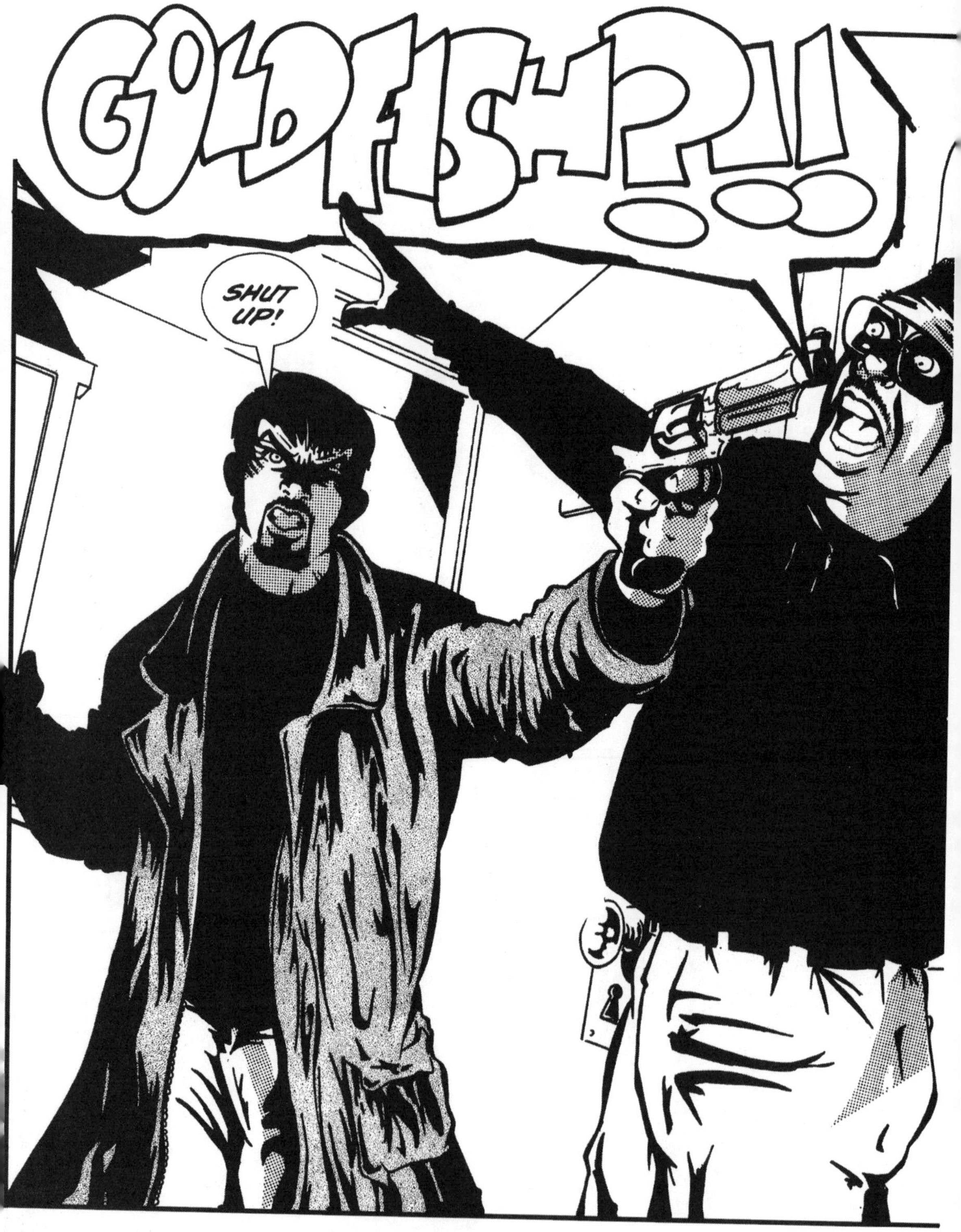
GOLDFISH?!!
SHUT UP!

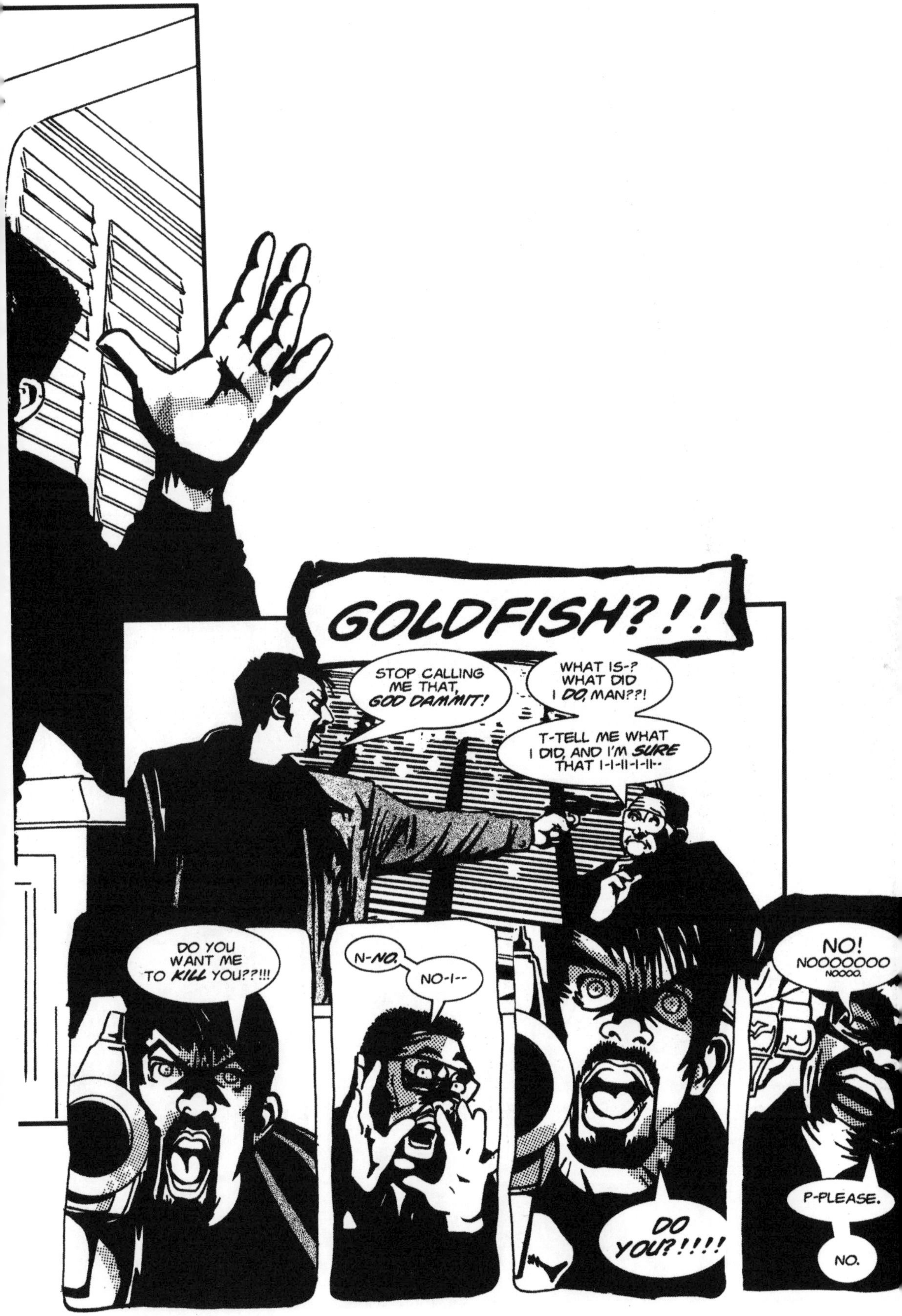
GOLDFISH?!!
STOP CALLING ME THAT, GOD DAMMIT!
WHAT IS-? WHAT DID I DO, MAN??!
T-TELL ME WHAT I DID, AND I'M SURE THAT I-I-II-I-II--
DO YOU WANT ME TO KILL YOU??!!!
N-NO,
NO-I--
DO YOU?!!!!
NO! NOOOOOOO NOOOO.
P-PLEASE.
NO.

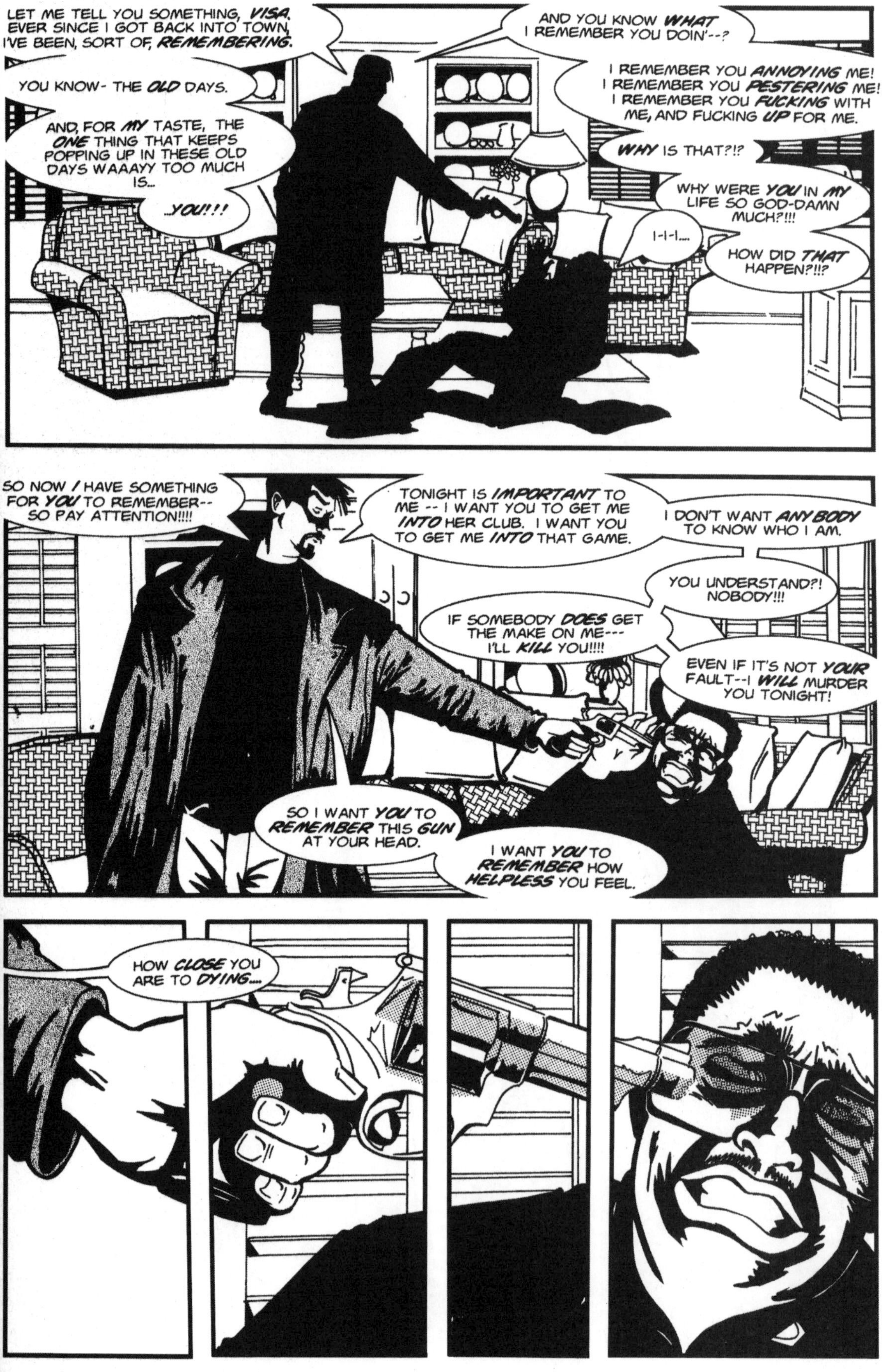
LET ME TELL YOU SOMETHING, VISA. EVER SINCE I GOT BACK INTO TOWN, I'VE BEEN, SORT OF, REMEMBERING.
YOU KNOW- THE OLD DAYS.
AND, FOR MY TASTE, THE ONE THING THAT KEEPS POPPING UP IN THESE OLD DAYS WAAAYY TOO MUCH IS...
...YOU!!!
AND YOU KNOW WHAT I REMEMBER YOU DOIN'--?
I REMEMBER YOU ANNOYING ME! I REMEMBER YOU PESTERING ME! I REMEMBER YOU FUCKING WITH ME, AND FUCKING UP FOR ME.
WHY IS THAT?!?
WHY WERE YOU IN MY LIFE SO GOD-DAMN MUCH?!!!
I-I-I....
HOW DID THAT HAPPEN?!!?
SO NOW I HAVE SOMETHING FOR YOU TO REMEMBER-- SO PAY ATTENTION!!!!
TONIGHT IS IMPORTANT TO ME -- I WANT YOU TO GET ME INTO HER CLUB. I WANT YOU TO GET ME INTO THAT GAME.
I DON'T WANT ANYBODY TO KNOW WHO I AM.
YOU UNDERSTAND?! NOBODY!!!
IF SOMEBODY DOES GET THE MAKE ON ME--- I'LL KILL YOU!!!!
EVEN IF IT'S NOT YOUR FAULT--I WILL MURDER YOU TONIGHT!
SO I WANT YOU TO REMEMBER THIS GUN AT YOUR HEAD.
I WANT YOU TO REMEMBER HOW HELPLESS YOU FEEL.
HOW CLOSE YOU ARE TO DYING....

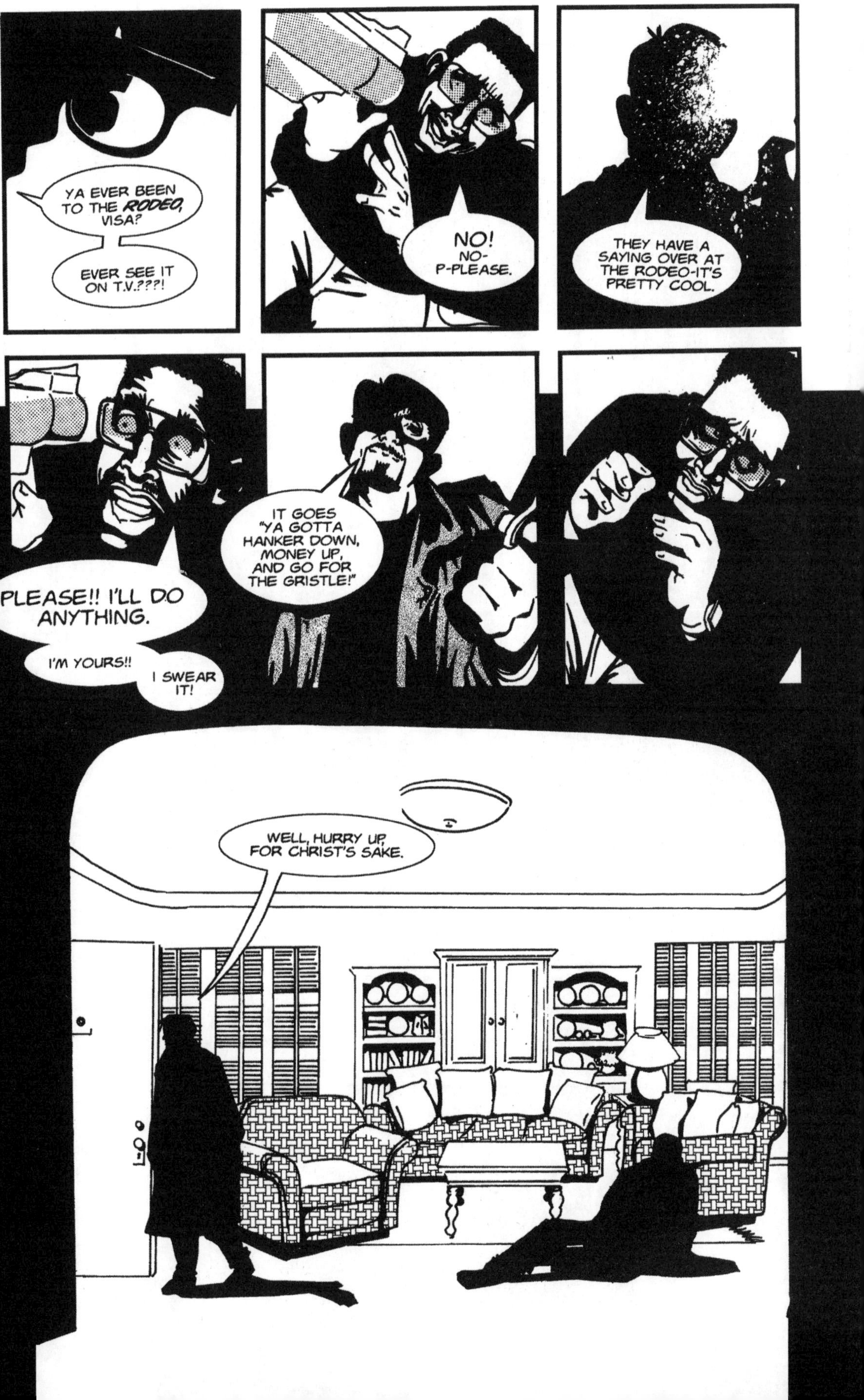
YA EVER BEEN TO THE RODEO, VISA?
EVER SEE IT ON T.V.???!
NO! NO- P-PLEASE.
THEY HAVE A SAYING OVER AT THE RODEO-IT'S PRETTY COOL.
PLEASE!! I'LL DO ANYTHING.
I'M YOURS!!
I SWEAR IT!
IT GOES "YA GOTTA HANKER DOWN, MONEY UP, AND GO FOR THE GRISTLE!"
WELL, HURRY UP, FOR CHRIST'S SAKE.

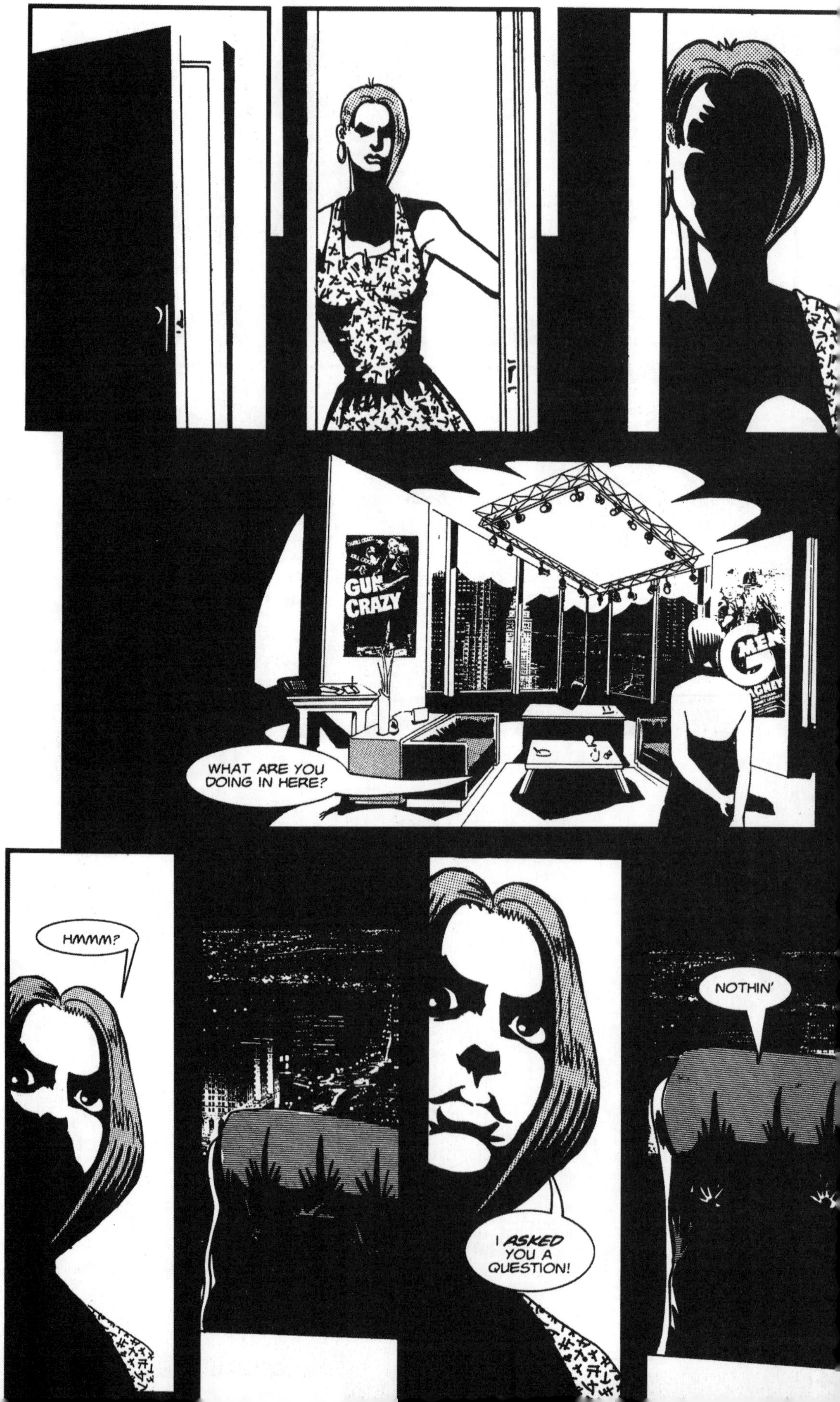
GUN CRAZY
G MEN
WHAT ARE YOU DOING IN HERE?
HMMM?
NOTHIN'
I ASKED YOU A QUESTION!

LET ME TELL YOU A STORY--

WHEN I WAS A LITTLE GIRL, REALLY, JUST A KID-

-I USED TO SPEND ONE WEEKEND A MONTH WITH MY *GRANDMA*.

I DON'T KNOW *WHY*. I GUESS MY PARENTS JUST GOT *SICK* OF ME.

ANYHOW, MY GRAM S WAS WHAT YOU'D CALL ONE OF THE REAL *OLD-TIME* MOB-GIRLS, ACTUALLY, SHE WAS SORT OF A *GROUNDBREAKER*, IN HER OWN WAY.

KIDS KNOW STUFF!! THEY PAY ATTENTION. MOST PEOPLE- MOST *ADULTS*-LIKE TO FEEL SUPERIOR, SO THEY JUST *IGNORE* LITTLE CHILDREN.

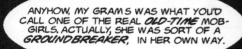

MY PARENTS, THE INCORRIGIBLE *SAPS* THAT THEY WERE, DIDN'T THINK I *KNEW* ABOUT GRAM'S ILLUSTRIOUS PAST. BUT I *DID*.

NOW GRAM S WASN'T *STILL* A BIG-TIME SMOKE. SHE'D GOTTEN UP IN THE YEARS, Y'KNOW?

BUT SHE *WAS* STILL-WHAT YOU'D CALL--

-IN!

SO, SATURDAY AFTERNOONS, SHE WOULD *DRINK* HERSELF INTO A *COMA* ON KEDEM, OR MANICHEVITZ, OR SOME OTHER CHEAP, CRAP, JEW WINE.

WHILE SHE SLEPT IT OFF, I'D SNEAK INTO HER CLOSETS AND TRY ON ALL OF HER OLD CLOTHES AND STUFF.

I'D PUT ON HER FLAPPER DRESSES AND SILLY HATS.

PEARLS.

I'D CLOMP AROUND IN HER GIANT HIGH HEEL SHOES AND I'D *PRETEND* I WAS *THERE.*

WORKING THE CROWD LIKE GRANDMA USED TO.

THEN ONE DAY-

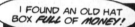

I FOUND AN OLD HAT BOX *FULL* OF *MONEY!*

PIN MONEY.

GRAM'S *STASH.* HER SOCIAL SECURITY.

AND I'M TELLIN' YA- THIS BOX WAS *FULL!!*

SO EVERY SATURDAY FOR *YEARS,* I WOULD GO UP INTO THAT CLOSET AND OPEN THAT HAT BOX AND JUST *BE* WITH THIS MAGNIFICENT TREASURE!

I WOULD JUST *SIT* THERE AND *INHALE* THAT OLD MONEY SMELL.

ON MY MORE ADVENTUROUS DAYS, I WOULD HOLD WADS OF IT IN MY LITTLE *FISTS!*

IT GOT TO THE POINT WHERE I THOUGHT ABOUT NOTHING ELSE.

I WOULD *DAYDREAM* AT SCHOOL ABOUT IT. I WOULD *SPEND* IT IN MY HEAD OVER AND OVER AGAIN.

AND EVEN THOUGH MY TEMPTATION -- GREATER THAN ANY I'D *EVER* KNOWN...

I *NEVER* TOOK ONE DOLLAR *OUT* OF THAT BOX.

Y'KNOW *WHY?* BECAUSE I KNEW IF I *DID*-MY GRAM'S WOULD *KNOW.*

AND IF I WAS *LUCKY*- SHE'D BREAK MY ARM.

SHE'D BREAK MY ARM RIGHT IN *HALF* -AND TELL MY PARENTS I TRIPPED AND FELL DOWN THE STAIRS OR SOME FUCKING THING!

-AND IT WOULDN'T MATTER IF I GOT UP THE NERVE TO TELL ON HER OR NOT--

-NOBODY LISTENS TO LITTLE KIDS.

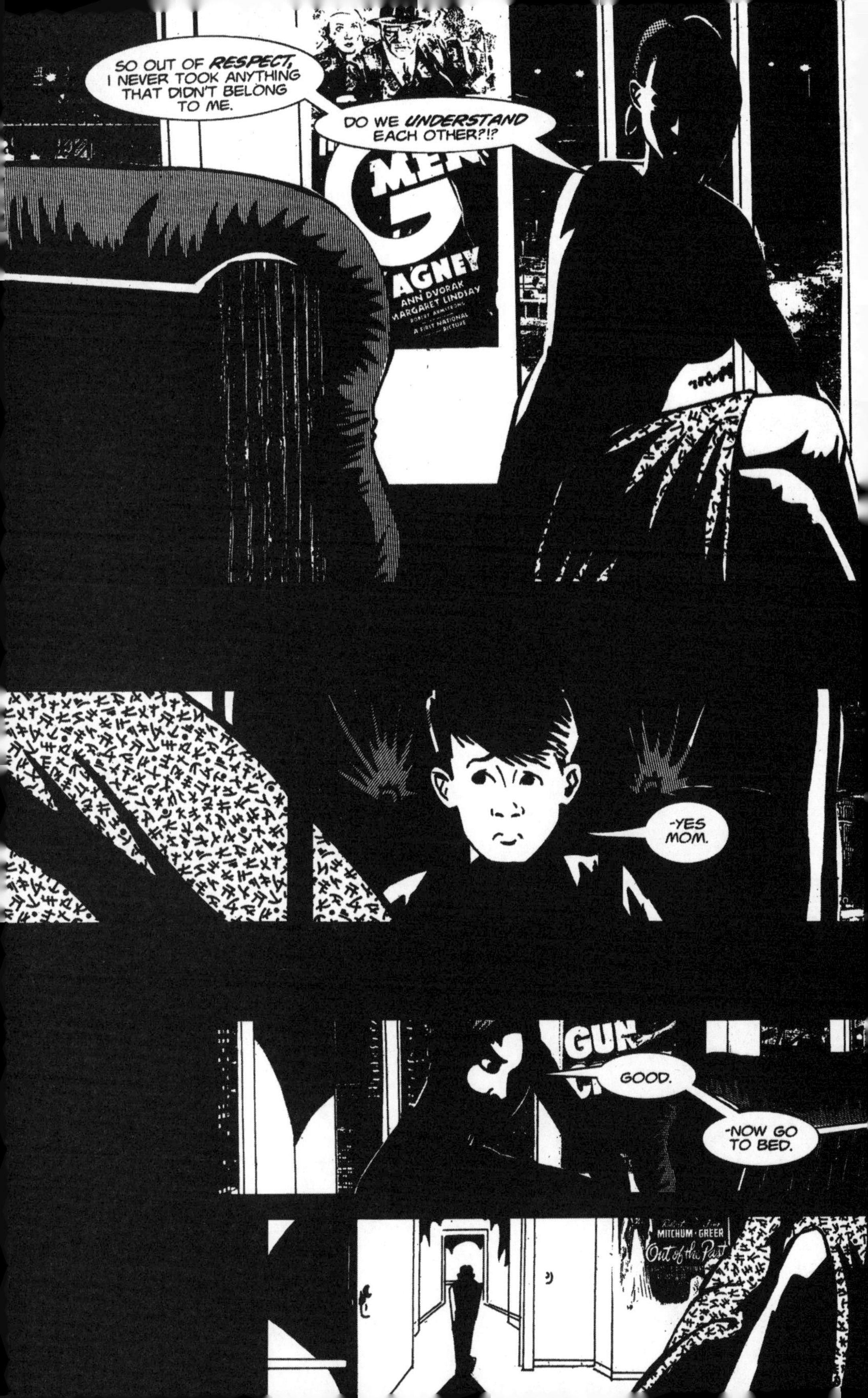
SO OUT OF *RESPECT*, I NEVER TOOK ANYTHING THAT DIDN'T BELONG TO ME.
DO WE *UNDERSTAND* EACH OTHER?!?
MEN
AGNEY
ANN DVORAK
MARGARET LINDSAY
-YES MOM.
GUN
GOOD.
-NOW GO TO BED.
MITCHUM · GREER
Out of the Past

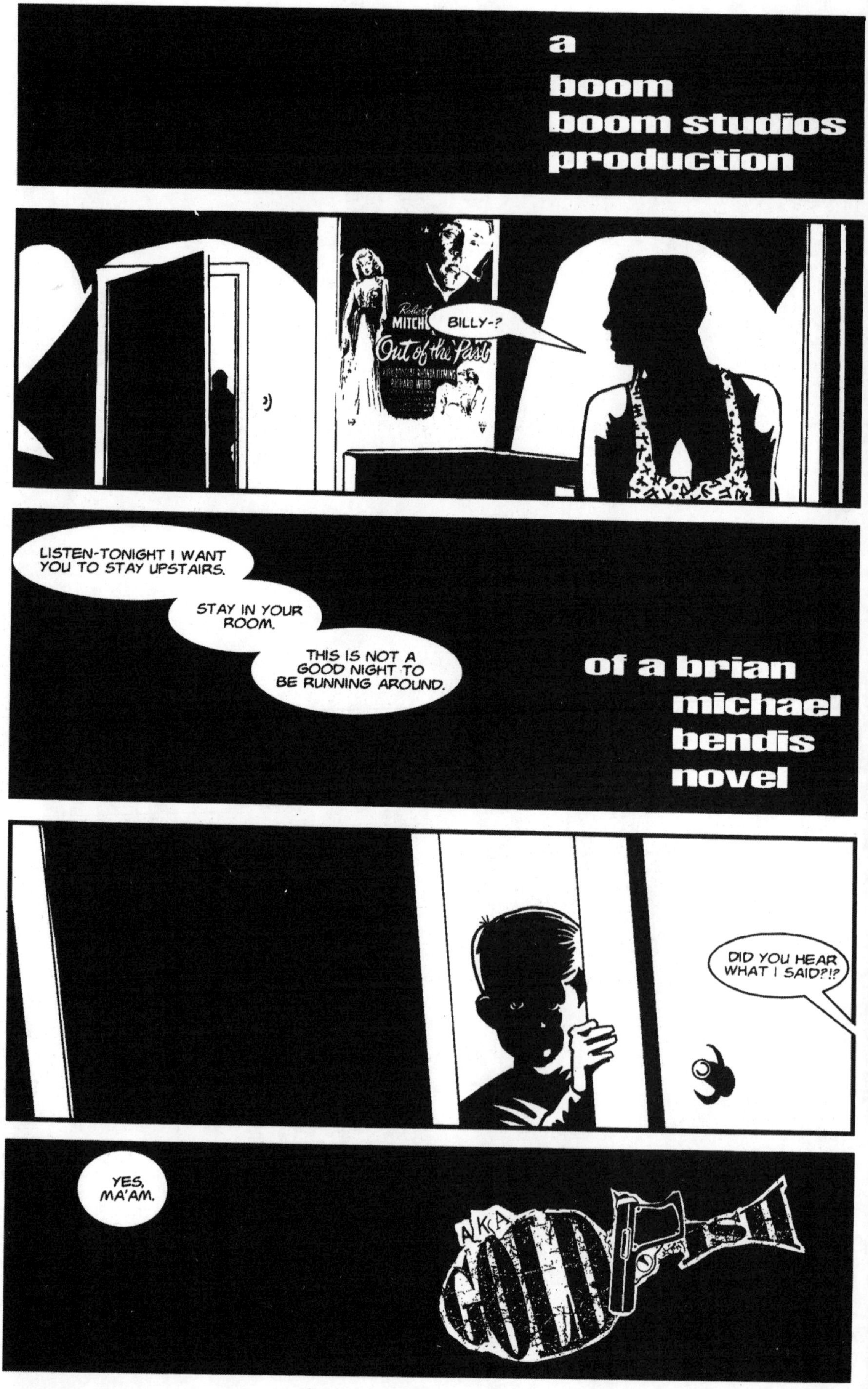
a
boom
boom studios
production
Out of the Past
BILLY-?
LISTEN-TONIGHT I WANT YOU TO STAY UPSTAIRS.
STAY IN YOUR ROOM.
THIS IS NOT A GOOD NIGHT TO BE RUNNING AROUND.
of a brian
michael
bendis
novel
DID YOU HEAR WHAT I SAID?!?
YES, MA'AM.
AKA

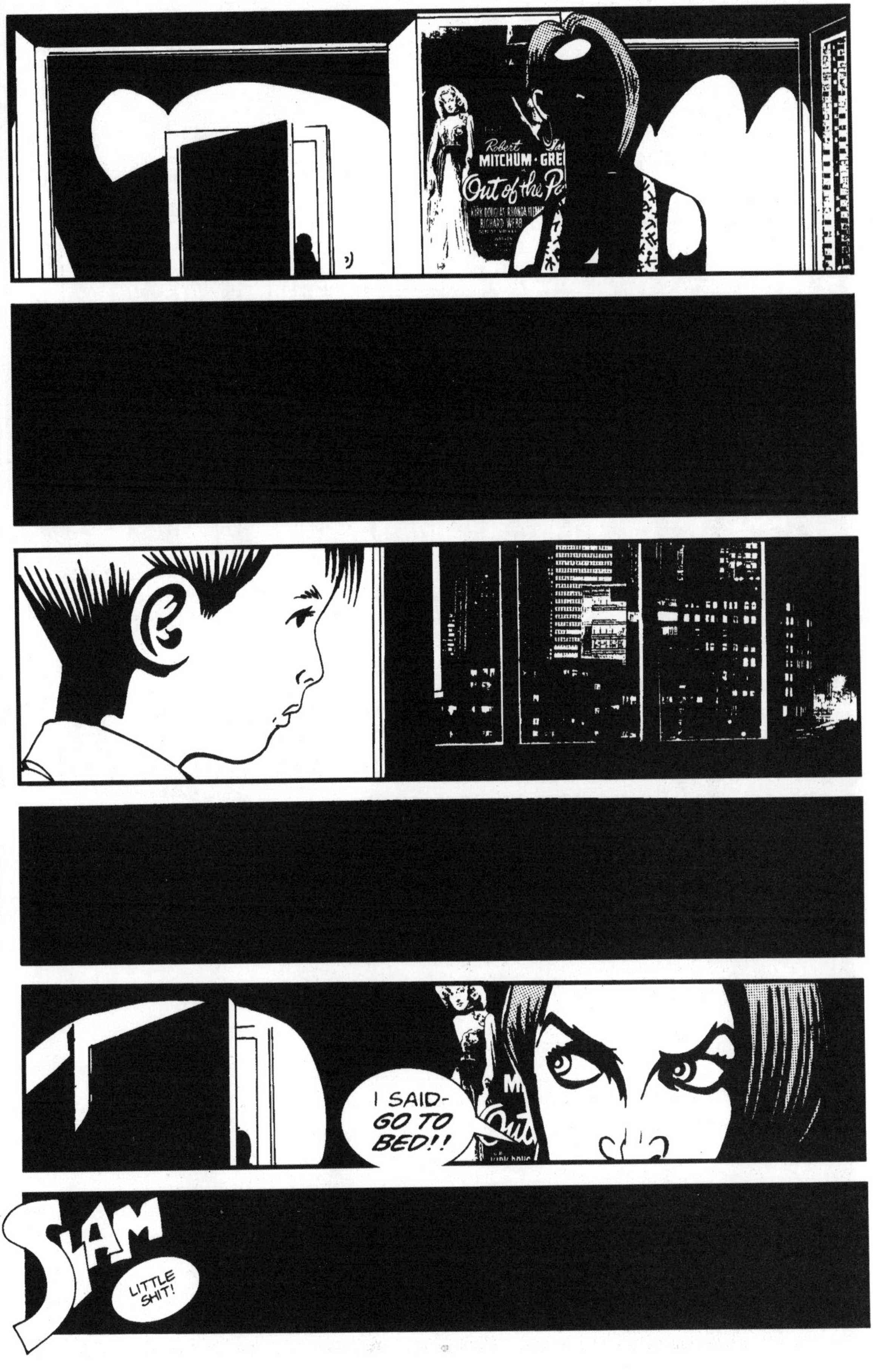

Robert
MITCHUM
KIRK DOUGLAS
RICHARD WEBB
I SAID- GO TO BED!!
SLAM
LITTLE SHIT!

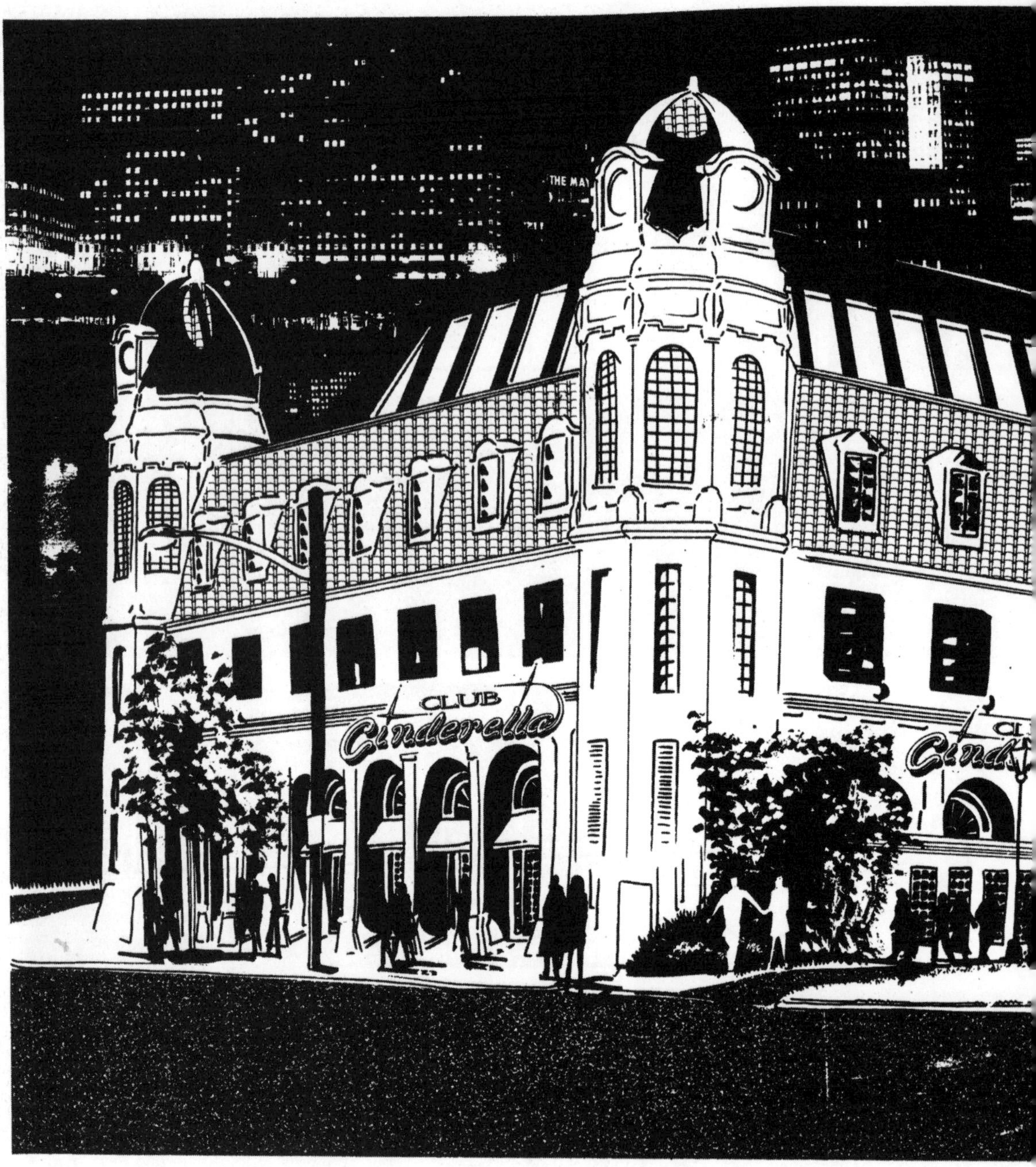
CLUB
Cinderella

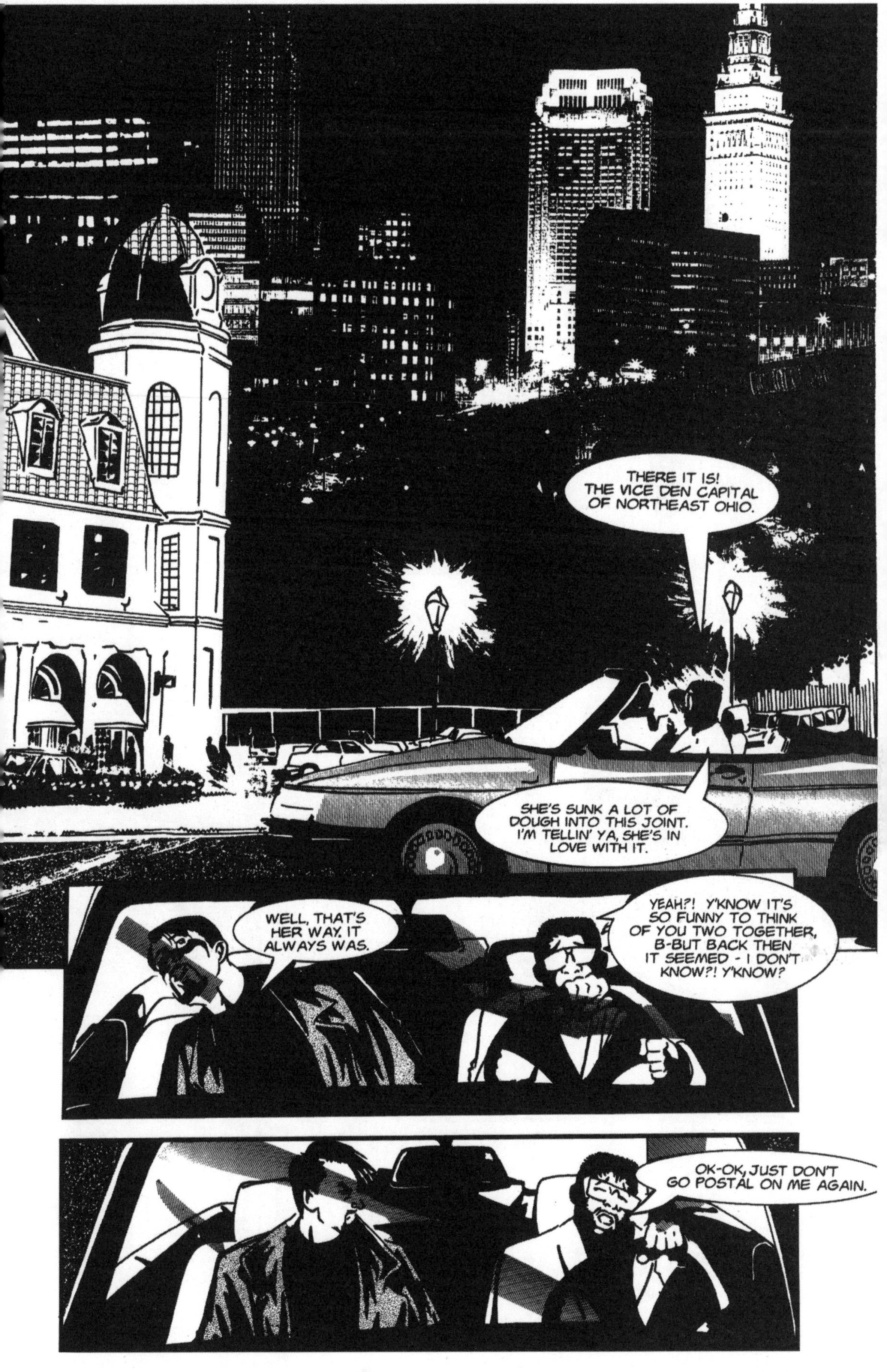
THERE IT IS! THE VICE DEN CAPITAL OF NORTHEAST OHIO.
SHE'S SUNK A LOT OF DOUGH INTO THIS JOINT. I'M TELLIN' YA, SHE'S IN LOVE WITH IT.
WELL, THAT'S HER WAY. IT ALWAYS WAS.
YEAH?! Y'KNOW IT'S SO FUNNY TO THINK OF YOU TWO TOGETHER, B-BUT BACK THEN IT SEEMED - I DON'T KNOW?! Y'KNOW?
OK-OK, JUST DON'T GO POSTAL ON ME AGAIN.

Speech bubbles: "HEY! THIS IS *NICE*, BUT IT ISN'T ALL THAT!" "WELL-THIS IS JUST THE CLUB-" "WHA-?"

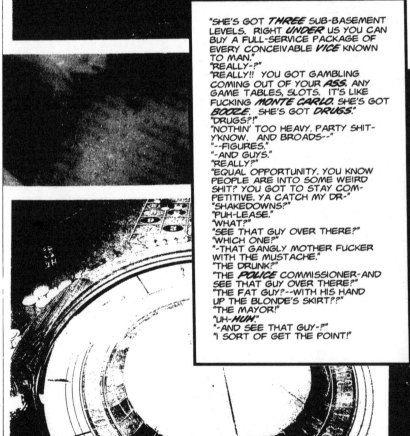

"SHE'S GOT *THREE* SUB-BASEMENT LEVELS. RIGHT *UNDER* US YOU CAN BUY A FULL-SERVICE PACKAGE OF EVERY CONCEIVABLE *VICE* KNOWN TO MAN."

"REALLY-?"

"REALLY!! YOU GOT GAMBLING COMING OUT OF YOUR *ASS*. ANY GAME TABLES, SLOTS. IT'S LIKE FUCKING *MONTE CARLO.* SHE'S GOT *BOOZE*. SHE'S GOT *DRUGS*."

"DRUGS?!"

"NOTHIN' TOO HEAVY. PARTY SHIT-Y'KNOW. AND BROADS--"

"--FIGURES."

"-AND GUYS."

"REALLY?"

"EQUAL OPPORTUNITY. YOU KNOW PEOPLE ARE INTO SOME WEIRD SHIT? YOU GOT TO STAY COM-PETITIVE. YA CATCH MY DR-"

"SHAKEDOWNS?"

"PUH-LEASE."

"WHAT?"

"SEE THAT GUY OVER THERE?"

"WHICH ONE?"

"-THAT GANGLY MOTHER FUCKER WITH THE MUSTACHE."

"THE DRUNK?"

"THE *POLICE* COMMISSIONER-AND SEE THAT GUY OVER THERE?"

"THE FAT GUY?--WITH HIS HAND UP THE BLONDE'S SKIRT??"

"THE MAYOR!"

"UH-*HUH.*"

"-AND SEE THAT GUY-?"

"I SORT OF GET THE POINT!"

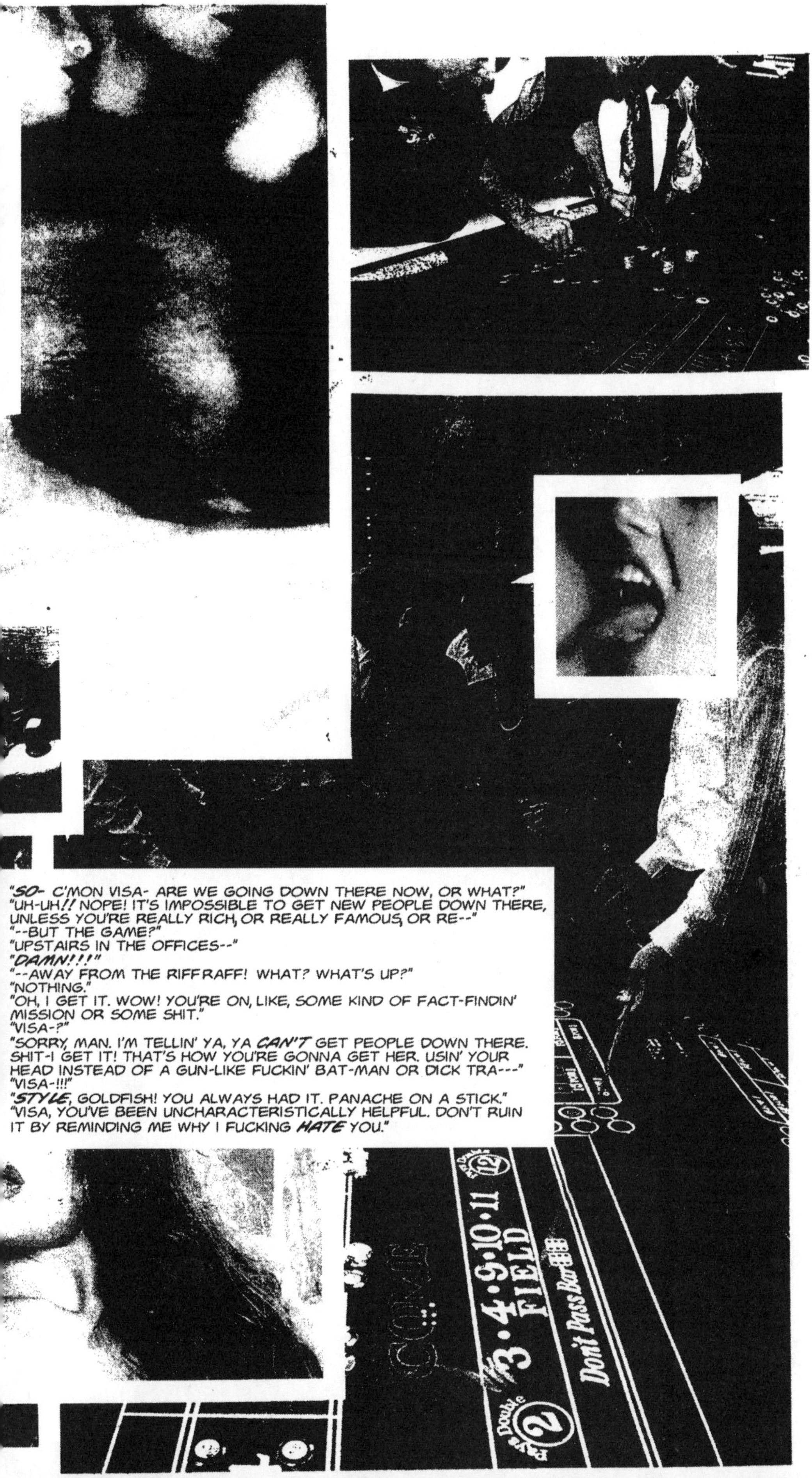
"SO- C'MON VISA- ARE WE GOING DOWN THERE NOW, OR WHAT?"
"UH-UH!! NOPE! IT'S IMPOSSIBLE TO GET NEW PEOPLE DOWN THERE, UNLESS YOU'RE REALLY RICH, OR REALLY FAMOUS, OR RE--"
"--BUT THE GAME?"
"UPSTAIRS IN THE OFFICES--"
"DAMN!!!"
"--AWAY FROM THE RIFFRAFF! WHAT? WHAT'S UP?"
"NOTHING."
"OH, I GET IT. WOW! YOU'RE ON, LIKE, SOME KIND OF FACT-FINDIN' MISSION OR SOME SHIT."
"VISA-?"
"SORRY, MAN. I'M TELLIN' YA, YA CAN'T GET PEOPLE DOWN THERE. SHIT-I GET IT! THAT'S HOW YOU'RE GONNA GET HER. USIN' YOUR HEAD INSTEAD OF A GUN-LIKE FUCKIN' BAT-MAN OR DICK TRA---"
"VISA-!!!"
"STYLE, GOLDFISH! YOU ALWAYS HAD IT. PANACHE ON A STICK."
"VISA, YOU'VE BEEN UNCHARACTERISTICALLY HELPFUL. DON'T RUIN IT BY REMINDING ME WHY I FUCKING HATE YOU."
3 · 4 · 9 · 10 · 11
FIELD
Don't Pass Bar
Pays Double 2

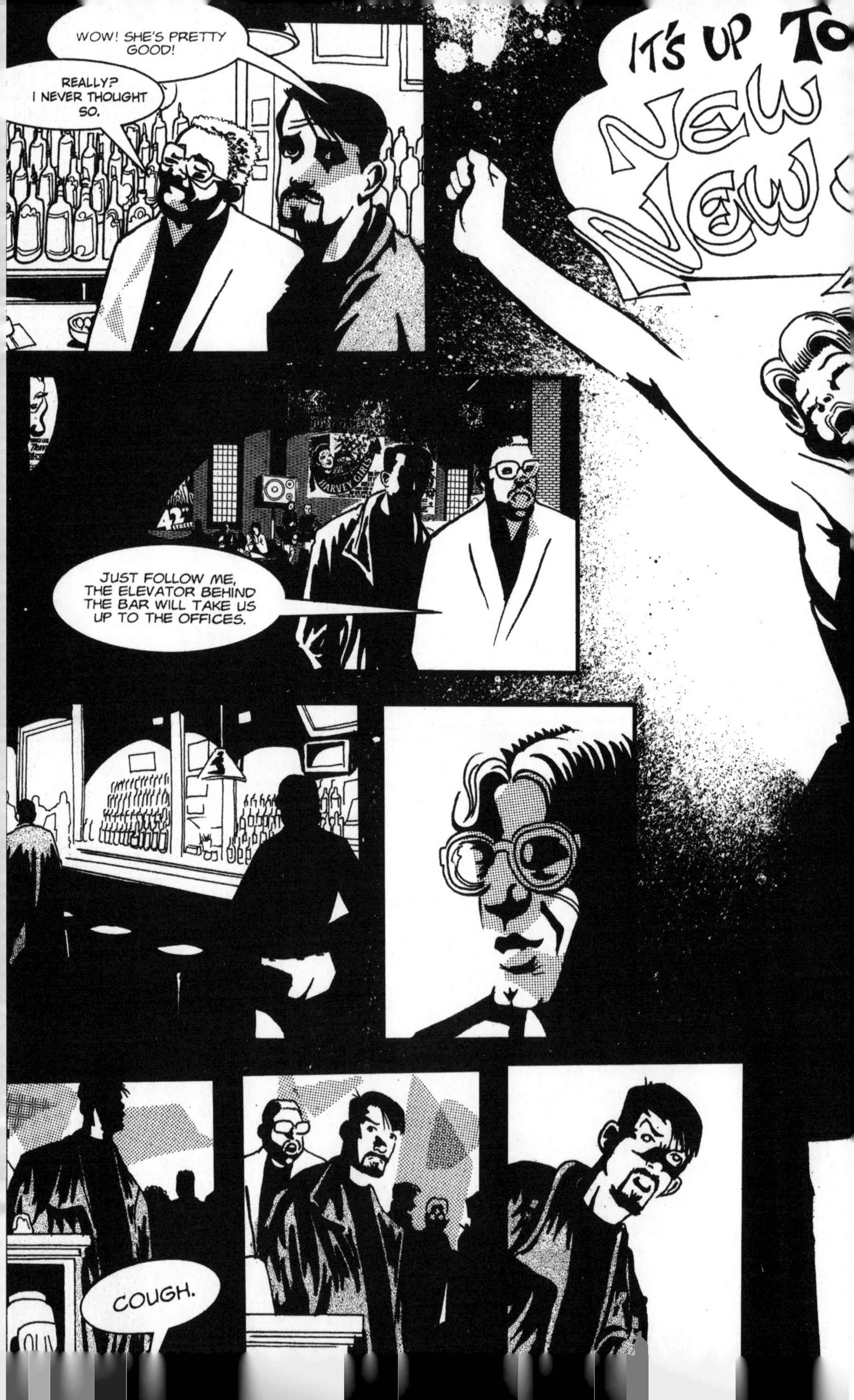
WOW! SHE'S PRETTY GOOD!
REALLY? I NEVER THOUGHT SO.
IT'S UP TO
NEW
NEW
HARVEY GIRLS
42nd STREET
JUST FOLLOW ME, THE ELEVATOR BEHIND THE BAR WILL TAKE US UP TO THE OFFICES.
COUGH.

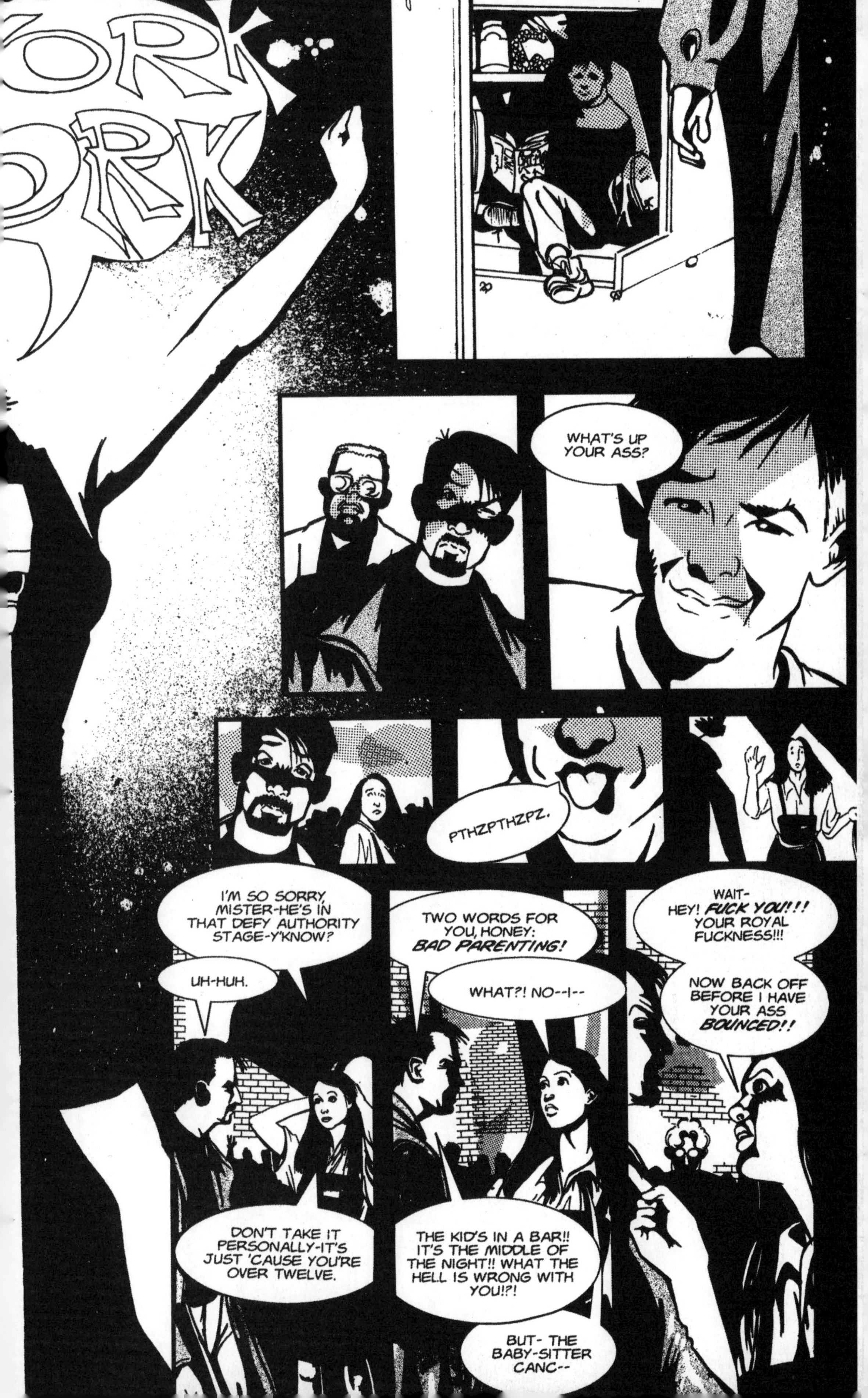
WHAT'S UP YOUR ASS?
PTHZPTHZPZ.
I'M SO SORRY, MISTER-HE'S IN THAT DEFY AUTHORITY STAGE-Y'KNOW?
UH-HUH.
DON'T TAKE IT PERSONALLY-IT'S JUST 'CAUSE YOU'RE OVER TWELVE.
TWO WORDS FOR YOU, HONEY: BAD PARENTING!
WHAT?! NO--I--
THE KID'S IN A BAR!! IT'S THE MIDDLE OF THE NIGHT!! WHAT THE HELL IS WRONG WITH YOU!?!
BUT- THE BABY-SITTER CANC--
WAIT- HEY! FUCK YOU!!! YOUR ROYAL FUCKNESS!!!
NOW BACK OFF BEFORE I HAVE YOUR ASS BOUNCED!!

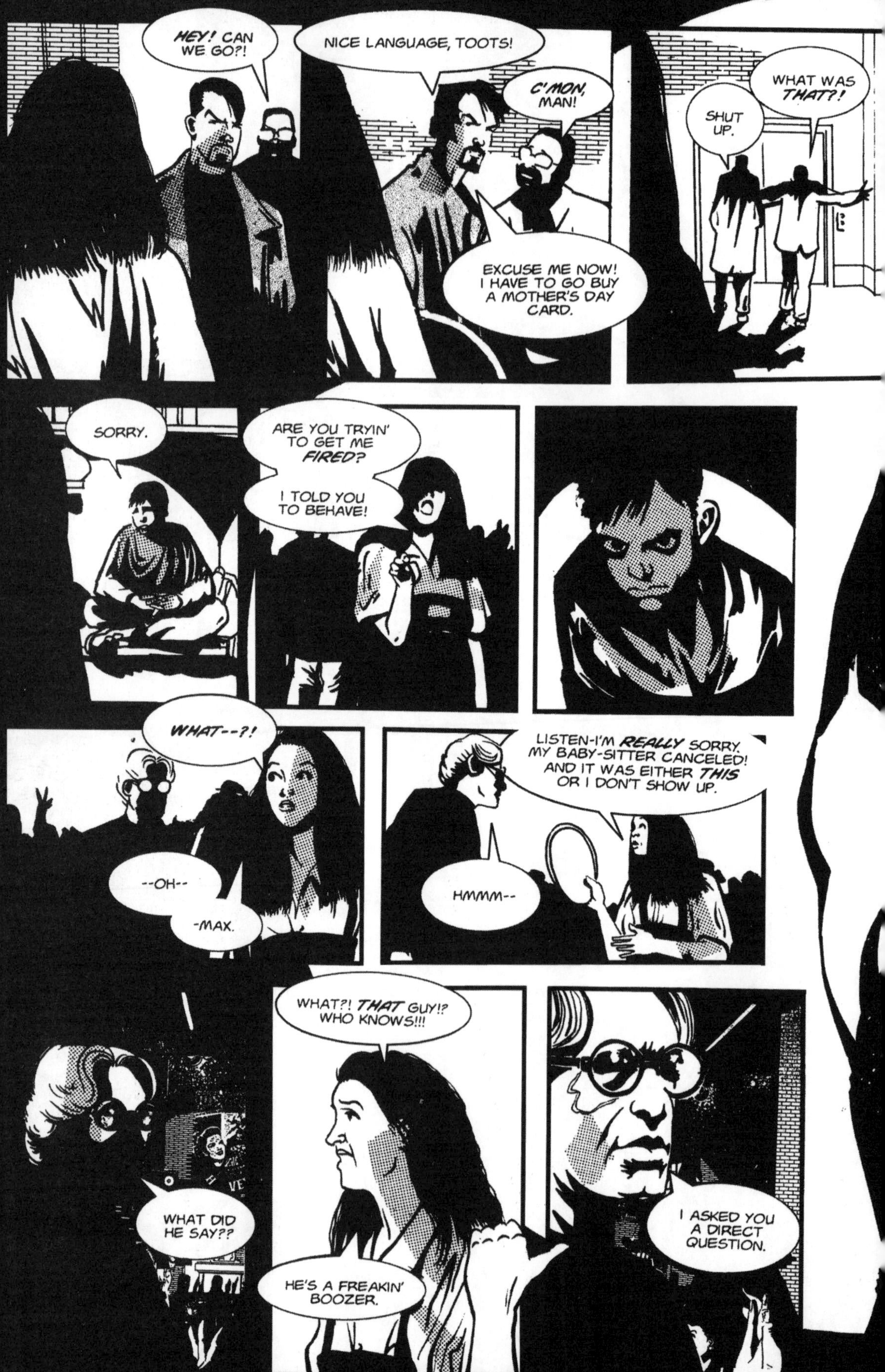
HEY! CAN WE GO?!
NICE LANGUAGE, TOOTS!
C'MON, MAN!
EXCUSE ME NOW! I HAVE TO GO BUY A MOTHER'S DAY CARD.
SHUT UP.
WHAT WAS THAT?!
SORRY.
ARE YOU TRYIN' TO GET ME FIRED?
I TOLD YOU TO BEHAVE!
WHAT--?!
--OH--
-MAX.
LISTEN-I'M REALLY SORRY. MY BABY-SITTER CANCELED! AND IT WAS EITHER THIS OR I DON'T SHOW UP.
HMMM--
WHAT DID HE SAY??
WHAT?! THAT GUY!? WHO KNOWS!!!
HE'S A FREAKIN' BOOZER.
I ASKED YOU A DIRECT QUESTION.

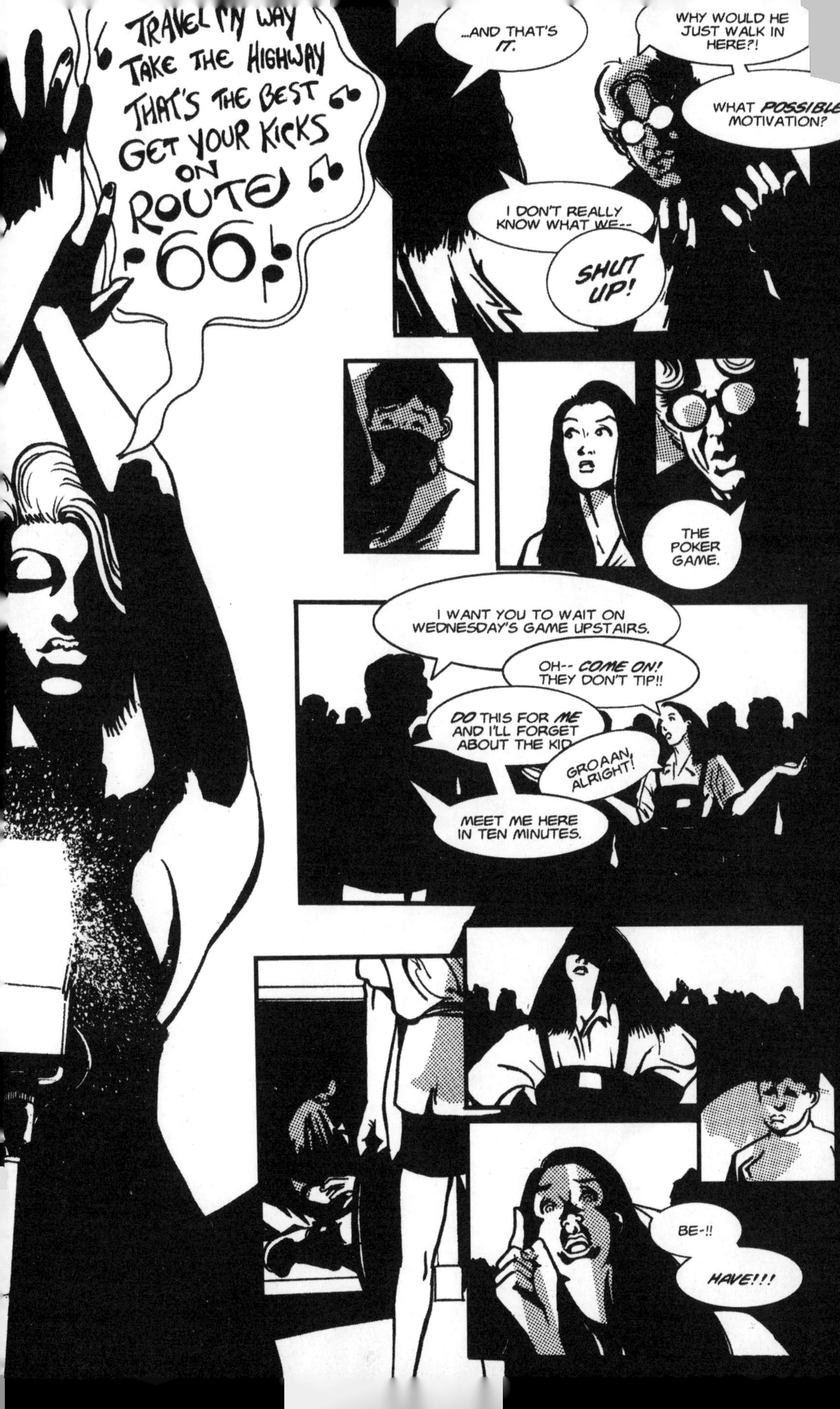
TRAVEL MY WAY TAKE THE HIGHWAY THAT'S THE BEST GET YOUR KICKS ON ROUTE 66
...AND THAT'S IT.
WHY WOULD HE JUST WALK IN HERE?!
WHAT POSSIBLE MOTIVATION?
I DON'T REALLY KNOW WHAT WE--
SHUT UP!
THE POKER GAME.
I WANT YOU TO WAIT ON WEDNESDAY'S GAME UPSTAIRS.
OH-- COME ON! THEY DON'T TIP!!
DO THIS FOR ME AND I'LL FORGET ABOUT THE KID.
GROAAN, ALRIGHT!
MEET ME HERE IN TEN MINUTES.
BE-!!
HAVE!!!

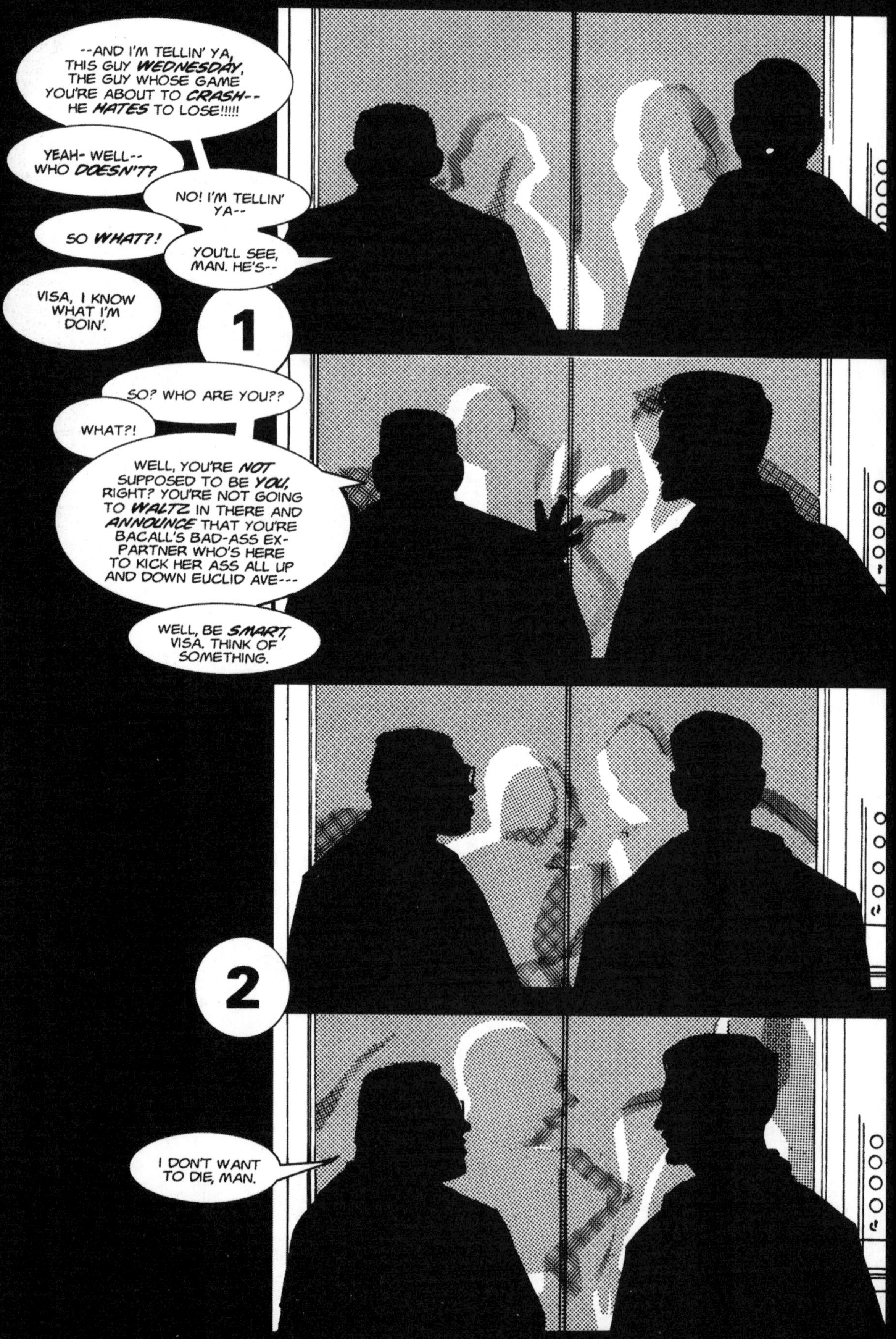
--AND I'M TELLIN' YA, THIS GUY WEDNESDAY, THE GUY WHOSE GAME YOU'RE ABOUT TO CRASH-- HE HATES TO LOSE!!!!!
YEAH- WELL-- WHO DOESN'T?
NO! I'M TELLIN' YA--
SO WHAT?!
YOU'LL SEE, MAN. HE'S--
VISA, I KNOW WHAT I'M DOIN'.
1
SO? WHO ARE YOU??
WHAT?!
WELL, YOU'RE NOT SUPPOSED TO BE YOU, RIGHT? YOU'RE NOT GOING TO WALTZ IN THERE AND ANNOUNCE THAT YOU'RE BACALL'S BAD-ASS EX-PARTNER WHO'S HERE TO KICK HER ASS ALL UP AND DOWN EUCLID AVE---
WELL, BE SMART, VISA. THINK OF SOMETHING.
2
I DON'T WANT TO DIE, MAN.

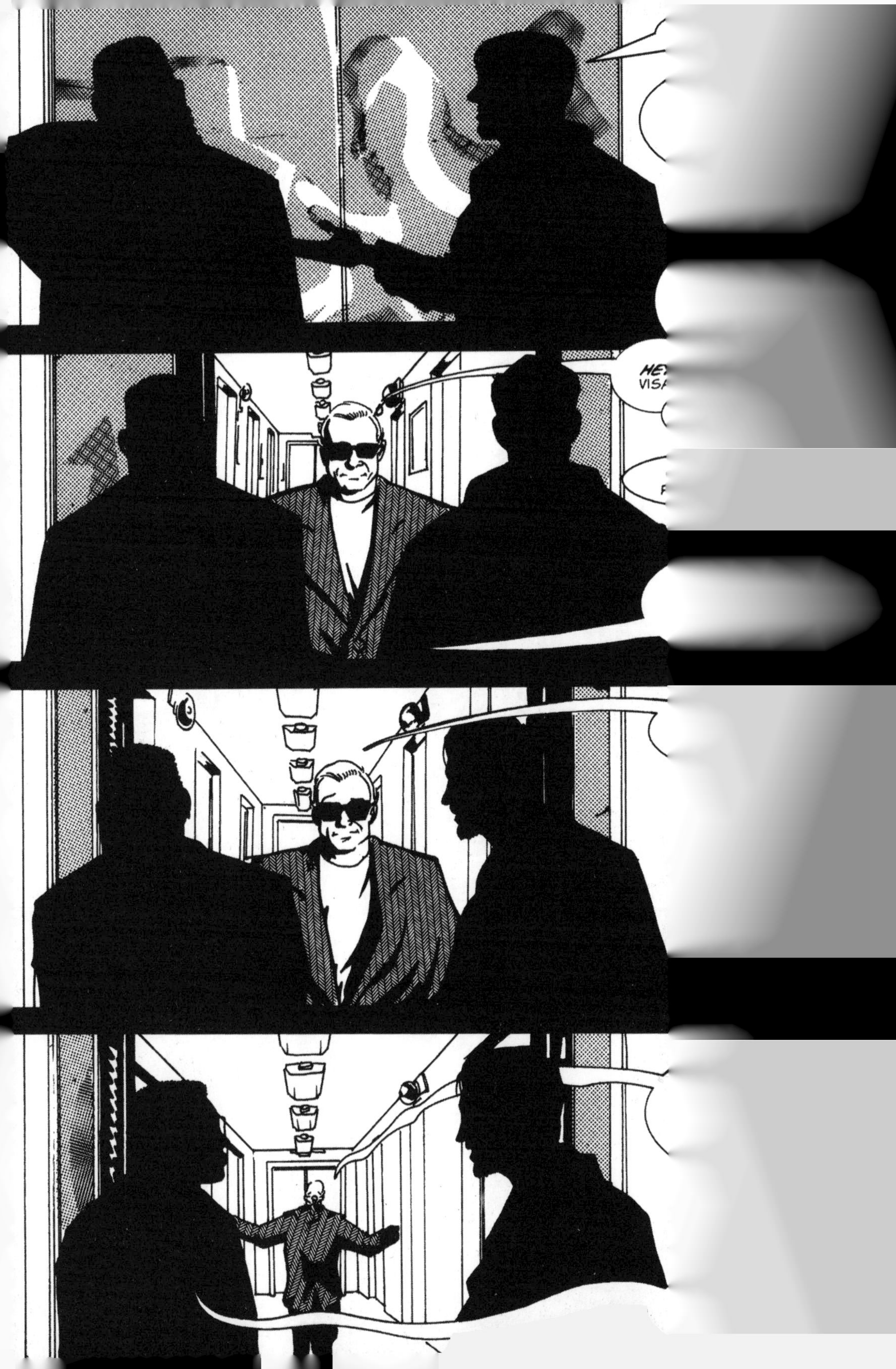

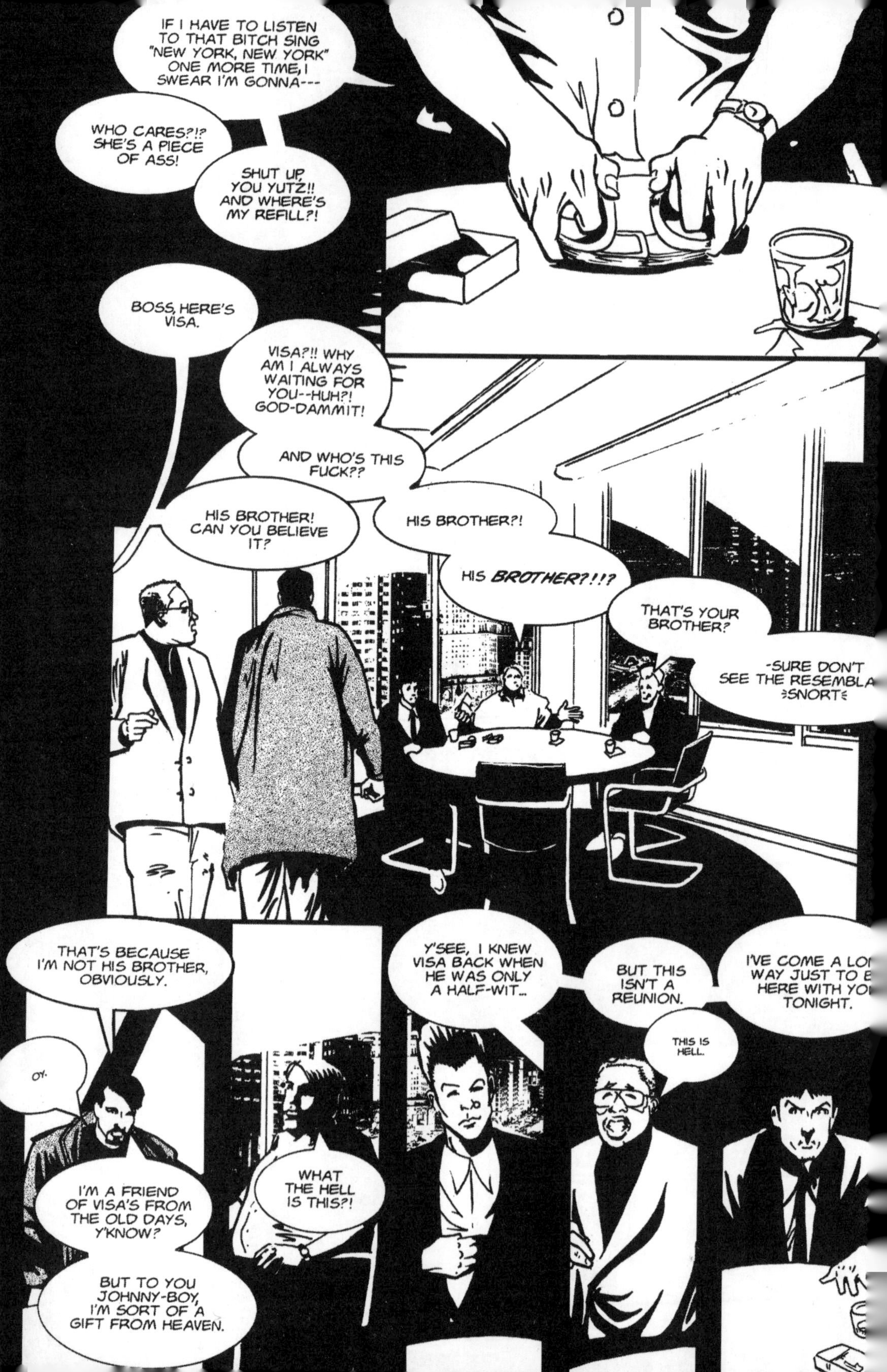

IF I HAVE TO LISTEN TO THAT BITCH SING "NEW YORK, NEW YORK" ONE MORE TIME, I SWEAR I'M GONNA---
WHO CARES?!? SHE'S A PIECE OF ASS!
SHUT UP YOU YUTZ!! AND WHERE'S MY REFILL?!
BOSS, HERE'S VISA.
VISA?!! WHY AM I ALWAYS WAITING FOR YOU--HUH?! GOD-DAMMIT!
AND WHO'S THIS FUCK??
HIS BROTHER! CAN YOU BELIEVE IT?
HIS BROTHER?!
HIS BROTHER?!!?
THAT'S YOUR BROTHER?
-SURE DON'T SEE THE RESEMBLA
=SNORT=
THAT'S BECAUSE I'M NOT HIS BROTHER, OBVIOUSLY.
OY.
I'M A FRIEND OF VISA'S FROM THE OLD DAYS, Y'KNOW?
BUT TO YOU JOHNNY-BOY, I'M SORT OF A GIFT FROM HEAVEN.
WHAT THE HELL IS THIS?!
Y'SEE, I KNEW VISA BACK WHEN HE WAS ONLY A HALF-WIT...
BUT THIS ISN'T A REUNION.
THIS IS HELL.
I'VE COME A LO
WAY JUST TO B
HERE WITH YO
TONIGHT.

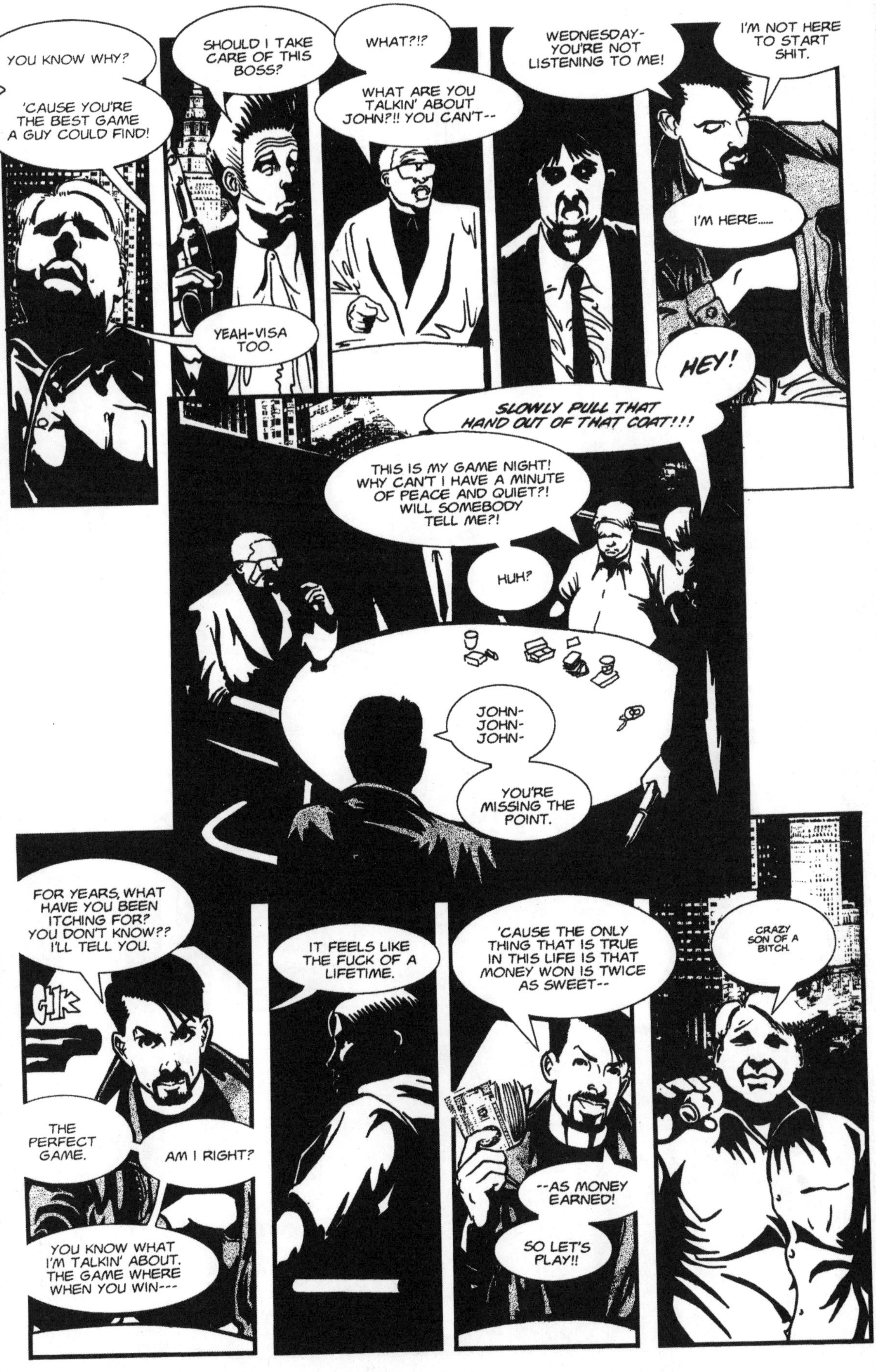

YOU KNOW WHY?
'CAUSE YOU'RE THE BEST GAME A GUY COULD FIND!
YEAH-VISA TOO.
SHOULD I TAKE CARE OF THIS BOSS?
WHAT?!?
WHAT ARE YOU TALKIN' ABOUT JOHN?!! YOU CAN'T--
WEDNESDAY- YOU'RE NOT LISTENING TO ME!
I'M NOT HERE TO START SHIT.
I'M HERE......
HEY!
SLOWLY PULL THAT HAND OUT OF THAT COAT!!!
THIS IS MY GAME NIGHT! WHY CAN'T I HAVE A MINUTE OF PEACE AND QUIET?! WILL SOMEBODY TELL ME?!
HUH?
JOHN- JOHN- JOHN-
YOU'RE MISSING THE POINT.
FOR YEARS, WHAT HAVE YOU BEEN ITCHING FOR? YOU DON'T KNOW?? I'LL TELL YOU.
CLIK
THE PERFECT GAME.
AM I RIGHT?
YOU KNOW WHAT I'M TALKIN' ABOUT. THE GAME WHERE WHEN YOU WIN---
IT FEELS LIKE THE FUCK OF A LIFETIME.
'CAUSE THE ONLY THING THAT IS TRUE IN THIS LIFE IS THAT MONEY WON IS TWICE AS SWEET--
--AS MONEY EARNED!
SO LET'S PLAY!!
CRAZY SON OF A BITCH.

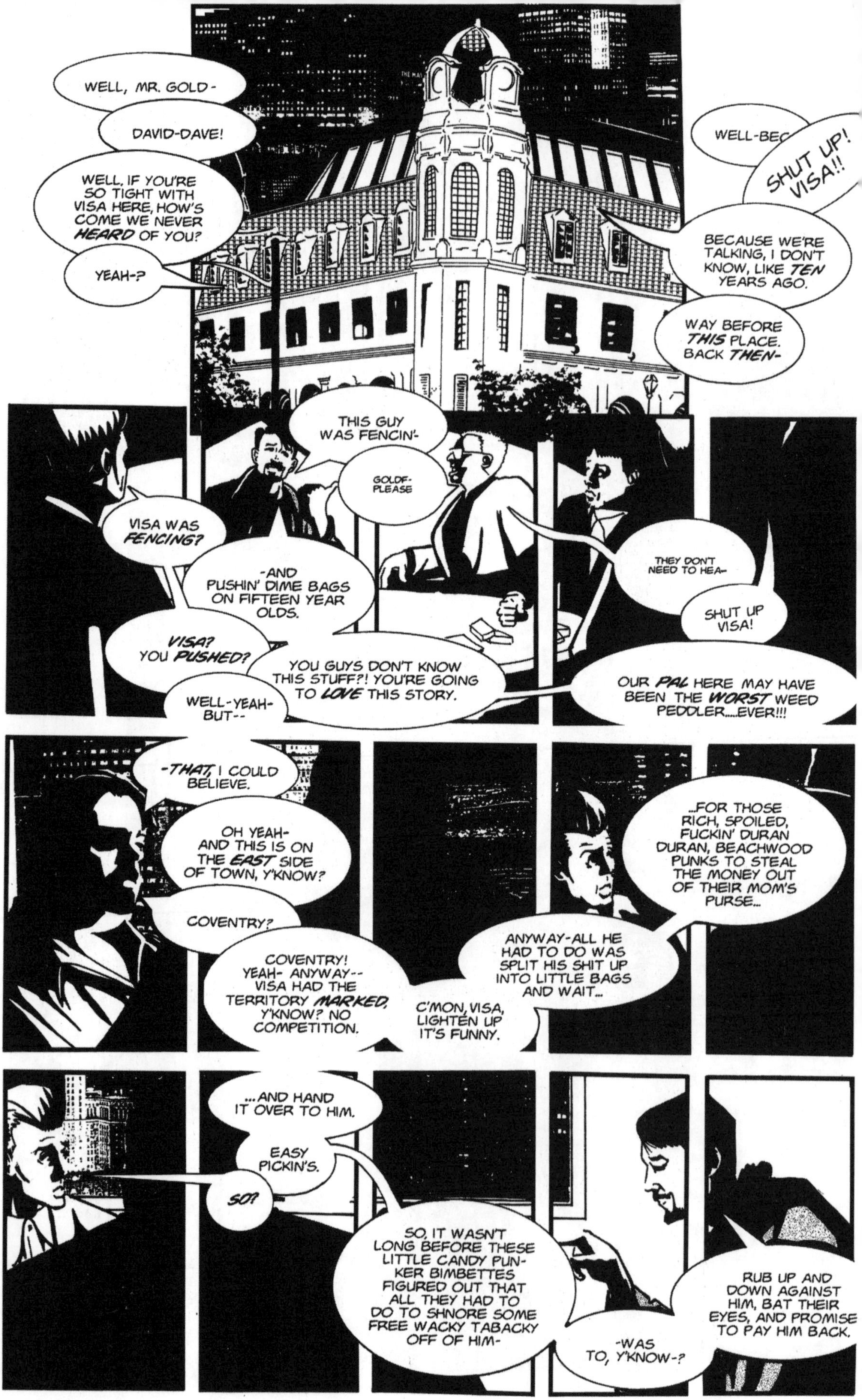
WELL, MR. GOLD-
DAVID-DAVE!
WELL, IF YOU'RE SO TIGHT WITH VISA HERE, HOW'S COME WE NEVER HEARD OF YOU?
YEAH-?
WELL-BEC
SHUT UP! VISA!!
BECAUSE WE'RE TALKING, I DON'T KNOW, LIKE TEN YEARS AGO.
WAY BEFORE THIS PLACE. BACK THEN-
THIS GUY WAS FENCIN'-
GOLDF-PLEASE
VISA WAS FENCING?
-AND PUSHIN' DIME BAGS ON FIFTEEN YEAR OLDS.
THEY DON'T NEED TO HEA-
SHUT UP VISA!
VISA? YOU PUSHED?
YOU GUYS DON'T KNOW THIS STUFF?! YOU'RE GOING TO LOVE THIS STORY.
WELL-YEAH-BUT--
OUR PAL HERE MAY HAVE BEEN THE WORST WEED PEDDLER....EVER!!!
-THAT, I COULD BELIEVE.
OH YEAH-AND THIS IS ON THE EAST SIDE OF TOWN, Y'KNOW?
COVENTRY?
COVENTRY! YEAH- ANYWAY--VISA HAD THE TERRITORY MARKED, Y'KNOW? NO COMPETITION.
C'MON, VISA, LIGHTEN UP IT'S FUNNY.
...FOR THOSE RICH, SPOILED, FUCKIN' DURAN DURAN, BEACHWOOD PUNKS TO STEAL THE MONEY OUT OF THEIR MOM'S PURSE...
ANYWAY-ALL HE HAD TO DO WAS SPLIT HIS SHIT UP INTO LITTLE BAGS AND WAIT...
...AND HAND IT OVER TO HIM.
EASY PICKIN'S.
SO?
SO, IT WASN'T LONG BEFORE THESE LITTLE CANDY PUNKER BIMBETTES FIGURED OUT THAT ALL THEY HAD TO DO TO SHNORE SOME FREE WACKY TABACKY OFF OF HIM-
-WAS TO, Y'KNOW-?
RUB UP AND DOWN AGAINST HIM, BAT THEIR EYES, AND PROMISE TO PAY HIM BACK.

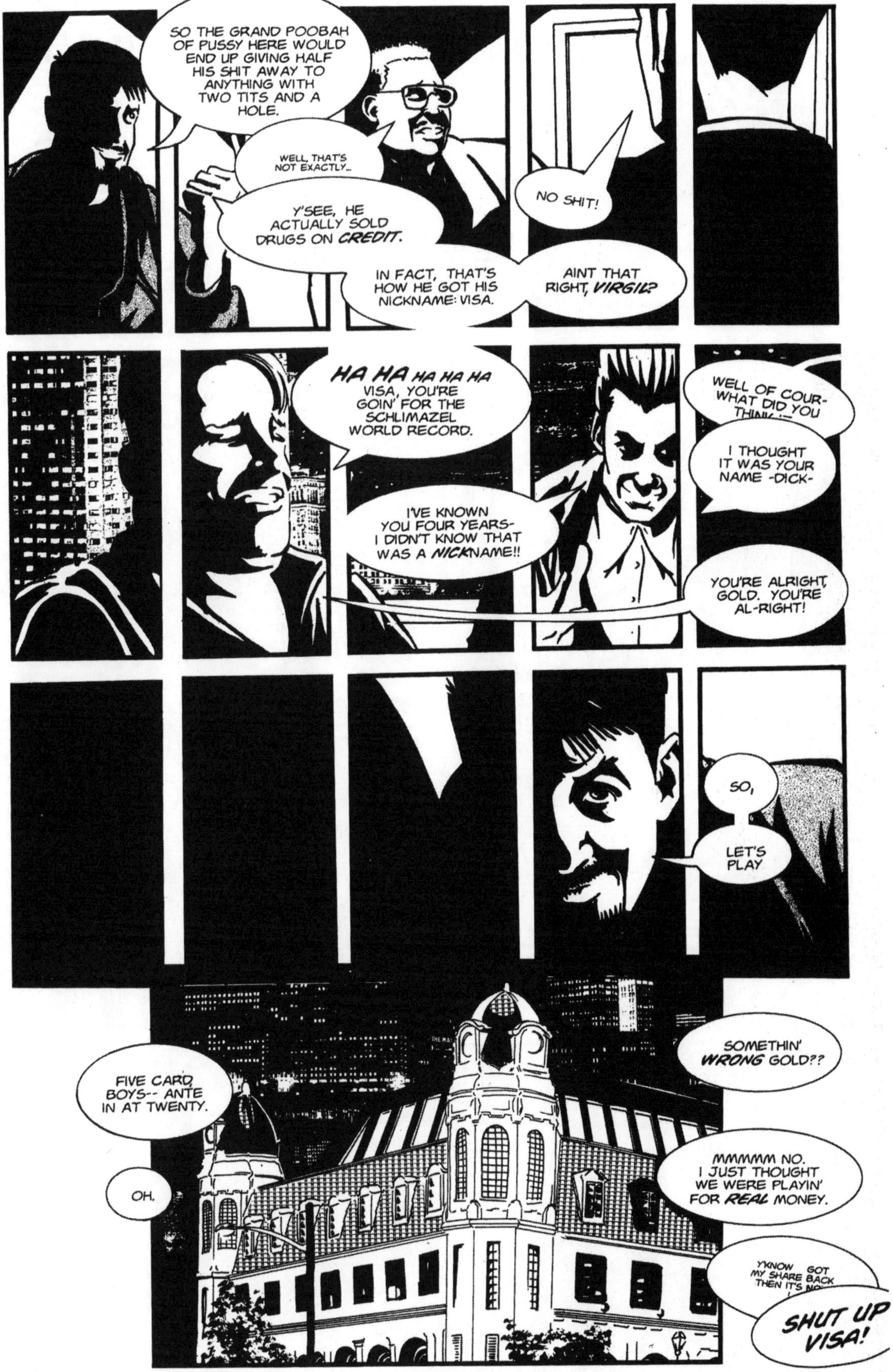

SO THE GRAND POOBAH OF PUSSY HERE WOULD END UP GIVING HALF HIS SHIT AWAY TO ANYTHING WITH TWO TITS AND A HOLE.
WELL, THAT'S NOT EXACTLY...
Y'SEE, HE ACTUALLY SOLD DRUGS ON CREDIT.
NO SHIT!
IN FACT, THAT'S HOW HE GOT HIS NICKNAME: VISA.
AINT THAT RIGHT, VIRGIL?
HA HA HA HA HA VISA, YOU'RE GOIN' FOR THE SCHLIMAZEL WORLD RECORD.
I'VE KNOWN YOU FOUR YEARS- I DIDN'T KNOW THAT WAS A NICKNAME!!
WELL OF COUR- WHAT DID YOU
I THOUGHT IT WAS YOUR NAME -DICK-
YOU'RE ALRIGHT, GOLD. YOU'RE AL-RIGHT!
SO,
LET'S PLAY
FIVE CARD, BOYS-- ANTE IN AT TWENTY.
SOMETHIN' WRONG GOLD??
OH.
MMMMM NO. I JUST THOUGHT WE WERE PLAYIN' FOR REAL MONEY.
Y'KNOW GOT MY SHARE BACK THEN IT'S
SHUT UP VISA!

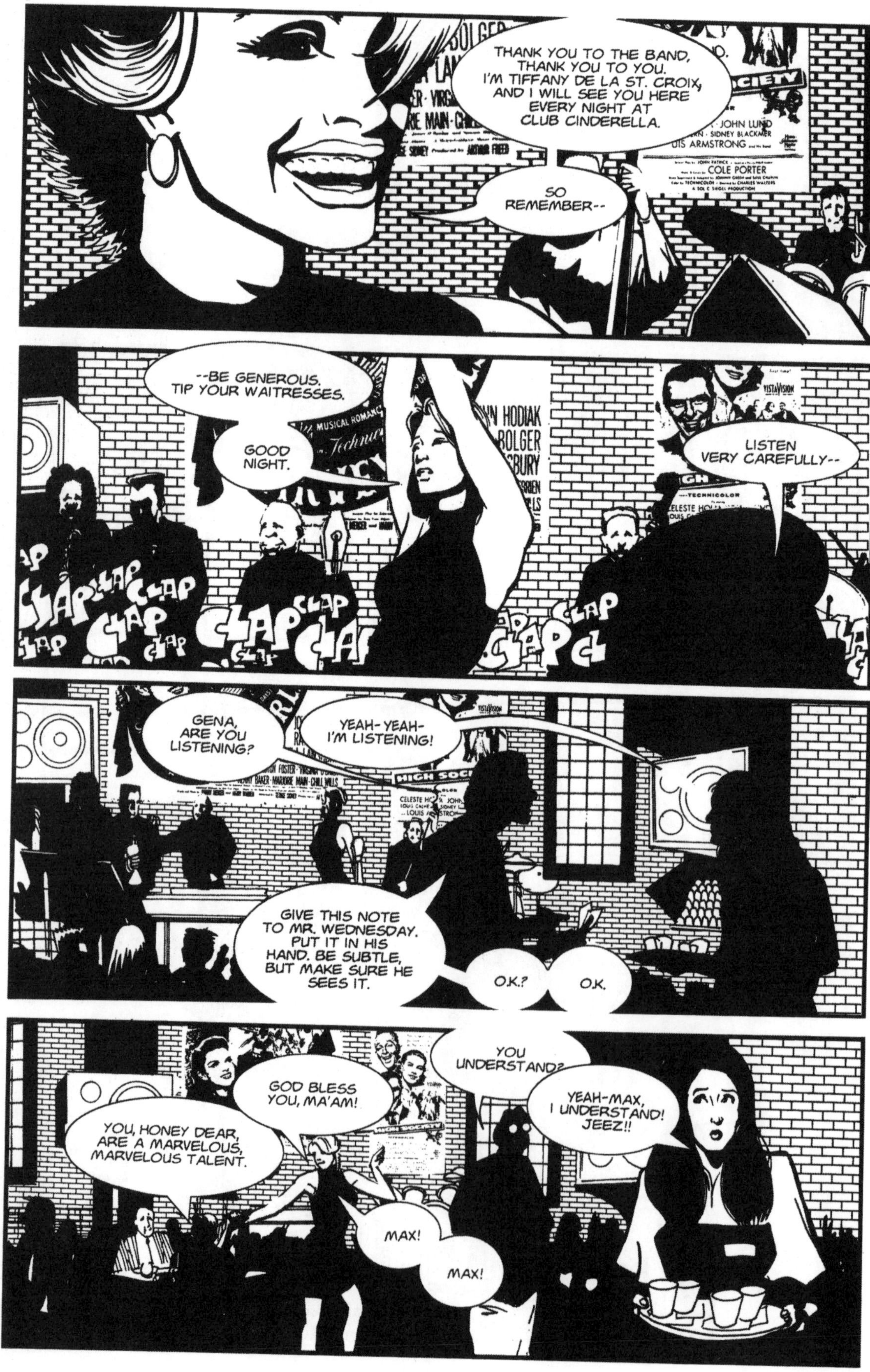
THANK YOU TO THE BAND, THANK YOU TO YOU. I'M TIFFANY DE LA ST. CROIX, AND I WILL SEE YOU HERE EVERY NIGHT AT CLUB CINDERELLA.
SO REMEMBER--
JOHN LUND
SIDNEY BLACKMER
COLE PORTER
--BE GENEROUS. TIP YOUR WAITRESSES.
GOOD NIGHT.
LISTEN VERY CAREFULLY--
CLAP CLAP CLAP CLAP CLAP CLAP CLAP
HIGH SOCIETY
GENA, ARE YOU LISTENING?
YEAH-YEAH- I'M LISTENING!
GIVE THIS NOTE TO MR. WEDNESDAY. PUT IT IN HIS HAND. BE SUBTLE, BUT MAKE SURE HE SEES IT.
O.K.?
O.K.
YOU, HONEY DEAR, ARE A MARVELOUS, MARVELOUS TALENT.
GOD BLESS YOU, MA'AM!
YOU UNDERSTAND?
YEAH-MAX, I UNDERSTAND! JEEZ!!
MAX!
MAX!

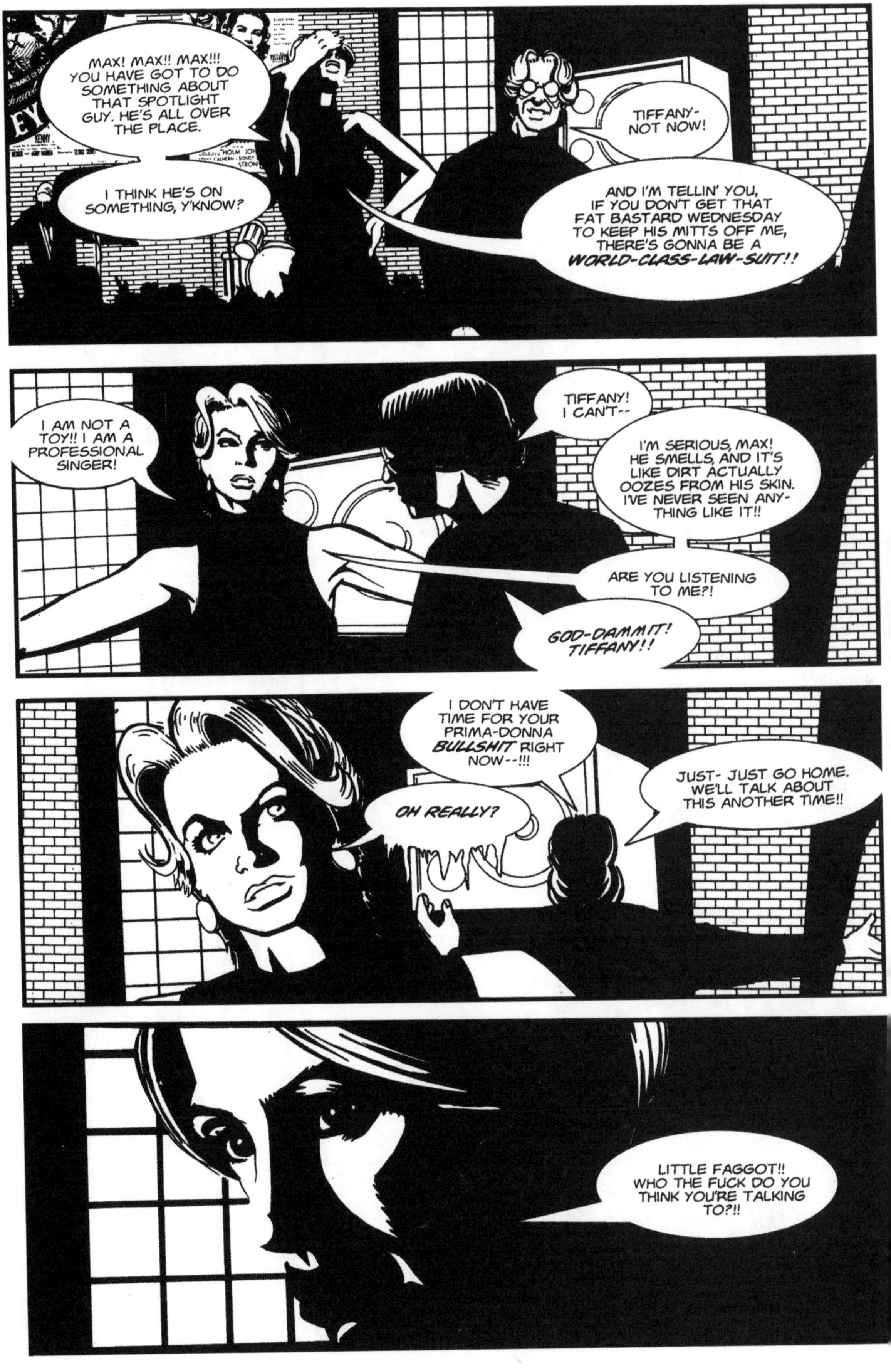
MAX! MAX!! MAX!!! YOU HAVE GOT TO DO SOMETHING ABOUT THAT SPOTLIGHT GUY. HE'S ALL OVER THE PLACE.
I THINK HE'S ON SOMETHING, Y'KNOW?
TIFFANY- NOT NOW!
AND I'M TELLIN' YOU, IF YOU DON'T GET THAT FAT BASTARD WEDNESDAY TO KEEP HIS MITTS OFF ME, THERE'S GONNA BE A WORLD-CLASS-LAW-SUIT!!
I AM NOT A TOY!! I AM A PROFESSIONAL SINGER!
TIFFANY! I CAN'T--
I'M SERIOUS, MAX! HE SMELLS, AND IT'S LIKE DIRT ACTUALLY OOZES FROM HIS SKIN. I'VE NEVER SEEN ANYTHING LIKE IT!!
ARE YOU LISTENING TO ME?!
GOD-DAMMIT! TIFFANY!!
I DON'T HAVE TIME FOR YOUR PRIMA-DONNA BULLSHIT RIGHT NOW--!!!
OH REALLY?
JUST- JUST GO HOME. WE'LL TALK ABOUT THIS ANOTHER TIME!!
LITTLE FAGGOT!! WHO THE FUCK DO YOU THINK YOU'RE TALKING TO?!!

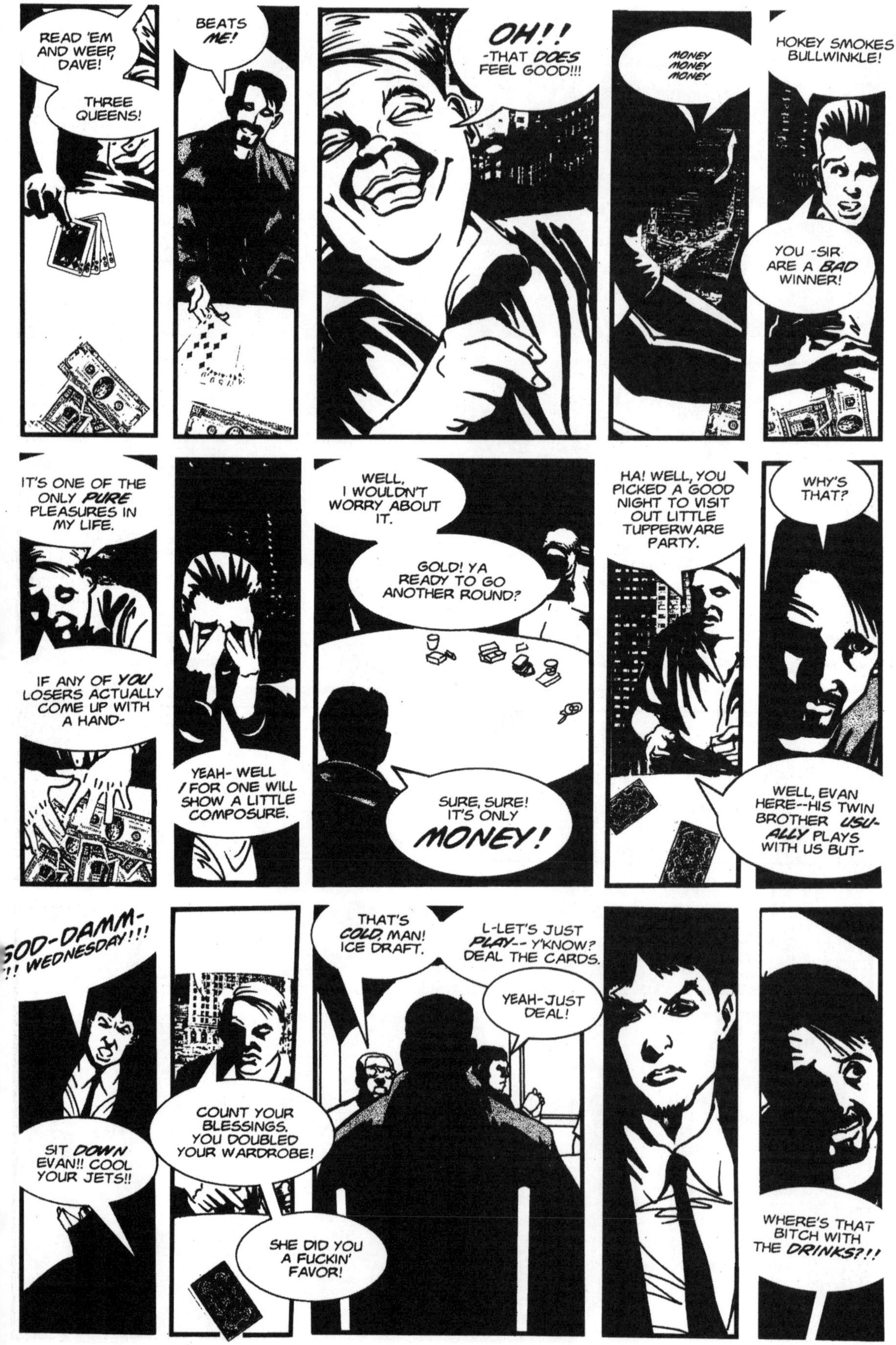

READ 'EM AND WEEP, DAVE!
THREE QUEENS!
BEATS *ME!*
OH!! -THAT *DOES* FEEL GOOD!!!
MONEY MONEY MONEY
HOKEY SMOKES BULLWINKLE!
YOU -SIR ARE A *BAD* WINNER!
IT'S ONE OF THE ONLY *PURE* PLEASURES IN MY LIFE.
IF ANY OF *YOU* LOSERS ACTUALLY COME UP WITH A HAND-
YEAH- WELL *I* FOR ONE WILL SHOW A LITTLE COMPOSURE.
WELL, I WOULDN'T WORRY ABOUT IT.
GOLD! YA READY TO GO ANOTHER ROUND?
SURE, SURE! IT'S ONLY *MONEY!*
HA! WELL, YOU PICKED A GOOD NIGHT TO VISIT OUT LITTLE TUPPERWARE PARTY.
WHY'S THAT?
WELL, EVAN HERE--HIS TWIN BROTHER *USU-ALLY* PLAYS WITH US BUT-
GOD-DAMM-!! WEDNESDAY!!!
SIT *DOWN* EVAN!! COOL YOUR JETS!!
COUNT YOUR BLESSINGS. YOU DOUBLED YOUR WARDROBE!
SHE DID YOU A FUCKIN' FAVOR!
THAT'S *COLD,* MAN! ICE DRAFT.
L-LET'S JUST *PLAY*-- Y'KNOW? DEAL THE CARDS.
YEAH-JUST DEAL!
WHERE'S THAT BITCH WITH THE *DRINKS?!!*

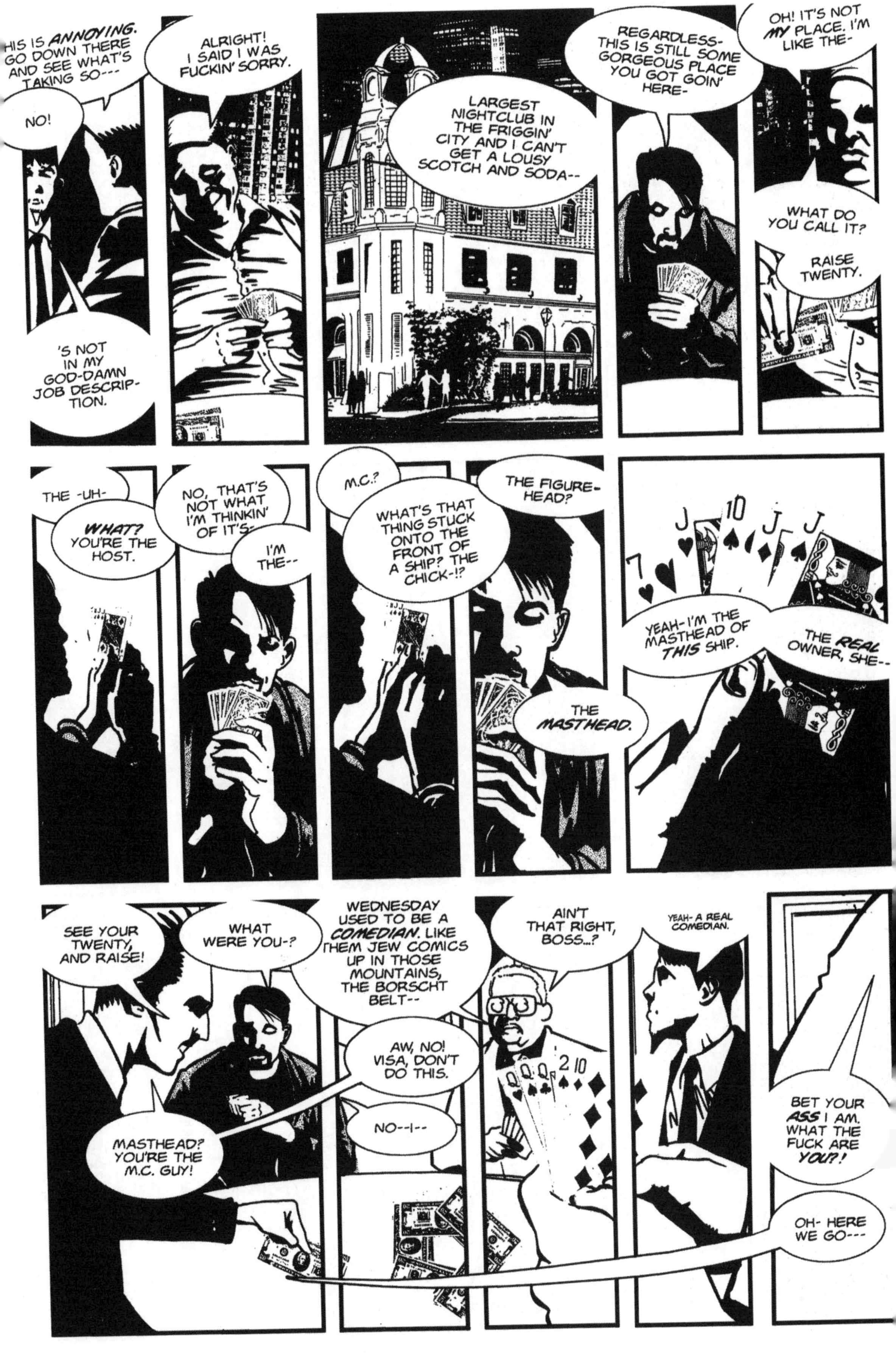
HIS IS ANNOYING. GO DOWN THERE AND SEE WHAT'S TAKING SO---
NO!
'S NOT IN MY GOD-DAMN JOB DESCRIPTION.
ALRIGHT! I SAID I WAS FUCKIN' SORRY.
LARGEST NIGHTCLUB IN THE FRIGGIN' CITY AND I CAN'T GET A LOUSY SCOTCH AND SODA--
REGARDLESS- THIS IS STILL SOME GORGEOUS PLACE YOU GOT GOIN' HERE-
OH! IT'S NOT MY PLACE. I'M LIKE THE-
WHAT DO YOU CALL IT?
RAISE TWENTY.
THE -UH-
WHAT? YOU'RE THE HOST.
NO, THAT'S NOT WHAT I'M THINKIN' OF IT'S-
I'M THE--
M.C.?
WHAT'S THAT THING STUCK ONTO THE FRONT OF A SHIP? THE CHICK-!?
THE FIGURE-HEAD?
THE MASTHEAD.
YEAH- I'M THE MASTHEAD OF THIS SHIP.
THE REAL OWNER, SHE--
SEE YOUR TWENTY, AND RAISE!
WHAT WERE YOU-?
MASTHEAD? YOU'RE THE M.C. GUY!
WEDNESDAY USED TO BE A COMEDIAN. LIKE THEM JEW COMICS UP IN THOSE MOUNTAINS, THE BORSCHT BELT--
AW, NO! VISA, DON'T DO THIS.
NO--I--
AIN'T THAT RIGHT, BOSS...?
YEAH- A REAL COMEDIAN.
BET YOUR ASS I AM. WHAT THE FUCK ARE YOU?!
OH- HERE WE GO---

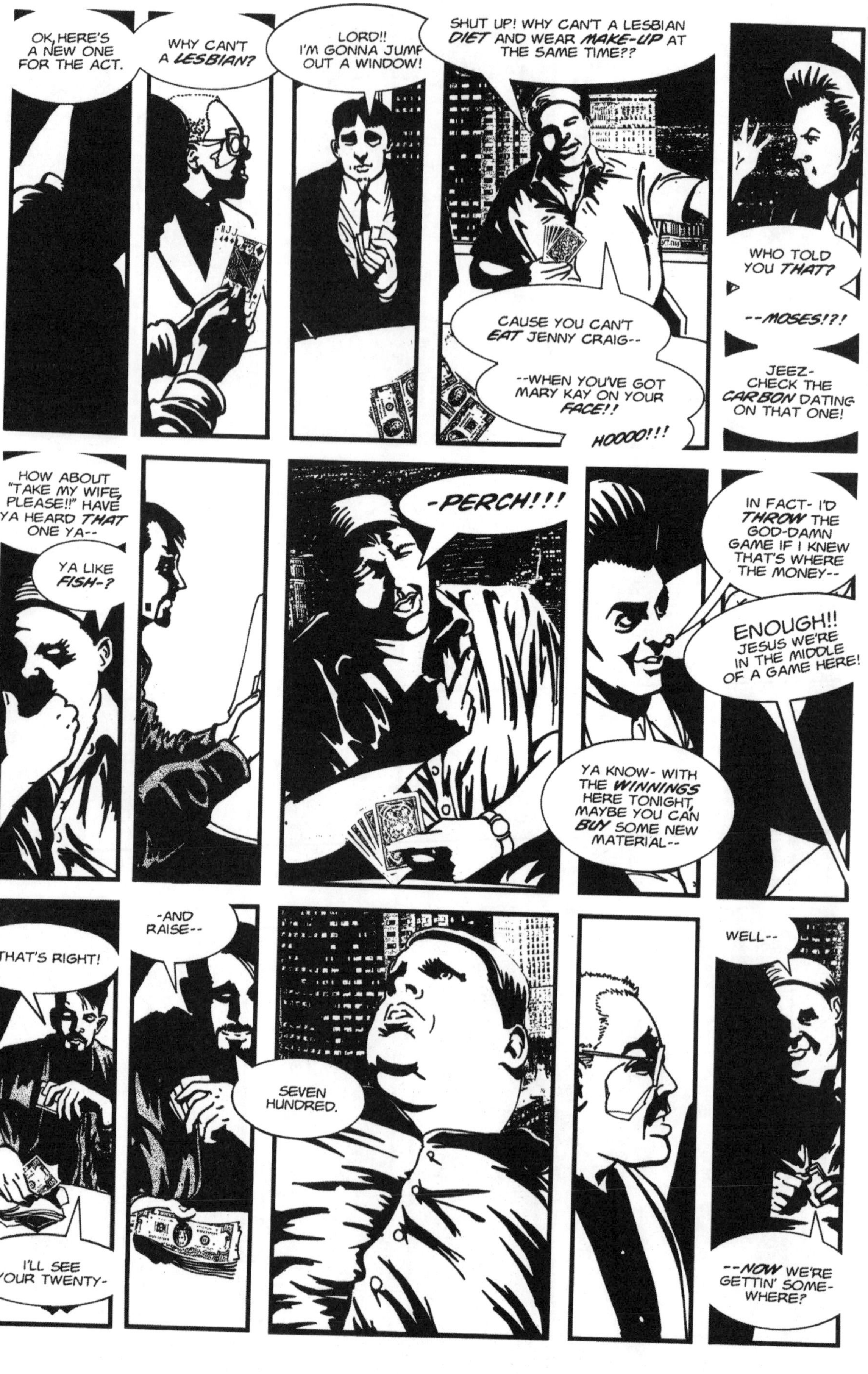
OK, HERE'S A NEW ONE FOR THE ACT.
WHY CAN'T A *LESBIAN*?
LORD!! I'M GONNA JUMP OUT A WINDOW!
SHUT UP! WHY CAN'T A LESBIAN *DIET* AND WEAR *MAKE-UP* AT THE SAME TIME??
CAUSE YOU CAN'T *EAT* JENNY CRAIG--
--WHEN YOU'VE GOT MARY KAY ON YOUR *FACE!!*
HOOOO!!!
WHO TOLD YOU *THAT?*
--MOSES!?!
JEEZ- CHECK THE *CARBON* DATING ON THAT ONE!
HOW ABOUT "TAKE MY WIFE, PLEASE!!" HAVE YA HEARD *THAT* ONE YA--
YA LIKE *FISH-?*
-PERCH!!!
IN FACT- I'D *THROW* THE GOD-DAMN GAME IF I KNEW THAT'S WHERE THE MONEY--
ENOUGH!! JESUS WE'RE IN THE MIDDLE OF A GAME HERE!
YA KNOW- WITH THE *WINNINGS* HERE TONIGHT, MAYBE YOU CAN *BUY* SOME NEW MATERIAL--
THAT'S RIGHT!
I'LL SEE YOUR TWENTY-
-AND RAISE--
SEVEN HUNDRED.
WELL--
--NOW WE'RE GETTIN' SOME-WHERE?

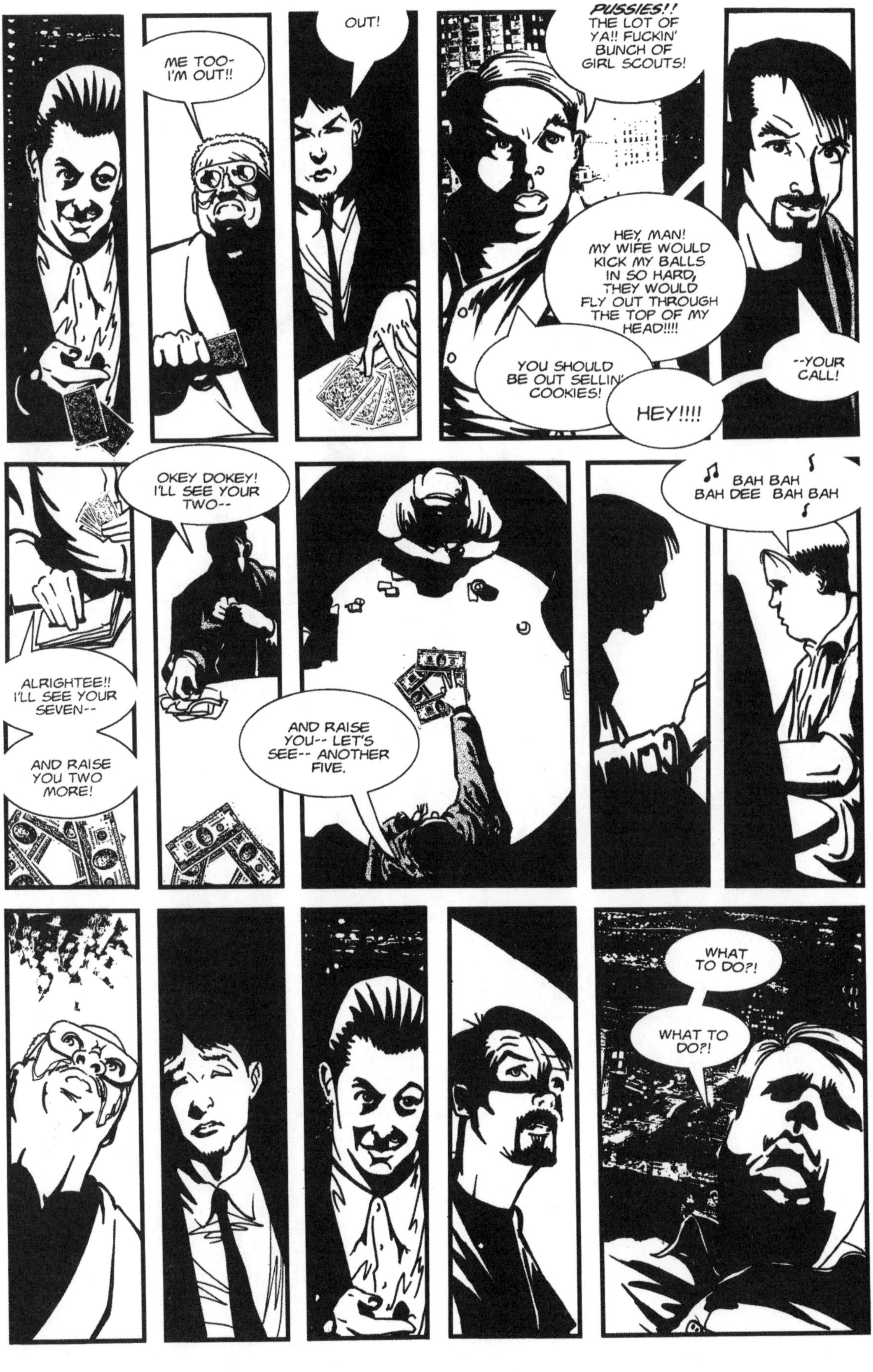
ME TOO-
I'M OUT!!
OUT!
PUSSIES!! THE LOT OF YA!! FUCKIN' BUNCH OF GIRL SCOUTS!
YOU SHOULD BE OUT SELLIN' COOKIES!
HEY, MAN! MY WIFE WOULD KICK MY BALLS IN SO HARD, THEY WOULD FLY OUT THROUGH THE TOP OF MY HEAD!!!!
HEY!!!!
--YOUR CALL!
OKEY DOKEY! I'LL SEE YOUR TWO--
ALRIGHTEE!! I'LL SEE YOUR SEVEN--
AND RAISE YOU TWO MORE!
AND RAISE YOU-- LET'S SEE-- ANOTHER FIVE.
BAH BAH BAH DEE BAH BAH
WHAT TO DO?!
WHAT TO DO?!

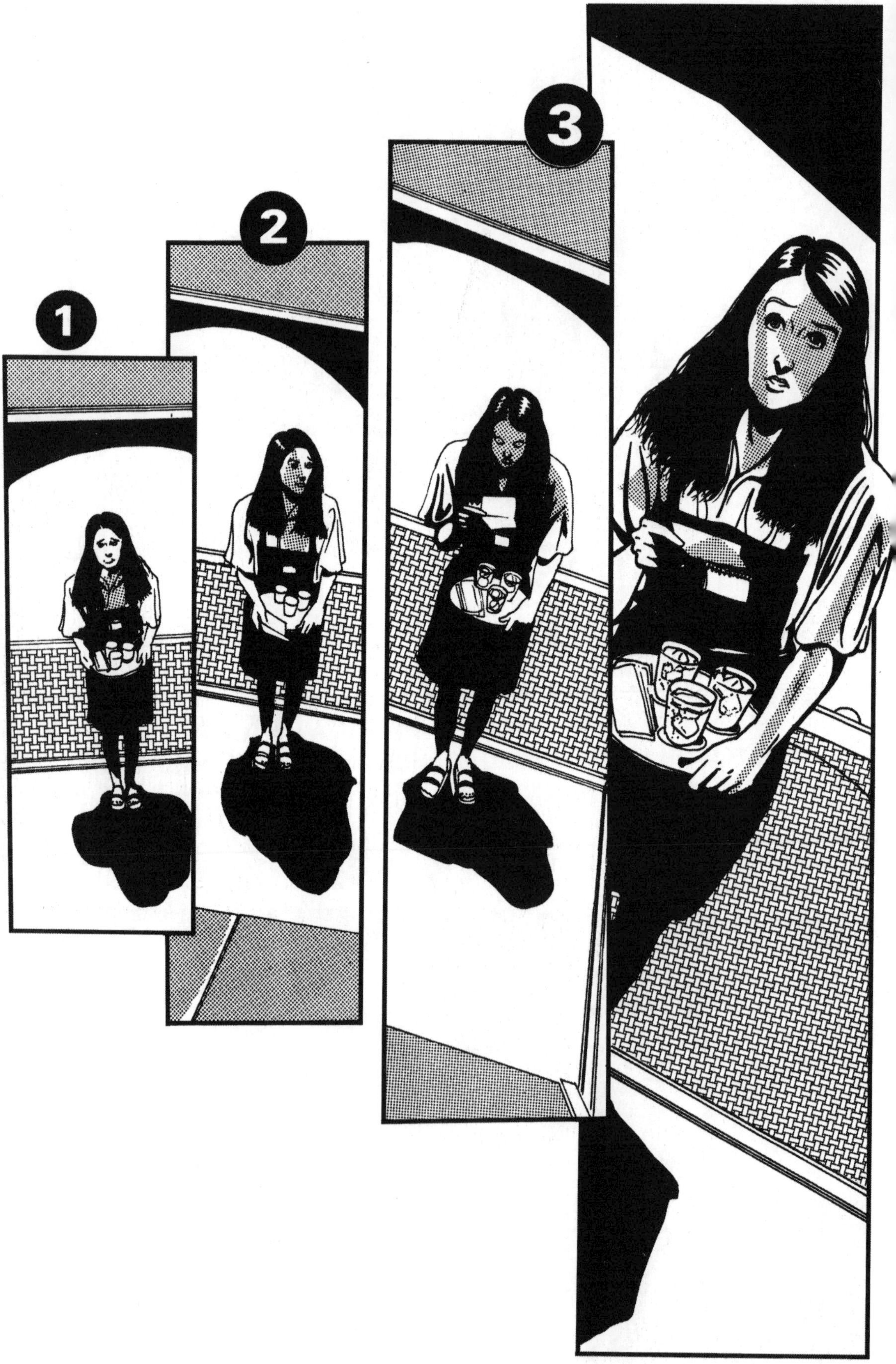
1
2
3

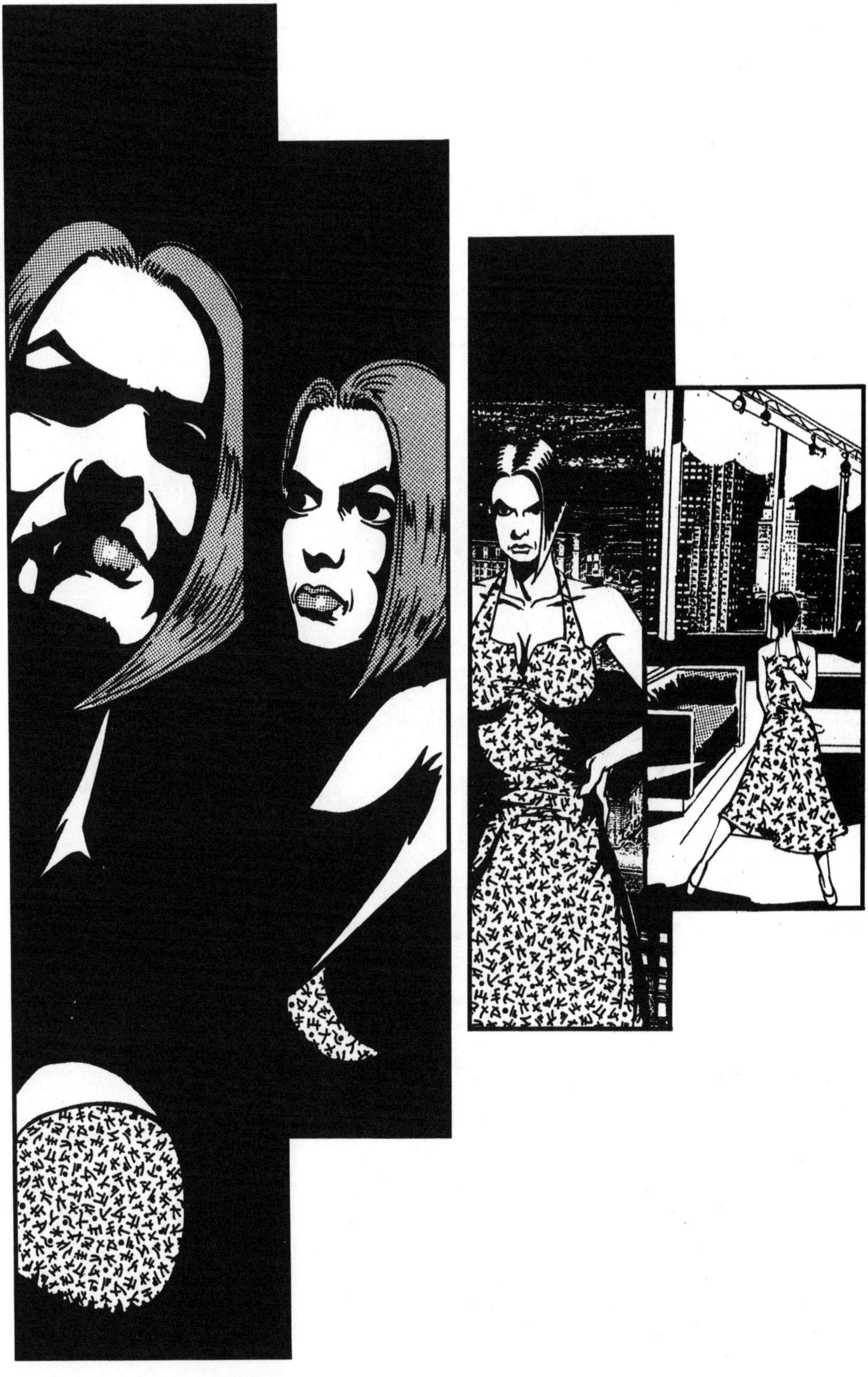

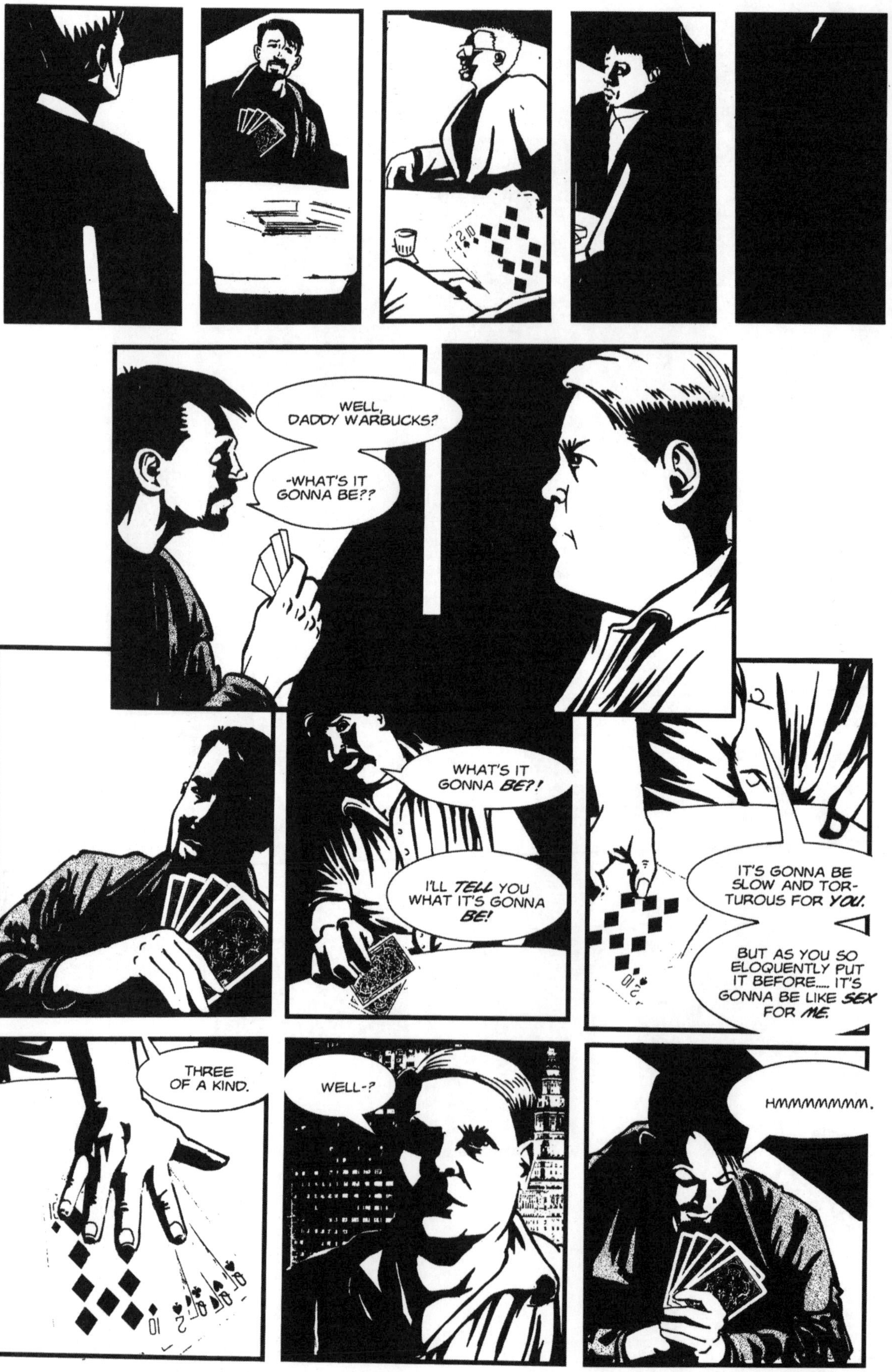
WELL, DADDY WARBUCKS?
-WHAT'S IT GONNA BE??
WHAT'S IT GONNA BE?!
I'LL TELL YOU WHAT IT'S GONNA BE!
IT'S GONNA BE SLOW AND TOR-TUROUS FOR YOU.
BUT AS YOU SO ELOQUENTLY PUT IT BEFORE..... IT'S GONNA BE LIKE SEX FOR ME.
THREE OF A KIND.
WELL-?
HMMMMMMMM.

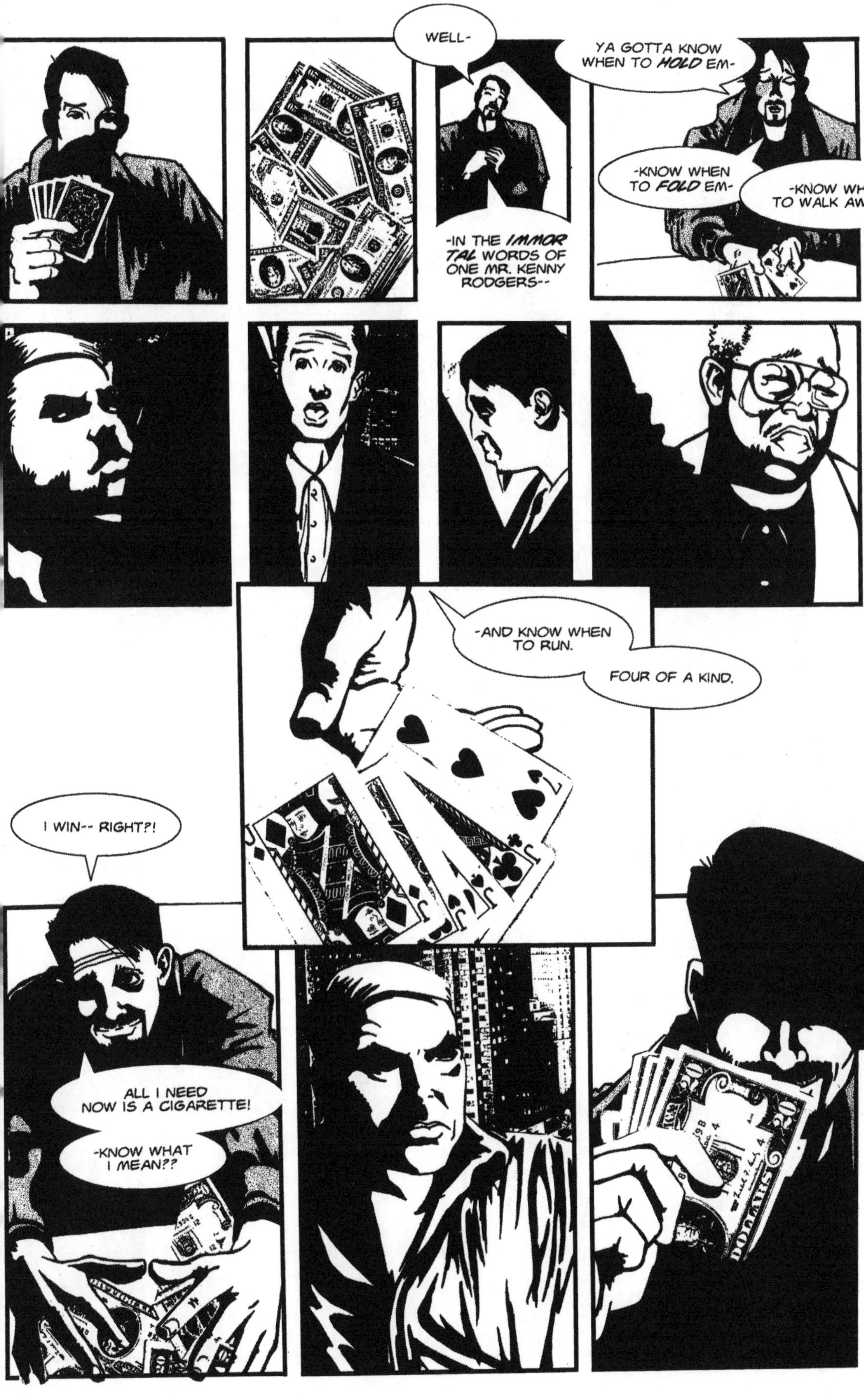
WELL-
-IN THE IMMORTAL WORDS OF ONE MR. KENNY RODGERS--
YA GOTTA KNOW WHEN TO HOLD EM-
-KNOW WHEN TO FOLD EM-
-KNOW WHEN TO WALK AWAY....
-AND KNOW WHEN TO RUN.
FOUR OF A KIND.
I WIN-- RIGHT?!
ALL I NEED NOW IS A CIGARETTE!
-KNOW WHAT I MEAN??

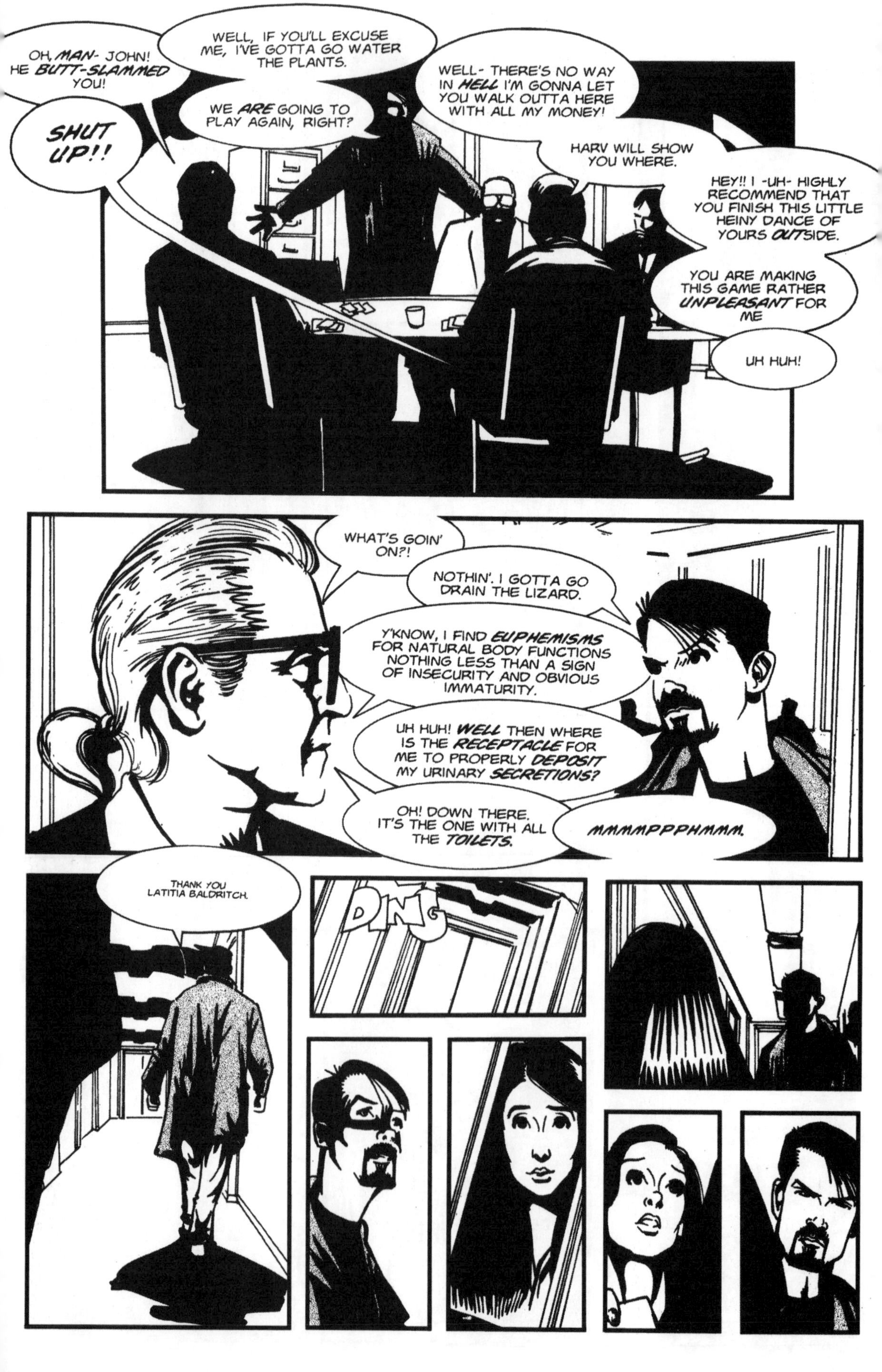
OH, MAN- JOHN! HE BUTT-SLAMMED YOU!
WELL, IF YOU'LL EXCUSE ME, I'VE GOTTA GO WATER THE PLANTS.
SHUT UP!!
WE ARE GOING TO PLAY AGAIN, RIGHT?
WELL- THERE'S NO WAY IN HELL I'M GONNA LET YOU WALK OUTTA HERE WITH ALL MY MONEY!
HARV WILL SHOW YOU WHERE.
HEY!! I -UH- HIGHLY RECOMMEND THAT YOU FINISH THIS LITTLE HEINY DANCE OF YOURS OUTSIDE.
YOU ARE MAKING THIS GAME RATHER UNPLEASANT FOR ME
UH HUH!
WHAT'S GOIN' ON?!
NOTHIN'. I GOTTA GO DRAIN THE LIZARD.
Y'KNOW, I FIND EUPHEMISMS FOR NATURAL BODY FUNCTIONS NOTHING LESS THAN A SIGN OF INSECURITY AND OBVIOUS IMMATURITY.
UH HUH! WELL THEN WHERE IS THE RECEPTACLE FOR ME TO PROPERLY DEPOSIT MY URINARY SECRETIONS?
OH! DOWN THERE. IT'S THE ONE WITH ALL THE TOILETS.
MMMMPPPHMMM.
THANK YOU LATITIA BALDRITCH.
DING

Jon,

This is important. Vis, prise guest is a unwa d visitor from Laure st. I don't know what s doing here, but he uldn't be. Detain him thout harm. Take car of visa once and for all.

MAX

This is impor prise guest d visitor fro st, I don't kn s doing her uldn't be de thout harm. f visa once

MAX

THESE VAGABOND

SHOOOOOEES

ARE YA DA

DA DA!

EXCUSE ME, HOPPALONG.

WHY ARE YOU?

THIS *IS* A WALKWAY!

SORRY.

YEAH— I'D SAY.

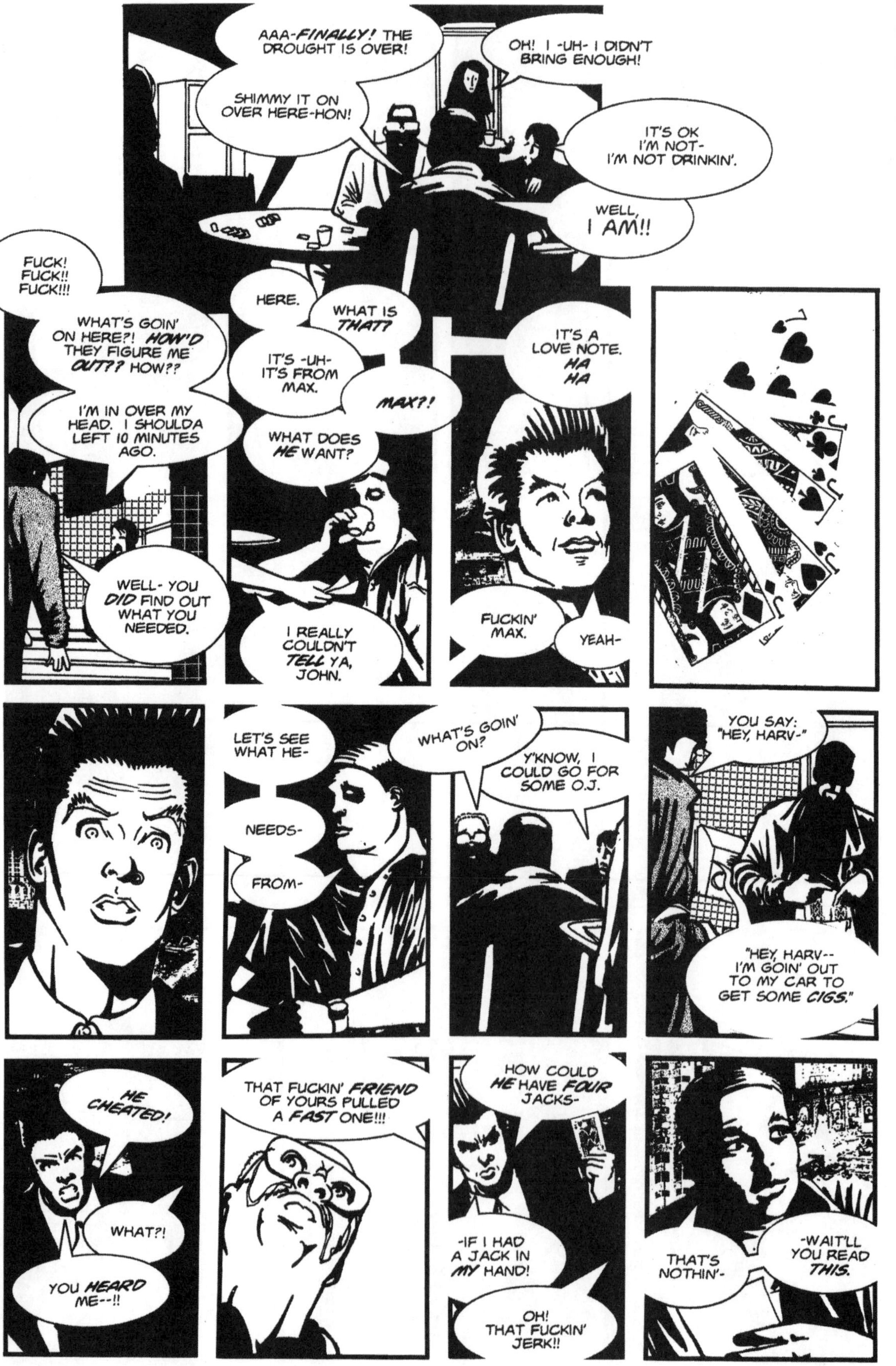
AAA-FINALLY! THE DROUGHT IS OVER!
SHIMMY IT ON OVER HERE-HON!
OH! I -UH- I DIDN'T BRING ENOUGH!
IT'S OK I'M NOT- I'M NOT DRINKIN'.
WELL, I AM!!
FUCK! FUCK!! FUCK!!!
WHAT'S GOIN' ON HERE?! HOW'D THEY FIGURE ME OUT?? HOW??
I'M IN OVER MY HEAD. I SHOULDA LEFT 10 MINUTES AGO.
WELL- YOU DID FIND OUT WHAT YOU NEEDED.
HERE.
WHAT IS THAT?
IT'S -UH- IT'S FROM MAX.
MAX?!
WHAT DOES HE WANT?
I REALLY COULDN'T TELL YA, JOHN.
IT'S A LOVE NOTE. HA HA
FUCKIN' MAX.
YEAH-
LET'S SEE WHAT HE-
NEEDS-
FROM-
WHAT'S GOIN' ON?
Y'KNOW, I COULD GO FOR SOME O.J.
YOU SAY: "HEY, HARV-"
"HEY, HARV-- I'M GOIN' OUT TO MY CAR TO GET SOME CIGS."
HE CHEATED!
WHAT?!
YOU HEARD ME--!!
THAT FUCKIN' FRIEND OF YOURS PULLED A FAST ONE!!!
HOW COULD HE HAVE FOUR JACKS-
-IF I HAD A JACK IN MY HAND!
OH! THAT FUCKIN' JERK!!
THAT'S NOTHIN'-
-WAIT'LL YOU READ THIS.

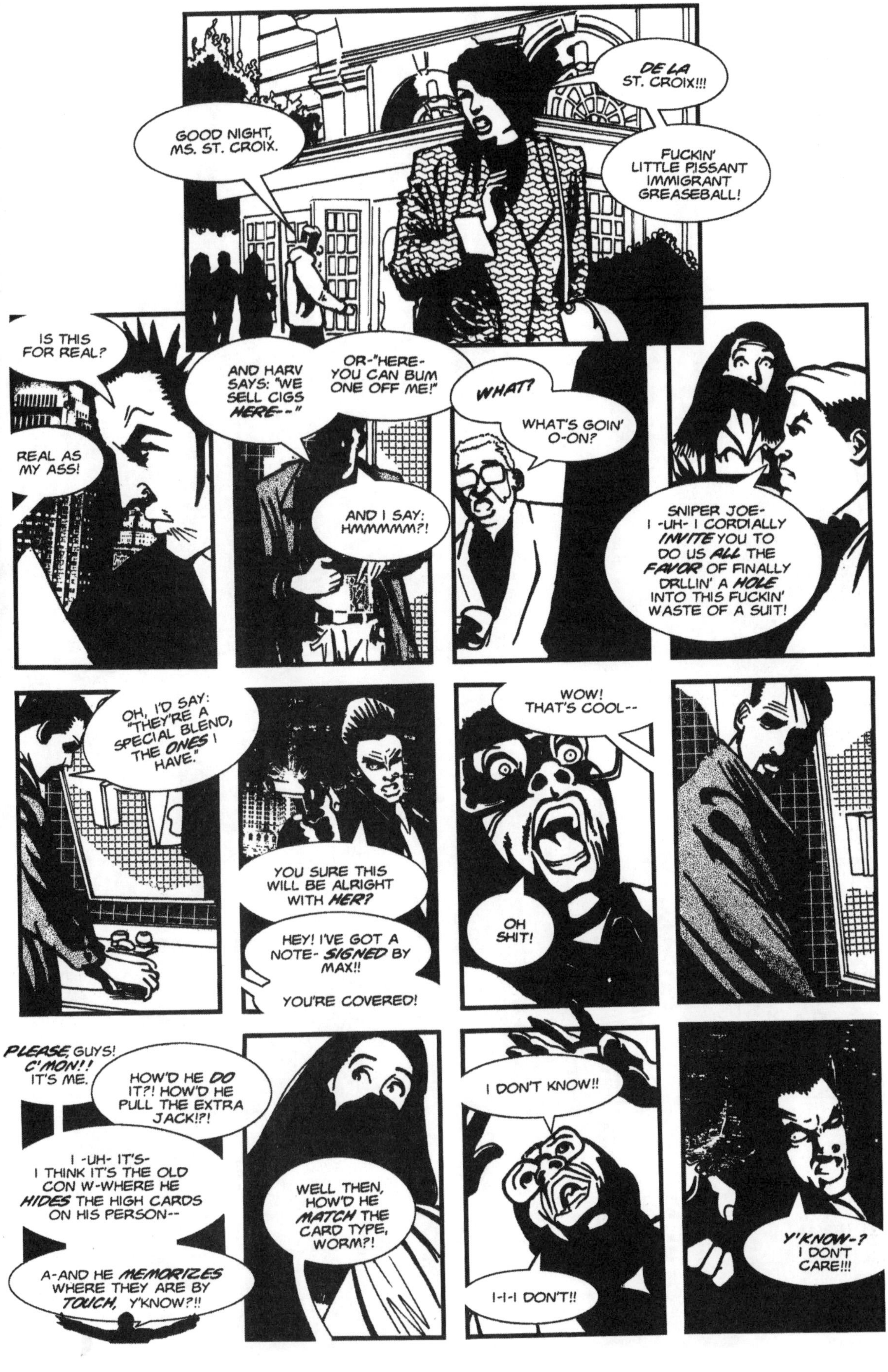
GOOD NIGHT, MS. ST. CROIX.
DE LA ST. CROIX!!!
FUCKIN' LITTLE PISSANT IMMIGRANT GREASEBALL!
IS THIS FOR REAL?
REAL AS MY ASS!
AND HARV SAYS: "WE SELL CIGS HERE--"
OR-"HERE- YOU CAN BUM ONE OFF ME!"
AND I SAY: HMMMMM?!
WHAT?
WHAT'S GOIN' O-ON?
SNIPER JOE- I -UH- I CORDIALLY INVITE YOU TO DO US ALL THE FAVOR OF FINALLY DRLLIN' A HOLE INTO THIS FUCKIN' WASTE OF A SUIT!
OH, I'D SAY: "THEY'RE A SPECIAL BLEND, THE ONES I HAVE."
YOU SURE THIS WILL BE ALRIGHT WITH HER?
HEY! I'VE GOT A NOTE- SIGNED BY MAX!!
YOU'RE COVERED!
WOW! THAT'S COOL--
OH SHIT!
PLEASE, GUYS! C'MON!! IT'S ME.
HOW'D HE DO IT?! HOW'D HE PULL THE EXTRA JACK!?!
I -UH- IT'S- I THINK IT'S THE OLD CON W-WHERE HE HIDES THE HIGH CARDS ON HIS PERSON--
A-AND HE MEMORIZES WHERE THEY ARE BY TOUCH, Y'KNOW?!!
WELL THEN, HOW'D HE MATCH THE CARD TYPE, WORM?!
I DON'T KNOW!!
I-I-I DON'T!!
Y'KNOW-? I DON'T CARE!!!

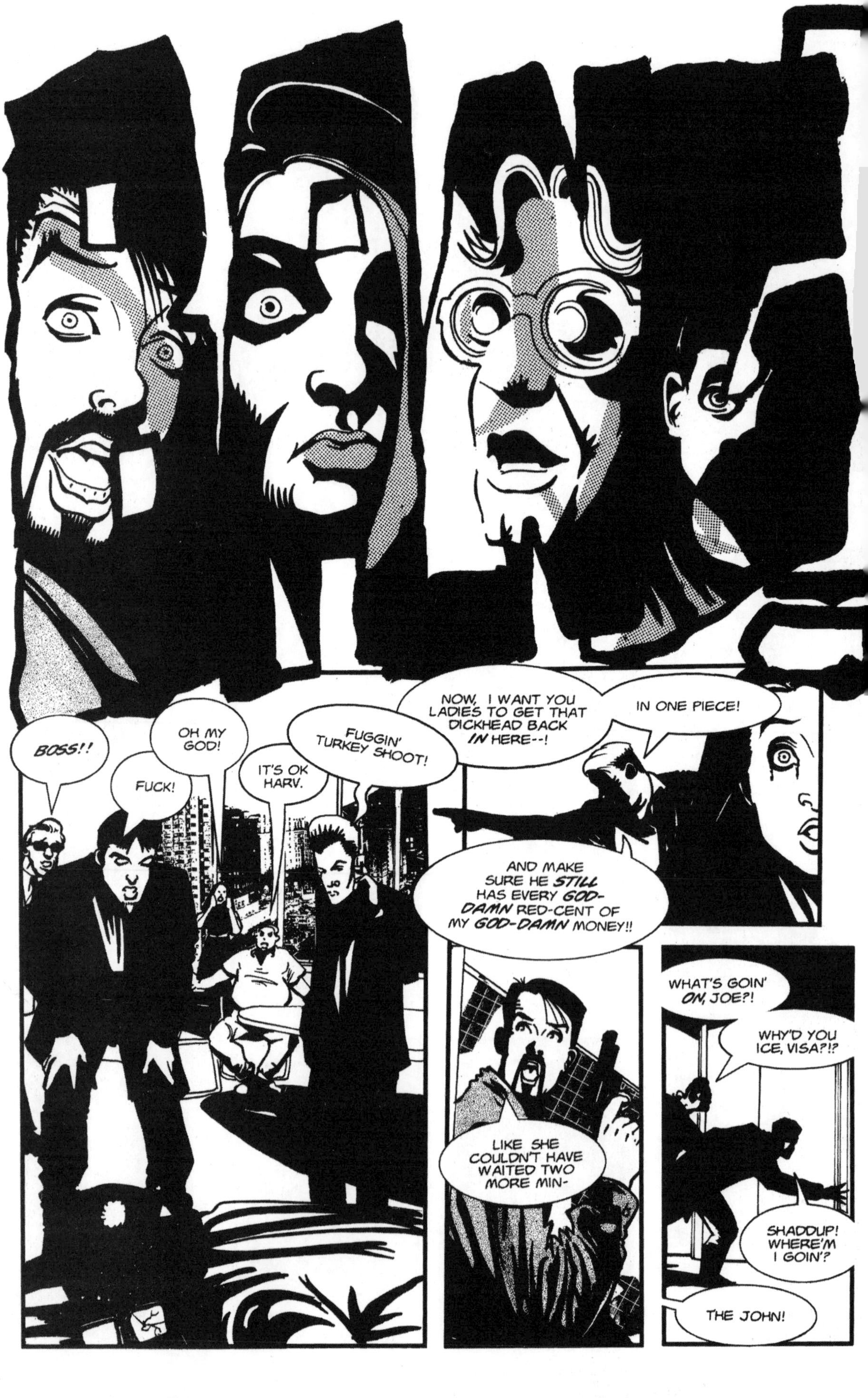
BOSS!!
FUCK!
OH MY GOD!
IT'S OK HARV.
FUGGIN' TURKEY SHOOT!
NOW, I WANT YOU LADIES TO GET THAT DICKHEAD BACK IN HERE--!
IN ONE PIECE!
AND MAKE SURE HE STILL HAS EVERY GOD-DAMN RED-CENT OF MY GOD-DAMN MONEY!!
LIKE SHE COULDN'T HAVE WAITED TWO MORE MIN-
WHAT'S GOIN' ON, JOE?!
WHY'D YOU ICE, VISA?!?
SHADDUP! WHERE'M I GOIN'?
THE JOHN!

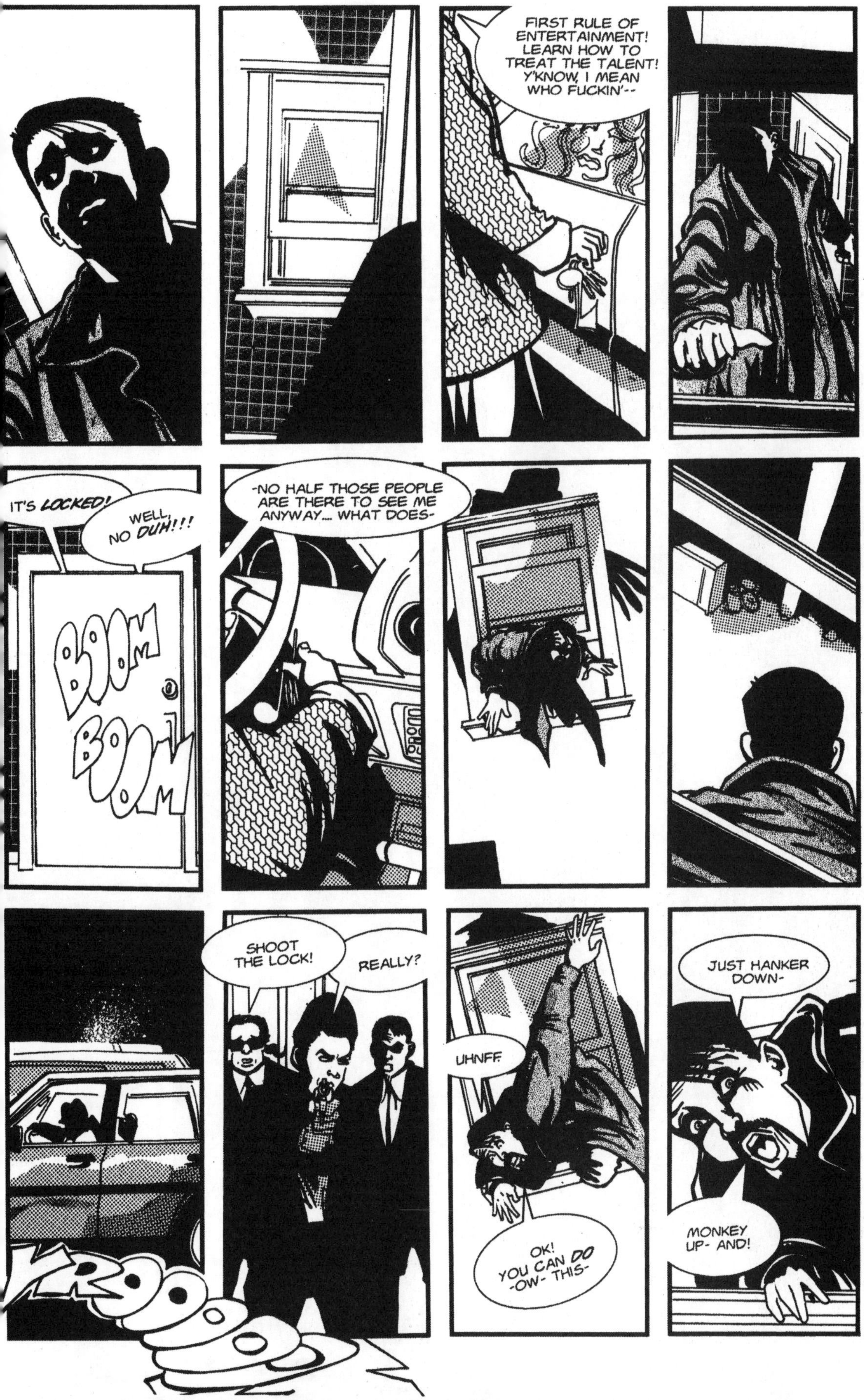
FIRST RULE OF ENTERTAINMENT! LEARN HOW TO TREAT THE TALENT! Y'KNOW, I MEAN WHO FUCKIN'--
IT'S LOCKED!
WELL, NO DUH!!!
BOOM BOOM
-NO HALF THOSE PEOPLE ARE THERE TO SEE ME ANYWAY.... WHAT DOES-
VROOOOO
SHOOT THE LOCK!
REALLY?
UHNFF.
OK! YOU CAN DO -OW- THIS-
JUST HANKER DOWN-
MONKEY UP- AND!

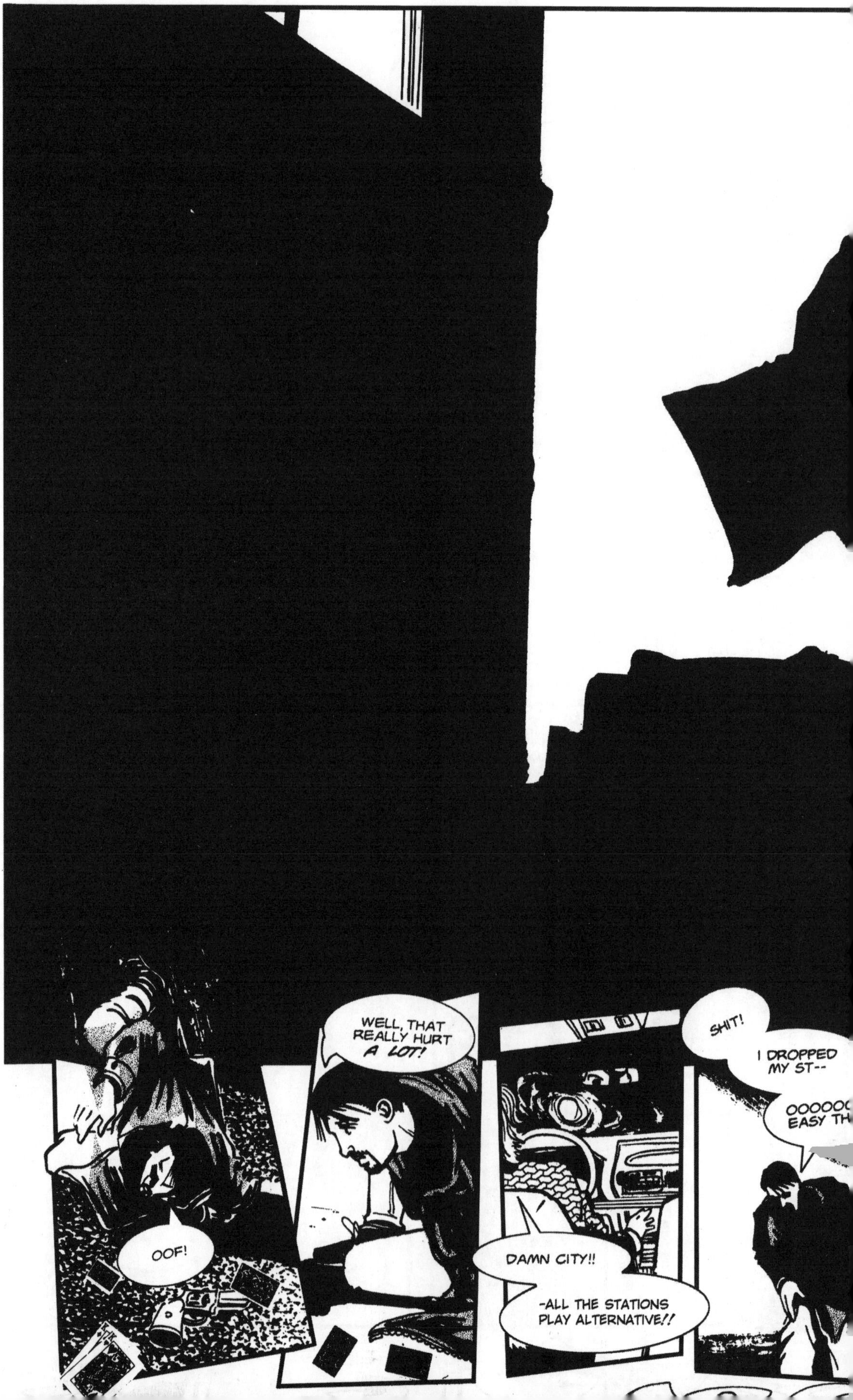
OOF!
WELL, THAT REALLY HURT A LOT!
DAMN CITY!!
-ALL THE STATIONS PLAY ALTERNATIVE!!
SHIT!
I DROPPED MY ST--
OOOOOC EASY TH

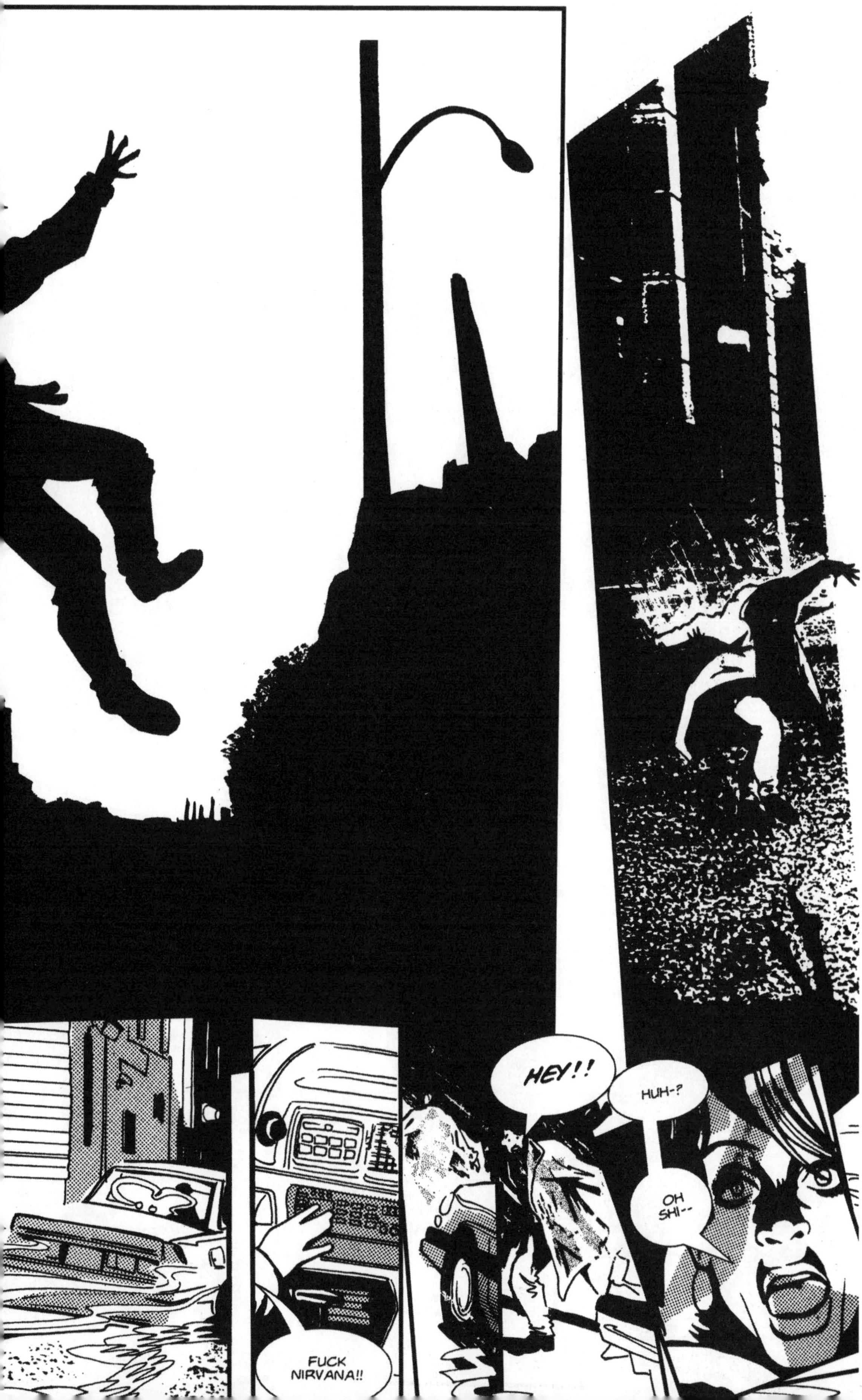
FUCK
NIRVANA!!
HEY!!
HUH-?
OH
SHI--

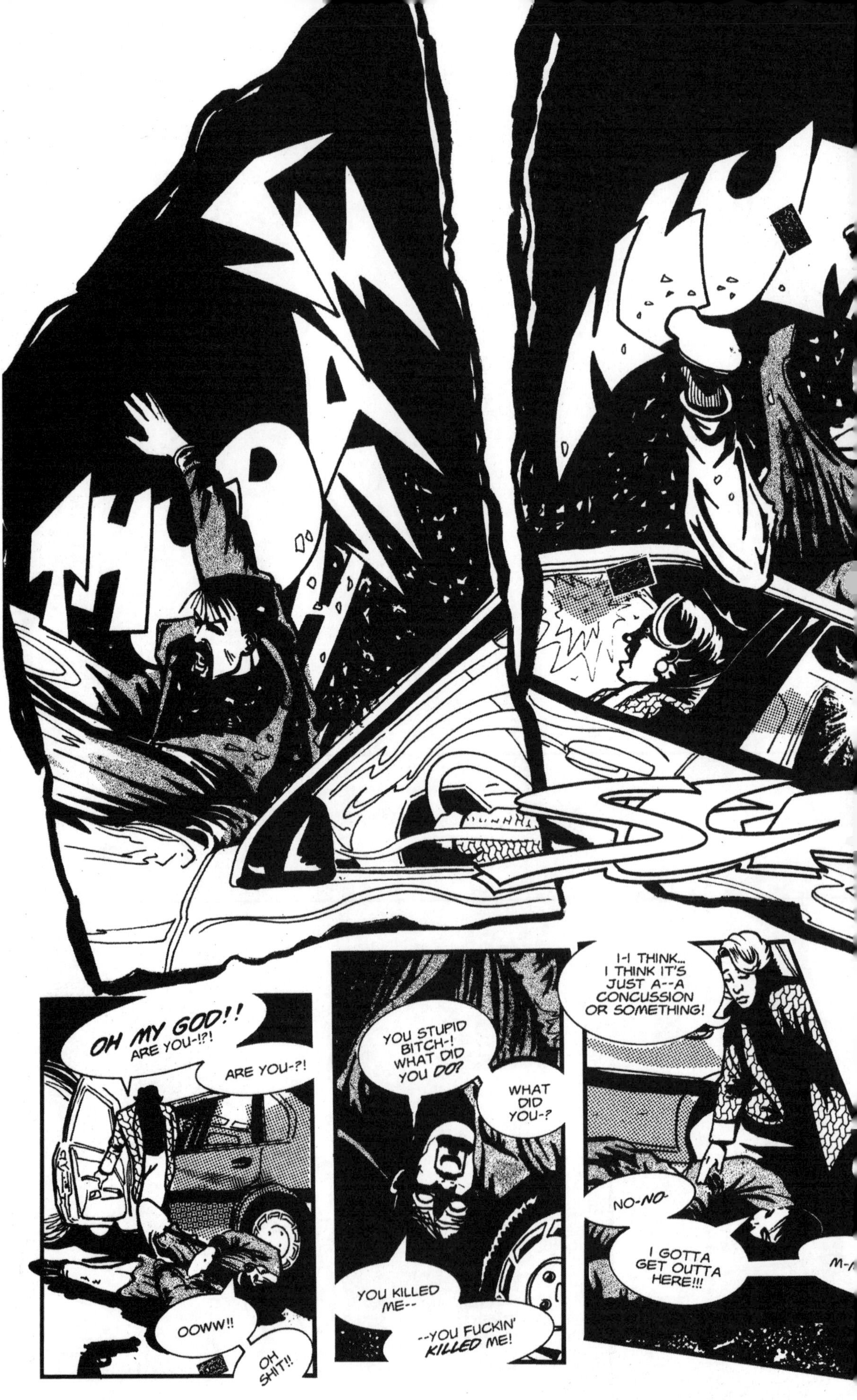
OH MY GOD!! ARE YOU-!?!
ARE YOU-?!
OOWW!!
OH SHIT!!
YOU STUPID BITCH-! WHAT DID YOU DO?
WHAT DID YOU-?
YOU KILLED ME--
--YOU FUCKIN' KILLED ME!
I-I THINK... I THINK IT'S JUST A--A CONCUSSION OR SOMETHING!
NO-NO-
I GOTTA GET OUTTA HERE!!!

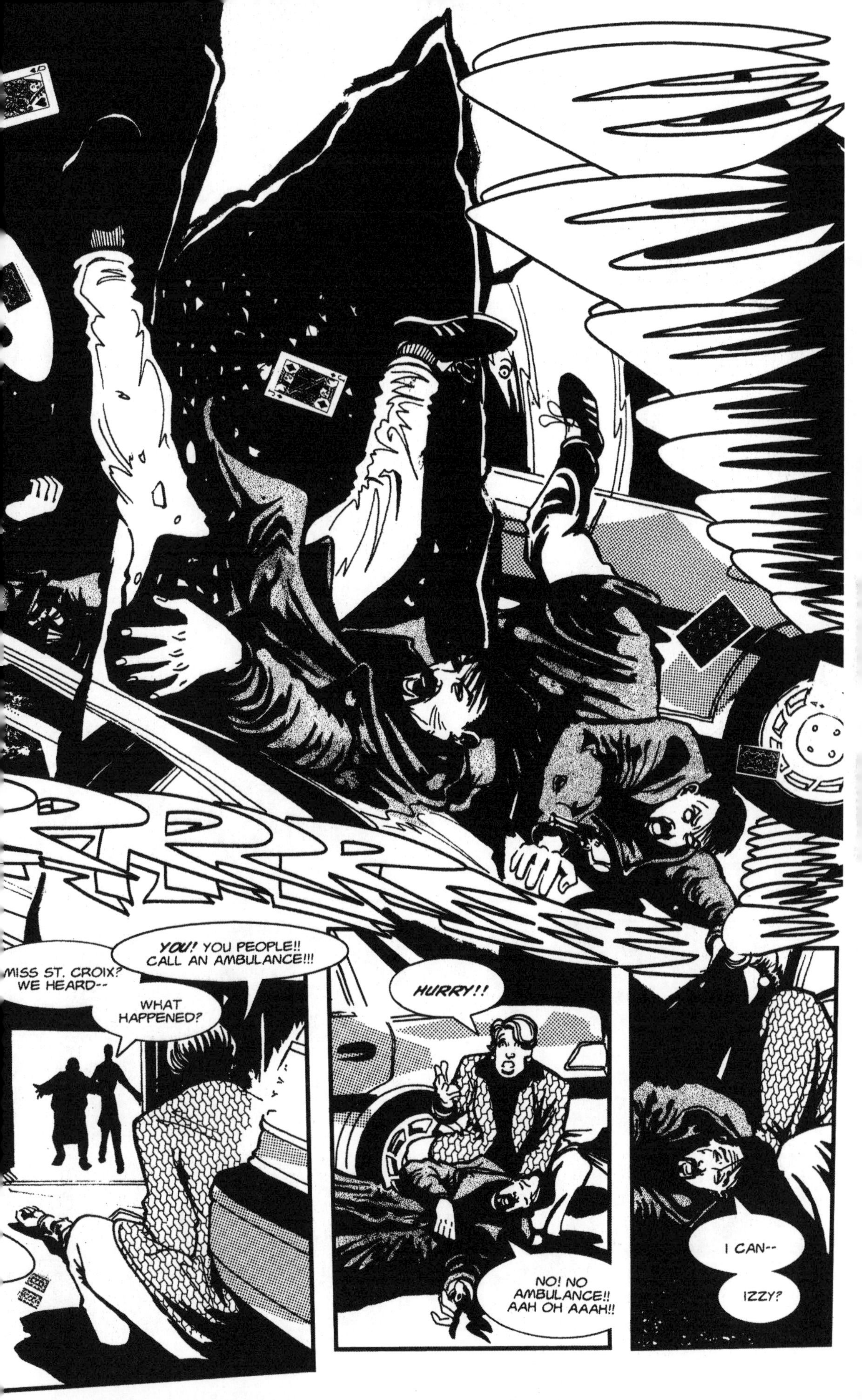
MISS ST. CROIX? WE HEARD--
WHAT HAPPENED?
YOU! YOU PEOPLE!! CALL AN AMBULANCE!!!
HURRY!!
NO! NO AMBULANCE!! AAH OH AAAH!!
I CAN--
IZZY?

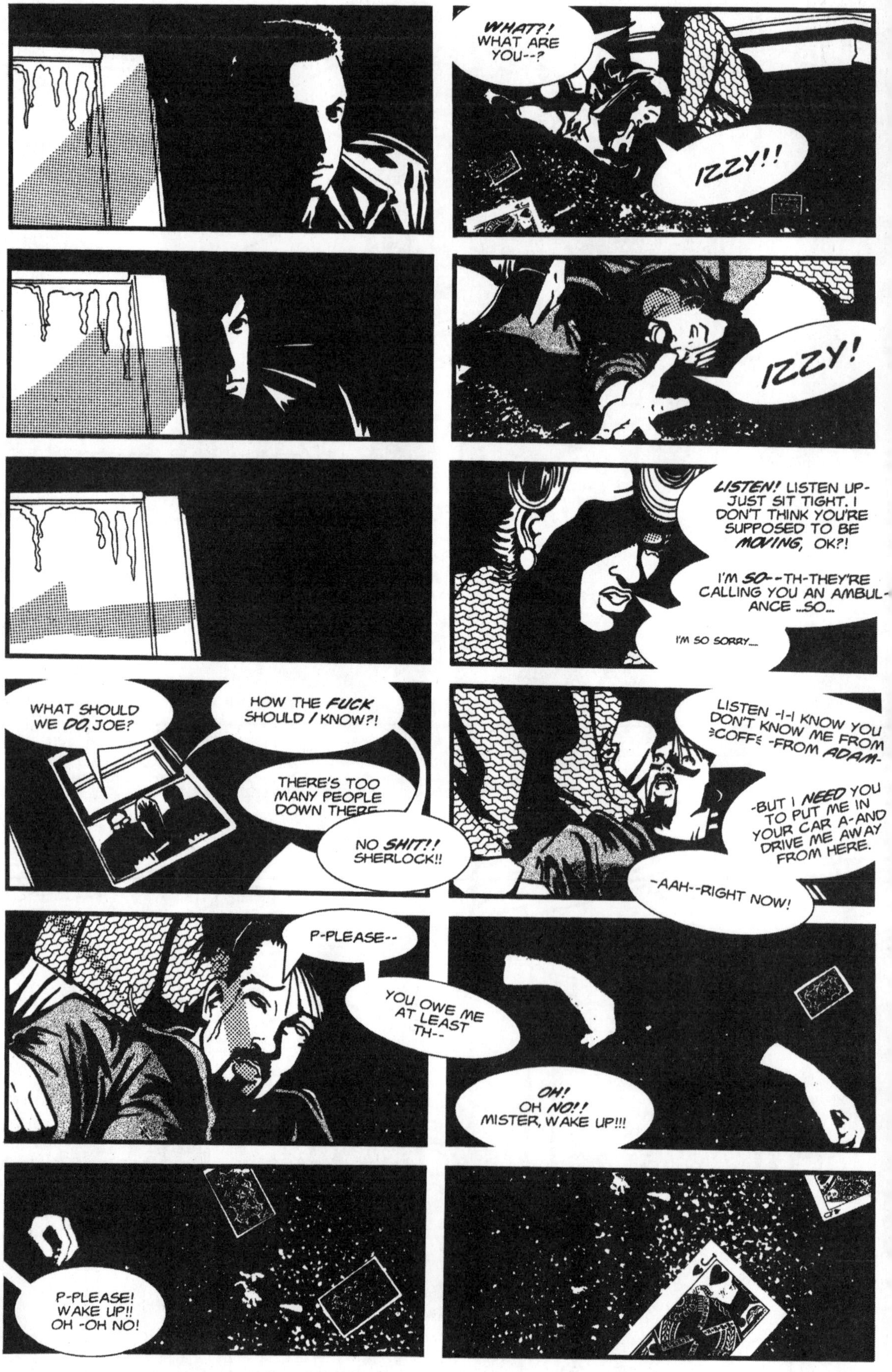
WHAT?! WHAT ARE YOU--?
IZZY!!
IZZY!
LISTEN! LISTEN UP- JUST SIT TIGHT. I DON'T THINK YOU'RE SUPPOSED TO BE MOVING, OK?!
I'M SO--TH-THEY'RE CALLING YOU AN AMBUL-ANCE ...SO...
I'M SO SORRY....
WHAT SHOULD WE DO, JOE?
HOW THE FUCK SHOULD I KNOW?!
THERE'S TOO MANY PEOPLE DOWN THERE
NO SHIT!! SHERLOCK!!
LISTEN -I-I KNOW YOU DON'T KNOW ME FROM COFF -FROM ADAM-
-BUT I NEED YOU TO PUT ME IN YOUR CAR A-AND DRIVE ME AWAY FROM HERE.
-AAH--RIGHT NOW!
P-PLEASE--
YOU OWE ME AT LEAST TH--
OH! OH NO!! MISTER, WAKE UP!!!
P-PLEASE! WAKE UP!! OH -OH NO!

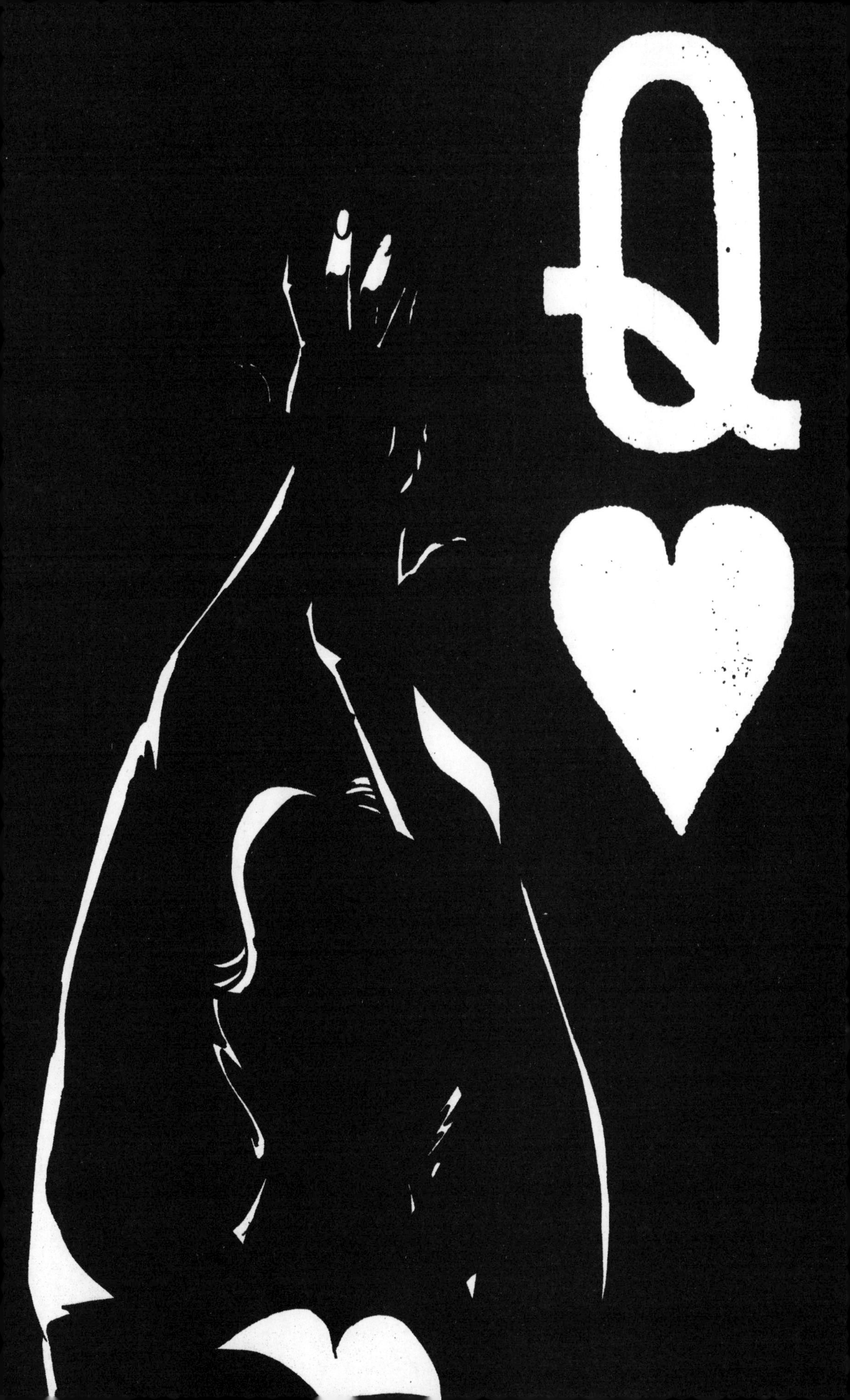
Q

"OH DAVE! *DAVE?!* IT'S *AMAZING!!!!*"

" I *THOUGHT* YOU'D..... "

"REALLY!!"

"...LIKE IT."

"WHERE?..."

"WHAT?"

"WHERE DID YOU GET IT?"

"WHAT DO YOU MEAN?"

"*WHERE* DID YOU...?"

"I *GOT* IT."

"I KNOW, I..."

"I GOT IT. IT'S *GOT*"

"YOU JUST DON'T GO OUT AND *GET* THIS. THIS IS *REAL*, RIGHT?"

"WHAT?"

"IT'S REAL?"

"OF *COURSE* IT'S REAL. IS IT *REAL?* PLEASE."

" THAT COST SOME...."

"YEP."

"...SOME BUCKS"

"DAMN STRAIGHT, HONEY! THIS IS A FIRST-PRINT CINDERELLA LOBBY
POSTER, I MEAN *-FIRST RUN*, IT'S SO RARE, *SO* RARE, THAT YOU
CAN'T EVEN FIND, LIKE, A PICTURE OF IT IN A BOOK."

"OH! DAVID, IT'S... IT'S *BEAUTIFUL*. HOW'D YOU?... -C'MON -WHERE DID
YOU GET IT? I MEAN...."

"OH, DON'T WORRY. I *SCAMMED* IT. SCAMMED THE *PANTS* OFF
SOMEONE. IT JUST TOOK, Y'KNOW, *A LOT* TO FIND THE RIGHT PANTS
TO SCAM."

"WELL, MY HEART IS GOIN' A PITTER-PATTER. IT'S-- IT'S JUST, Y'KNOW PEOPLE BUY PRESENTS FOR PEOPLE ALL THE TIME, EVERY DAY OF THE WEEK, RIGHT? BUT HOW OFTEN IS IT A REALLY *GOOD* PRESENT? DAVE, *THIS* IS A *REALLY* GOOD PRESENT. I LOVE THIS."

"WELL, HAPPY KANOOKAH LAUREN."

"I DO, I LOVE THIS."

"*MAJOR* BROWNIE POINTS?"

"OH YAH!"

"*WELL?*"

"WELL?"

"WELL? COUGH IT UP, BABE."

"*WHAT?*"

"WHERE *IS* IT? WHERE'S *MINE?*"

"IT'S HERE. IT'S RIGHT HERE. SETTLE DOWN."

"WELL?"

"OH, Y'KNOW, I DON'T KNOW."

"WHAT?"

"IT'S NOT AS GOOD AS YOURS."

"OH *STOP!*"

"WELL IT'S..."

"*STOP* IT! IT'S NOT A CONTEST."

"I KNOW, I..."

"SO GIMME. *GIMME! GIMME! GIMME!*....OOH! IT'S HEAVY!"

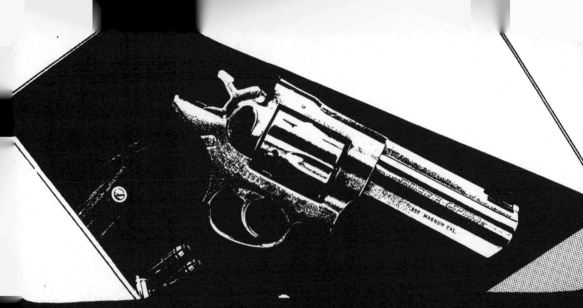

"OH MAN....!"

"HUH? *HUH?!* DO YOU LIKE IT?"

"LAUREN, WHAT'S THE MATTER WITH YOU?! WHAT.... WHAT DID I SAY?!"

"OH, I KNOW, BUT...."

"I SAID I DON'T WANT TO CARRY A PIECE!"

"HOW DO YOU KNOW? DO YOU...?"

"HOW DO I *KNOW?*"

"YOU'VE *NEVER* CARRIED....."

"I'VE HELD A GUN!"

"IT'S NOT THE SAME."

"I CAN'T BELIEVE YOU! YOU NEVER LISTEN, *NEVER!*"

"I LISTEN. I LISTEN MORE THAN YOU KNOW, C'MON!!!! YOU WANT TO PISS
WITH THE BIG BOYS? WELL, EVENTUALLY YOU'RE GONNA HAVE TO,
Y'KNOW, BE READY FOR ANYTHING."

"NO! NO.... THIS ISN'T...."

"C'MON, YOU WANNA BE DOIN' *CARD* TRICKS FOR THE REST OF YOUR
LIFE? YOU'LL END UP LIKE FUCKIN' KRESKIN, Y'KNOW?"

"I DON'T WANT A GUN!"

"PICK IT UP."

"NO!"

"C'MON, PICK IT UP."

"*NO!!!!!!!!*"

"THESE AREN'T *CHEAP,* Y'KNOW? THAT'S A NICE PIECE."

"I DON'T MEAN TO SOUND *UNGRATEFUL,* BUT, WE *TALKED* ABOUT
THIS LAUREN, AND....."

"YEAH? YEAH, WE DID. WE TALKED ABOUT *A LOT* OF THINGS. WE TALKED
ABOUT DRAGGING OURSELVES OUT OF THIS FUCKING MUD. WE TALKED
ABOUT NOT EATING *RAMEN* AND FUCKIN' *SPAGHETTI-O'S* FOUR DAYS
A WEEK. WE TALKED ABOUT LIVIN' OFF MORE THAN JUST CHUMP
CHANGE THAT WE SQUEEZE OFF THE PROVERBIAL CHUMPS."

"WELL? LET'S GO FOR IT. THE *BIG TIME*! LET'S START PLANNIN'. WHAT ARE YOU *SCARED* OF, HUH? WE'LL DO IT TOGETHER. I'M NOT.... YOU'RE NOT *ALONE* HERE. I'M NOT ASKIN' YOU TO GO OUT AND START ROBBIN' 7-11'S FOR ME."

"I KNOW..."

"C'MON! *THIS*.... THIS IS OUR *LIVES*, Y'KNOW? THIS ISN'T A REHEARSAL. IT'S GOING ON RIGHT NOW! LET EVERYBODY ELSE DRIFT FROM DAY TO DAY IN A *FOG* OF THEIR OWN CREATION. CAN YOU EVEN FOR A SECOND FATHOM THE AMOUNT, THE SHEER VOLUME OF PEOPLE THAT ARE OUT THERE SITTING IN THEIR CRAPPY LITTLE HOUSES WITH THEIR CRAPPY LITTLE LIVES? THEY SIT THERE DULLING EVERY UNIQUE FEELING AND EMOTION THEY HAVE, EVERYTHING THAT MAKES THEM INTERESTING, WITH *TV* AND SHIT. THEY SIT THERE AND NEVER FACE THEIR FEAR OR WHATEVER IT IS. THEY NEVER RISE TO THE CHALLENGES THAT FATE HAS BROUGHT THEIR WAY. 'OH-*ONE* OF THESE DAYS I'M GONNA BLAH BLAH BLAH! AND *THEN* MY LIFE WILL TURN AROUND, AND *THEN* MY LIFE WILL BE MY OWN!' ...BUT DAYS TURN INTO MONTHS, AND MONTHS TURN INTO A GIANT FUCKING *TUMOR* FROM ALL THAT REPRESSION. AND THEN ---- *DEAD!* AND THEY NEVER *EVER* DID ANYTHING TO ACCOUNT FOR LIVIN' THE BIOLOGICAL MIRACLE THAT IS LIFE. WELL, Y'KNOW WHAT? *FUCK 'EM!* FUCK 'EM ALL. LET THEM ALL DROP OFF THE FACE OF THE EARTH. BUT YOU AND ME? LET'S BE THE ELITE. LET'S BE THE *MOD SQUAD*. LET'S BE THE ONES THAT OTHERS LOOK AT AS MORE THAN HUMAN. UNTOUCHABLE. LET'S BE THE ONES THAT DO SOMETHING."

"WHAT? WHAT DO YOU WANT? WHAT DO WANT FROM ME?"

"WHAT DO I *WANT*?" HOW LONG HAVE YOU KNOWN ME? LET'S, Y'KNOW? SCAM EVERY CENT WE CAN OFF EVERY LUMP WE MEET. LET'S GO AFTER THE BIG SCORE. LET'S LIVE WITH MONEY IN OUR POCKETS, FUCK 'TIL WE'RE BLUE IN THE FACE, AND GO TO THE MOVIES."

"ARE YOU PROPOSING?"

"PICK IT UP....... YEAH- THAT'S IT"

"IT IS NICE."

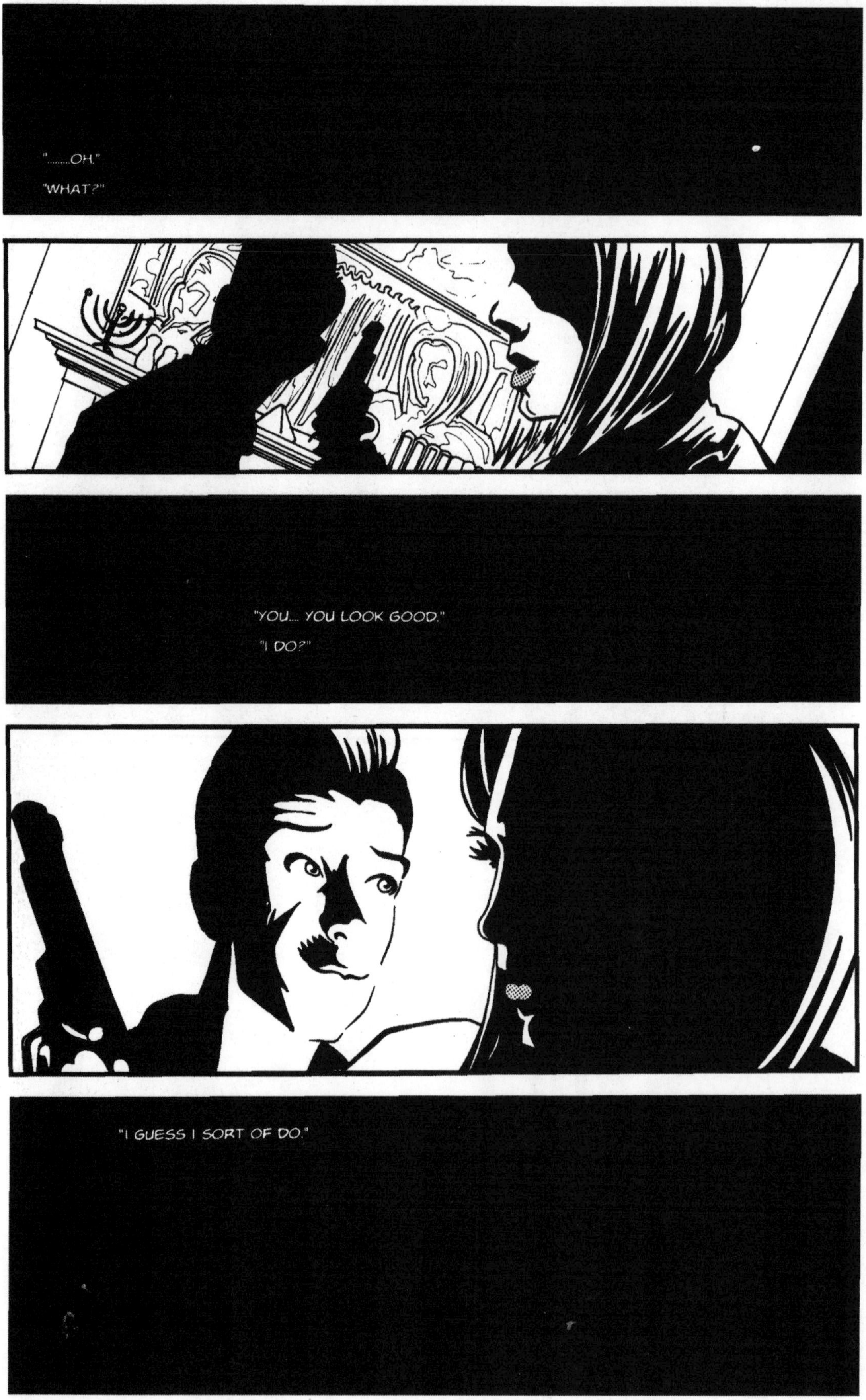
"........OH."
"WHAT?"
"YOU.... YOU LOOK GOOD."
"I DO?"
"I GUESS I SORT OF DO."

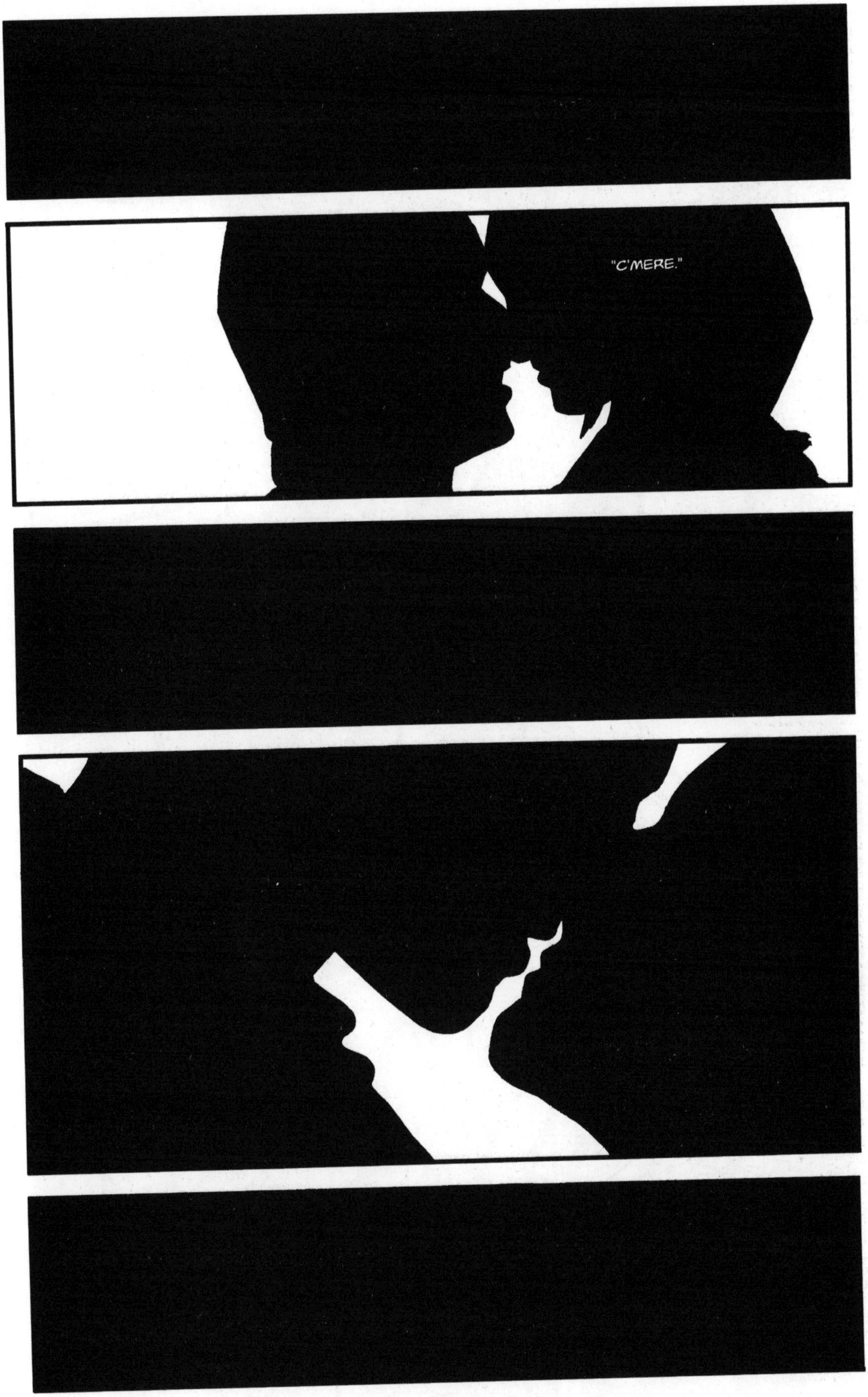
"C'MERE."

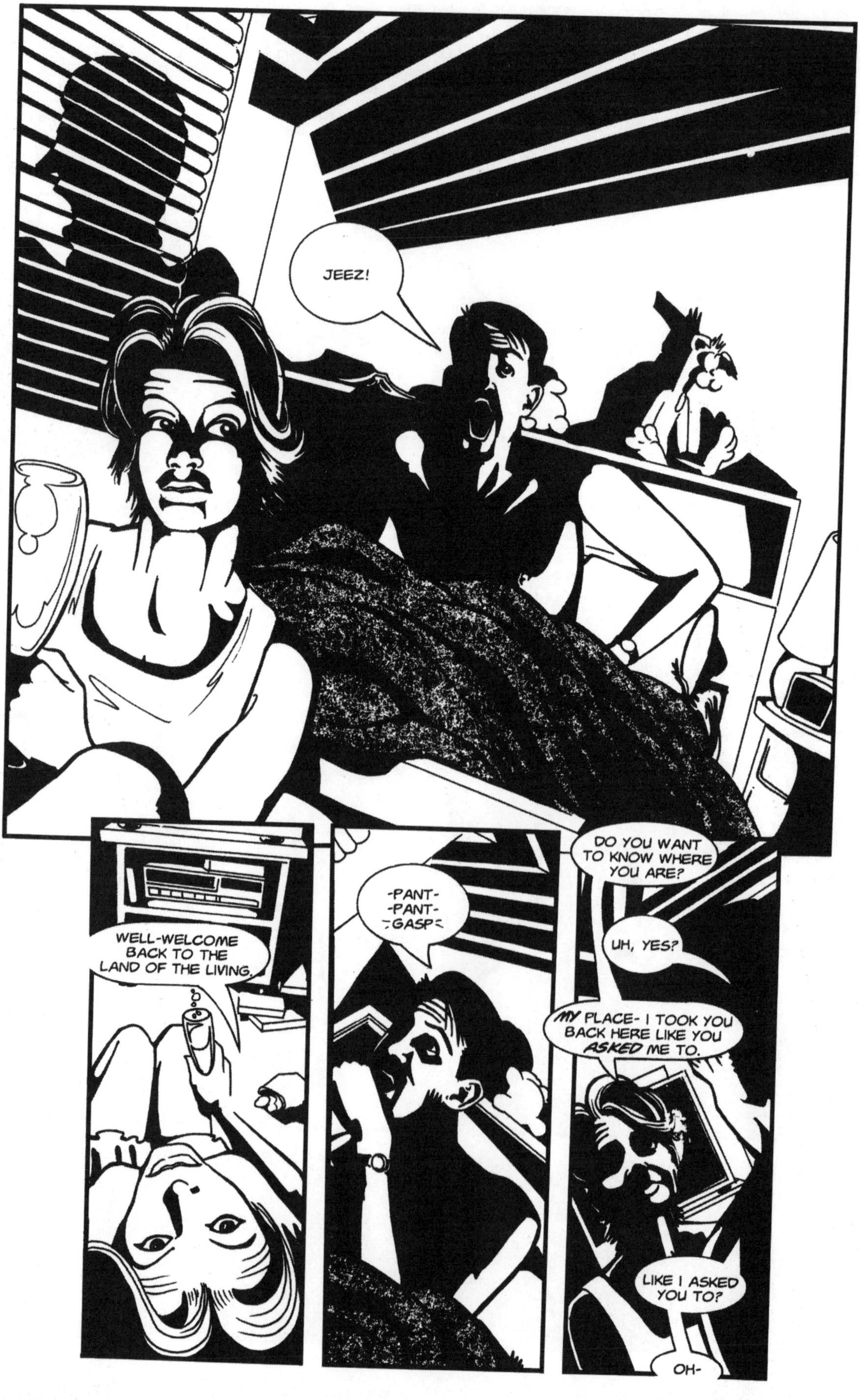
JEEZ!
WELL-WELCOME BACK TO THE LAND OF THE LIVING.
-PANT- -PANT- GASP
DO YOU WANT TO KNOW WHERE YOU ARE?
UH, YES?
MY PLACE- I TOOK YOU BACK HERE LIKE YOU ASKED ME TO.
LIKE I ASKED YOU TO?
OH-

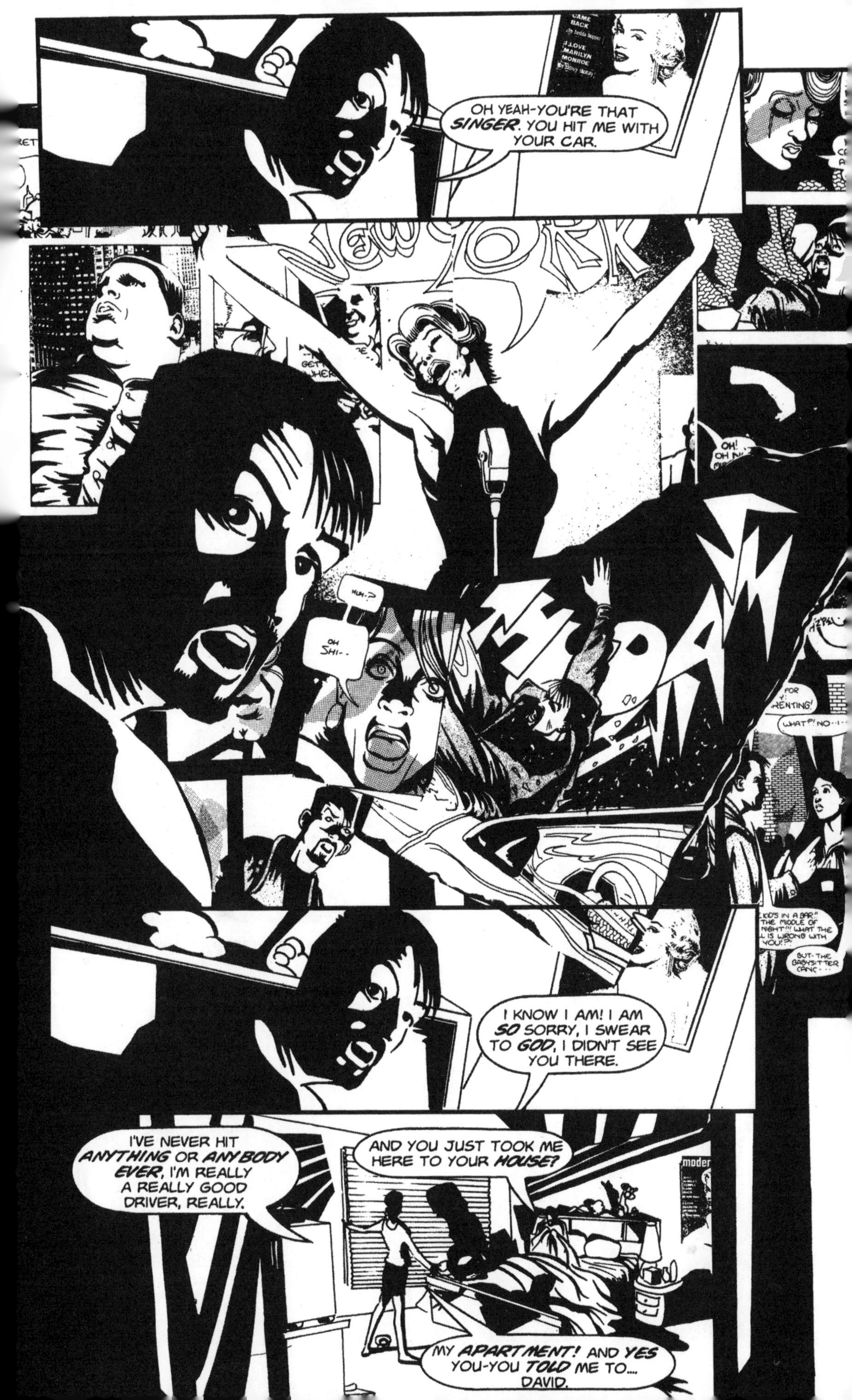

CAME BACK
I LOVE MARILYN MONROE
OH YEAH-YOU'RE THAT **SINGER**. YOU HIT ME WITH YOUR CAR.
HUH-?
OH SHI--
WHAT?! NO--
BUT- THE BABYSITTER CANC...
I KNOW I AM! I AM **SO** SORRY, I SWEAR TO **GOD**, I DIDN'T SEE YOU THERE.
I'VE NEVER HIT **ANYTHING** OR **ANYBODY EVER**, I'M REALLY A REALLY GOOD DRIVER, REALLY.
AND YOU JUST TOOK ME HERE TO YOUR **HOUSE**?
MY **APARTMENT**! AND **YES** YOU-YOU **TOLD** ME TO.... DAVID.

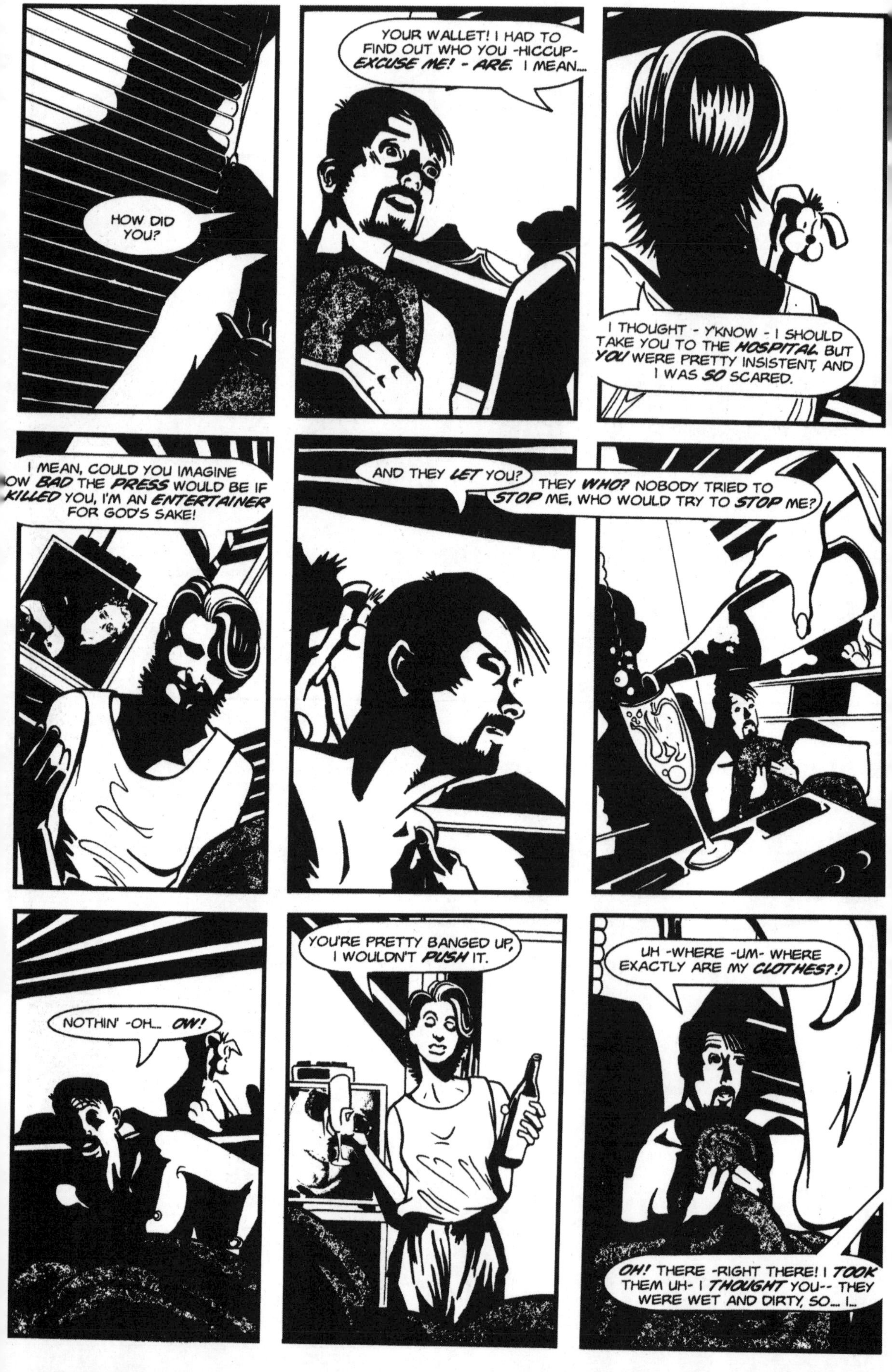
HOW DID YOU?
YOUR WALLET! I HAD TO FIND OUT WHO YOU -HICCUP- EXCUSE ME! - ARE. I MEAN...
I THOUGHT - Y'KNOW - I SHOULD TAKE YOU TO THE HOSPITAL BUT YOU WERE PRETTY INSISTENT, AND I WAS SO SCARED.
I MEAN, COULD YOU IMAGINE OW BAD THE PRESS WOULD BE IF KILLED YOU, I'M AN ENTERTAINER FOR GOD'S SAKE!
AND THEY LET YOU?
THEY WHO? NOBODY TRIED TO STOP ME, WHO WOULD TRY TO STOP ME?
NOTHIN' -OH... OW!
YOU'RE PRETTY BANGED UP, I WOULDN'T PUSH IT.
UH -WHERE -UM- WHERE EXACTLY ARE MY CLOTHES?!
OH! THERE -RIGHT THERE! I TOOK THEM UH- I THOUGHT YOU-- THEY WERE WET AND DIRTY, SO... I...

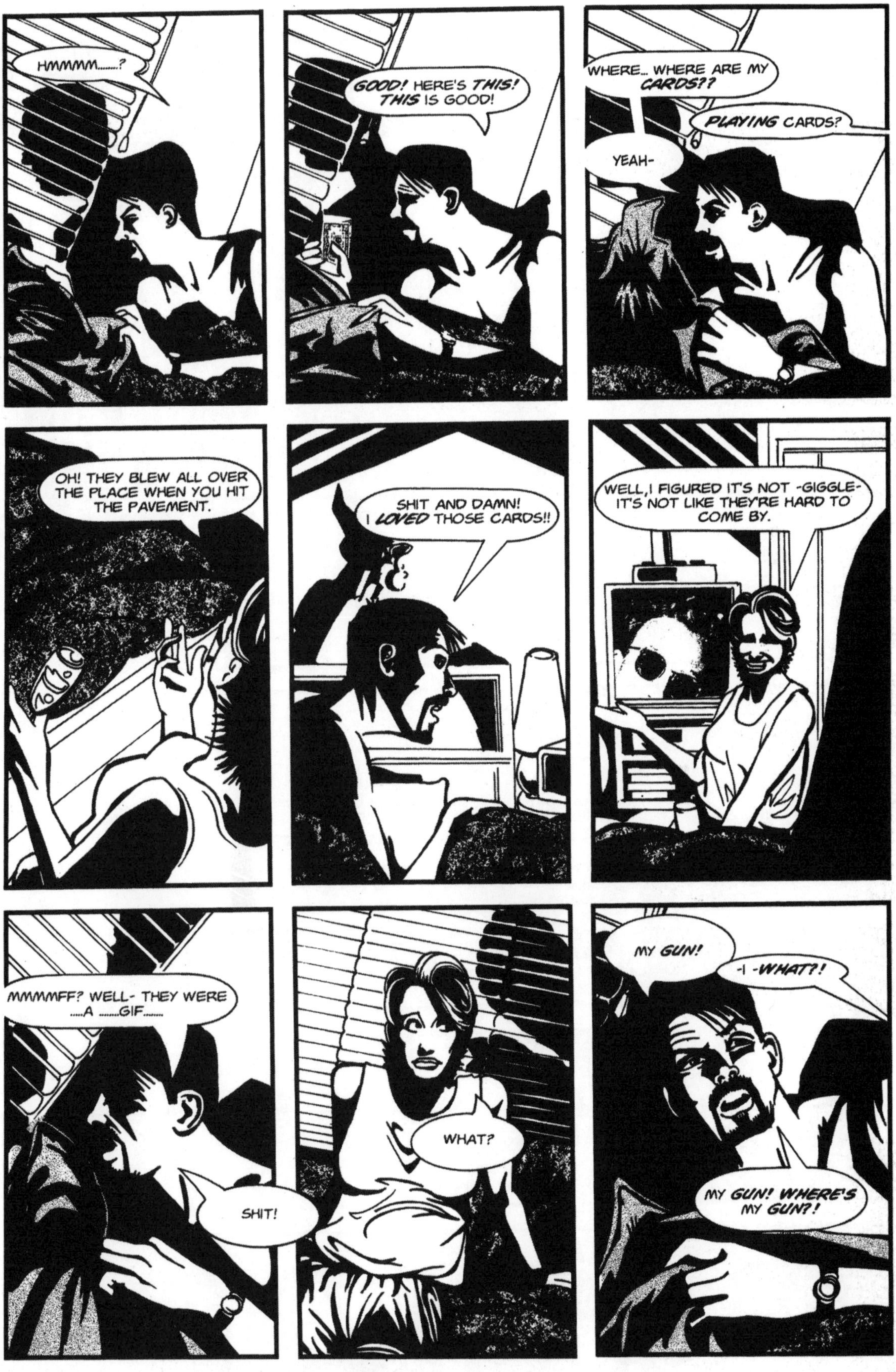
HMMMM.......?
GOOD! HERE'S THIS! THIS IS GOOD!
WHERE... WHERE ARE MY CARDS??
PLAYING CARDS?
YEAH-
OH! THEY BLEW ALL OVER THE PLACE WHEN YOU HIT THE PAVEMENT.
SHIT AND DAMN! I LOVED THOSE CARDS!!
WELL, I FIGURED IT'S NOT -GIGGLE- IT'S NOT LIKE THEY'RE HARD TO COME BY.
MMMMFF? WELL- THEY WERE .....A ....GIF.......
SHIT!
WHAT?
MY GUN!
-I -WHAT?!
MY GUN! WHERE'S MY GUN?!

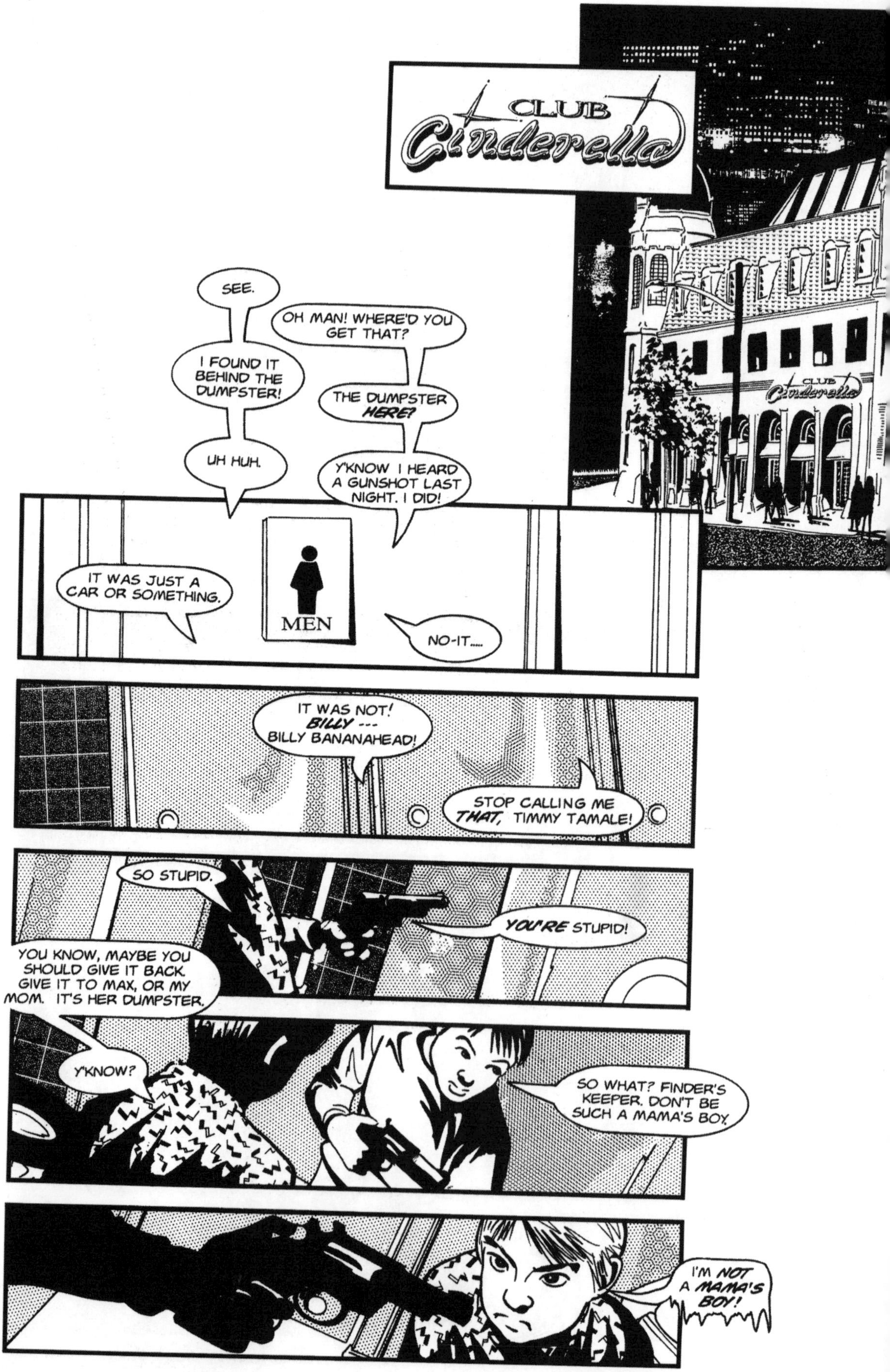
CLUB Cinderella
CLUB Cinderella
SEE.
OH MAN! WHERE'D YOU GET THAT?
I FOUND IT BEHIND THE DUMPSTER!
THE DUMPSTER HERE?
UH HUH.
Y'KNOW I HEARD A GUNSHOT LAST NIGHT. I DID!
MEN
IT WAS JUST A CAR OR SOMETHING.
NO-IT.....
IT WAS NOT! BILLY --- BILLY BANANAHEAD!
STOP CALLING ME THAT, TIMMY TAMALE!
SO STUPID.
YOU'RE STUPID!
YOU KNOW, MAYBE YOU SHOULD GIVE IT BACK. GIVE IT TO MAX, OR MY MOM. IT'S HER DUMPSTER.
Y'KNOW?
SO WHAT? FINDER'S KEEPER. DON'T BE SUCH A MAMA'S BOY.
I'M NOT A MAMA'S BOY!

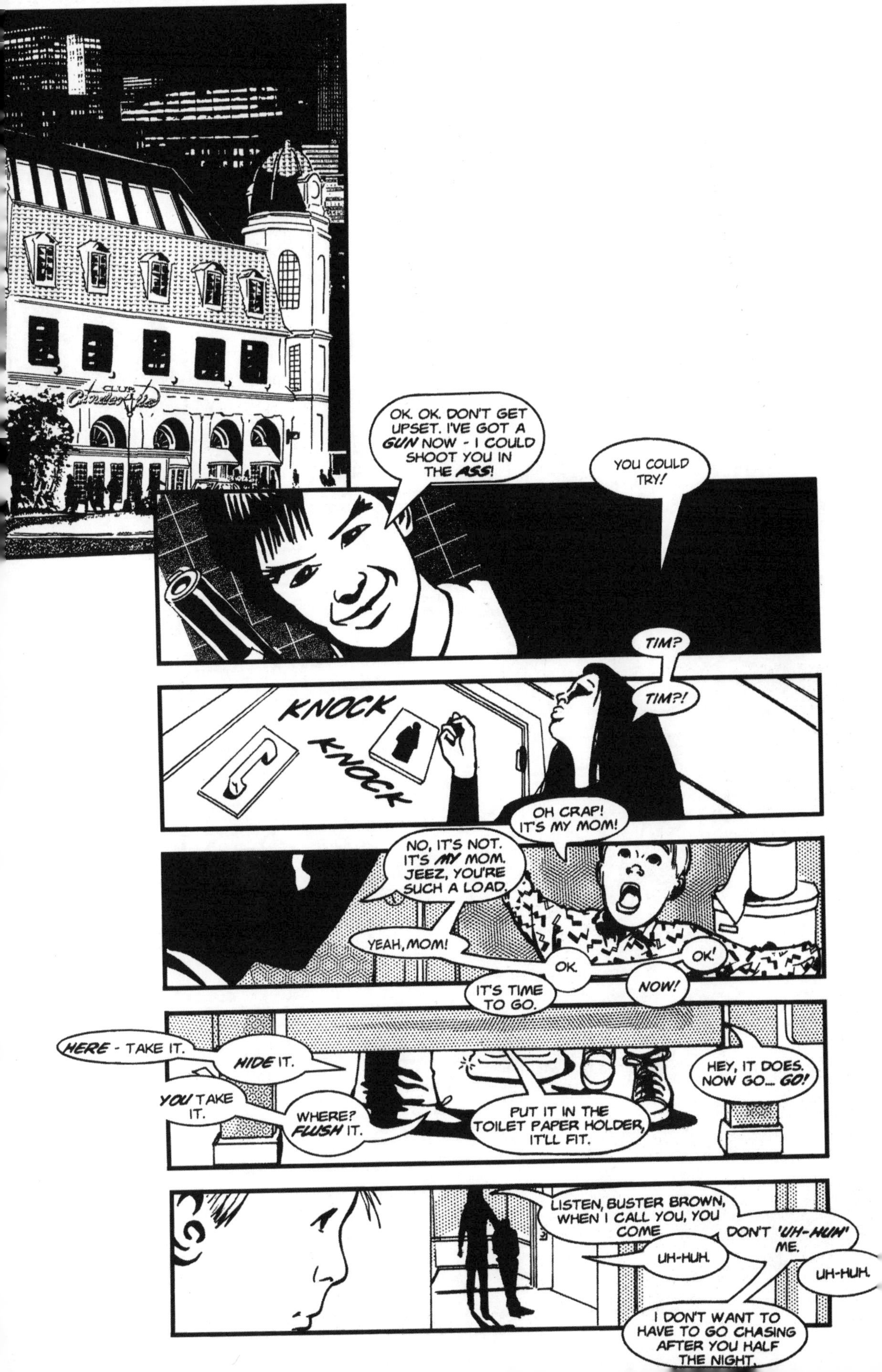
CLUB Cinderella
OK. OK. DON'T GET UPSET. I'VE GOT A GUN NOW - I COULD SHOOT YOU IN THE ASS!
YOU COULD TRY!
TIM?
TIM?!
KNOCK
KNOCK
OH CRAP! IT'S MY MOM!
NO, IT'S NOT. IT'S MY MOM. JEEZ, YOU'RE SUCH A LOAD.
YEAH, MOM!
OK.
OK!
IT'S TIME TO GO.
NOW!
HERE - TAKE IT.
HIDE IT.
YOU TAKE IT.
WHERE? FLUSH IT.
PUT IT IN THE TOILET PAPER HOLDER, IT'LL FIT.
HEY, IT DOES. NOW GO... GO!
LISTEN, BUSTER BROWN, WHEN I CALL YOU, YOU COME.
UH-HUH.
DON'T 'UH-HUH' ME.
UH-HUH.
I DON'T WANT TO HAVE TO GO CHASING AFTER YOU HALF THE NIGHT.

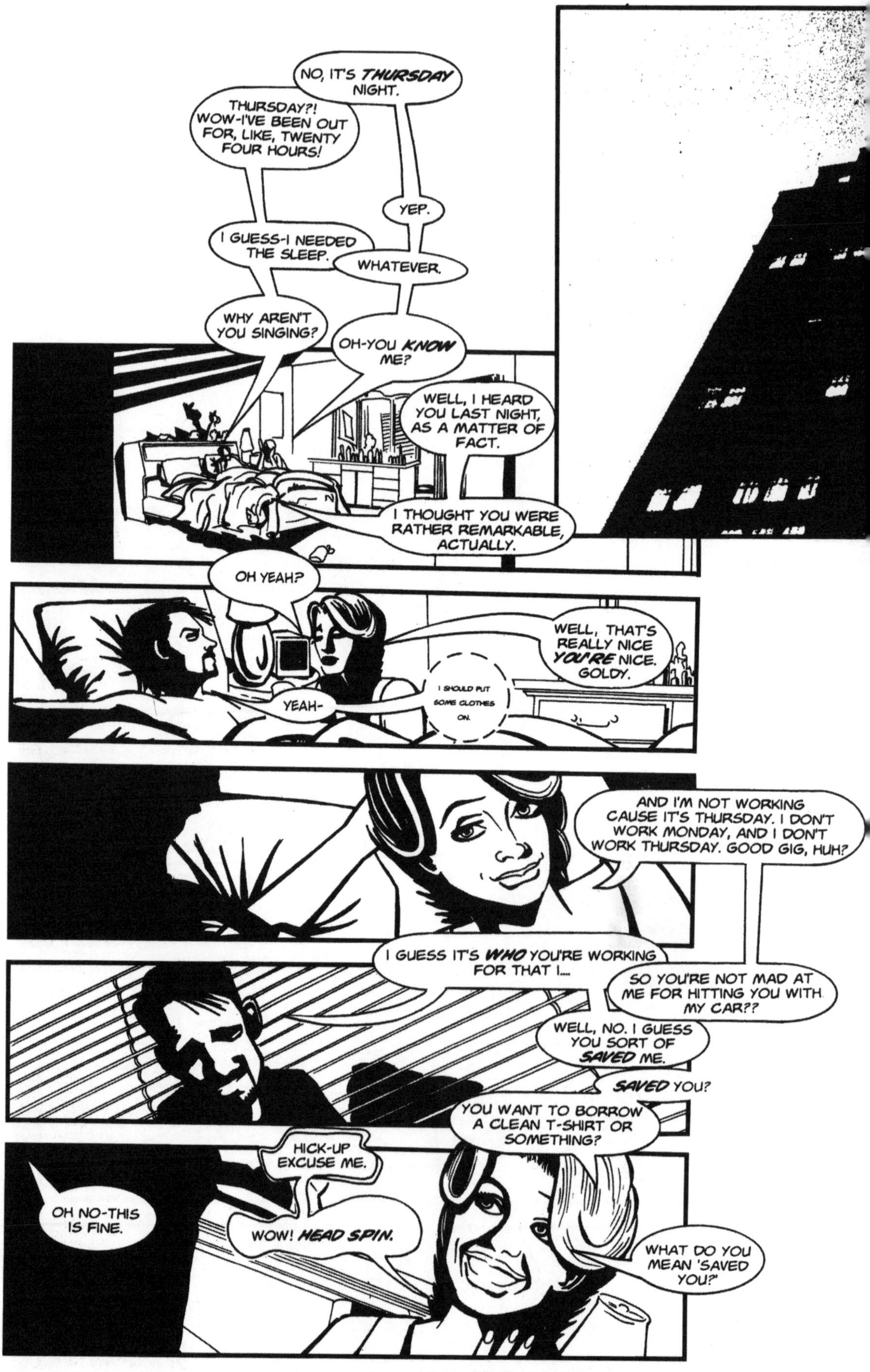
NO, IT'S THURSDAY NIGHT.
THURSDAY?! WOW-I'VE BEEN OUT FOR, LIKE, TWENTY FOUR HOURS!
YEP.
I GUESS-I NEEDED THE SLEEP.
WHATEVER.
WHY AREN'T YOU SINGING?
OH-YOU KNOW ME?
WELL, I HEARD YOU LAST NIGHT, AS A MATTER OF FACT.
I THOUGHT YOU WERE RATHER REMARKABLE, ACTUALLY.
OH YEAH?
WELL, THAT'S REALLY NICE YOU'RE NICE. GOLDY.
YEAH-
I SHOULD PUT SOME CLOTHES ON.
AND I'M NOT WORKING CAUSE IT'S THURSDAY. I DON'T WORK MONDAY, AND I DON'T WORK THURSDAY. GOOD GIG, HUH?
I GUESS IT'S WHO YOU'RE WORKING FOR THAT I....
SO YOU'RE NOT MAD AT ME FOR HITTING YOU WITH MY CAR??
WELL, NO. I GUESS YOU SORT OF SAVED ME.
SAVED YOU?
YOU WANT TO BORROW A CLEAN T-SHIRT OR SOMETHING?
HICK-UP EXCUSE ME.
OH NO-THIS IS FINE.
WOW! HEAD SPIN.
WHAT DO YOU MEAN 'SAVED YOU?'

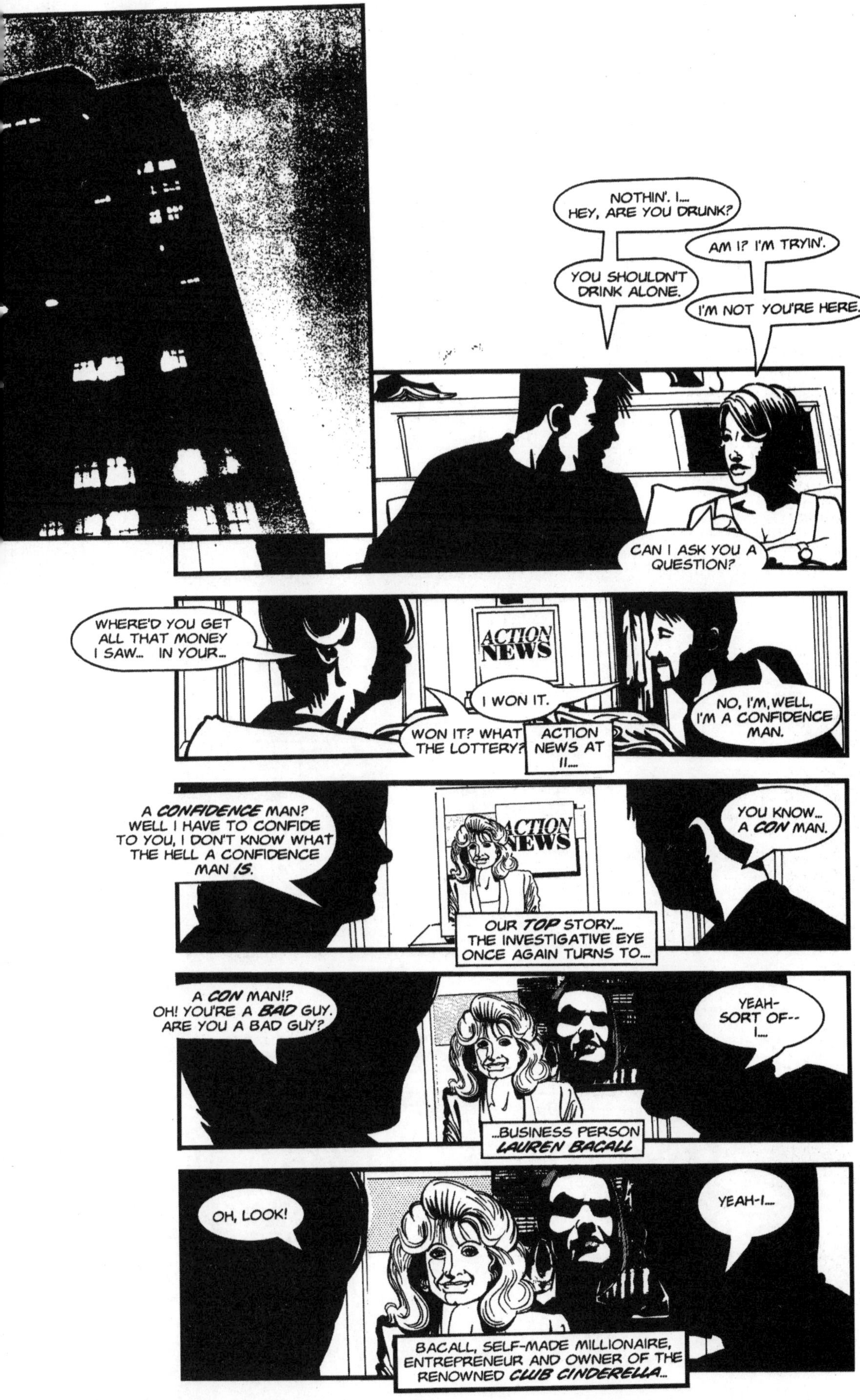
NOTHIN'. I...
HEY, ARE YOU DRUNK?
AM I? I'M TRYIN'.
YOU SHOULDN'T DRINK ALONE.
I'M NOT YOU'RE HERE.
CAN I ASK YOU A QUESTION?
WHERE'D YOU GET ALL THAT MONEY I SAW... IN YOUR...
ACTION NEWS
I WON IT.
WON IT? WHAT THE LOTTERY?
ACTION NEWS AT 11...
NO, I'M, WELL, I'M A CONFIDENCE MAN.
A CONFIDENCE MAN? WELL I HAVE TO CONFIDE TO YOU, I DON'T KNOW WHAT THE HELL A CONFIDENCE MAN IS.
ACTION NEWS
YOU KNOW... A CON MAN.
OUR TOP STORY... THE INVESTIGATIVE EYE ONCE AGAIN TURNS TO...
A CON MAN!? OH! YOU'RE A BAD GUY. ARE YOU A BAD GUY?
YEAH- SORT OF-- I...
...BUSINESS PERSON LAUREN BACALL
OH, LOOK!
YEAH-I...
BACALL, SELF-MADE MILLIONAIRE, ENTREPRENEUR AND OWNER OF THE RENOWNED CLUB CINDERELLA...

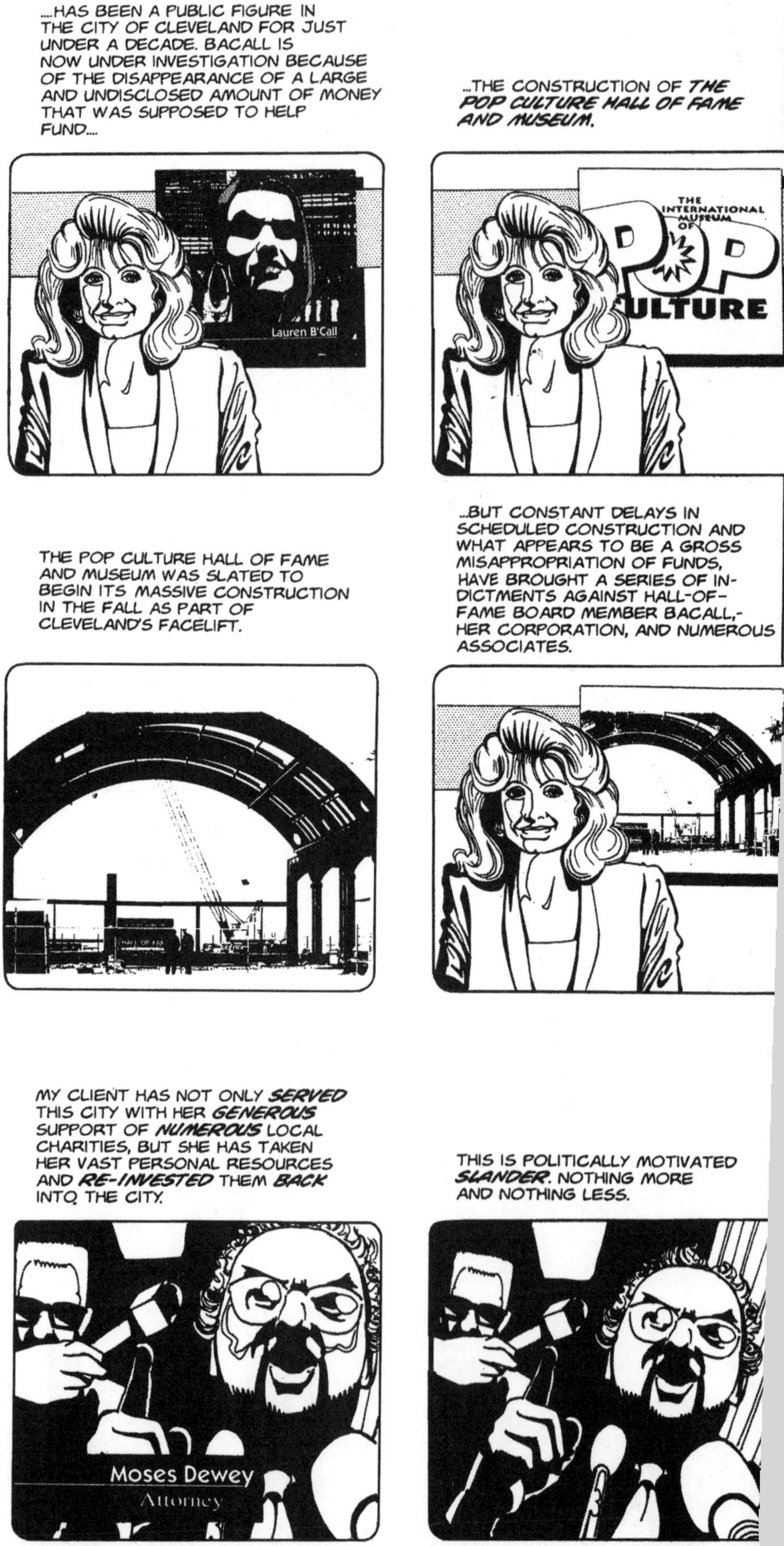
...HAS BEEN A PUBLIC FIGURE IN THE CITY OF CLEVELAND FOR JUST UNDER A DECADE. BACALL IS NOW UNDER INVESTIGATION BECAUSE OF THE DISAPPEARANCE OF A LARGE AND UNDISCLOSED AMOUNT OF MONEY THAT WAS SUPPOSED TO HELP FUND....
Lauren B'Call
...THE CONSTRUCTION OF *THE POP CULTURE HALL OF FAME AND MUSEUM.*
THE INTERNATIONAL MUSEUM OF POP CULTURE
THE POP CULTURE HALL OF FAME AND MUSEUM WAS SLATED TO BEGIN ITS MASSIVE CONSTRUCTION IN THE FALL AS PART OF CLEVELAND'S FACELIFT.
...BUT CONSTANT DELAYS IN SCHEDULED CONSTRUCTION AND WHAT APPEARS TO BE A GROSS MISAPPROPRIATION OF FUNDS, HAVE BROUGHT A SERIES OF INDICTMENTS AGAINST HALL-OF-FAME BOARD MEMBER BACALL,- HER CORPORATION, AND NUMEROUS ASSOCIATES.
MY CLIENT HAS NOT ONLY *SERVED* THIS CITY WITH HER *GENEROUS* SUPPORT OF *NUMEROUS* LOCAL CHARITIES, BUT SHE HAS TAKEN HER VAST PERSONAL RESOURCES AND *RE-INVESTED* THEM *BACK* INTO THE CITY.
Moses Dewey
Attorney
THIS IS POLITICALLY MOTIVATED *SLANDER*. NOTHING MORE AND NOTHING LESS.

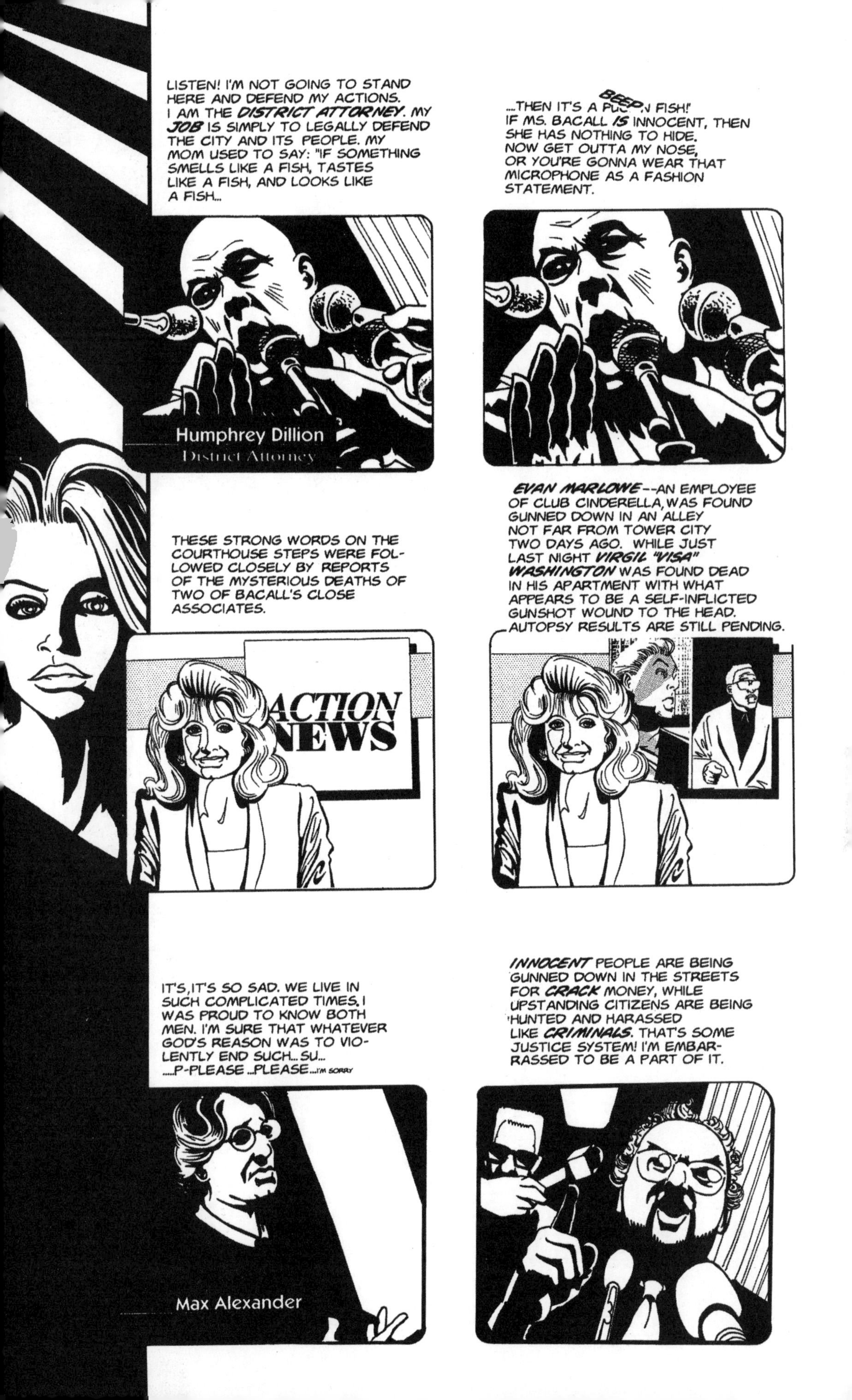
LISTEN! I'M NOT GOING TO STAND HERE AND DEFEND MY ACTIONS. I AM THE DISTRICT ATTORNEY. MY JOB IS SIMPLY TO LEGALLY DEFEND THE CITY AND ITS PEOPLE. MY MOM USED TO SAY: "IF SOMETHING SMELLS LIKE A FISH, TASTES LIKE A FISH, AND LOOKS LIKE A FISH...
Humphrey Dillion
District Attorney
...THEN IT'S A BEEP FISH!" IF MS. BACALL IS INNOCENT, THEN SHE HAS NOTHING TO HIDE. NOW GET OUTTA MY NOSE, OR YOU'RE GONNA WEAR THAT MICROPHONE AS A FASHION STATEMENT.
THESE STRONG WORDS ON THE COURTHOUSE STEPS WERE FOLLOWED CLOSELY BY REPORTS OF THE MYSTERIOUS DEATHS OF TWO OF BACALL'S CLOSE ASSOCIATES.
ACTION NEWS
EVAN MARLOWE--AN EMPLOYEE OF CLUB CINDERELLA, WAS FOUND GUNNED DOWN IN AN ALLEY NOT FAR FROM TOWER CITY TWO DAYS AGO. WHILE JUST LAST NIGHT VIRGIL "VISA" WASHINGTON WAS FOUND DEAD IN HIS APARTMENT WITH WHAT APPEARS TO BE A SELF-INFLICTED GUNSHOT WOUND TO THE HEAD. AUTOPSY RESULTS ARE STILL PENDING.
IT'S, IT'S SO SAD. WE LIVE IN SUCH COMPLICATED TIMES. I WAS PROUD TO KNOW BOTH MEN. I'M SURE THAT WHATEVER GOD'S REASON WAS TO VIOLENTLY END SUCH... SU... ....P-PLEASE ...PLEASE ...I'M SORRY
Max Alexander
INNOCENT PEOPLE ARE BEING GUNNED DOWN IN THE STREETS FOR CRACK MONEY, WHILE UPSTANDING CITIZENS ARE BEING HUNTED AND HARASSED LIKE CRIMINALS. THAT'S SOME JUSTICE SYSTEM! I'M EMBARRASSED TO BE A PART OF IT.

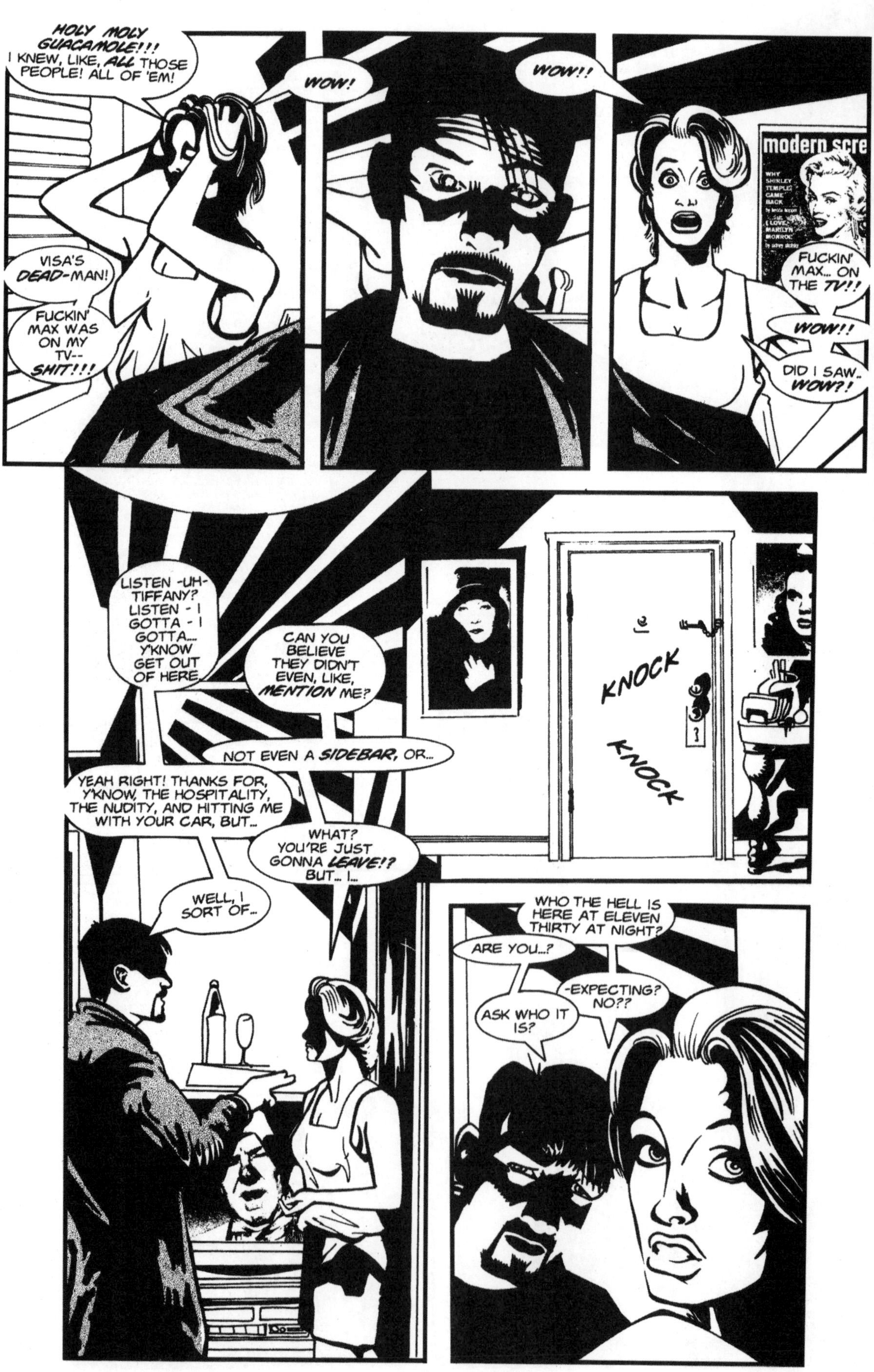
HOLY MOLY GUACAMOLE!!! I KNEW, LIKE, ALL THOSE PEOPLE! ALL OF 'EM!
VISA'S DEAD-MAN!
FUCKIN' MAX WAS ON MY TV-- SHIT!!!
WOW!
WOW!!
modern scre
WHY SHIRLEY TEMPLE CAME BACK
I LOVE MARILYN MONROE
FUCKIN' MAX... ON THE TV!!
WOW!!
DID I SAW.. WOW?!
LISTEN -UH- TIFFANY? LISTEN - I GOTTA - I GOTTA... Y'KNOW GET OUT OF HERE.
CAN YOU BELIEVE THEY DIDN'T EVEN, LIKE, MENTION ME?
NOT EVEN A SIDEBAR, OR...
YEAH RIGHT! THANKS FOR, Y'KNOW, THE HOSPITALITY, THE NUDITY, AND HITTING ME WITH YOUR CAR, BUT...
WHAT? YOU'RE JUST GONNA LEAVE!? BUT... I...
KNOCK
KNOCK
WELL, I SORT OF...
WHO THE HELL IS HERE AT ELEVEN THIRTY AT NIGHT?
ARE YOU...?
-EXPECTING? NO??
ASK WHO IT IS?

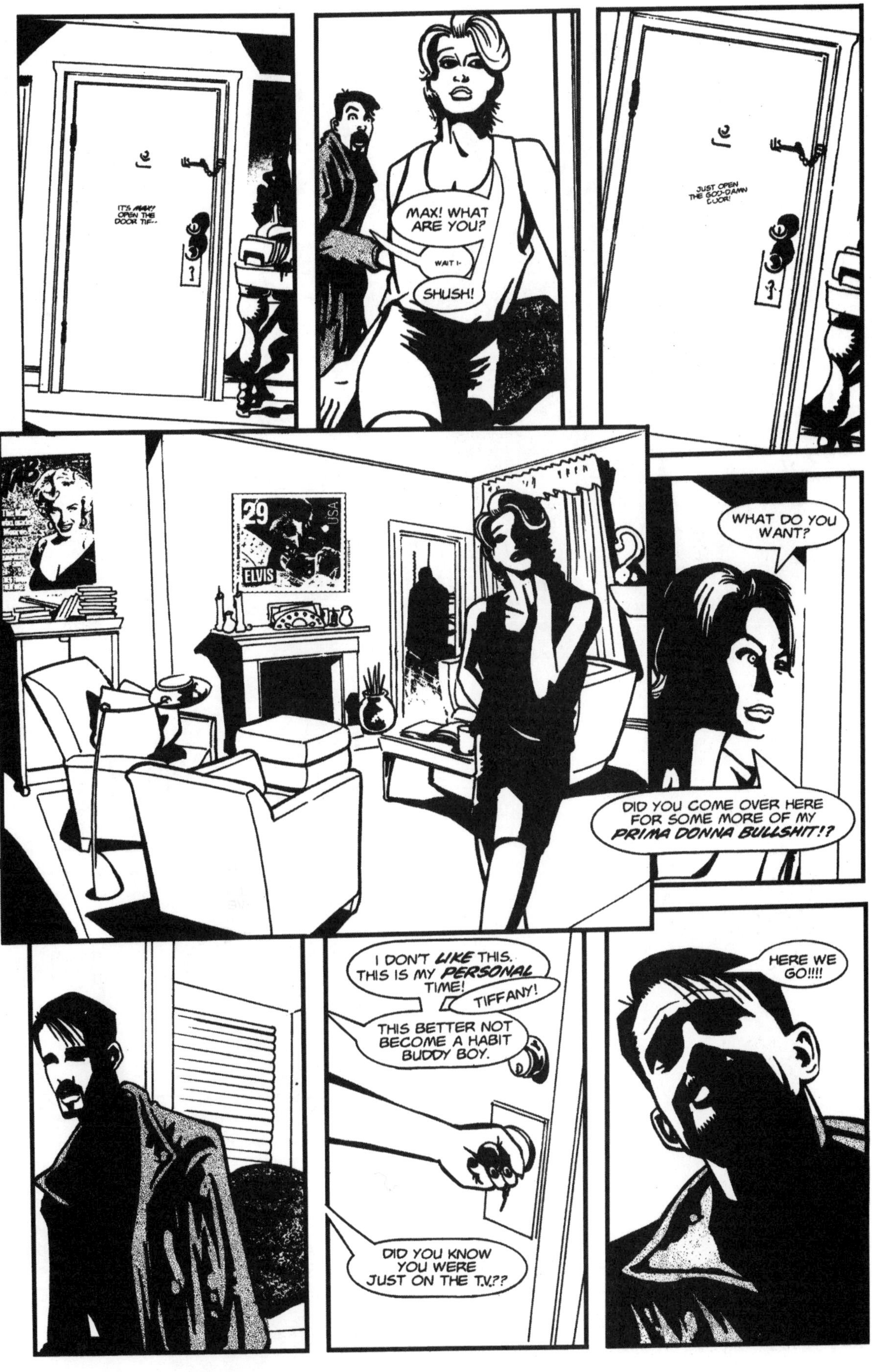
IT'S MAX!! OPEN THE DOOR TIF--
MAX! WHAT ARE YOU?
WAIT I-
SHUSH!
JUST OPEN THE GOD-DAMN DOOR!
29 USA
ELVIS
WHAT DO YOU WANT?
DID YOU COME OVER HERE FOR SOME MORE OF MY PRIMA DONNA BULLSHIT!?
I DON'T LIKE THIS. THIS IS MY PERSONAL TIME!
TIFFANY!
THIS BETTER NOT BECOME A HABIT BUDDY BOY.
DID YOU KNOW YOU WERE JUST ON THE T.V.??
HERE WE GO!!!!

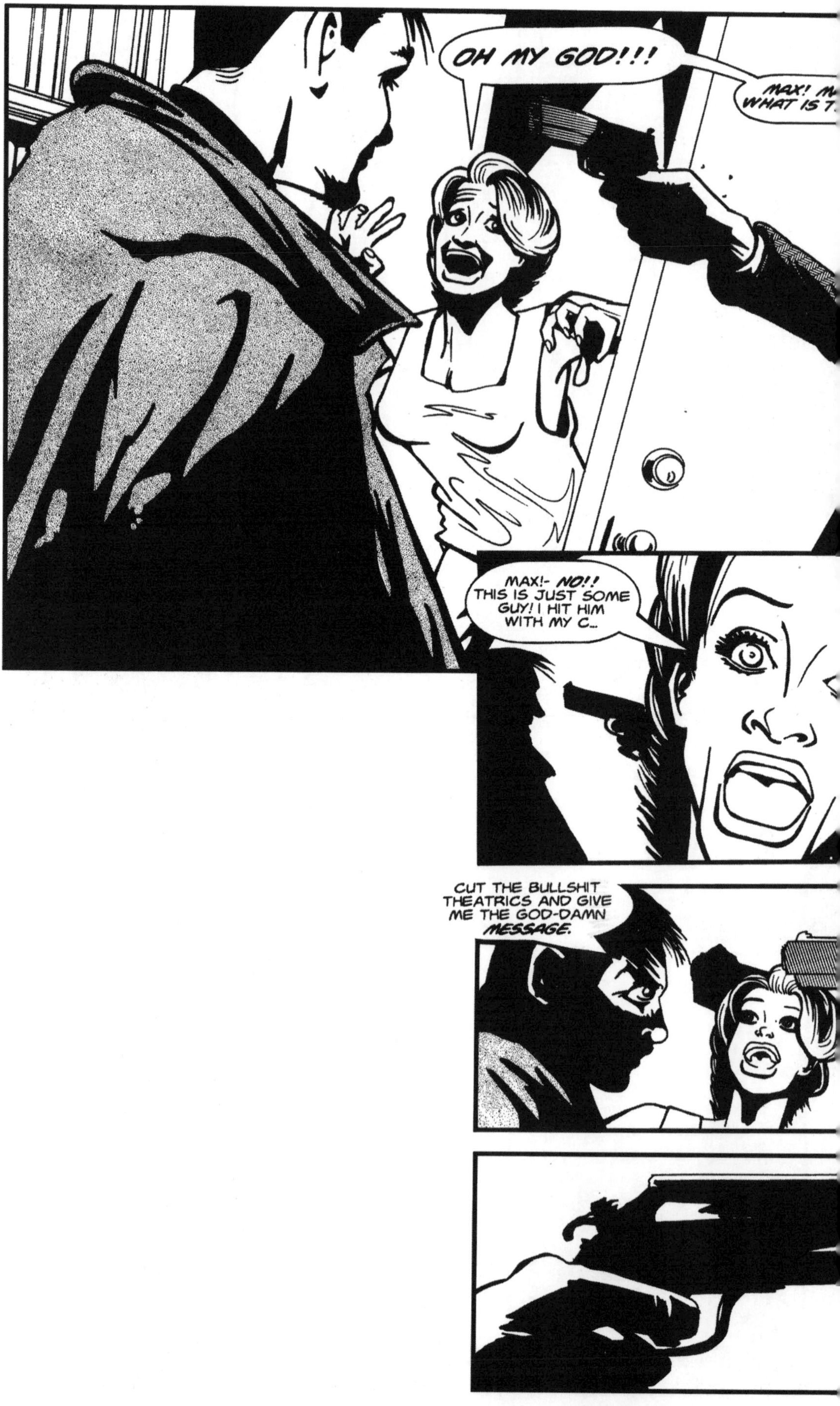
OH MY GOD!!!
MAX!
WHAT IS
MAX!- NO!! THIS IS JUST SOME GUY! I HIT HIM WITH MY C...
CUT THE BULLSHIT THEATRICS AND GIVE ME THE GOD-DAMN MESSAGE.

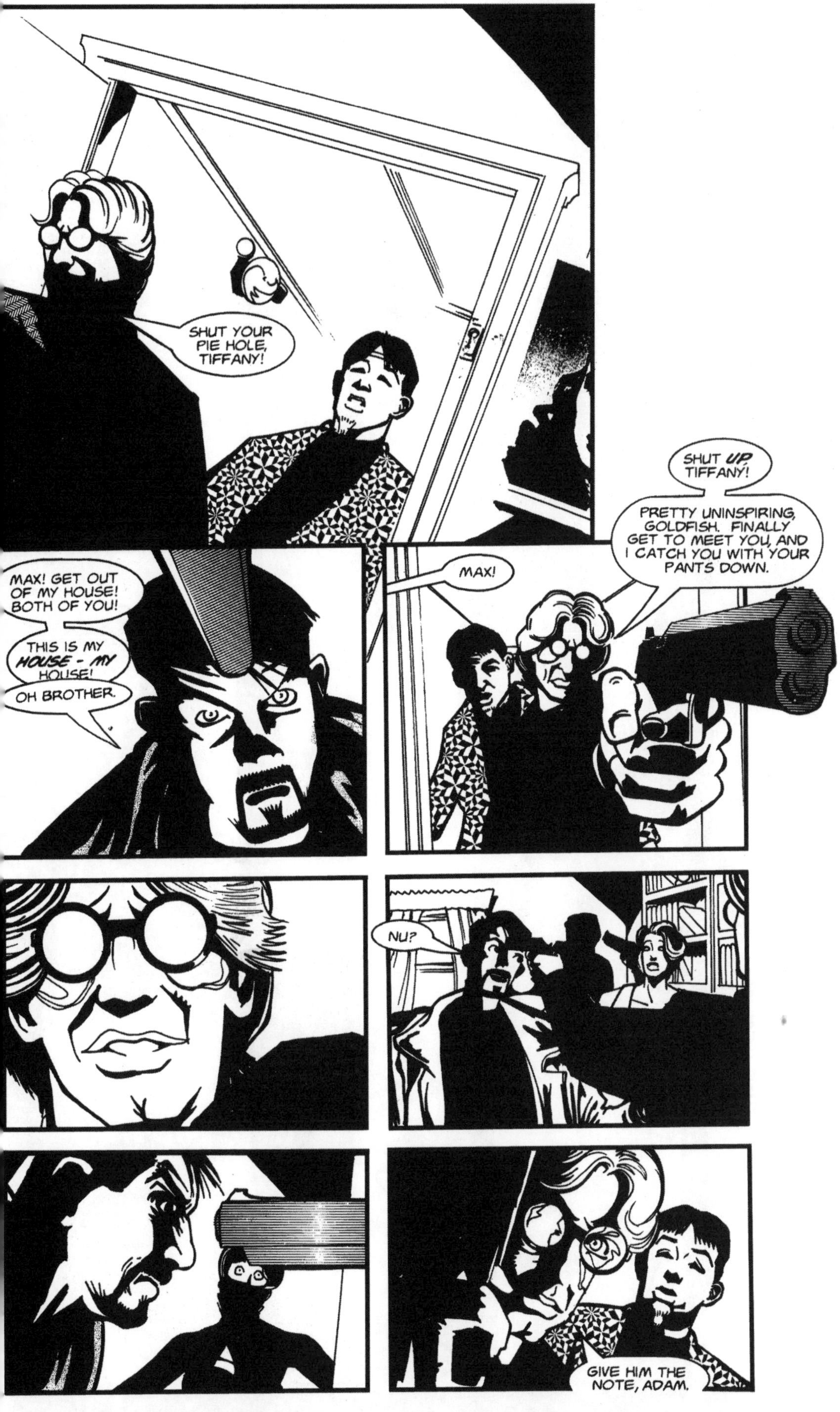
SHUT YOUR PIE HOLE, TIFFANY!
SHUT UP, TIFFANY!
PRETTY UNINSPIRING, GOLDFISH. FINALLY GET TO MEET YOU, AND I CATCH YOU WITH YOUR PANTS DOWN.
MAX! GET OUT OF MY HOUSE! BOTH OF YOU!
THIS IS MY HOUSE - MY HOUSE!
OH BROTHER.
MAX!
NU?
GIVE HIM THE NOTE, ADAM.

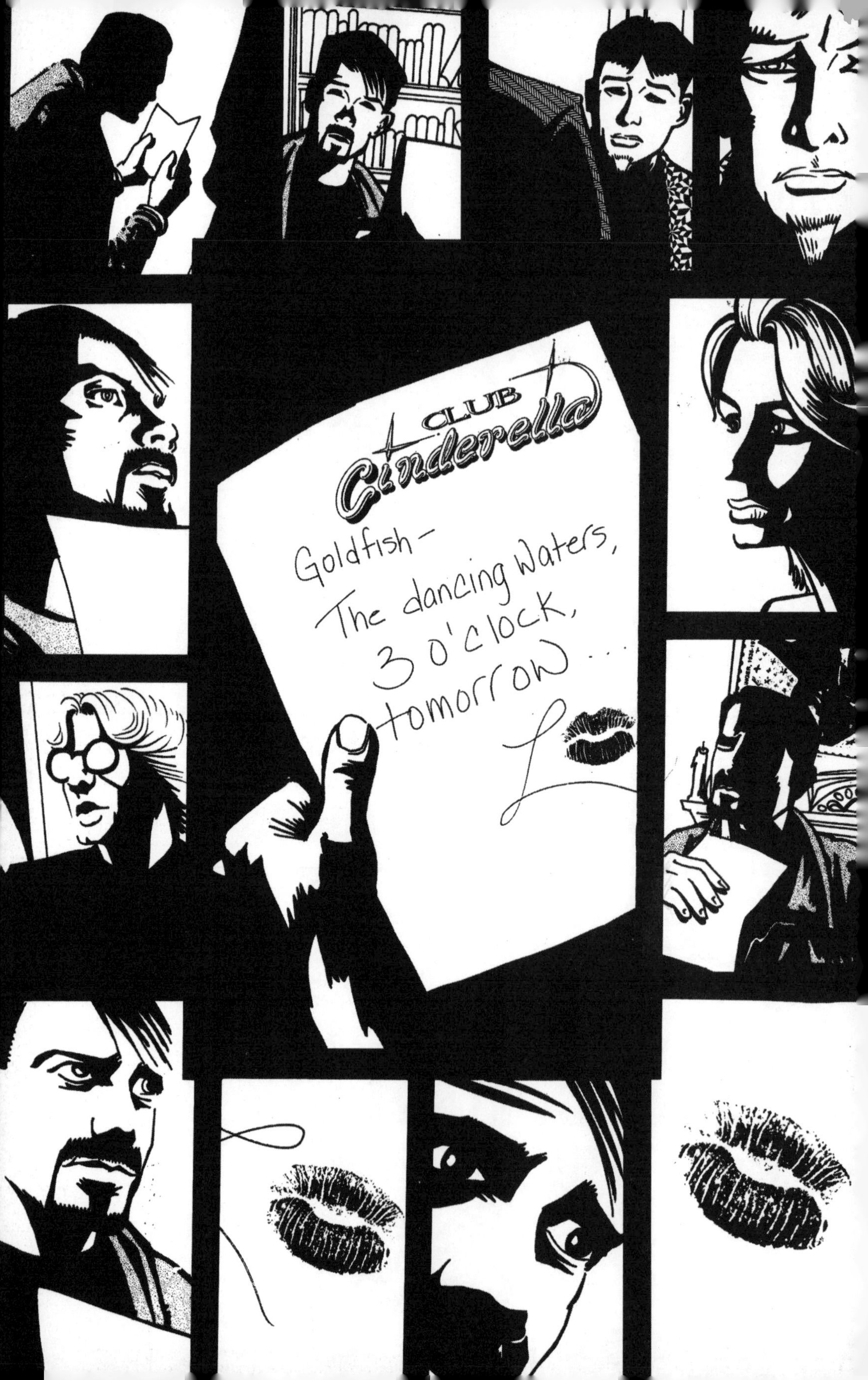
CLUB Cinderella
Goldfish -
The dancing Waters,
3 o'clock,
tomorrow . . .
L

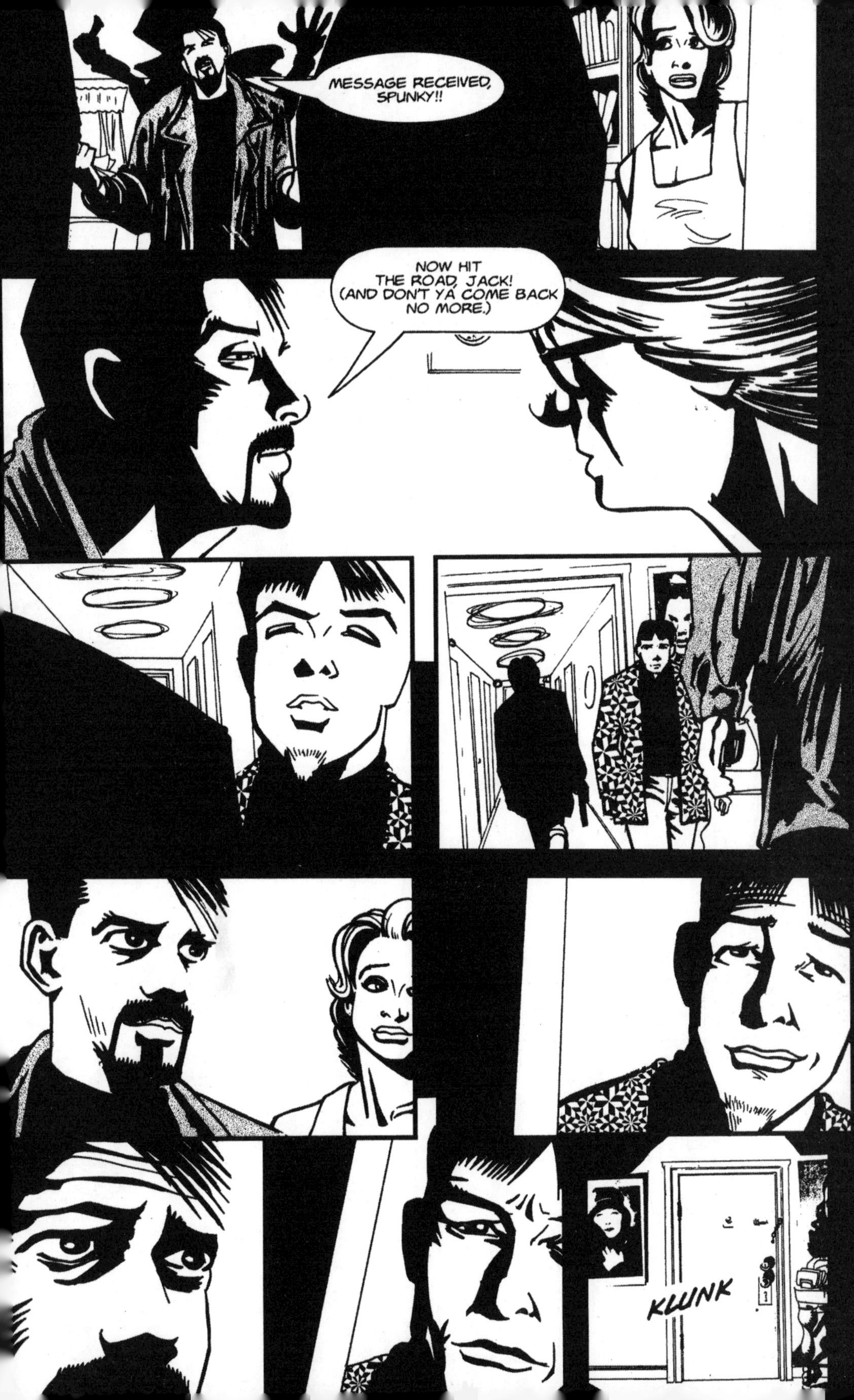
MESSAGE RECEIVED, SPUNKY!!
NOW HIT THE ROAD, JACK! (AND DON'T YA COME BACK NO MORE.)
KLUNK

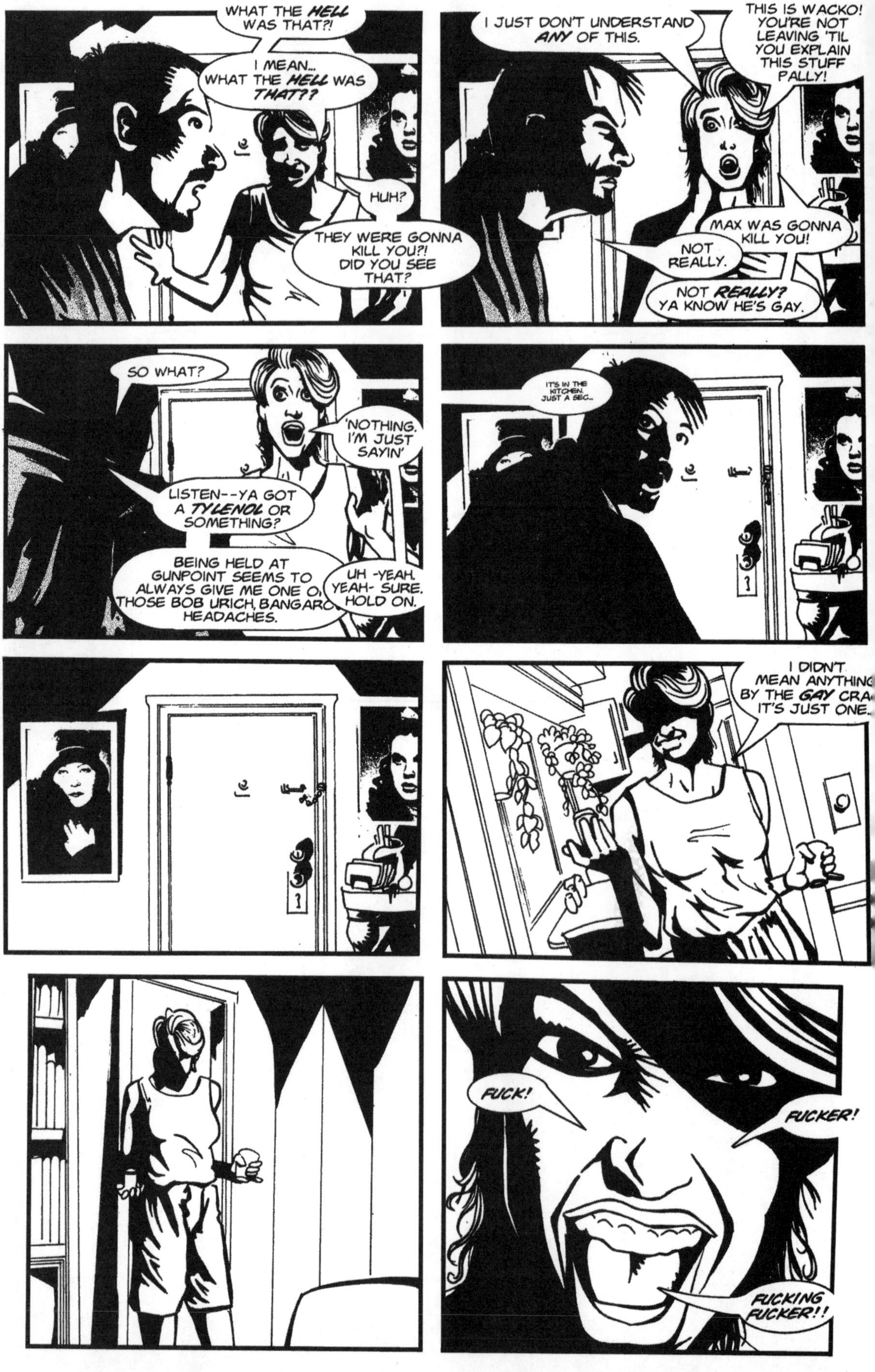
WHAT THE HELL WAS THAT?!
I MEAN... WHAT THE HELL WAS THAT??
HUH?
THEY WERE GONNA KILL YOU?! DID YOU SEE THAT?
I JUST DON'T UNDERSTAND ANY OF THIS.
THIS IS WACKO! YOU'RE NOT LEAVING 'TIL YOU EXPLAIN THIS STUFF PALLY!
MAX WAS GONNA KILL YOU!
NOT REALLY.
NOT REALLY? YA KNOW HE'S GAY.
SO WHAT?
'NOTHING. I'M JUST SAYIN'
LISTEN--YA GOT A TYLENOL OR SOMETHING?
BEING HELD AT GUNPOINT SEEMS TO ALWAYS GIVE ME ONE O THOSE BOB URICH, BANGARO HEADACHES.
UH -YEAH. YEAH- SURE. HOLD ON.
IT'S IN THE KITCHEN. JUST A SEC...
I DIDN'T MEAN ANYTHING BY THE GAY CRA IT'S JUST ONE...
FUCK!
FUCKER!
FUCKING FUCKER!!

JINGLE-
JINGLE.

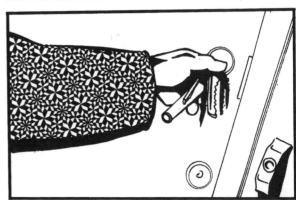

QUITE A
WEEK,
HUH?

WHO SAID
THAT?

WHO'S THERE?!?

SHE DID IT.
DIDN'T SHE?

SHE KILLED
YOUR BROTHER.

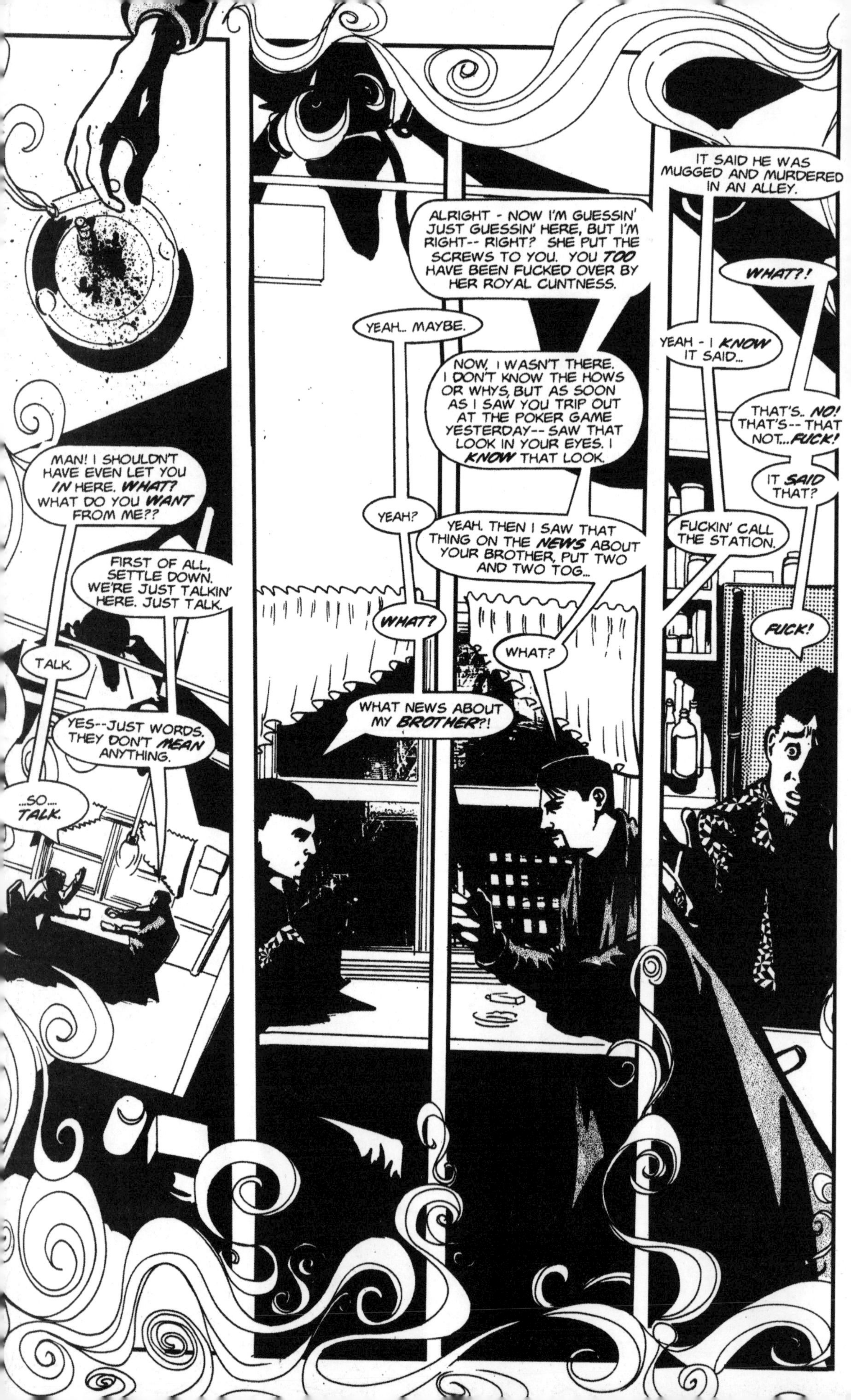
MAN! I SHOULDN'T HAVE EVEN LET YOU *IN* HERE. *WHAT?* WHAT DO YOU *WANT* FROM ME??
FIRST OF ALL, SETTLE DOWN. WE'RE JUST TALKIN' HERE. JUST TALK.
TALK.
YES--JUST WORDS. THEY DON'T *MEAN* ANYTHING.
...SO.... *TALK.*
ALRIGHT - NOW I'M GUESSIN' JUST GUESSIN' HERE, BUT I'M RIGHT-- RIGHT? SHE PUT THE SCREWS TO YOU. YOU *TOO* HAVE BEEN FUCKED OVER BY HER ROYAL CUNTNESS.
YEAH.. MAYBE.
NOW, I WASN'T THERE. I DON'T KNOW THE HOWS OR WHYS, BUT AS SOON AS I SAW YOU TRIP OUT AT THE POKER GAME YESTERDAY-- SAW THAT LOOK IN YOUR EYES. I *KNOW* THAT LOOK.
YEAH?
YEAH. THEN I SAW THAT THING ON THE *NEWS* ABOUT YOUR BROTHER, PUT TWO AND TWO TOG...
WHAT?
WHAT?
WHAT NEWS ABOUT MY *BROTHER*?!
IT SAID HE WAS MUGGED AND MURDERED IN AN ALLEY.
WHAT?!
YEAH - I *KNOW* IT SAID...
THAT'S.. *NO!* THAT'S-- THAT NOT...*FUCK!*
IT *SAID* THAT?
FUCKIN' CALL THE STATION.
FUCK!

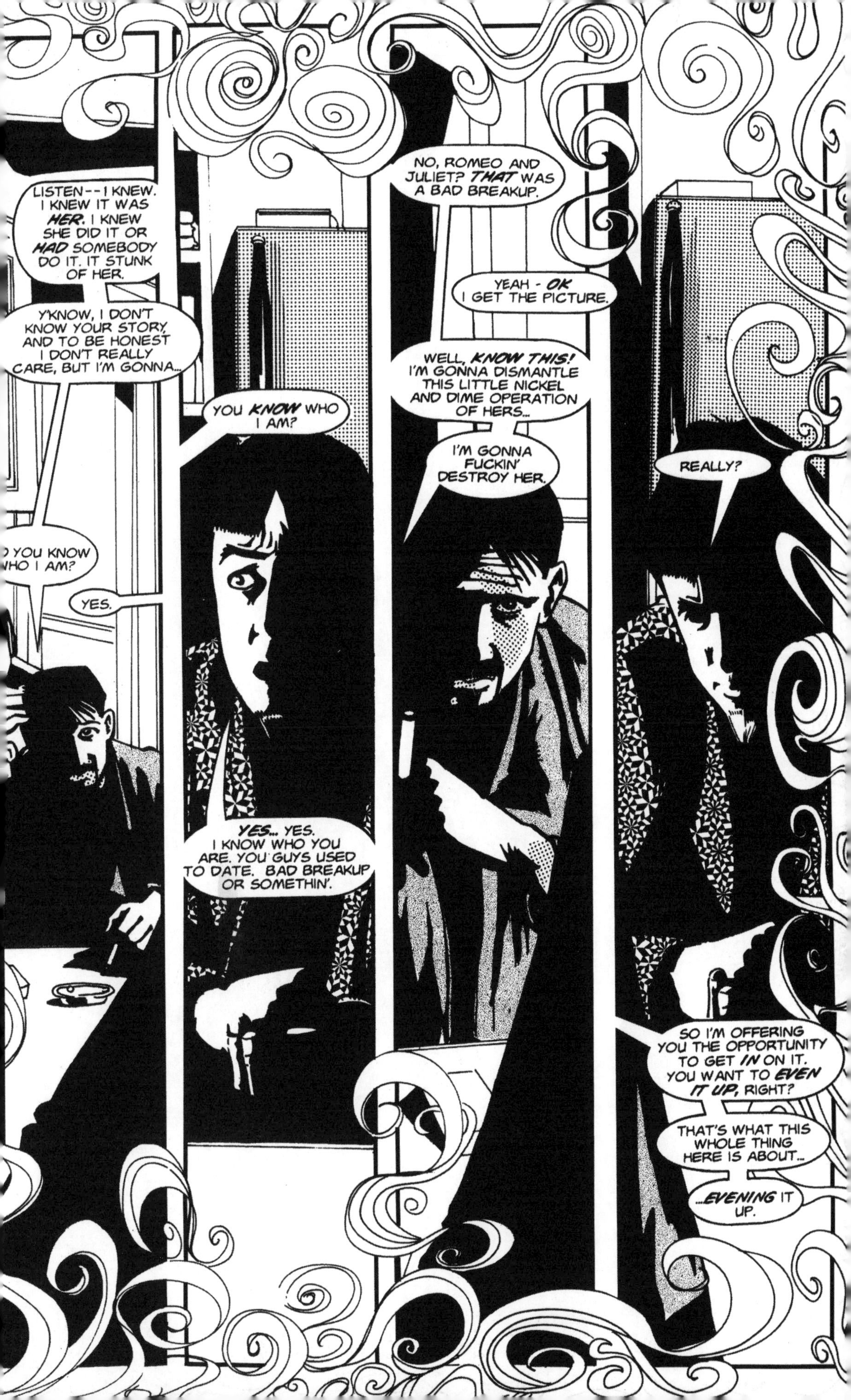
LISTEN--I KNEW. I KNEW IT WAS HER. I KNEW SHE DID IT OR HAD SOMEBODY DO IT. IT STUNK OF HER.
Y'KNOW, I DON'T KNOW YOUR STORY, AND TO BE HONEST I DON'T REALLY CARE, BUT I'M GONNA...
YOU KNOW WHO I AM?
YES.
YOU KNOW WHO I AM?
YES... YES. I KNOW WHO YOU ARE. YOU GUYS USED TO DATE. BAD BREAKUP OR SOMETHIN'.
NO, ROMEO AND JULIET? THAT WAS A BAD BREAKUP.
YEAH - OK I GET THE PICTURE.
WELL, KNOW THIS! I'M GONNA DISMANTLE THIS LITTLE NICKEL AND DIME OPERATION OF HERS...
I'M GONNA FUCKIN' DESTROY HER.
REALLY?
SO I'M OFFERING YOU THE OPPORTUNITY TO GET IN ON IT. YOU WANT TO EVEN IT UP, RIGHT?
THAT'S WHAT THIS WHOLE THING HERE IS ABOUT...
...EVENING IT UP.

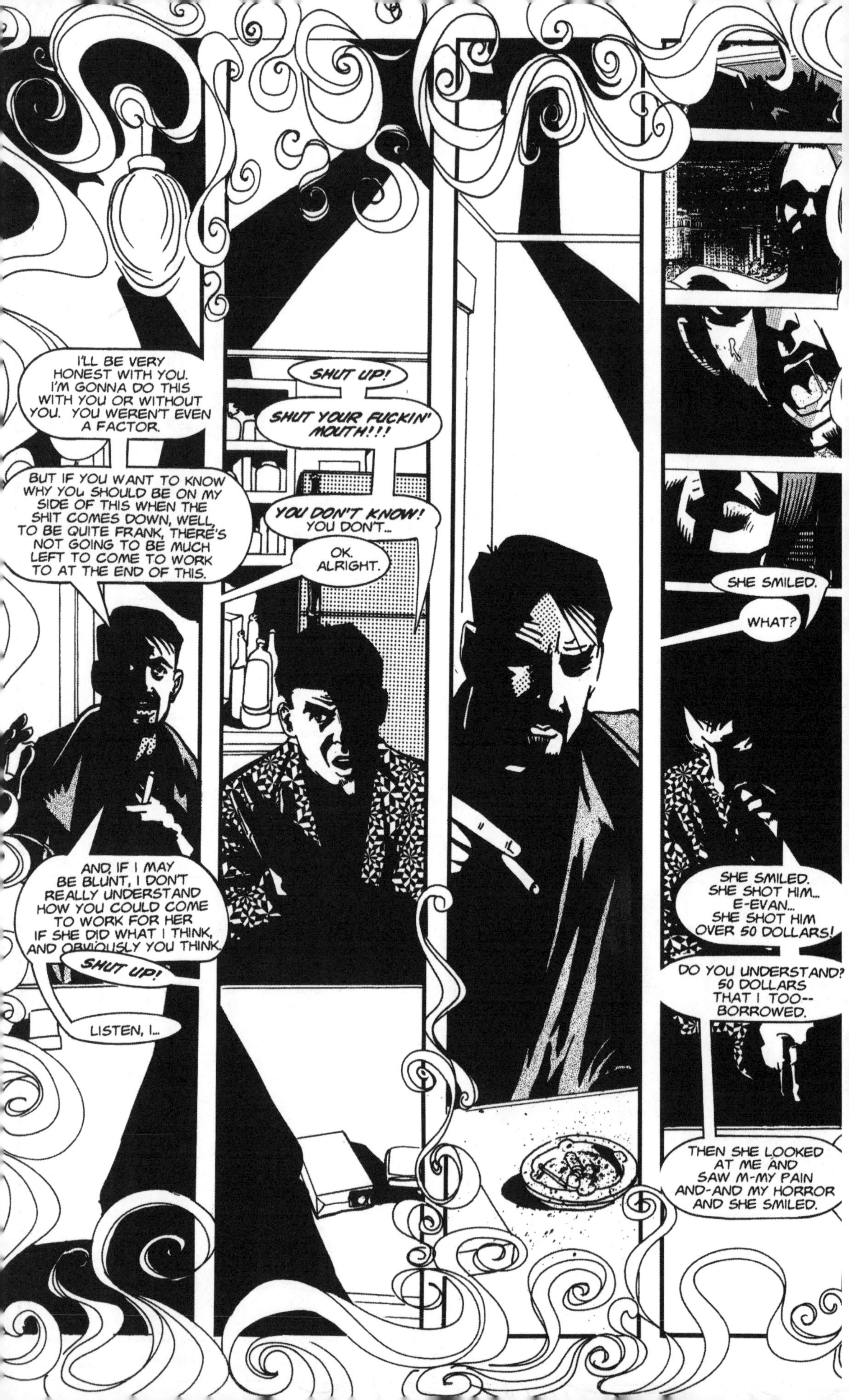
I'LL BE VERY HONEST WITH YOU. I'M GONNA DO THIS WITH YOU OR WITHOUT YOU. YOU WEREN'T EVEN A FACTOR.
BUT IF YOU WANT TO KNOW WHY YOU SHOULD BE ON MY SIDE OF THIS WHEN THE SHIT COMES DOWN, WELL, TO BE QUITE FRANK, THERE'S NOT GOING TO BE MUCH LEFT TO COME TO WORK TO AT THE END OF THIS.
SHUT UP!
SHUT YOUR FUCKIN' MOUTH!!!
YOU DON'T KNOW! YOU DON'T...
OK. ALRIGHT.
AND, IF I MAY BE BLUNT, I DON'T REALLY UNDERSTAND HOW YOU COULD COME TO WORK FOR HER IF SHE DID WHAT I THINK, AND OBVIOUSLY YOU THINK.
SHUT UP!
LISTEN, I...
SHE SMILED.
WHAT?
SHE SMILED. SHE SHOT HIM... E-EVAN... SHE SHOT HIM OVER 50 DOLLARS!
DO YOU UNDERSTAND? 50 DOLLARS THAT I TOO-- BORROWED.
THEN SHE LOOKED AT ME AND SAW M-MY PAIN AND-AND MY HORROR AND SHE SMILED.

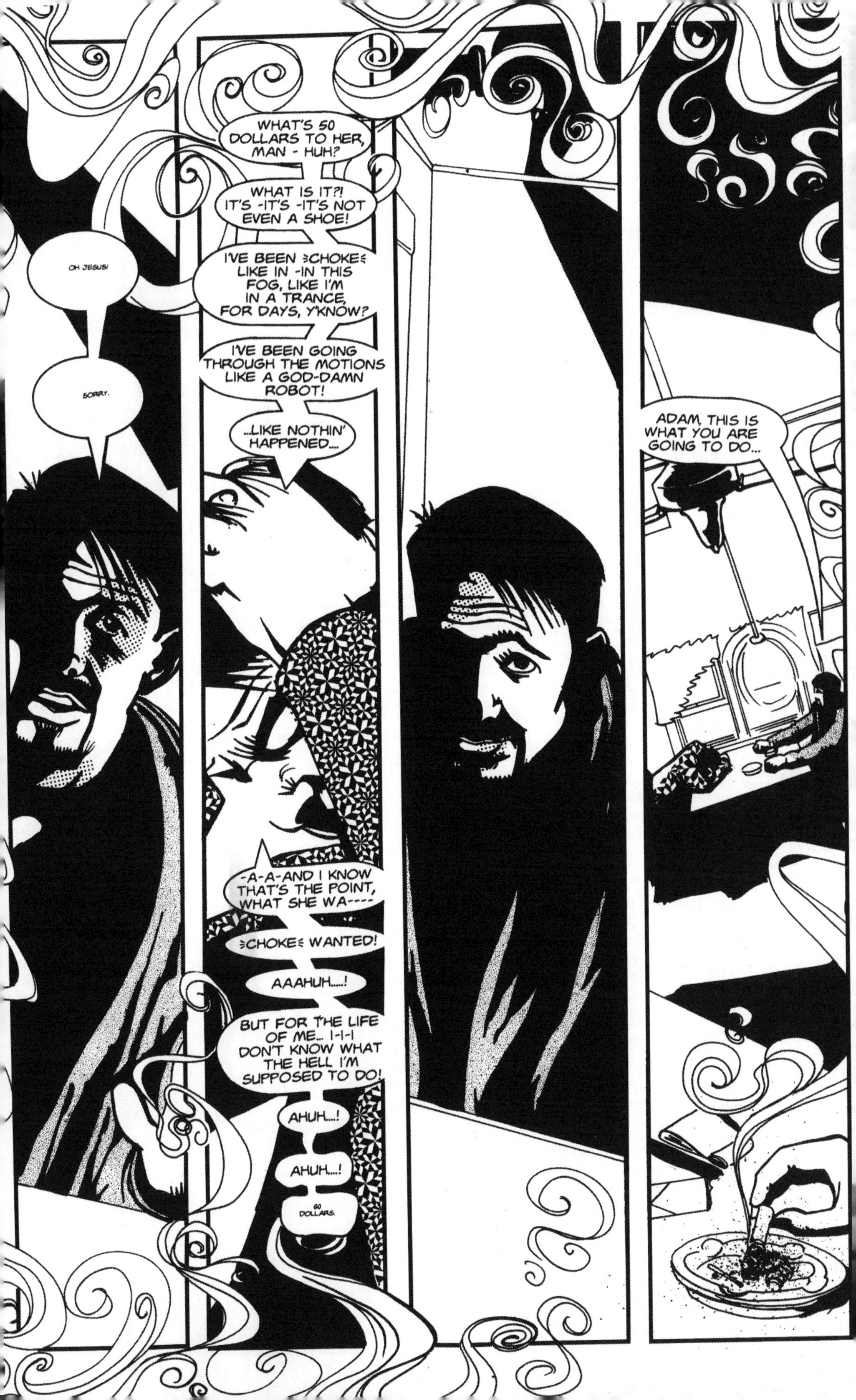
OH JESUS!
SORRY.
WHAT'S 50 DOLLARS TO HER, MAN - HUH?
WHAT IS IT?! IT'S -IT'S -IT'S NOT EVEN A SHOE!
I'VE BEEN ≥CHOKE≤ LIKE IN -IN THIS FOG, LIKE I'M IN A TRANCE, FOR DAYS, Y'KNOW?
I'VE BEEN GOING THROUGH THE MOTIONS LIKE A GOD-DAMN ROBOT!
...LIKE NOTHIN' HAPPENED...
-A-A-AND I KNOW THAT'S THE POINT, WHAT SHE WA----
≥CHOKE≤ WANTED!
AAAHUH.....!
BUT FOR THE LIFE OF ME... I-I-I DON'T KNOW WHAT THE HELL I'M SUPPOSED TO DO!
AHUH....!
AHUH....!
50 DOLLARS.
ADAM, THIS IS WHAT YOU ARE GOING TO DO...

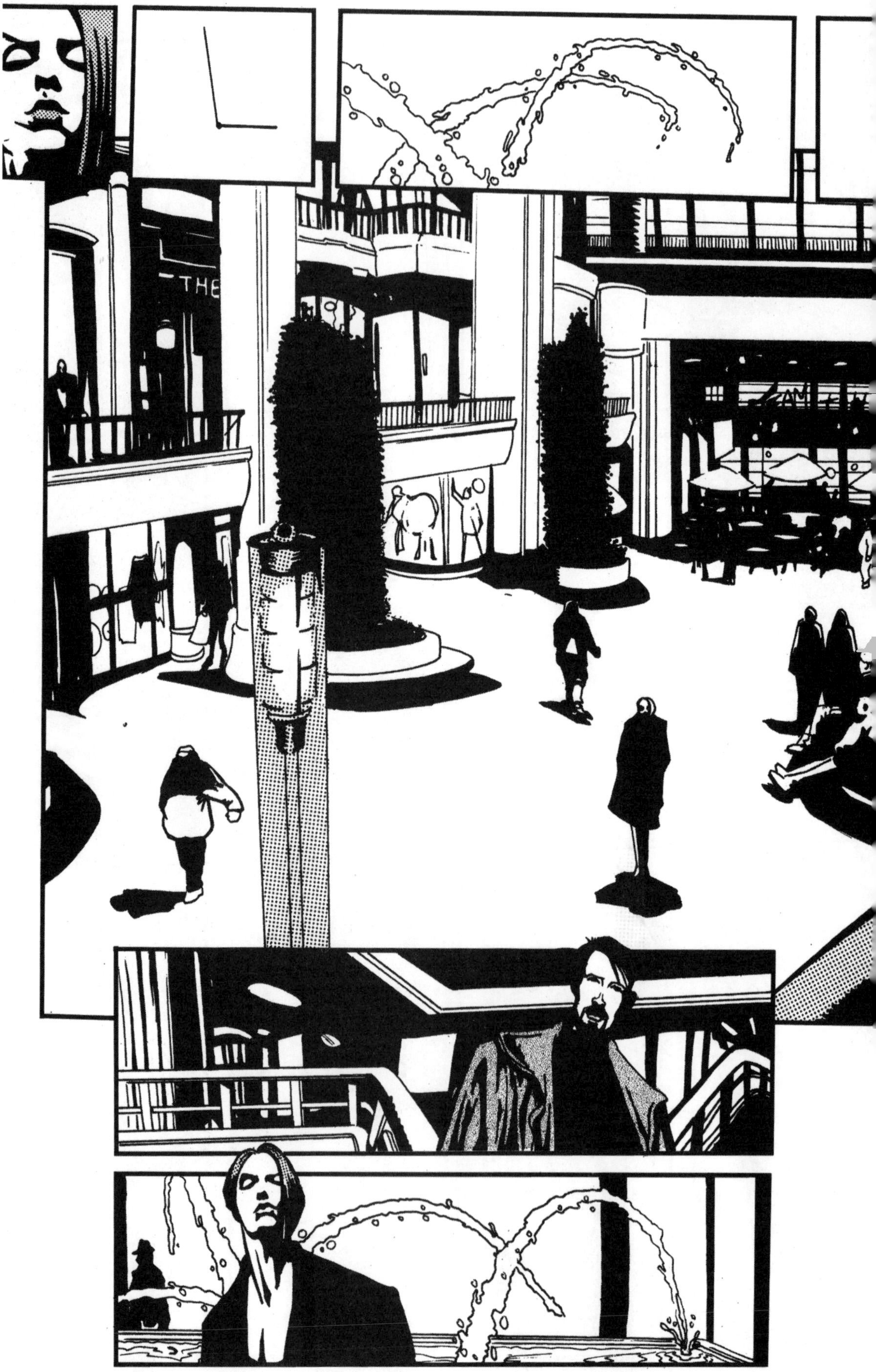
THE

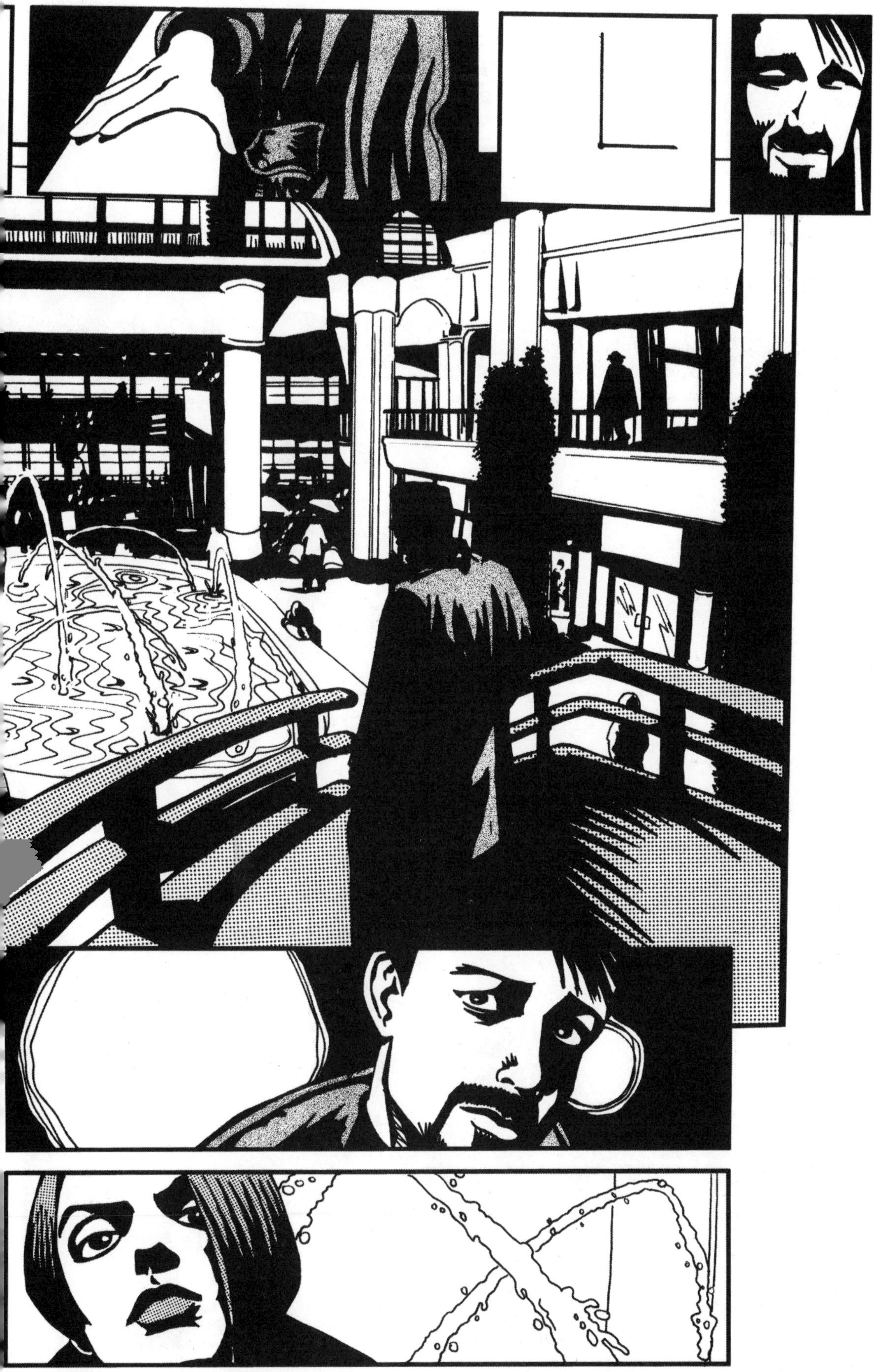

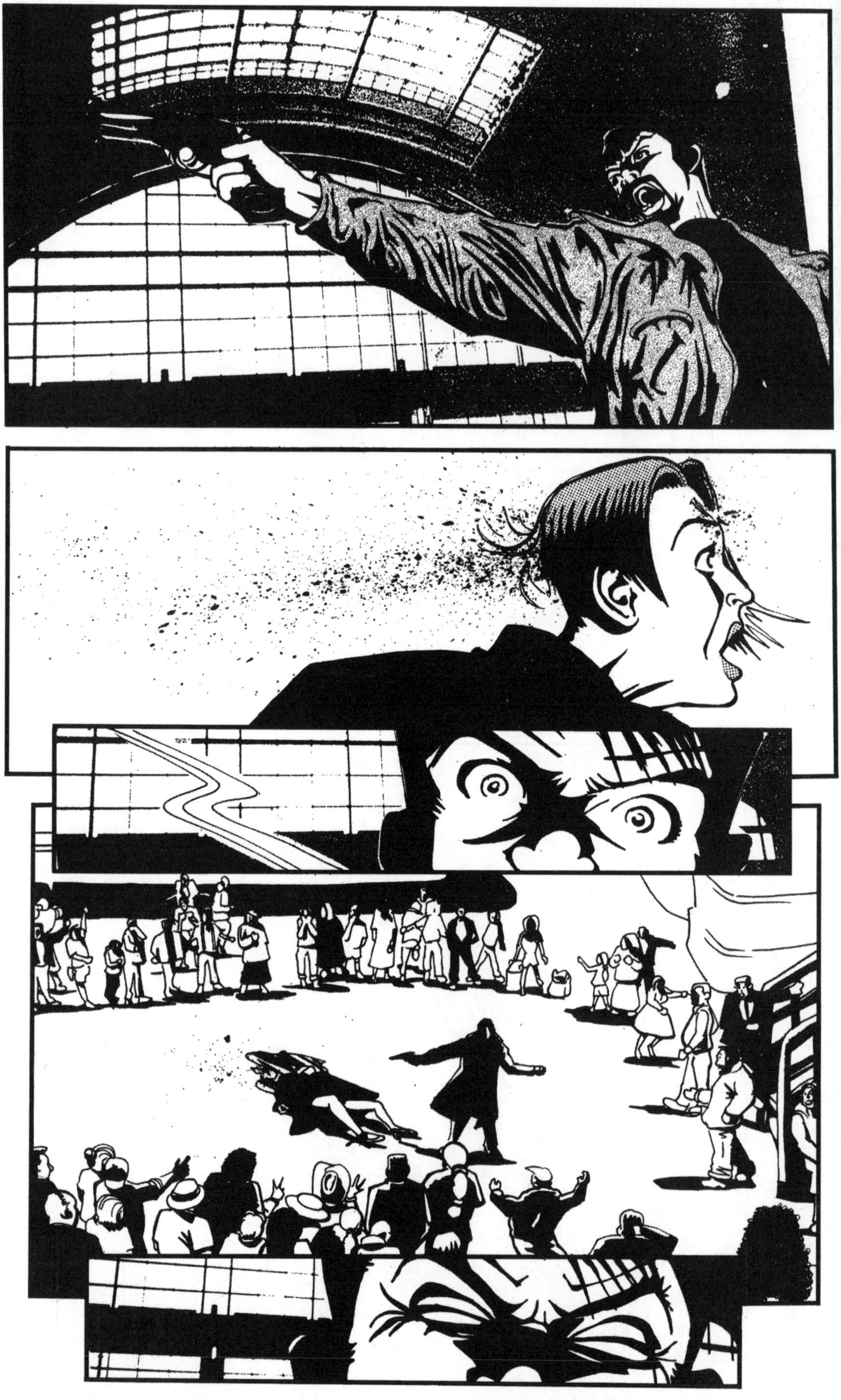

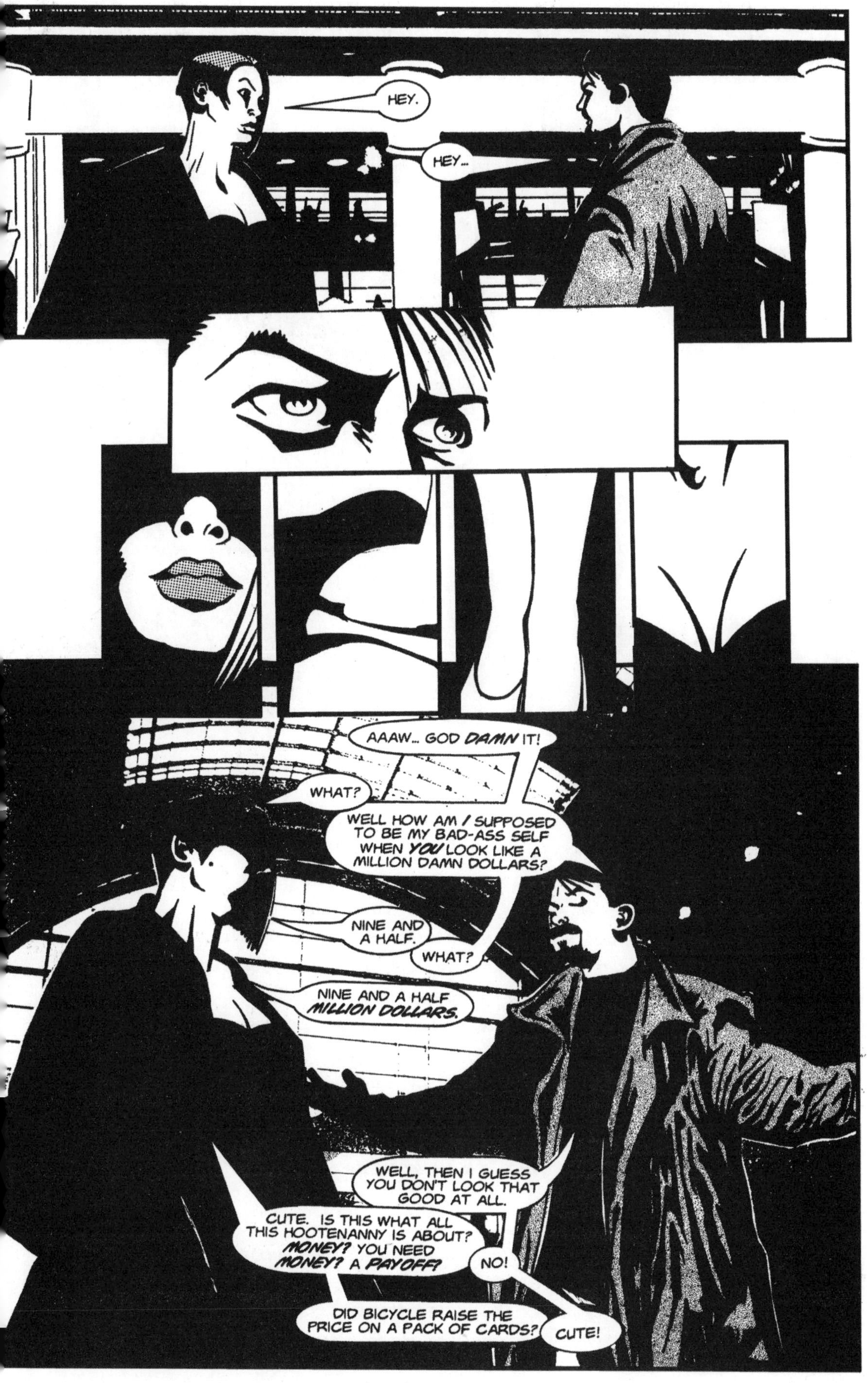
HEY.
HEY...
AAAW... GOD DAMN IT!
WHAT?
WELL HOW AM I SUPPOSED TO BE MY BAD-ASS SELF WHEN YOU LOOK LIKE A MILLION DAMN DOLLARS?
NINE AND A HALF.
WHAT?
NINE AND A HALF MILLION DOLLARS.
WELL, THEN I GUESS YOU DON'T LOOK THAT GOOD AT ALL.
CUTE. IS THIS WHAT ALL THIS HOOTENANNY IS ABOUT? MONEY? YOU NEED MONEY? A PAYOFF?
NO!
DID BICYCLE RAISE THE PRICE ON A PACK OF CARDS?
CUTE!

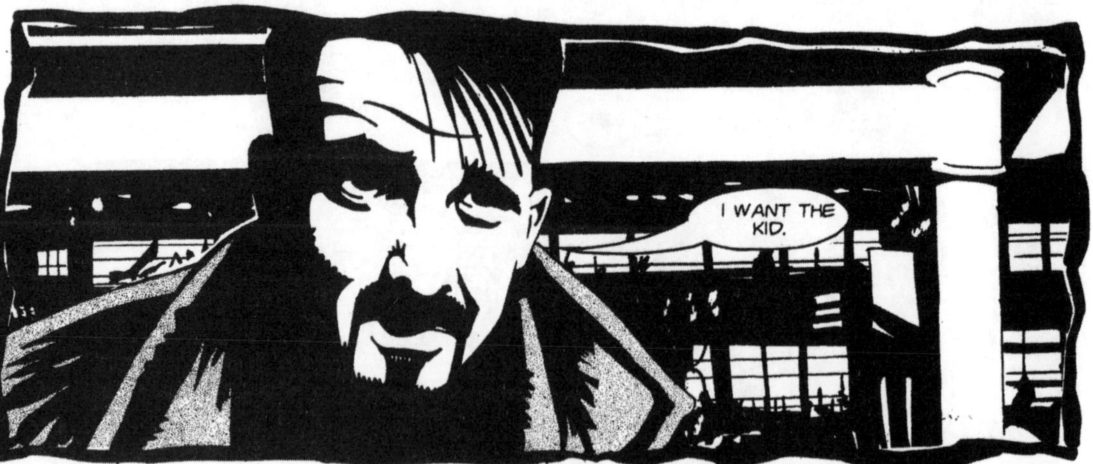
I WANT THE KID.

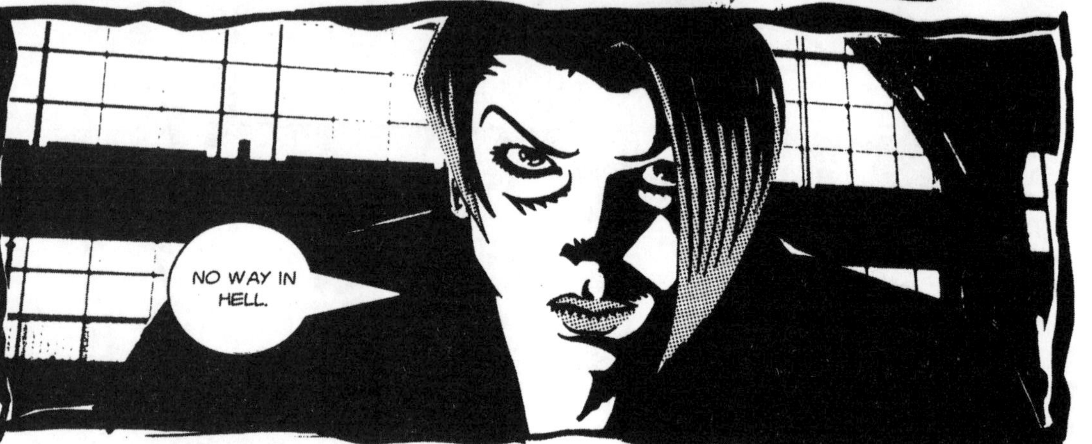
NO WAY IN HELL.

"IT'S SIMPLE, LAUREN. GIVE ME THE KID, I WALK AWAY. YOU NEVER SEE ME AGAIN. I'M ***HOFFA***. IF YOU DON'T, WELL...."

"...***WELL?***"

"WELL... LET THE GAMES BEGIN."

"GOLDFISH, I... I COULD FUCKIN' ***SQUASH*** YOU!!!"

"MMMM. INTERESTING THING IS YOU ***HAVEN'T***. GRANTED, YOU ***COULD***, ***SURE!*** YOU'RE QUEEN OF THE NORTH COAST, PRINCESS OF PARMA, YET YOU ***HAVEN'T***. I THINK THAT IF YOU WERE GOING TO, YOU ***WOULD*** HAVE BY NOW. ***WHY*** IS THAT? I WONDER? I HAVE A COUPLE OF ***THEORIES***, A LITTLE ***CONJECTURE*** ON WHY YOU ARE ACTING SO UNLIKE YOUR...."

"***COCKY LITTLE FUCK!*** MAYBE I JUST WANTED TO DO IT FACE TO FACE WITH MY ***OWN*** HANDS."

"WELL ***THAT*** WOULD BE A FIRST!"

"OH! WHY DON'T YOU ***GROW THE FUCK UP ALREADY AND LET IT GO!***"

"LET IT GO?"

"YEAH!! I MEAN... ***JESUS FUCK!*** YOU REALLY OUGHTA THINK ABOUT GETTING A LIFE. I HEAR THEY'RE ALL THE RAGE. IT'S BEEN--LET'S CHECK THE CALENDAR--OH MY GOD! ***A WHOLE DECADE!***"

"LET IT GO, HUH? HMMM, LIKE ***YOU***, I SUPPOSE?"

"WHAT?"

"YOU HEARD ME."

"WHAT'S THAT SUPPOSED TO MEAN? I...."

"YOU KNOW."

"*GOD!* YOU ARE SUCH A FUCKIN...."

"THIS IS MY THEORY ON WHY THIS MEETING IS TAKING PLACE. IT'S A *THEORY*, MIND YOU, BUT I THINK IT'S A GOOD ONE."

"OH--YOU'VE PREPARED A SPEECH. OK, LET'S HEAR--"

"YOU'RE STILL IN LOVE WITH ME."

"OH PU-LEASE! THAT'S IT? THAT'S THE BEST YOU'VE GOT?!?"

"WELL I KNOW IT'S WHY I'M NOT LAYING ON TOP OF VISA RIGHT NOW IN A SHALLOW GRAVE OUTSIDE OF TOWN. AND DON'T GET ME WRONG-- THIS IS NOT ARROGANCE TALKING, I KNOW YOU'RE NOT IN LOVE WITH *ME*. YOU DON'T EVEN *KNOW* ME. YOU'RE IN LOVE WITH WHAT I *REPRESENT*, SEE? DO YOU SEE? I MEAN, YOU GO THROUGH OBSTACLES-*ANY* OBSTACLE-LIKE, Y'KNOW? THEY'RE NOT *OBSTACLES*. BUT HERE YOU ARE, WITH ME, HANGIN' OUT AT THE MALL. I LOOK IN YOUR EYES-RIGHT NOW-I LOOK IN YOUR EYES AND I KNOW I'M RIGHT."

"*OH MY GOD! COULD YOU BE MORE FULL OF SHIT?!*"

"PROBABLY, BUT IT'S HARDLY THE POINT. JUST GIVE ME THE KID."

"THE KID IS MINE. I HAVE THE SCAR TO PROVE IT."

"WHAT'S WITH YOU? YOU *HATE* HIM. YOU KICK HIM AROUND. YOU TREAT HIM LIKE A RETARDED COCKER SPANIEL THAT CONSTANTLY PEES ON THE RUG. HE'S A GOOD KID. HE'S A *SMART* KID. LET ME HAVE HIM. LET ME TAKE HIM AWAY FROM YOU AND ALL OF THIS. HE'LL GROW UP LOVED AND HEALTHY, OR AS CLOSE AS ANYBODY CAN, AND THIS, THIS *THING* BETWEEN US-IT ENDS."

"YOU'VE *TALKED* TO HIM! YOU-*HE* FOUND *YOU*, DIDN'T HE?"

"LET'S JUST SAY WE FOUND EACH OTHER. HE'S A SMART KID."

"WHOOOOO!! THAT LITTLE SHIT. JUST LIKE...."

"...HIS FATHER? SEE, THAT'S PART OF MY THEORY. HERE'S THE BOY! YOU ***HATE*** THE BOY! WHY? BECAUSE, HE REMINDS YOU OF ***ME.*** ***REPRESENTS*** ME. YOU COULD HAVE ABORTED HIM, YOU COULD HAVE GOTTEN RID OF HIM--LORD KNOWS YOU'RE CAPABLE. BUT YOU ***DIDN'T.*** I MEAN, I WASN'T EVEN PHYSICALLY THERE DURING THE PREGNANCY--YOU MADE SURE OF ***THAT.*** YOU COULD HAVE GIVEN HIM AWAY. BUT YOU DIDN'T. SO HE, THE BOY, IS YOUR OWN LITTLE PRISON. THIS IS YOU PUNISHING YOURSELF FOR WHAT YOU DID TO ME. YOU WANTED US TO WORK--YOU ***ALWAYS*** WANTED US TO WORK-- AND IT ***DIDN'T,*** SO YOU'RE PUNISHING YOURSELF."

"THIS IS ***SO*** WARPED."

"OH, I ***KNOW!*** BUT IT'S STILL THE DAMN TRUTH."

"NO... IT...."

"THEN LET ME, THE MAN YOU SUPPOSEDLY HATE, TAKE THE BOY, WHO YOU SUPPOSEDLY HATE, AND WE'LL BOTH GO. ***NO-MORE-HATE.***"

"NO! NO! THIS IS NOT A ...."

"IT'S BECAUSE YOU ARE SO FAR IN ***DENIAL,*** YOU'RE IN THE ***SUEZ.***"

"WE DIDN'T WORK BECAUSE ***YOU*** ARE A ***LIAR!***"

"WE DIDN'T WORK BECAUSE ***YOU*** COULDN'T ***CONTROL ME.***"

"***YOU LIED*** TO ***ME!!!***"

"***GOD, LAUREN! THAT REALLY BURNS MY ASS!!*** I WAS ***ALWAYS*** THERE FOR YOU! I ***ADORED*** YOU! I EVEN LIKED THIS TWISTED, FUCKED-UP MORALITY OF YOURS. I MEAN, YOU... YOU... NEEDED ME... I WAS THERE. SUPPORT--YOURS. LOVE--YOURS. EVERYTHING I SAID TO YOU BY DEFINITION WAS ABSOLUTE ***TRUTH.*** COULD YOU SAY THE SAME ABOUT ***YOURSELF?*** YOU SAY ***I'M*** A LIAR?"

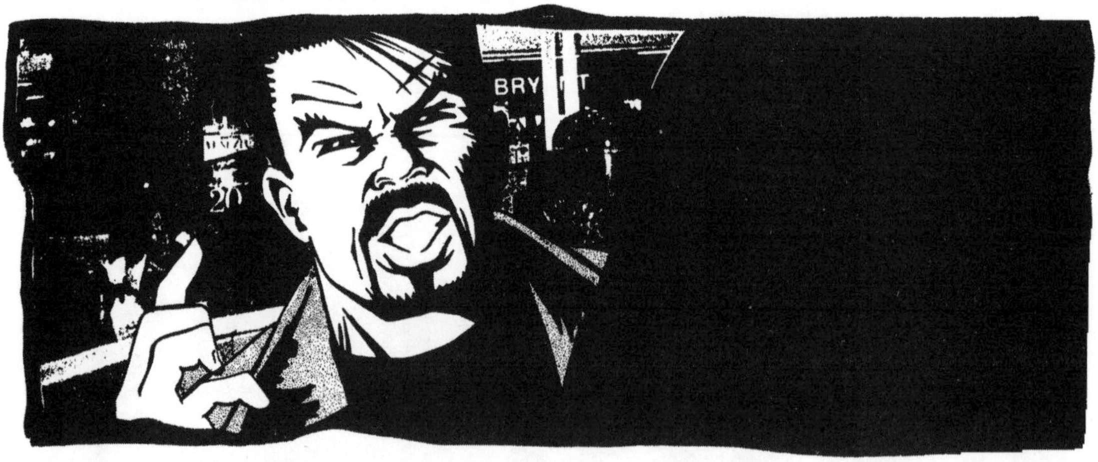
BRY

"YOU NEVER...."

"AND YOU KNOW WHAT? YOU KNOW WHAT NIGHT KEEPS RUNNING OVER IN MY HEAD?"

"WHAT ARE YOU--?"

"THAT NIGHT YOU WANTED TO GET ***MARRIED***-- HUH? I MEAN, WHAT ***WAS*** THAT?! WHY? WHAT WAS THAT?"

"DON'T YOU D--!"

"WE'RE LYING THERE THAT NIGHT, AND YOU ASKED ME IF I COULD EVER
IMAGINE BEING *MARRIED* TO YOU. I LOOKED IN YOUR EYES AND I SAW
THAT YOU NEEDED TO HEAR IT, RIGHT THEN. YOU HAD TO HEAR THAT
YOU MEANT *THAT* MUCH TO ME, TO *SOMEONE.* I DIDN'T THINK ABOUT
MARRIAGE AND STUFF. IT'S JUST NOT HOW MY BRAIN WORKED. BUT I
SAID *YES.* I MEAN-*SURE*-WE'D BEEN GOING OUT FOR MONTHS AND
NEVER EVEN HAD A FIGHT. YOU WERE THE GREATEST INVENTION SINCE
SLICED BREAD, SO, SURE I COULD *SEE* IT."

"OH--LIKE YOU WERE DOING ME A *FAVOR!*"

"THAT'S NOT THE POINT!"

"*YOU* SAID-"

"*NO!* IT'S *NOT* THE POINT. THE POINT IS, I SAY-NO MATTER WHAT *SPIN*
YOU PUT ON IT. NO MATTER HOW MUCH YOU TRY TO *DEFACE* IT--BOTH
YOU AND I KNOW *WE WORKED. YOU* FUCKED IT UP, YOU SEE? YOU HAD
ME SAY ALL THOSE WORDS AND THEN YOU HAD THEM FLOAT THERE IN
THE AIR."

"WHY ARE WE TALKING ABOUT THIS?"

"WHAT DO YOU WANT TO TALK ABOUT? THE ECONOMY?"

"NO! WHY ARE WE TALKING BOUT *THIS?*"

"BECAUSE THE DAY YOU SAID THE '*M*' WORD IS THE DAY I SHOULD HAVE
BAILED. I SHOULD HAVE RUN SCREAMING FROM THE ROOM, BECAUSE I
SHOULD HAVE KNOWN THAT SOMEBODY AS FUCKED UP AS YOU
ALWAYS HAS SOMETHING *ELSE* UP THEIR SLEEVE."

"HOW COULD YOU...?"

"SO I SAY THE WORDS AND THEY HANG IN THE AIR. THEN THE NEXT DAY YOU GIVE ME A ***GUN***. YOU GAVE ME A GUN AND SAID 'IF YOU ***REALLY*** LOVED ME, YOU'D DO ***THIS!***'"

"I ***NEVER*** SAID THAT."

"***I KNOW! THAT'S THE POINT!!!*** YOU NEVER ***SAID ANYTHING***! YOU ***BAMBOOZLED*** ME INTO IT! ***YOU SCAMMED ME!!! ME!!!***"

"THAT NOT TRUE, I...!"

"IT'S NOT?! IT'S ***NOT?!*** YOU SEE, I KNOW WHAT YOU ***THINK*** I'M ANGRY AT YOU FOR. BUT ***THIS***, WHAT I'VE JUST TOLD YOU, ***THIS*** IS WHAT I'M MAD ABOUT. AM I MAD AT ***YOU?***-SURE, YOU'RE A RAVING ***BITCH***. BUT I'M MADDER AT MYSELF BECAUSE THE MINUTE I LET YOU SUCKER ME INTO DOING SOMETHING I KNEW WAS WRONG, WRONG FOR ***ME***, I... I..."

"YOU WHAT?"

"WELL, I'M SMARTER THAN THAT."

"OBVIOUSLY NOT."

"I--YOU PLAYED ME LIKE A PIANO. IT WAS SO DELICATE, SO SUBTLE, SO PRECISE--A PERFECT HUSTLE."

"NO."

"NO?"

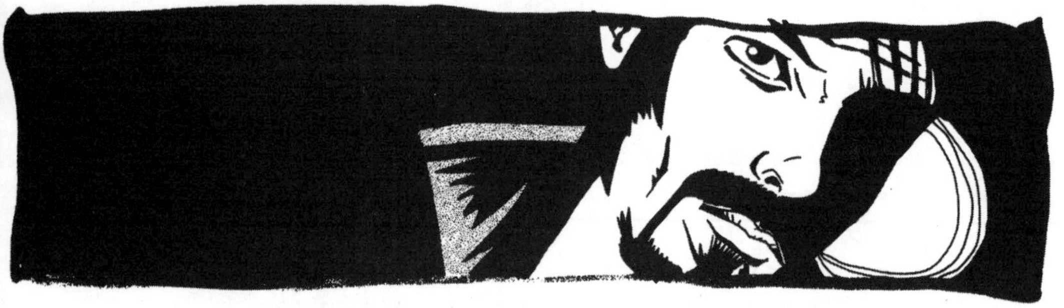

"YOU'RE READING TOO MUCH INTO IT. YOU'RE REMEMBERING ***WRONG***. YOU SAID YOU'D TAKE THE GUN, AND YOU ***DIDN'T***. YOU LIED TO ME."

"IT WAS A BUST-UP SCAM, LAUREN. IT WAS JUST MONEY. IT WASN'T WORTH ***KILLING*** OVER."

"SAYS ***YOU***."

"THAT'S RIGHT--SAYS ***ME***."

"IF YOU HAD A CHOICE NOW, DON'T YOU WISH..."

"IT'S A STUPID QUESTION!!"

"NO MORE STUPID THAN THIS CONVER..."

"ONE QUESTION! THEN, Y'KNOW, I'LL BE ON MY MERRY WAY. NO-NO. MAKE THAT ***TWO*** QUESTIONS. IF I WAS SUCH A LIAR, AND YOU WERE SO BETRAYED, WHY COULDN'T YOU JUST ***BREAK UP*** WITH ME? OTHER PEOPLE Y'KNOW, THEY ***BREAK UP*** IF IT'S NOT WORKING OUT. THEY ***TALK*** IT OUT, YELL AT EACH OTHER. BUT YOU-YOU PUT THE SCREWS TO ME, MAN. IZZY WAS RIGHT. FUCKIN' IZZY."

"IZZY! ***IZZY***: 'THE COP'."

"HMMMM, SO I ***HEAR***. SO THAT'S IT-THAT'S YOUR RATIONALIZATION FOR SETTIN' ME UP AND KNOCKIN ME DOWN, HUH?"

"WHAT DO YOU WANT? I TOLD YOU EARLY ON, EVEN BEFORE WE KISSED, '***NEVER*** LIE TO ME."

"*OY!* THIS IS LIKE TALKIN' TO THE GREAT WALL OF CHINA! Y'SEE, I KNOW YOU KNOW YOU'RE FULL OF SHIT BECAUSE WE WOULDN'T EVEN BE HAVING THIS CONVERSATION IF YOU EVEN HALF BELIEVED WHAT YOU WERE SAYING. YOU ***FREAKED*** ON ME-YOU ***SNAPPED***. AND THE NEXT DAY, YOU FOUND YOURSELF WEIGHTED WITH THIS INCREDIBLE PLANET OF REMORSE. YOU WERE SO SET IN YOUR WAYS, IN HOW YOU DEALT WITH PEOPLE, THAT YOU COULDN'T EVEN STOP YOURSELF IF YOU TRIED. I JUST... I JUST WISH I COULD HAVE BEEN THERE TO SEE THE LOOK ON YOUR FACE WHEN YOU FOUND OUT YOU WERE PREGNANT. I MEAN IT. I BET THAT WAS A KODAK MOME..."

"WHAT'S THE SECOND?"

"HMMMM?"

"***WHAT'S THE SECOND QUESTION?***"

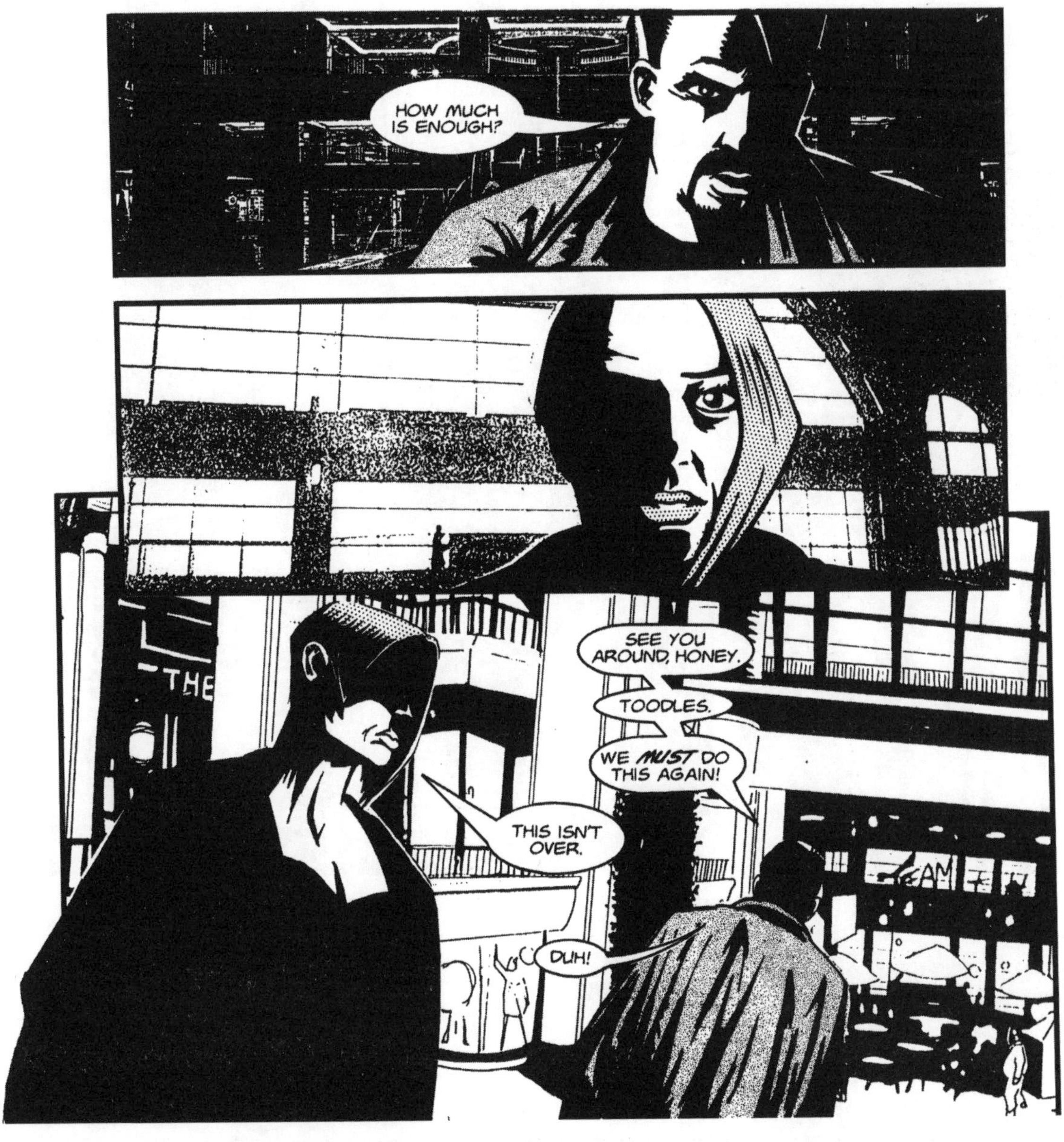
HOW MUCH IS ENOUGH?
SEE YOU AROUND, HONEY.
TOODLES.
WE *MUST* DO THIS AGAIN!
THIS ISN'T OVER.
DUH!

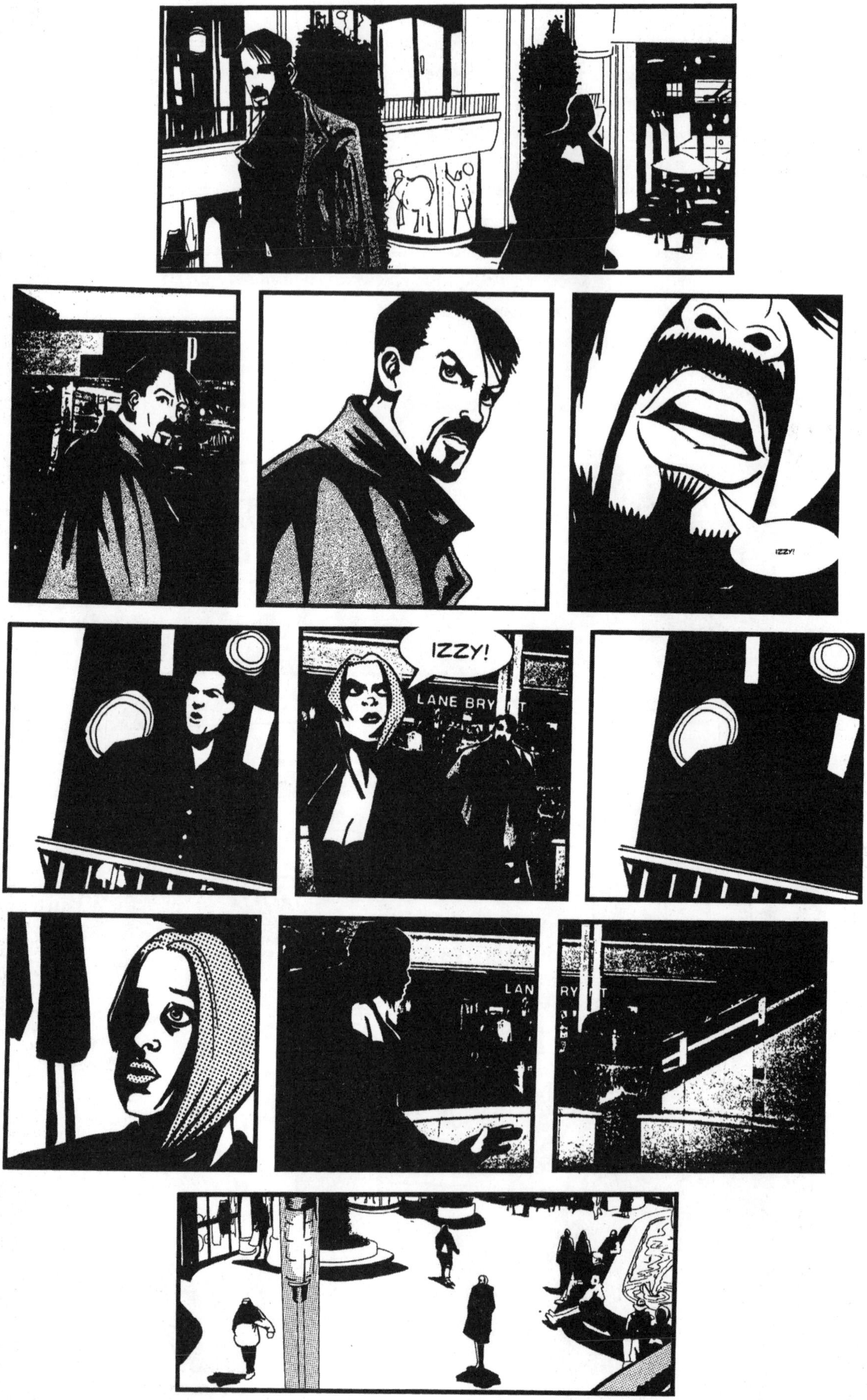
IZZY!
IZZY!

CRRREEAKK
CLUB Cinderella
GUN CRAZY
CRAZY
TAP
TAP
TAP
TAP
PASSWORD
GLASS SLIPPER--
THE PASSWORD...
IT'S 'GLASS SLIPPER'.
PASSWORD ACCEPTED
PRINTING

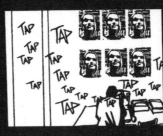

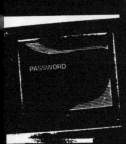

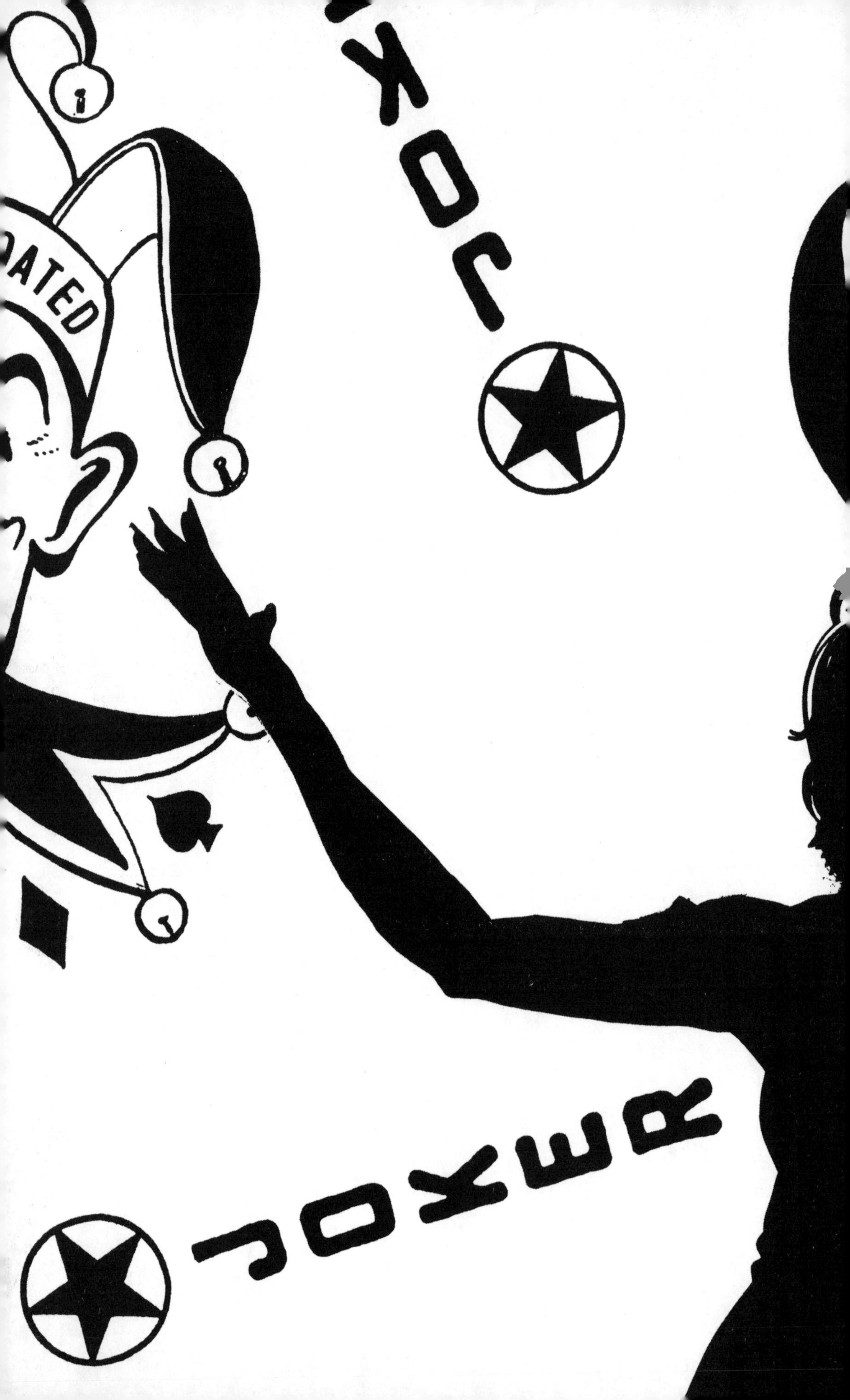
JOKER

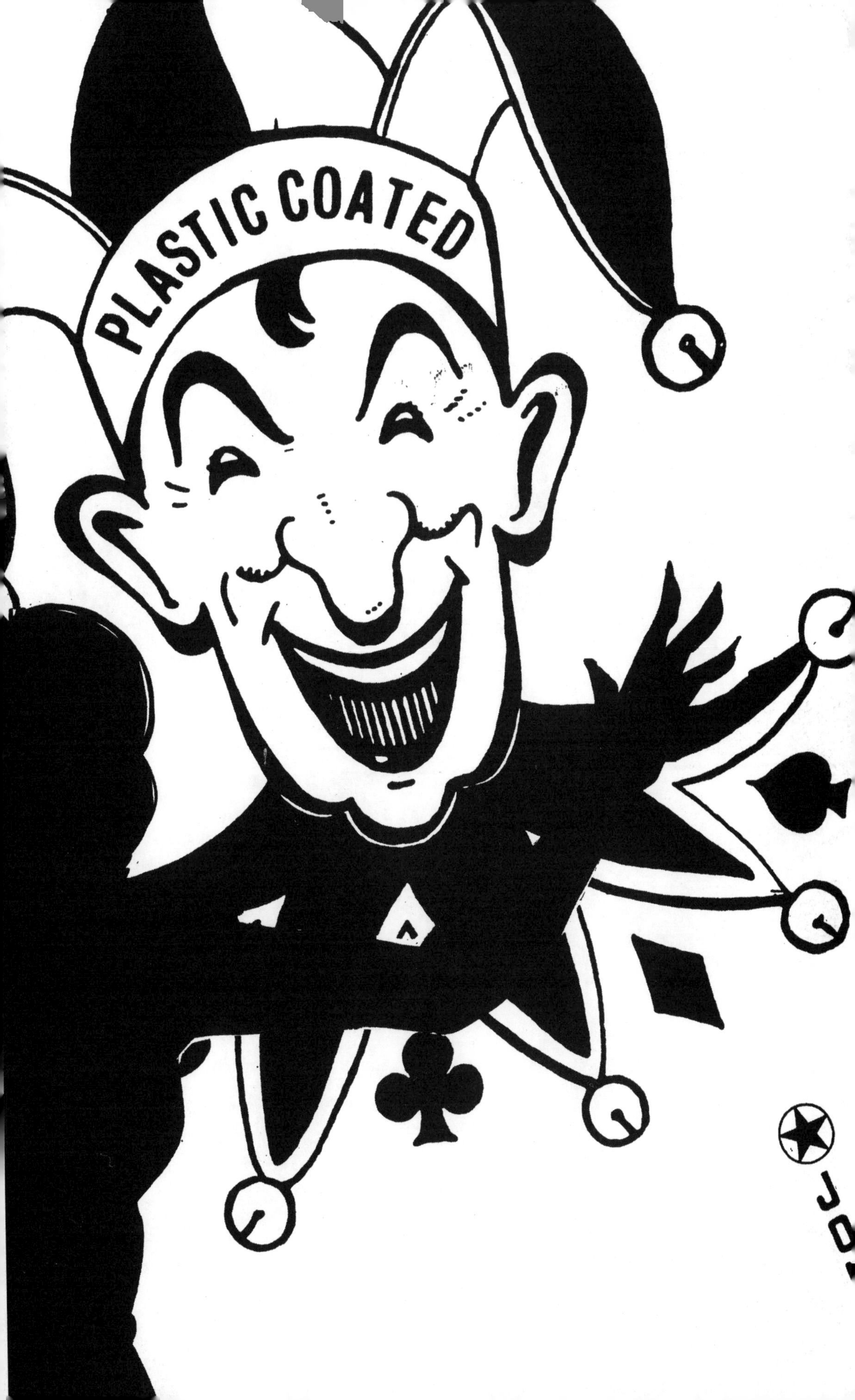
PLASTIC COATED

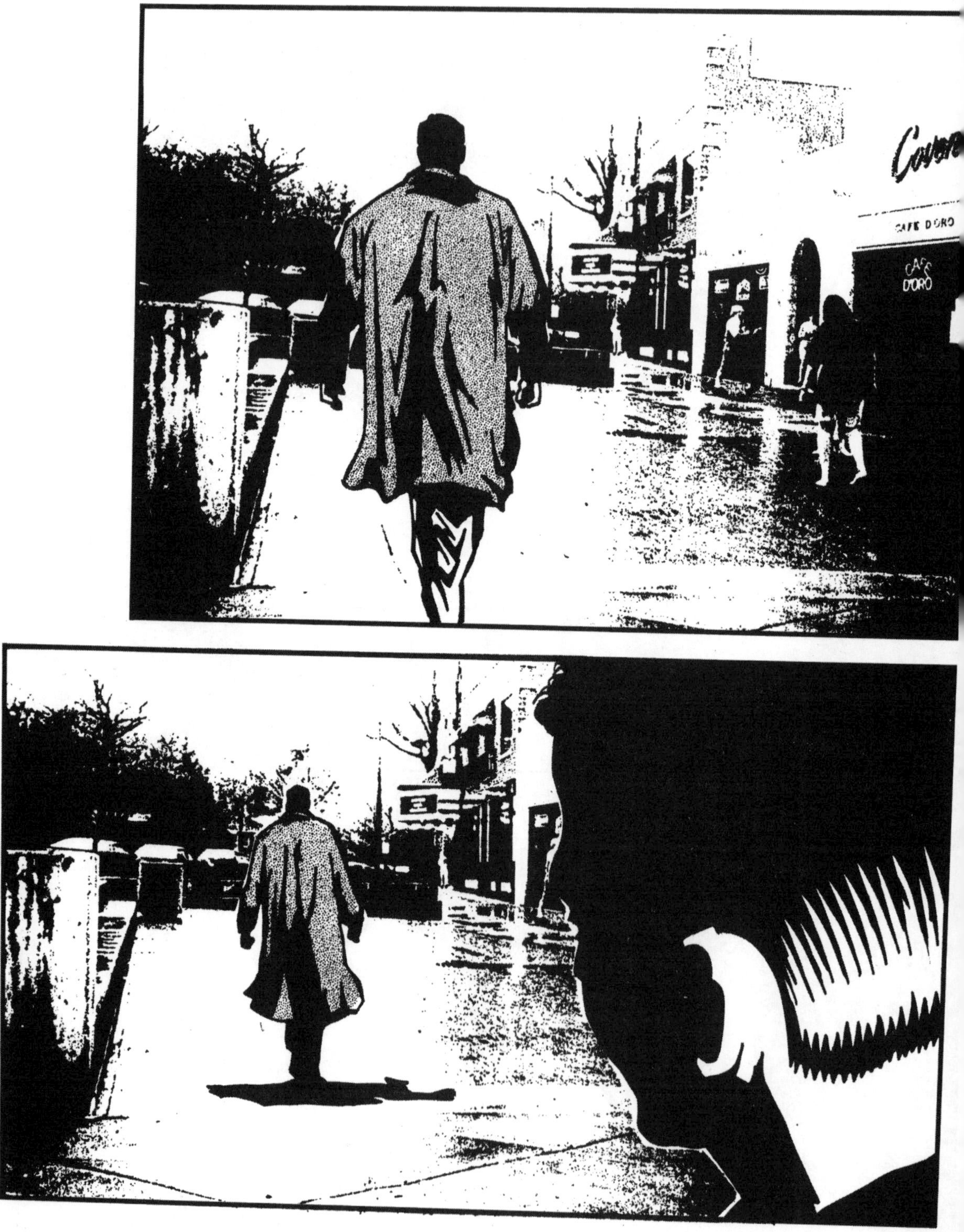
CAFE D'ORO
CAFE D'ORO

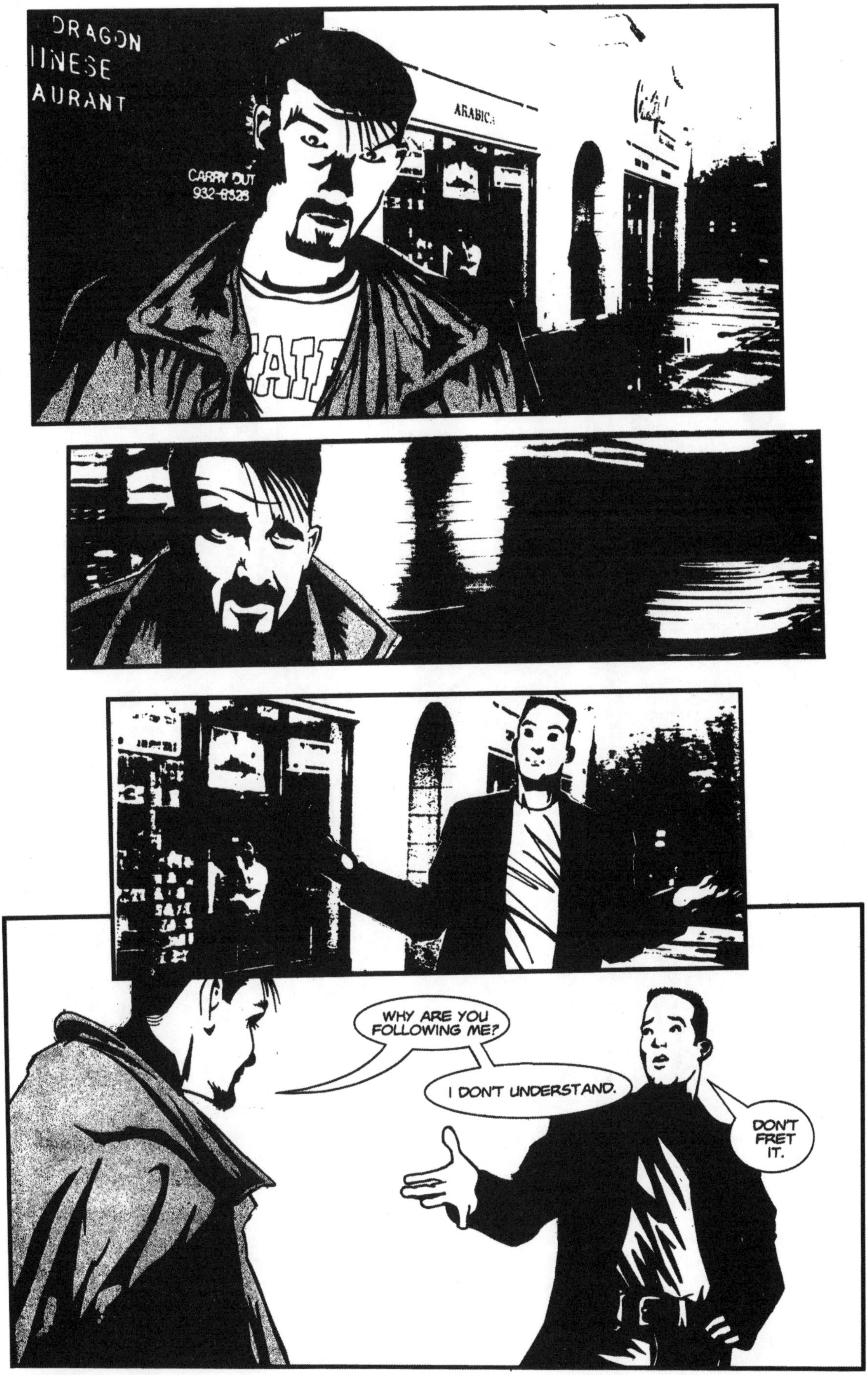
WHY ARE YOU FOLLOWING ME?
I DON'T UNDERSTAND.
DON'T FRET IT.

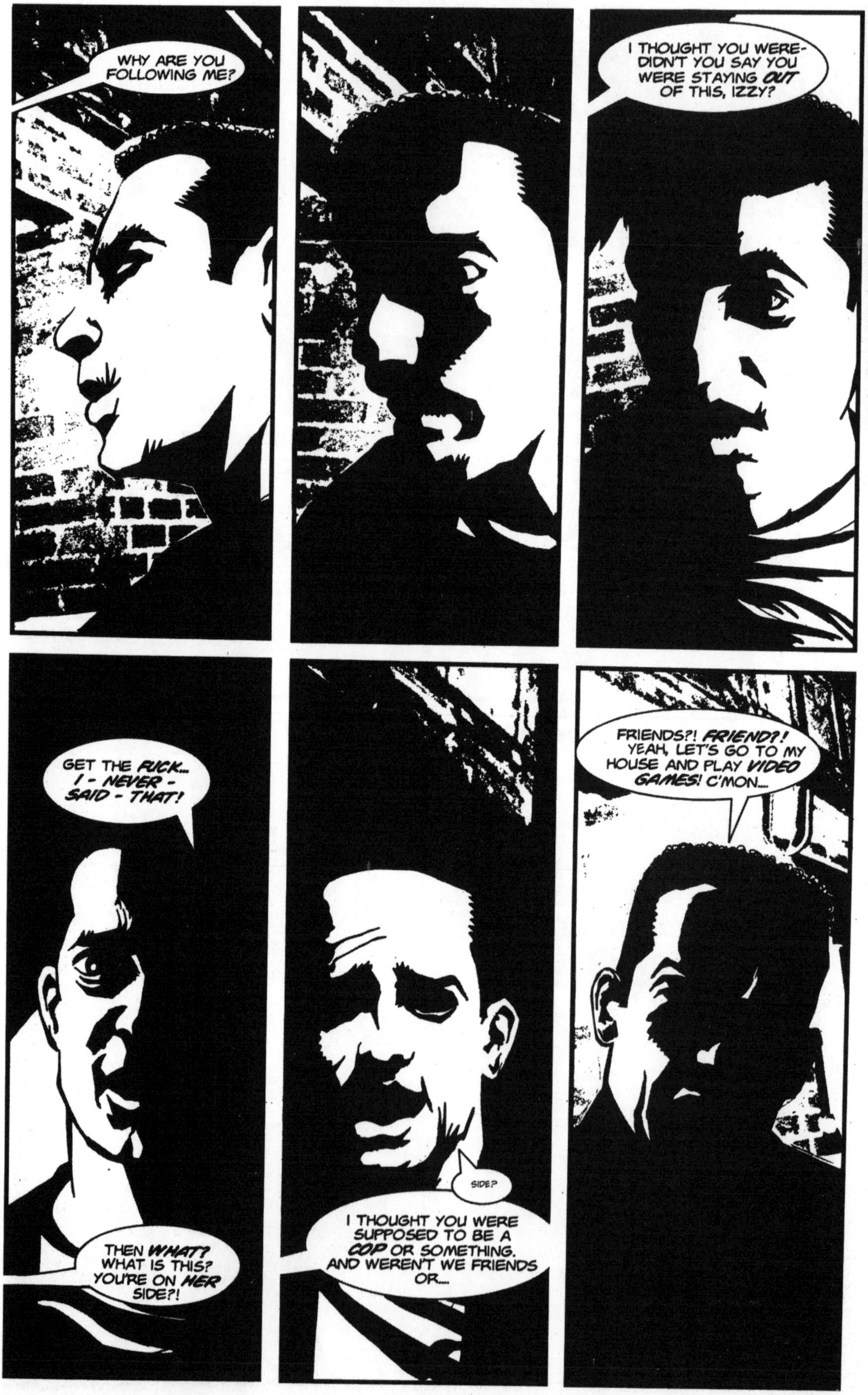
WHY ARE YOU FOLLOWING ME?
I THOUGHT YOU WERE- DIDN'T YOU SAY YOU WERE STAYING OUT OF THIS, IZZY?
GET THE FUCK... I - NEVER - SAID - THAT!
THEN WHAT? WHAT IS THIS? YOU'RE ON HER SIDE?!
SIDE?
I THOUGHT YOU WERE SUPPOSED TO BE A COP OR SOMETHING. AND WEREN'T WE FRIENDS OR...
FRIENDS?! FRIEND?! YEAH, LET'S GO TO MY HOUSE AND PLAY VIDEO GAMES! C'MON...

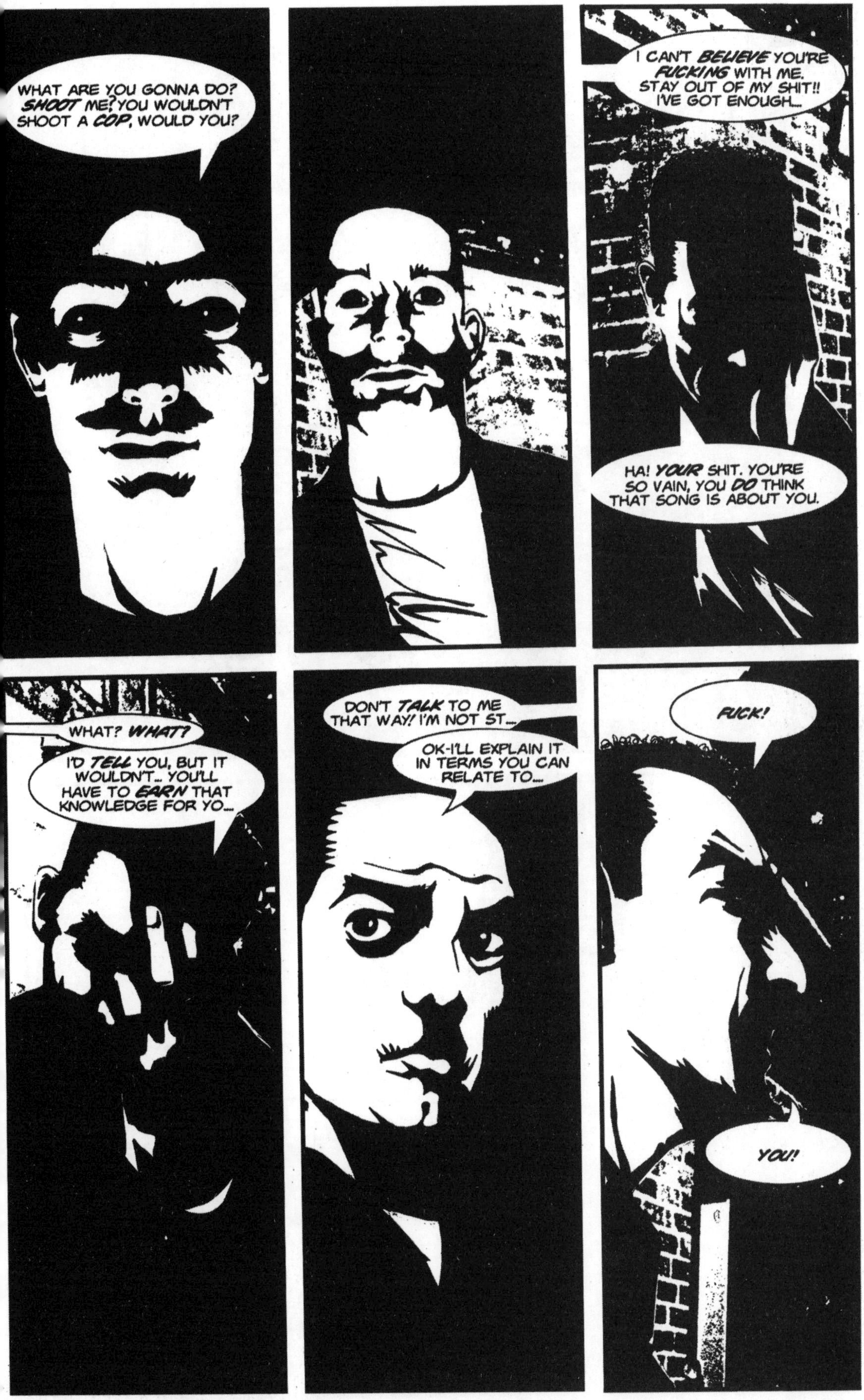
WHAT ARE YOU GONNA DO? SHOOT ME? YOU WOULDN'T SHOOT A COP, WOULD YOU?
I CAN'T BELIEVE YOU'RE FUCKING WITH ME. STAY OUT OF MY SHIT!! I'VE GOT ENOUGH...
HA! YOUR SHIT. YOU'RE SO VAIN, YOU DO THINK THAT SONG IS ABOUT YOU.
WHAT? WHAT?
I'D TELL YOU, BUT IT WOULDN'T... YOU'LL HAVE TO EARN THAT KNOWLEDGE FOR YO...
DON'T TALK TO ME THAT WAY! I'M NOT ST...
OK-I'LL EXPLAIN IT IN TERMS YOU CAN RELATE TO...
FUCK!
YOU!

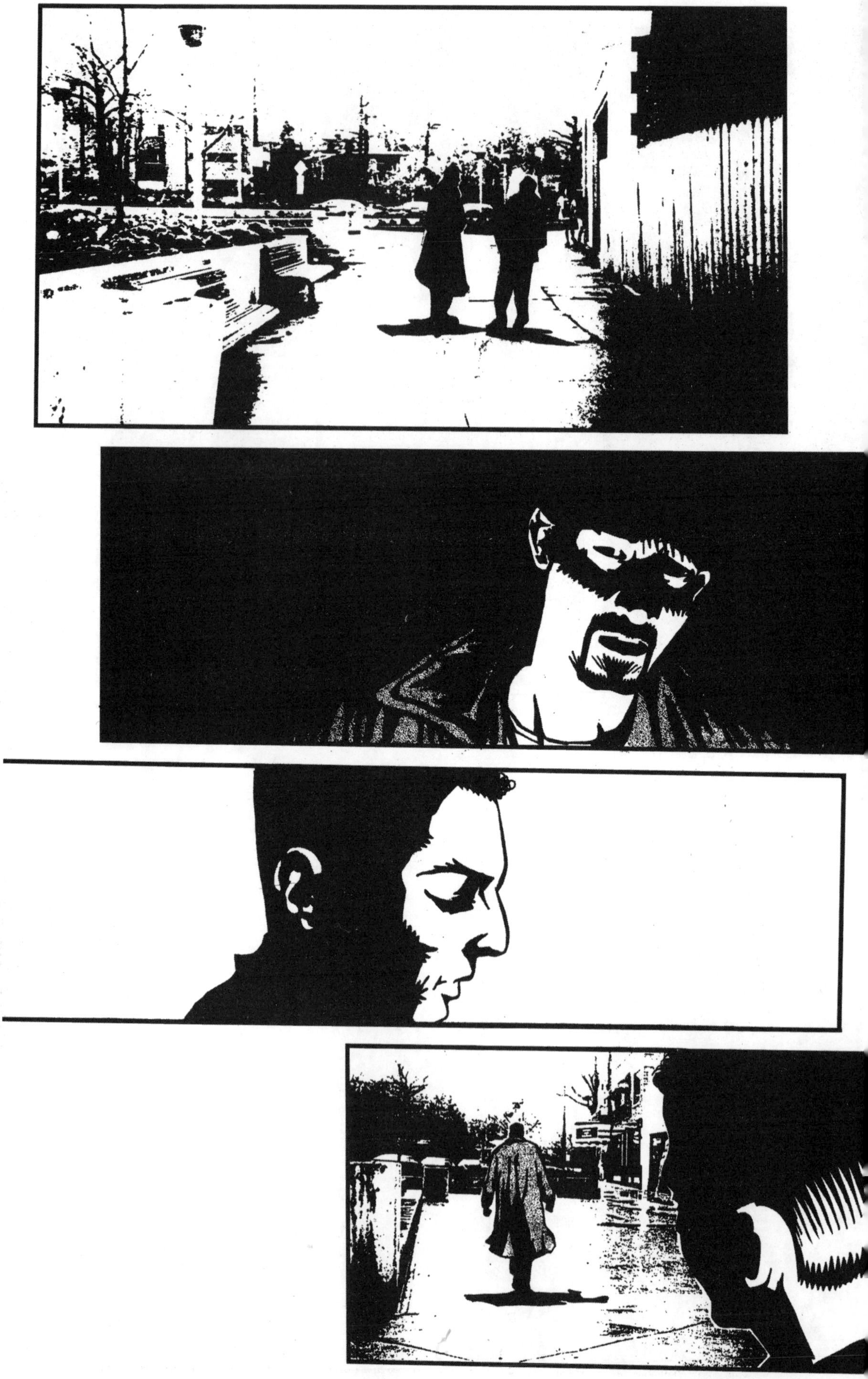

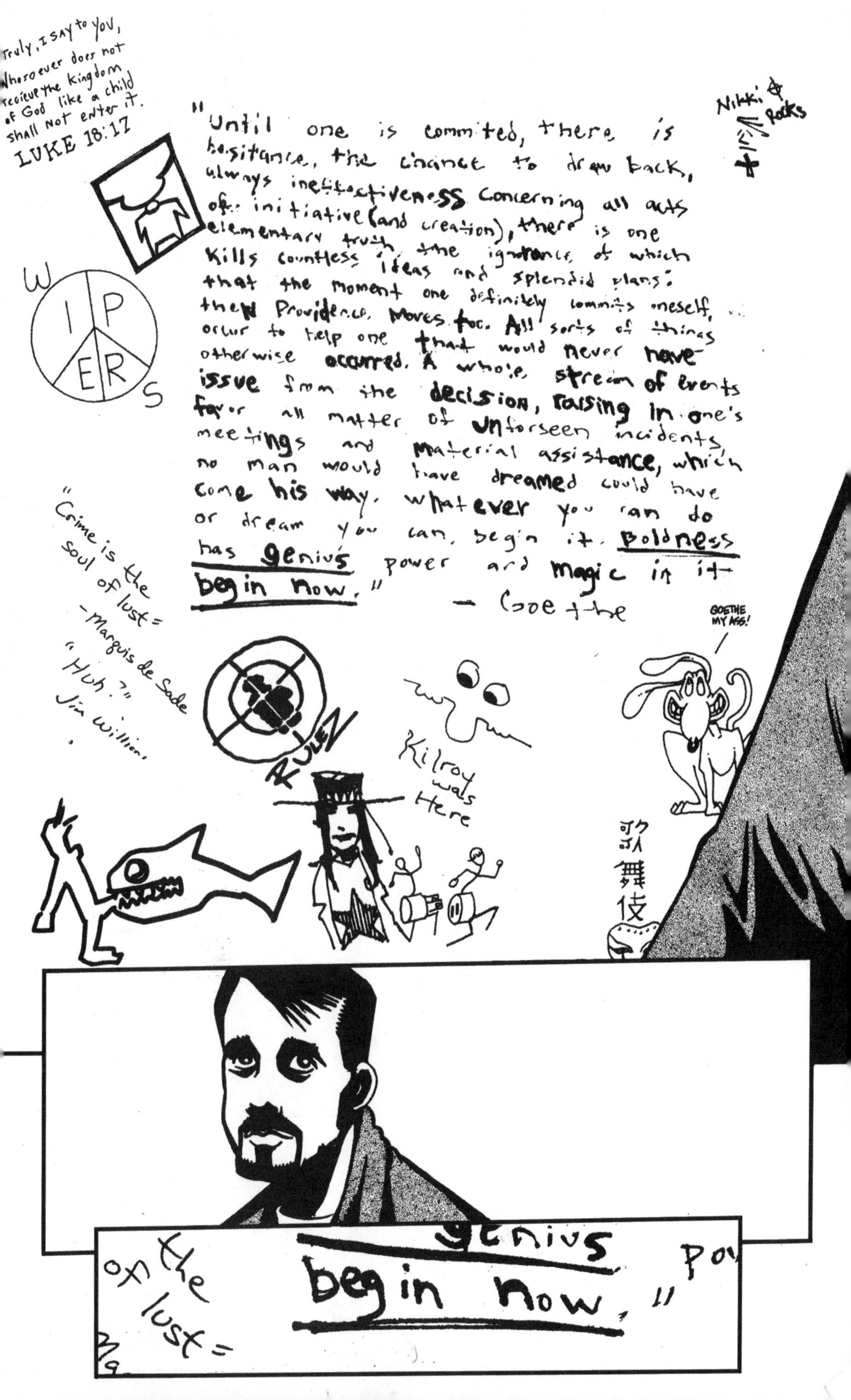
Truly, I SAY to you, Whosoever does not receive the kingdom of God like a child shall not enter it. LUKE 18:17
"Until one is commited, there is hesitance, the chance to draw back, always ineffectiveness concerning all acts of initiative (and creation), there is one elementary truth, the ignorance of which kills countless ideas and splendid plans: that the moment one definitely commits oneself, then Providence moves too. All sorts of things occur to help one that would never otherwise occurred. A whole stream of events issue from the decision, raising in one's favor all matter of unforseen incidents, meetings and material assistance, which no man would have dreamed could have come his way. Whatever you can do or dream you can, begin it. Boldness has genius, power and magic in it. begin now." — Goethe
Nikki Rocks
W I P E R S
"Crime is the soul of lust" — Marquis de Sade
"Huh?" Jim Williams
RULEZ
Kilroy was Here
GOETHE MY ASS!
歌舞伎
genius
begin now,"
the of lust

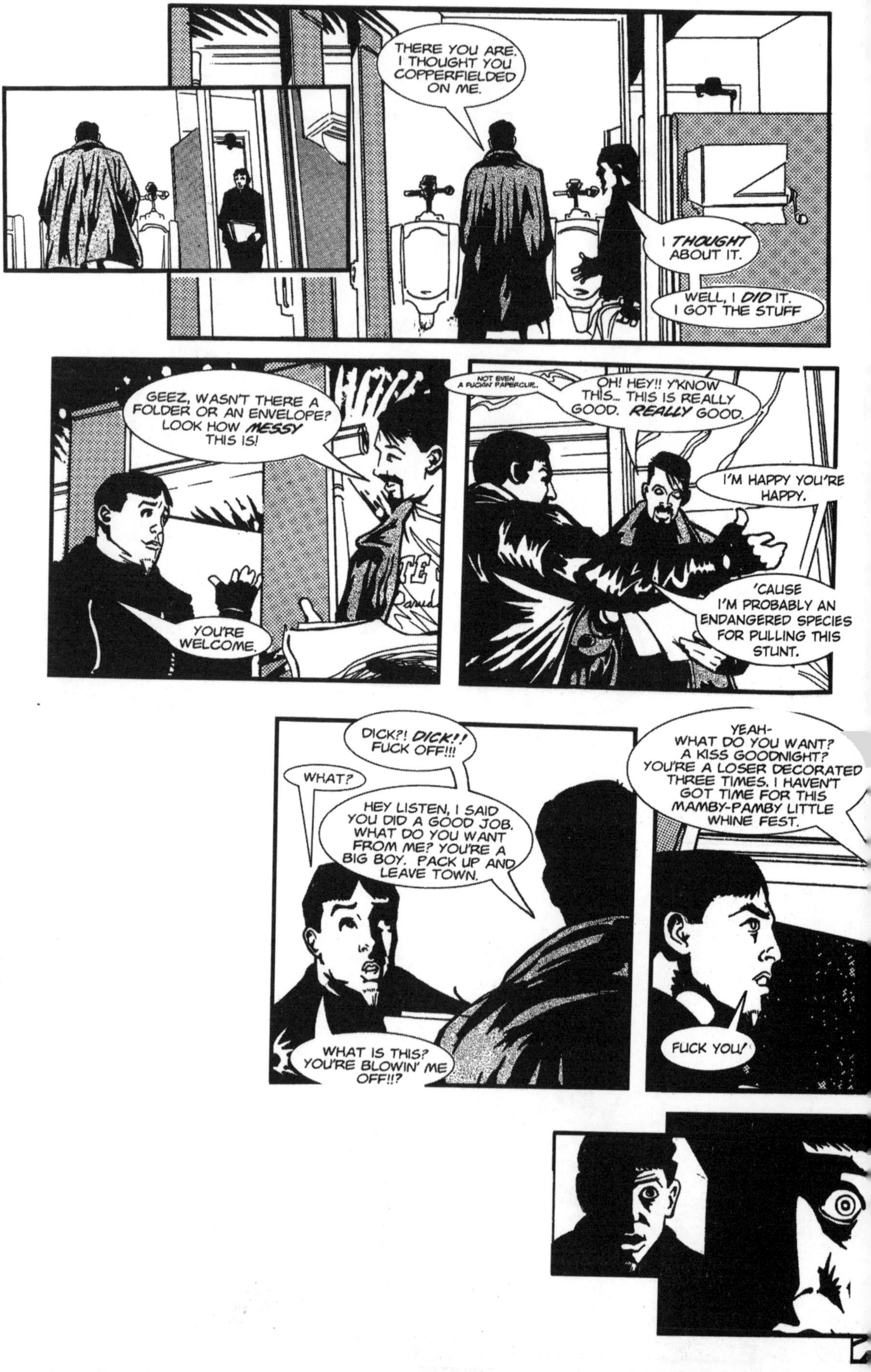
THERE YOU ARE. I THOUGHT YOU COPPERFIELDED ON ME.
I THOUGHT ABOUT IT.
WELL, I DID IT. I GOT THE STUFF
GEEZ, WASN'T THERE A FOLDER OR AN ENVELOPE? LOOK HOW MESSY THIS IS!
YOU'RE WELCOME.
NOT EVEN A FUCKIN' PAPERCLIP..
OH! HEY!! Y'KNOW THIS.. THIS IS REALLY GOOD. REALLY GOOD.
I'M HAPPY YOU'RE HAPPY.
'CAUSE I'M PROBABLY AN ENDANGERED SPECIES FOR PULLING THIS STUNT.
DICK?! DICK!! FUCK OFF!!!
WHAT?
HEY LISTEN, I SAID YOU DID A GOOD JOB. WHAT DO YOU WANT FROM ME? YOU'RE A BIG BOY. PACK UP AND LEAVE TOWN.
WHAT IS THIS? YOU'RE BLOWIN' ME OFF!!?
YEAH- WHAT DO YOU WANT? A KISS GOODNIGHT? YOU'RE A LOSER DECORATED THREE TIMES. I HAVEN'T GOT TIME FOR THIS MAMBY-PAMBY LITTLE WHINE FEST.
FUCK YOU!

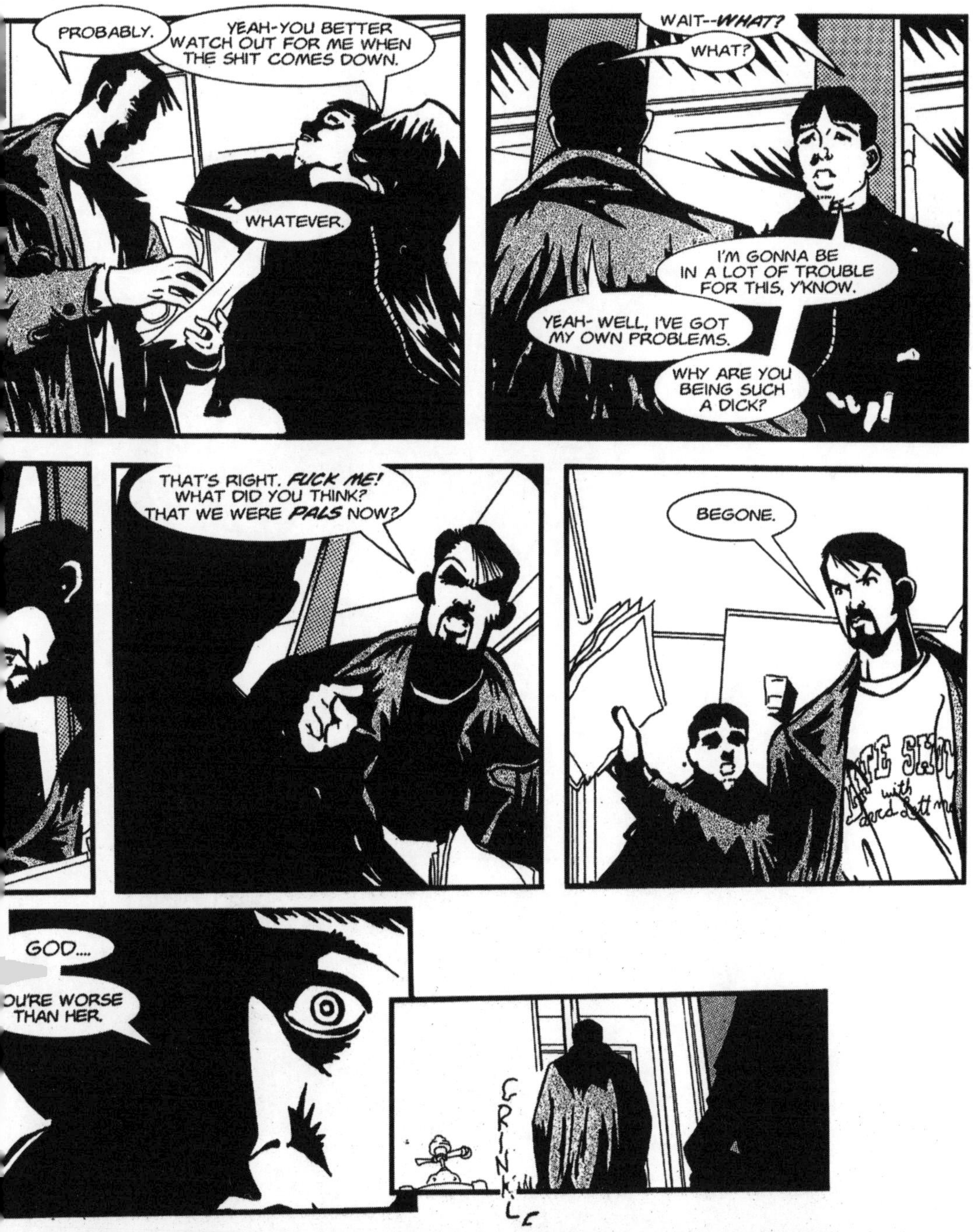
PROBABLY.
YEAH-YOU BETTER WATCH OUT FOR ME WHEN THE SHIT COMES DOWN.
WHATEVER.
WAIT--WHAT?
WHAT?
I'M GONNA BE IN A LOT OF TROUBLE FOR THIS, Y'KNOW.
YEAH- WELL, I'VE GOT MY OWN PROBLEMS.
WHY ARE YOU BEING SUCH A DICK?
THAT'S RIGHT. FUCK ME! WHAT DID YOU THINK? THAT WE WERE PALS NOW?
BEGONE.
GOD....
OU'RE WORSE THAN HER.
GRINKLE

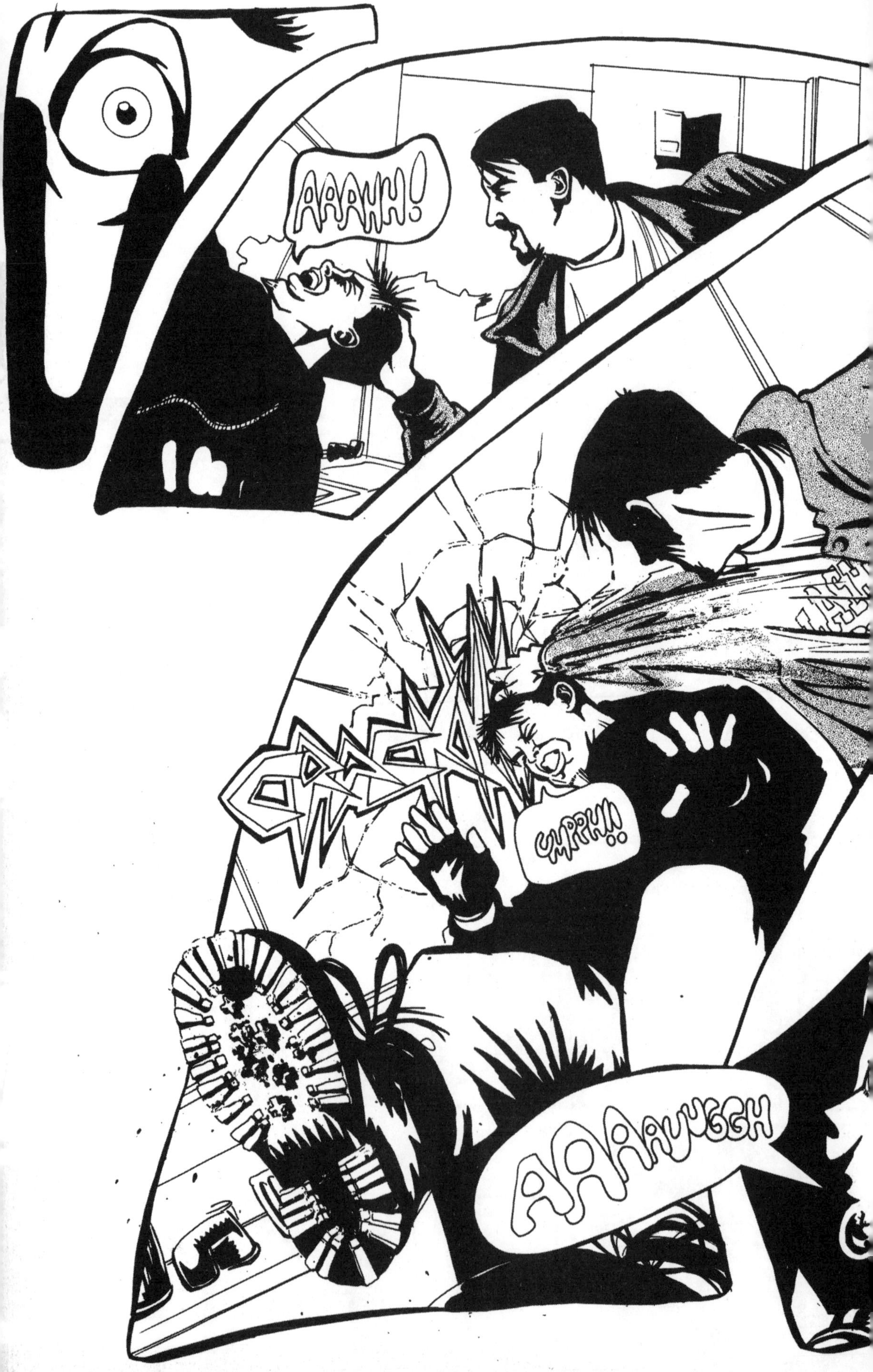
AAAHH!
UMPPH!!
AAAAUUGGH

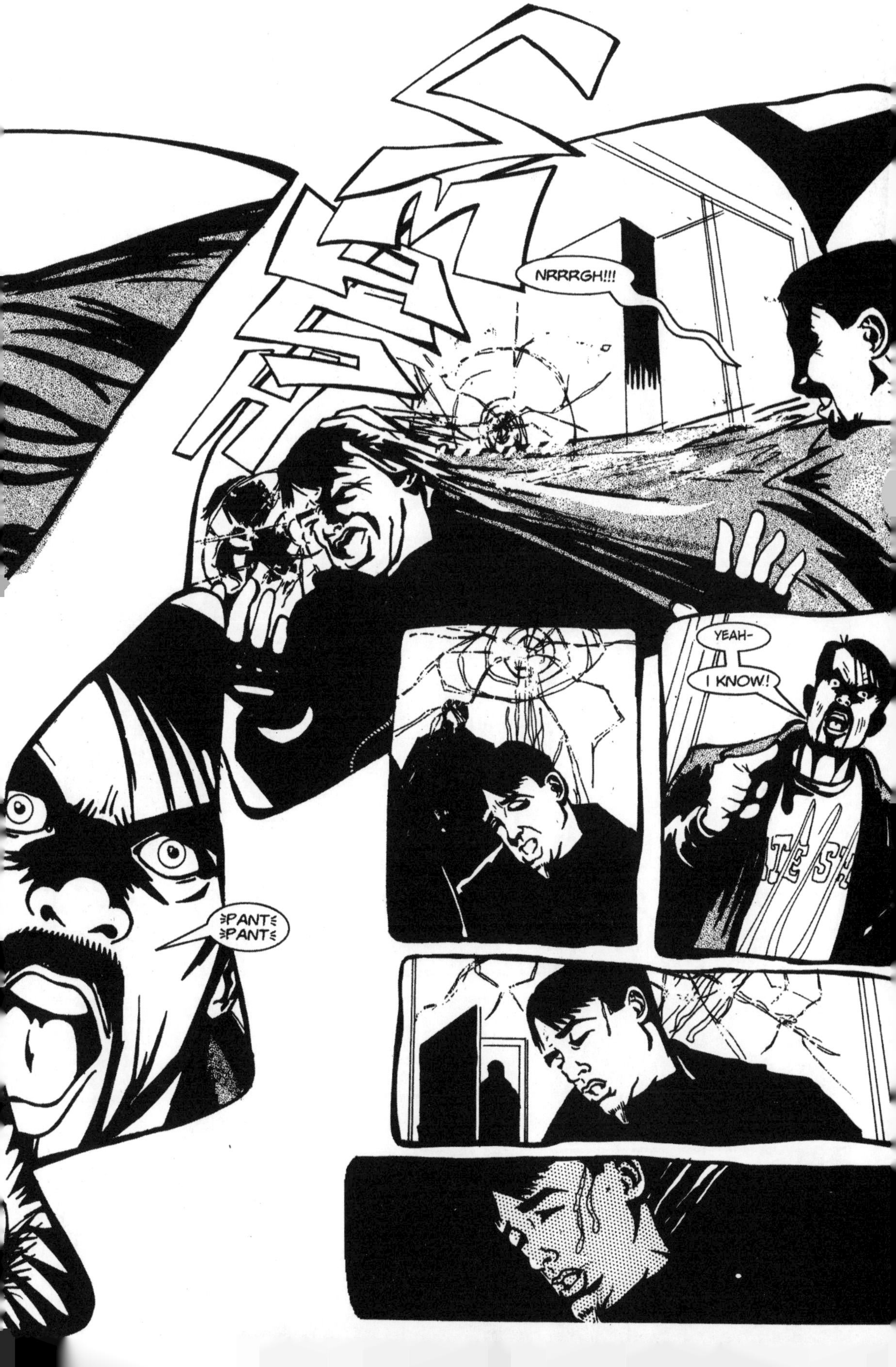
NRRRGH!!!
YEAH-
I KNOW!
PANT
PANT

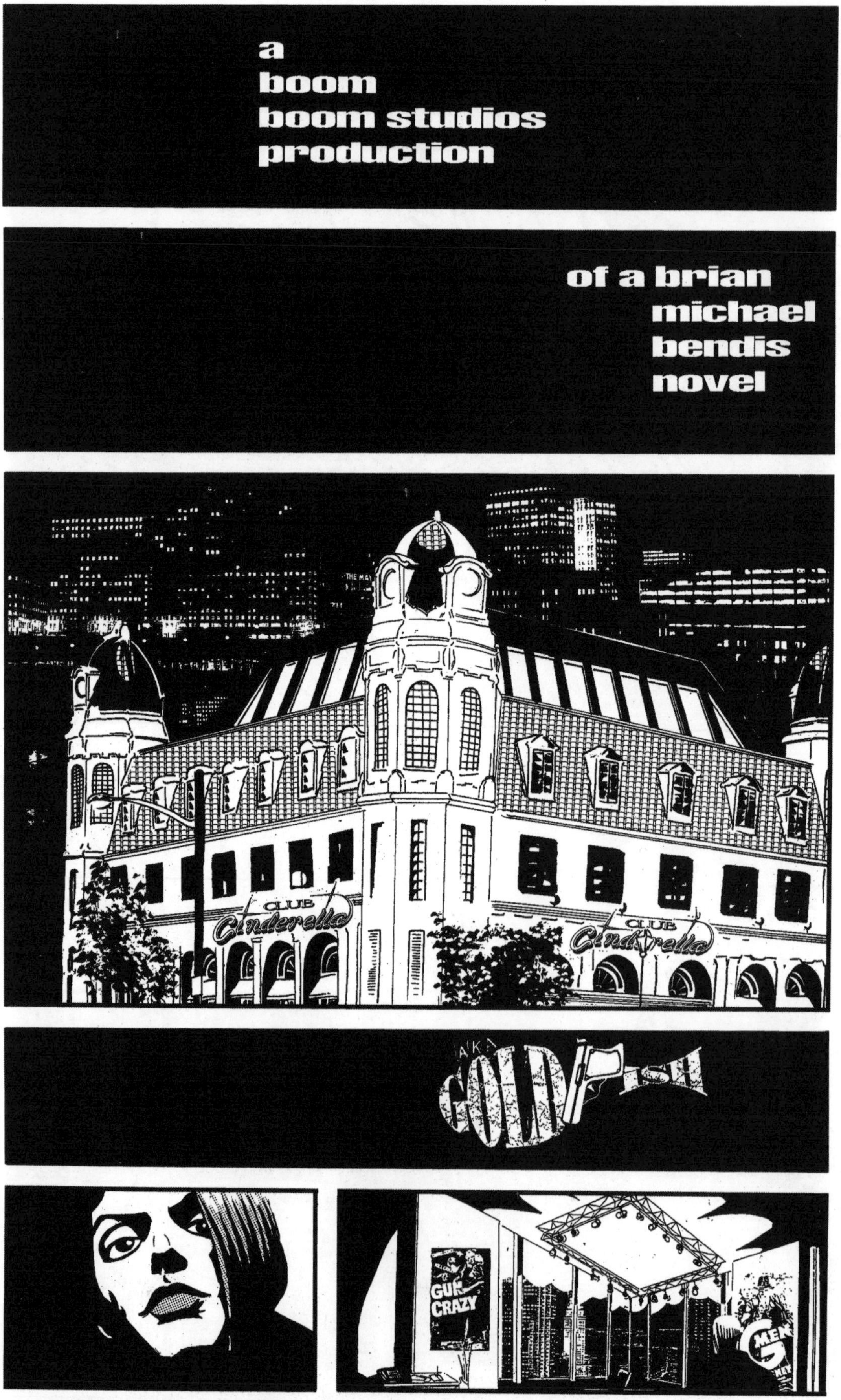
a
boom
boom studios
production
of a brian
michael
bendis
novel
CLUB
Cinderella
CLUB
Cinderella
A.K.A.
GOLDFISH
GUN
CRAZY
G MEN

typography by **rick conrad**

lettering by **jared bendis**

edited by **kim l. bushman**

FILE ACCESSED

GUN CRAZY
G MEN
CAGNEY

created and executed by **brian michael bendis**

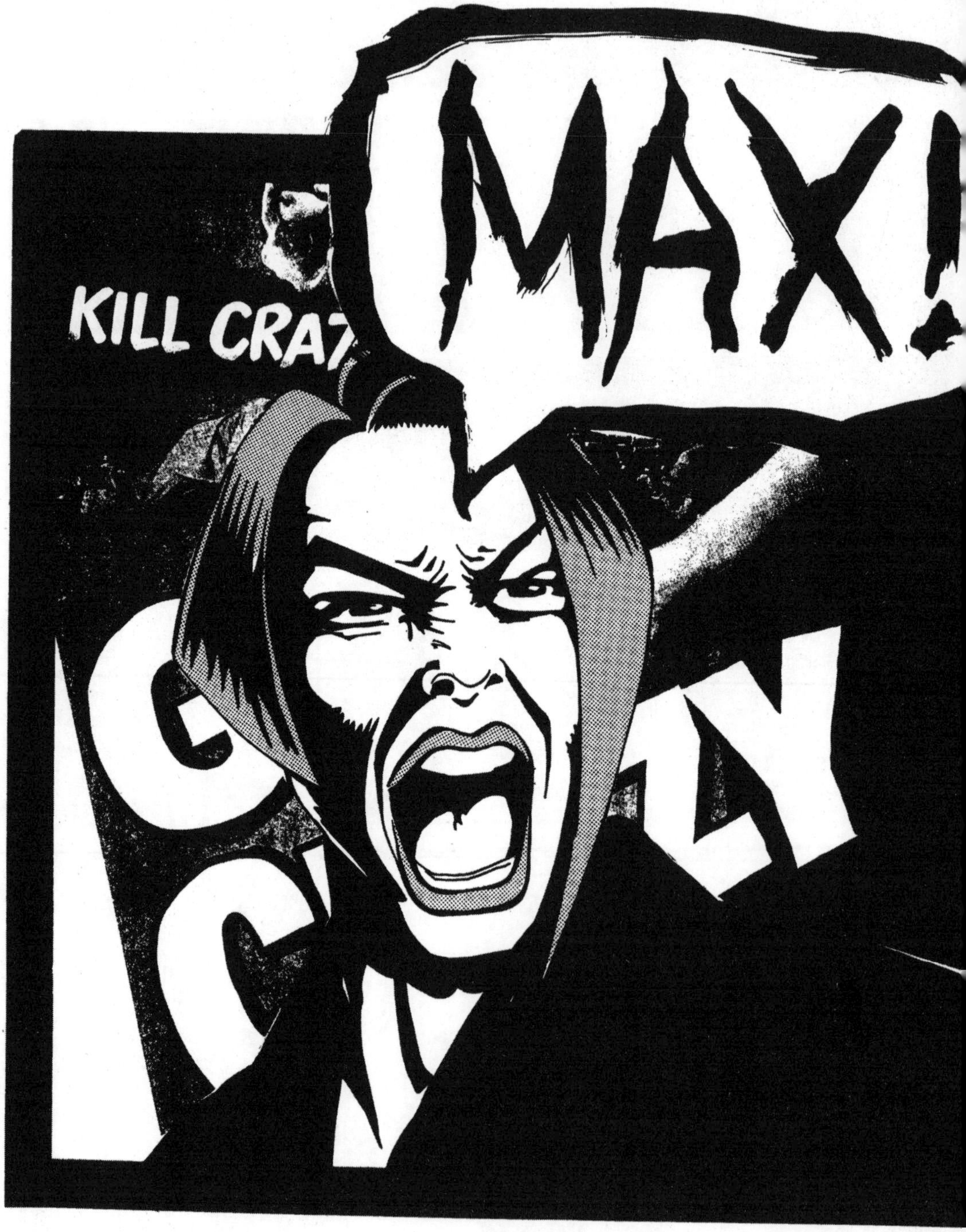
MAX!
KILL CRAZ

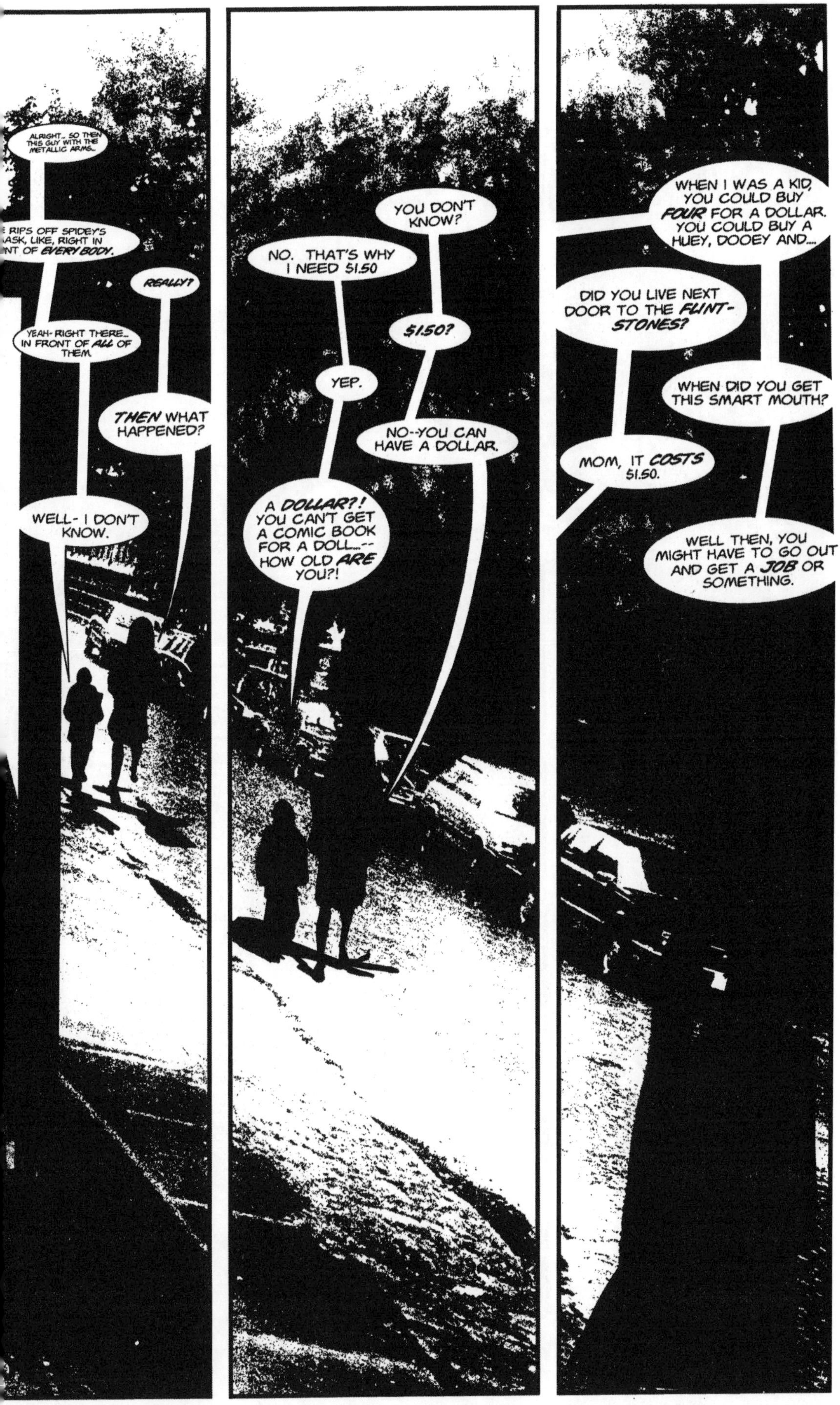
ALRIGHT... SO THEN THIS GUY WITH THE METALLIC ARMS...
RIPS OFF SPIDEY'S
ASK, LIKE, RIGHT IN
NT OF EVERYBODY.
REALLY?
YEAH- RIGHT THERE... IN FRONT OF ALL OF THEM.
THEN WHAT HAPPENED?
WELL- I DON'T KNOW.
YOU DON'T KNOW?
NO. THAT'S WHY I NEED $1.50
$1.50?
YEP.
NO--YOU CAN HAVE A DOLLAR.
A DOLLAR?! YOU CAN'T GET A COMIC BOOK FOR A DOLL...-- HOW OLD ARE YOU?!
WHEN I WAS A KID, YOU COULD BUY FOUR FOR A DOLLAR. YOU COULD BUY A HUEY, DOOEY AND...
DID YOU LIVE NEXT DOOR TO THE FLINT-STONES?
WHEN DID YOU GET THIS SMART MOUTH?
MOM, IT COSTS $1.50.
WELL THEN, YOU MIGHT HAVE TO GO OUT AND GET A JOB OR SOMETHING.

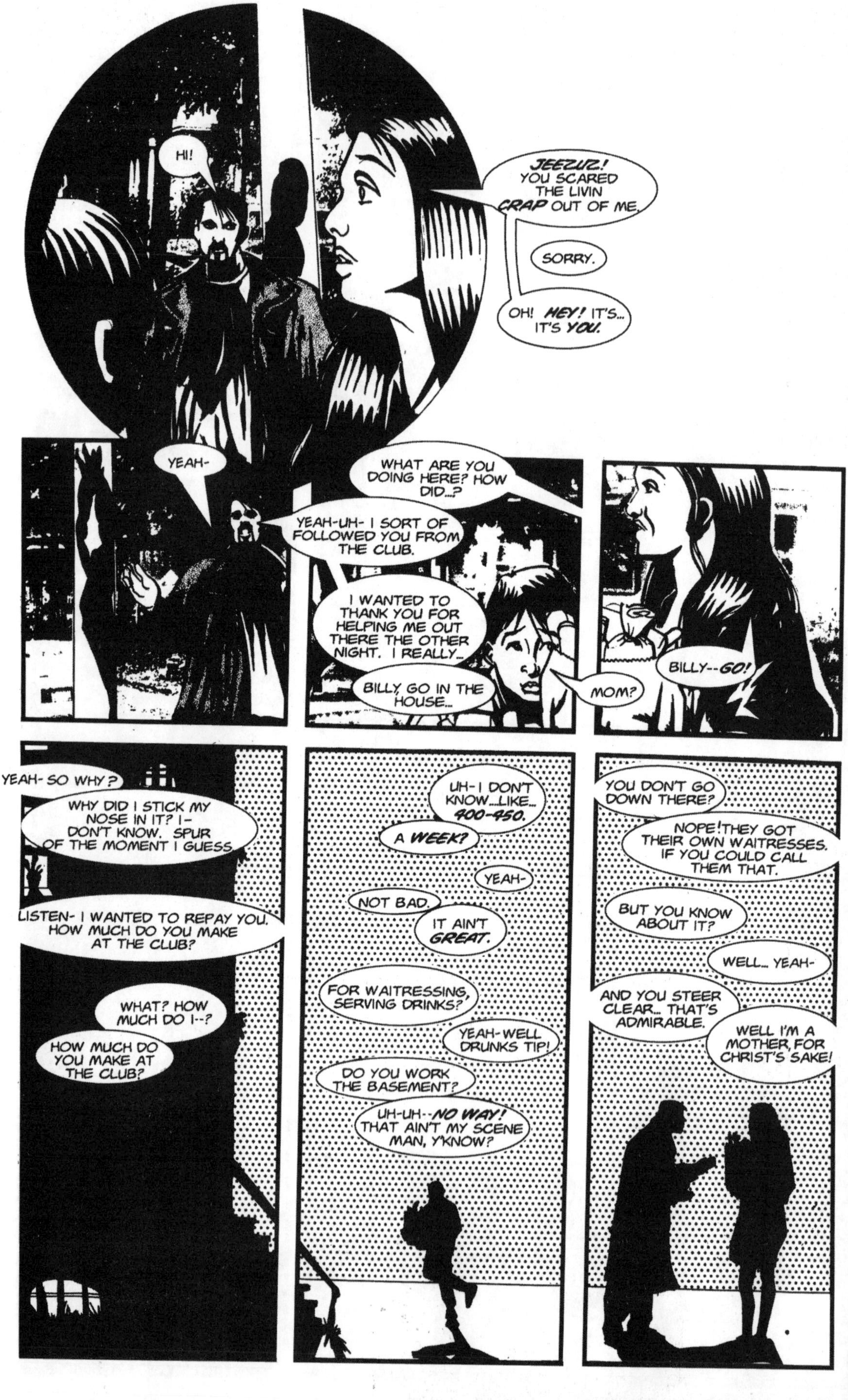
HI!
JEEZUZ! YOU SCARED THE LIVIN CRAP OUT OF ME.
SORRY.
OH! HEY! IT'S... IT'S YOU.
YEAH-
WHAT ARE YOU DOING HERE? HOW DID...?
YEAH-UH- I SORT OF FOLLOWED YOU FROM THE CLUB.
I WANTED TO THANK YOU FOR HELPING ME OUT THERE THE OTHER NIGHT. I REALLY...
BILLY, GO IN THE HOUSE...
MOM?
BILLY--GO!
YEAH- SO WHY?
WHY DID I STICK MY NOSE IN IT? I- DON'T KNOW. SPUR OF THE MOMENT I GUESS.
LISTEN- I WANTED TO REPAY YOU. HOW MUCH DO YOU MAKE AT THE CLUB?
WHAT? HOW MUCH DO I--?
HOW MUCH DO YOU MAKE AT THE CLUB?
UH- I DON'T KNOW...LIKE... 400-450.
A WEEK?
YEAH-
NOT BAD.
IT AIN'T GREAT.
FOR WAITRESSING, SERVING DRINKS?
YEAH-WELL DRUNKS TIP!
DO YOU WORK THE BASEMENT?
UH-UH--NO WAY! THAT AIN'T MY SCENE MAN, Y'KNOW?
YOU DON'T GO DOWN THERE?
NOPE! THEY GOT THEIR OWN WAITRESSES. IF YOU COULD CALL THEM THAT.
BUT YOU KNOW ABOUT IT?
WELL... YEAH-
AND YOU STEER CLEAR... THAT'S ADMIRABLE.
WELL I'M A MOTHER, FOR CHRIST'S SAKE!

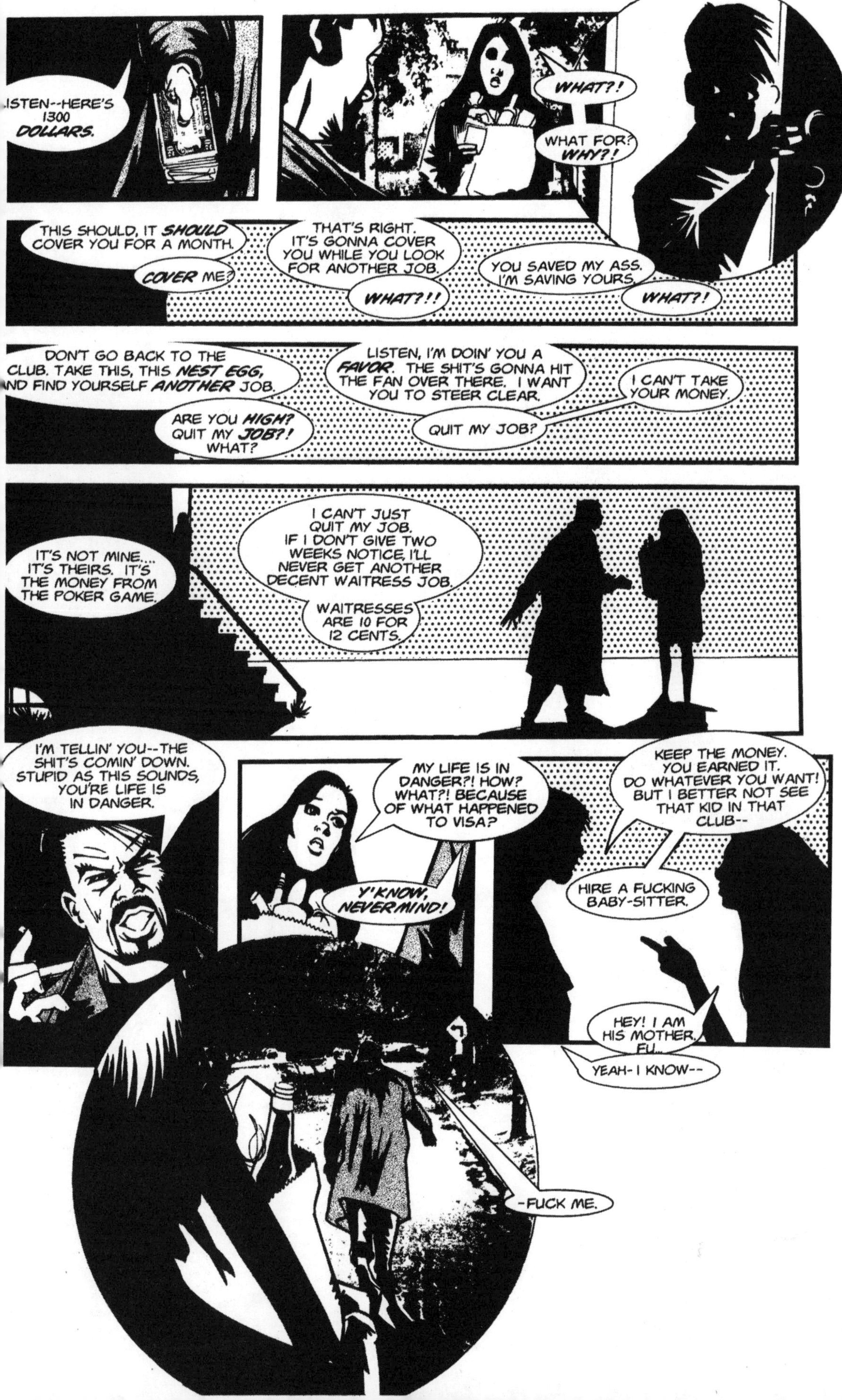

LISTEN--HERE'S 1300 DOLLARS.
WHAT?!
WHAT FOR? WHY?!
THIS SHOULD, IT SHOULD COVER YOU FOR A MONTH.
COVER ME?
THAT'S RIGHT. IT'S GONNA COVER YOU WHILE YOU LOOK FOR ANOTHER JOB.
WHAT?!!
YOU SAVED MY ASS. I'M SAVING YOURS.
WHAT?!
DON'T GO BACK TO THE CLUB. TAKE THIS, THIS NEST EGG, AND FIND YOURSELF ANOTHER JOB.
ARE YOU HIGH? QUIT MY JOB?! WHAT?
LISTEN, I'M DOIN' YOU A FAVOR. THE SHIT'S GONNA HIT THE FAN OVER THERE. I WANT YOU TO STEER CLEAR.
QUIT MY JOB?
I CAN'T TAKE YOUR MONEY.
IT'S NOT MINE... IT'S THEIRS. IT'S THE MONEY FROM THE POKER GAME.
I CAN'T JUST QUIT MY JOB. IF I DON'T GIVE TWO WEEKS NOTICE, I'LL NEVER GET ANOTHER DECENT WAITRESS JOB.
WAITRESSES ARE 10 FOR 12 CENTS.
I'M TELLIN' YOU--THE SHIT'S COMIN' DOWN. STUPID AS THIS SOUNDS, YOU'RE LIFE IS IN DANGER.
MY LIFE IS IN DANGER?! HOW? WHAT?! BECAUSE OF WHAT HAPPENED TO VISA?
Y'KNOW, NEVERMIND!
KEEP THE MONEY. YOU EARNED IT. DO WHATEVER YOU WANT! BUT I BETTER NOT SEE THAT KID IN THAT CLUB--
HIRE A FUCKING BABY-SITTER.
HEY! I AM HIS MOTHER, FU...
YEAH- I KNOW--
-FUCK ME.

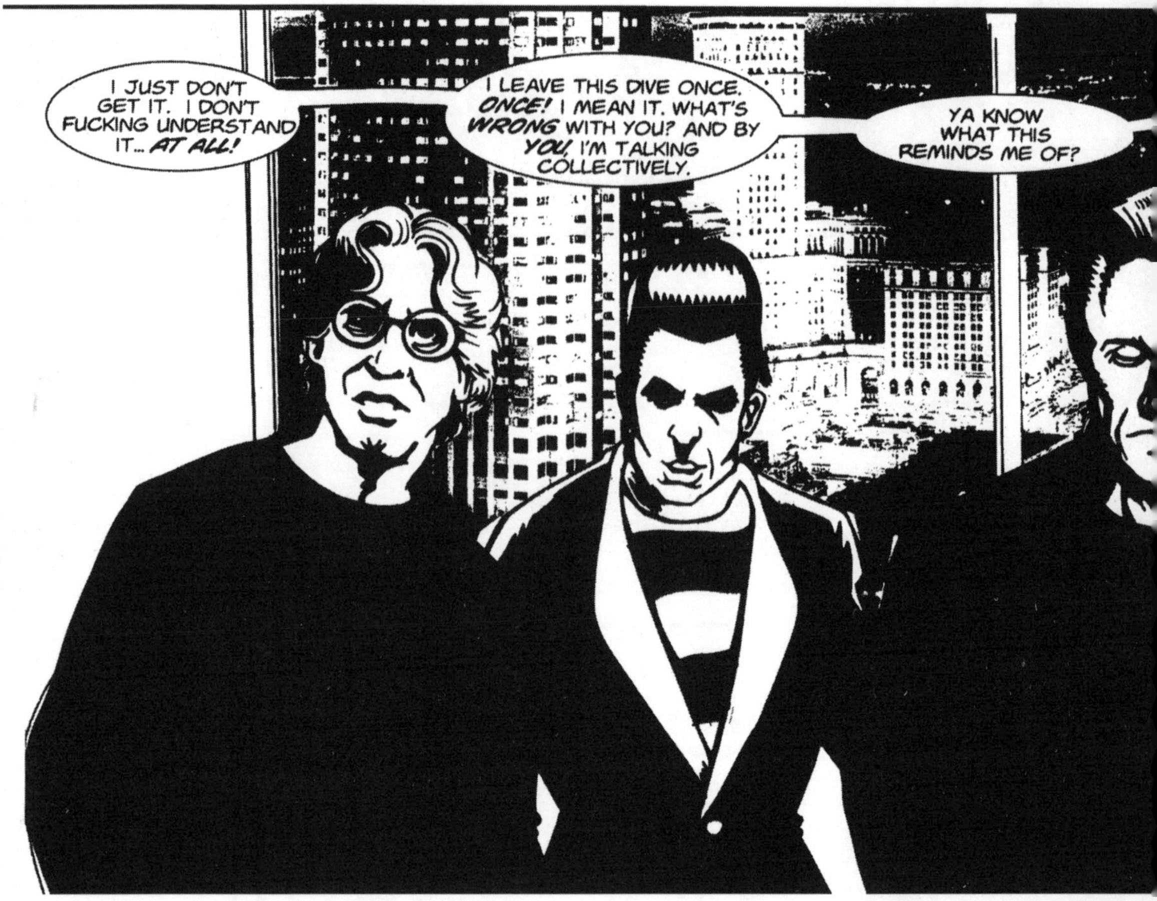
I JUST DON'T GET IT. I DON'T FUCKING UNDERSTAND IT... AT ALL!
I LEAVE THIS DIVE ONCE. ONCE! I MEAN IT. WHAT'S WRONG WITH YOU? AND BY YOU, I'M TALKING COLLECTIVELY.
YA KNOW WHAT THIS REMINDS ME OF?

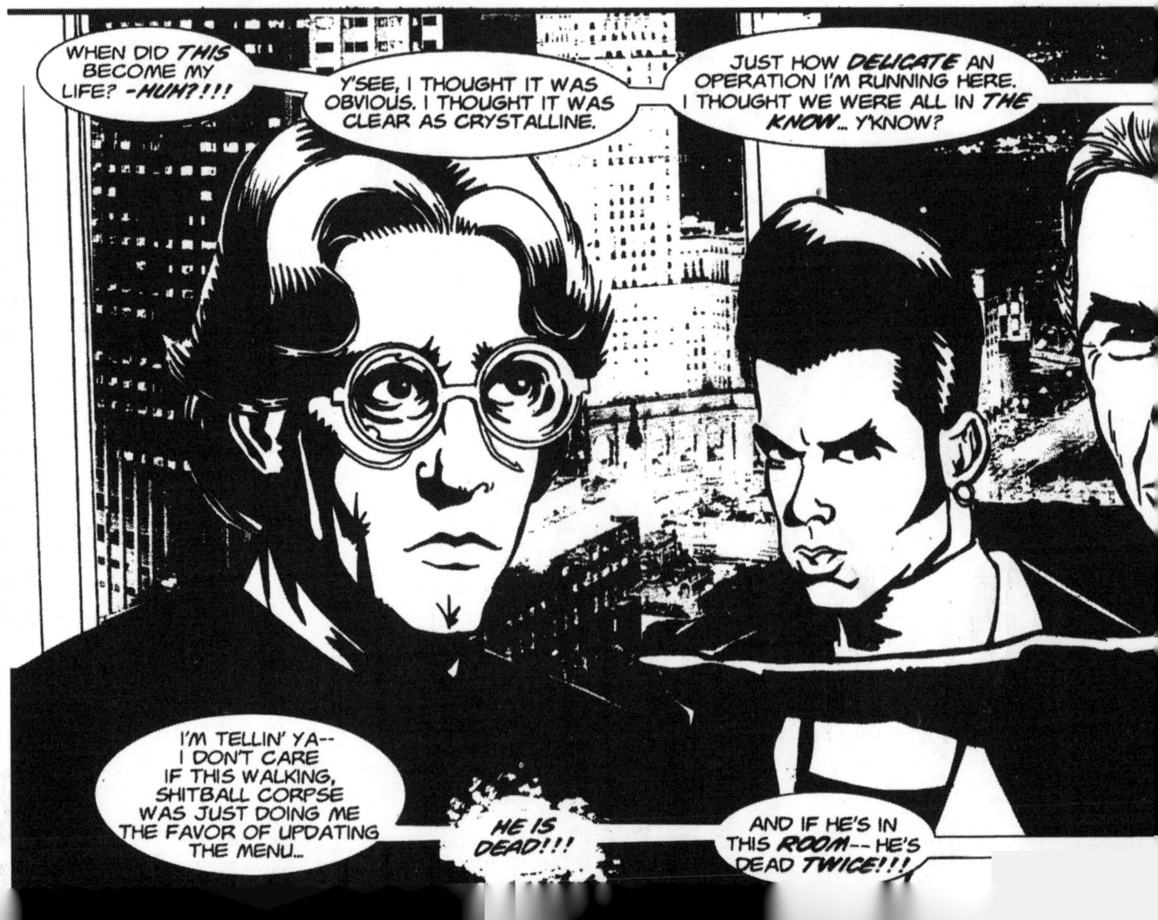
WHEN DID THIS BECOME MY LIFE? -HUH?!!!
Y'SEE, I THOUGHT IT WAS OBVIOUS. I THOUGHT IT WAS CLEAR AS CRYSTALLINE.
JUST HOW DELICATE AN OPERATION I'M RUNNING HERE. I THOUGHT WE WERE ALL IN THE KNOW... Y'KNOW?
I'M TELLIN' YA-- I DON'T CARE IF THIS WALKING, SHITBALL CORPSE WAS JUST DOING ME THE FAVOR OF UPDATING THE MENU...
HE IS DEAD!!!
AND IF HE'S IN THIS ROOM-- HE'S DEAD TWICE!!!

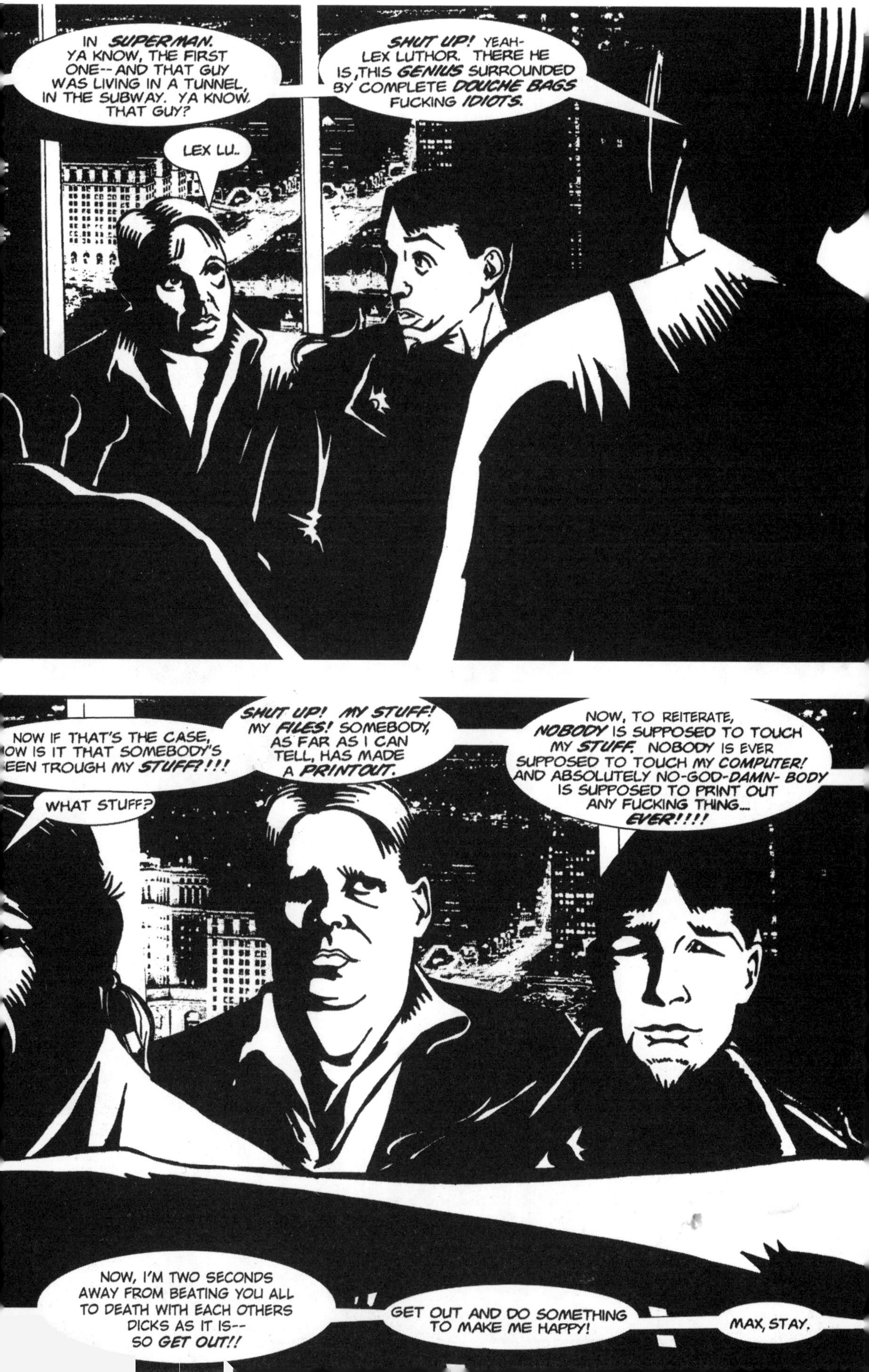
IN SUPERMAN. YA KNOW, THE FIRST ONE-- AND THAT GUY WAS LIVING IN A TUNNEL, IN THE SUBWAY. YA KNOW. THAT GUY?
LEX LU..
SHUT UP! YEAH- LEX LUTHOR. THERE HE IS, THIS GENIUS SURROUNDED BY COMPLETE DOUCHE BAGS FUCKING IDIOTS.
NOW IF THAT'S THE CASE, OW IS IT THAT SOMEBODY'S EEN TROUGH MY STUFF?!!!
WHAT STUFF?
SHUT UP! MY STUFF! MY FILES! SOMEBODY, AS FAR AS I CAN TELL, HAS MADE A PRINTOUT.
NOW, TO REITERATE, NOBODY IS SUPPOSED TO TOUCH MY STUFF. NOBODY IS EVER SUPPOSED TO TOUCH MY COMPUTER! AND ABSOLUTELY NO-GOD-DAMN- BODY IS SUPPOSED TO PRINT OUT ANY FUCKING THING... EVER!!!!
NOW, I'M TWO SECONDS AWAY FROM BEATING YOU ALL TO DEATH WITH EACH OTHERS DICKS AS IT IS-- SO GET OUT!!
GET OUT AND DO SOMETHING TO MAKE ME HAPPY!
MAX, STAY.

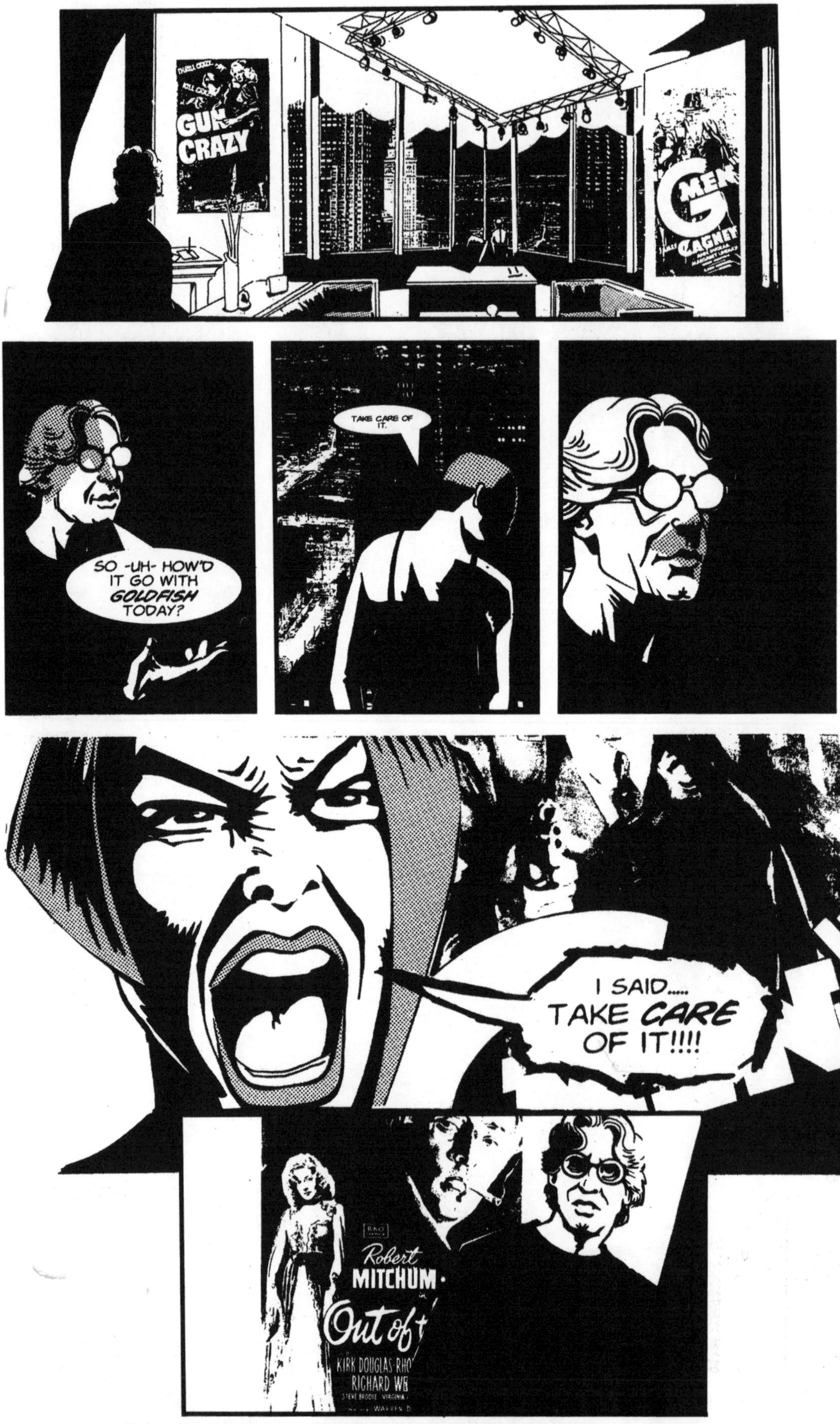
GUN CRAZY
G MEN
CAGNEY
SO -UH- HOW'D IT GO WITH GOLDFISH TODAY?
TAKE CARE OF IT.
I SAID..... TAKE CARE OF IT!!!!!
Robert MITCHUM
KIRK DOUGLAS

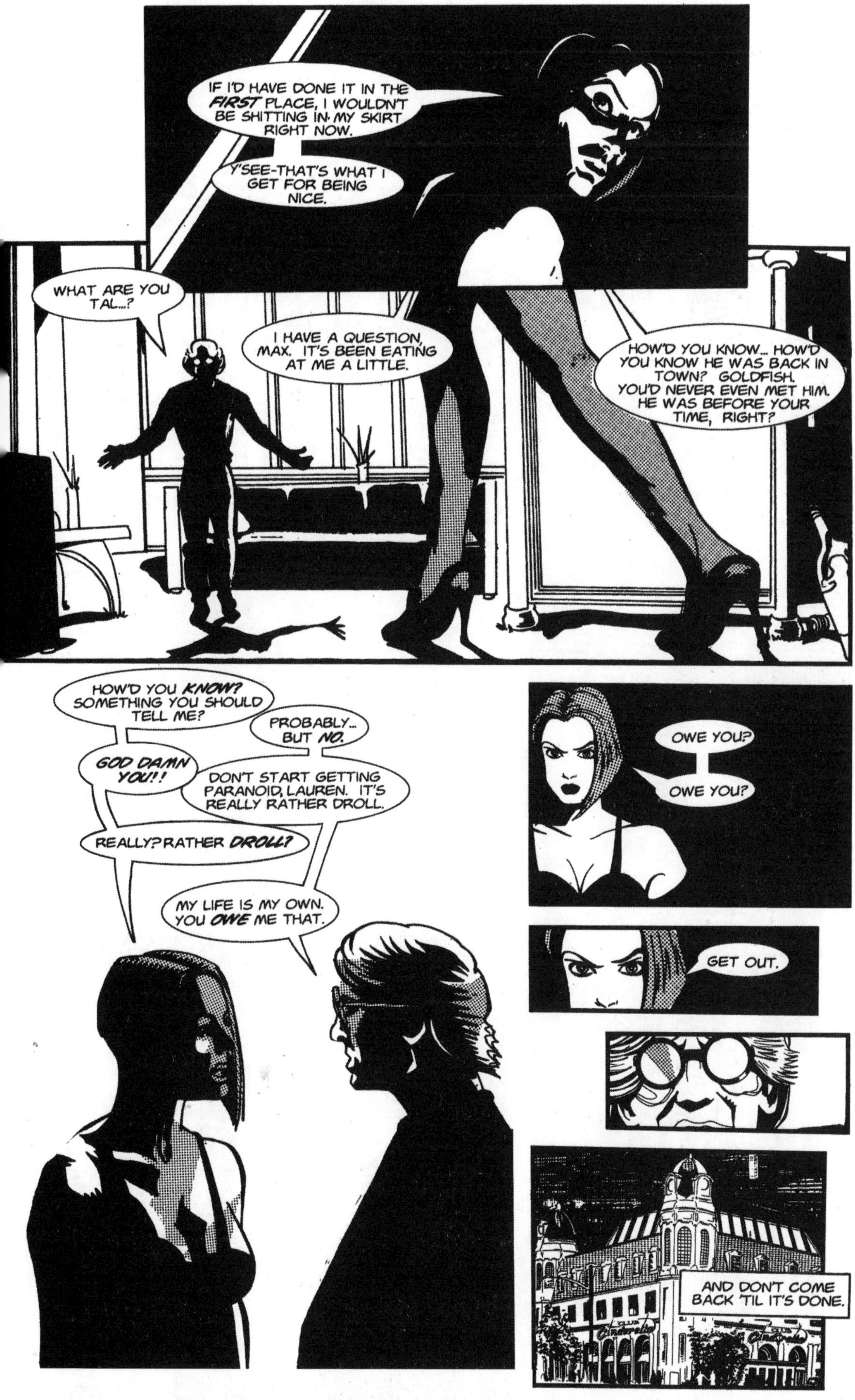
IF I'D HAVE DONE IT IN THE FIRST PLACE, I WOULDN'T BE SHITTING IN MY SKIRT RIGHT NOW.
Y'SEE-THAT'S WHAT I GET FOR BEING NICE.
WHAT ARE YOU TAL...?
I HAVE A QUESTION, MAX. IT'S BEEN EATING AT ME A LITTLE.
HOW'D YOU KNOW... HOW'D YOU KNOW HE WAS BACK IN TOWN? GOLDFISH. YOU'D NEVER EVEN MET HIM. HE WAS BEFORE YOUR TIME, RIGHT?
HOW'D YOU KNOW? SOMETHING YOU SHOULD TELL ME?
PROBABLY... BUT NO.
GOD DAMN YOU!!
DON'T START GETTING PARANOID, LAUREN. IT'S REALLY RATHER DROLL.
REALLY? RATHER DROLL?
MY LIFE IS MY OWN. YOU OWE ME THAT.
OWE YOU?
OWE YOU?
GET OUT.
AND DON'T COME BACK 'TIL IT'S DONE.

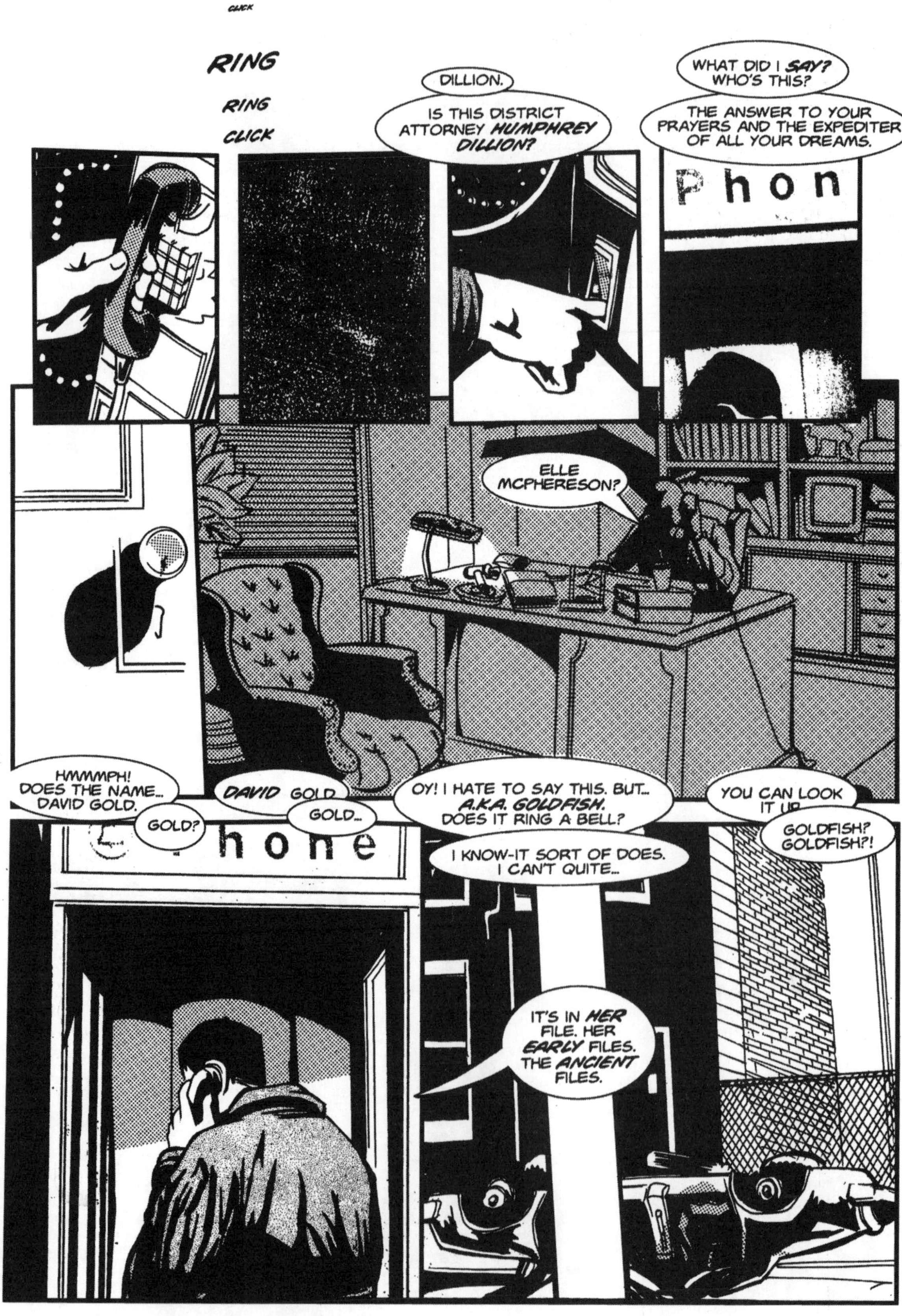
CLICK
RING
RING
CLICK
DILLION.
IS THIS DISTRICT ATTORNEY HUMPHREY DILLION?
WHAT DID I SAY? WHO'S THIS?
THE ANSWER TO YOUR PRAYERS AND THE EXPEDITER OF ALL YOUR DREAMS.
Phon
ELLE MCPHERESON?
HMMMPH! DOES THE NAME... DAVID GOLD.
GOLD?
DAVID GOLD
GOLD...
hone
OY! I HATE TO SAY THIS. BUT... A.K.A. GOLDFISH. DOES IT RING A BELL?
I KNOW-IT SORT OF DOES. I CAN'T QUITE...
YOU CAN LOOK IT UP
GOLDFISH? GOLDFISH?!
IT'S IN HER FILE. HER EARLY FILES. THE ANCIENT FILES.

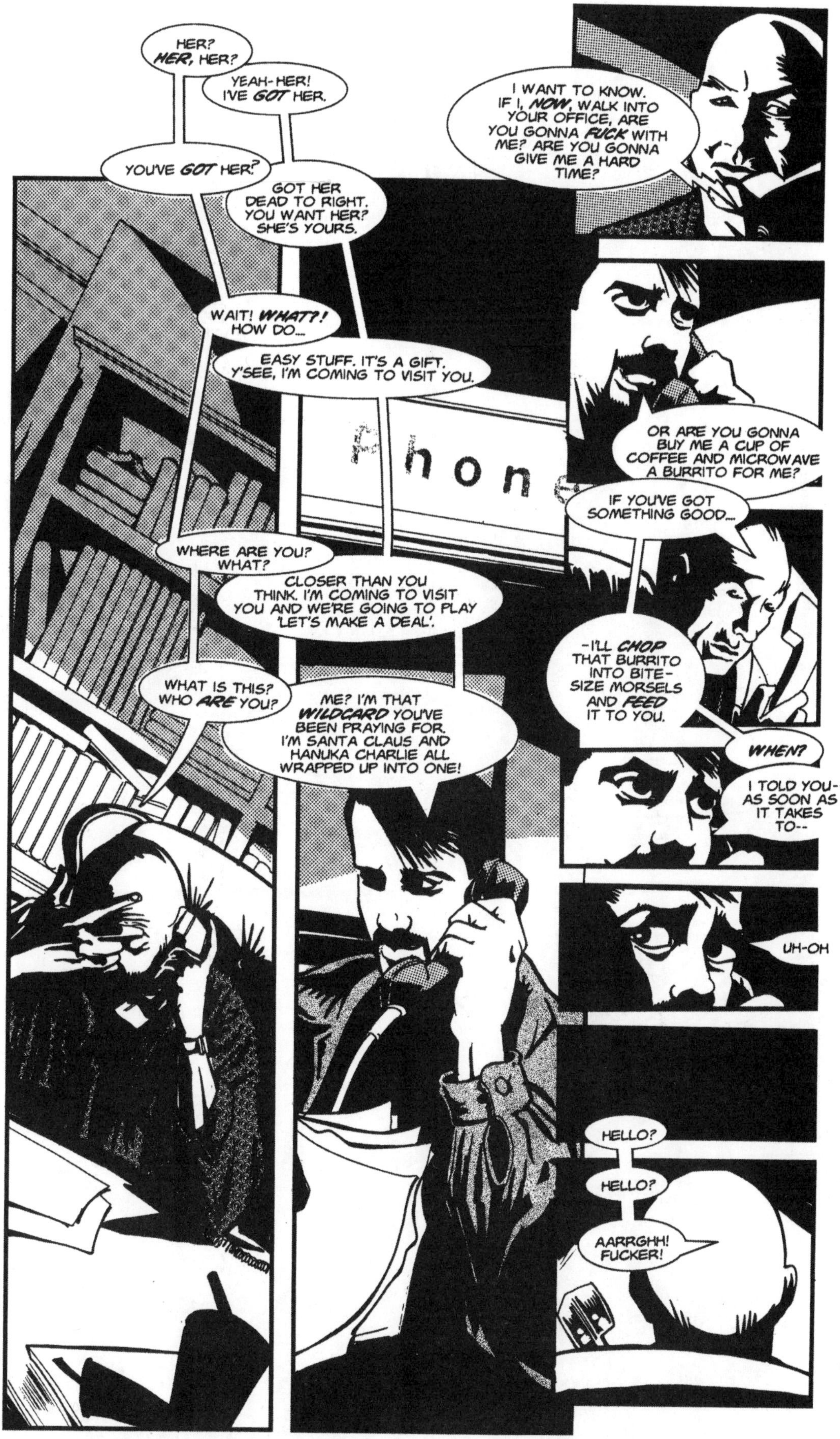

HER? HER, HER?
YEAH-HER! I'VE GOT HER.
YOU'VE GOT HER?
GOT HER DEAD TO RIGHT. YOU WANT HER? SHE'S YOURS.
WAIT! WHAT?! HOW DO....
EASY STUFF. IT'S A GIFT. Y'SEE, I'M COMING TO VISIT YOU.
Phone
WHERE ARE YOU? WHAT?
CLOSER THAN YOU THINK. I'M COMING TO VISIT YOU AND WE'RE GOING TO PLAY 'LET'S MAKE A DEAL'.
WHAT IS THIS? WHO ARE YOU?
ME? I'M THAT WILDCARD YOU'VE BEEN PRAYING FOR. I'M SANTA CLAUS AND HANUKA CHARLIE ALL WRAPPED UP INTO ONE!
I WANT TO KNOW. IF I, NOW, WALK INTO YOUR OFFICE, ARE YOU GONNA FUCK WITH ME? ARE YOU GONNA GIVE ME A HARD TIME?
OR ARE YOU GONNA BUY ME A CUP OF COFFEE AND MICROWAVE A BURRITO FOR ME?
IF YOU'VE GOT SOMETHING GOOD....
-I'LL CHOP THAT BURRITO INTO BITE-SIZE MORSELS AND FEED IT TO YOU.
WHEN?
I TOLD YOU-- AS SOON AS IT TAKES TO--
UH-OH
HELLO?
HELLO?
AARRGHH! FUCKER!

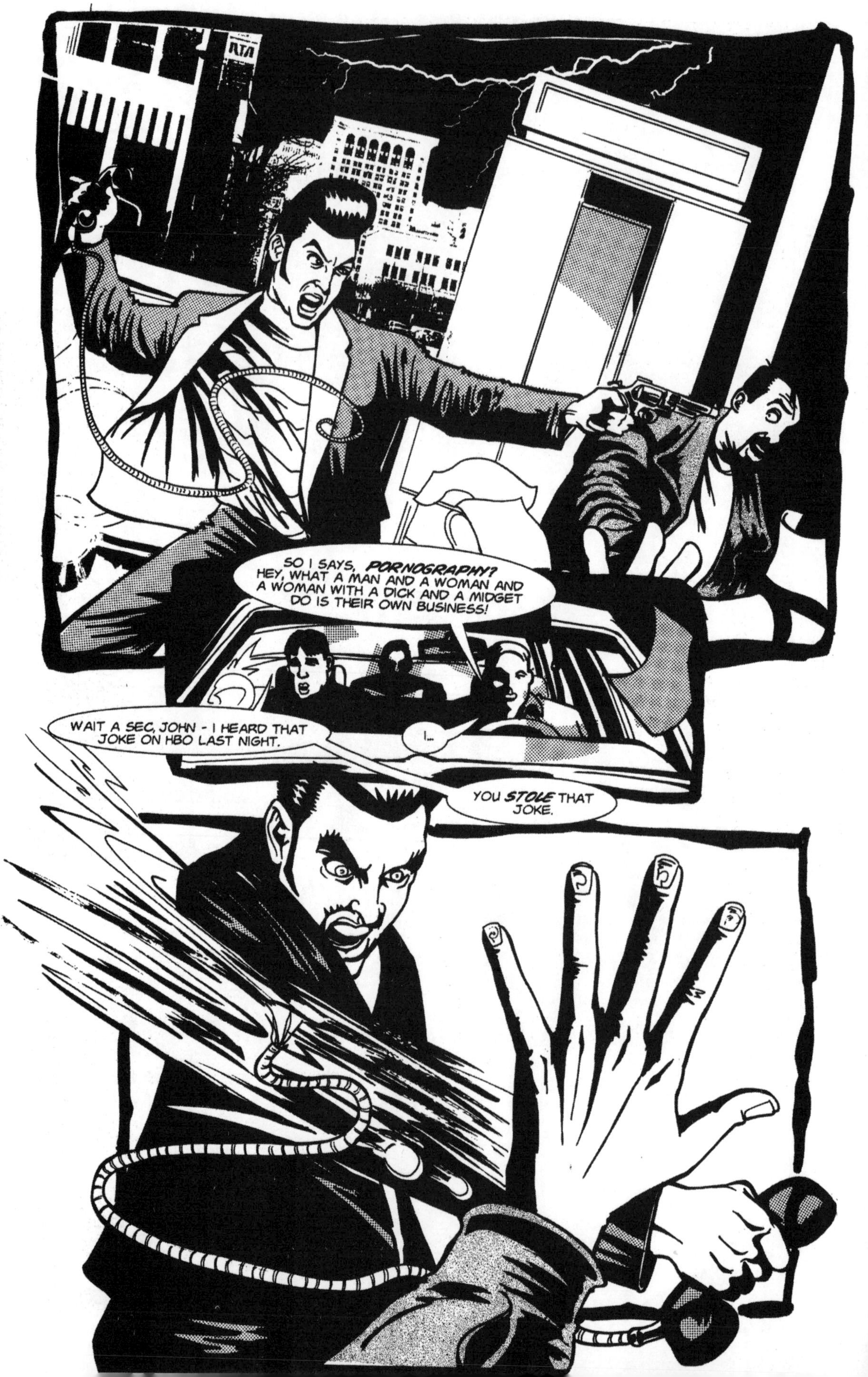
SO I SAYS, PORNOGRAPHY? HEY, WHAT A MAN AND A WOMAN AND A WOMAN WITH A DICK AND A MIDGET DO IS THEIR OWN BUSINESS!
WAIT A SEC, JOHN - I HEARD THAT JOKE ON HBO LAST NIGHT.
I...
YOU STOLE THAT JOKE.

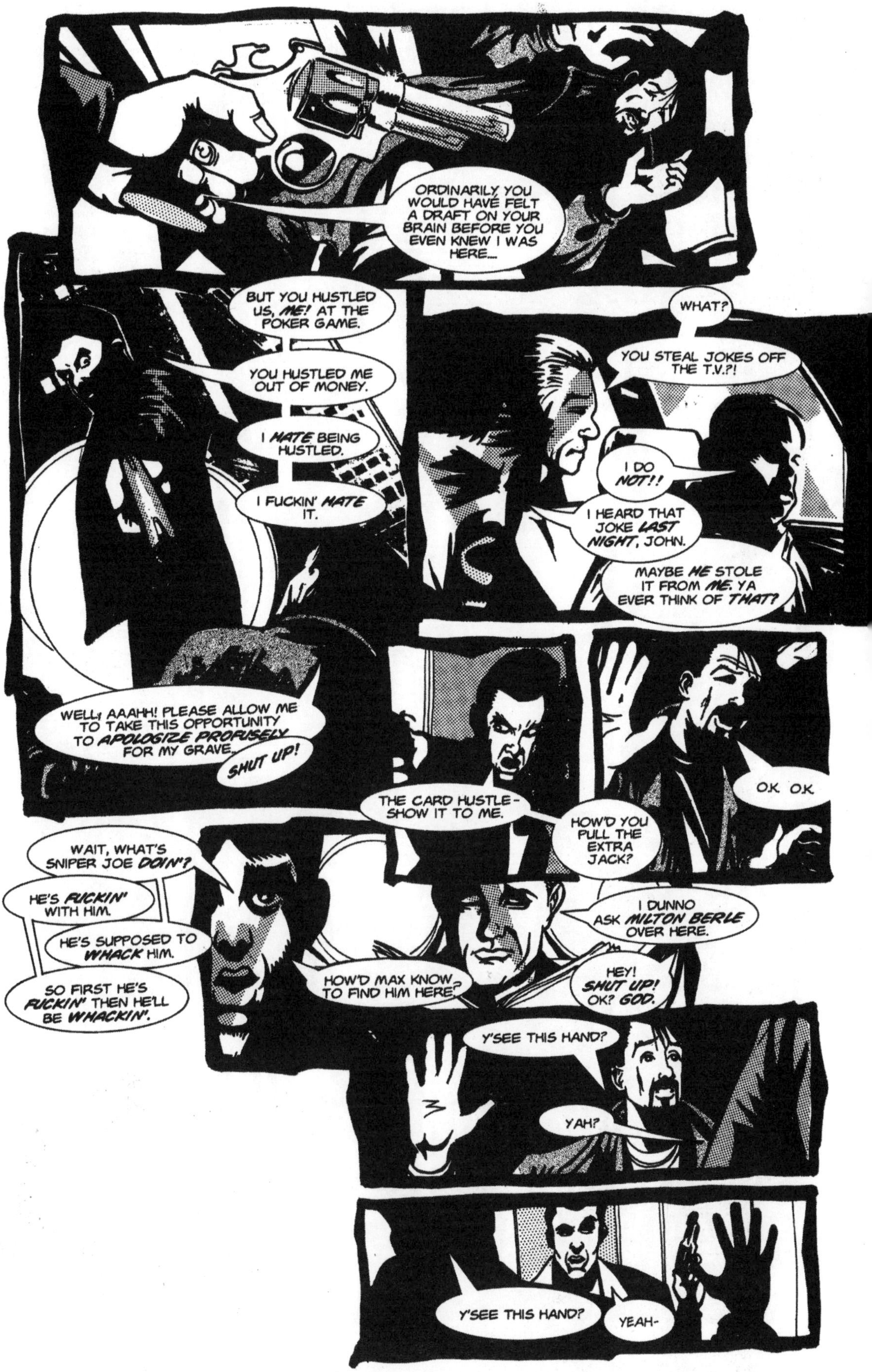
ORDINARILY, YOU WOULD HAVE FELT A DRAFT ON YOUR BRAIN BEFORE YOU EVEN KNEW I WAS HERE...
BUT YOU HUSTLED US, ME! AT THE POKER GAME.
YOU HUSTLED ME OUT OF MONEY.
I HATE BEING HUSTLED.
I FUCKIN' HATE IT.
WHAT?
YOU STEAL JOKES OFF THE T.V.?!
I DO NOT!!
I HEARD THAT JOKE LAST NIGHT, JOHN.
MAYBE HE STOLE IT FROM ME. YA EVER THINK OF THAT?
WELL, AAAHH! PLEASE ALLOW ME TO TAKE THIS OPPORTUNITY TO APOLOGIZE PROFUSELY FOR MY GRAVE...
SHUT UP!
O.K. O.K.
THE CARD HUSTLE- SHOW IT TO ME.
HOW'D YOU PULL THE EXTRA JACK?
WAIT, WHAT'S SNIPER JOE DOIN'?
HE'S FUCKIN' WITH HIM.
HE'S SUPPOSED TO WHACK HIM.
SO FIRST HE'S FUCKIN' THEN HE'LL BE WHACKIN'.
I DUNNO ASK MILTON BERLE OVER HERE.
HOW'D MAX KNOW TO FIND HIM HERE?
HEY! SHUT UP! OK? GOD.
Y'SEE THIS HAND?
YAH?
Y'SEE THIS HAND?
YEAH-

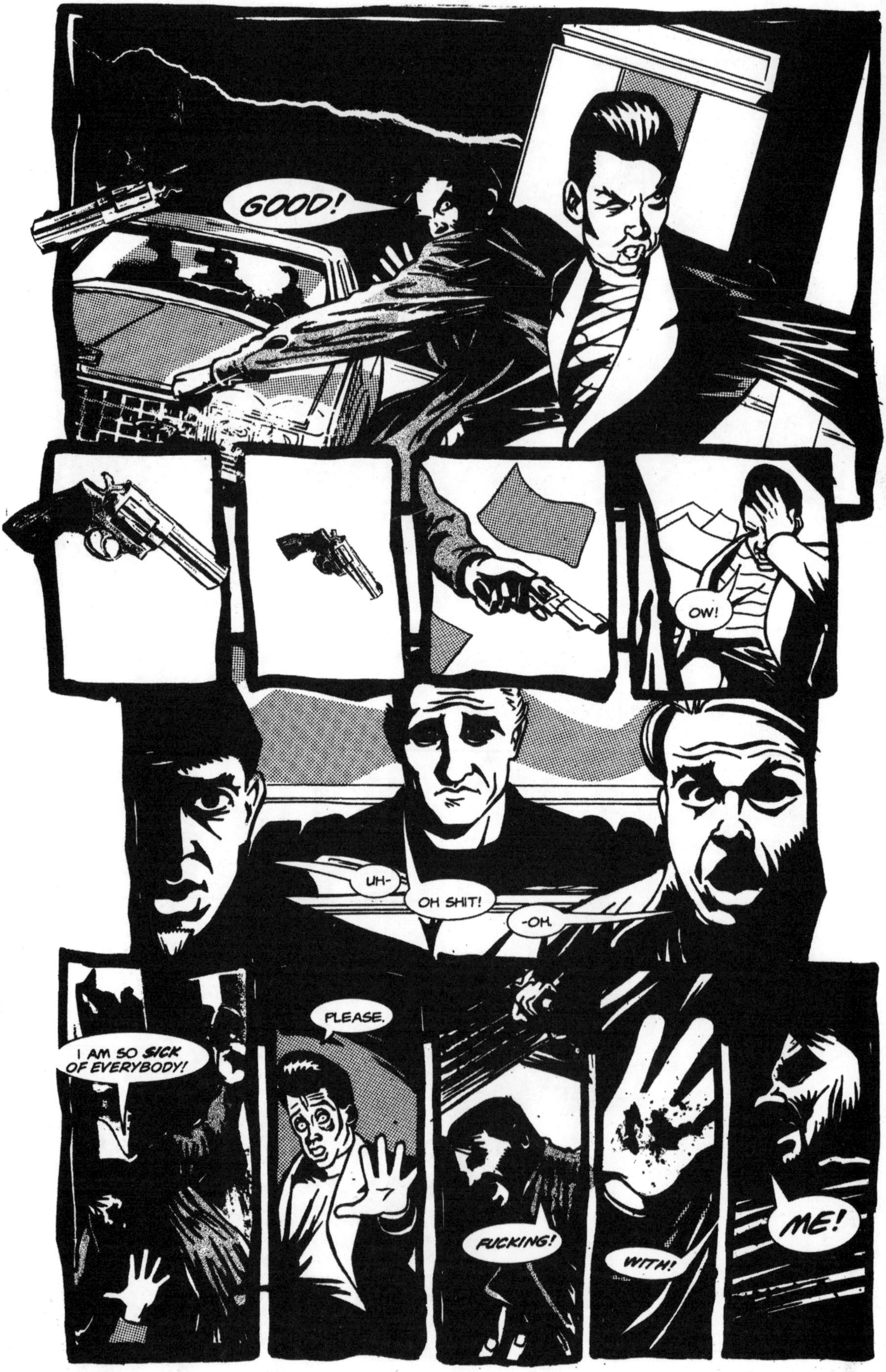
GOOD!
OW!
UH-
OH SHIT!
-OH.
I AM SO SICK OF EVERYBODY!
PLEASE.
FUCKING!
WITH!
ME!

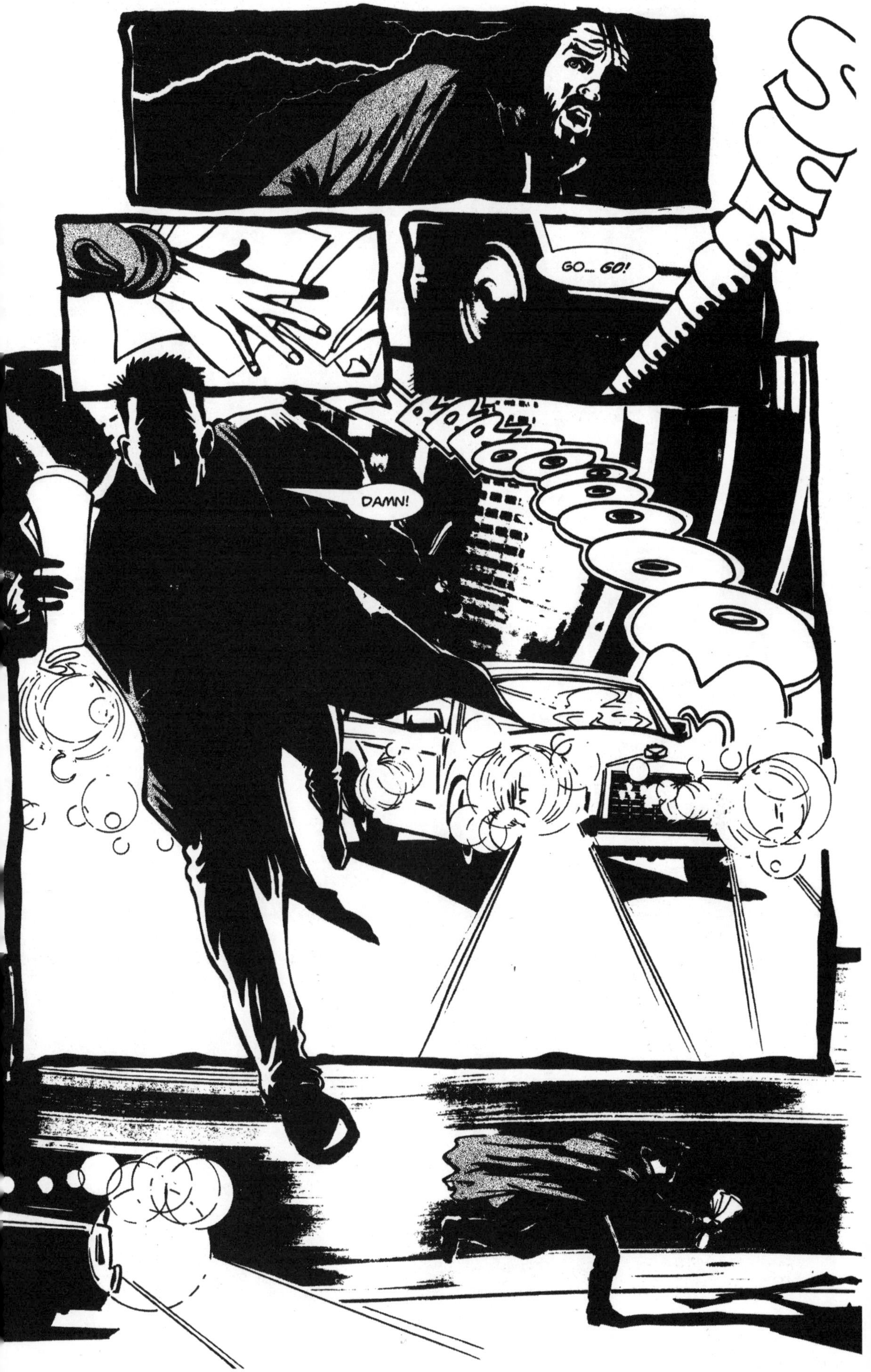
GO... GO!
DAMN!

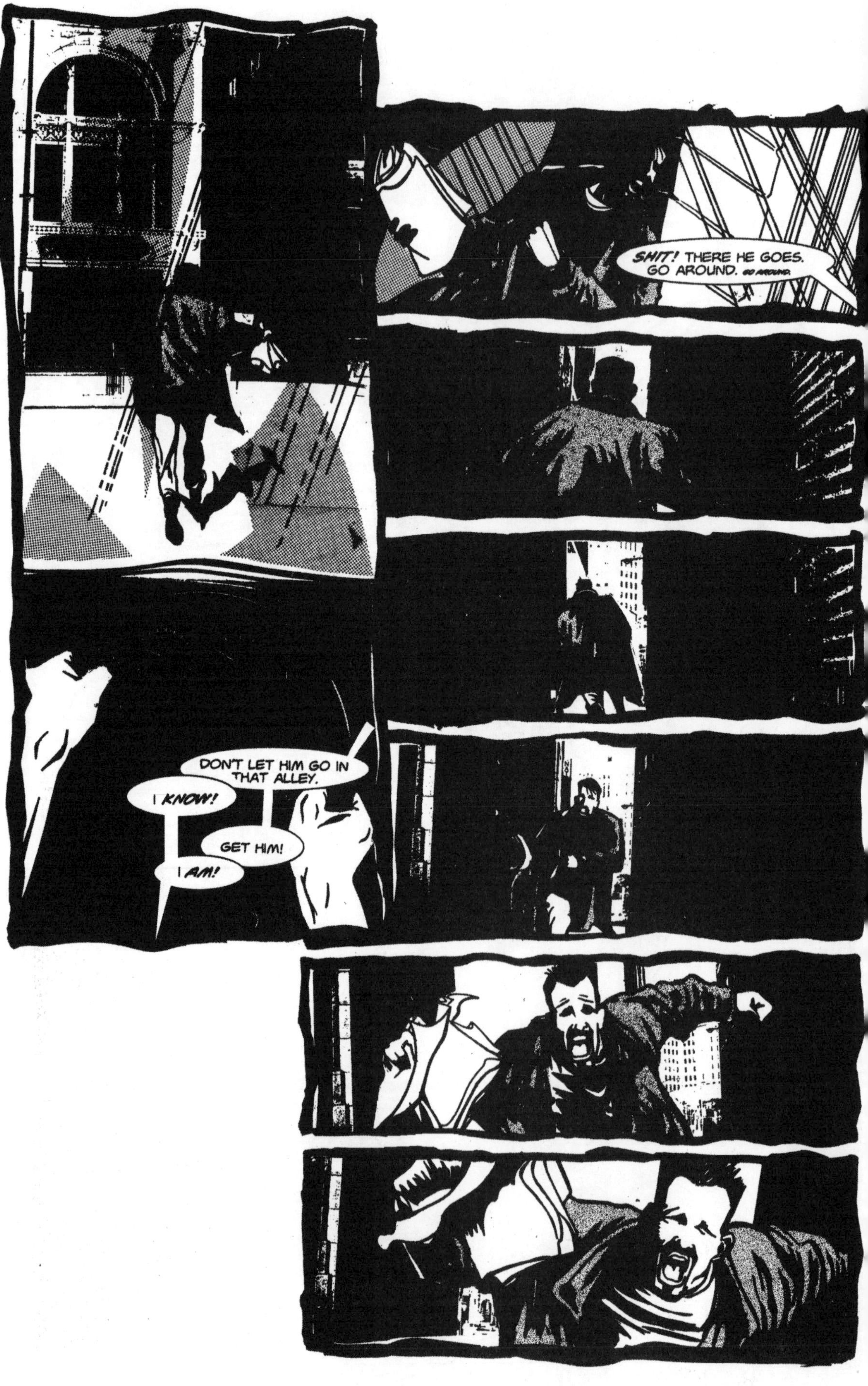
SHIT! THERE HE GOES. GO AROUND. GO AROUND.
DON'T LET HIM GO IN THAT ALLEY.
I KNOW!
GET HIM!
I AM!

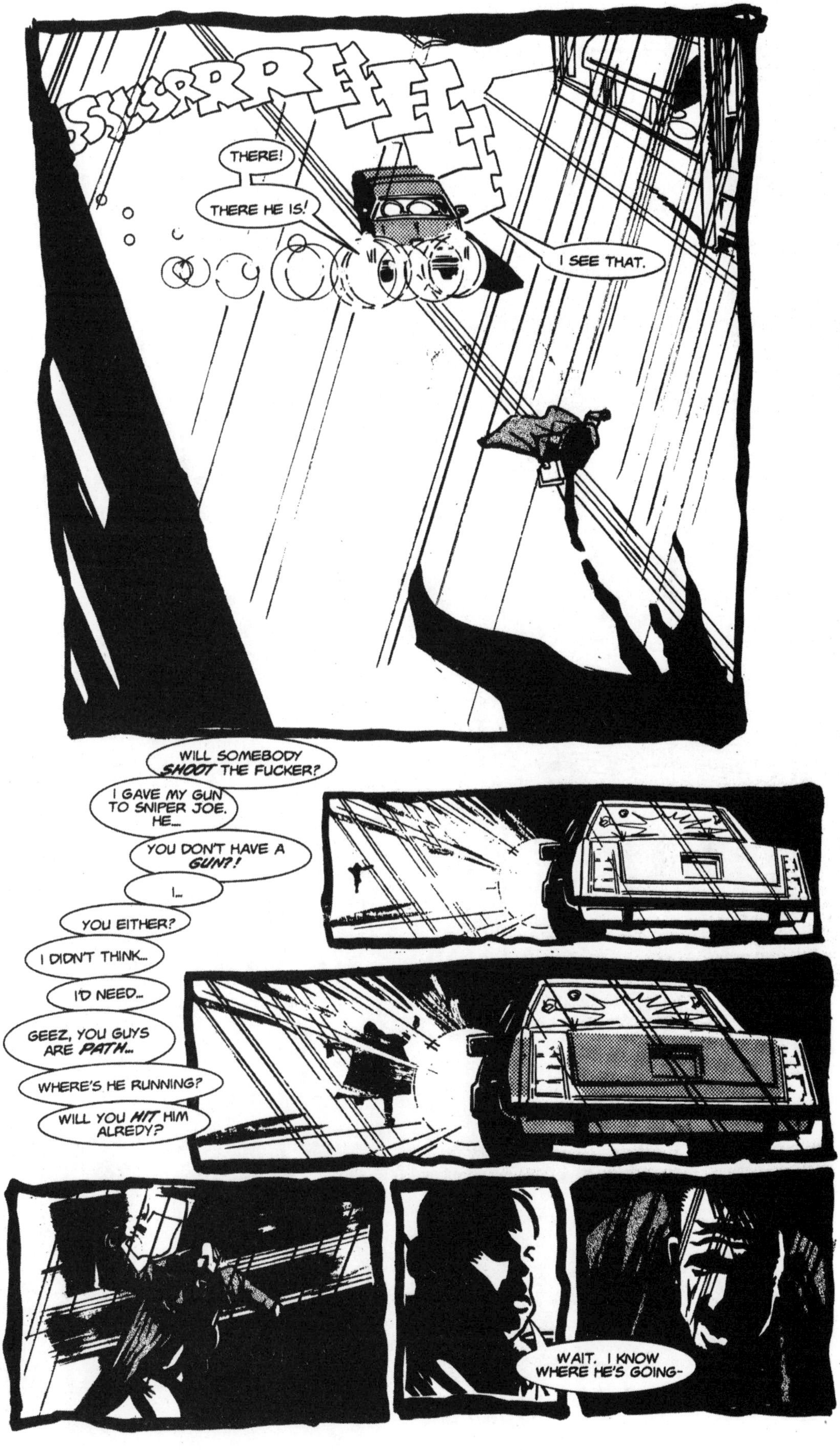
SSKKRRREEEE
THERE!
THERE HE IS!
I SEE THAT.
WILL SOMEBODY SHOOT THE FUCKER?
I GAVE MY GUN TO SNIPER JOE. HE...
YOU DON'T HAVE A GUN?!
I...
YOU EITHER?
I DIDN'T THINK...
I'D NEED...
GEEZ, YOU GUYS ARE PATH...
WHERE'S HE RUNNING?
WILL YOU HIT HIM ALREDY?
WAIT. I KNOW WHERE HE'S GOING-

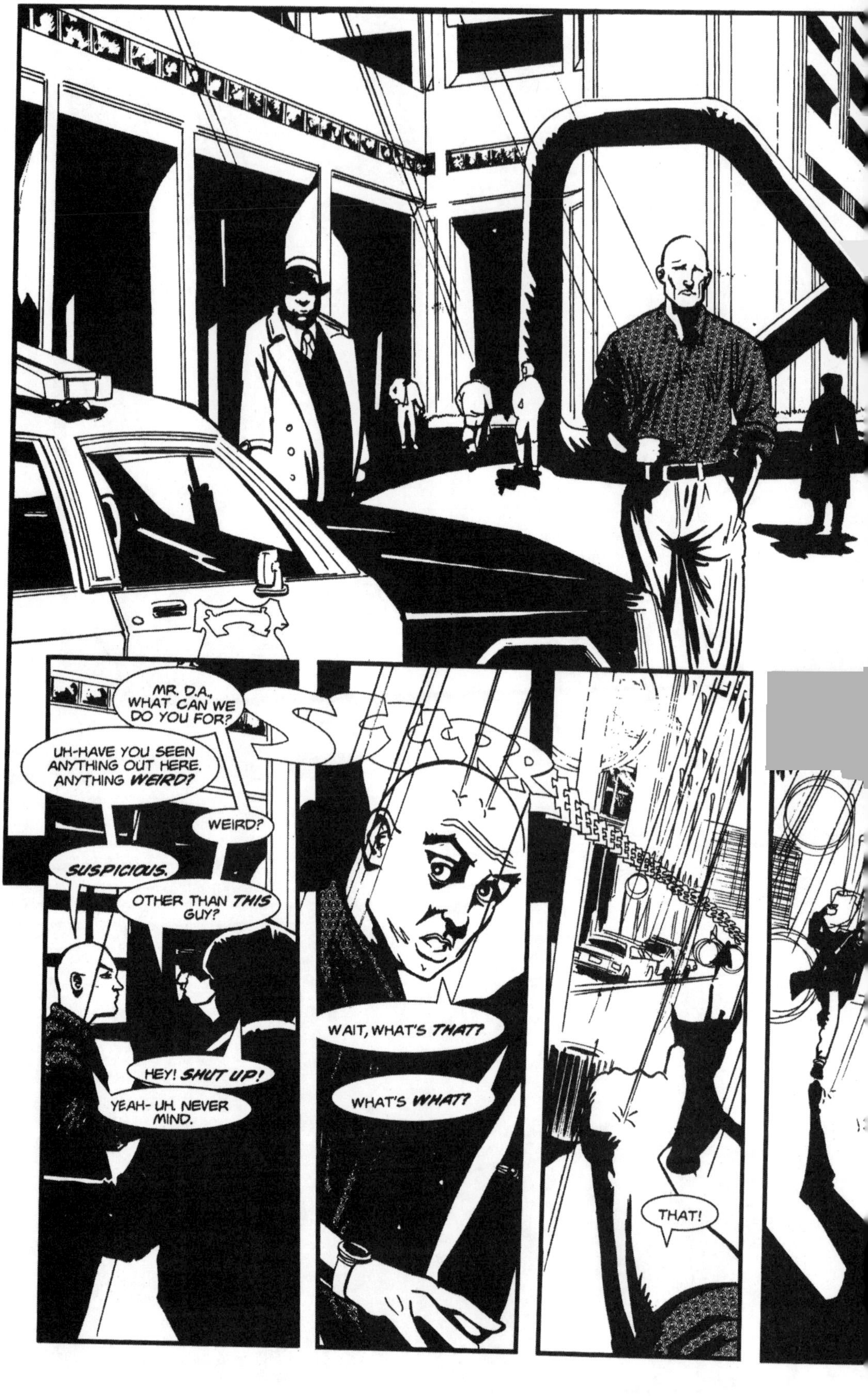
MR. D.A., WHAT CAN WE DO YOU FOR?
UH-HAVE YOU SEEN ANYTHING OUT HERE. ANYTHING WEIRD?
WEIRD?
SUSPICIOUS.
OTHER THAN THIS GUY?
HEY! SHUT UP!
YEAH- UH. NEVER MIND.
SCREEEEEE
WAIT, WHAT'S THAT?
WHAT'S WHAT?
THAT!

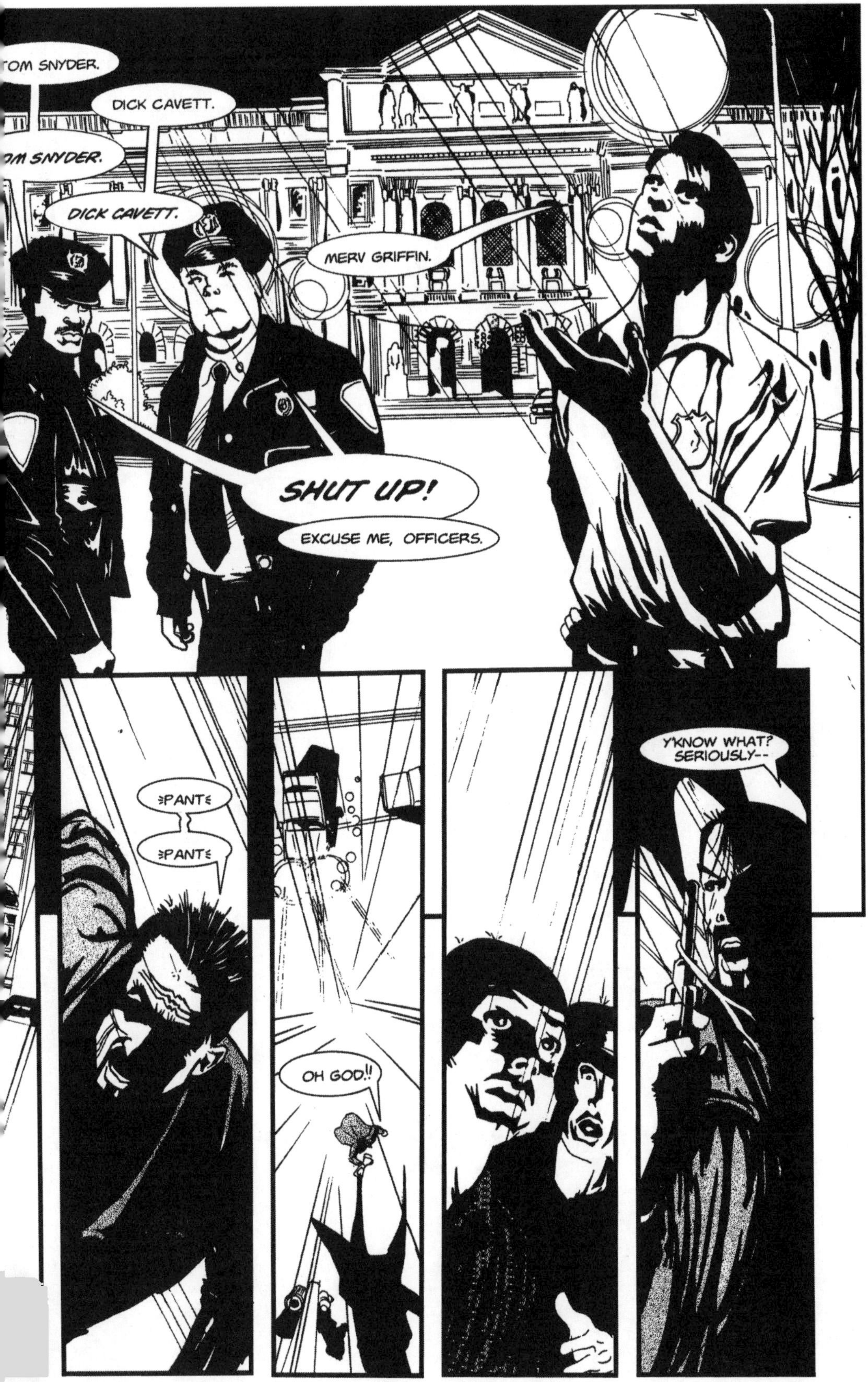
TOM SNYDER.
DICK CAVETT.
OM SNYDER.
DICK CAVETT.
MERV GRIFFIN.
SHUT UP!
EXCUSE ME, OFFICERS.
PANT
PANT
OH GOD!!
Y'KNOW WHAT? SERIOUSLY--

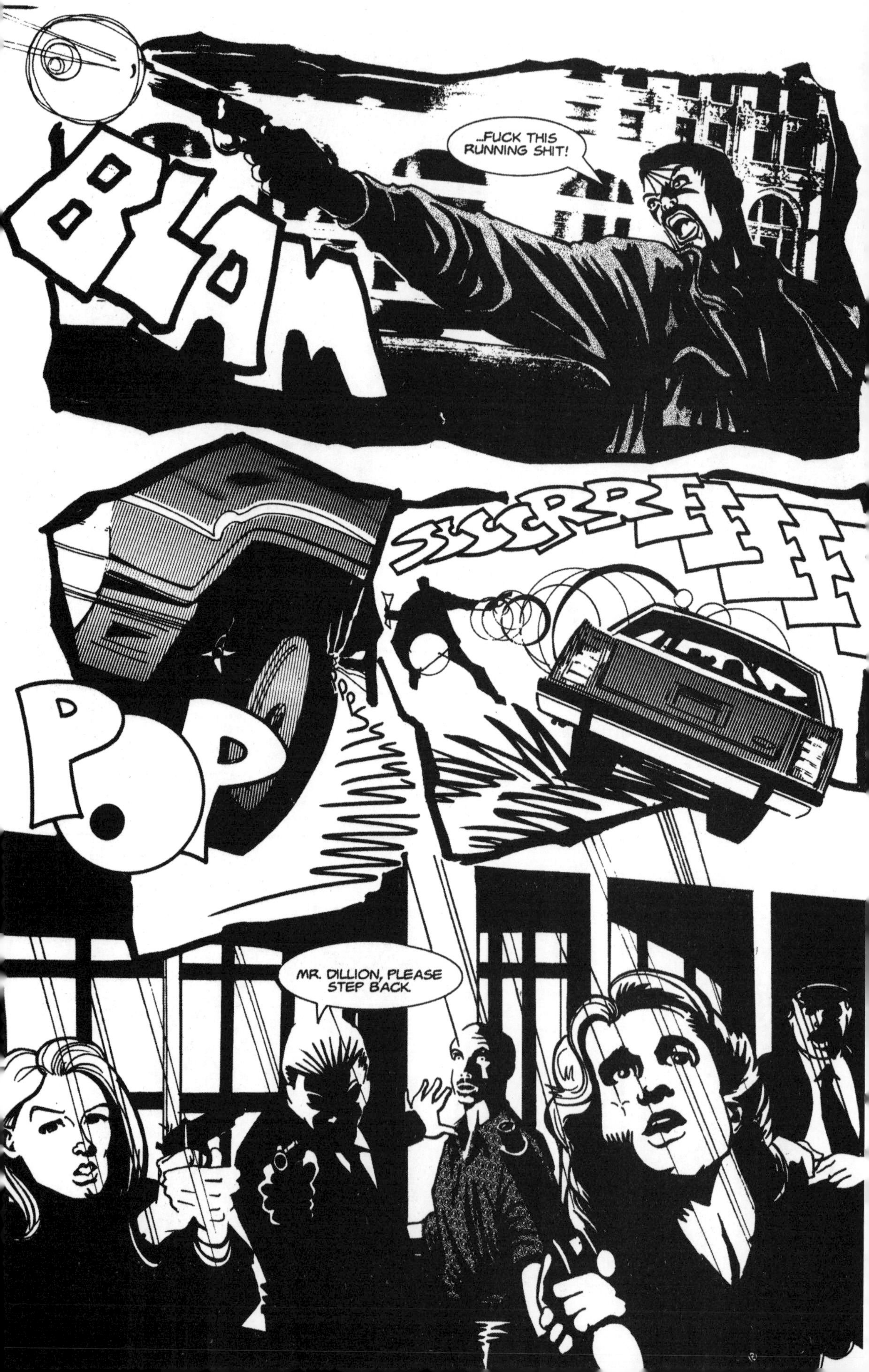

BLAM
...FUCK THIS RUNNING SHIT!
POP
SSSS
SSCRREEEE
MR. DILLION, PLEASE STEP BACK.

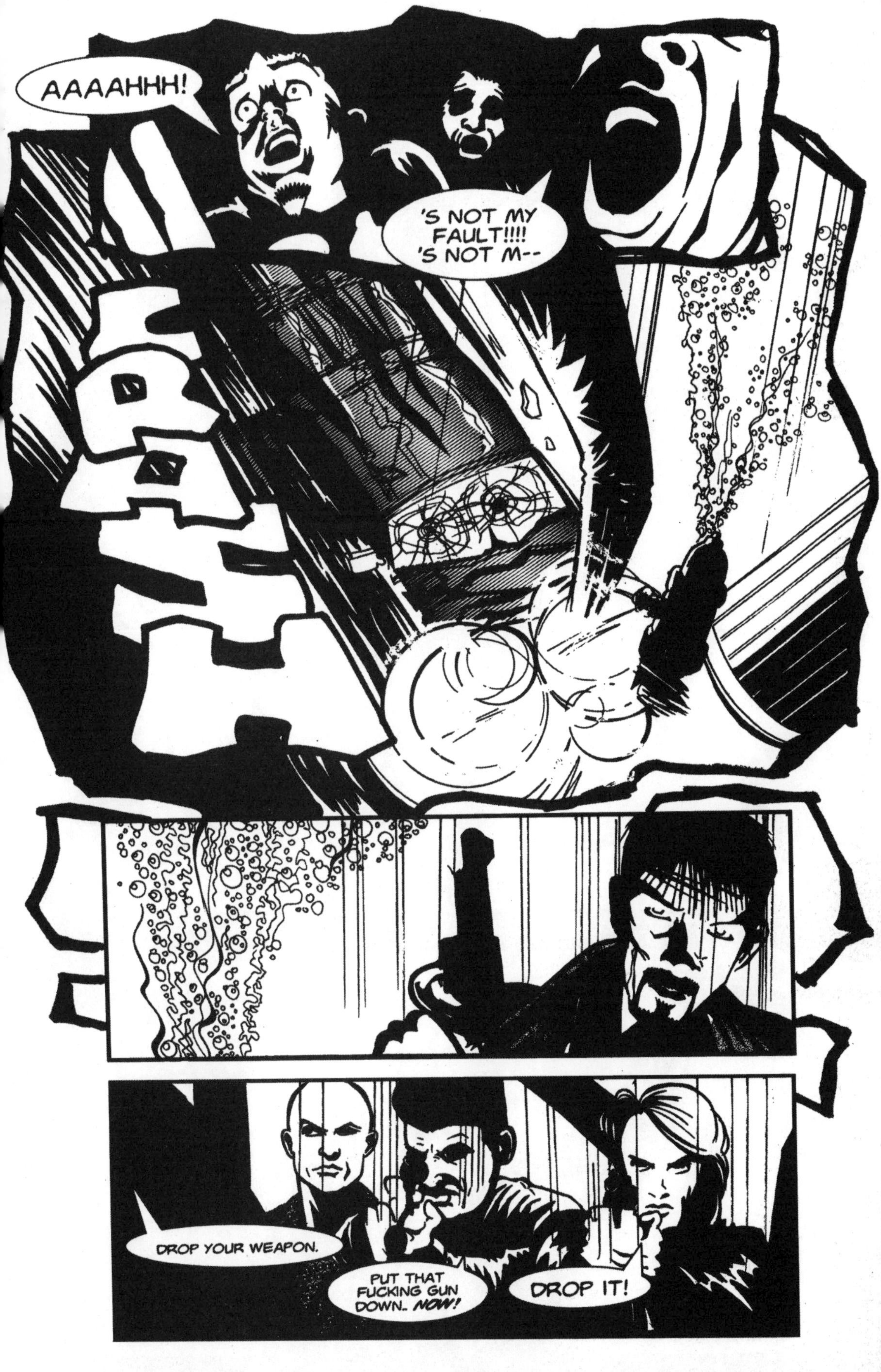
AAAAHHH!
'S NOT MY FAULT!!!! 'S NOT M--
DROP YOUR WEAPON.
PUT THAT FUCKING GUN DOWN.. NOW!
DROP IT!

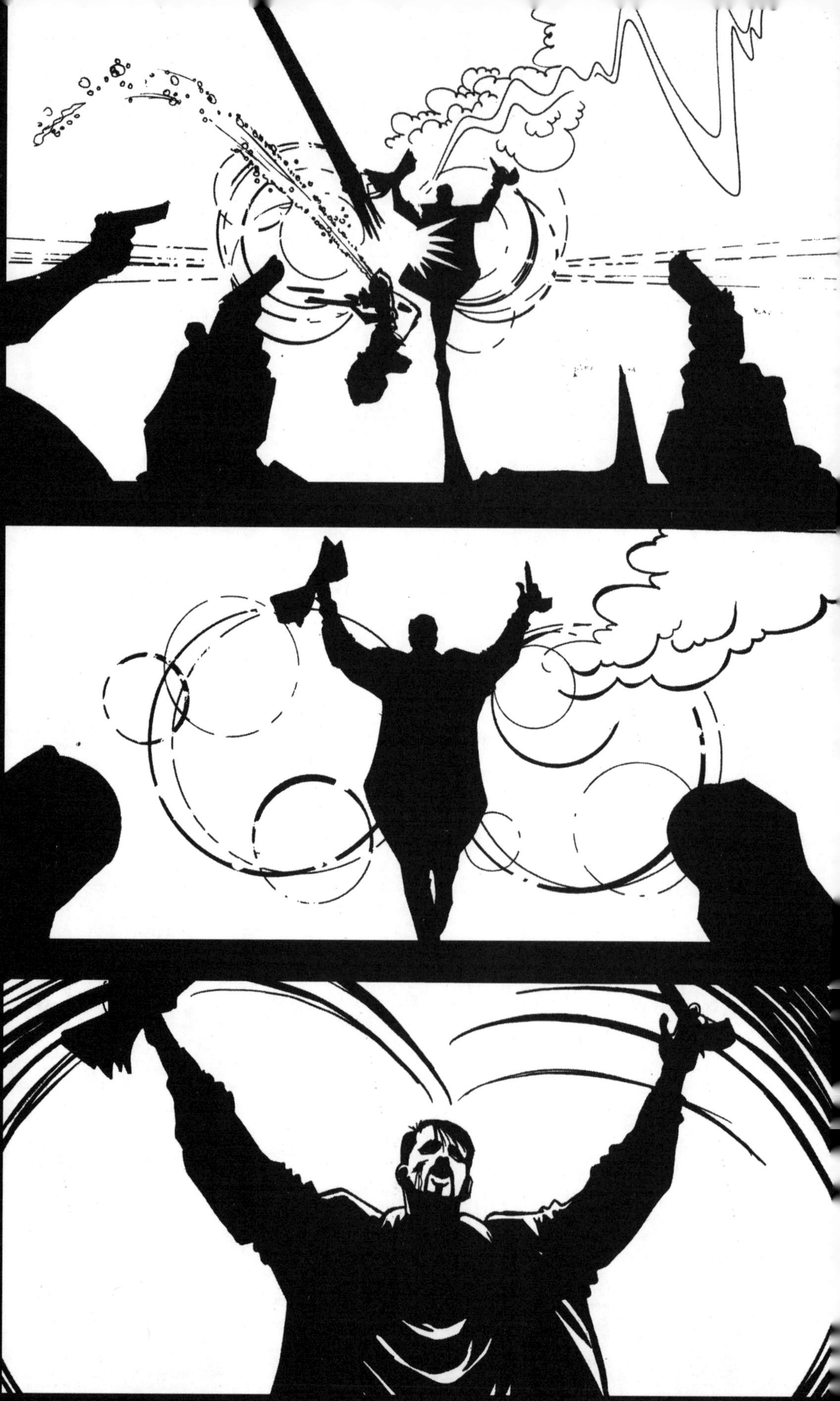

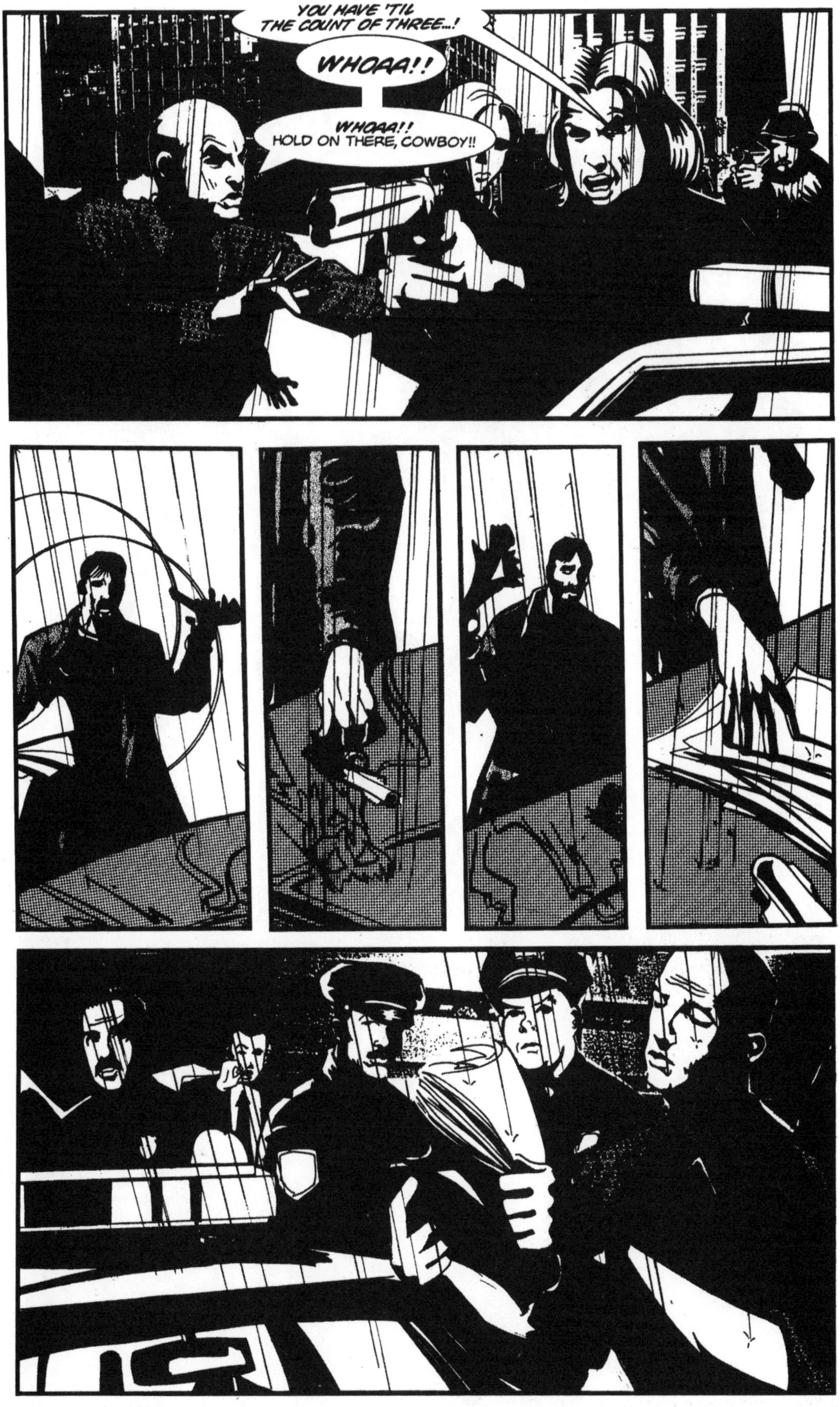
YOU HAVE 'TIL THE COUNT OF THREE...!
WHOAA!!
WHOAA!! HOLD ON THERE, COWBOY!!

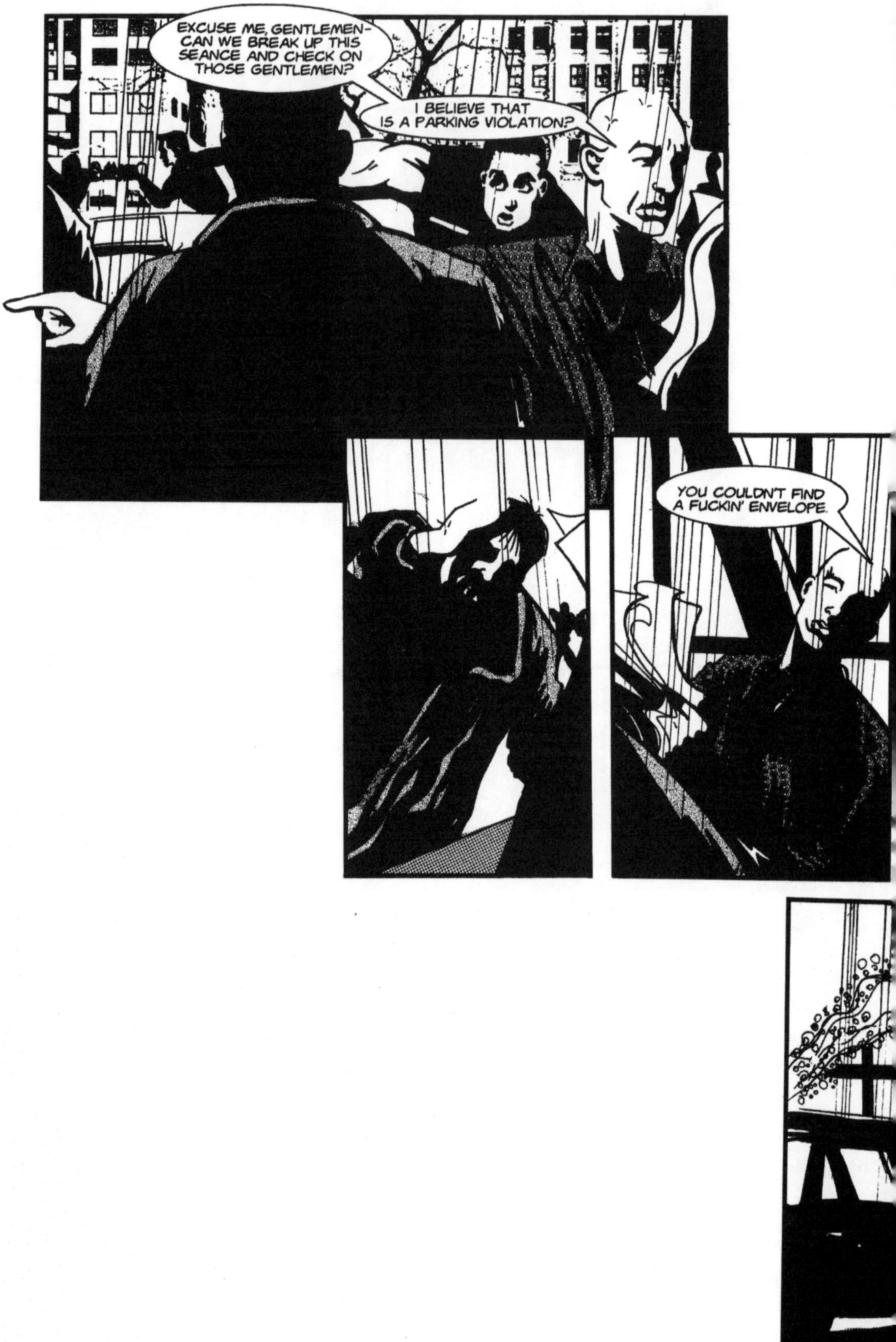
EXCUSE ME, GENTLEMEN-
CAN WE BREAK UP THIS
SEANCE AND CHECK ON
THOSE GENTLEMEN?
I BELIEVE THAT
IS A PARKING VIOLATION?
YOU COULDN'T FIND
A FUCKIN' ENVELOPE.

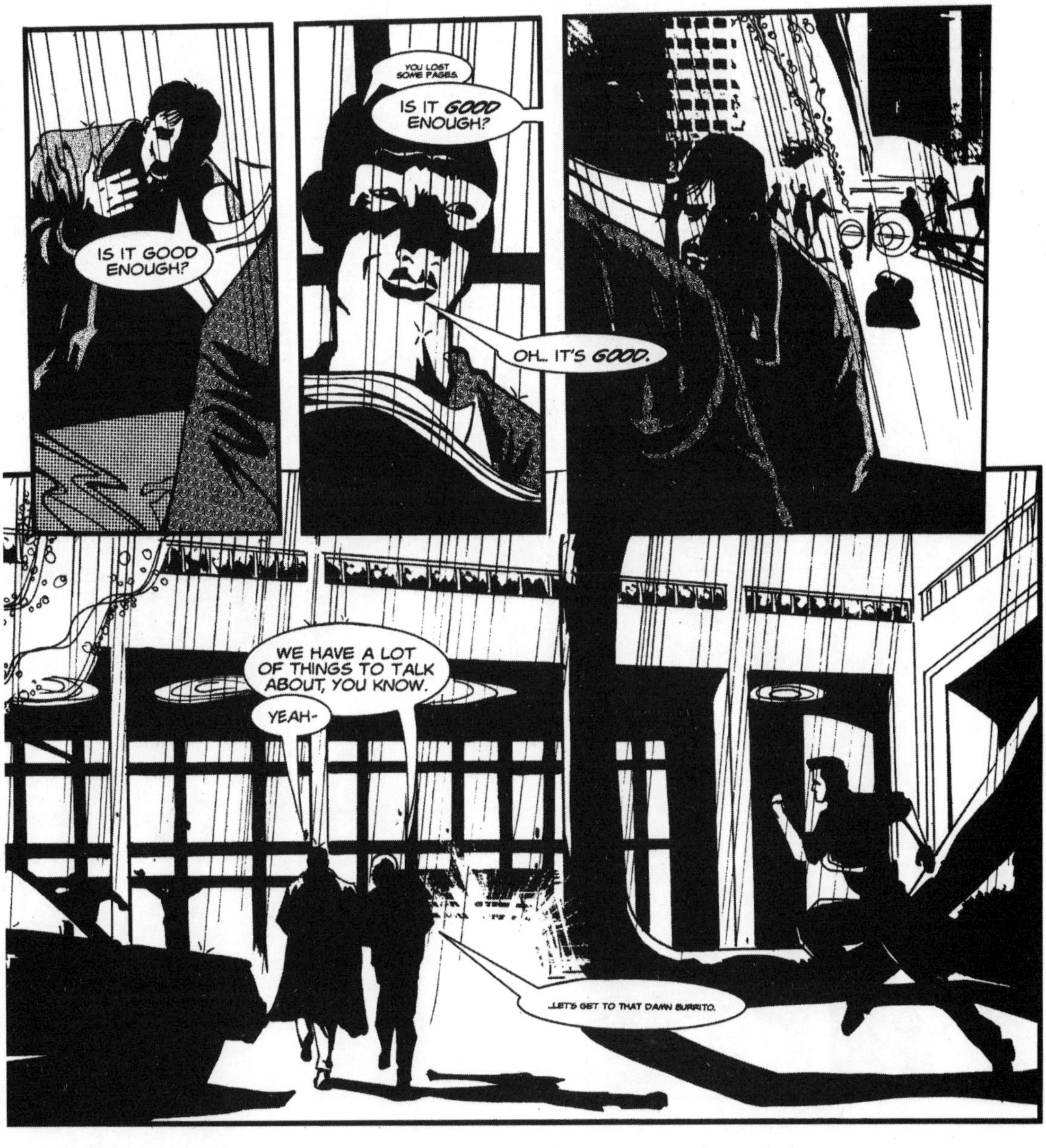
IS IT GOOD ENOUGH?
YOU LOST SOME PAGES.
IS IT *GOOD* ENOUGH?
OH.. IT'S *GOOD*.
WE HAVE A LOT OF THINGS TO TALK ABOUT, YOU KNOW.
YEAH-
..LET'S GET TO THAT DAMN BURRITO.

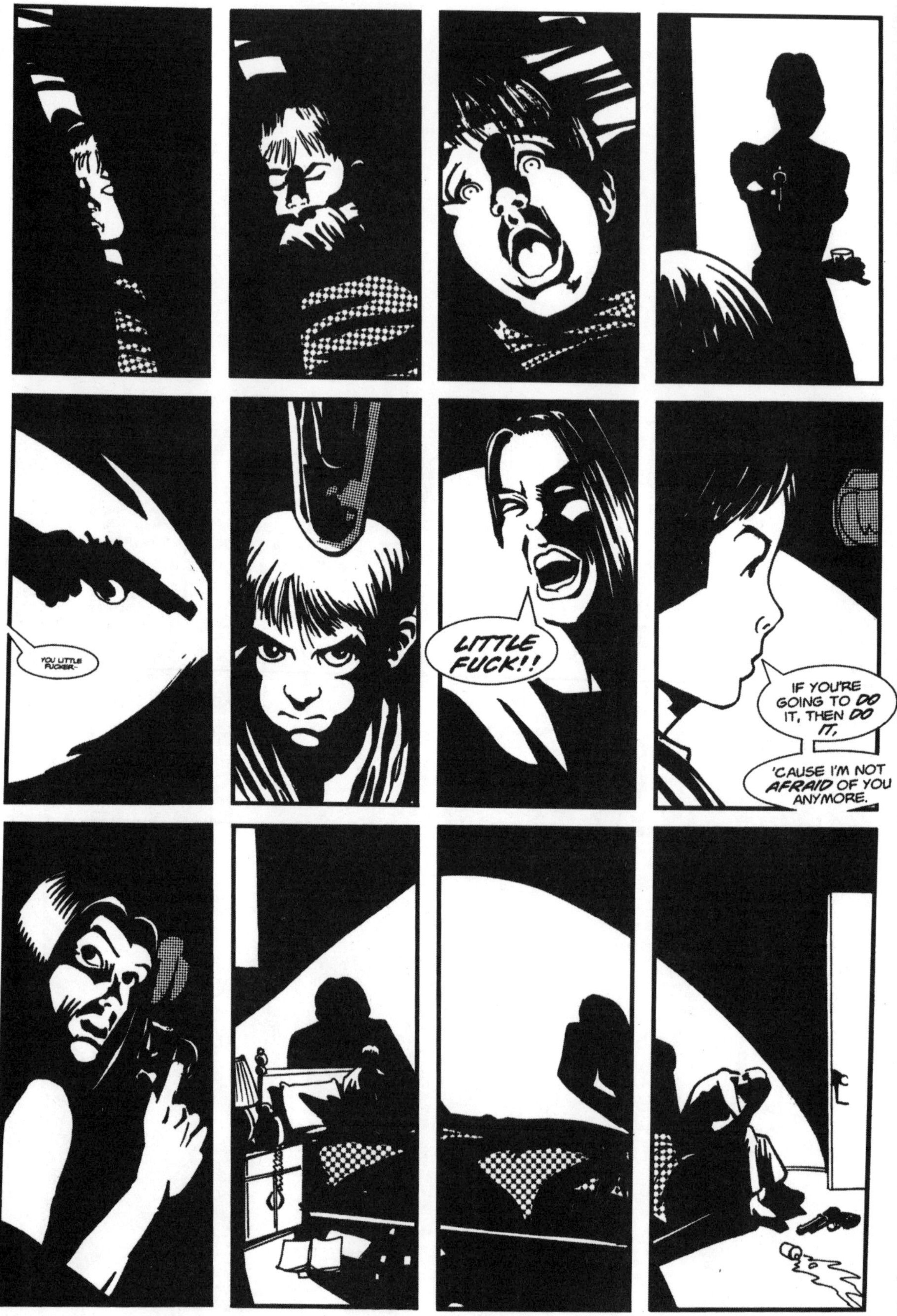
YOU LITTLE FUCKER--
LITTLE FUCK!!
IF YOU'RE GOING TO DO IT, THEN DO IT,
'CAUSE I'M NOT AFRAID OF YOU ANYMORE.

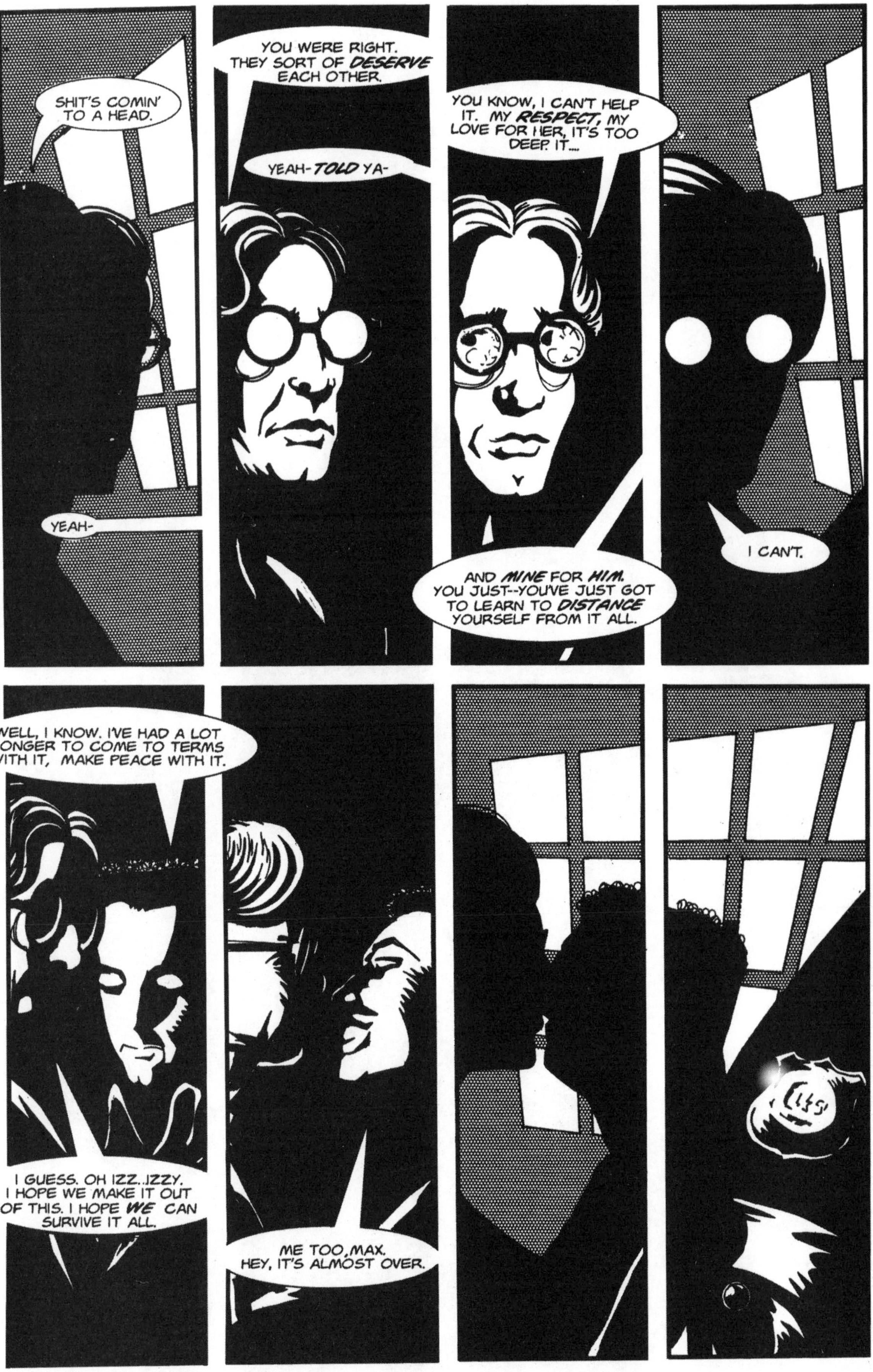
SHIT'S COMIN' TO A HEAD.
YEAH-
YOU WERE RIGHT. THEY SORT OF DESERVE EACH OTHER.
YEAH-TOLD YA-
YOU KNOW, I CAN'T HELP IT. MY RESPECT, MY LOVE FOR HER, IT'S TOO DEEP. IT...
AND MINE FOR HIM. YOU JUST--YOU'VE JUST GOT TO LEARN TO DISTANCE YOURSELF FROM IT ALL.
I CAN'T.
WELL, I KNOW. I'VE HAD A LOT LONGER TO COME TO TERMS WITH IT, MAKE PEACE WITH IT.
I GUESS. OH IZZ..IZZY. I HOPE WE MAKE IT OUT OF THIS. I HOPE WE CAN SURVIVE IT ALL.
ME TOO, MAX. HEY, IT'S ALMOST OVER.

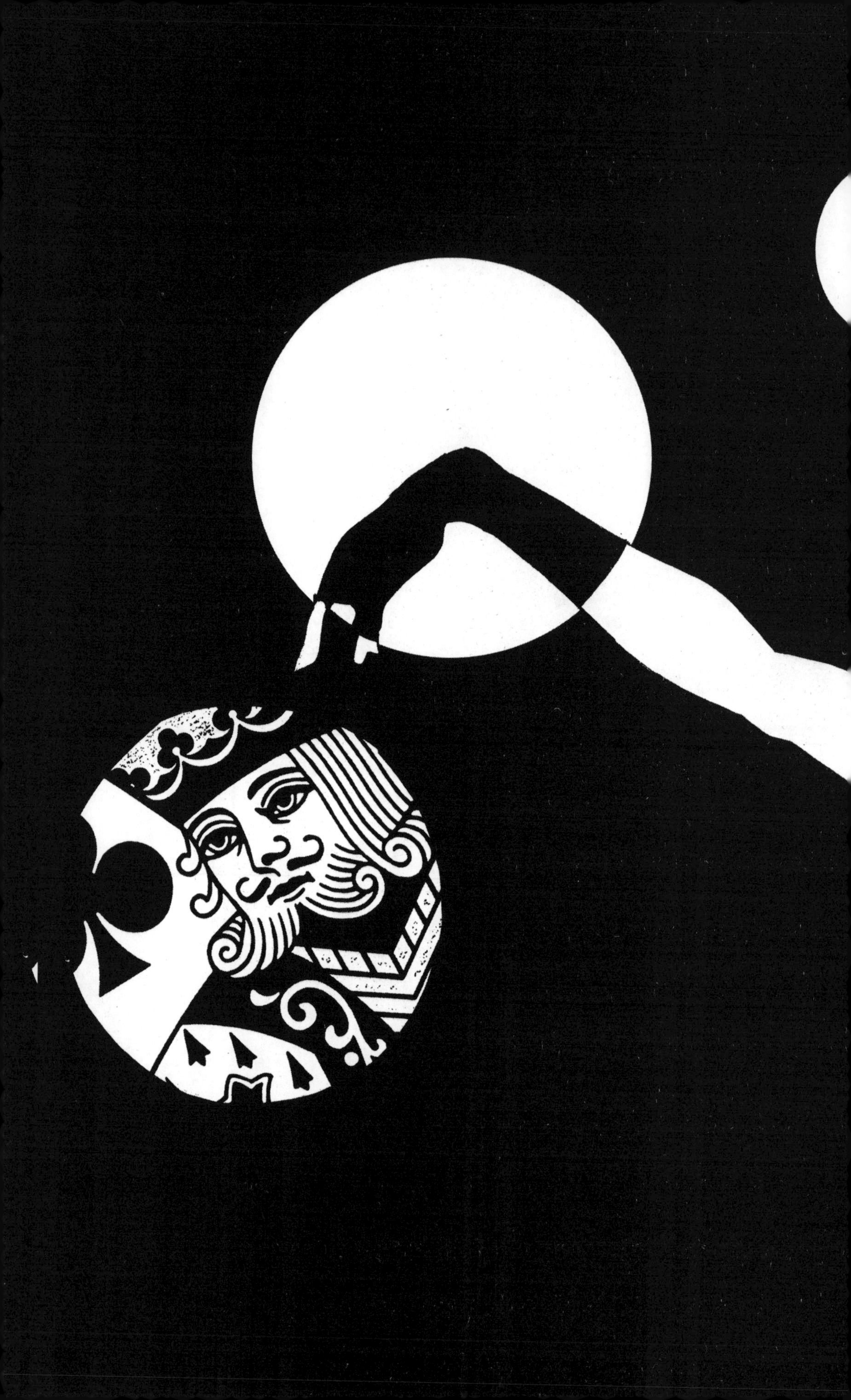

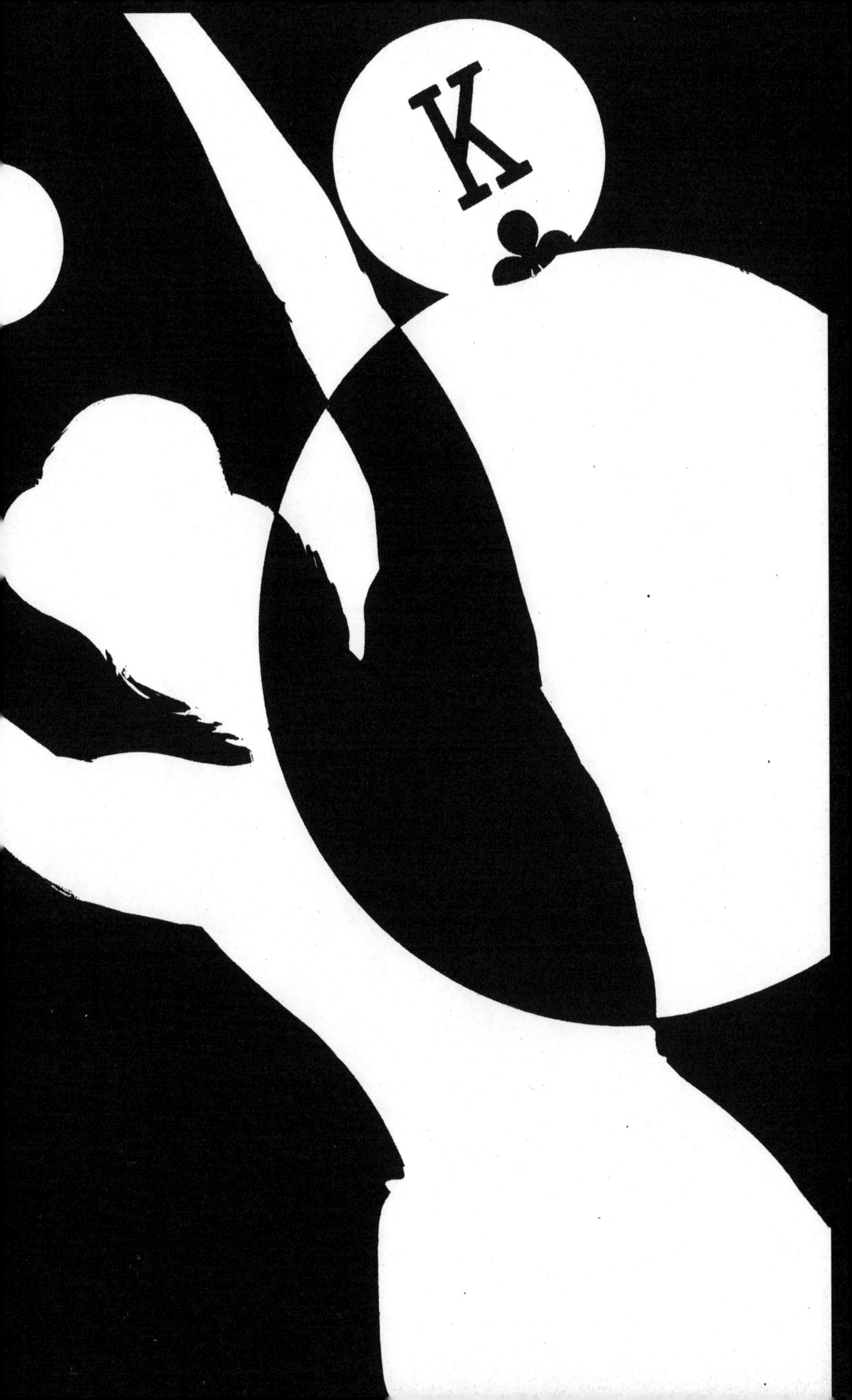
K

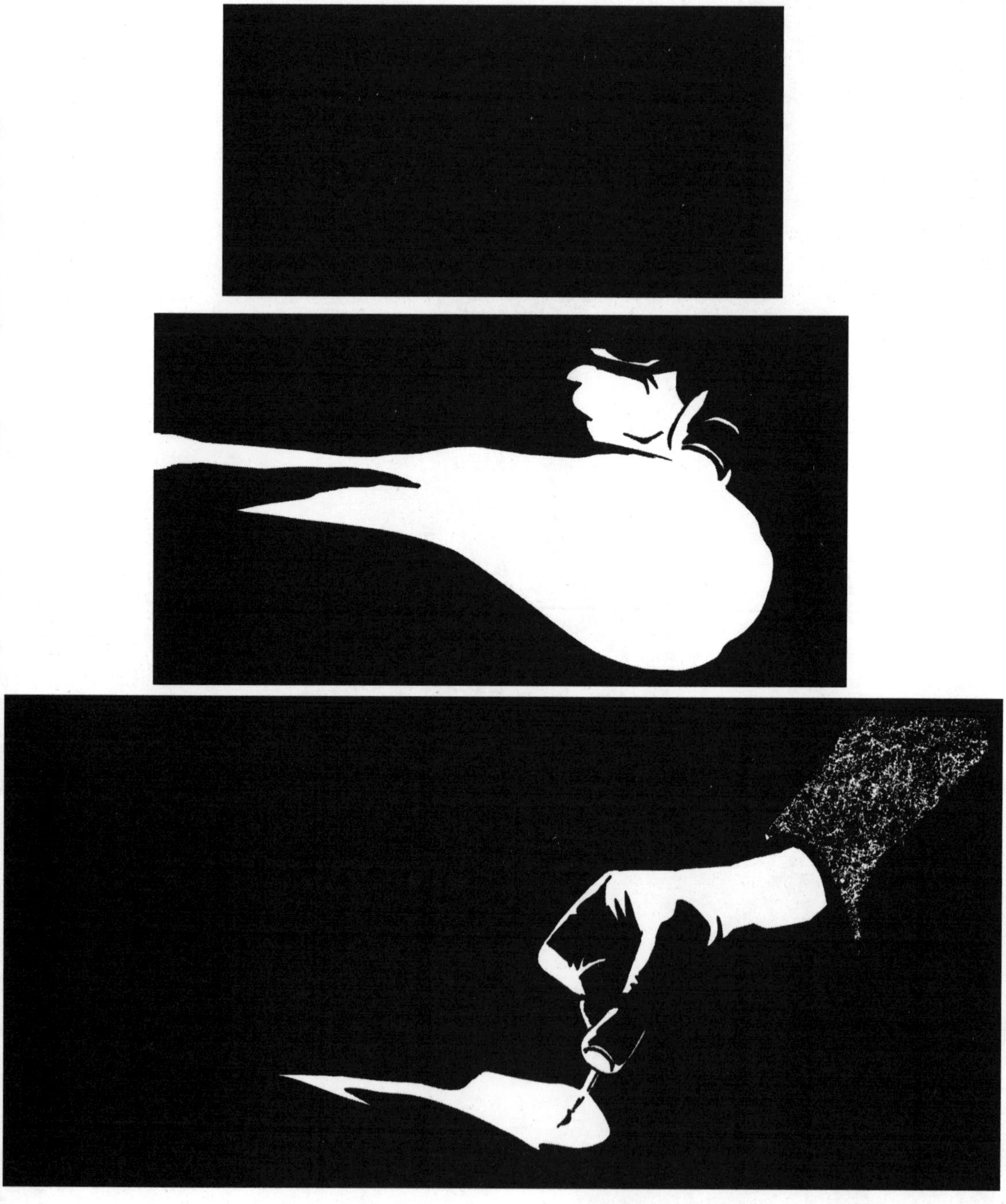

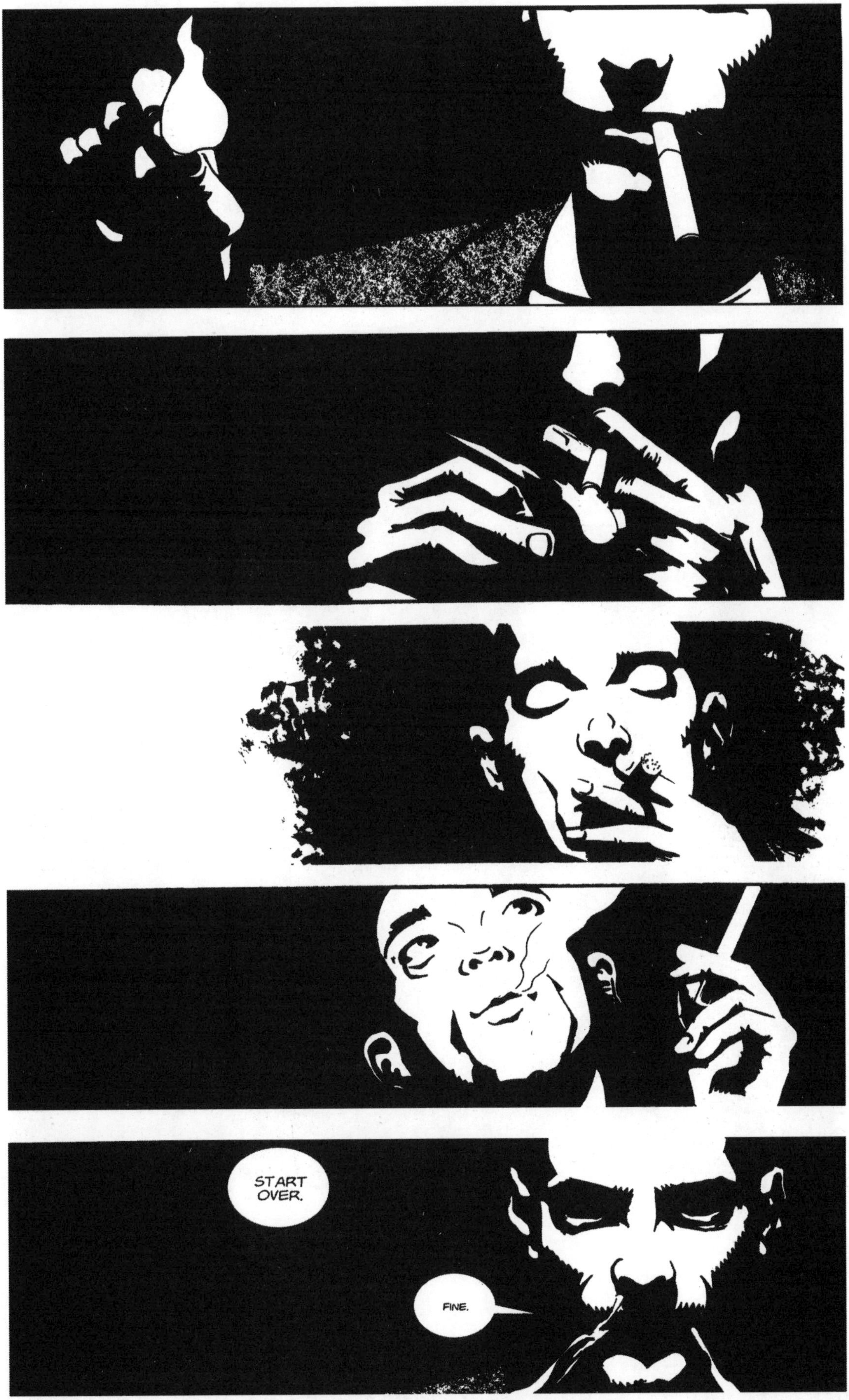
START OVER.
FINE.

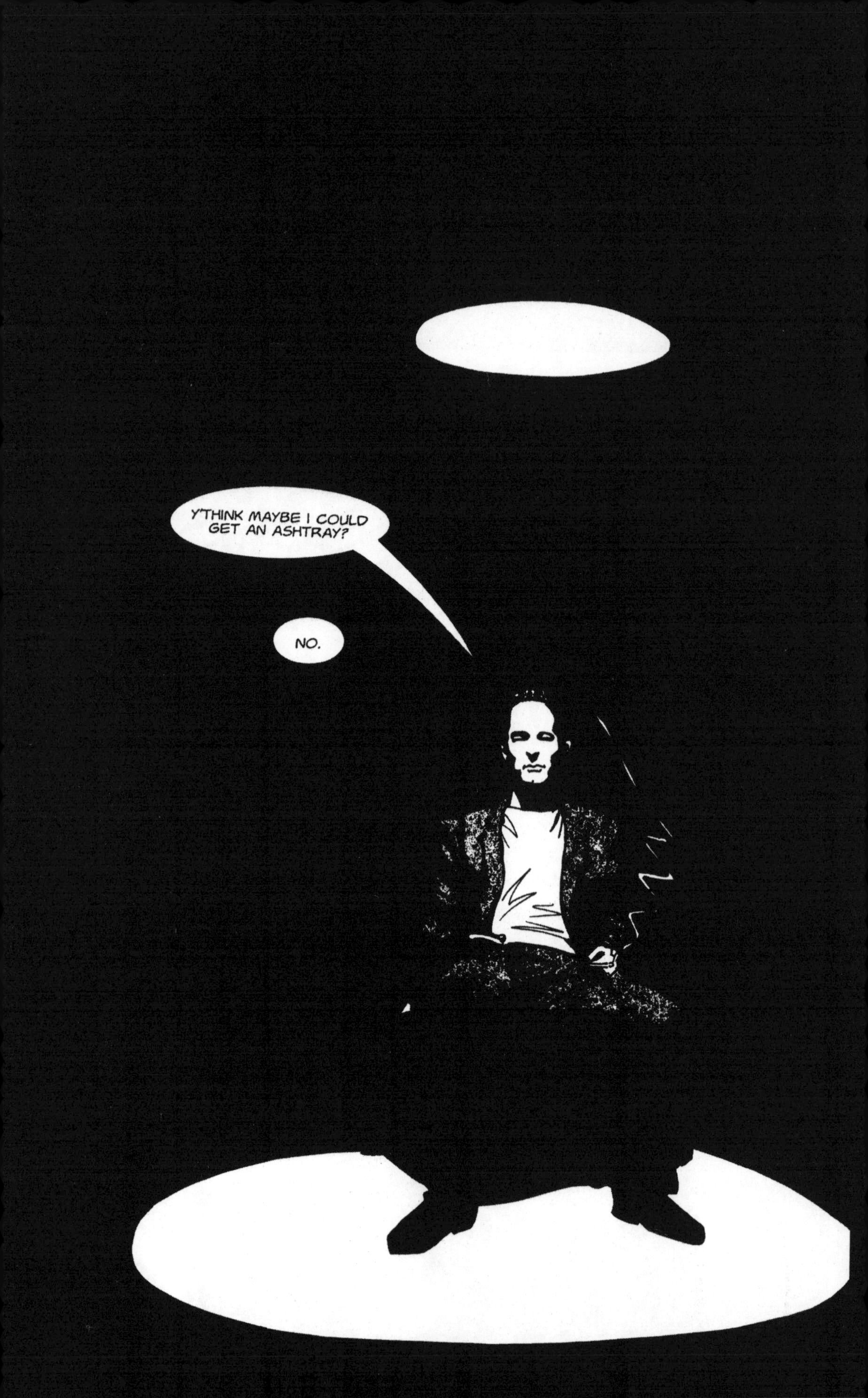
Y'THINK MAYBE I COULD GET AN ASHTRAY?
NO.

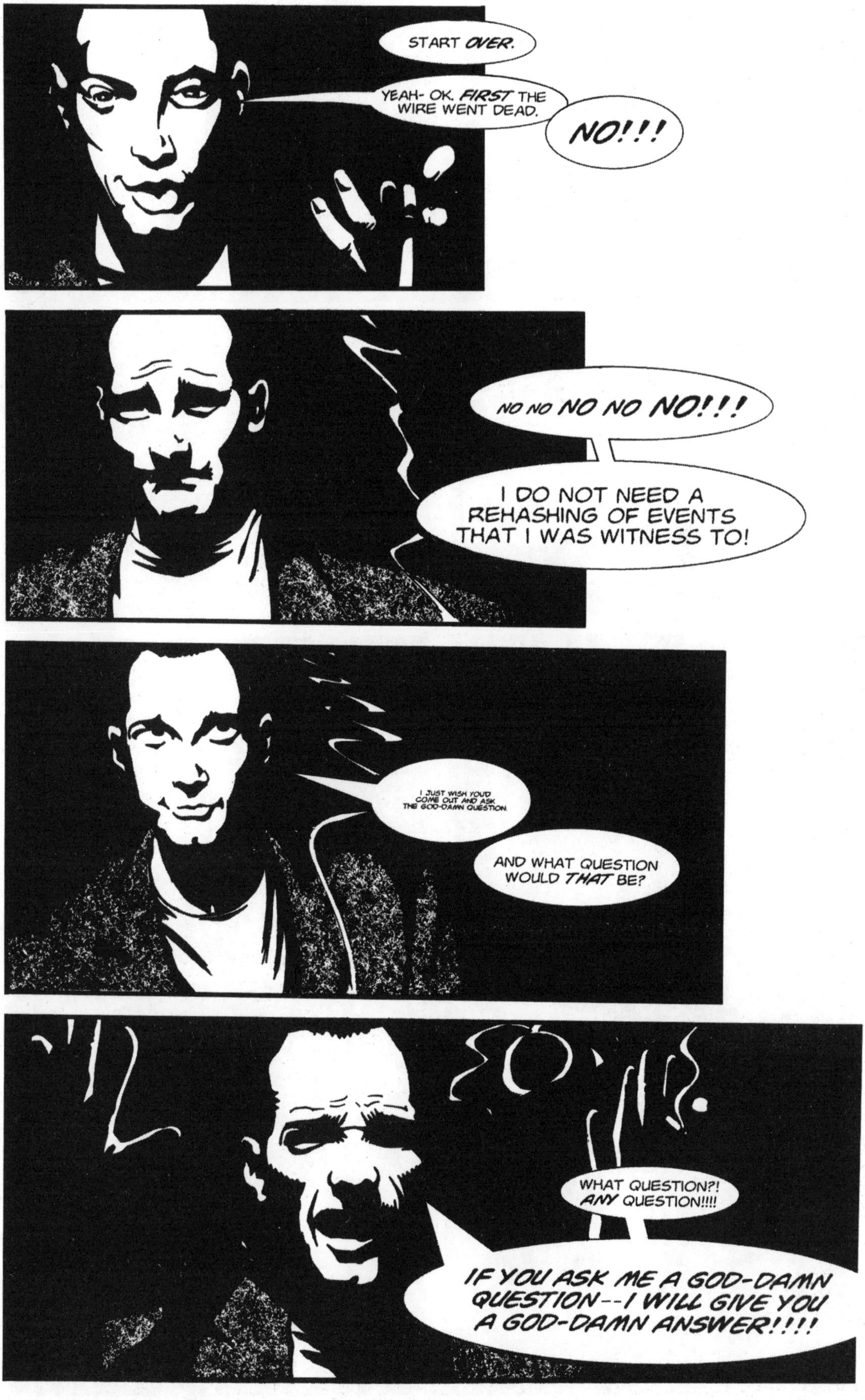
START OVER.
YEAH- OK. FIRST THE WIRE WENT DEAD.
NO!!!
NO NO NO NO NO!!!
I DO NOT NEED A REHASHING OF EVENTS THAT I WAS WITNESS TO!
I JUST WISH YOU'D COME OUT AND ASK THE GOD-DAMN QUESTION.
AND WHAT QUESTION WOULD THAT BE?
WHAT QUESTION?! ANY QUESTION!!!!
IF YOU ASK ME A GOD-DAMN QUESTION--I WILL GIVE YOU A GOD-DAMN ANSWER!!!!

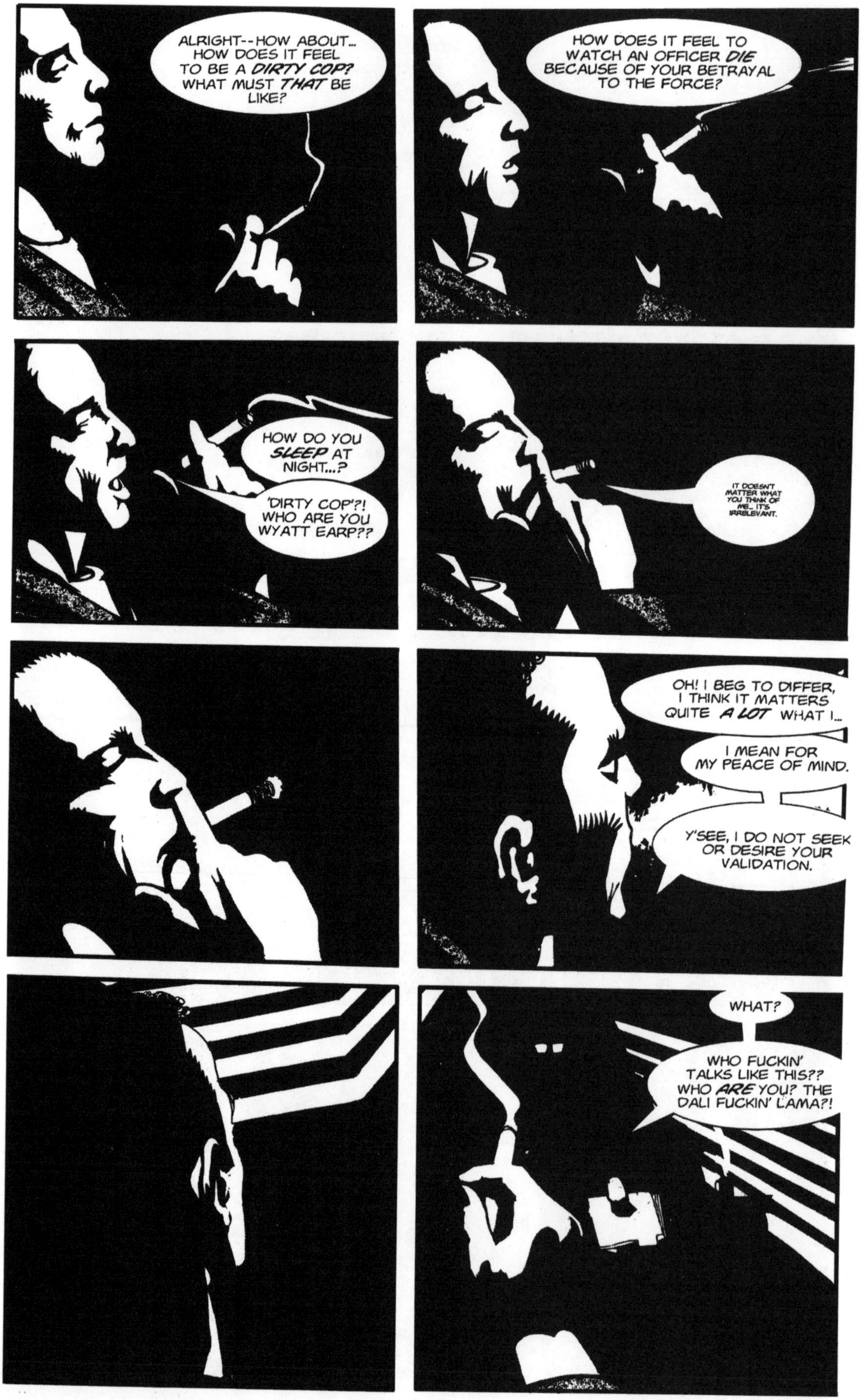
ALRIGHT--HOW ABOUT... HOW DOES IT FEEL TO BE A DIRTY COP? WHAT MUST THAT BE LIKE?
HOW DOES IT FEEL TO WATCH AN OFFICER DIE BECAUSE OF YOUR BETRAYAL TO THE FORCE?
HOW DO YOU SLEEP AT NIGHT...?
'DIRTY COP'?! WHO ARE YOU WYATT EARP??
IT DOESN'T MATTER WHAT YOU THINK OF ME... IT'S IRRELEVANT.
OH! I BEG TO DIFFER, I THINK IT MATTERS QUITE A LOT WHAT I...
I MEAN FOR MY PEACE OF MIND.
Y'SEE, I DO NOT SEEK OR DESIRE YOUR VALIDATION.
WHAT?
WHO FUCKIN' TALKS LIKE THIS?? WHO ARE YOU? THE DALI FUCKIN' LAMA?!

I'VE READ YOUR FILE. I'VE READ IT FIVE TIMES.

REALLY?

YEAH- WELL, YOU *MYSTIFY* ME.

NO, I.... YOU JUST DON'T COME OFF AS MUCH OF A READER.

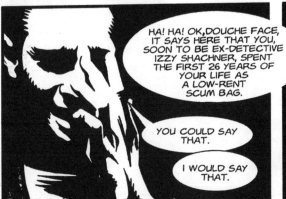

HA! HA! OK, DOUCHE FACE, IT SAYS HERE THAT YOU, SOON TO BE EX-DETECTIVE IZZY SHACHNER, SPENT THE FIRST 26 YEARS OF YOUR LIFE AS A LOW-RENT SCUM BAG.

YOU COULD SAY THAT.

I WOULD SAY THAT.

ONE MISDEMEANOR AFTER ANOTHER- THEN ALL OF A SUDDEN...

OUT OF THE BLUE, YOU DO A 180. YOU WEASEL YOUR WAY INTO POLICE WORK, YOU FALSIFY RECORDS. YOU LIE.

SO?

SO WHY BE A COP? WHY GO TO ALL THE TROUBLE OF GETTING ON THE FORCE AND KEEPING UP APPEARANCES IF YOU'RE JUST GOING TO KEEP ON BEING A SCUMBAG?

I KNOW YOU'LL FIND THIS HARD TO STOMACH AND MAKE IT A POINT OF RIDICULE, BUT UP UNTIL RECENT EVENTS....

I PRIDED MYSELF ON BEING AN *EXCELLENT* DETECTIVE.

OY! ARE YOU GIVING ME A HEADACHE IN MY EYE.

LET'S MOVE ON, SHALL WE?

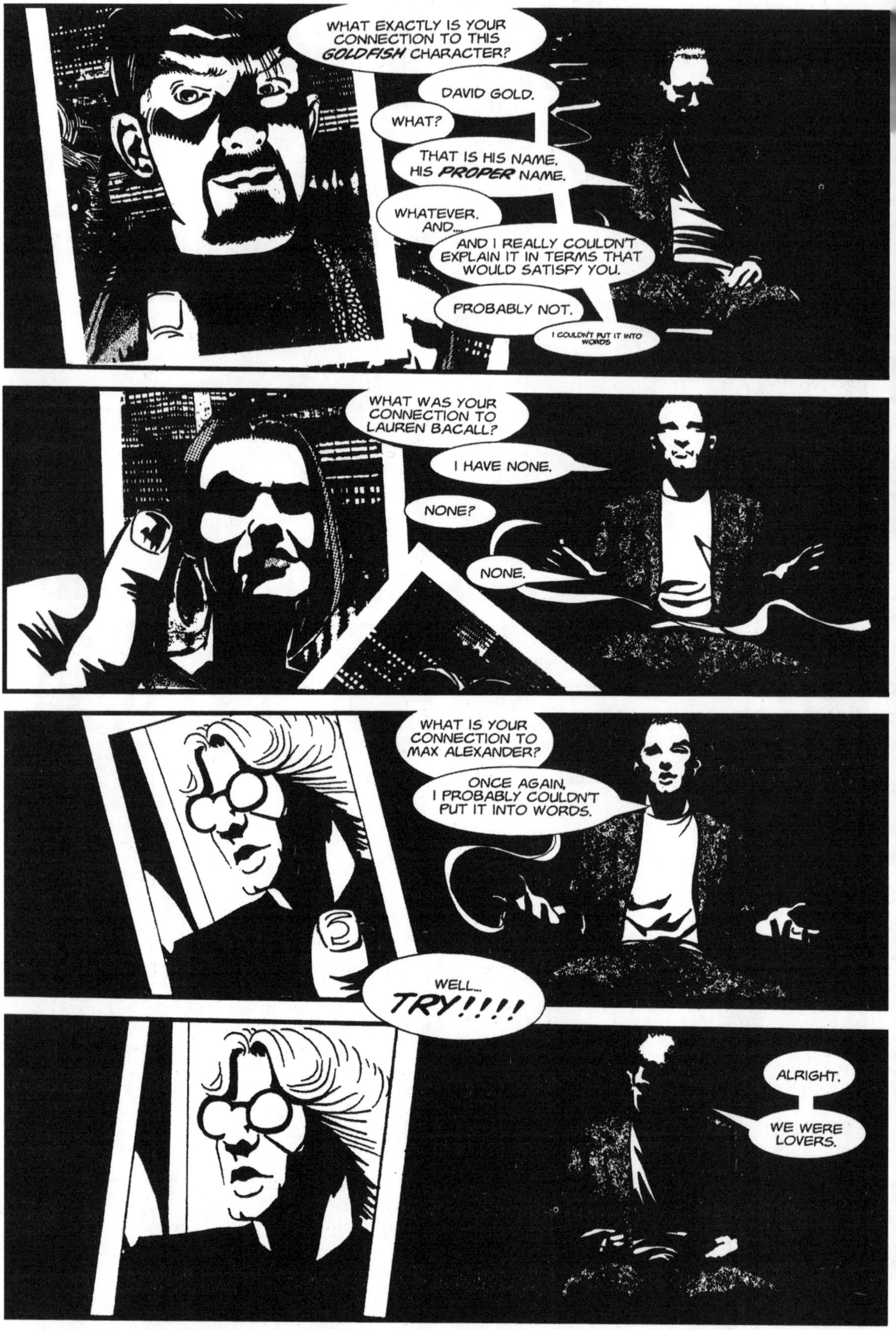
WHAT EXACTLY IS YOUR CONNECTION TO THIS *GOLDFISH* CHARACTER?
DAVID GOLD.
WHAT?
THAT IS HIS NAME. HIS *PROPER* NAME.
WHATEVER. AND...
AND I REALLY COULDN'T EXPLAIN IT IN TERMS THAT WOULD SATISFY YOU.
PROBABLY NOT.
I COULDN'T PUT IT INTO WORDS
WHAT WAS YOUR CONNECTION TO LAUREN BACALL?
I HAVE NONE.
NONE?
NONE.
WHAT IS YOUR CONNECTION TO MAX ALEXANDER?
ONCE AGAIN, I PROBABLY COULDN'T PUT IT INTO WORDS.
WELL... *TRY!!!!*
ALRIGHT.
WE WERE LOVERS.

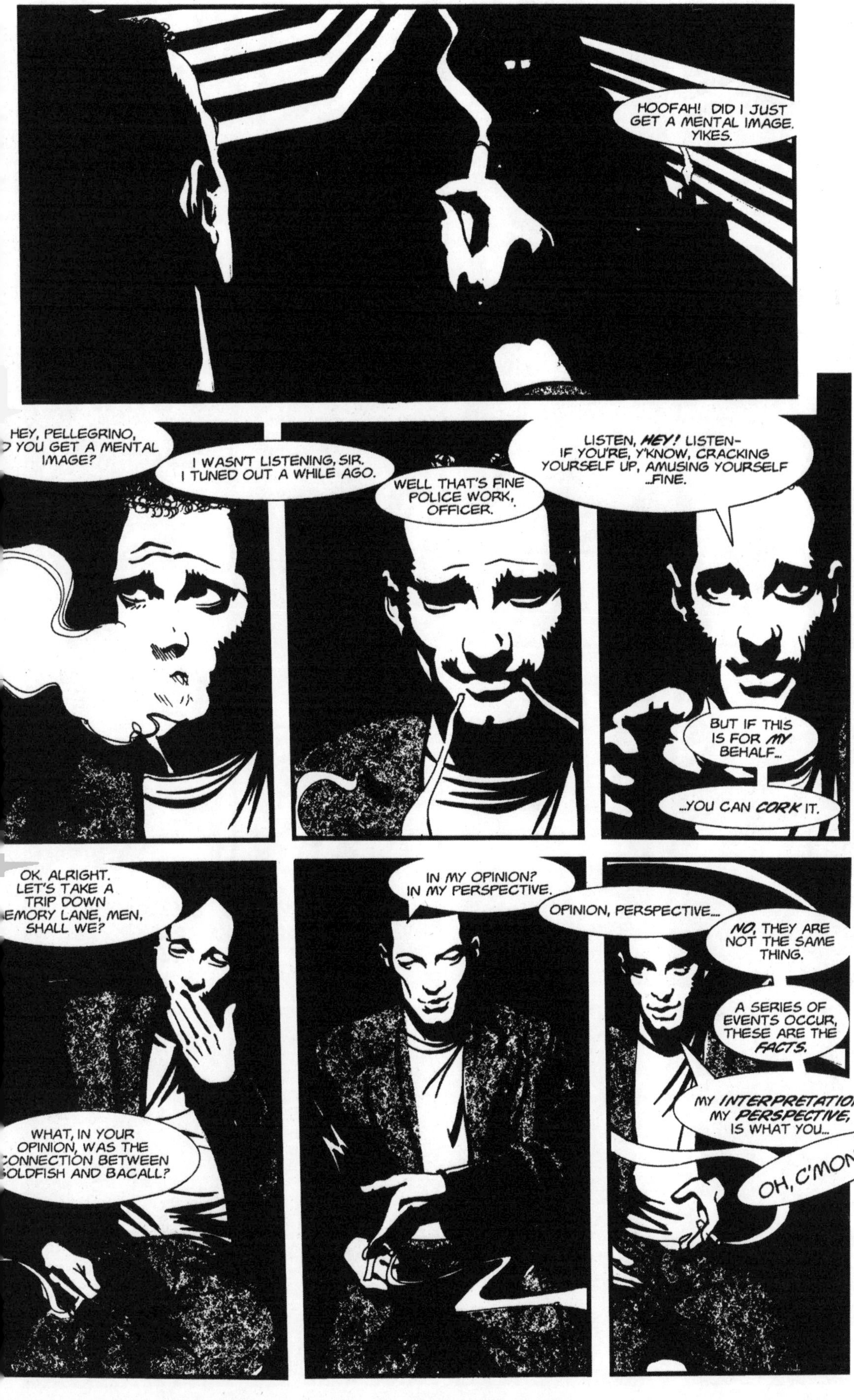
HOOFAH! DID I JUST GET A MENTAL IMAGE. YIKES.
HEY, PELLEGRINO, D YOU GET A MENTAL IMAGE?
I WASN'T LISTENING, SIR. I TUNED OUT A WHILE AGO.
WELL THAT'S FINE POLICE WORK, OFFICER.
LISTEN, HEY! LISTEN- IF YOU'RE, Y'KNOW, CRACKING YOURSELF UP, AMUSING YOURSELF ..FINE.
BUT IF THIS IS FOR MY BEHALF...
...YOU CAN CORK IT.
OK. ALRIGHT. LET'S TAKE A TRIP DOWN EMORY LANE, MEN, SHALL WE?
WHAT, IN YOUR OPINION, WAS THE ONNECTION BETWEEN OLDFISH AND BACALL?
IN MY OPINION? IN MY PERSPECTIVE.
OPINION, PERSPECTIVE....
NO, THEY ARE NOT THE SAME THING.
A SERIES OF EVENTS OCCUR, THESE ARE THE FACTS.
MY INTERPRETATION, MY PERSPECTIVE, IS WHAT YOU...
OH, C'MON!!!

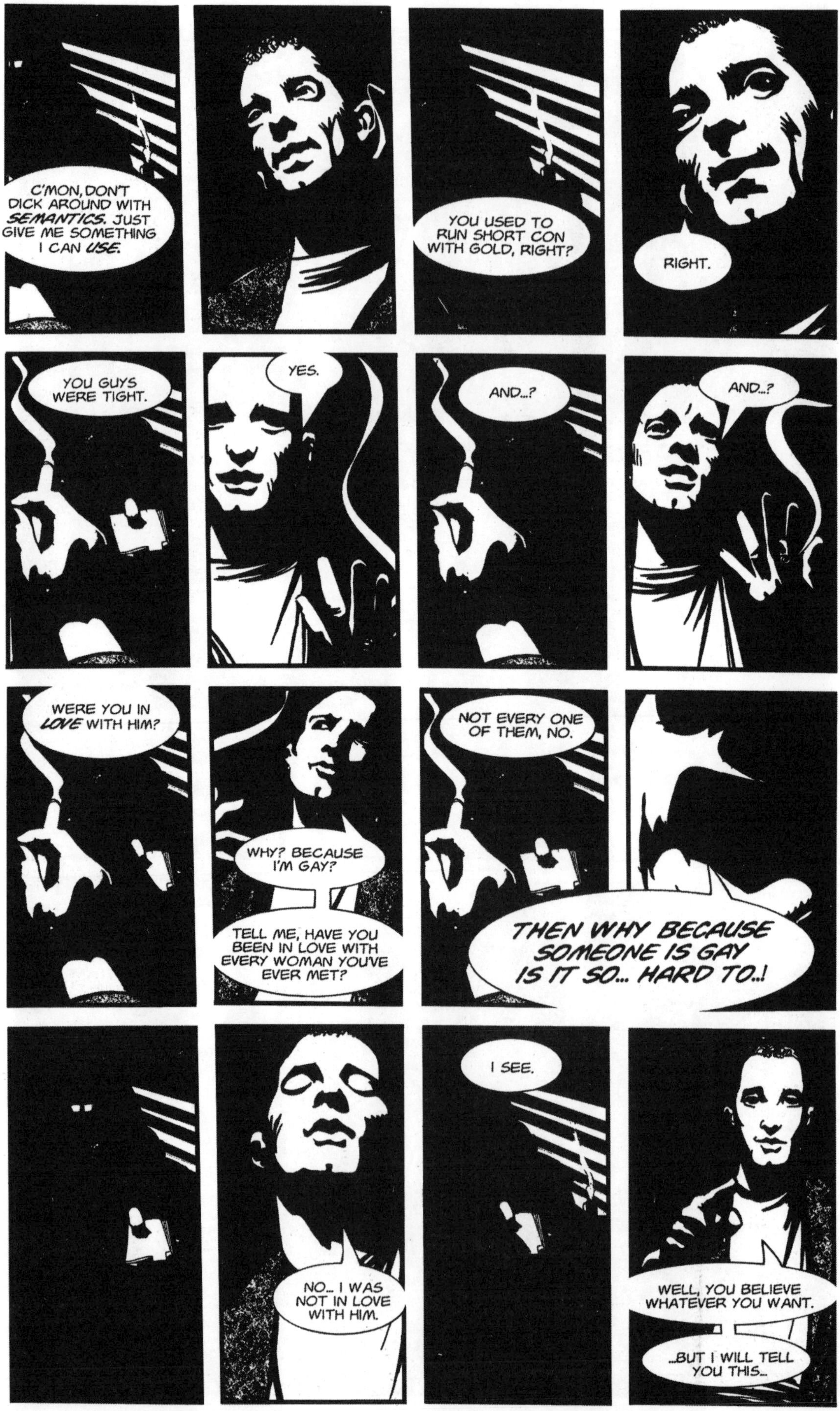
C'MON, DON'T DICK AROUND WITH SEMANTICS. JUST GIVE ME SOMETHING I CAN USE.
YOU USED TO RUN SHORT CON WITH GOLD, RIGHT?
RIGHT.
YOU GUYS WERE TIGHT.
YES.
AND...?
AND...?
WERE YOU IN LOVE WITH HIM?
WHY? BECAUSE I'M GAY?
TELL ME, HAVE YOU BEEN IN LOVE WITH EVERY WOMAN YOU'VE EVER MET?
NOT EVERY ONE OF THEM, NO.
THEN WHY BECAUSE SOMEONE IS GAY IS IT SO... HARD TO..!
NO... I WAS NOT IN LOVE WITH HIM.
I SEE.
WELL, YOU BELIEVE WHATEVER YOU WANT.
...BUT I WILL TELL YOU THIS...

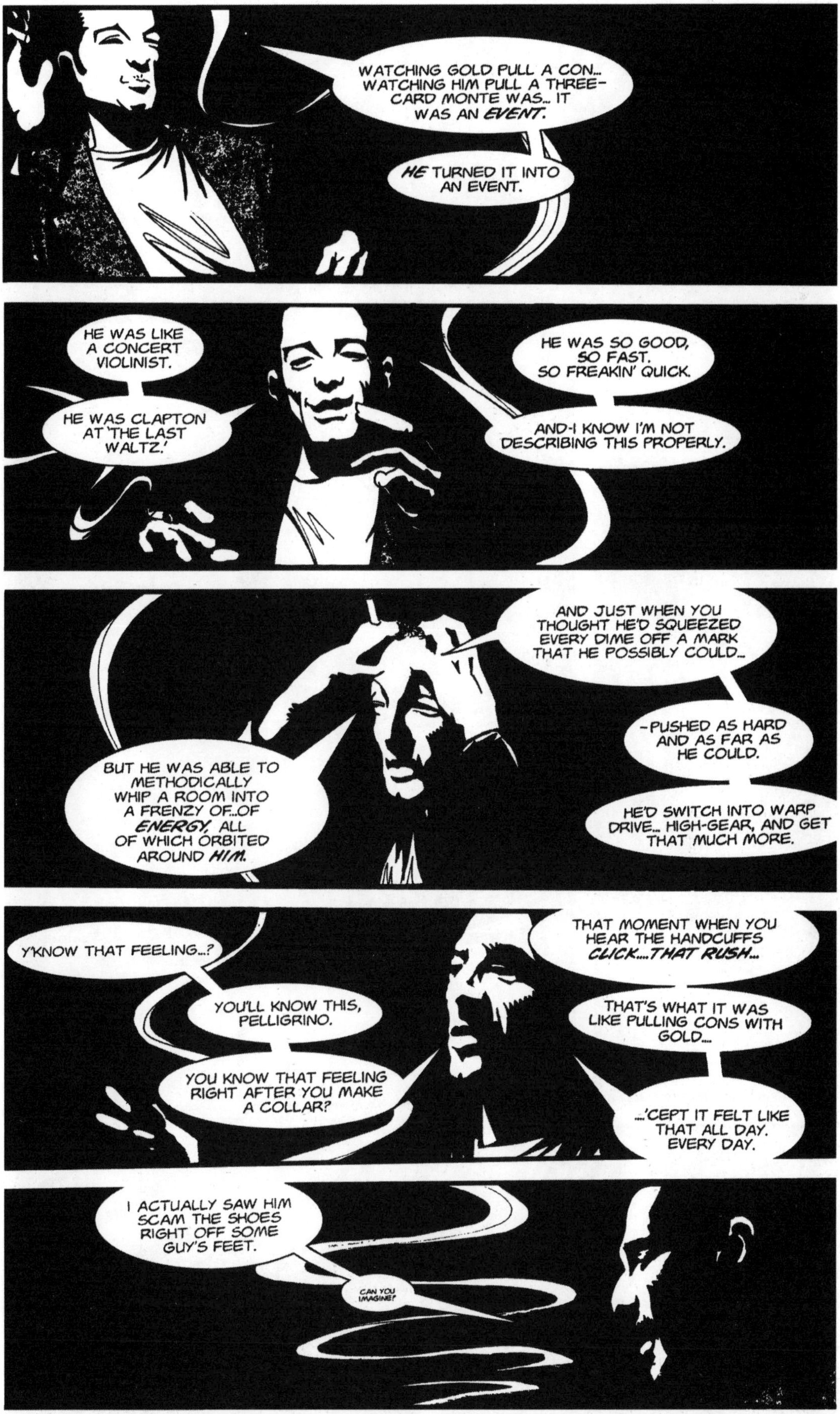
WATCHING GOLD PULL A CON... WATCHING HIM PULL A THREE-CARD MONTE WAS... IT WAS AN EVENT.
HE TURNED IT INTO AN EVENT.
HE WAS LIKE A CONCERT VIOLINIST.
HE WAS CLAPTON AT 'THE LAST WALTZ.'
HE WAS SO GOOD, SO FAST. SO FREAKIN' QUICK.
AND-I KNOW I'M NOT DESCRIBING THIS PROPERLY.
BUT HE WAS ABLE TO METHODICALLY WHIP A ROOM INTO A FRENZY OF...OF ENERGY, ALL OF WHICH ORBITED AROUND HIM.
AND JUST WHEN YOU THOUGHT HE'D SQUEEZED EVERY DIME OFF A MARK THAT HE POSSIBLY COULD...
-PUSHED AS HARD AND AS FAR AS HE COULD.
HE'D SWITCH INTO WARP DRIVE... HIGH-GEAR, AND GET THAT MUCH MORE.
Y'KNOW THAT FEELING...?
YOU'LL KNOW THIS, PELLIGRINO.
YOU KNOW THAT FEELING RIGHT AFTER YOU MAKE A COLLAR?
THAT MOMENT WHEN YOU HEAR THE HANDCUFFS CLICK....THAT RUSH...
THAT'S WHAT IT WAS LIKE PULLING CONS WITH GOLD....
...'CEPT IT FELT LIKE THAT ALL DAY. EVERY DAY.
I ACTUALLY SAW HIM SCAM THE SHOES RIGHT OFF SOME GUY'S FEET.
CAN YOU IMAGINE?

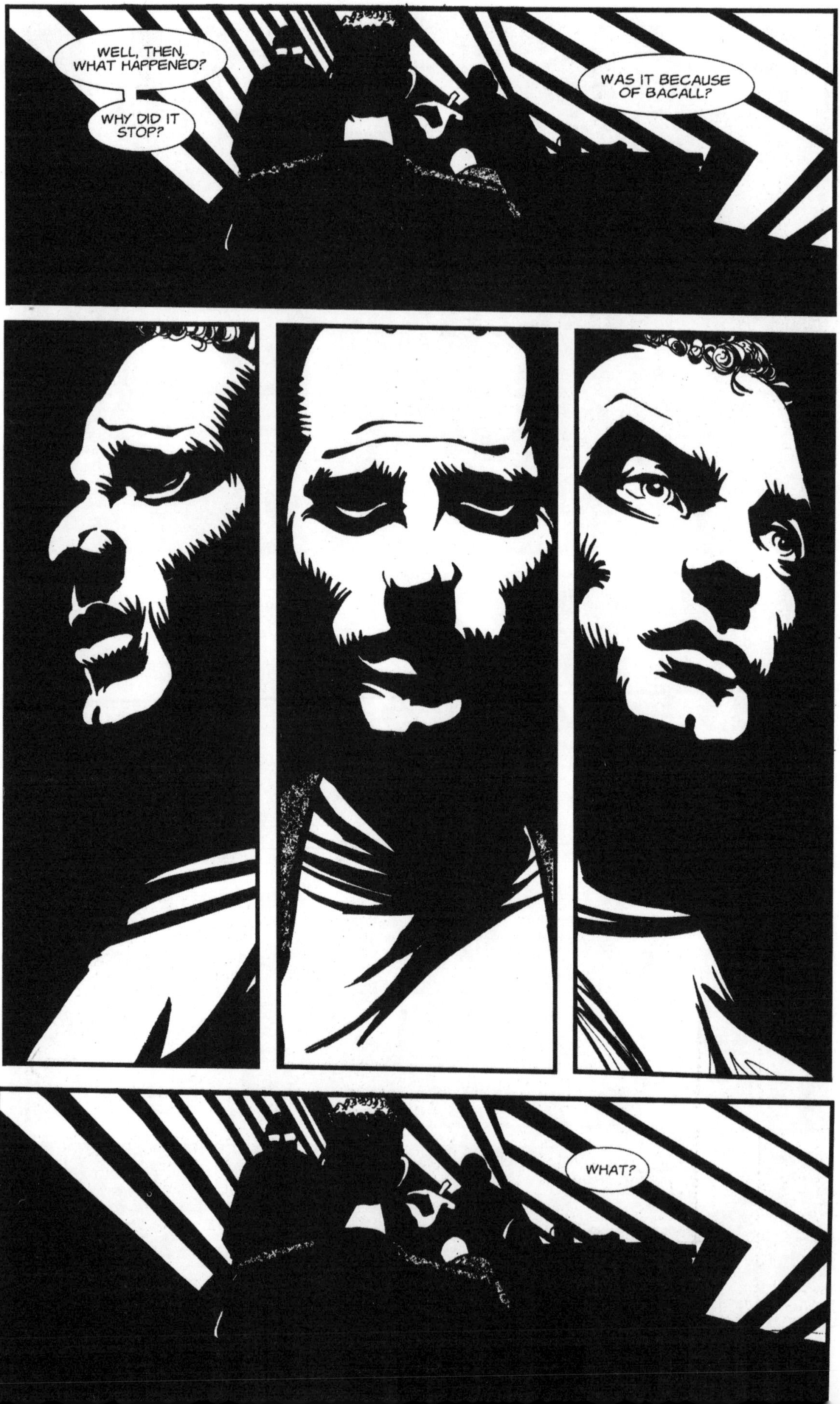
WELL, THEN, WHAT HAPPENED?
WHY DID IT STOP?
WAS IT BECAUSE OF BACALL?
WHAT?

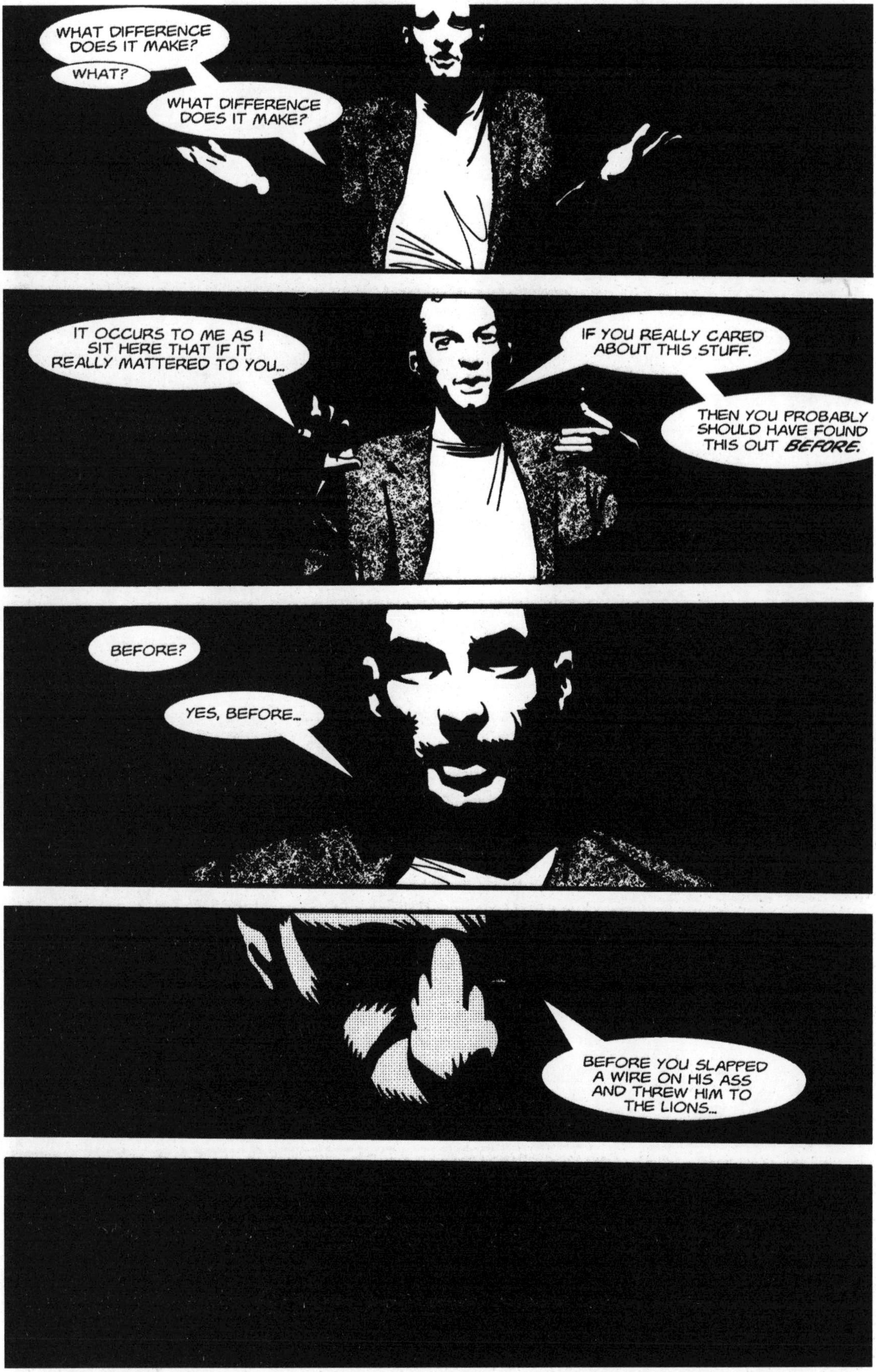
WHAT DIFFERENCE DOES IT MAKE?
WHAT?
WHAT DIFFERENCE DOES IT MAKE?
IT OCCURS TO ME AS I SIT HERE THAT IF IT REALLY MATTERED TO YOU...
IF YOU REALLY CARED ABOUT THIS STUFF.
THEN YOU PROBABLY SHOULD HAVE FOUND THIS OUT *BEFORE.*
BEFORE?
YES, BEFORE...
BEFORE YOU SLAPPED A WIRE ON HIS ASS AND THREW HIM TO THE LIONS...

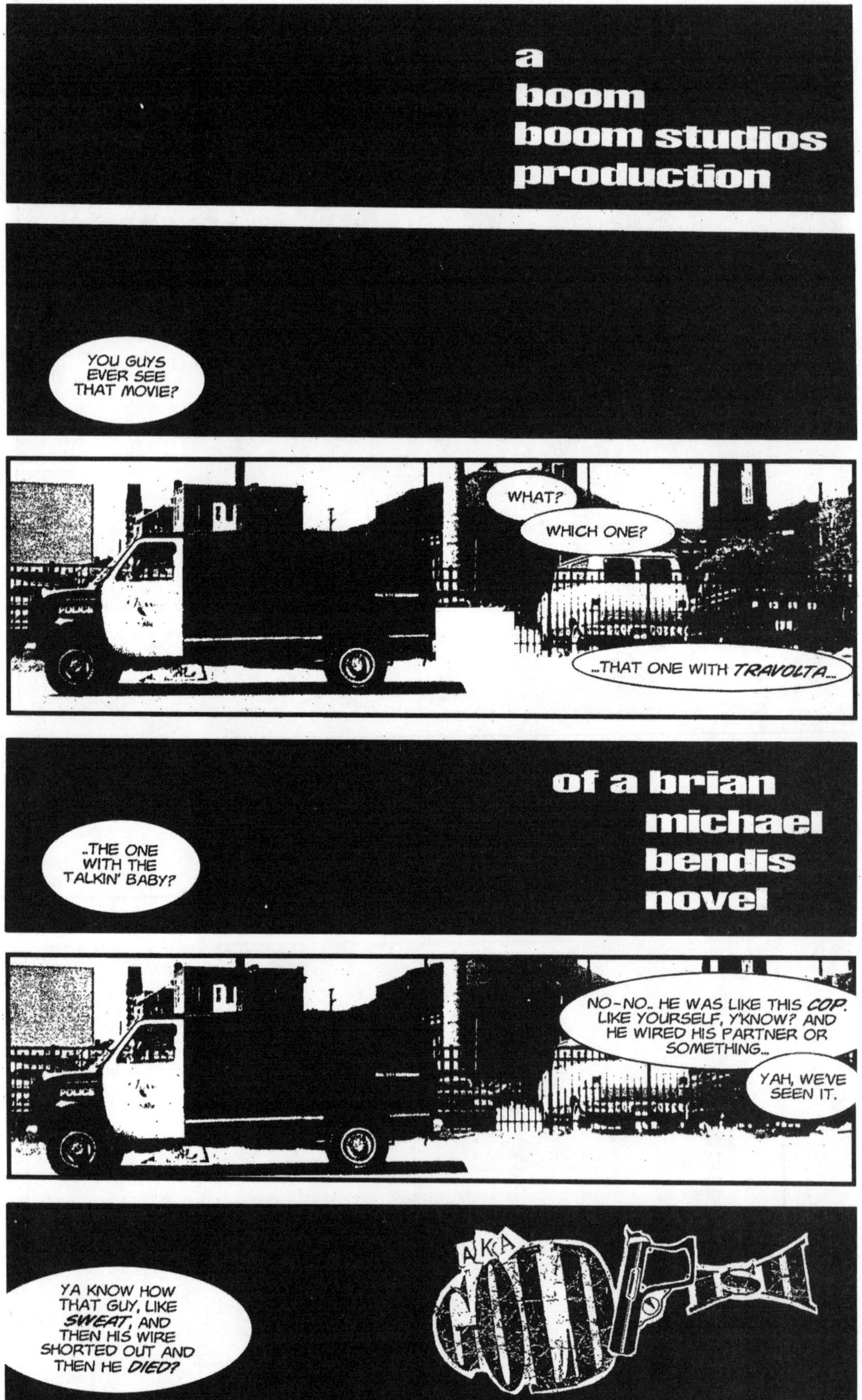
a boom boom studios production
YOU GUYS EVER SEE THAT MOVIE?
WHAT?
WHICH ONE?
...THAT ONE WITH TRAVOLTA...
of a brian michael bendis novel
..THE ONE WITH THE TALKIN' BABY?
NO-NO.. HE WAS LIKE THIS COP. LIKE YOURSELF, Y'KNOW? AND HE WIRED HIS PARTNER OR SOMETHING...
YAH, WE'VE SEEN IT.
YA KNOW HOW THAT GUY, LIKE SWEAT, AND THEN HIS WIRE SHORTED OUT AND THEN HE DIED?
A.K.A. GOLDFISH

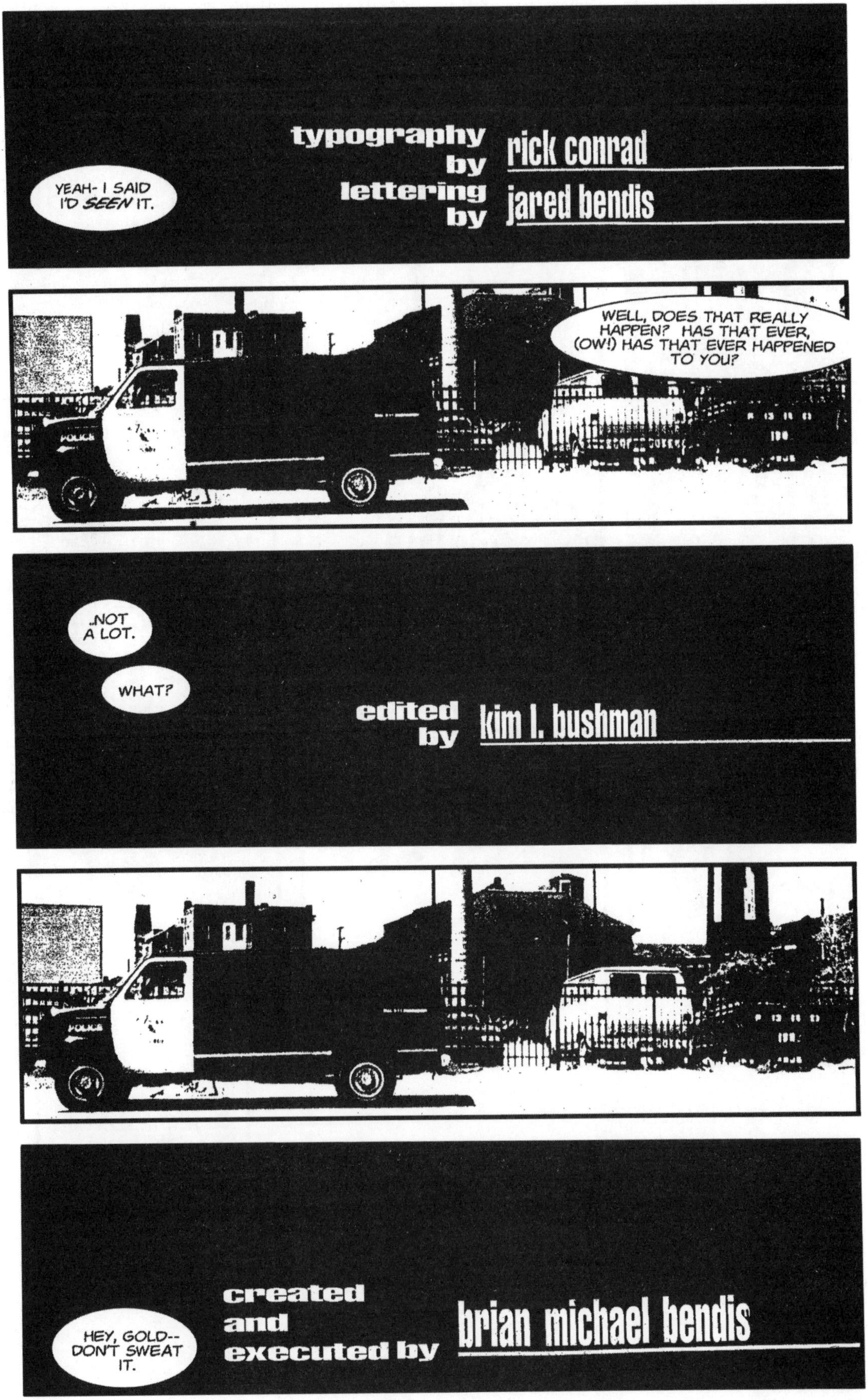
typography by
rick conrad
lettering by
jared bendis
YEAH- I SAID I'D SEEN IT.
WELL, DOES THAT REALLY HAPPEN? HAS THAT EVER, (OW!) HAS THAT EVER HAPPENED TO YOU?
POLICE
..NOT A LOT.
WHAT?
edited by
kim l. bushman
POLICE
created and executed by
brian michael bendis
HEY, GOLD-- DON'T SWEAT IT.

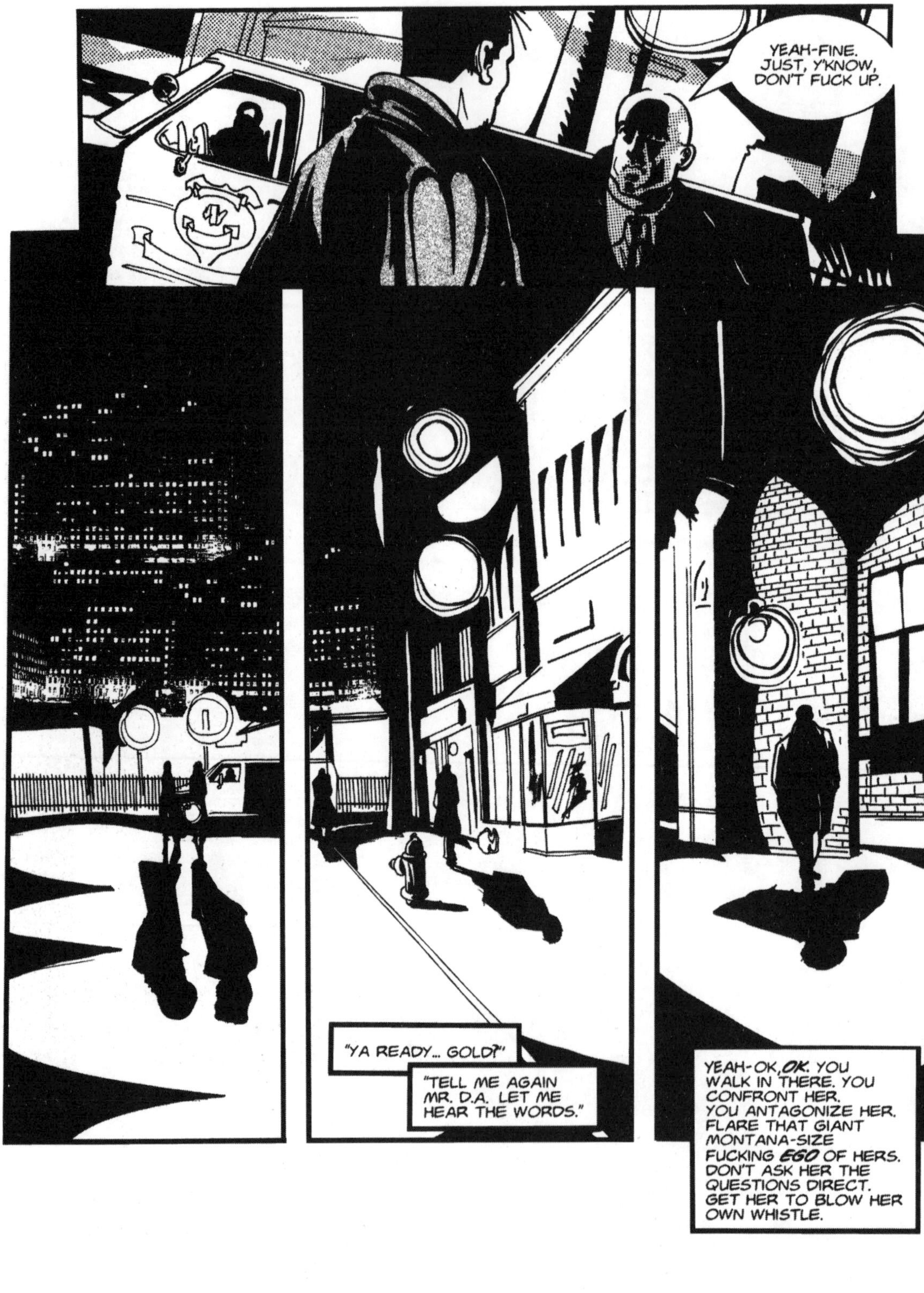
YEAH-FINE. JUST, Y'KNOW, DON'T FUCK UP.
"YA READY... GOLD?"
"TELL ME AGAIN MR. D.A. LET ME HEAR THE WORDS."
YEAH-OK, OK. YOU WALK IN THERE. YOU CONFRONT HER. YOU ANTAGONIZE HER. FLARE THAT GIANT MONTANA-SIZE FUCKING EGO OF HERS. DON'T ASK HER THE QUESTIONS DIRECT. GET HER TO BLOW HER OWN WHISTLE.

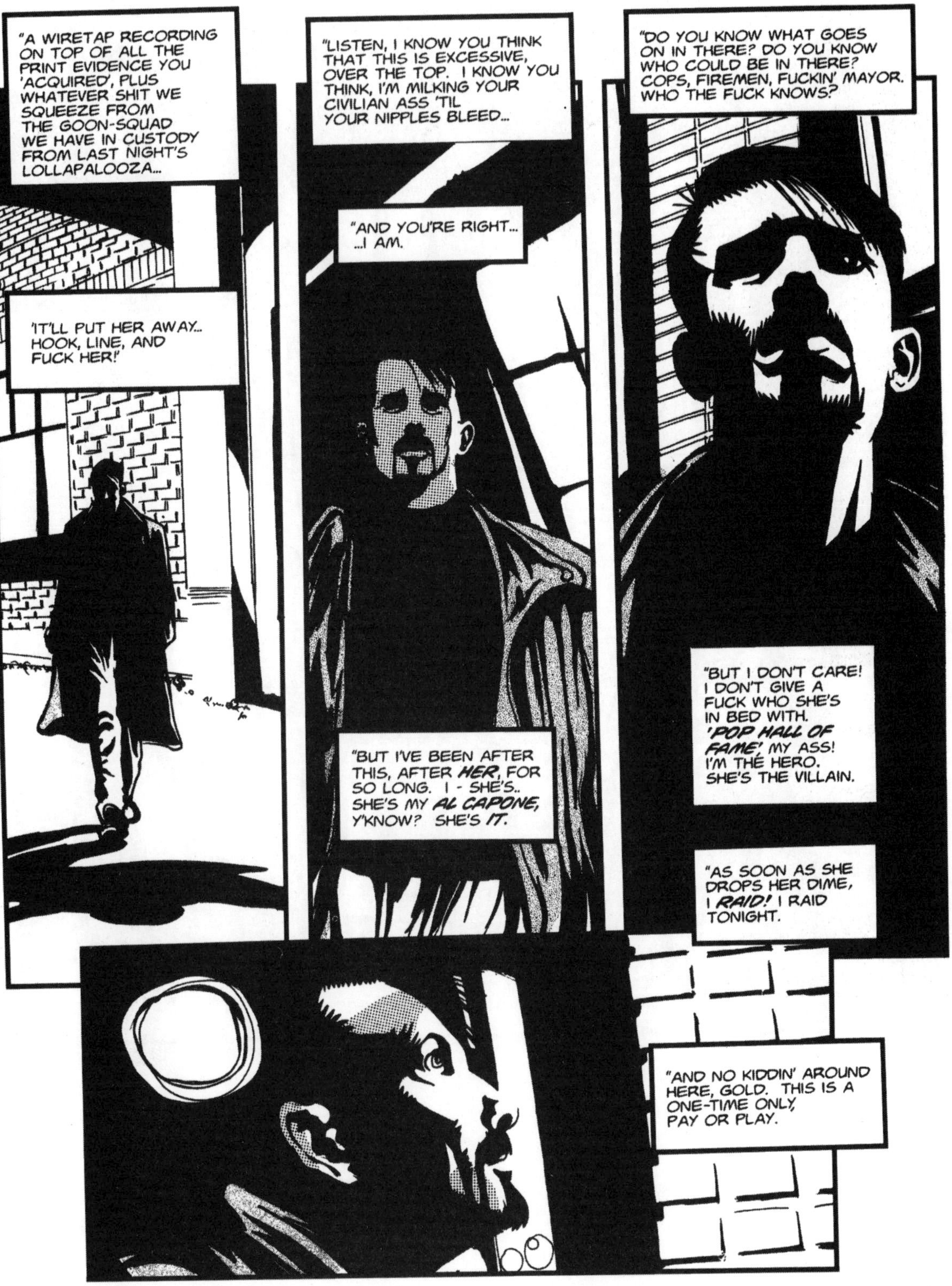
"A WIRETAP RECORDING ON TOP OF ALL THE PRINT EVIDENCE YOU 'ACQUIRED', PLUS WHATEVER SHIT WE SQUEEZE FROM THE GOON-SQUAD WE HAVE IN CUSTODY FROM LAST NIGHT'S LOLLAPALOOZA...
'IT'LL PUT HER AWAY... HOOK, LINE, AND FUCK HER!'
"LISTEN, I KNOW YOU THINK THAT THIS IS EXCESSIVE, OVER THE TOP. I KNOW YOU THINK, I'M MILKING YOUR CIVILIAN ASS 'TIL YOUR NIPPLES BLEED...
"AND YOU'RE RIGHT... ...I AM.
"BUT I'VE BEEN AFTER THIS, AFTER HER, FOR SO LONG. I - SHE'S.. SHE'S MY AL CAPONE, Y'KNOW? SHE'S IT.
"DO YOU KNOW WHAT GOES ON IN THERE? DO YOU KNOW WHO COULD BE IN THERE? COPS, FIREMEN, FUCKIN' MAYOR. WHO THE FUCK KNOWS?
"BUT I DON'T CARE! I DON'T GIVE A FUCK WHO SHE'S IN BED WITH. 'POP HALL OF FAME' MY ASS! I'M THÉ HERO. SHE'S THE VILLAIN.
"AS SOON AS SHE DROPS HER DIME, I RAID! I RAID TONIGHT.
"AND NO KIDDIN' AROUND HERE, GOLD. THIS IS A ONE-TIME ONLY, PAY OR PLAY.

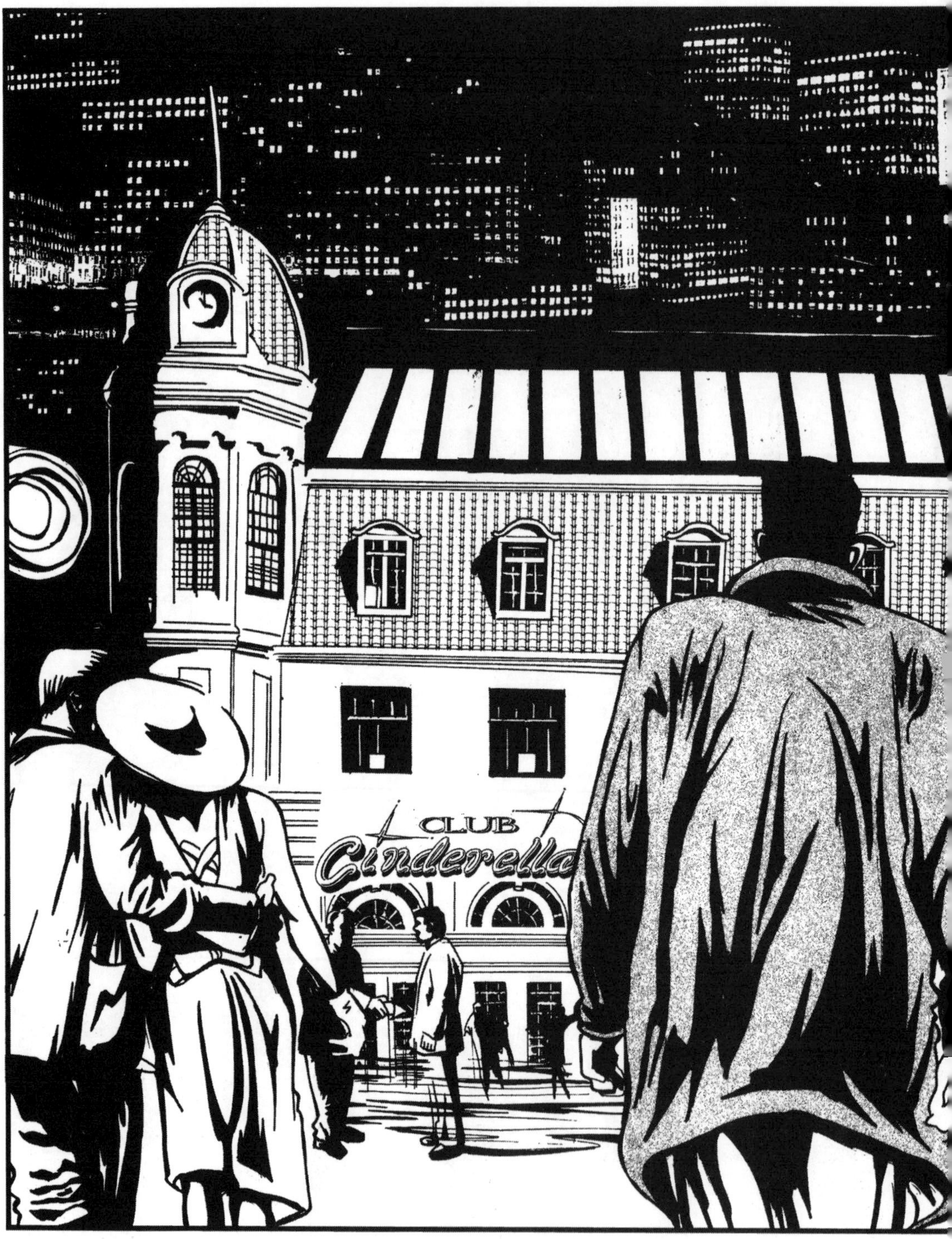
CLUB
Cinderella

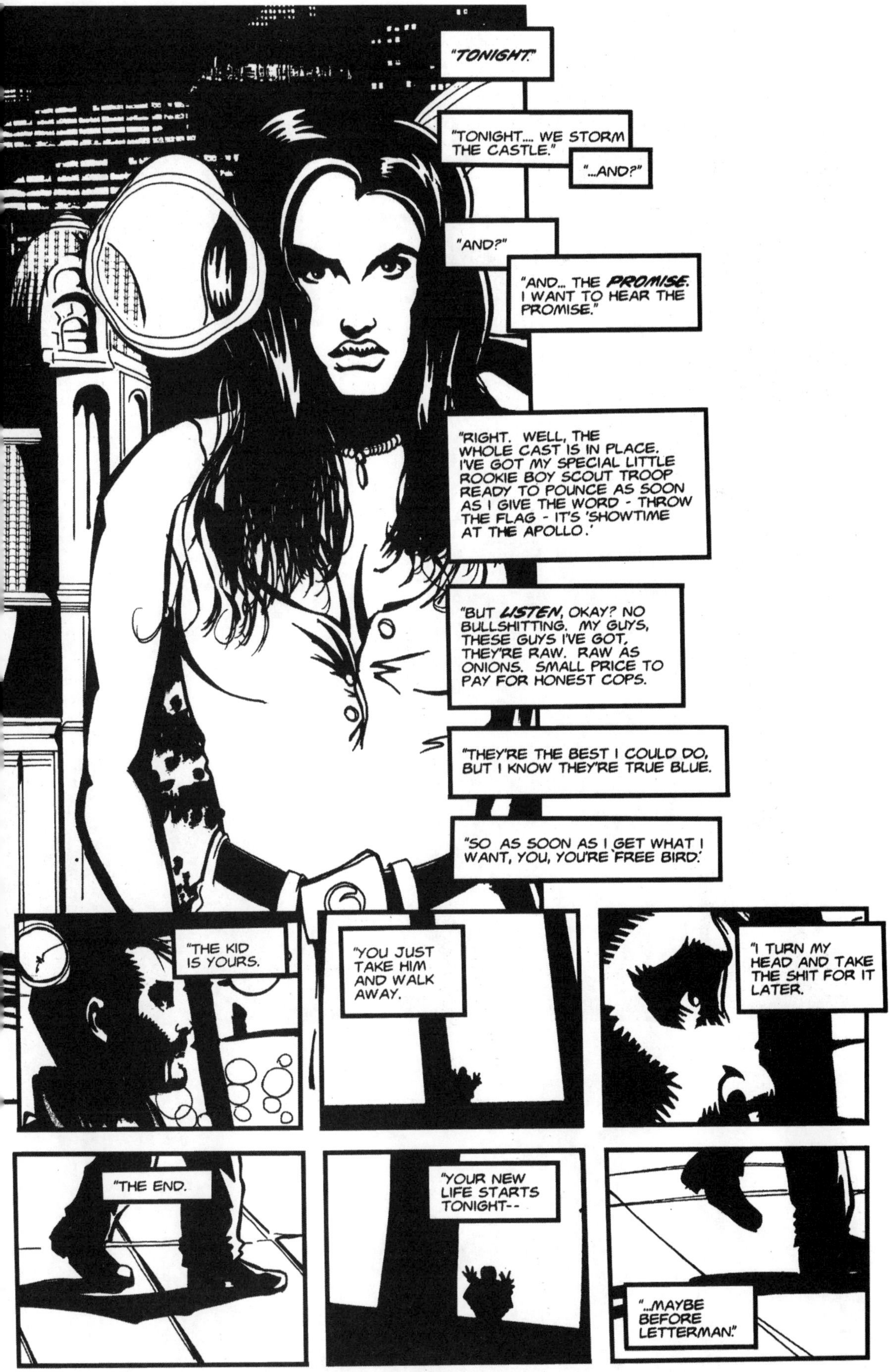
"TONIGHT."
"TONIGHT.... WE STORM THE CASTLE."
"...AND?"
"AND?"
"AND... THE PROMISE. I WANT TO HEAR THE PROMISE."
"RIGHT. WELL, THE WHOLE CAST IS IN PLACE. I'VE GOT MY SPECIAL LITTLE ROOKIE BOY SCOUT TROOP READY TO POUNCE AS SOON AS I GIVE THE WORD - THROW THE FLAG - IT'S 'SHOWTIME AT THE APOLLO.'
"BUT LISTEN, OKAY? NO BULLSHITTING. MY GUYS, THESE GUYS I'VE GOT, THEY'RE RAW. RAW AS ONIONS. SMALL PRICE TO PAY FOR HONEST COPS.
"THEY'RE THE BEST I COULD DO, BUT I KNOW THEY'RE TRUE BLUE.
"SO AS SOON AS I GET WHAT I WANT, YOU, YOU'RE 'FREE BIRD.'
"THE KID IS YOURS.
"YOU JUST TAKE HIM AND WALK AWAY.
"I TURN MY HEAD AND TAKE THE SHIT FOR IT LATER.
"THE END.
"YOUR NEW LIFE STARTS TONIGHT--
"...MAYBE BEFORE LETTERMAN."

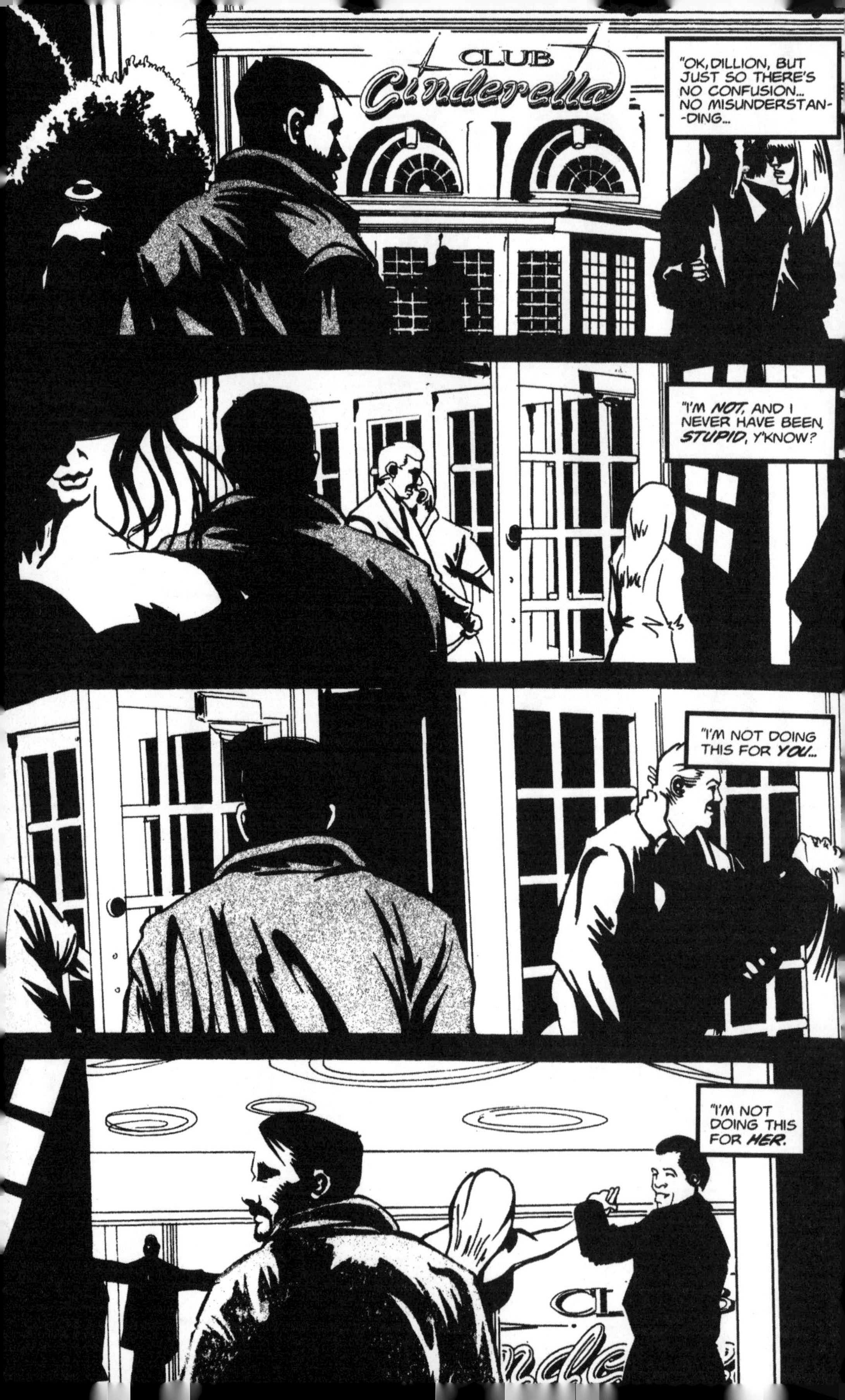
CLUB
Cinderella
"OK, DILLION, BUT JUST SO THERE'S NO CONFUSION... NO MISUNDERSTAN-DING...
"I'M NOT, AND I NEVER HAVE BEEN, STUPID, Y'KNOW?
"I'M NOT DOING THIS FOR YOU...
"I'M NOT DOING THIS FOR HER.

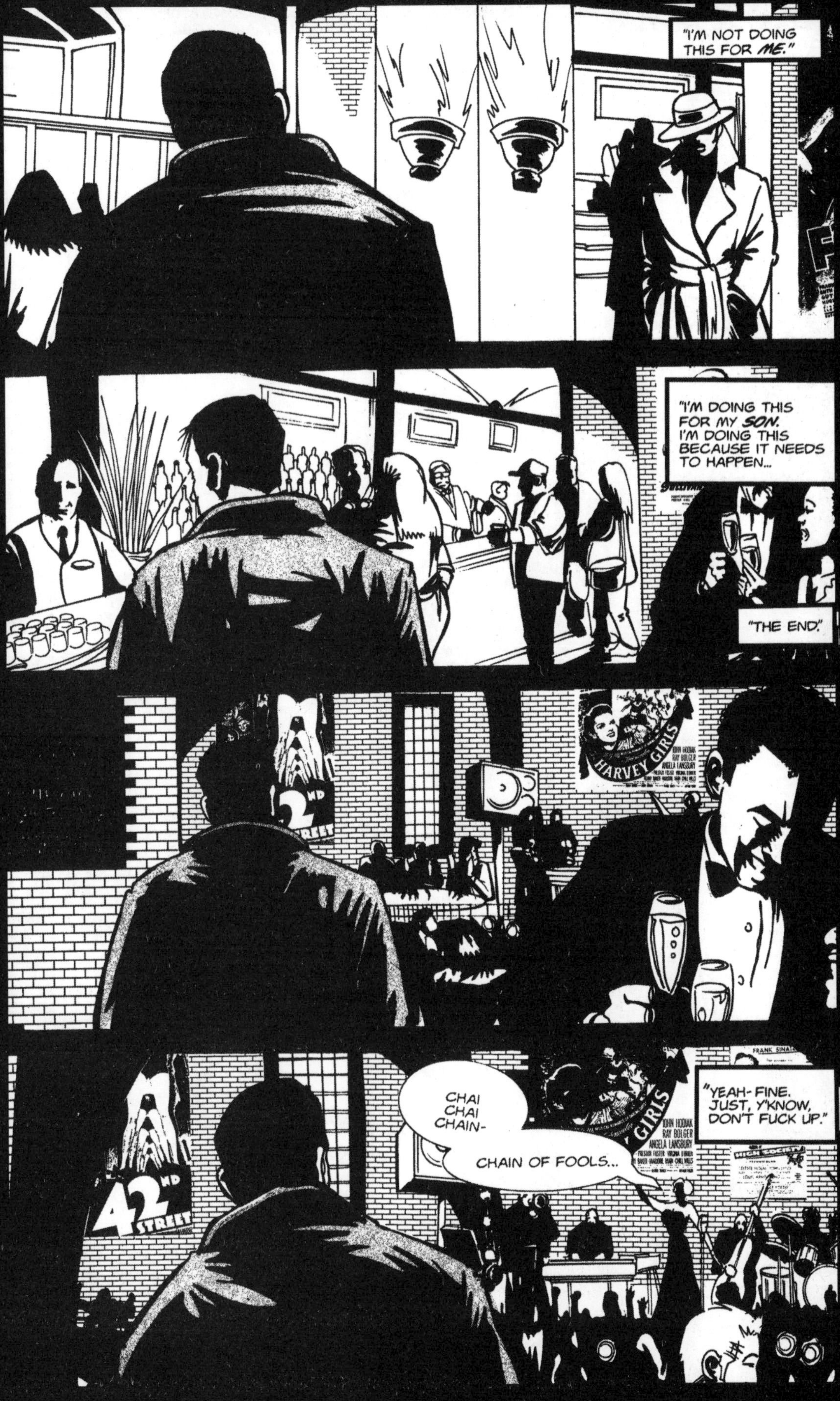
"I'M NOT DOING THIS FOR ME."
"I'M DOING THIS FOR MY SON. I'M DOING THIS BECAUSE IT NEEDS TO HAPPEN...
"THE END."
HARVEY GIRLS
JOHN HODIAK
RAY BOLGER
ANGELA LANSBURY
42ND STREET
CHAI CHAI CHAIN-
CHAIN OF FOOLS...
"YEAH- FINE. JUST, Y'KNOW, DON'T FUCK UP."

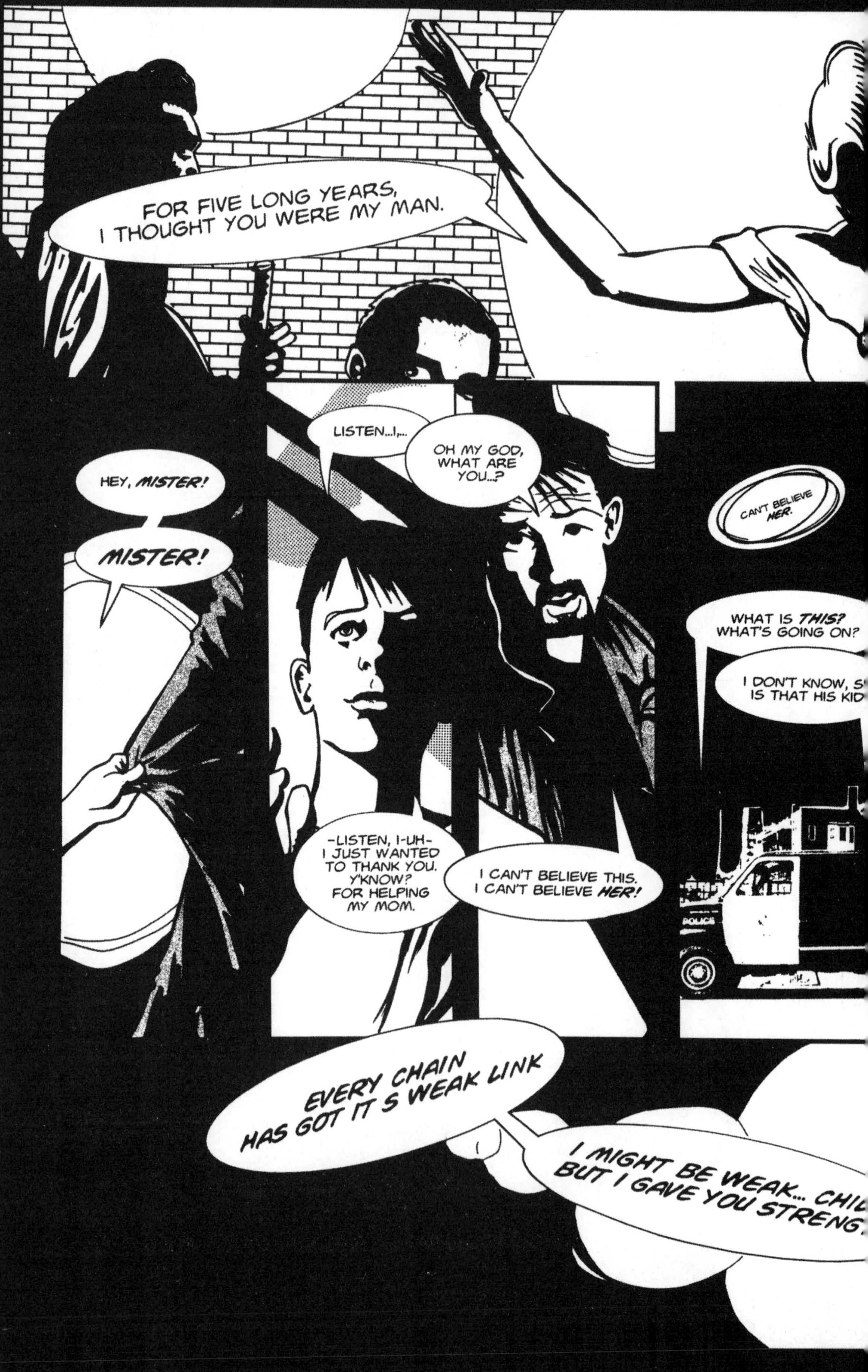
FOR FIVE LONG YEARS, I THOUGHT YOU WERE MY MAN.
HEY, *MISTER!*
MISTER!
LISTEN...I,...
OH MY GOD, WHAT ARE YOU...?
-LISTEN, I-UH- I JUST WANTED TO THANK YOU. Y'KNOW? FOR HELPING MY MOM.
I CAN'T BELIEVE THIS. I CAN'T BELIEVE *HER!*
CAN'T BELIEVE *HER.*
WHAT IS *THIS?* WHAT'S GOING ON?
I DON'T KNOW, IS THAT HIS
EVERY CHAIN HAS GOT IT S WEAK LINK
I MIGHT BE WEAK... BUT I GAVE YOU

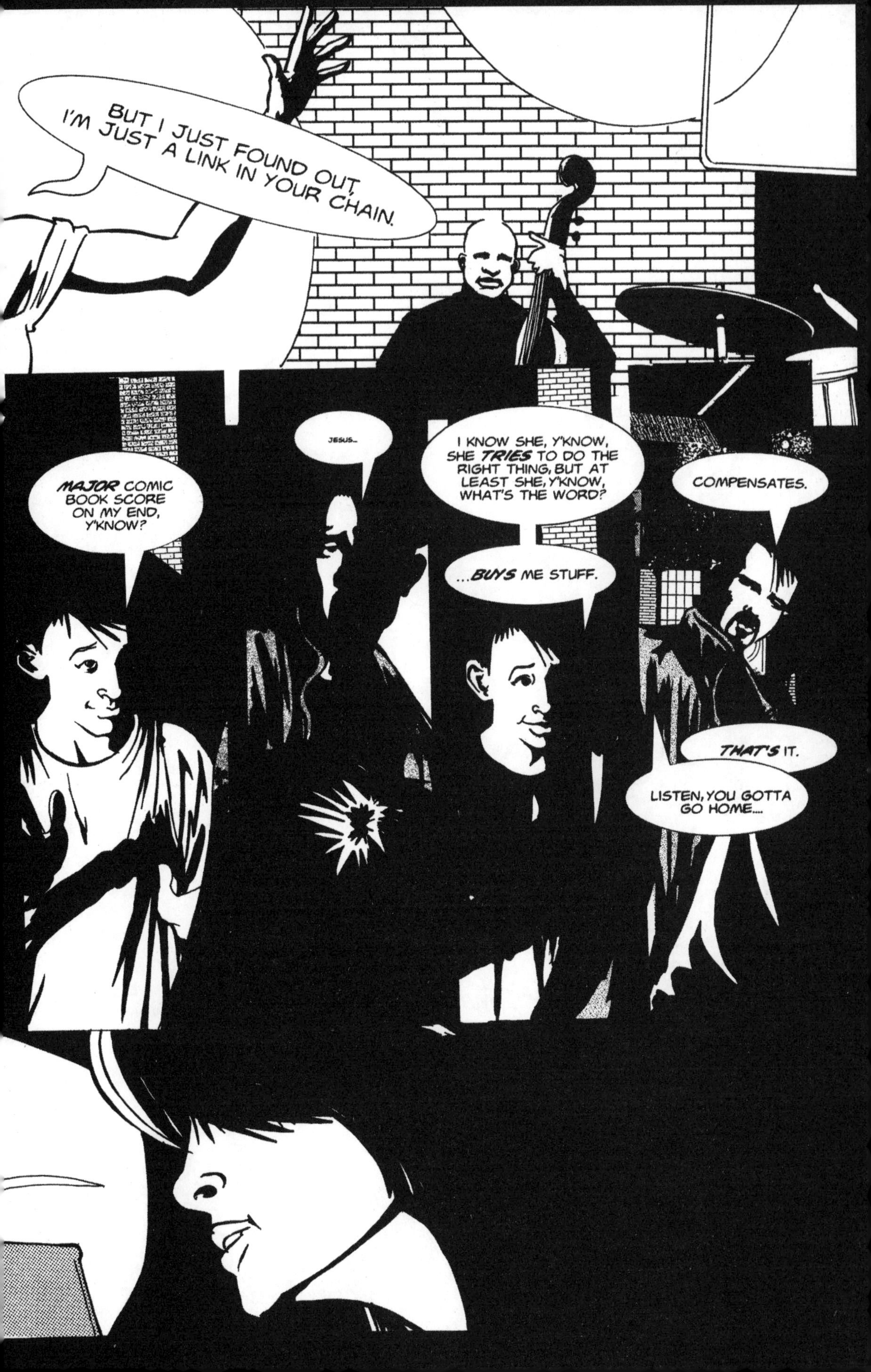
BUT I JUST FOUND OUT, I'M JUST A LINK IN YOUR CHAIN.
MAJOR COMIC BOOK SCORE ON MY END, Y'KNOW?
JESUS...
I KNOW SHE, Y'KNOW, SHE TRIES TO DO THE RIGHT THING, BUT AT LEAST SHE, Y'KNOW, WHAT'S THE WORD?
...BUYS ME STUFF.
COMPENSATES.
THAT'S IT.
LISTEN, YOU GOTTA GO HOME...

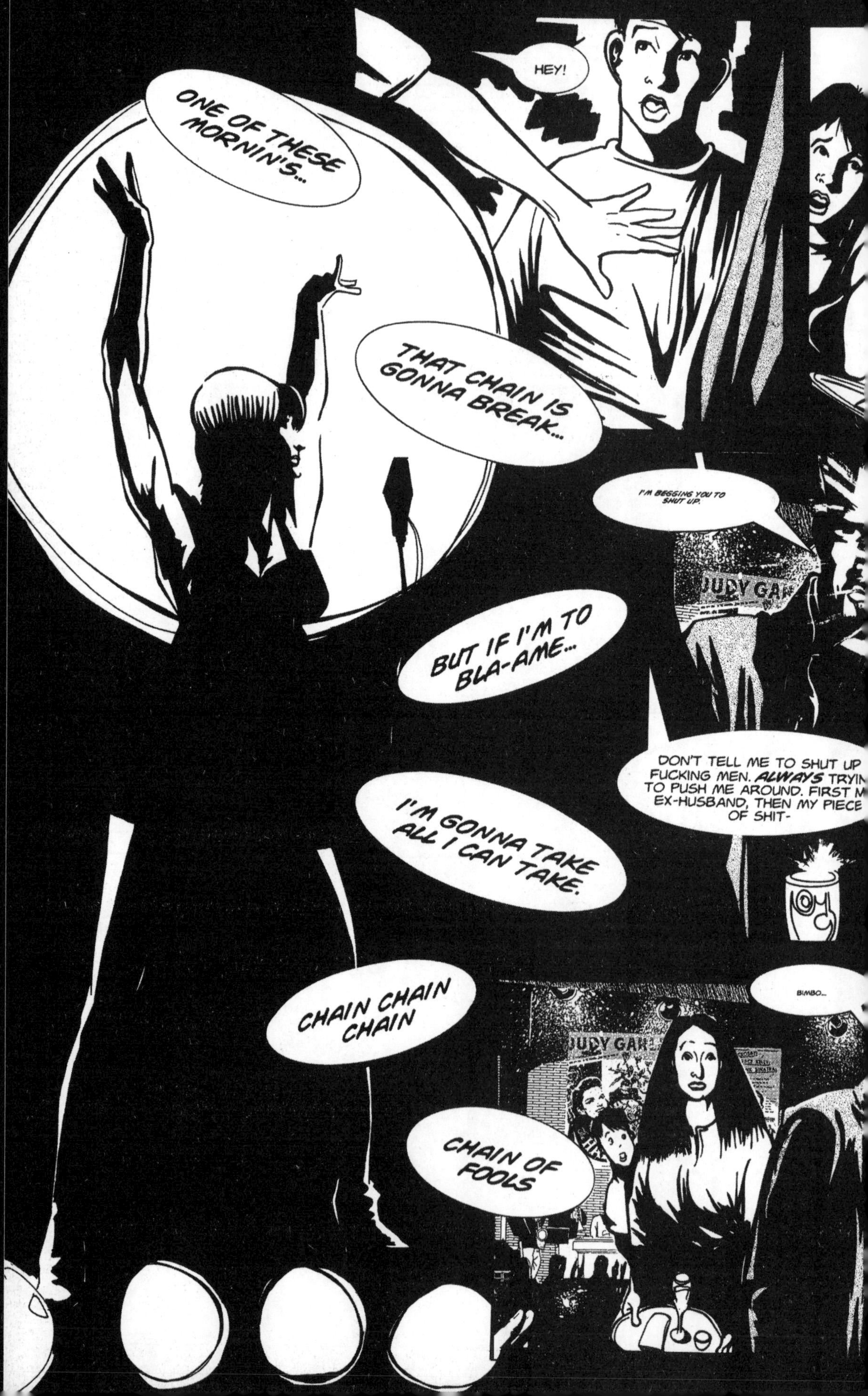
HEY!
ONE OF THESE MORNIN'S...
THAT CHAIN IS GONNA BREAK...
I'M BEGGING YOU TO SHUT UP.
BUT IF I'M TO BLA-AME...
DON'T TELL ME TO SHUT UP FUCKING MEN. *ALWAYS* TRYIN TO PUSH ME AROUND. FIRST M EX-HUSBAND, THEN MY PIECE OF SHIT-
I'M GONNA TAKE ALL I CAN TAKE.
BIMBO...
CHAIN CHAIN CHAIN
CHAIN OF FOOLS

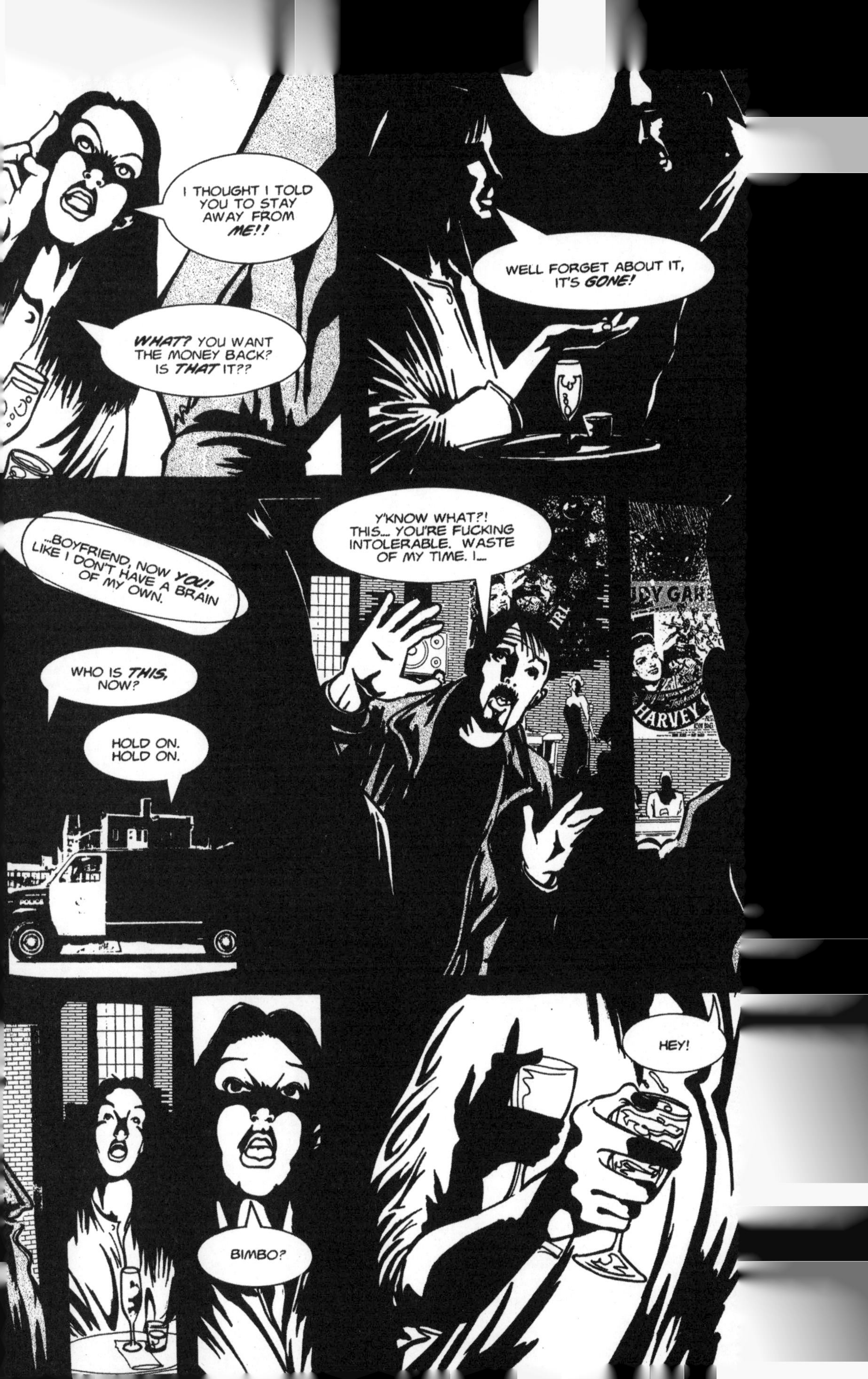
I THOUGHT I TOLD YOU TO STAY AWAY FROM *ME!!*
WELL FORGET ABOUT IT, IT'S *GONE!*
WHAT? YOU WANT THE MONEY BACK? IS *THAT* IT??
...BOYFRIEND, NOW *YOU!!* LIKE I DON'T HAVE A BRAIN OF MY OWN.
Y'KNOW WHAT?! THIS... YOU'RE FUCKING INTOLERABLE. WASTE OF MY TIME. I...
WHO IS *THIS,* NOW?
HOLD ON. HOLD ON.
POLICE
HARVEY
BIMBO?
HEY!

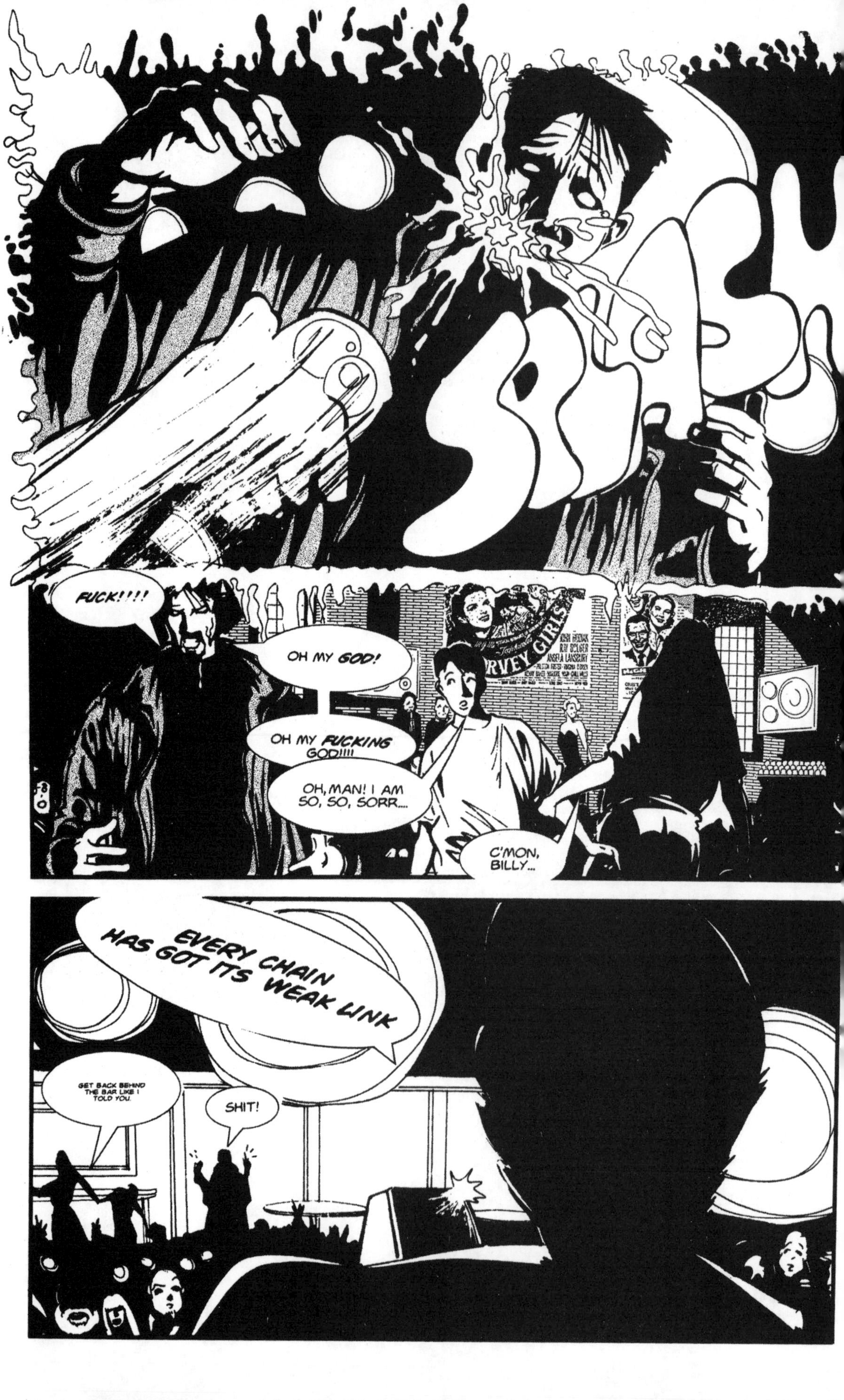

SPLASH
FUCK!!!!
OH MY GOD!
OH MY FUCKING GOD!!!!
OH, MAN! I AM SO, SO, SORR....
C'MON, BILLY...
EVERY CHAIN HAS GOT ITS WEAK LINK
GET BACK BEHIND THE BAR LIKE I TOLD YOU.
SHIT!

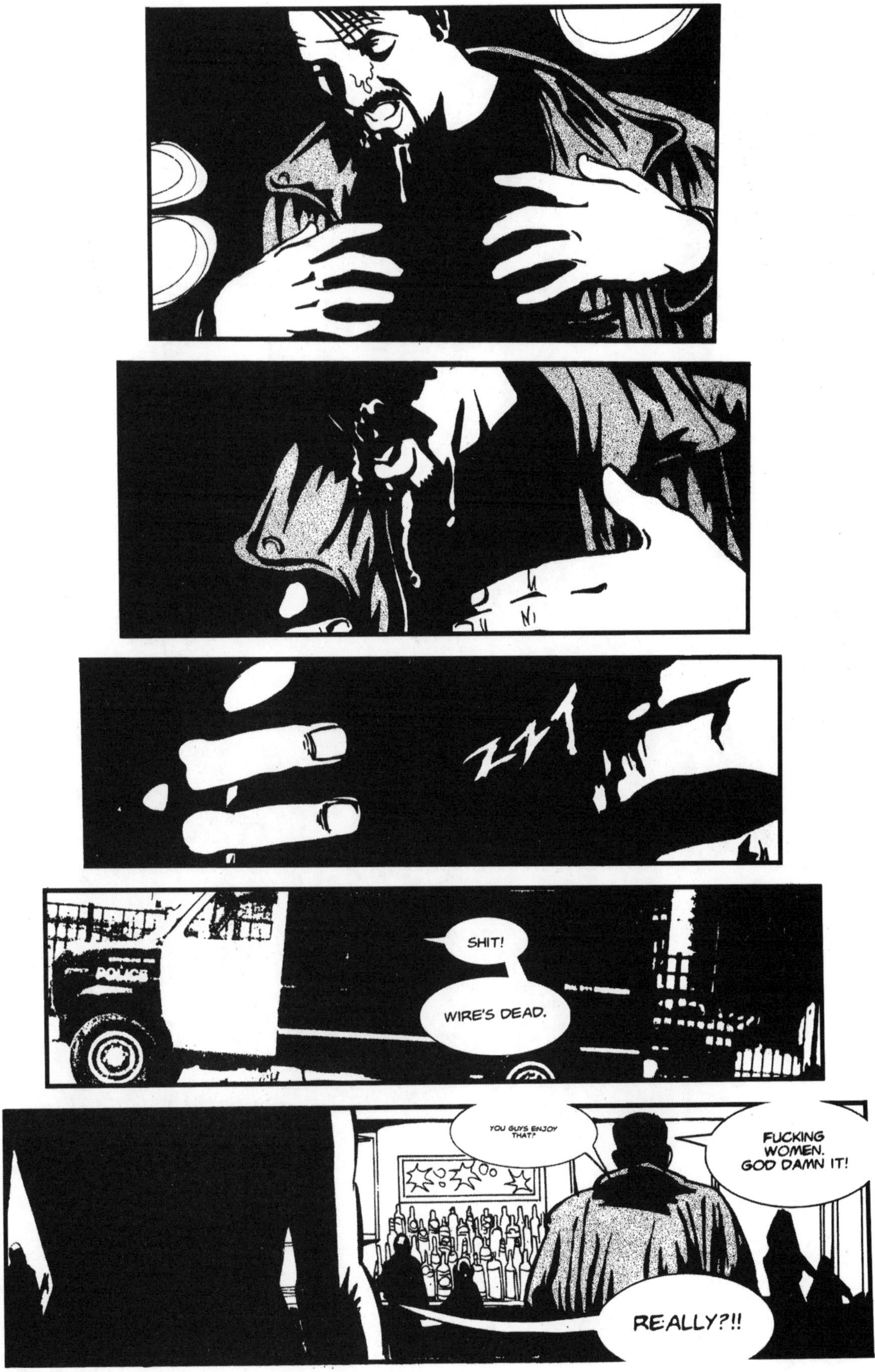
ZZT
POLICE
SHIT!
WIRE'S DEAD.
YOU GUYS ENJOY THAT?
FUCKING WOMEN. GOD DAMN IT!
REALLY?!!

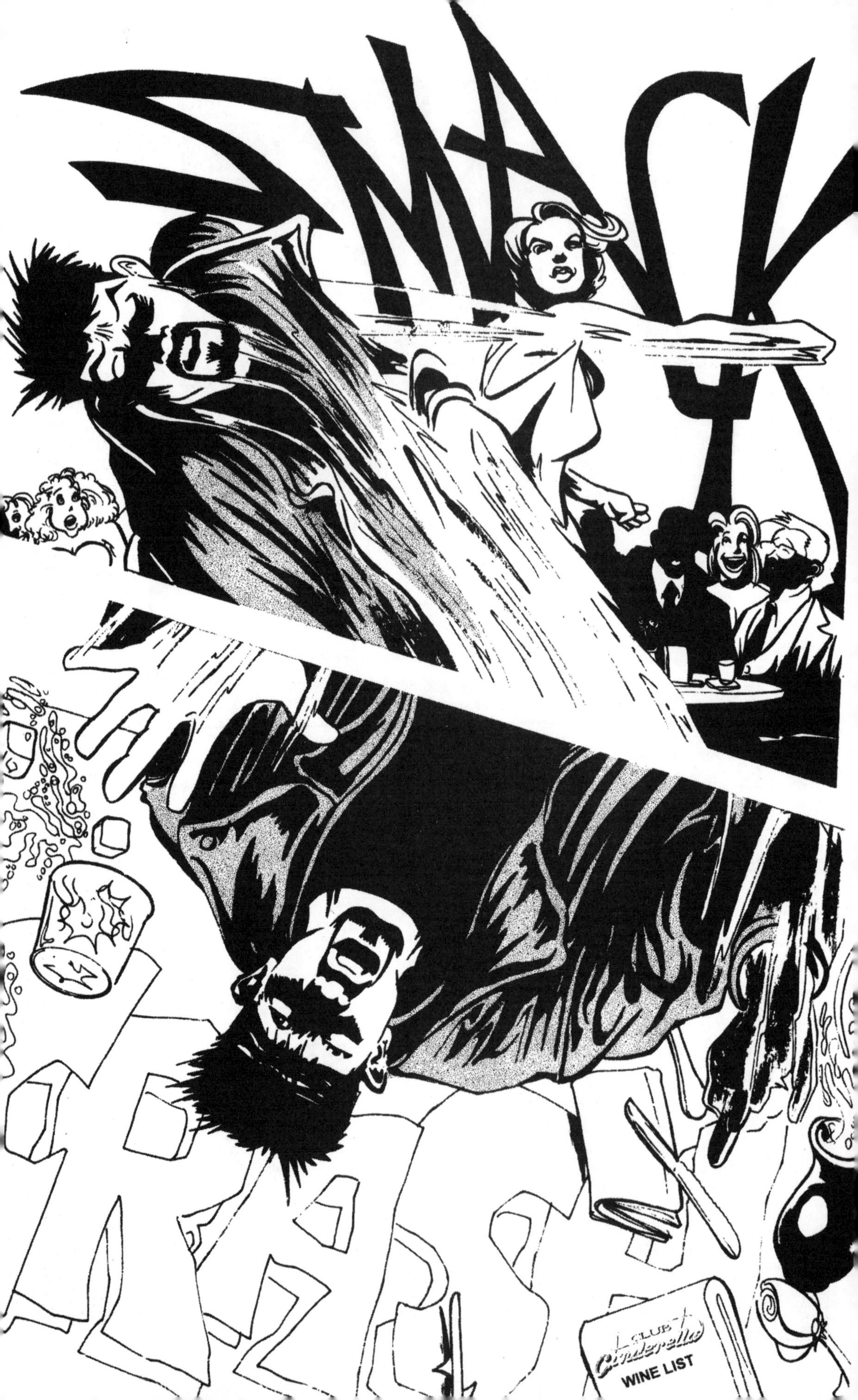
SMACK
KRASH
CLUB Cinderella
WINE LIST

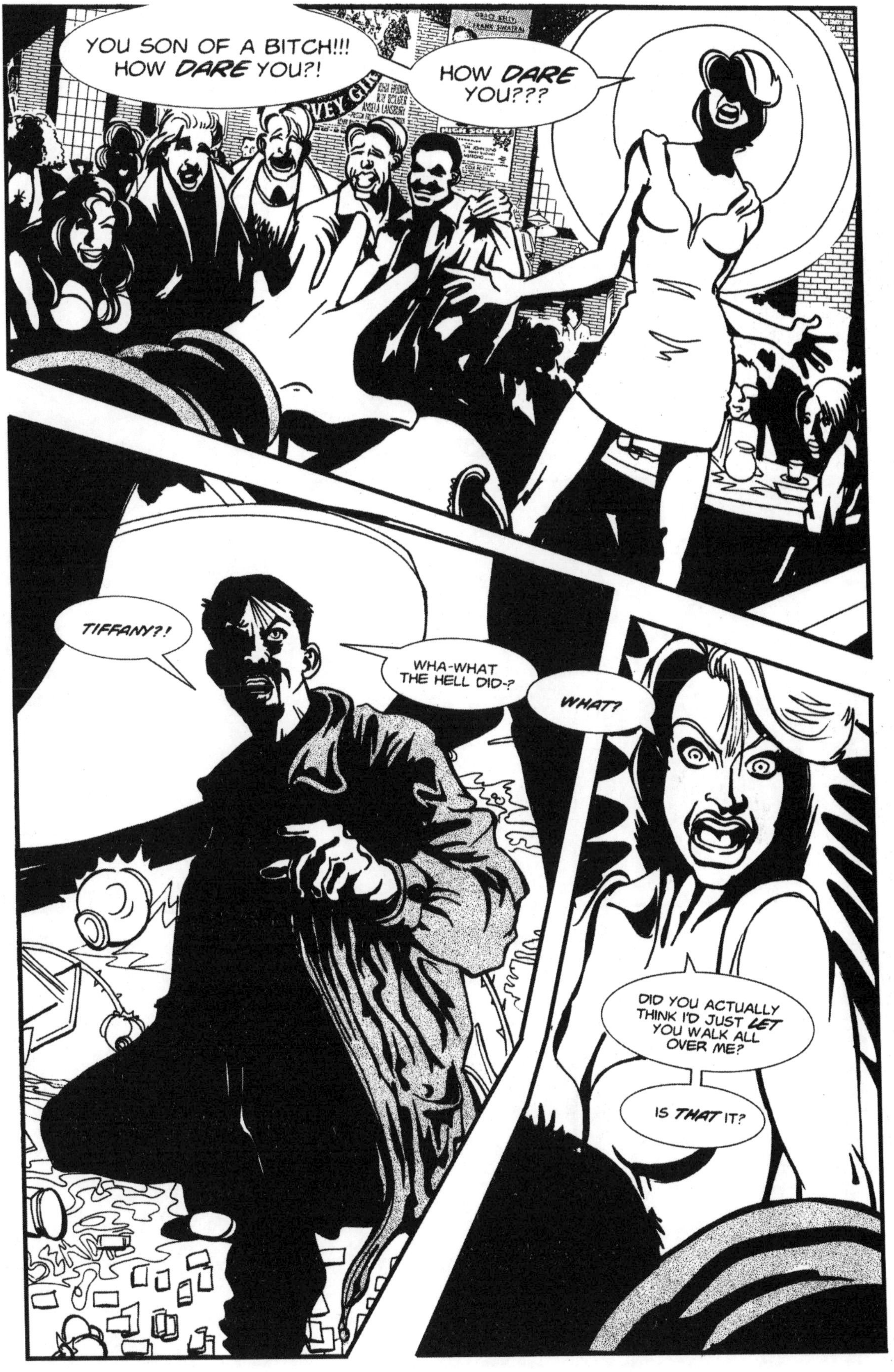
YOU SON OF A BITCH!!! HOW DARE YOU?!
HOW DARE YOU???
TIFFANY?!
WHA-WHAT THE HELL DID-?
WHAT?
DID YOU ACTUALLY THINK I'D JUST LET YOU WALK ALL OVER ME?
IS THAT IT?

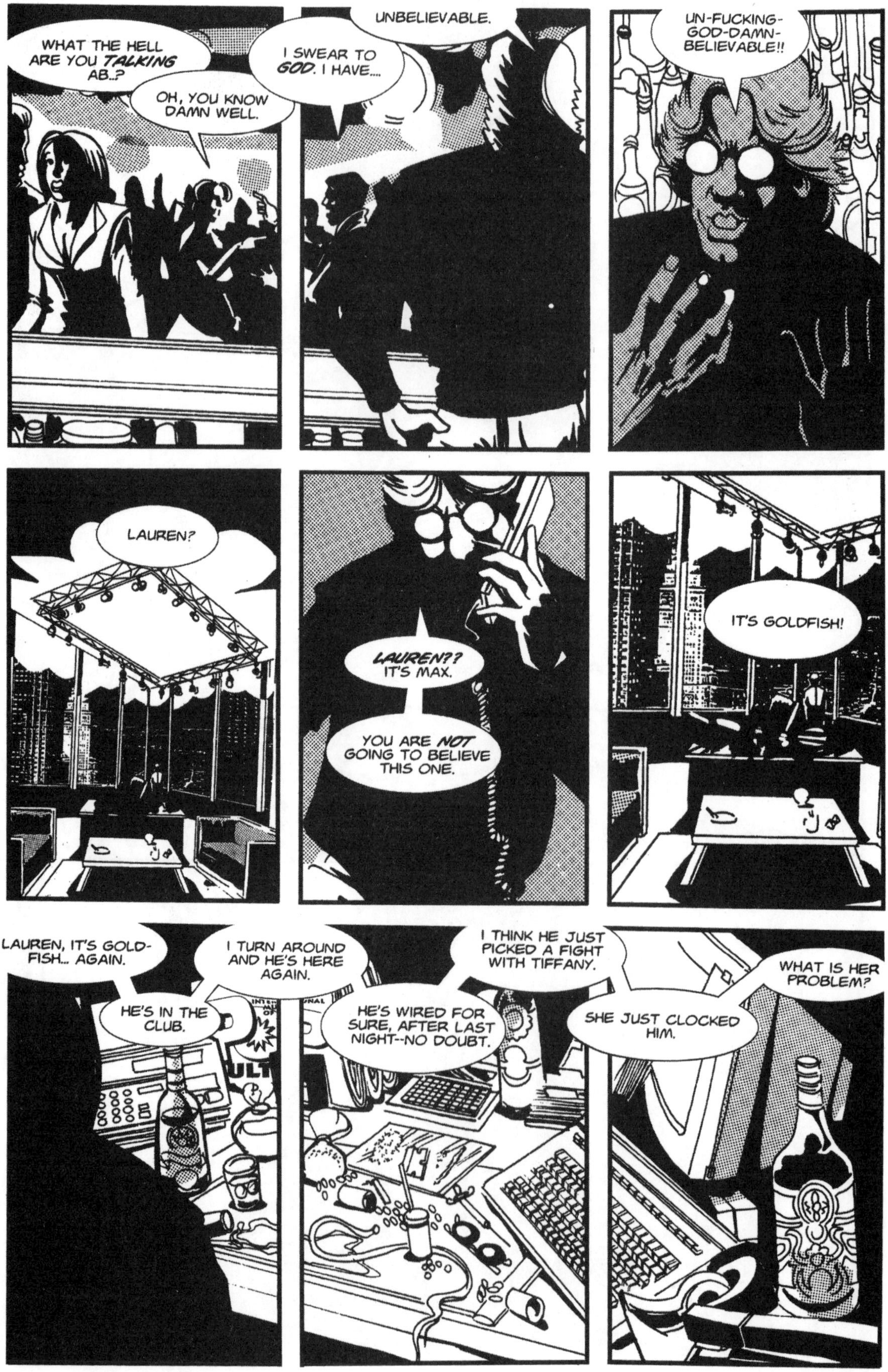
WHAT THE HELL ARE YOU *TALKING* AB..?
OH, YOU KNOW DAMN WELL.
I SWEAR TO *GOD*. I HAVE....
UNBELIEVABLE.
UN-FUCKING-GOD-DAMN-BELIEVABLE!!
LAUREN?
LAUREN?? IT'S MAX.
YOU ARE *NOT* GOING TO BELIEVE THIS ONE.
IT'S GOLDFISH!
LAUREN, IT'S GOLD-FISH... AGAIN.
HE'S IN THE CLUB.
I TURN AROUND AND HE'S HERE AGAIN.
HE'S WIRED FOR SURE, AFTER LAST NIGHT--NO DOUBT.
I THINK HE JUST PICKED A FIGHT WITH TIFFANY.
SHE JUST CLOCKED HIM.
WHAT IS HER PROBLEM?

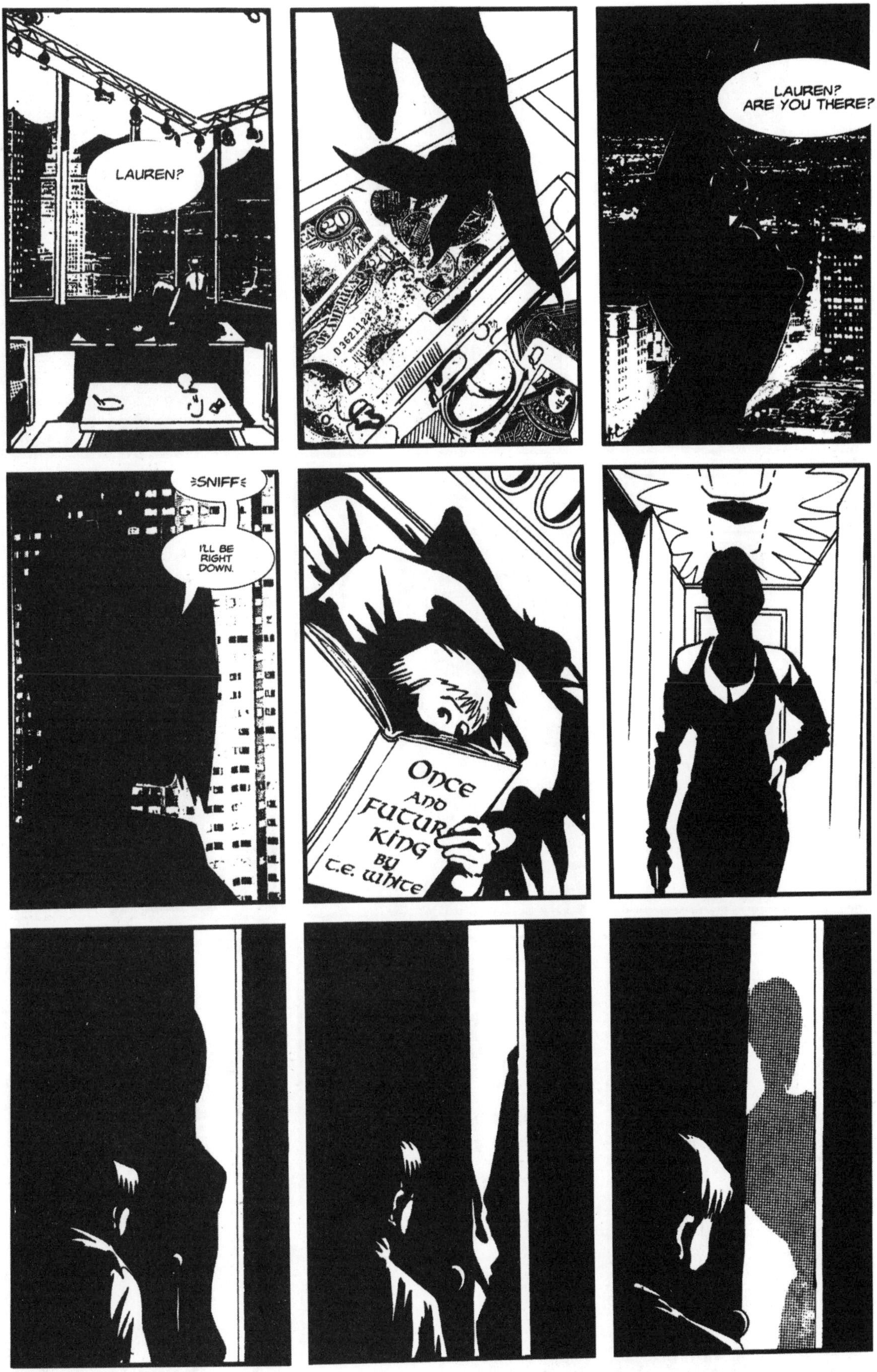
LAUREN?
LAUREN? ARE YOU THERE?
SNIFF
I'LL BE RIGHT DOWN.
ONCE AND FUTUR KING BY T.E. WHITE

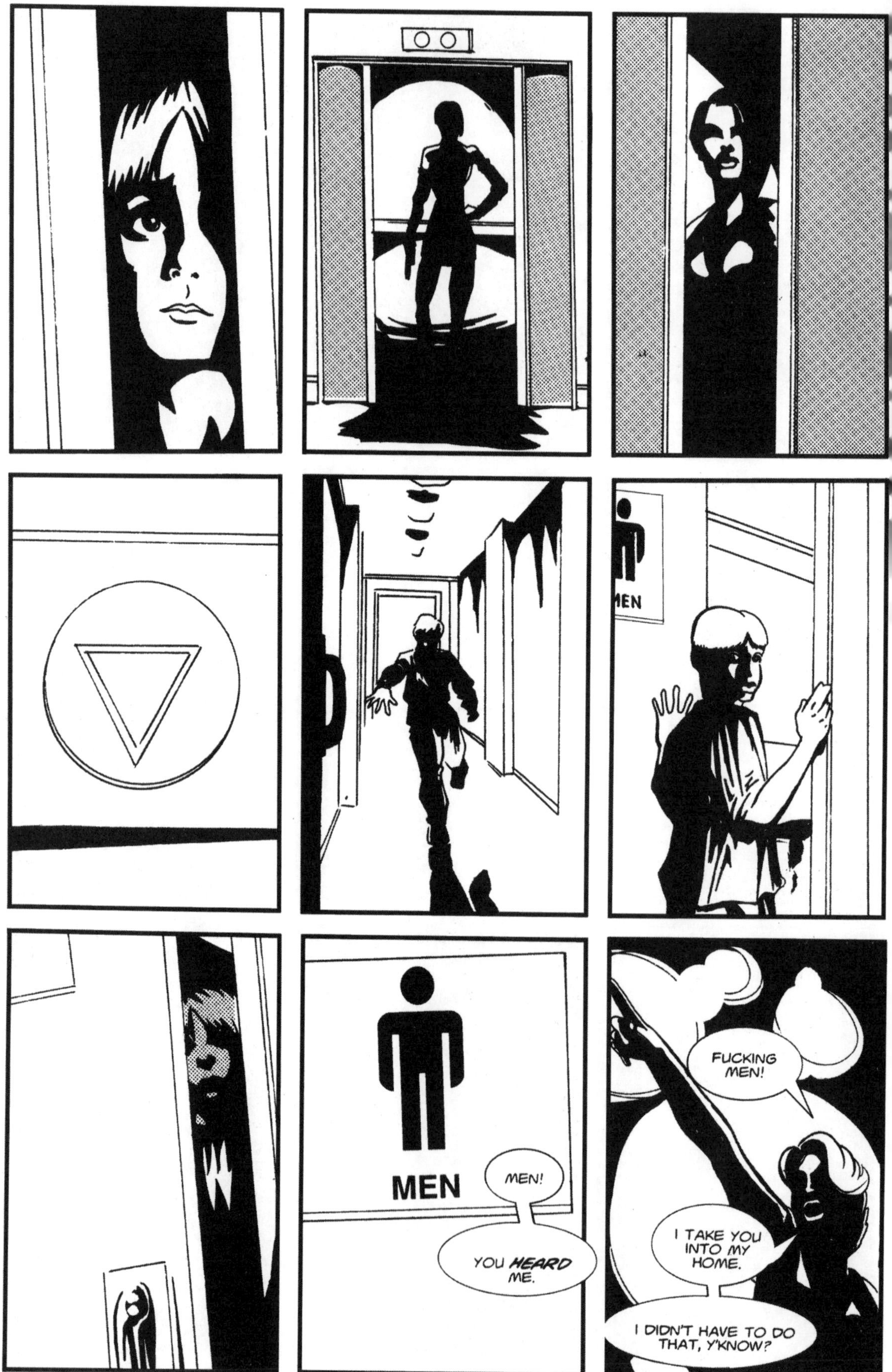
MEN
MEN
MEN!
YOU HEARD ME.
FUCKING MEN!
I TAKE YOU INTO MY HOME.
I DIDN'T HAVE TO DO THAT, Y'KNOW?

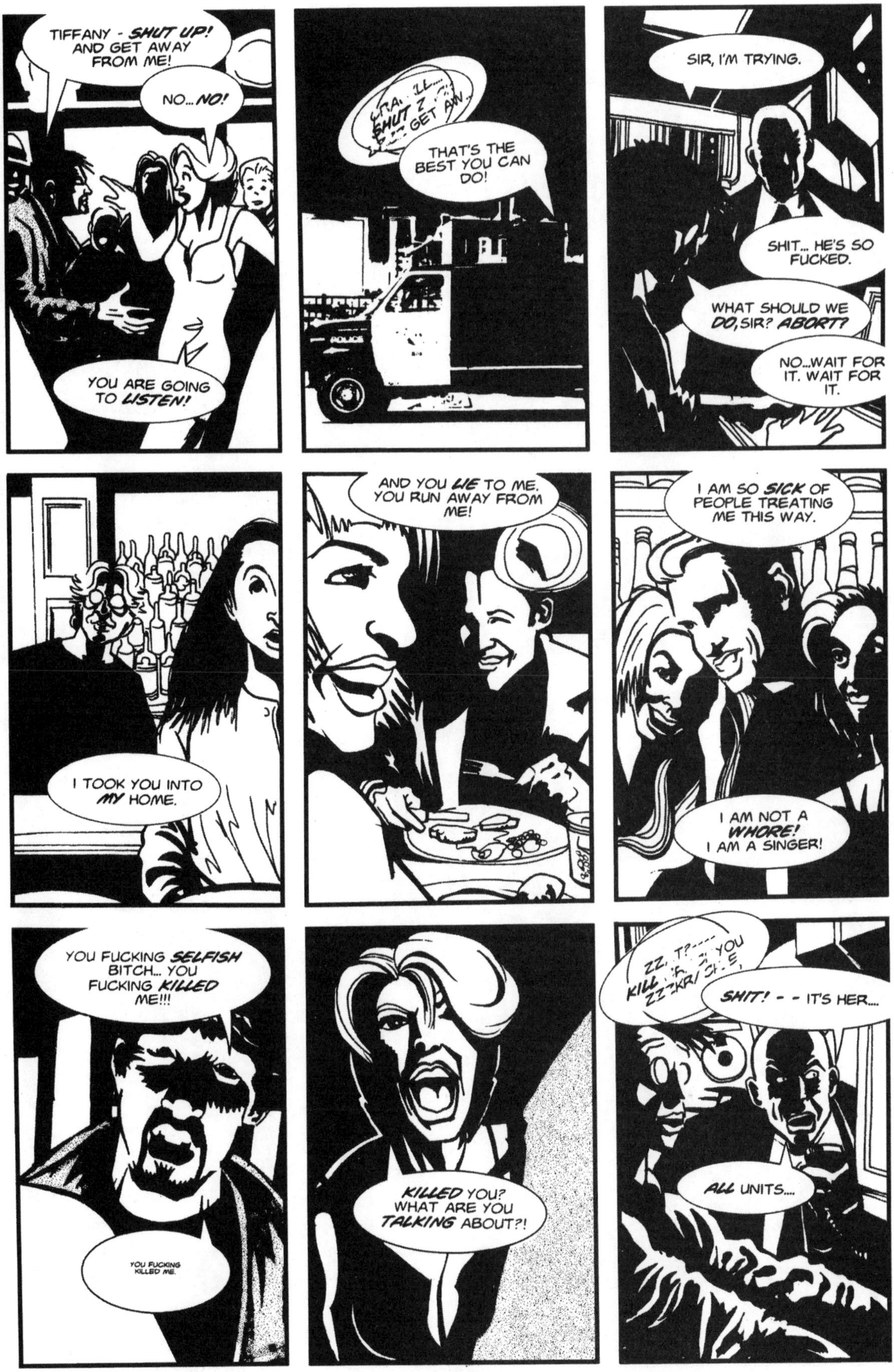
TIFFANY - SHUT UP! AND GET AWAY FROM ME!
NO... NO!
YOU ARE GOING TO LISTEN!
THAT'S THE BEST YOU CAN DO!
SIR, I'M TRYING.
SHIT... HE'S SO FUCKED.
WHAT SHOULD WE DO, SIR? ABORT?
NO...WAIT FOR IT. WAIT FOR IT.
I TOOK YOU INTO MY HOME.
AND YOU LIE TO ME. YOU RUN AWAY FROM ME!
I AM SO SICK OF PEOPLE TREATING ME THIS WAY.
I AM NOT A WHORE! I AM A SINGER!
YOU FUCKING SELFISH BITCH... YOU FUCKING KILLED ME!!!
YOU FUCKING KILLED ME.
KILLED YOU? WHAT ARE YOU TALKING ABOUT?!
SHIT! - - IT'S HER....
ALL UNITS....

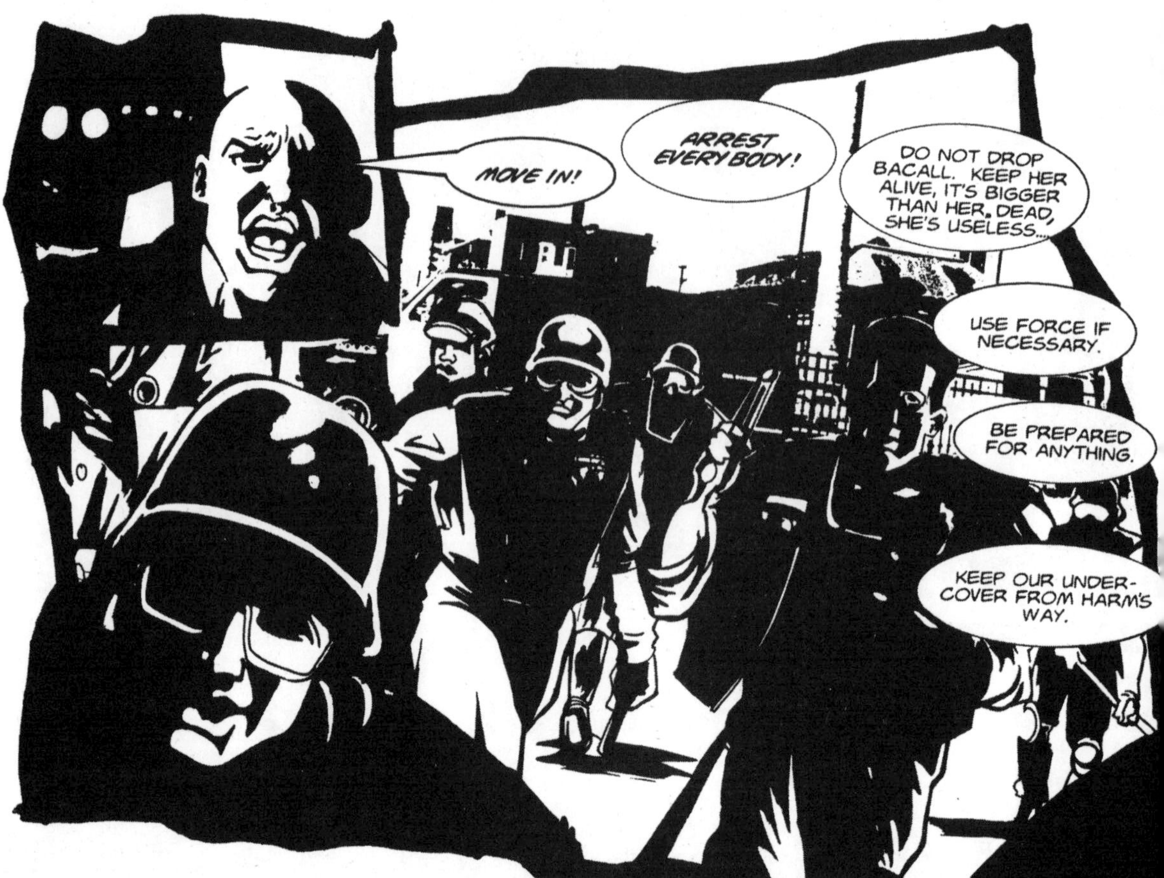
MOVE IN!
ARREST EVERYBODY!
DO NOT DROP BACALL. KEEP HER ALIVE, IT'S BIGGER THAN HER. DEAD, SHE'S USELESS...
USE FORCE IF NECESSARY.
BE PREPARED FOR ANYTHING.
KEEP OUR UNDER-COVER FROM HARM'S WAY.

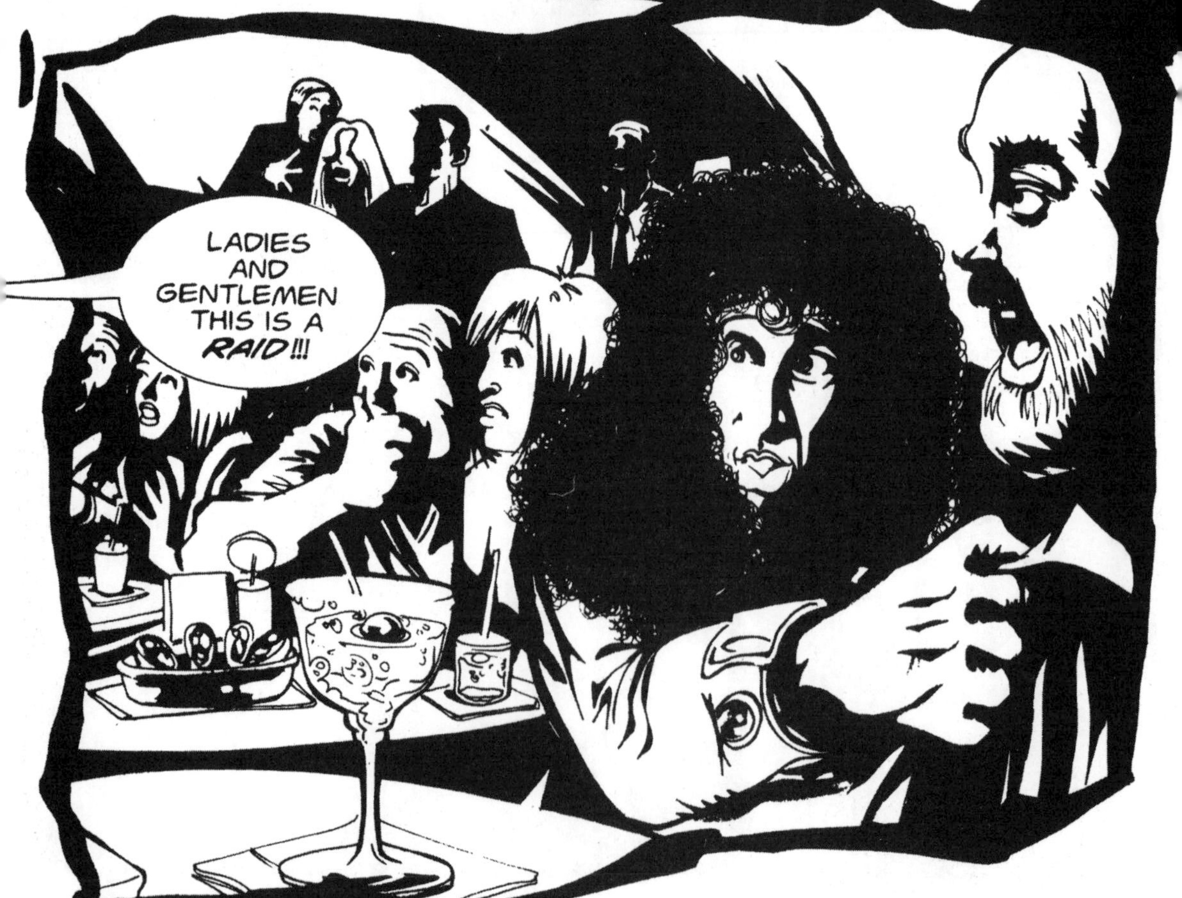
LADIES AND GENTLEMEN THIS IS A RAID!!!

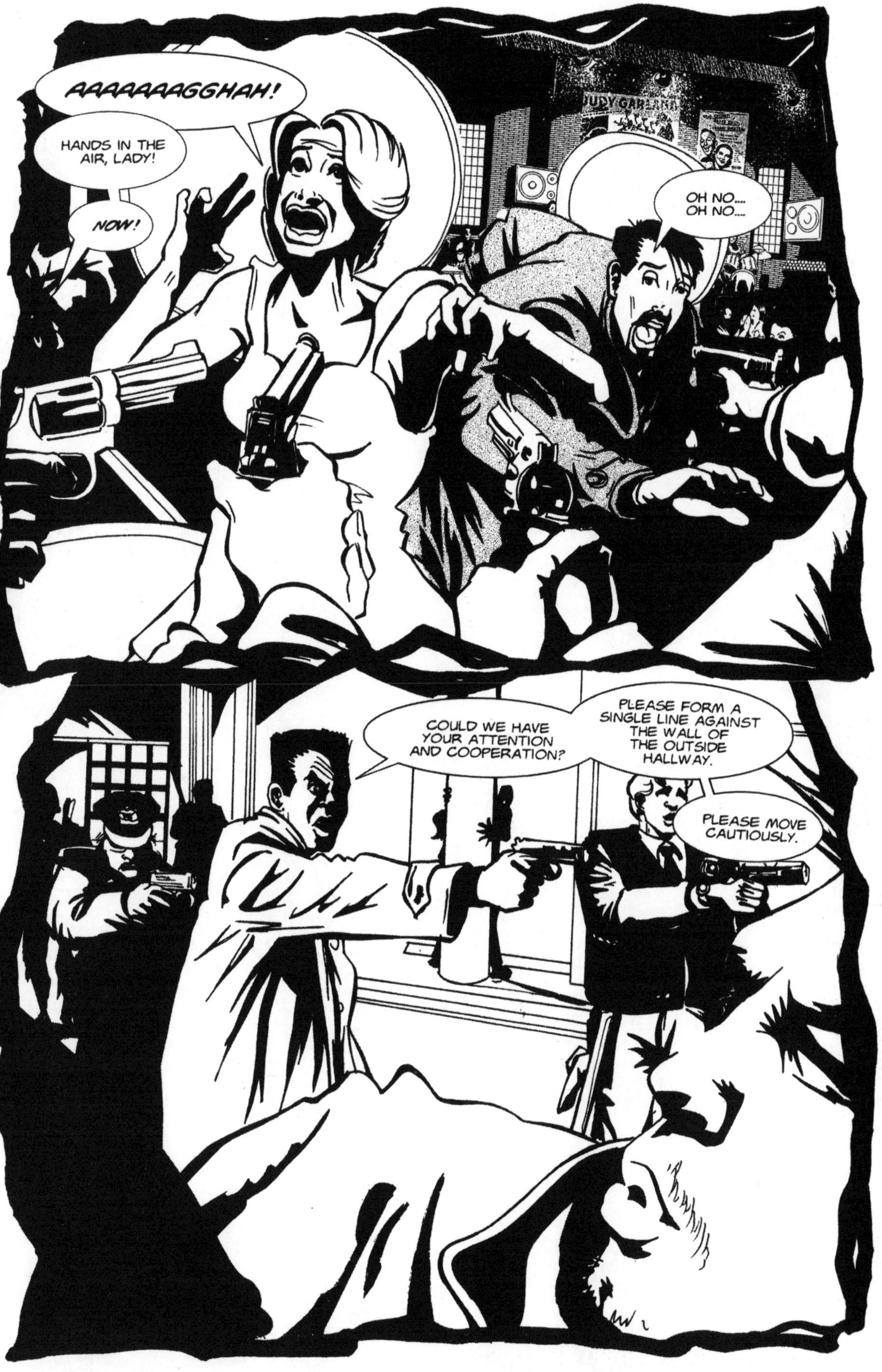
AAAAAAAGGHAH!
HANDS IN THE AIR, LADY!
NOW!
OH NO.... OH NO....
COULD WE HAVE YOUR ATTENTION AND COOPERATION?
PLEASE FORM A SINGLE LINE AGAINST THE WALL OF THE OUTSIDE HALLWAY.
PLEASE MOVE CAUTIOUSLY.

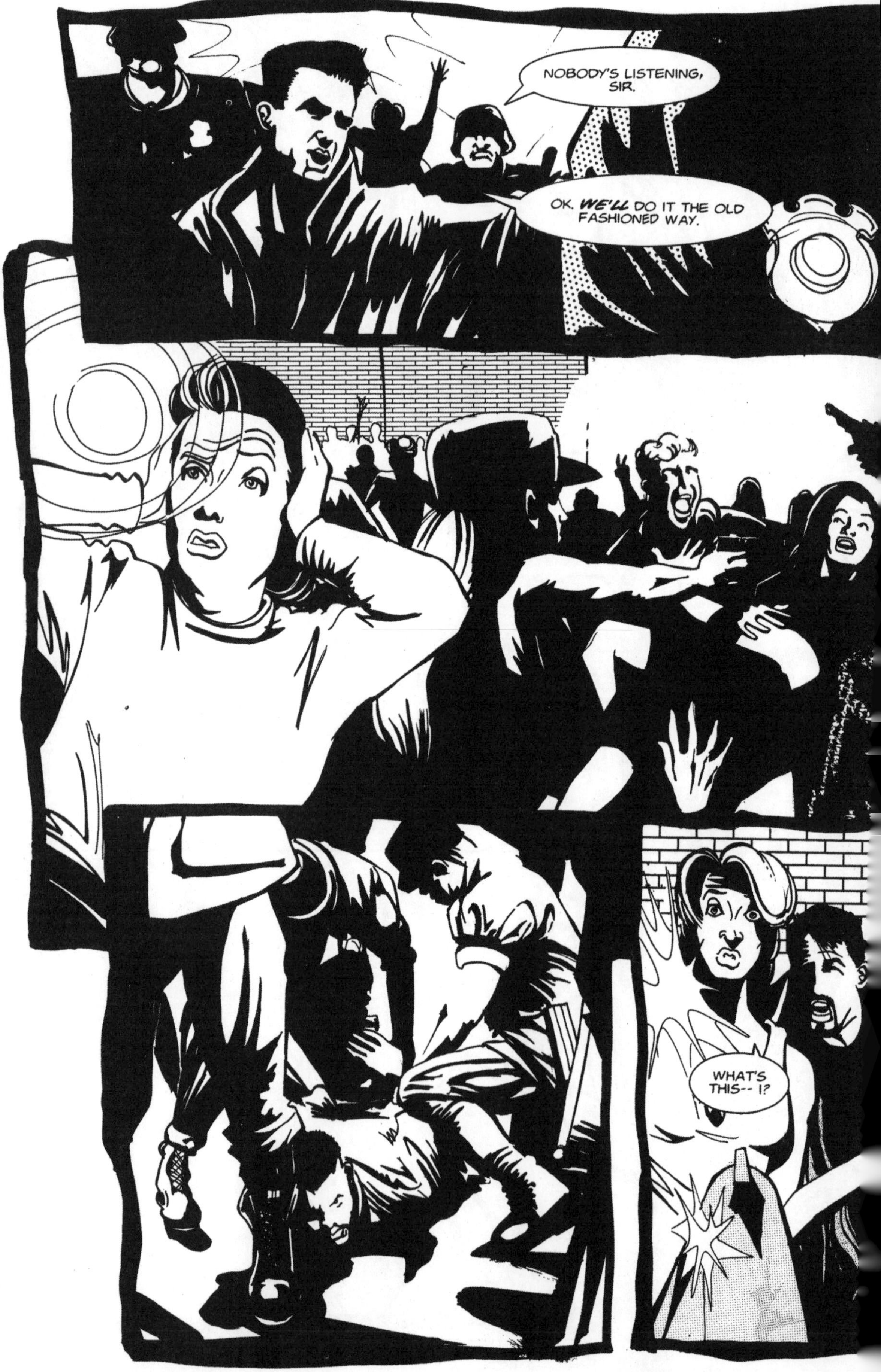
NOBODY'S LISTENING, SIR.
OK. WE'LL DO IT THE OLD FASHIONED WAY.
WHAT'S THIS-- !?

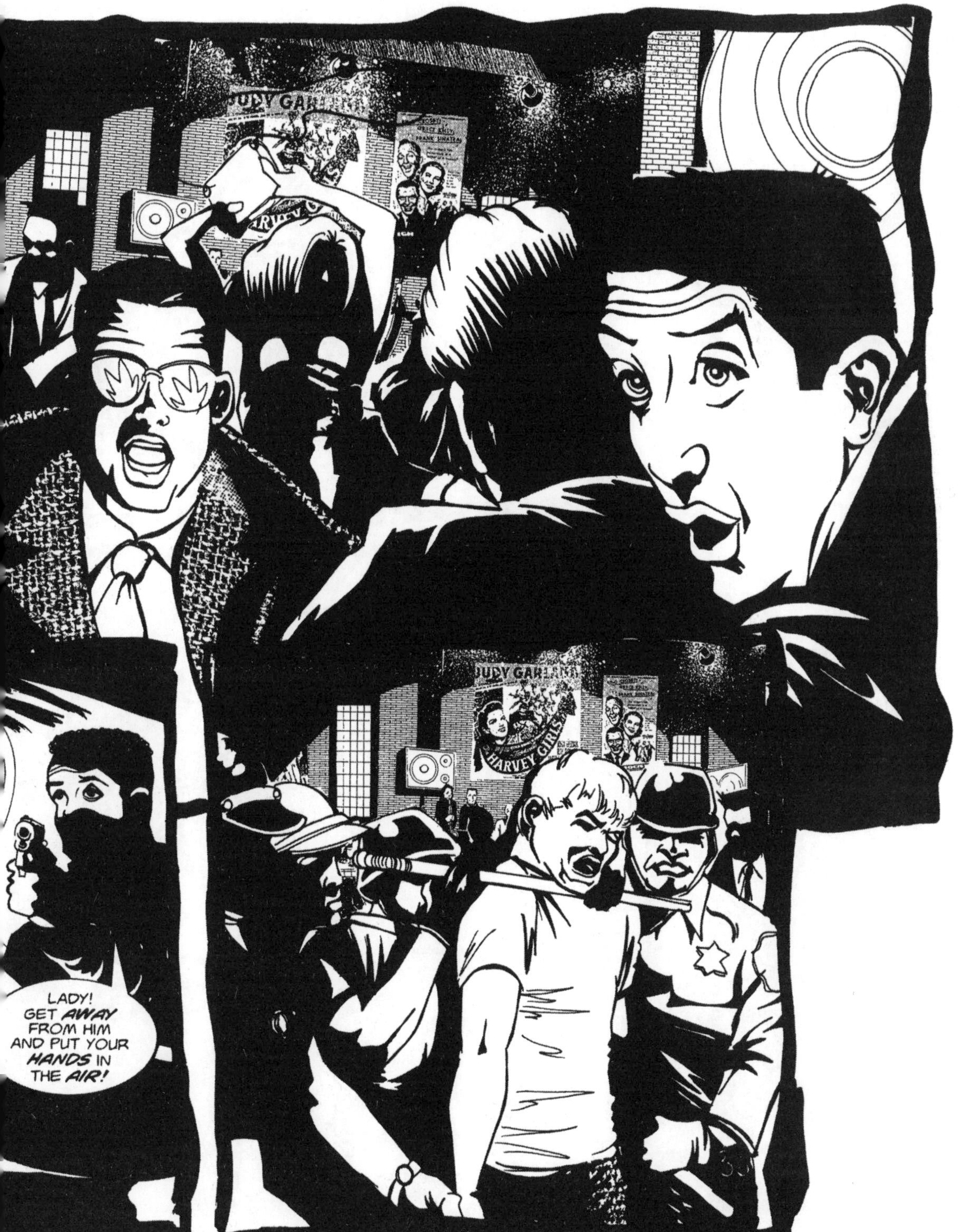
LADY! GET *AWAY* FROM HIM AND PUT YOUR *HANDS* IN THE *AIR!*

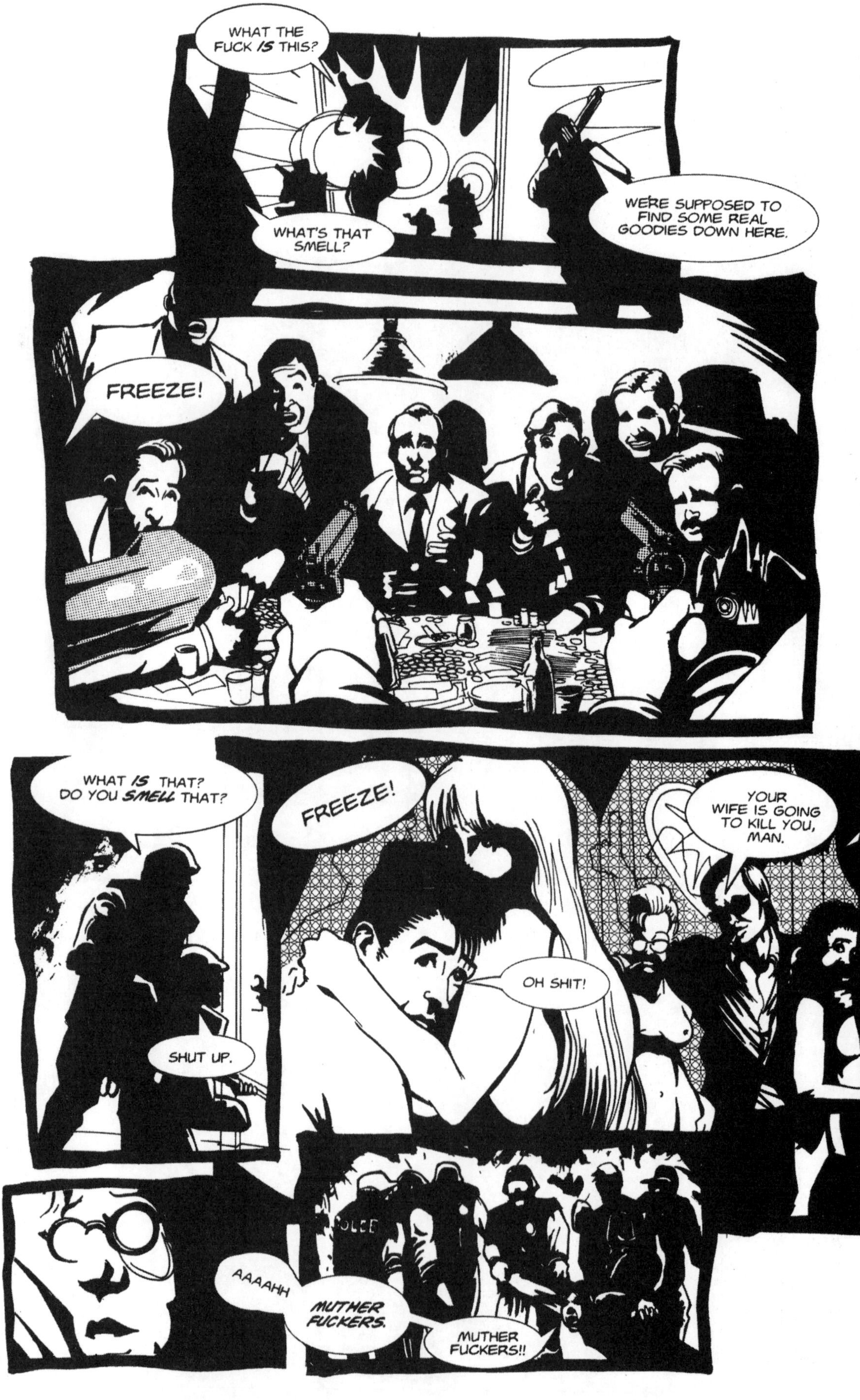

WHAT THE FUCK IS THIS?
WHAT'S THAT SMELL?
WE'RE SUPPOSED TO FIND SOME REAL GOODIES DOWN HERE.
FREEZE!
WHAT IS THAT? DO YOU SMELL THAT?
SHUT UP.
FREEZE!
YOUR WIFE IS GOING TO KILL YOU, MAN.
OH SHIT!
AAAAHH
MUTHER FUCKERS.
MUTHER FUCKERS!!

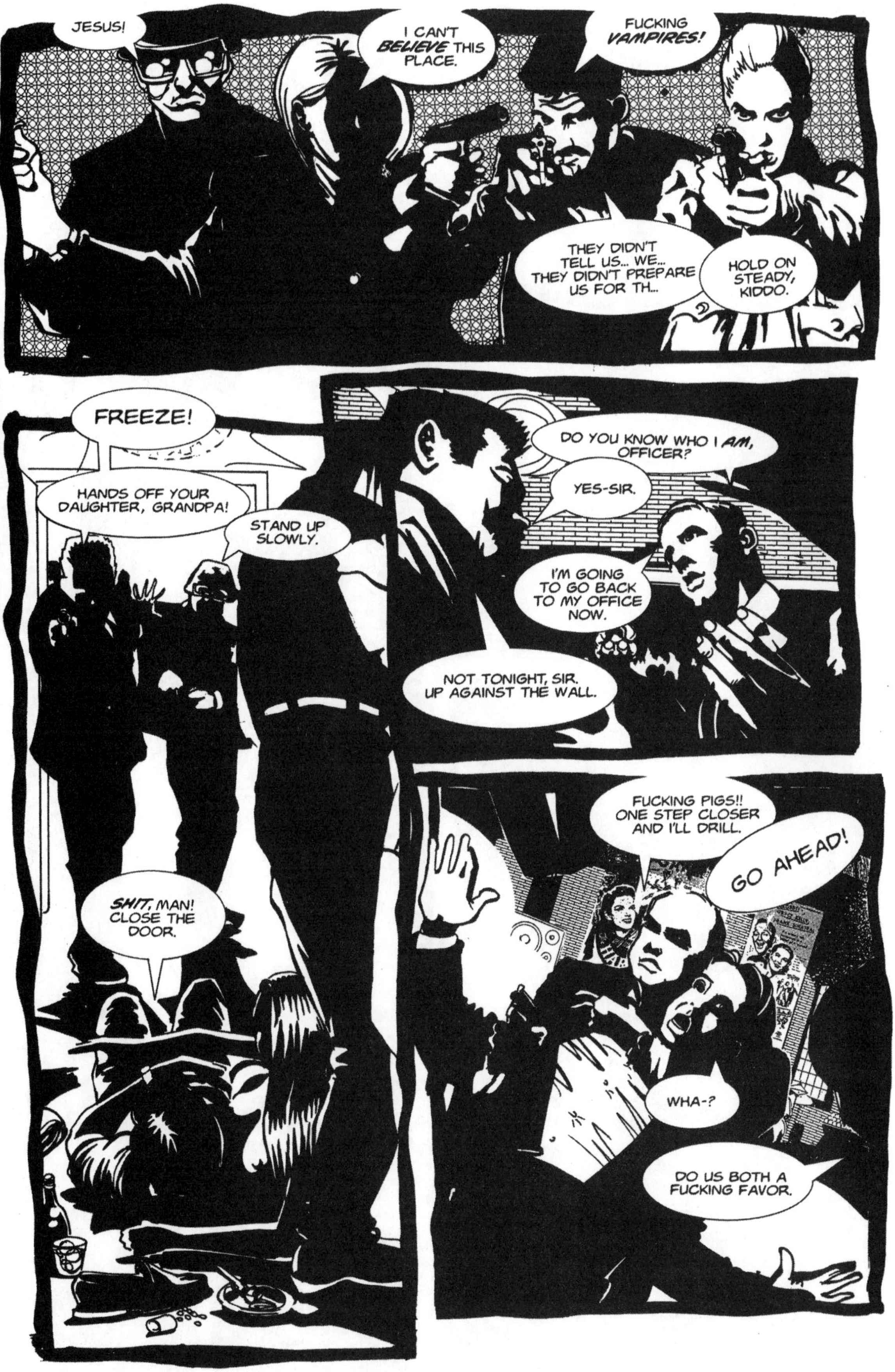
JESUS!
I CAN'T BELIEVE THIS PLACE.
FUCKING VAMPIRES!
THEY DIDN'T TELL US... WE... THEY DIDN'T PREPARE US FOR TH...
HOLD ON STEADY, KIDDO.
FREEZE!
HANDS OFF YOUR DAUGHTER, GRANDPA!
STAND UP SLOWLY.
SHIT, MAN! CLOSE THE DOOR.
DO YOU KNOW WHO I AM, OFFICER?
YES-SIR.
I'M GOING TO GO BACK TO MY OFFICE NOW.
NOT TONIGHT, SIR. UP AGAINST THE WALL.
FUCKING PIGS!! ONE STEP CLOSER AND I'LL DRILL.
GO AHEAD!
WHA-?
DO US BOTH A FUCKING FAVOR.

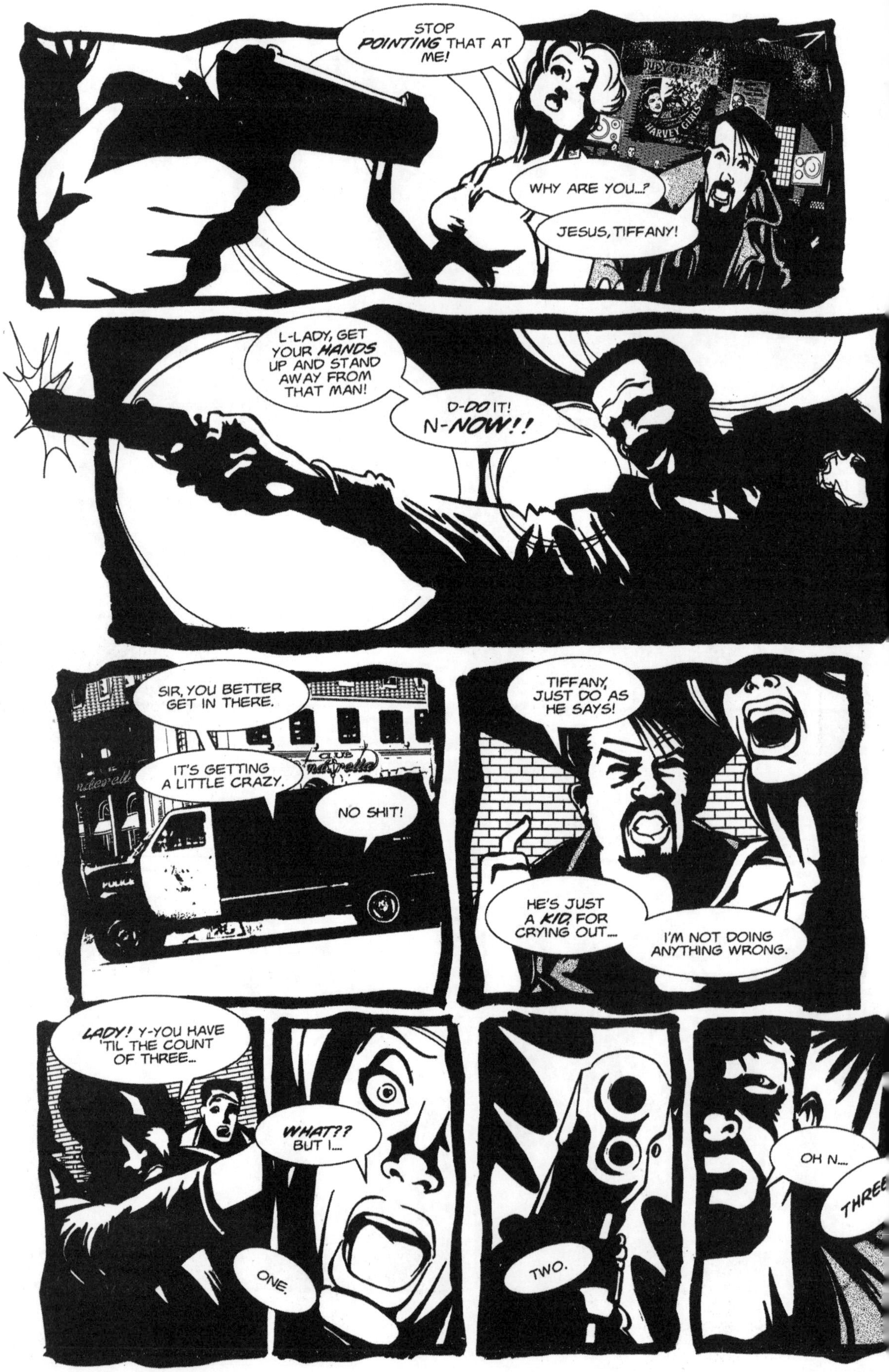
STOP POINTING THAT AT ME!
WHY ARE YOU...?
JESUS, TIFFANY!
L-LADY, GET YOUR HANDS UP AND STAND AWAY FROM THAT MAN!
D-DO IT! N-NOW!!
SIR, YOU BETTER GET IN THERE.
IT'S GETTING A LITTLE CRAZY.
NO SHIT!
TIFFANY, JUST DO AS HE SAYS!
HE'S JUST A KID, FOR CRYING OUT...
I'M NOT DOING ANYTHING WRONG.
LADY! Y-YOU HAVE 'TIL THE COUNT OF THREE...
ONE.
WHAT?? BUT I...
TWO.
OH N...

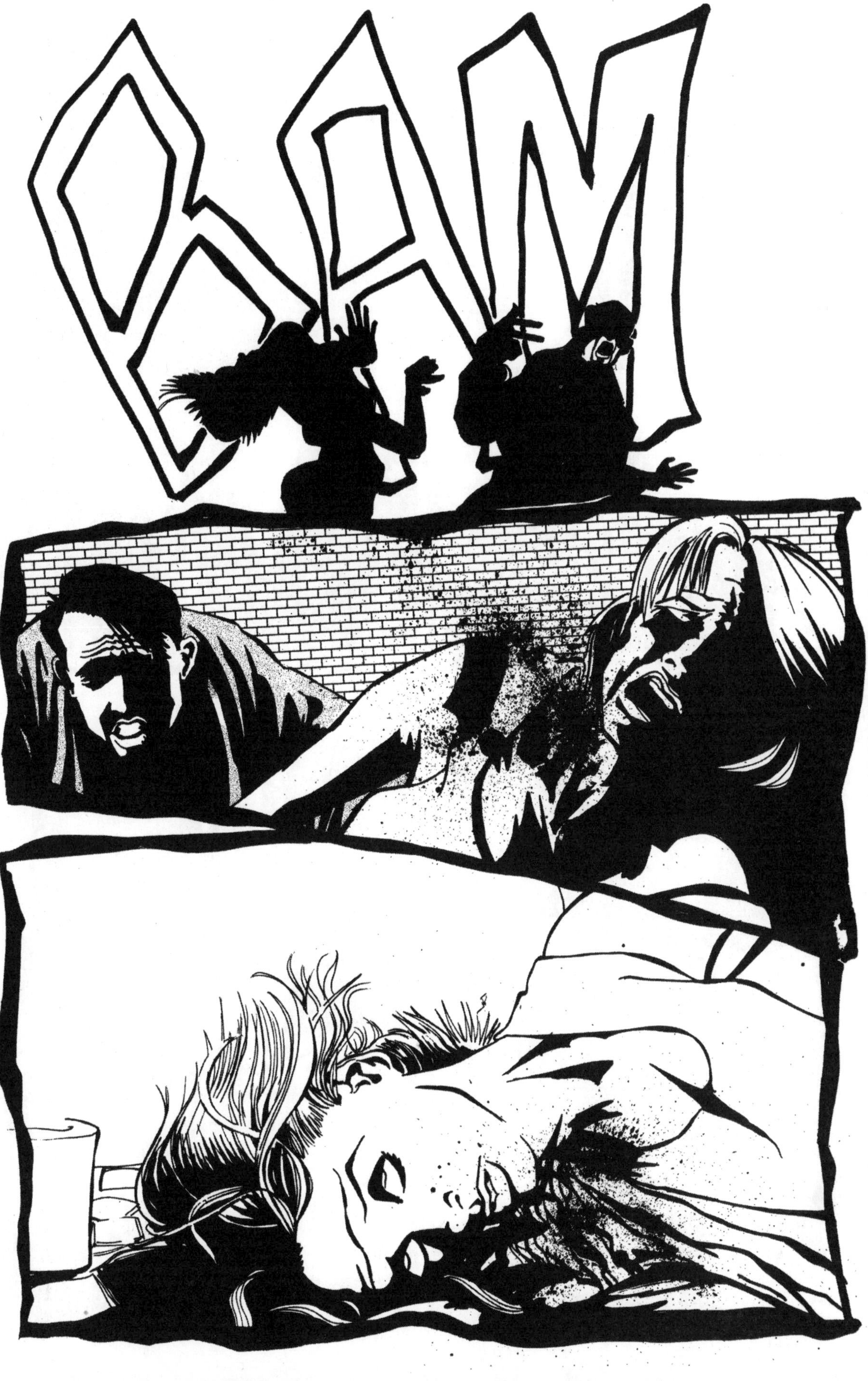
BAM

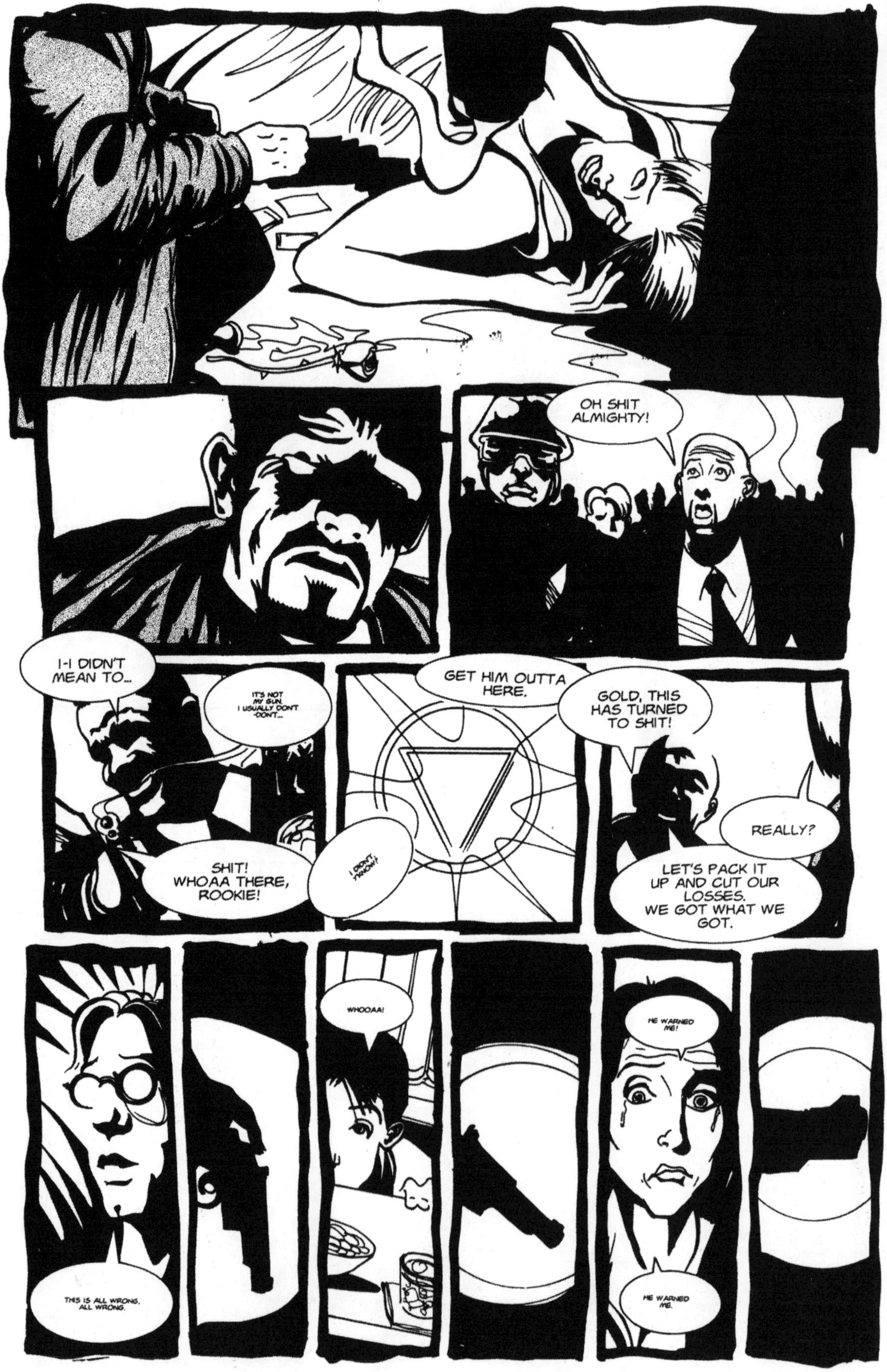
OH SHIT ALMIGHTY!
I-I DIDN'T MEAN TO...
IT'S NOT MY GUN. I USUALLY DON'T -DON'T...
SHIT! WHOAA THERE, ROOKIE!
I DIDN'T, Y'KNOW?
GET HIM OUTTA HERE.
GOLD, THIS HAS TURNED TO SHIT!
REALLY?
LET'S PACK IT UP AND CUT OUR LOSSES. WE GOT WHAT WE GOT.
THIS IS ALL WRONG, ALL WRONG.
WHOOAA!
HE WARNED ME!
HE WARNED ME.

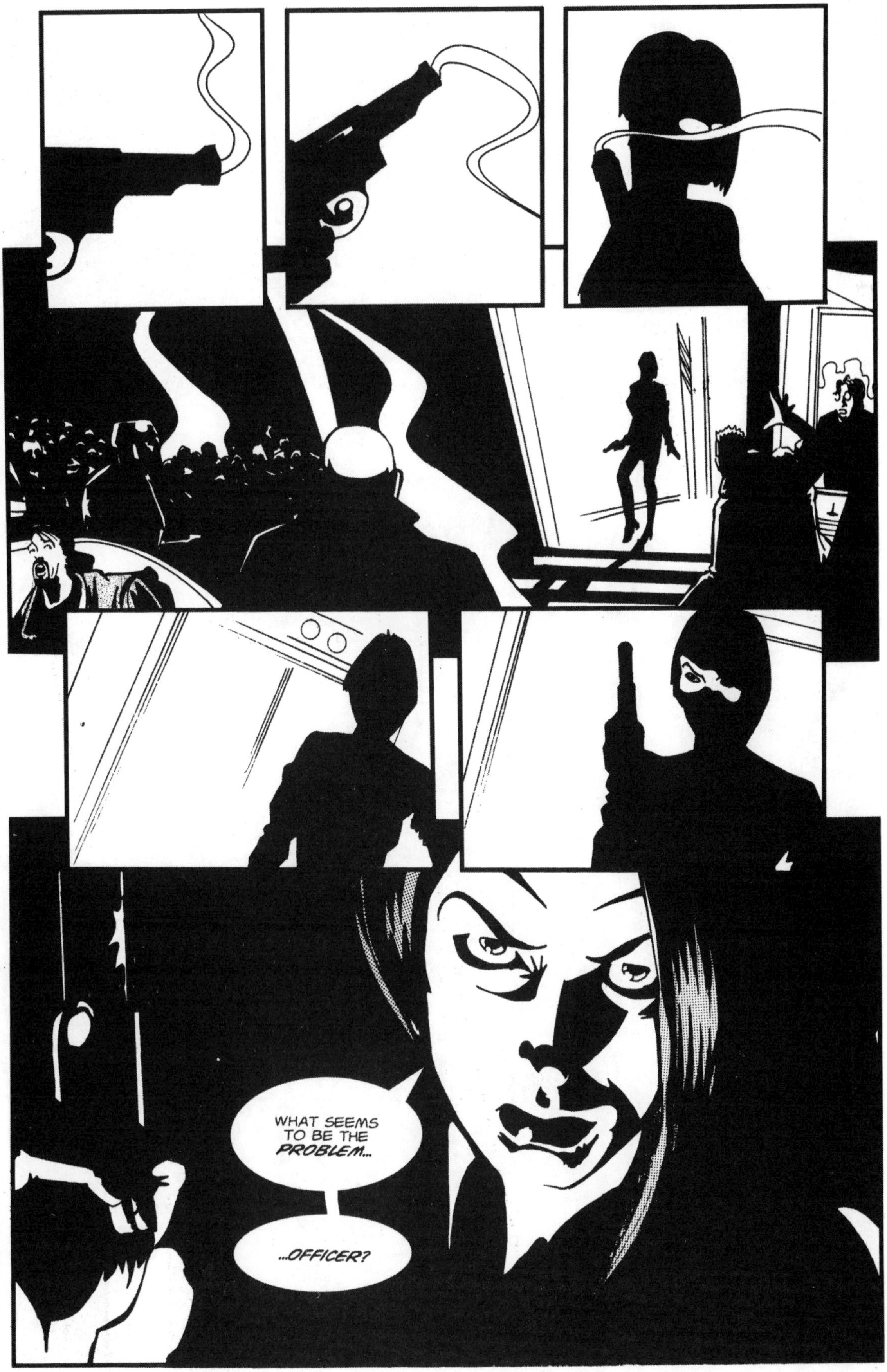
WHAT SEEMS TO BE THE PROBLEM...
...OFFICER?

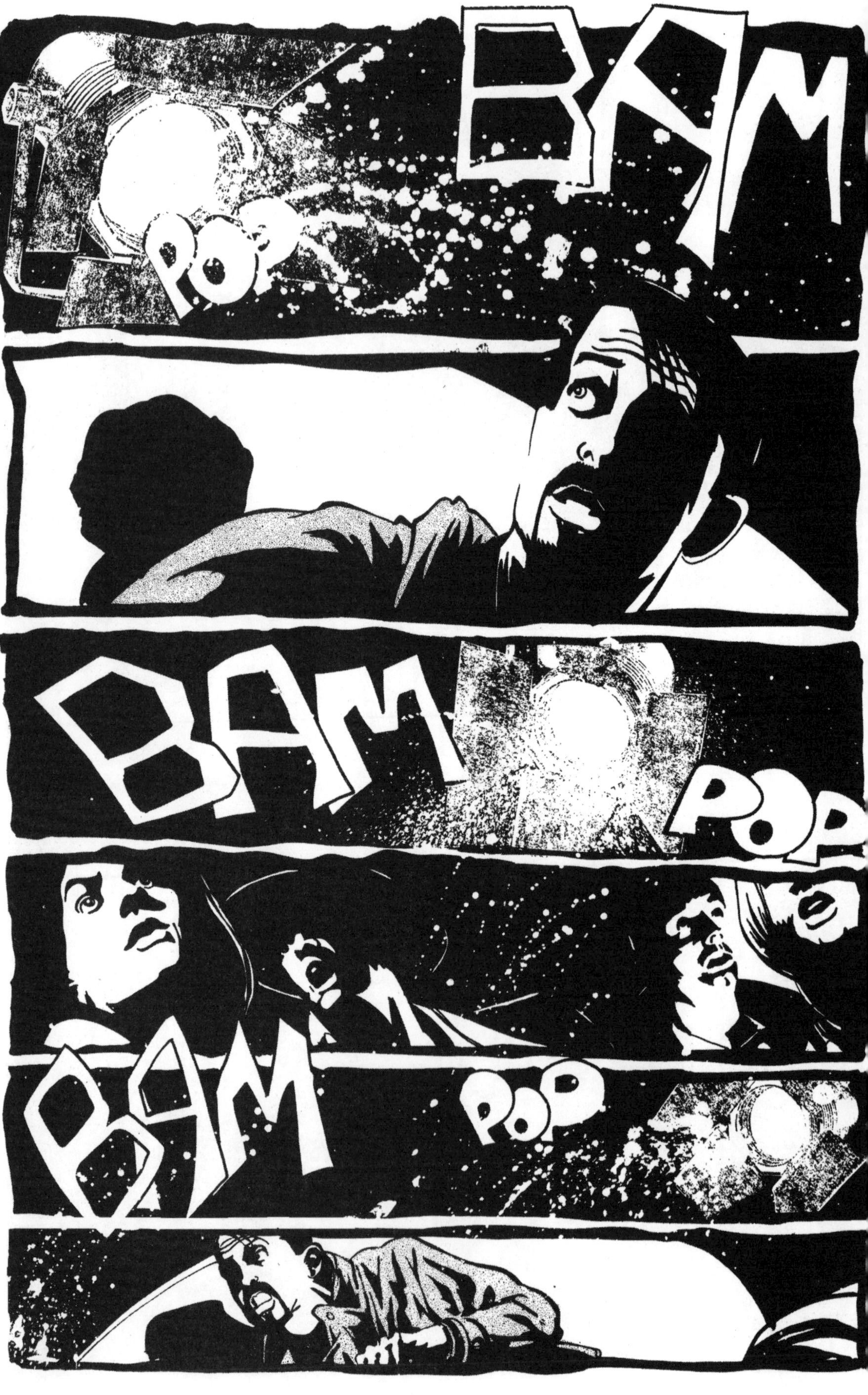
BAM
POP
BAM
POP
BAM
POP

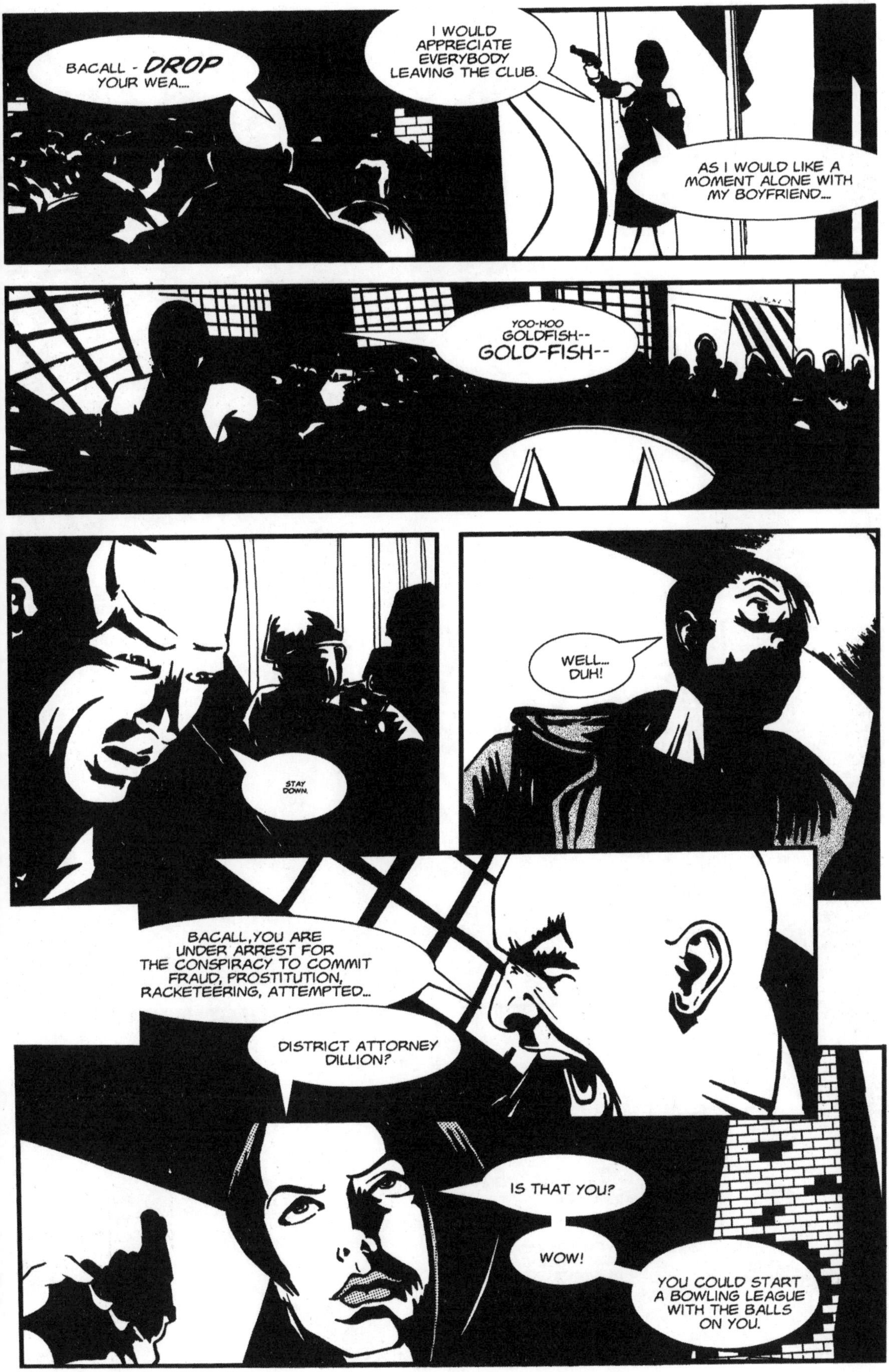
BACALL - DROP YOUR WEA....
I WOULD APPRECIATE EVERYBODY LEAVING THE CLUB.
AS I WOULD LIKE A MOMENT ALONE WITH MY BOYFRIEND...
YOO-HOO GOLDFISH-- GOLD-FISH--
STAY DOWN.
WELL... DUH!
BACALL, YOU ARE UNDER ARREST FOR THE CONSPIRACY TO COMMIT FRAUD, PROSTITUTION, RACKETEERING, ATTEMPTED...
DISTRICT ATTORNEY DILLION?
IS THAT YOU?
WOW!
YOU COULD START A BOWLING LEAGUE WITH THE BALLS ON YOU.

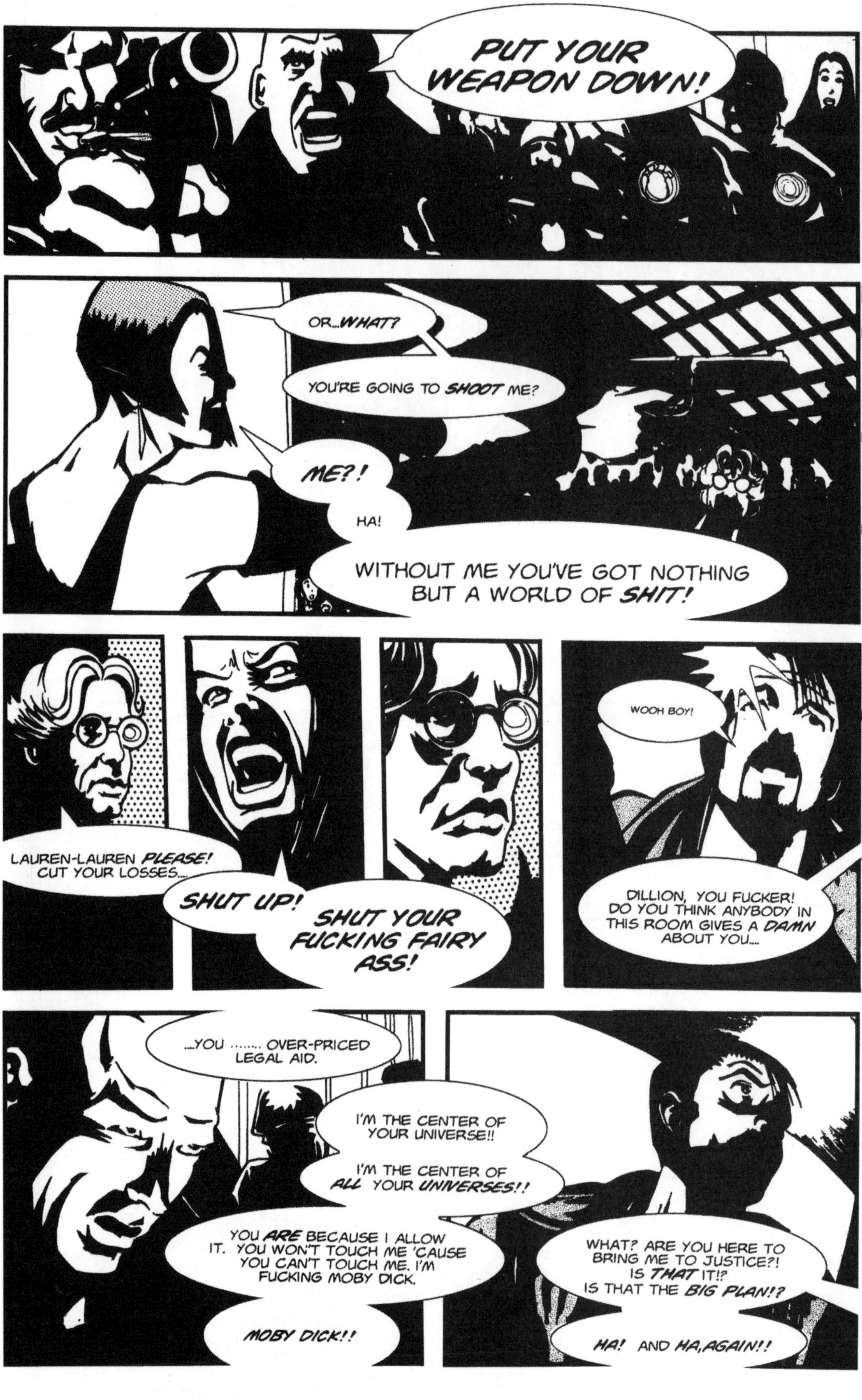
PUT YOUR WEAPON DOWN!
OR...WHAT?
YOU'RE GOING TO SHOOT ME?
ME?!
HA!
WITHOUT ME YOU'VE GOT NOTHING BUT A WORLD OF SHIT!
LAUREN-LAUREN PLEASE! CUT YOUR LOSSES....
SHUT UP!
SHUT YOUR FUCKING FAIRY ASS!
WOOH BOY!
DILLION, YOU FUCKER! DO YOU THINK ANYBODY IN THIS ROOM GIVES A DAMN ABOUT YOU....
...YOU .... OVER-PRICED LEGAL AID.
I'M THE CENTER OF YOUR UNIVERSE!!
I'M THE CENTER OF ALL YOUR UNIVERSES!!
YOU ARE BECAUSE I ALLOW IT. YOU WON'T TOUCH ME 'CAUSE YOU CAN'T TOUCH ME. I'M FUCKING MOBY DICK.
MOBY DICK!!
WHAT? ARE YOU HERE TO BRING ME TO JUSTICE?! IS THAT IT!? IS THAT THE BIG PLAN!?
HA! AND HA,AGAIN!!

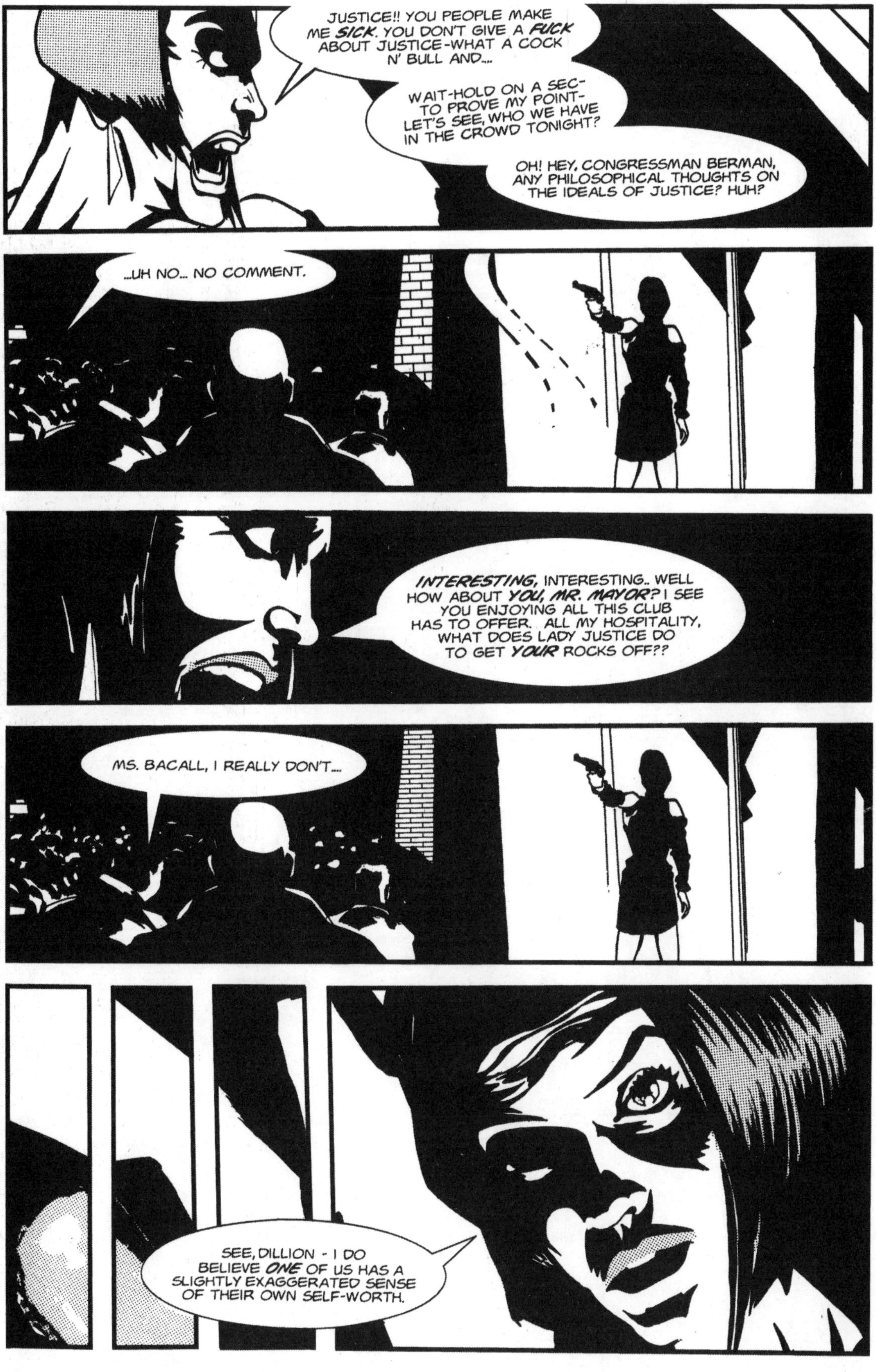
JUSTICE!! YOU PEOPLE MAKE ME SICK. YOU DON'T GIVE A FUCK ABOUT JUSTICE-WHAT A COCK N' BULL AND...
WAIT-HOLD ON A SEC-TO PROVE MY POINT-LET'S SEE, WHO WE HAVE IN THE CROWD TONIGHT?
OH! HEY, CONGRESSMAN BERMAN, ANY PHILOSOPHICAL THOUGHTS ON THE IDEALS OF JUSTICE? HUH?
...UH NO... NO COMMENT.
INTERESTING, INTERESTING.. WELL HOW ABOUT YOU, MR. MAYOR? I SEE YOU ENJOYING ALL THIS CLUB HAS TO OFFER. ALL MY HOSPITALITY, WHAT DOES LADY JUSTICE DO TO GET YOUR ROCKS OFF??
MS. BACALL, I REALLY DON'T....
SEE, DILLION - I DO BELIEVE ONE OF US HAS A SLIGHTLY EXAGGERATED SENSE OF THEIR OWN SELF-WORTH.

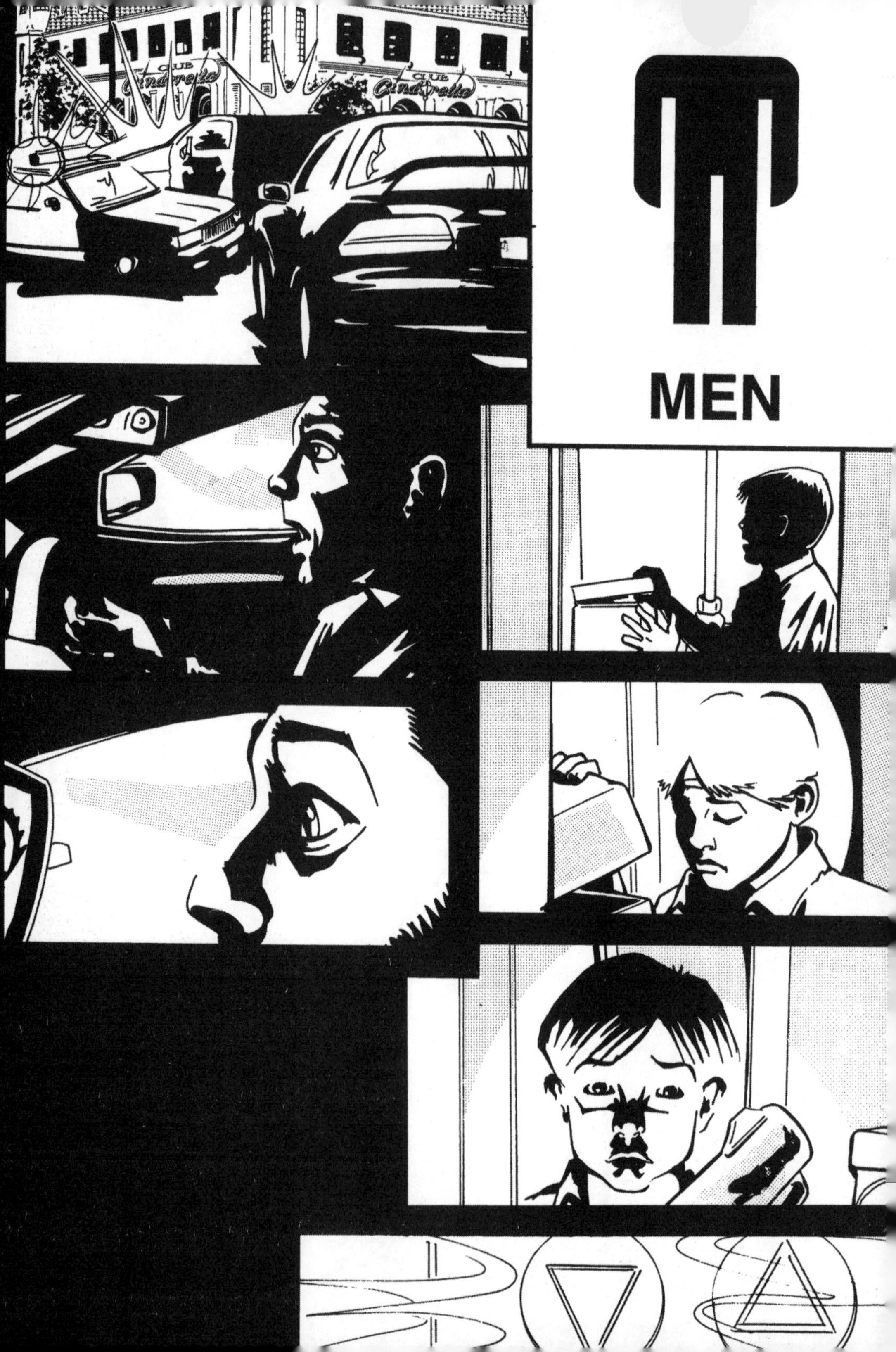
CLUB Cinderella
MEN

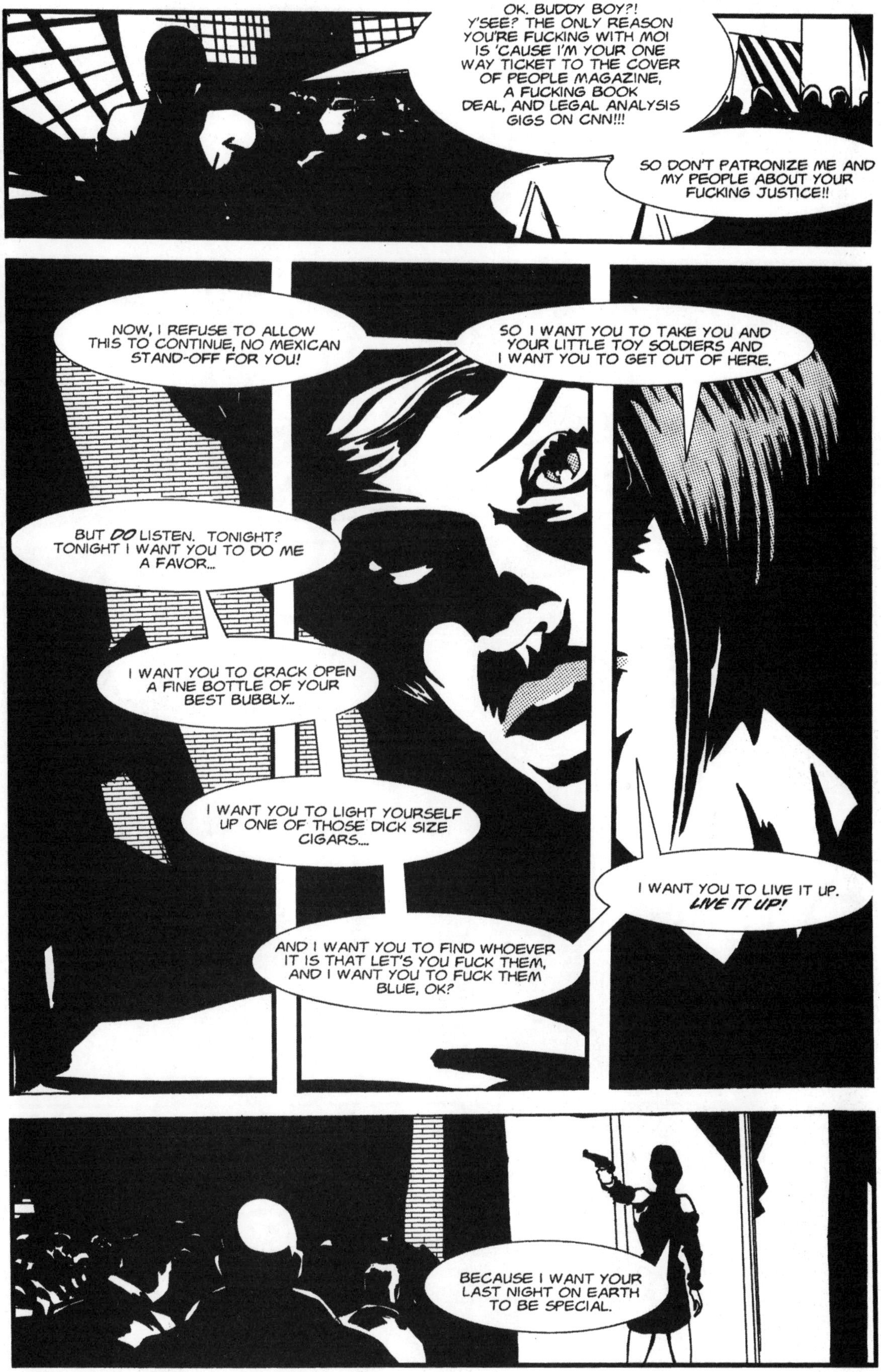
OK. BUDDY BOY?! Y'SEE? THE ONLY REASON YOU'RE FUCKING WITH MOI IS 'CAUSE I'M YOUR ONE WAY TICKET TO THE COVER OF PEOPLE MAGAZINE, A FUCKING BOOK DEAL, AND LEGAL ANALYSIS GIGS ON CNN!!!
SO DON'T PATRONIZE ME AND MY PEOPLE ABOUT YOUR FUCKING JUSTICE!!
NOW, I REFUSE TO ALLOW THIS TO CONTINUE, NO MEXICAN STAND-OFF FOR YOU!
SO I WANT YOU TO TAKE YOU AND YOUR LITTLE TOY SOLDIERS AND I WANT YOU TO GET OUT OF HERE.
BUT *DO* LISTEN. TONIGHT? TONIGHT I WANT YOU TO DO ME A FAVOR...
I WANT YOU TO CRACK OPEN A FINE BOTTLE OF YOUR BEST BUBBLY...
I WANT YOU TO LIGHT YOURSELF UP ONE OF THOSE DICK SIZE CIGARS....
I WANT YOU TO LIVE IT UP. *LIVE IT UP!*
AND I WANT YOU TO FIND WHOEVER IT IS THAT LET'S YOU FUCK THEM, AND I WANT YOU TO FUCK THEM BLUE, OK?
BECAUSE I WANT YOUR LAST NIGHT ON EARTH TO BE SPECIAL.

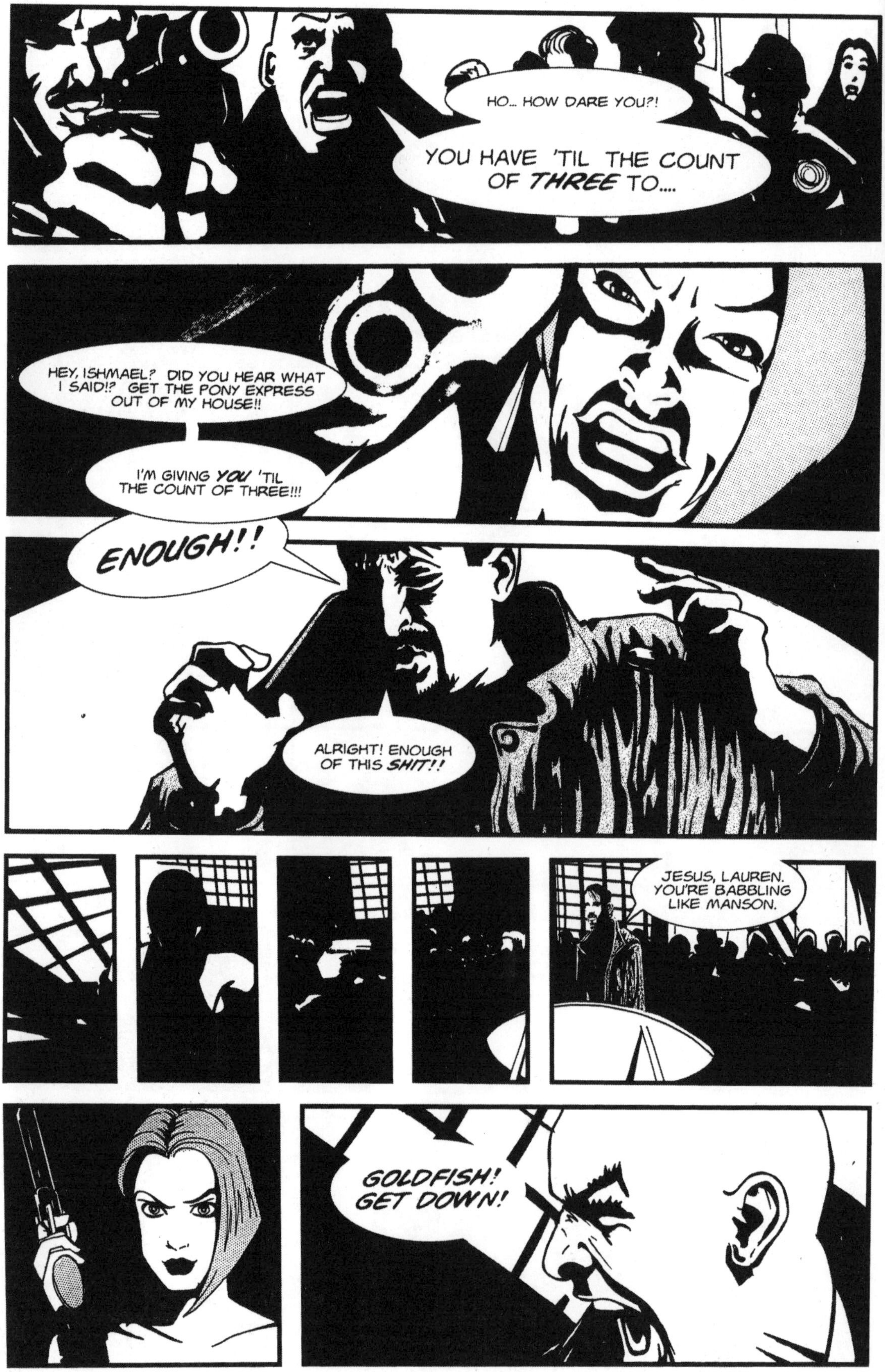
HO... HOW DARE YOU?!
YOU HAVE 'TIL THE COUNT OF *THREE* TO....
HEY, ISHMAEL? DID YOU HEAR WHAT I SAID!? GET THE PONY EXPRESS OUT OF MY HOUSE!!
I'M GIVING *YOU* 'TIL THE COUNT OF THREE!!!
ENOUGH!!
ALRIGHT! ENOUGH OF THIS *SHIT!!*
JESUS, LAUREN. YOU'RE BABBLING LIKE MANSON.
GOLDFISH! GET DOWN!

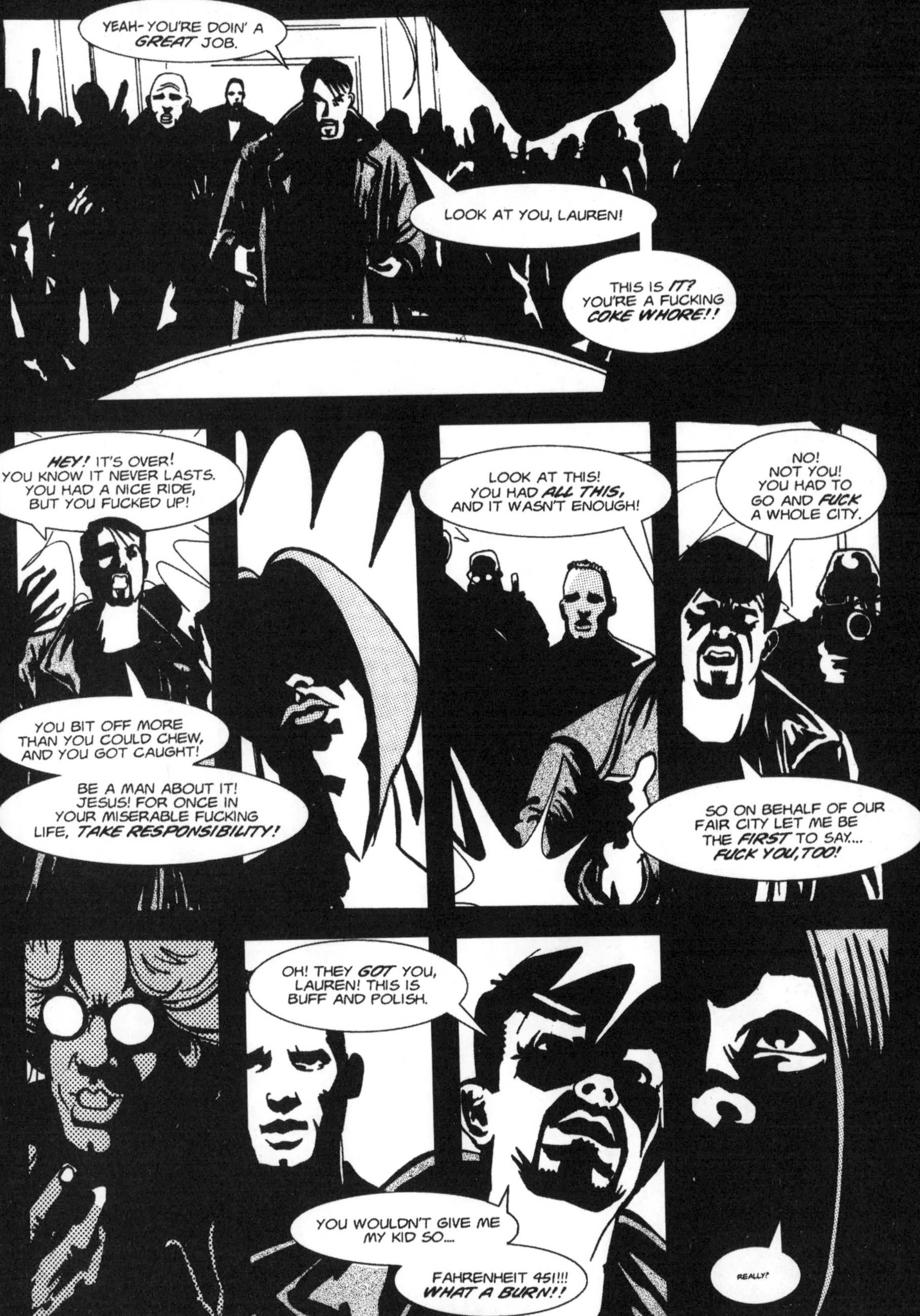

YEAH- YOU'RE DOIN' A GREAT JOB.
LOOK AT YOU, LAUREN!
THIS IS IT? YOU'RE A FUCKING COKE WHORE!!
HEY! IT'S OVER! YOU KNOW IT NEVER LASTS. YOU HAD A NICE RIDE, BUT YOU FUCKED UP!
YOU BIT OFF MORE THAN YOU COULD CHEW, AND YOU GOT CAUGHT!
BE A MAN ABOUT IT! JESUS! FOR ONCE IN YOUR MISERABLE FUCKING LIFE, TAKE RESPONSIBILITY!
LOOK AT THIS! YOU HAD ALL THIS, AND IT WASN'T ENOUGH!
NO! NOT YOU! YOU HAD TO GO AND FUCK A WHOLE CITY.
SO ON BEHALF OF OUR FAIR CITY LET ME BE THE FIRST TO SAY... FUCK YOU, TOO!
OH! THEY GOT YOU, LAUREN! THIS IS BUFF AND POLISH.
YOU WOULDN'T GIVE ME MY KID SO....
FAHRENHEIT 451!!! WHAT A BURN!!
REALLY?

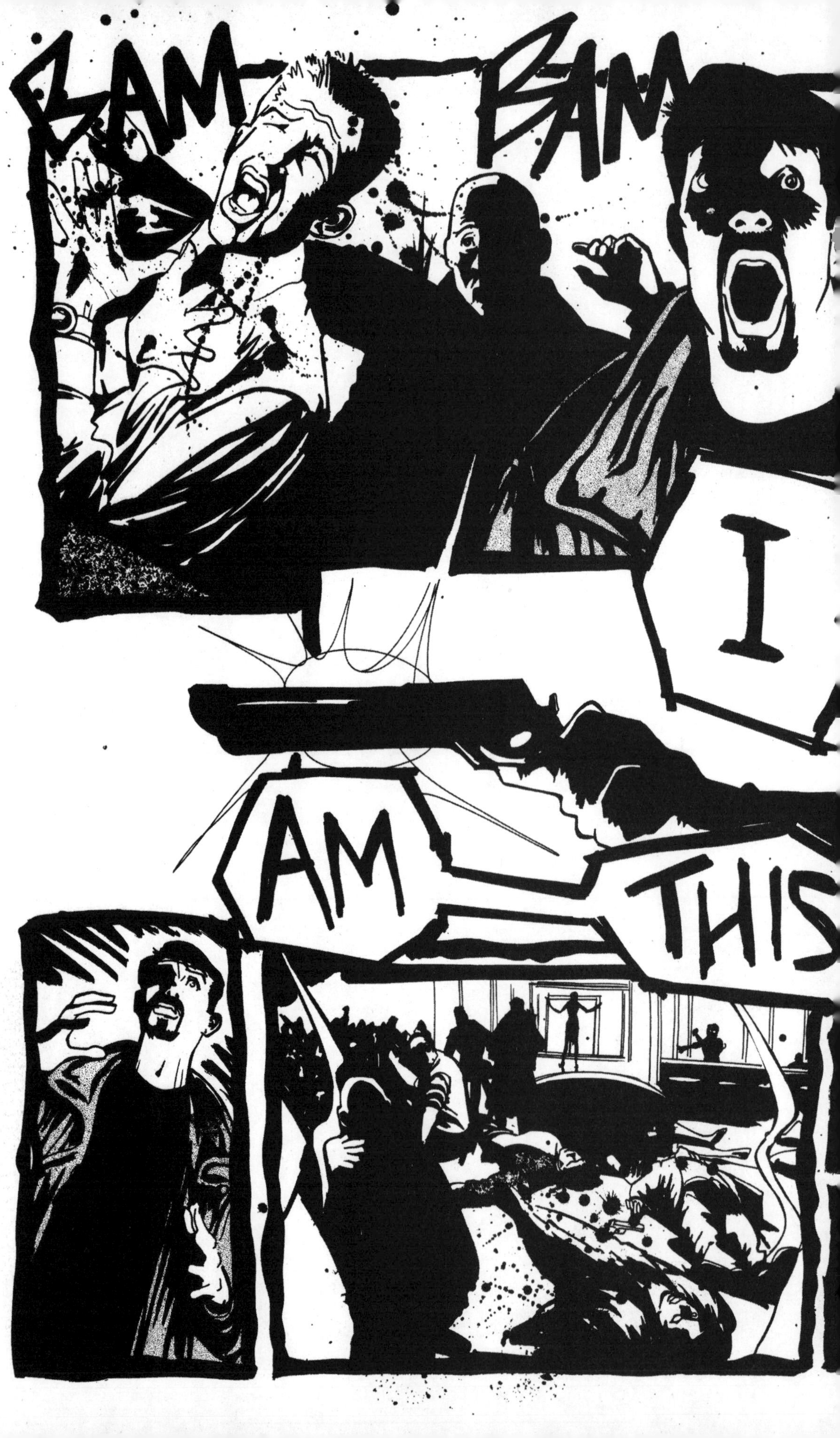
BAM
BAM
I
AM
THIS

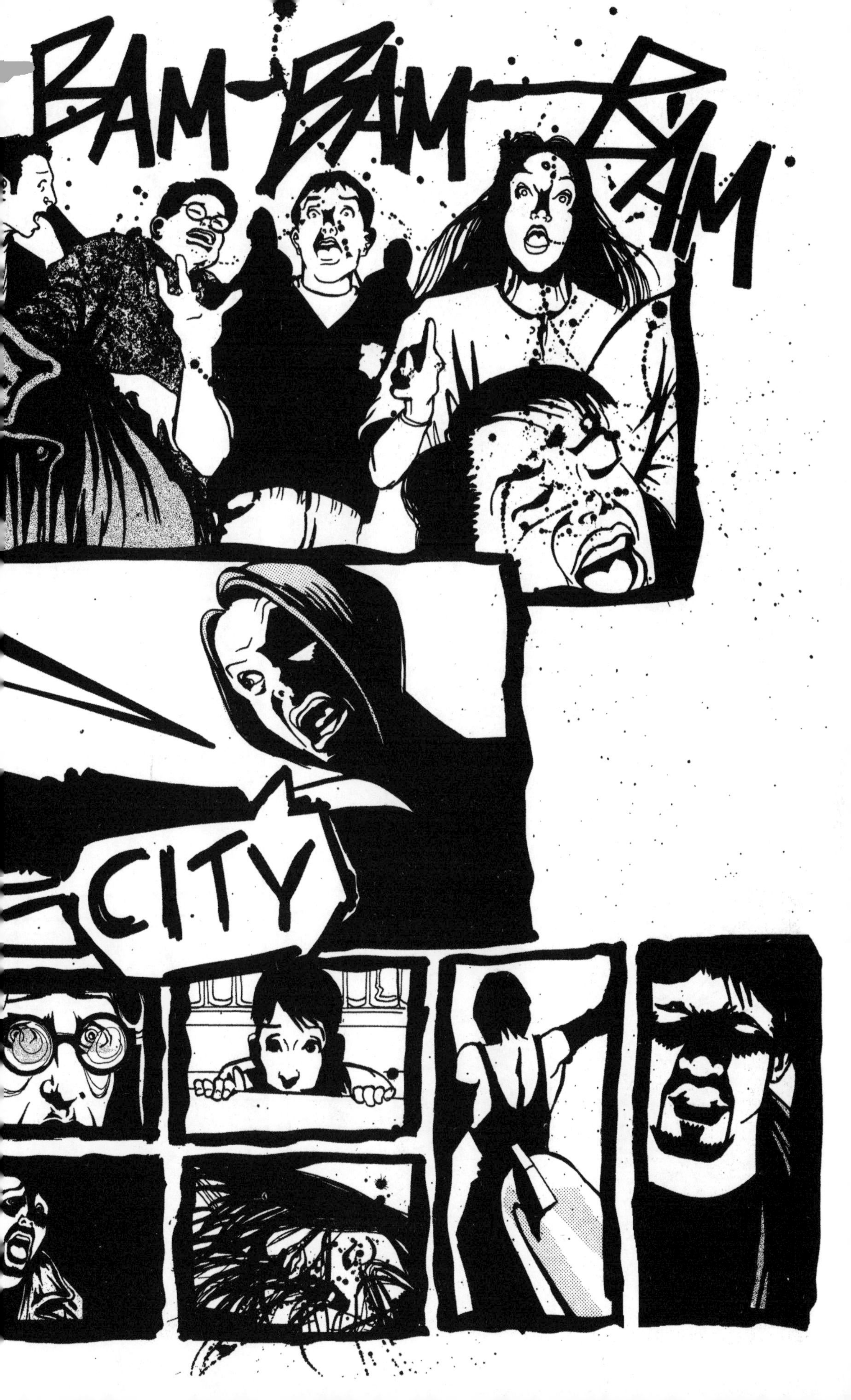
BAM BAM BAM
CITY

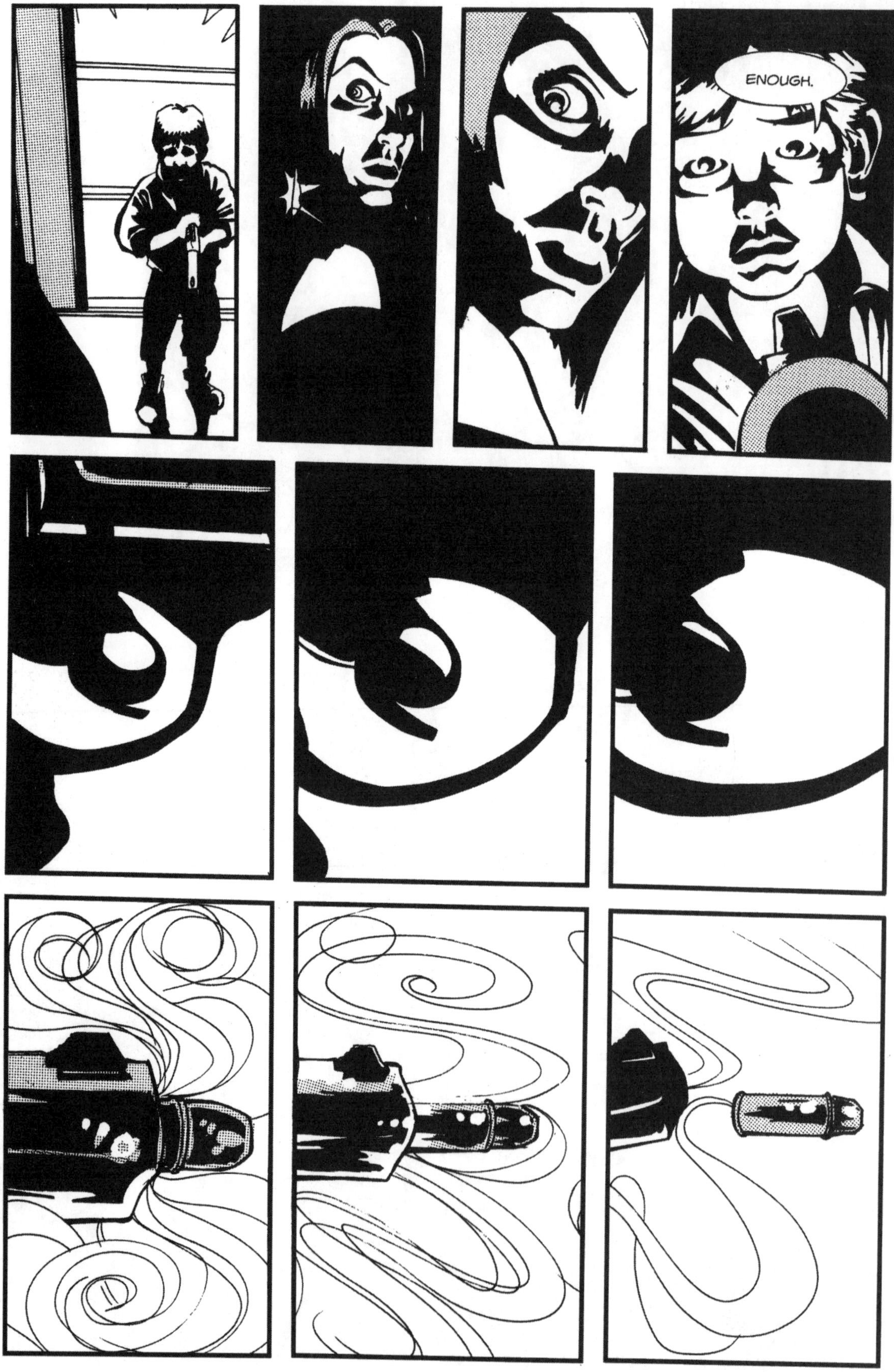
ENOUGH.

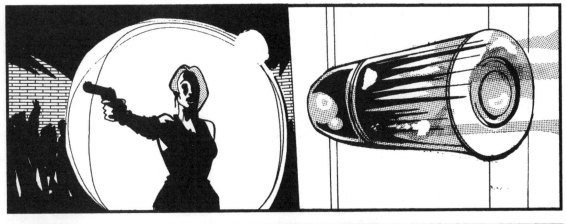

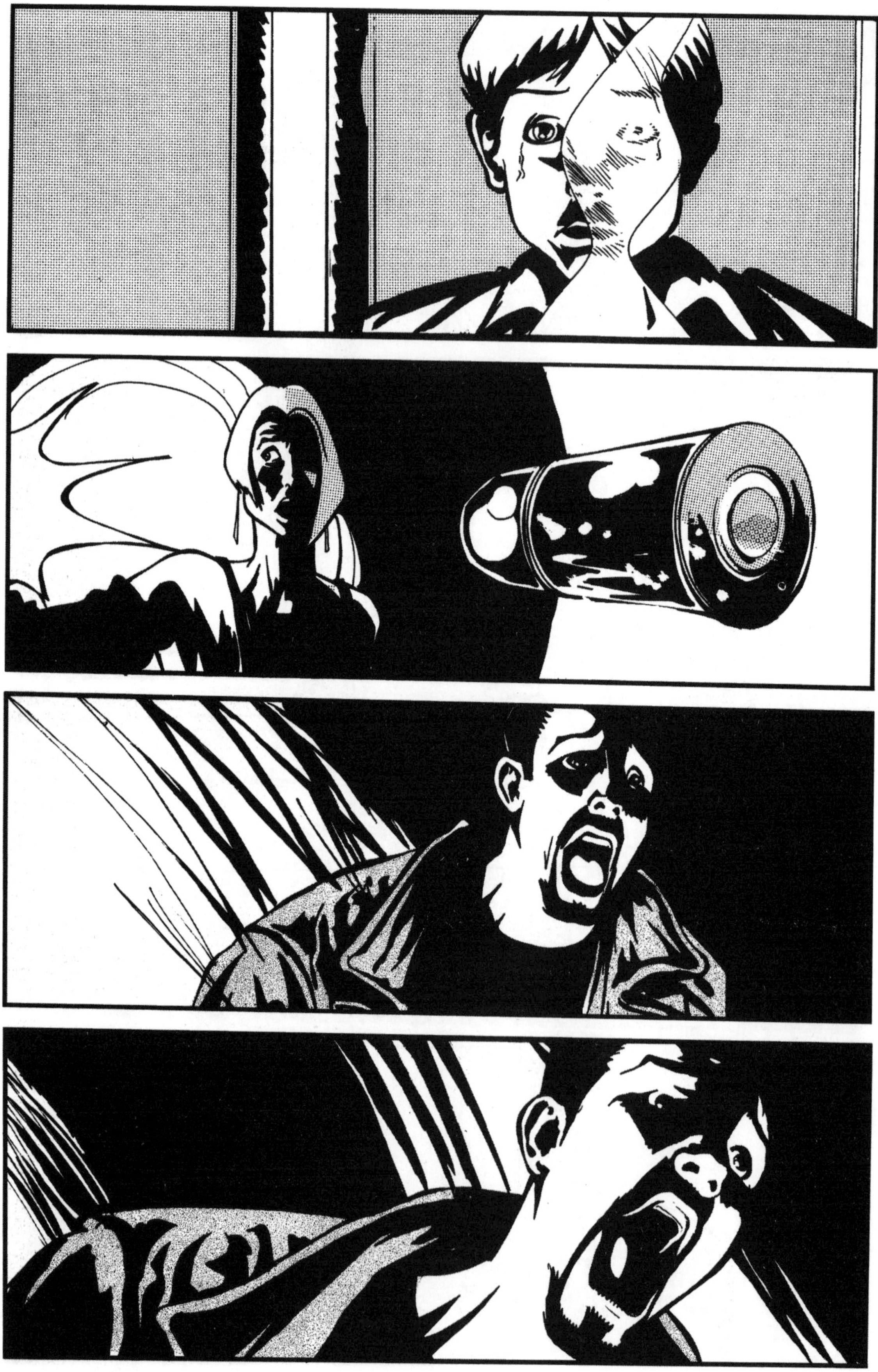

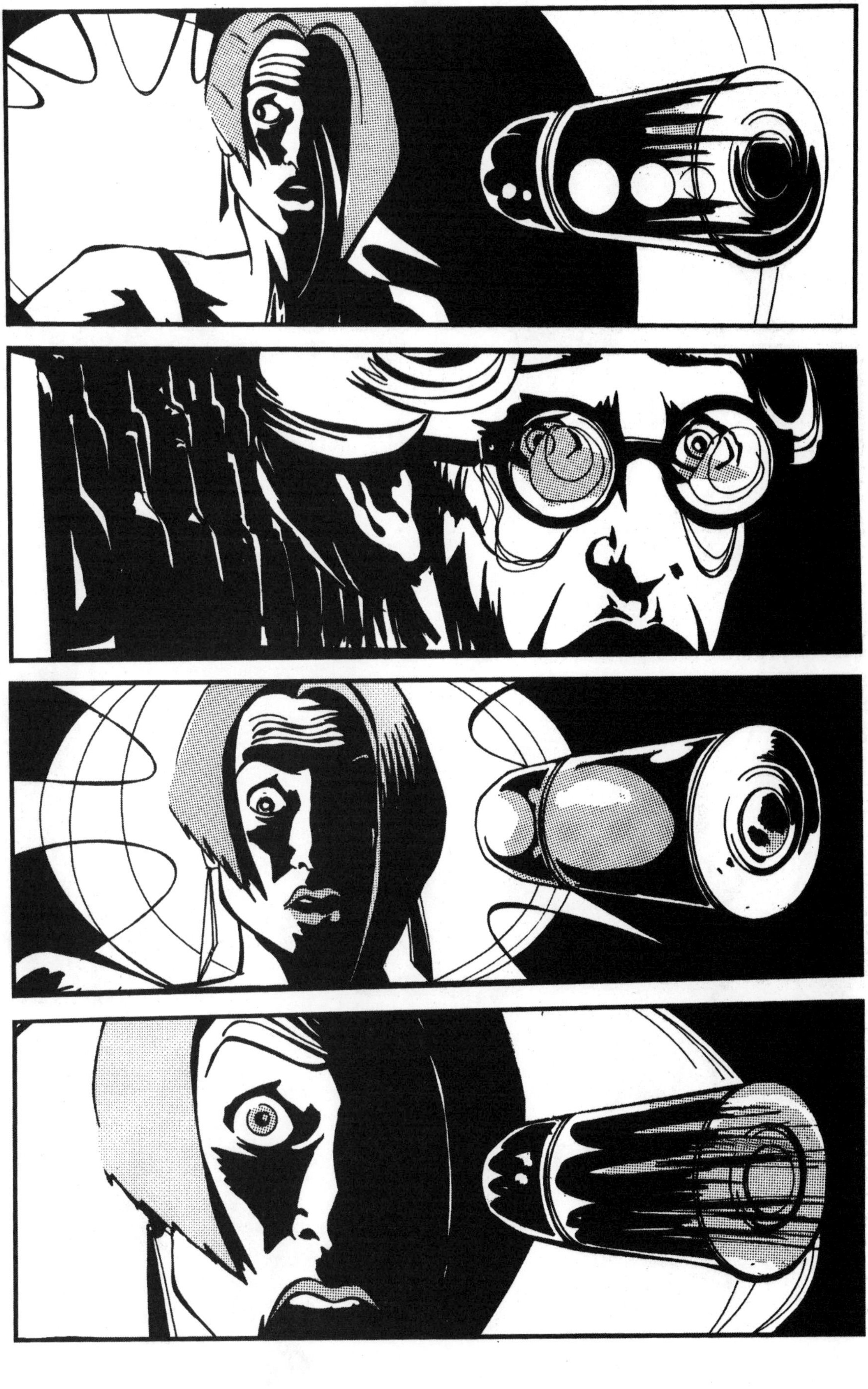

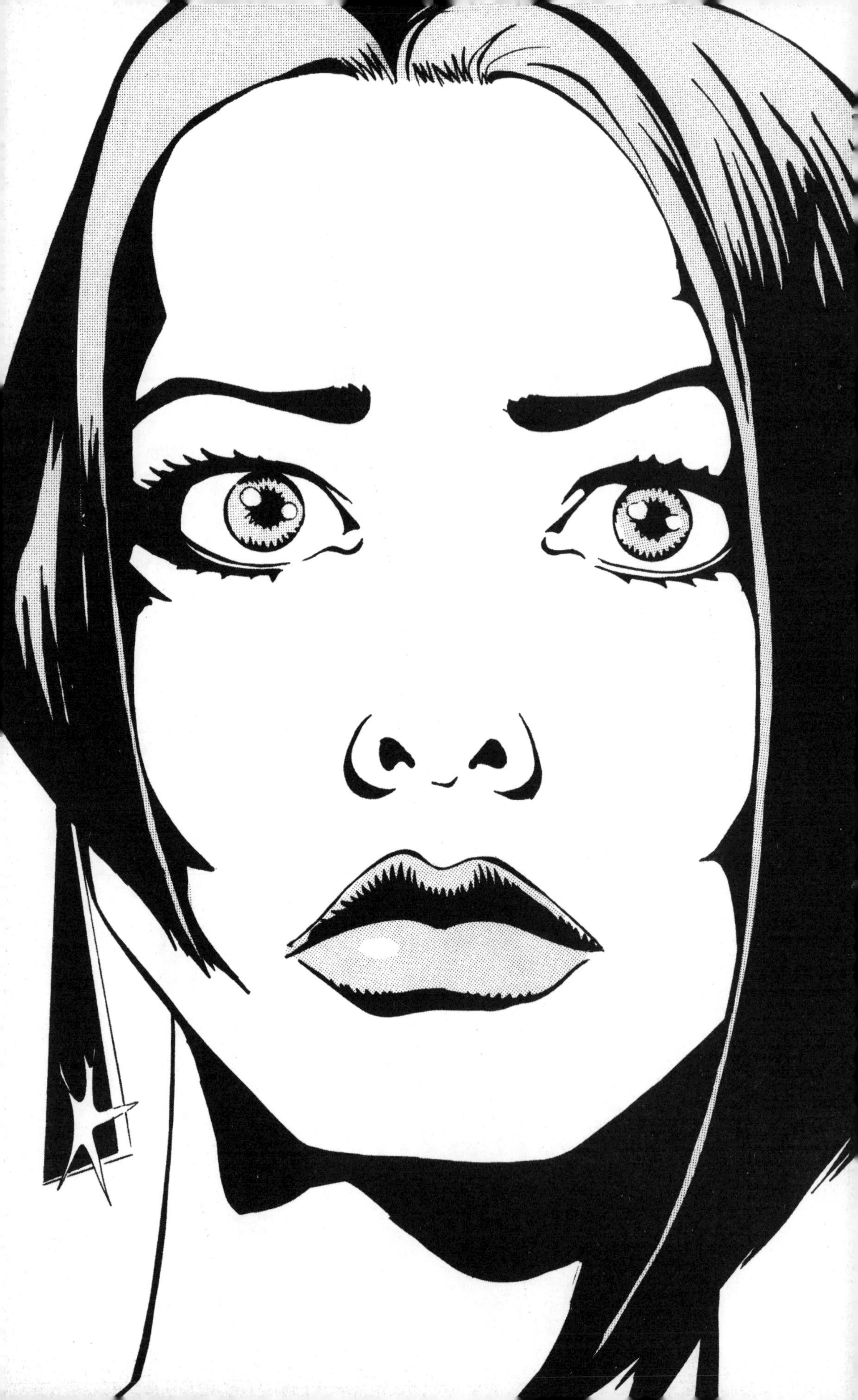

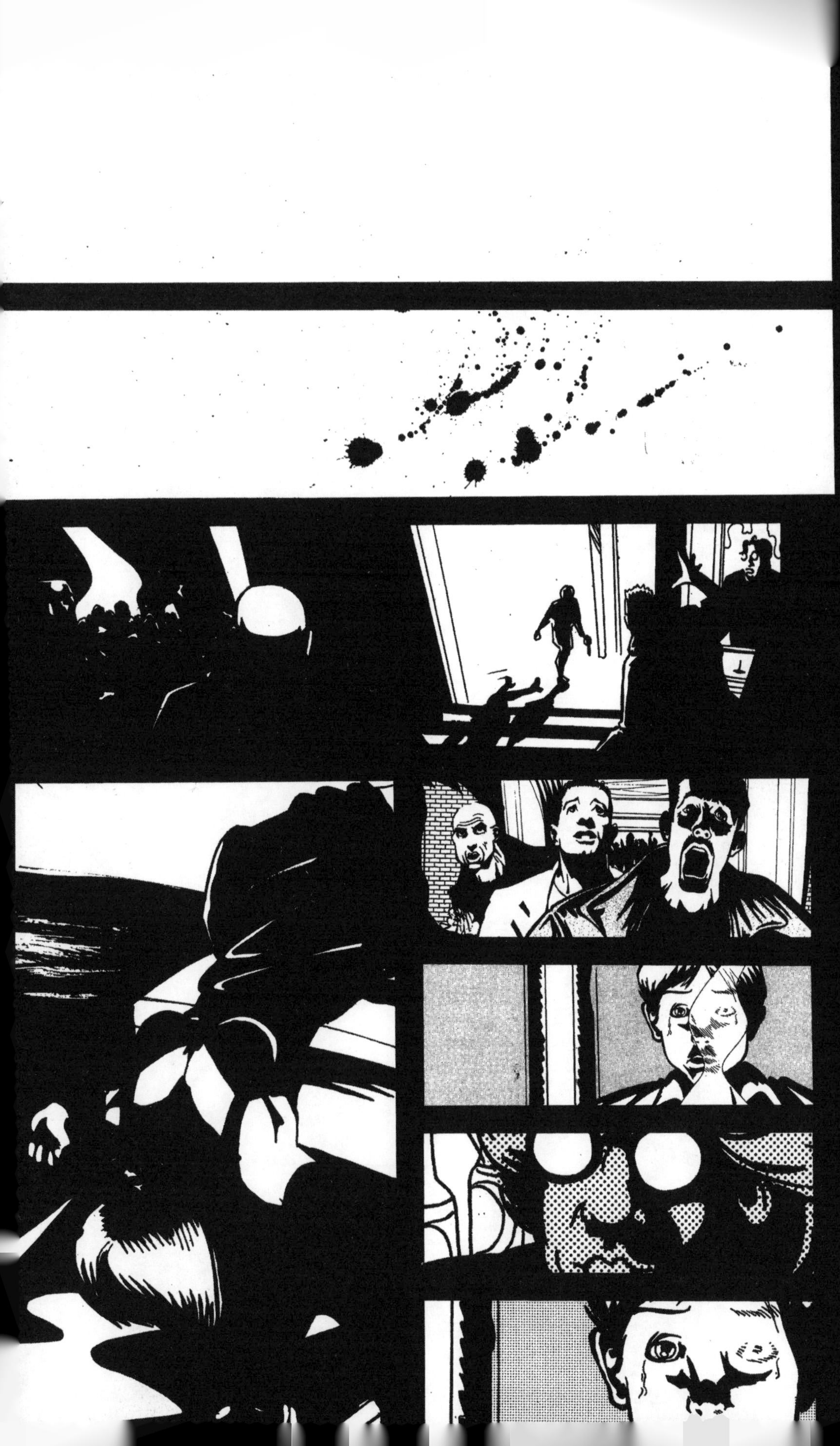

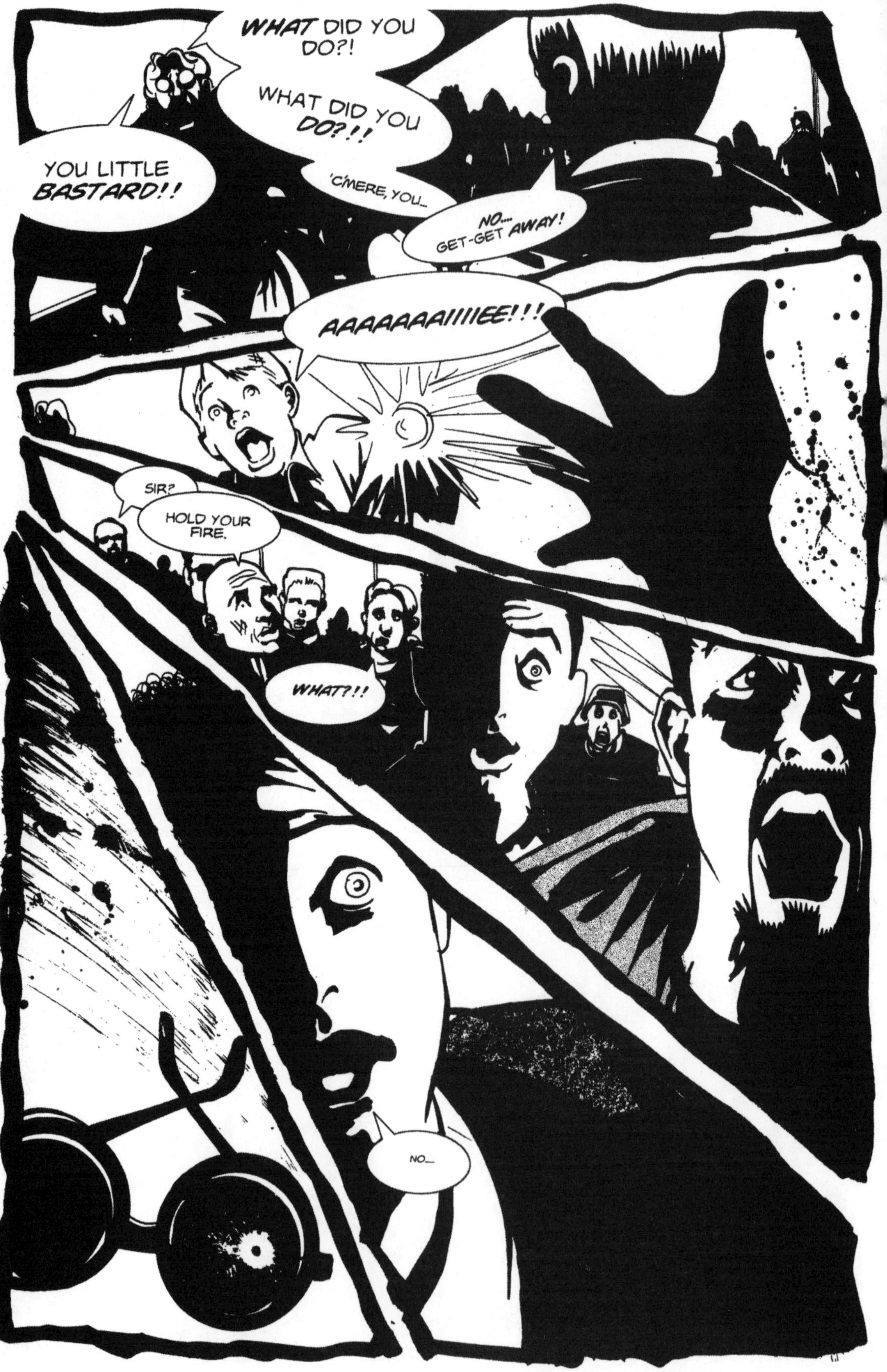
WHAT DID YOU DO?!
WHAT DID YOU DO?!!
YOU LITTLE BASTARD!!
'C'MERE, YOU...
NO.... GET-GET AWAY!
AAAAAAAIIIIIEE!!!
SIR?
HOLD YOUR FIRE.
WHAT?!!
NO.....

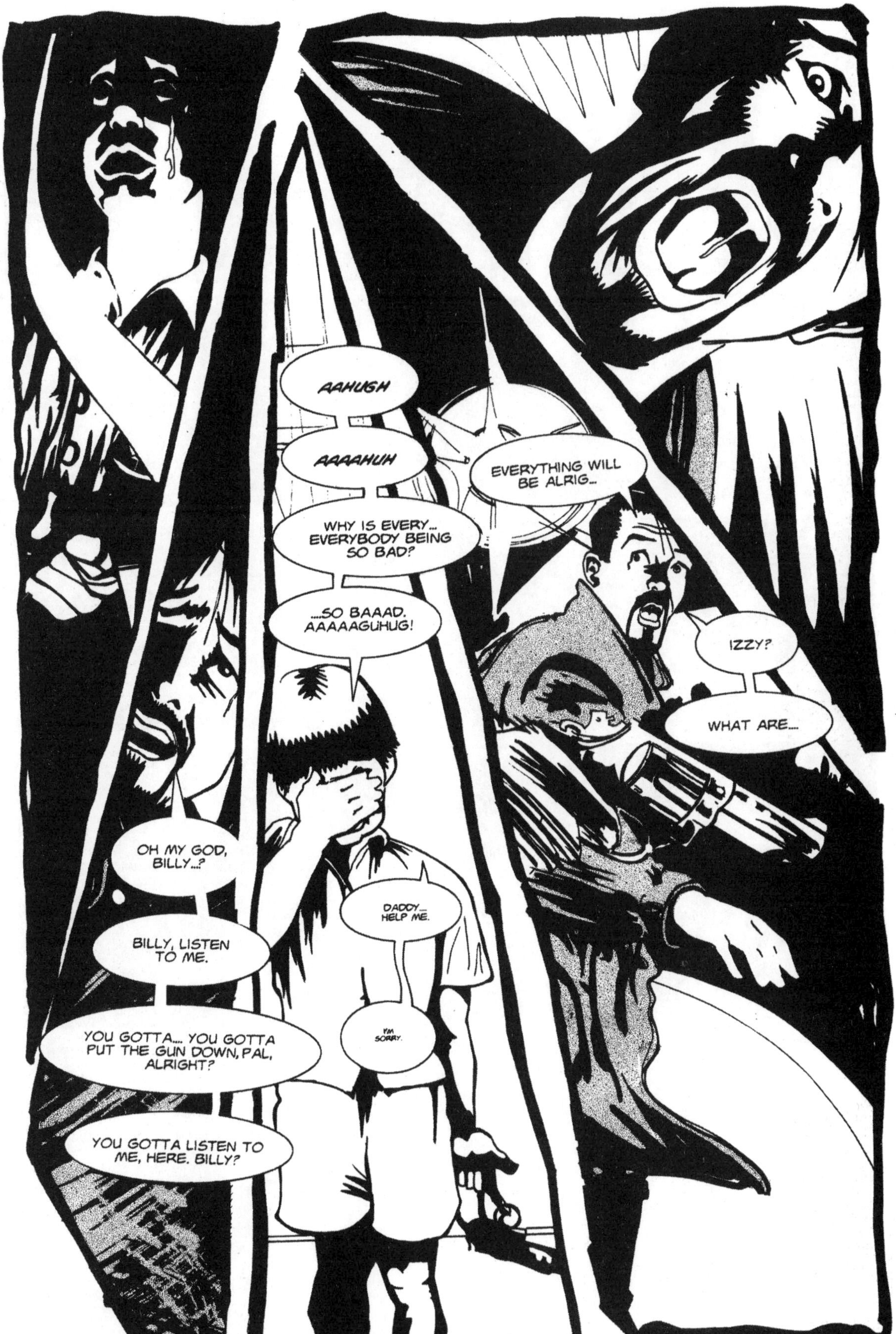

AAHUSH
AAAAHUH
WHY IS EVERY... EVERYBODY BEING SO BAD?
...SO BAAAD. AAAAAGUHUG!
EVERYTHING WILL BE ALRIG...
IZZY?
WHAT ARE...
OH MY GOD, BILLY...?
BILLY, LISTEN TO ME.
YOU GOTTA... YOU GOTTA PUT THE GUN DOWN, PAL, ALRIGHT?
YOU GOTTA LISTEN TO ME, HERE. BILLY?
DADDY... HELP ME.
I'M SORRY.

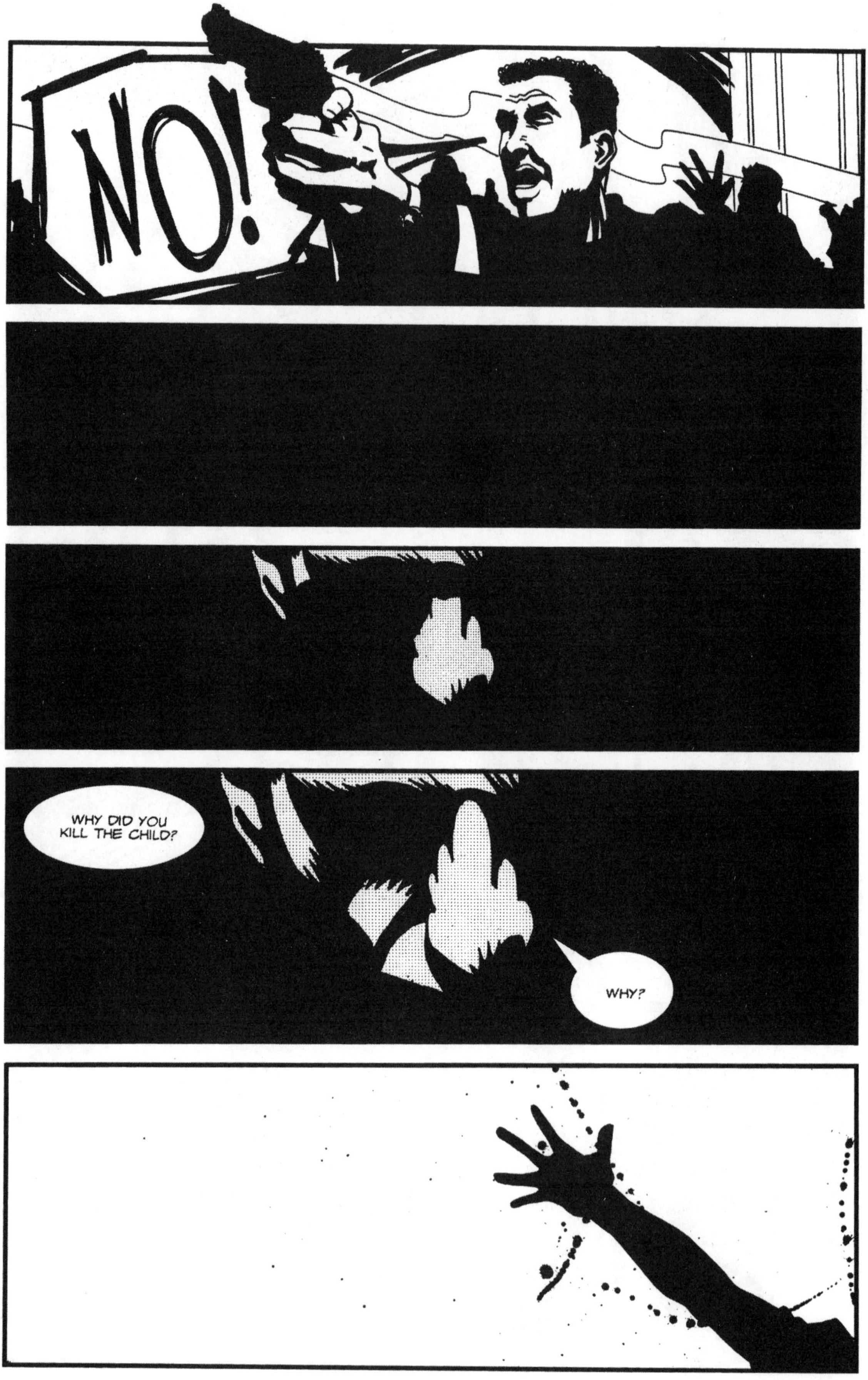
NO!
WHY DID YOU KILL THE CHILD?
WHY?

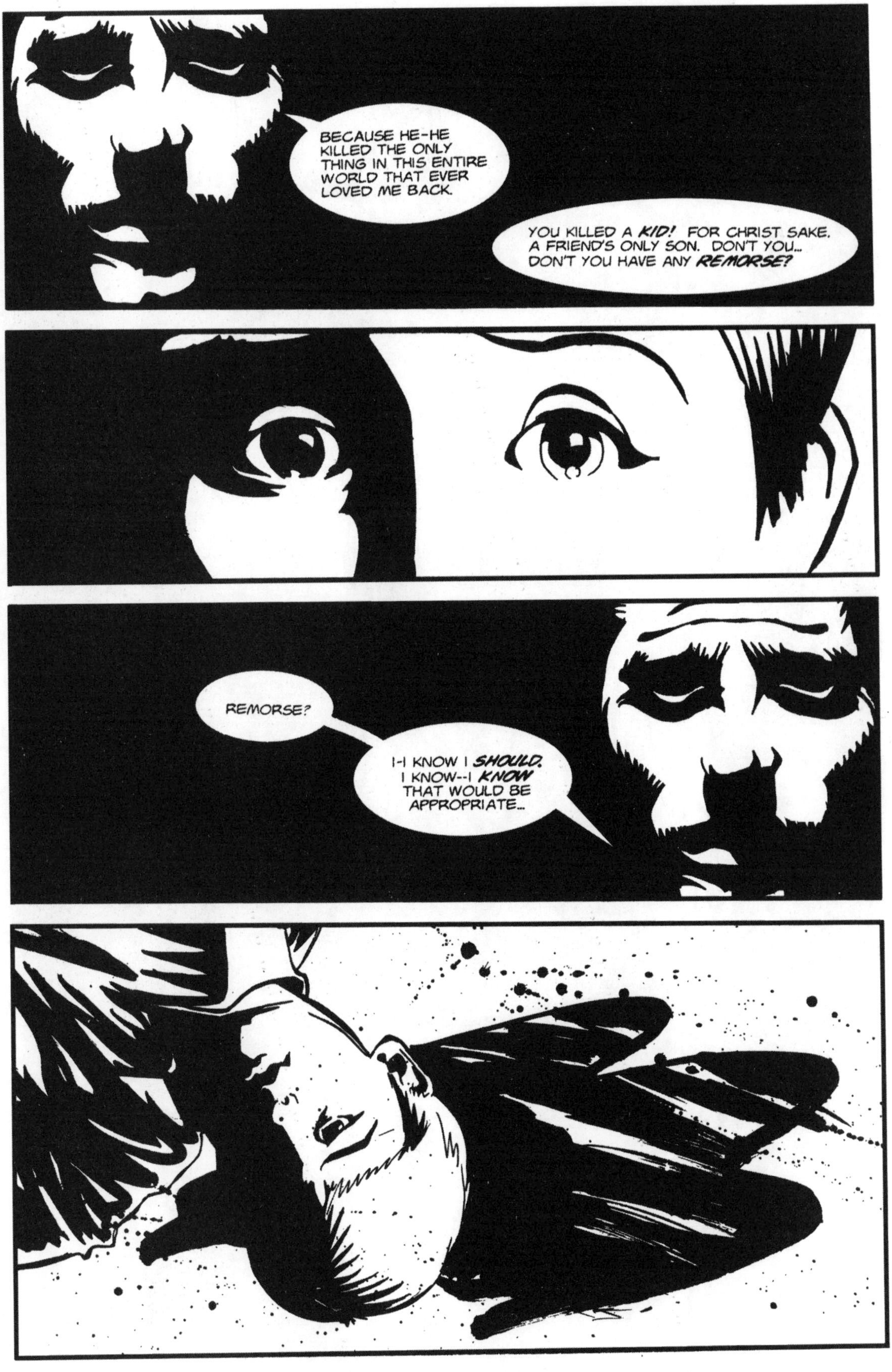
BECAUSE HE-HE KILLED THE ONLY THING IN THIS ENTIRE WORLD THAT EVER LOVED ME BACK.
YOU KILLED A KID! FOR CHRIST SAKE. A FRIEND'S ONLY SON. DON'T YOU... DON'T YOU HAVE ANY REMORSE?
REMORSE?
I-I KNOW I SHOULD. I KNOW--I KNOW THAT WOULD BE APPROPRIATE...

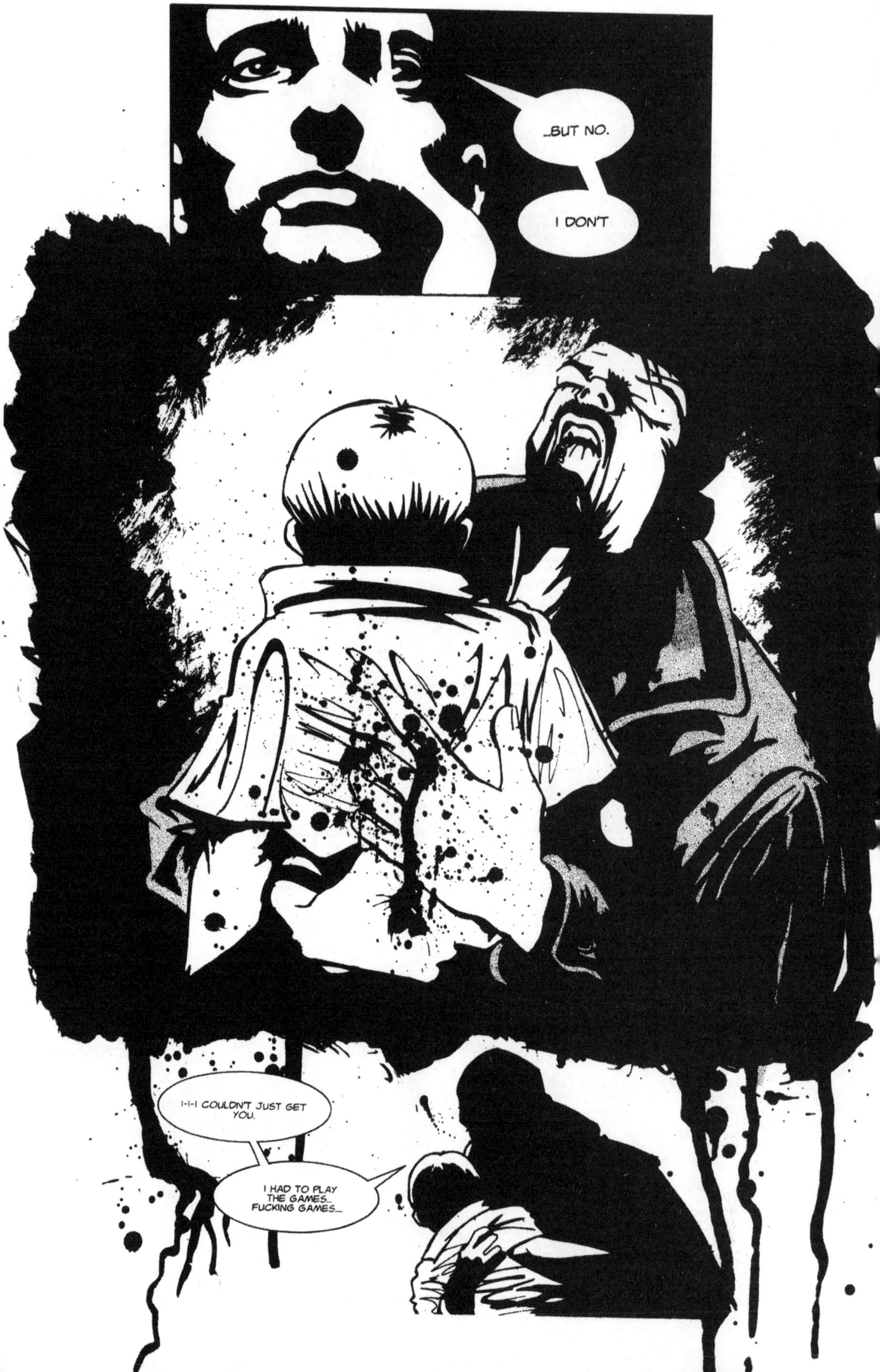
...BUT NO.
I DON'T
I-I-I COULDN'T JUST GET YOU.
I HAD TO PLAY THE GAMES... FUCKING GAMES....

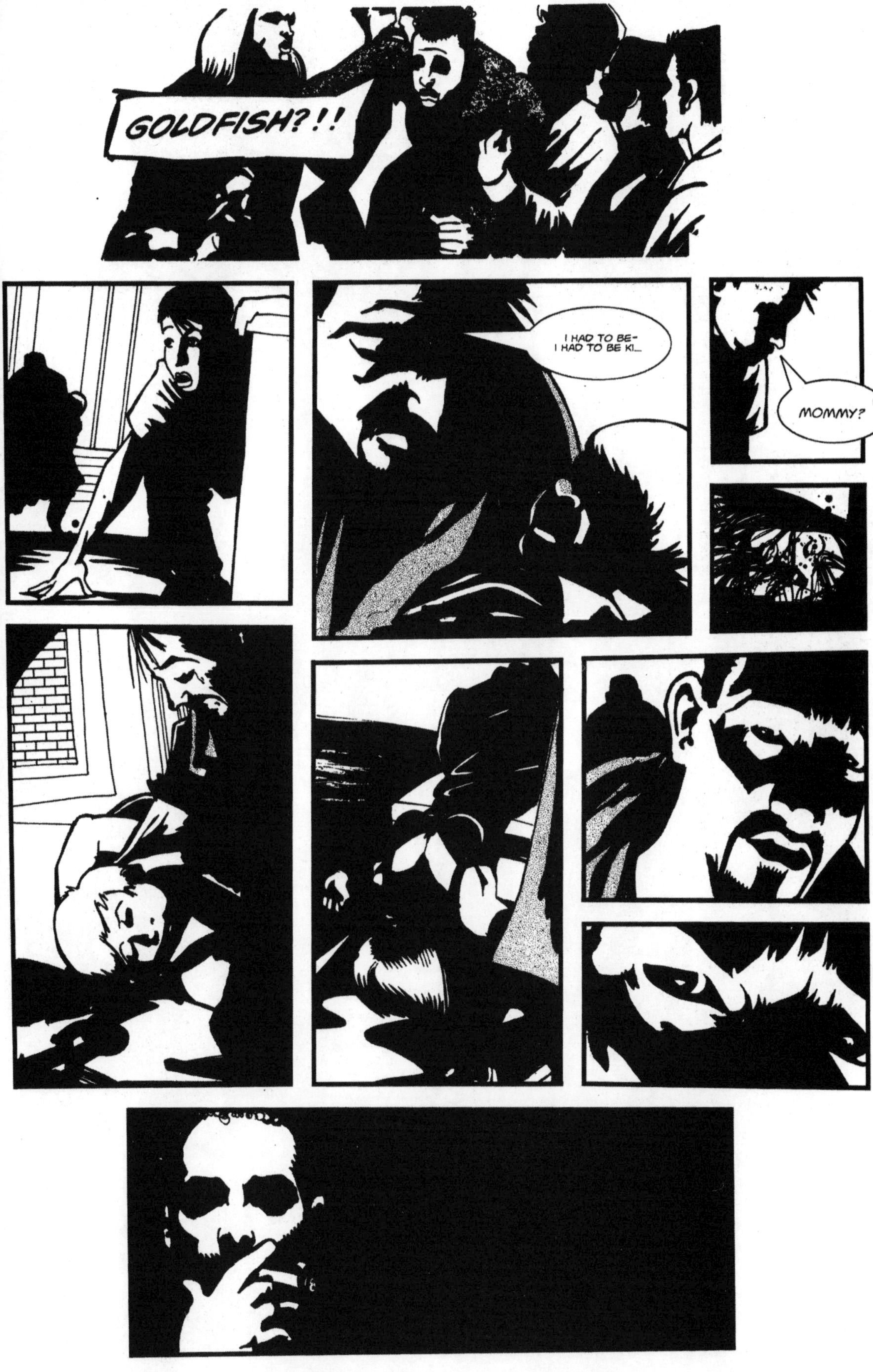
GOLDFISH?!!
I HAD TO BE-
I HAD TO BE KI...
MOMMY?

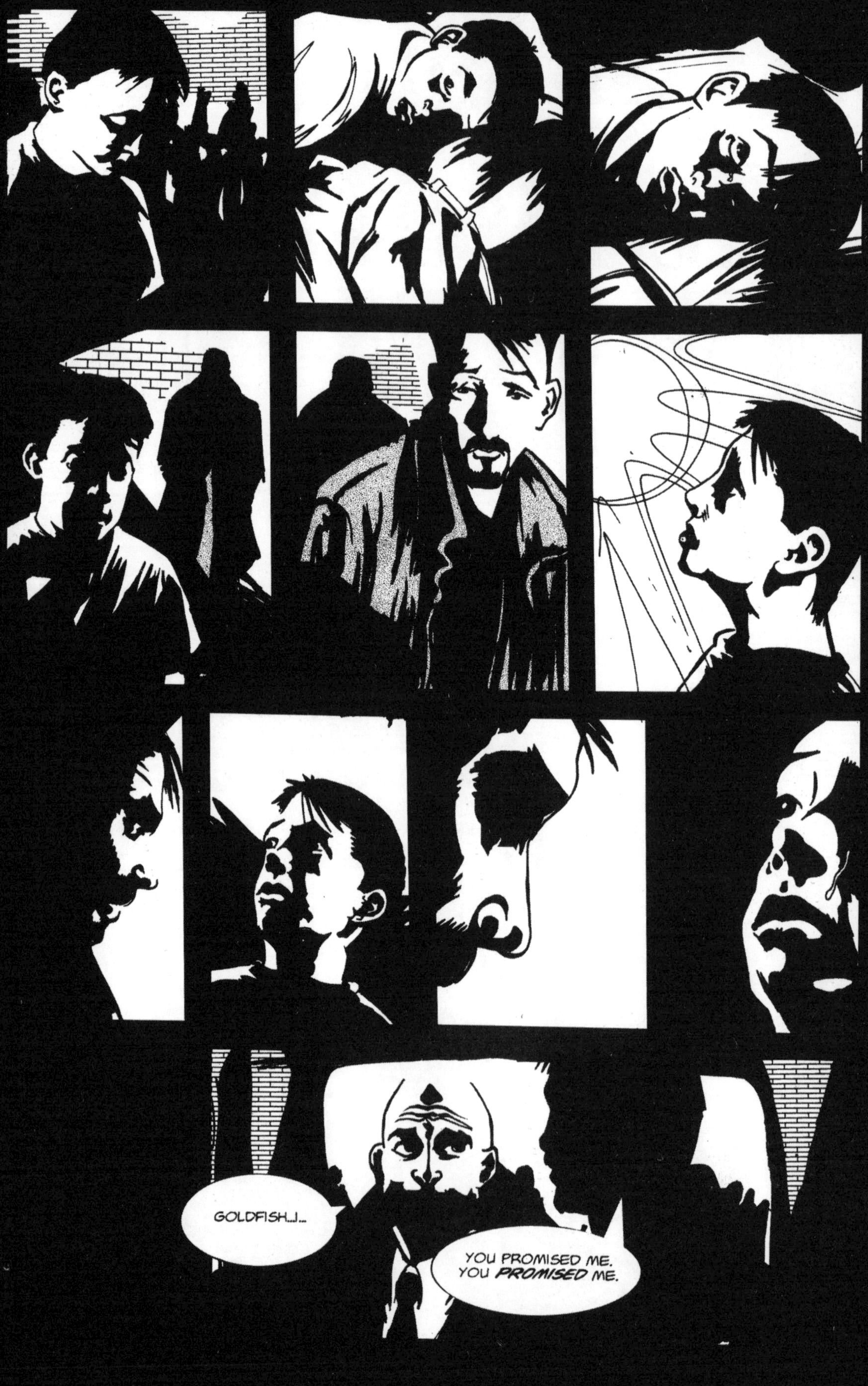
GOLDFISH...I...
YOU PROMISED ME. YOU *PROMISED* ME.

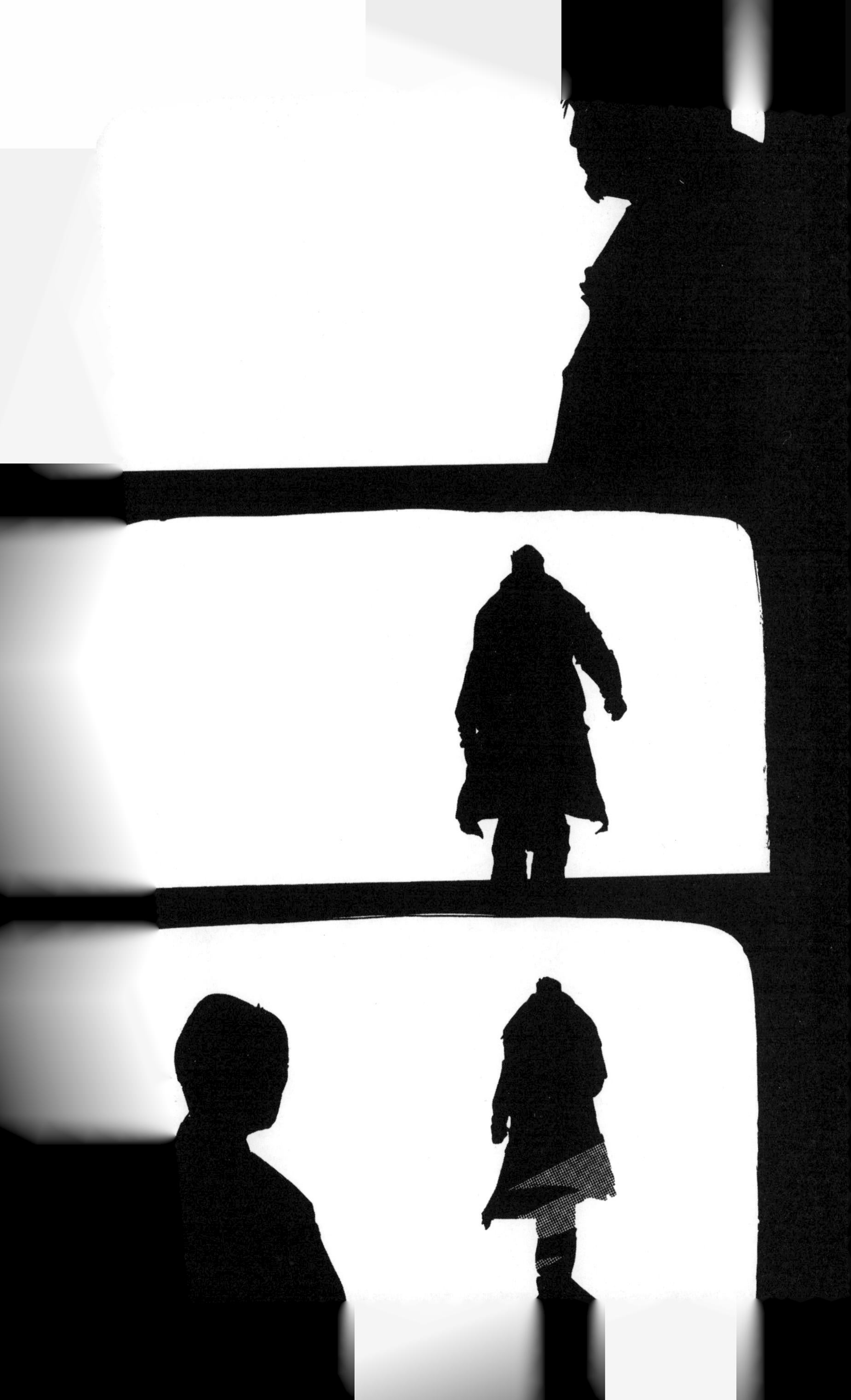

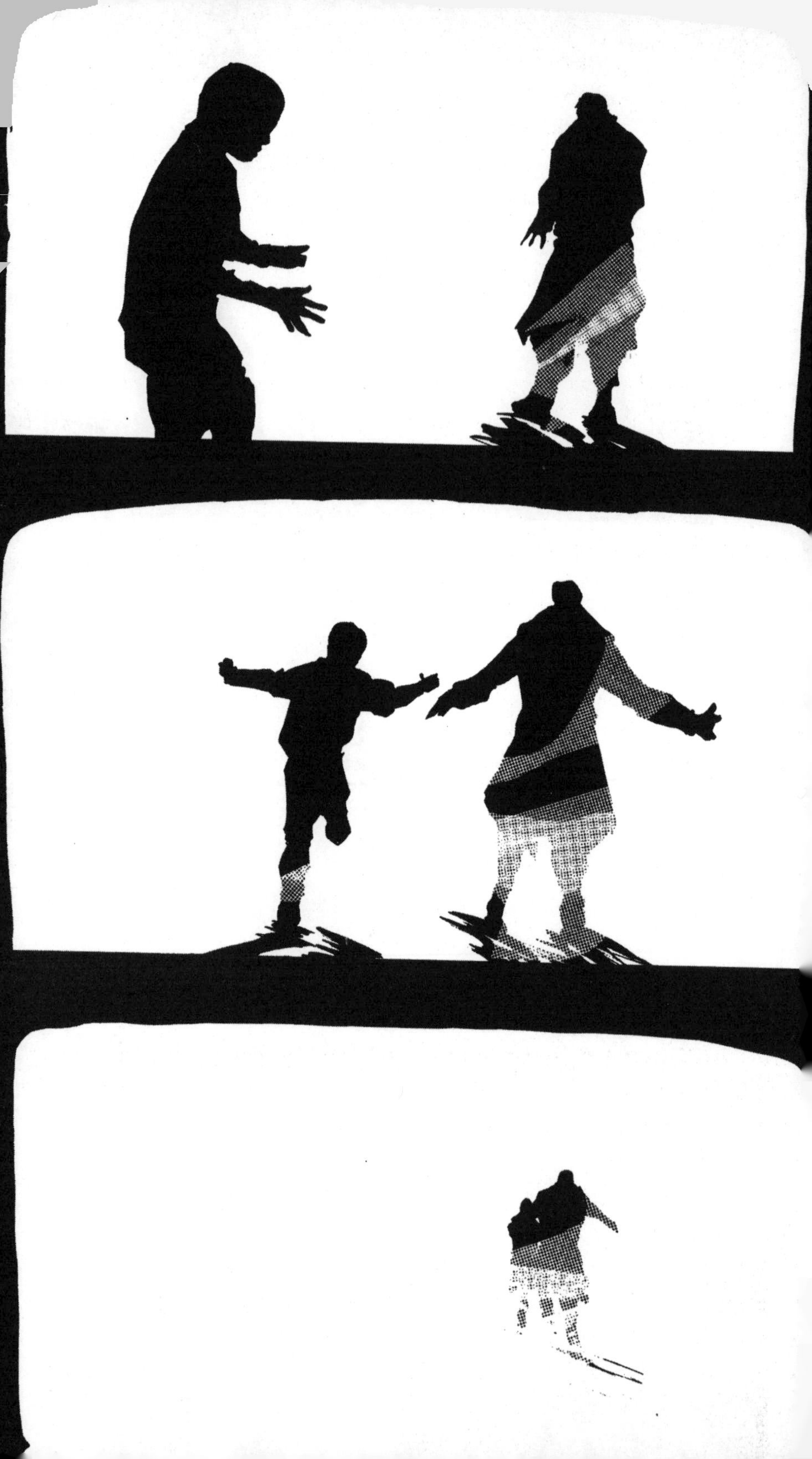

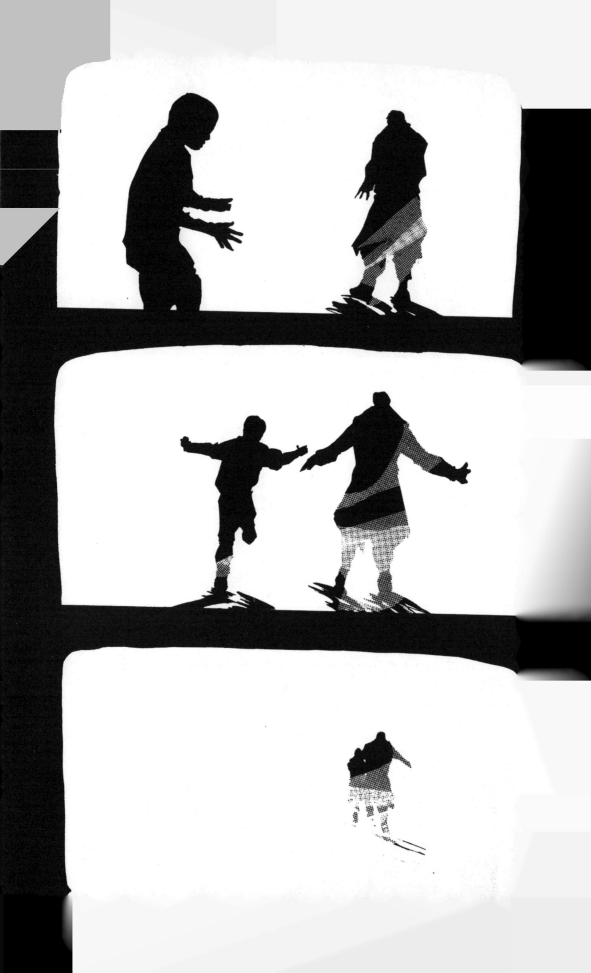

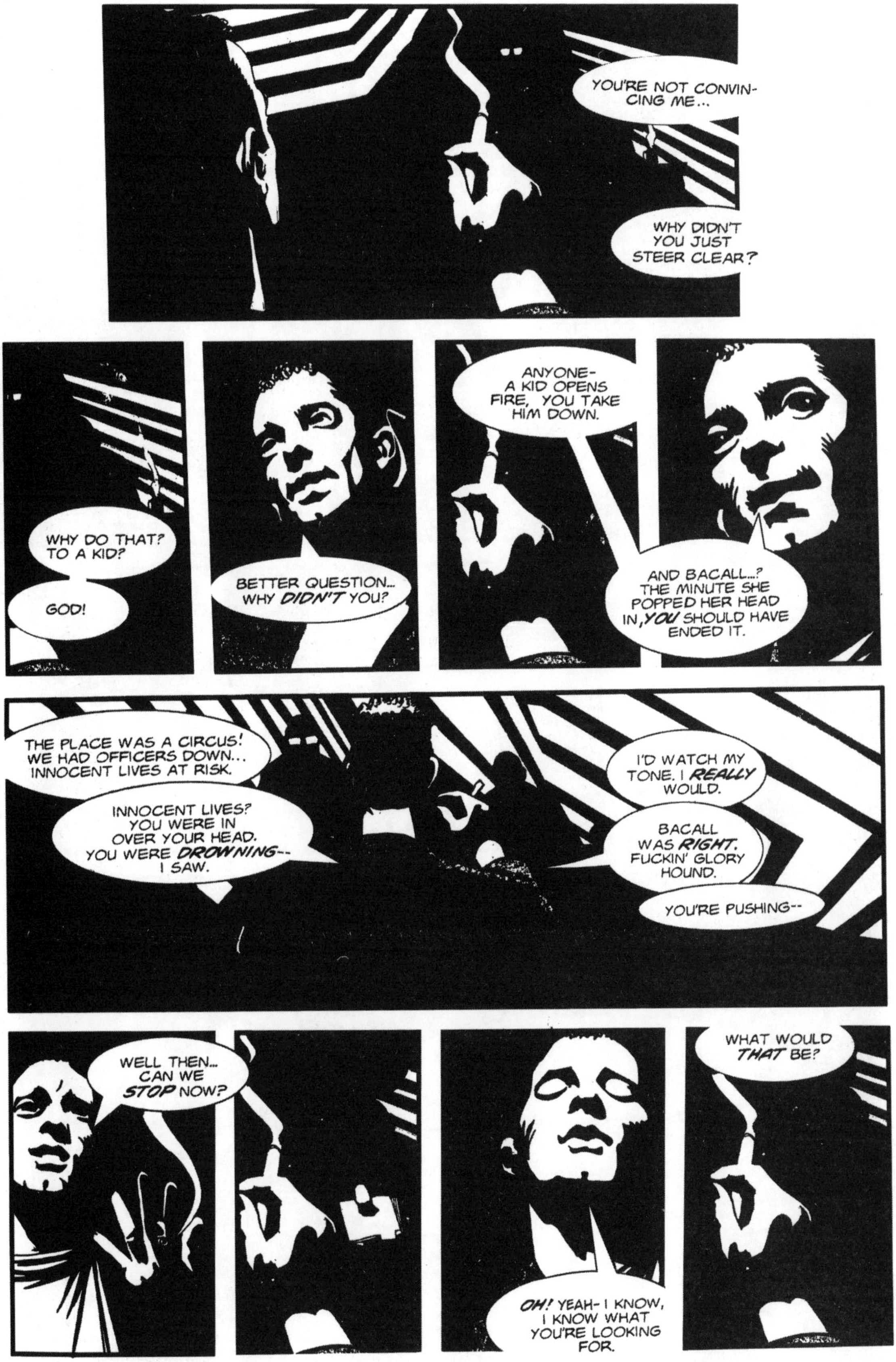
YOU'RE NOT CONVINCING ME...
WHY DIDN'T YOU JUST STEER CLEAR?
WHY DO THAT? TO A KID?
GOD!
BETTER QUESTION... WHY DIDN'T YOU?
ANYONE- A KID OPENS FIRE, YOU TAKE HIM DOWN.
AND BACALL...? THE MINUTE SHE POPPED HER HEAD IN, YOU SHOULD HAVE ENDED IT.
THE PLACE WAS A CIRCUS! WE HAD OFFICERS DOWN... INNOCENT LIVES AT RISK.
INNOCENT LIVES? YOU WERE IN OVER YOUR HEAD. YOU WERE DROWNING-- I SAW.
I'D WATCH MY TONE. I REALLY WOULD.
BACALL WAS RIGHT. FUCKIN' GLORY HOUND.
YOU'RE PUSHING--
WELL THEN... CAN WE STOP NOW?
OH! YEAH- I KNOW, I KNOW WHAT YOU'RE LOOKING FOR.
WHAT WOULD THAT BE?

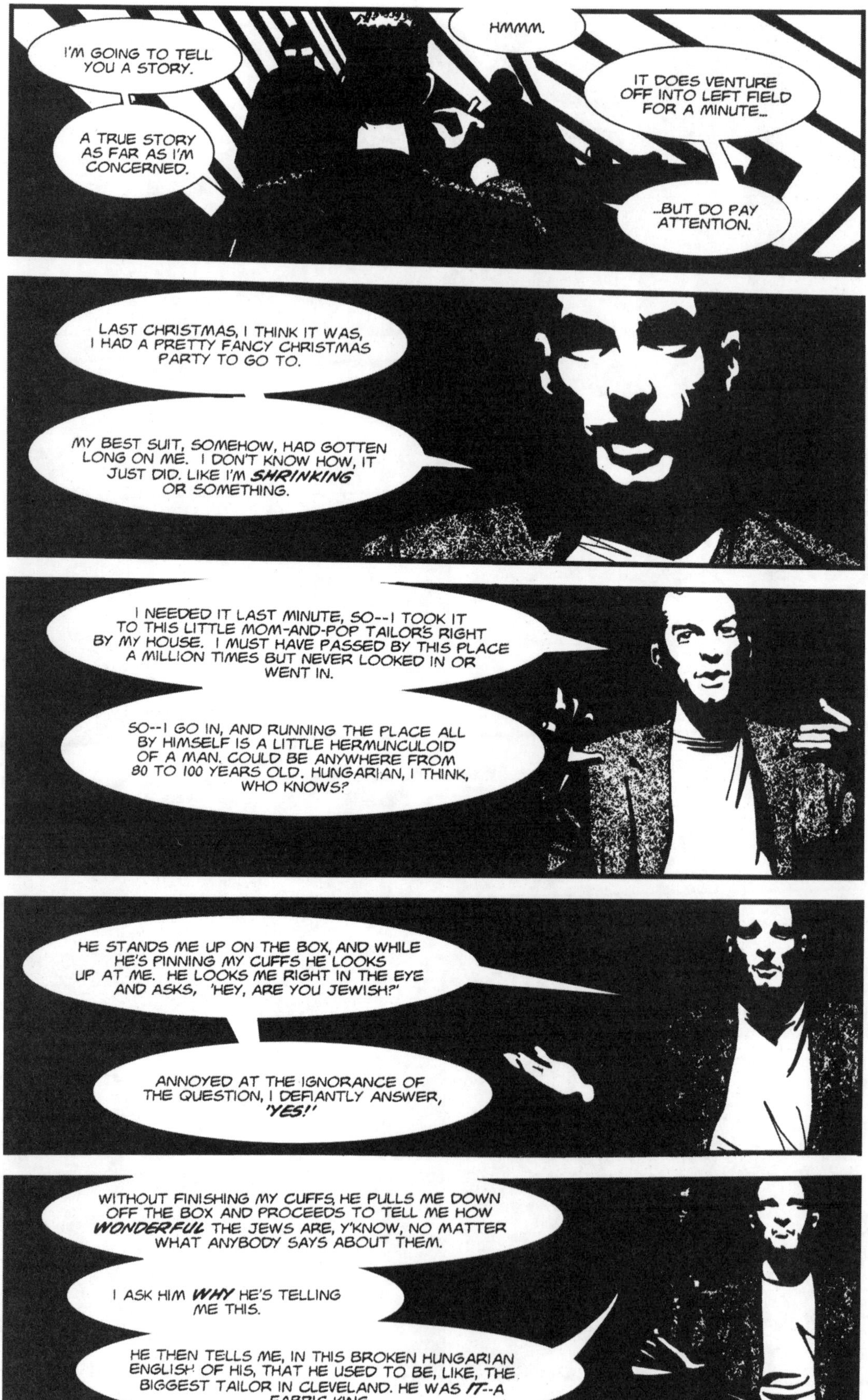
I'M GOING TO TELL YOU A STORY.
HMMM.
A TRUE STORY AS FAR AS I'M CONCERNED.
IT DOES VENTURE OFF INTO LEFT FIELD FOR A MINUTE...
...BUT DO PAY ATTENTION.
LAST CHRISTMAS, I THINK IT WAS, I HAD A PRETTY FANCY CHRISTMAS PARTY TO GO TO.
MY BEST SUIT, SOMEHOW, HAD GOTTEN LONG ON ME. I DON'T KNOW HOW, IT JUST DID. LIKE I'M *SHRINKING* OR SOMETHING.
I NEEDED IT LAST MINUTE, SO--I TOOK IT TO THIS LITTLE MOM-AND-POP TAILOR'S RIGHT BY MY HOUSE. I MUST HAVE PASSED BY THIS PLACE A MILLION TIMES BUT NEVER LOOKED IN OR WENT IN.
SO--I GO IN, AND RUNNING THE PLACE ALL BY HIMSELF IS A LITTLE HERMUNCULOID OF A MAN. COULD BE ANYWHERE FROM 80 TO 100 YEARS OLD. HUNGARIAN, I THINK, WHO KNOWS?
HE STANDS ME UP ON THE BOX, AND WHILE HE'S PINNING MY CUFFS HE LOOKS UP AT ME. HE LOOKS ME RIGHT IN THE EYE AND ASKS, 'HEY, ARE YOU JEWISH?'
ANNOYED AT THE IGNORANCE OF THE QUESTION, I DEFIANTLY ANSWER, *'YES!'*
WITHOUT FINISHING MY CUFFS, HE PULLS ME DOWN OFF THE BOX AND PROCEEDS TO TELL ME HOW *WONDERFUL* THE JEWS ARE, Y'KNOW, NO MATTER WHAT ANYBODY SAYS ABOUT THEM.
I ASK HIM *WHY* HE'S TELLING ME THIS.
HE THEN TELLS ME, IN THIS BROKEN HUNGARIAN ENGLISH OF HIS, THAT HE USED TO BE, LIKE, THE BIGGEST TAILOR IN CLEVELAND. HE WAS *IT*--A FABRIC KING.

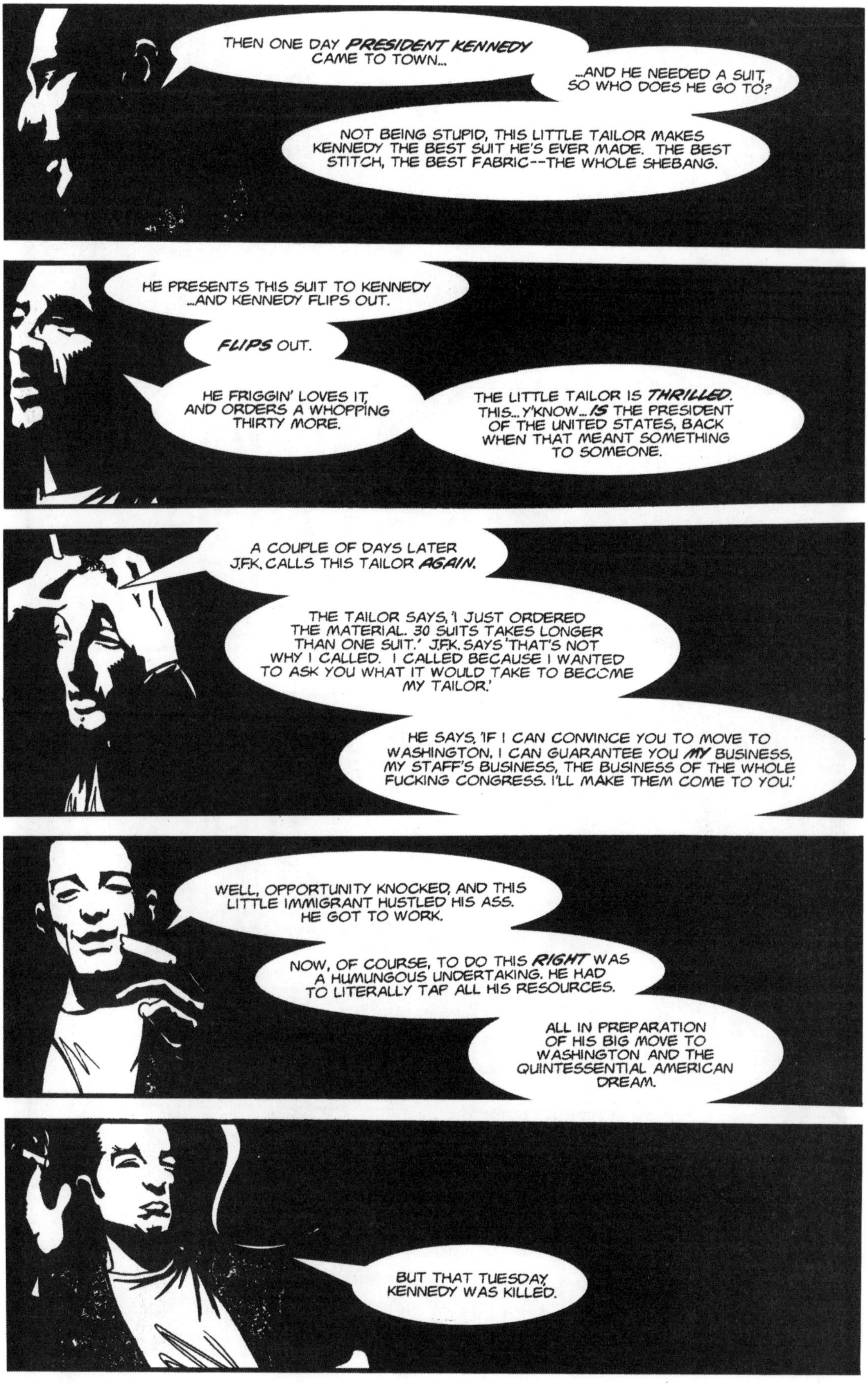
THEN ONE DAY PRESIDENT KENNEDY CAME TO TOWN...
...AND HE NEEDED A SUIT, SO WHO DOES HE GO TO?
NOT BEING STUPID, THIS LITTLE TAILOR MAKES KENNEDY THE BEST SUIT HE'S EVER MADE. THE BEST STITCH, THE BEST FABRIC--THE WHOLE SHEBANG.
HE PRESENTS THIS SUIT TO KENNEDY ...AND KENNEDY FLIPS OUT.
FLIPS OUT.
HE FRIGGIN' LOVES IT, AND ORDERS A WHOPPING THIRTY MORE.
THE LITTLE TAILOR IS THRILLED. THIS... Y'KNOW... IS THE PRESIDENT OF THE UNITED STATES, BACK WHEN THAT MEANT SOMETHING TO SOMEONE.
A COUPLE OF DAYS LATER J.F.K. CALLS THIS TAILOR AGAIN.
THE TAILOR SAYS, 'I JUST ORDERED THE MATERIAL. 30 SUITS TAKES LONGER THAN ONE SUIT.' J.F.K. SAYS 'THAT'S NOT WHY I CALLED. I CALLED BECAUSE I WANTED TO ASK YOU WHAT IT WOULD TAKE TO BECOME MY TAILOR.'
HE SAYS, 'IF I CAN CONVINCE YOU TO MOVE TO WASHINGTON, I CAN GUARANTEE YOU MY BUSINESS, MY STAFF'S BUSINESS, THE BUSINESS OF THE WHOLE FUCKING CONGRESS. I'LL MAKE THEM COME TO YOU.'
WELL, OPPORTUNITY KNOCKED, AND THIS LITTLE IMMIGRANT HUSTLED HIS ASS. HE GOT TO WORK.
NOW, OF COURSE, TO DO THIS RIGHT WAS A HUMUNGOUS UNDERTAKING. HE HAD TO LITERALLY TAP ALL HIS RESOURCES.
ALL IN PREPARATION OF HIS BIG MOVE TO WASHINGTON AND THE QUINTESSENTIAL AMERICAN DREAM.
BUT THAT TUESDAY, KENNEDY WAS KILLED.

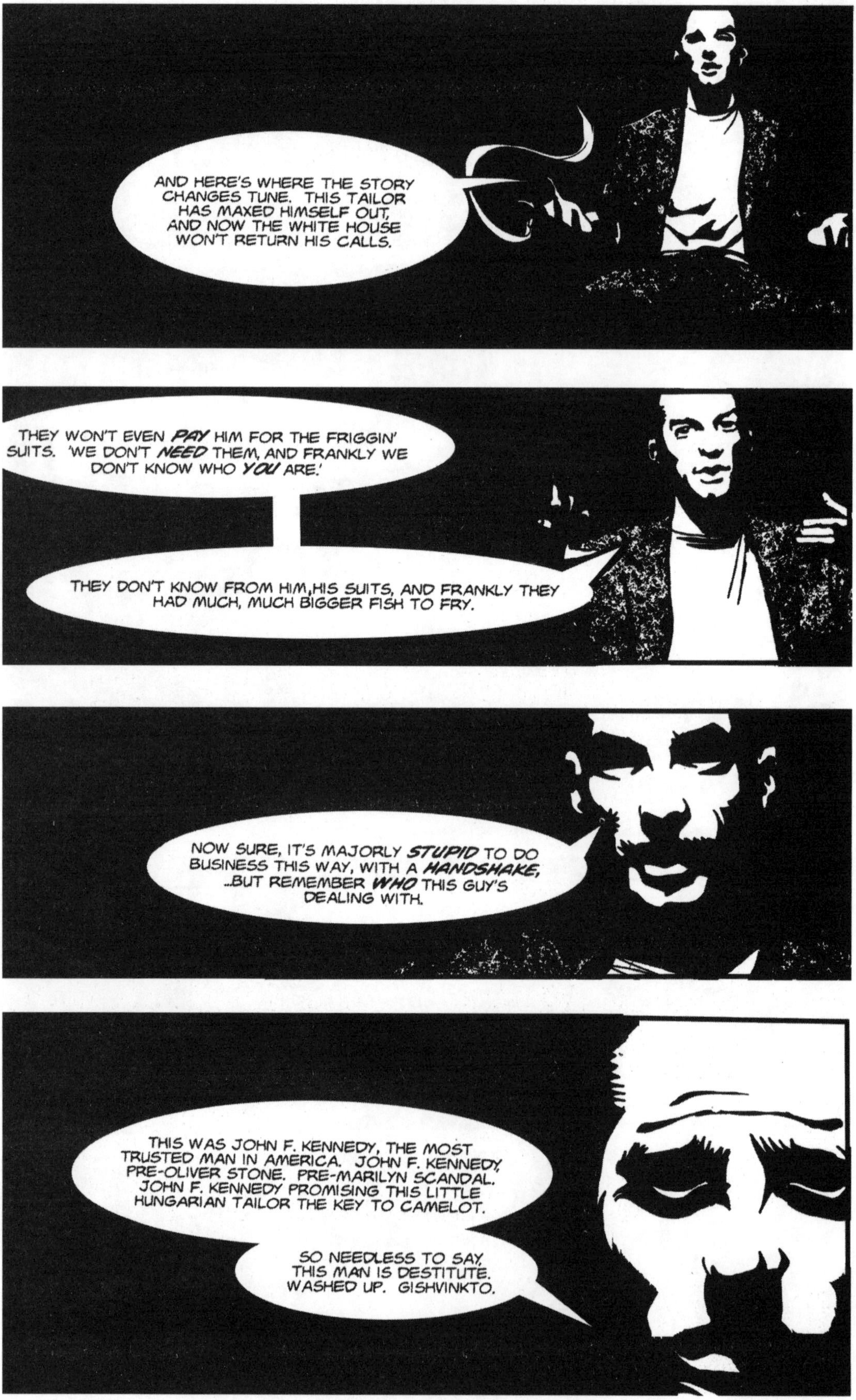
AND HERE'S WHERE THE STORY CHANGES TUNE. THIS TAILOR HAS MAXED HIMSELF OUT, AND NOW THE WHITE HOUSE WON'T RETURN HIS CALLS.
THEY WON'T EVEN *PAY* HIM FOR THE FRIGGIN' SUITS. 'WE DON'T *NEED* THEM, AND FRANKLY WE DON'T KNOW WHO *YOU* ARE.'
THEY DON'T KNOW FROM HIM,HIS SUITS, AND FRANKLY THEY HAD MUCH, MUCH BIGGER FISH TO FRY.
NOW SURE, IT'S MAJORLY *STUPID* TO DO BUSINESS THIS WAY, WITH A *HANDSHAKE*, ..BUT REMEMBER *WHO* THIS GUY'S DEALING WITH.
THIS WAS JOHN F. KENNEDY, THE MOST TRUSTED MAN IN AMERICA. JOHN F. KENNEDY. PRE-OLIVER STONE. PRE-MARILYN SCANDAL. JOHN F. KENNEDY PROMISING THIS LITTLE HUNGARIAN TAILOR THE KEY TO CAMELOT.
SO NEEDLESS TO SAY, THIS MAN IS DESTITUTE. WASHED UP. GISHVINKTO.

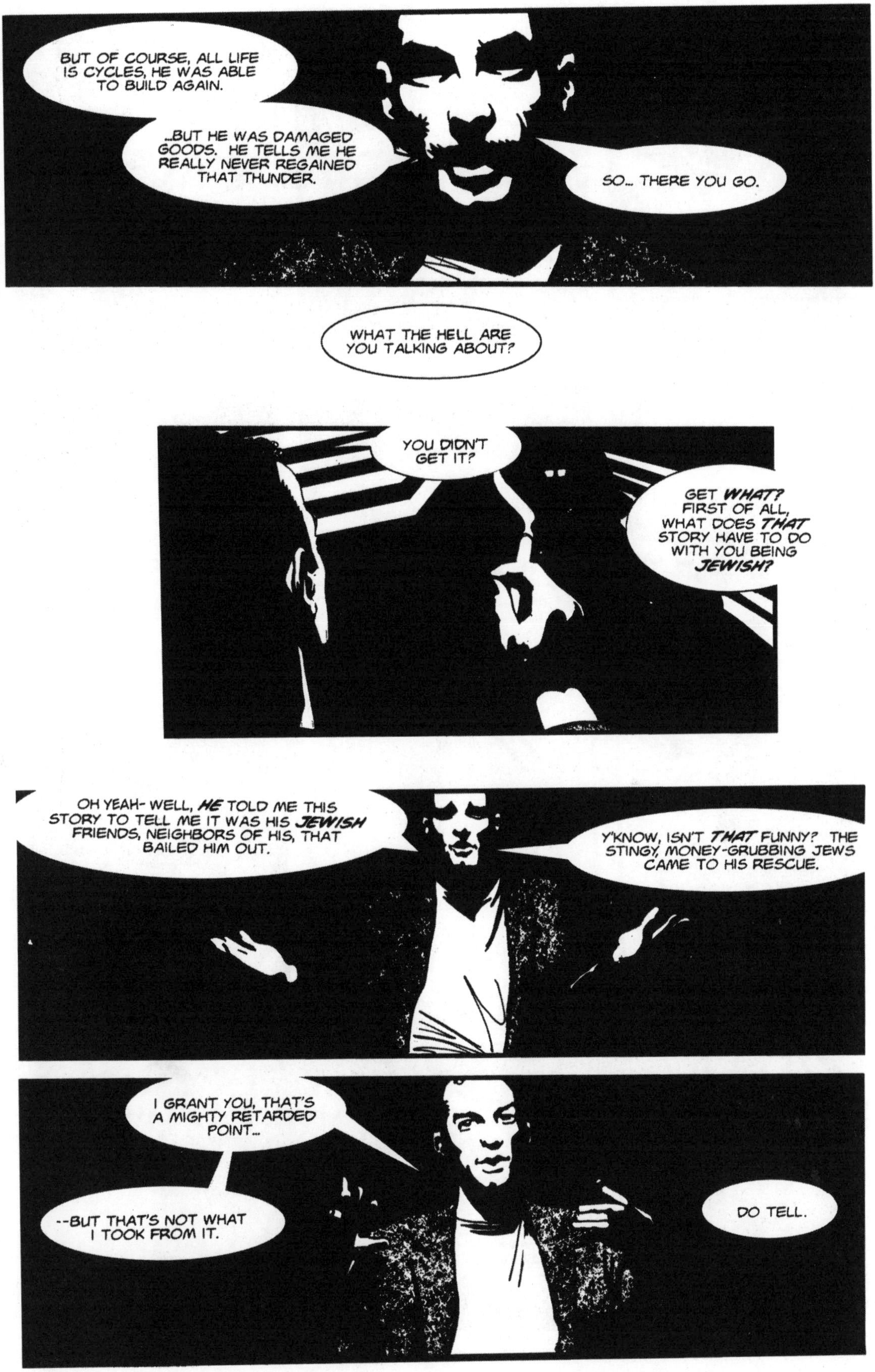
BUT OF COURSE, ALL LIFE IS CYCLES, HE WAS ABLE TO BUILD AGAIN.
..BUT HE WAS DAMAGED GOODS. HE TELLS ME HE REALLY NEVER REGAINED THAT THUNDER.
SO... THERE YOU GO.
WHAT THE HELL ARE YOU TALKING ABOUT?
YOU DIDN'T GET IT?
GET WHAT? FIRST OF ALL, WHAT DOES THAT STORY HAVE TO DO WITH YOU BEING JEWISH?
OH YEAH- WELL, HE TOLD ME THIS STORY TO TELL ME IT WAS HIS JEWISH FRIENDS, NEIGHBORS OF HIS, THAT BAILED HIM OUT.
Y'KNOW, ISN'T THAT FUNNY? THE STINGY, MONEY-GRUBBING JEWS CAME TO HIS RESCUE.
I GRANT YOU, THAT'S A MIGHTY RETARDED POINT...
--BUT THAT'S NOT WHAT I TOOK FROM IT.
DO TELL.

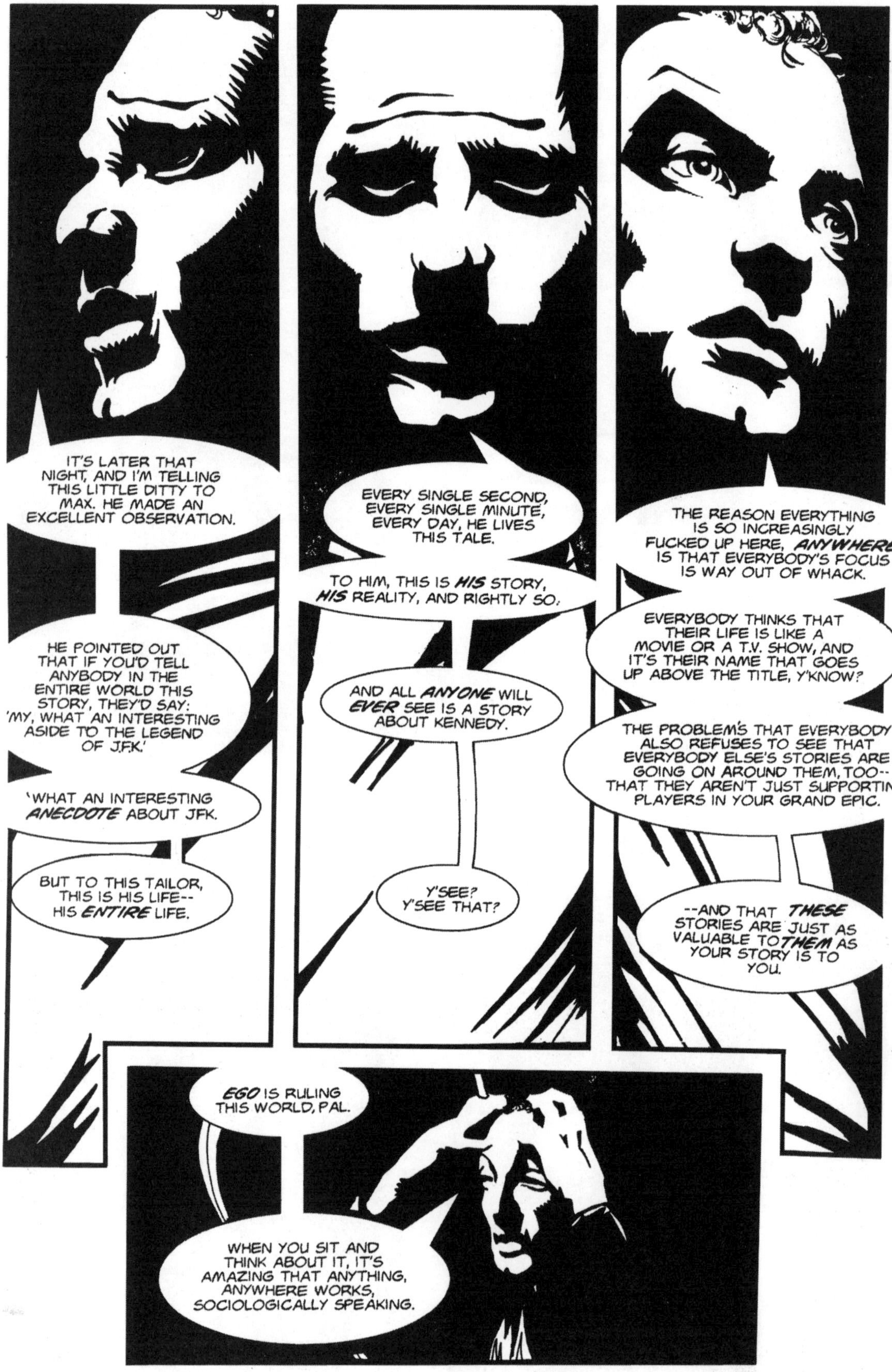
IT'S LATER THAT NIGHT, AND I'M TELLING THIS LITTLE DITTY TO MAX. HE MADE AN EXCELLENT OBSERVATION.
HE POINTED OUT THAT IF YOU'D TELL ANYBODY IN THE ENTIRE WORLD THIS STORY, THEY'D SAY: 'MY, WHAT AN INTERESTING ASIDE TO THE LEGEND OF J.F.K.'
'WHAT AN INTERESTING *ANECDOTE* ABOUT JFK.
BUT TO THIS TAILOR, THIS IS HIS LIFE-- HIS *ENTIRE* LIFE.
EVERY SINGLE SECOND, EVERY SINGLE MINUTE, EVERY DAY, HE LIVES THIS TALE.
TO HIM, THIS IS *HIS* STORY, *HIS* REALITY, AND RIGHTLY SO.
AND ALL *ANYONE* WILL *EVER* SEE IS A STORY ABOUT KENNEDY.
Y'SEE? Y'SEE THAT?
THE REASON EVERYTHING IS SO INCREASINGLY FUCKED UP HERE, *ANYWHERE,* IS THAT EVERYBODY'S FOCUS IS WAY OUT OF WHACK.
EVERYBODY THINKS THAT THEIR LIFE IS LIKE A MOVIE OR A T.V. SHOW, AND IT'S THEIR NAME THAT GOES UP ABOVE THE TITLE, Y'KNOW?
THE PROBLEM'S THAT EVERYBODY ALSO REFUSES TO SEE THAT EVERYBODY ELSE'S STORIES ARE GOING ON AROUND THEM, TOO-- THAT THEY AREN'T JUST SUPPORTING PLAYERS IN YOUR GRAND EPIC.
--AND THAT *THESE* STORIES ARE JUST AS VALUABLE TO *THEM* AS YOUR STORY IS TO YOU.
EGO IS RULING THIS WORLD, PAL.
WHEN YOU SIT AND THINK ABOUT IT, IT'S AMAZING THAT ANYTHING, ANYWHERE WORKS, SOCIOLOGICALLY SPEAKING.

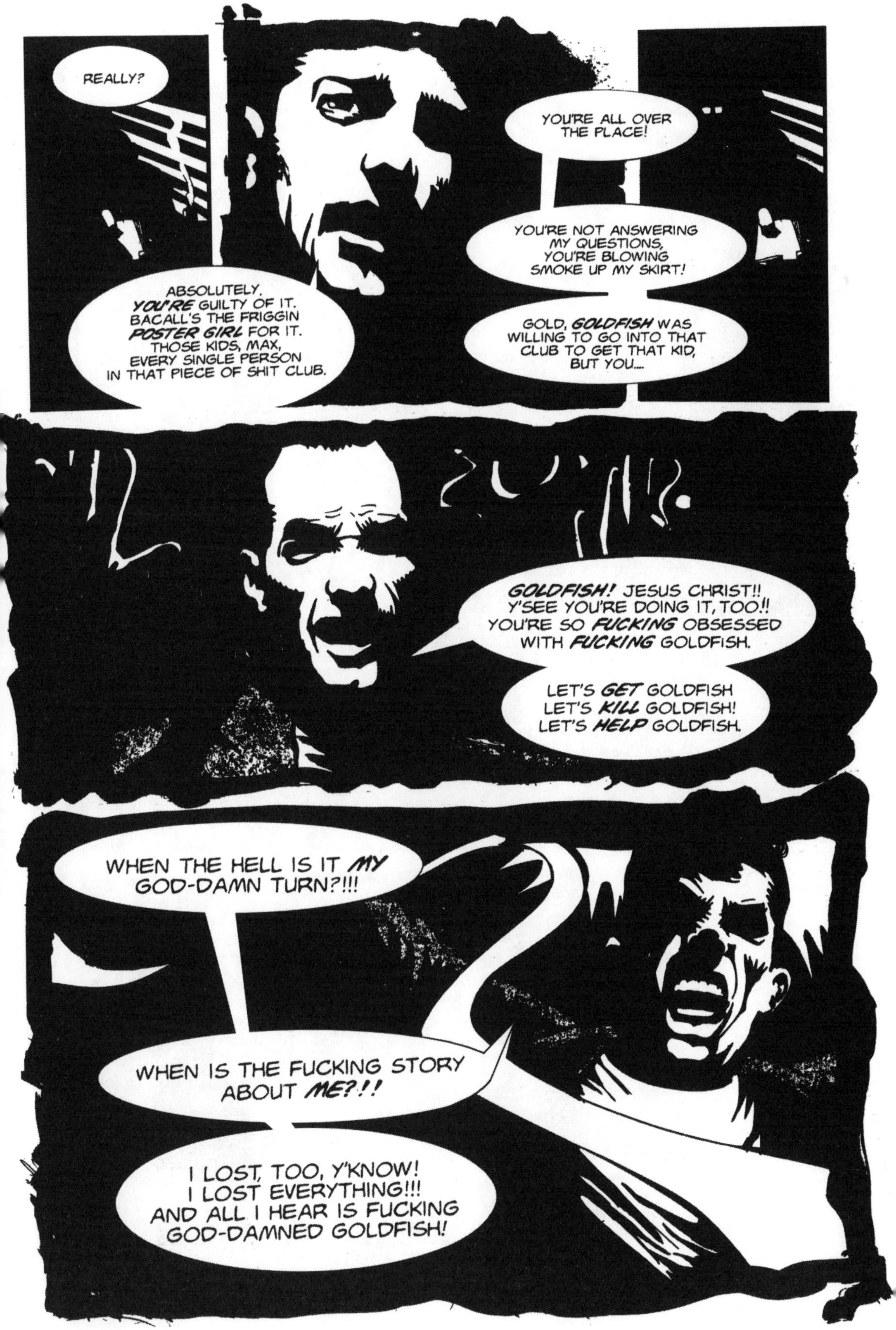
REALLY?
ABSOLUTELY. YOU'RE GUILTY OF IT. BACALL'S THE FRIGGIN POSTER GIRL FOR IT. THOSE KIDS, MAX, EVERY SINGLE PERSON IN THAT PIECE OF SHIT CLUB.
YOU'RE ALL OVER THE PLACE!
YOU'RE NOT ANSWERING MY QUESTIONS, YOU'RE BLOWING SMOKE UP MY SKIRT!
GOLD, GOLDFISH WAS WILLING TO GO INTO THAT CLUB TO GET THAT KID, BUT YOU...
GOLDFISH! JESUS CHRIST!! Y'SEE YOU'RE DOING IT, TOO!! YOU'RE SO FUCKING OBSESSED WITH FUCKING GOLDFISH.
LET'S GET GOLDFISH LET'S KILL GOLDFISH! LET'S HELP GOLDFISH.
WHEN THE HELL IS IT MY GOD-DAMN TURN?!!!
WHEN IS THE FUCKING STORY ABOUT ME?!!
I LOST, TOO, Y'KNOW! I LOST EVERYTHING!!! AND ALL I HEAR IS FUCKING GOD-DAMNED GOLDFISH!

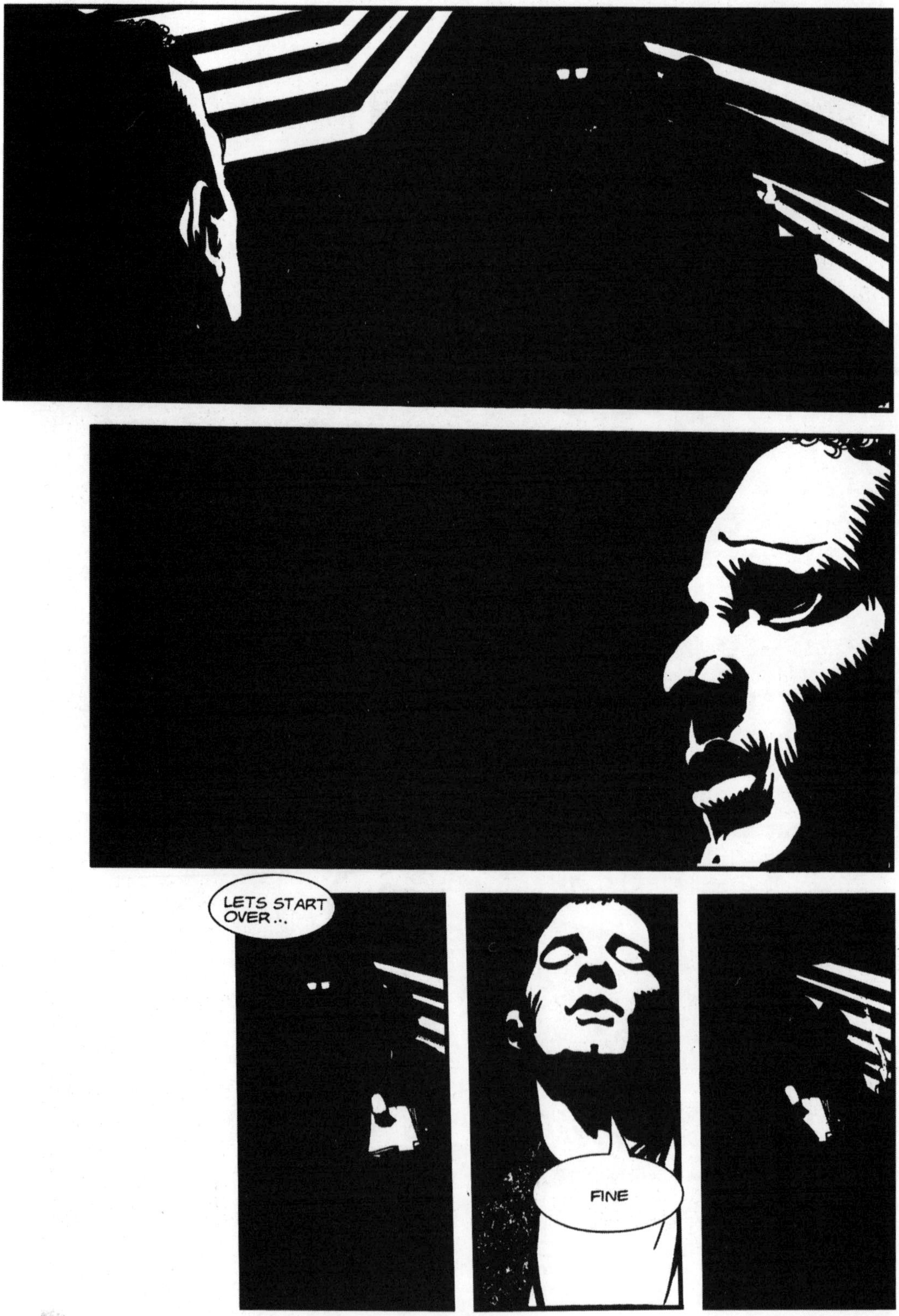
LETS START OVER...
FINE

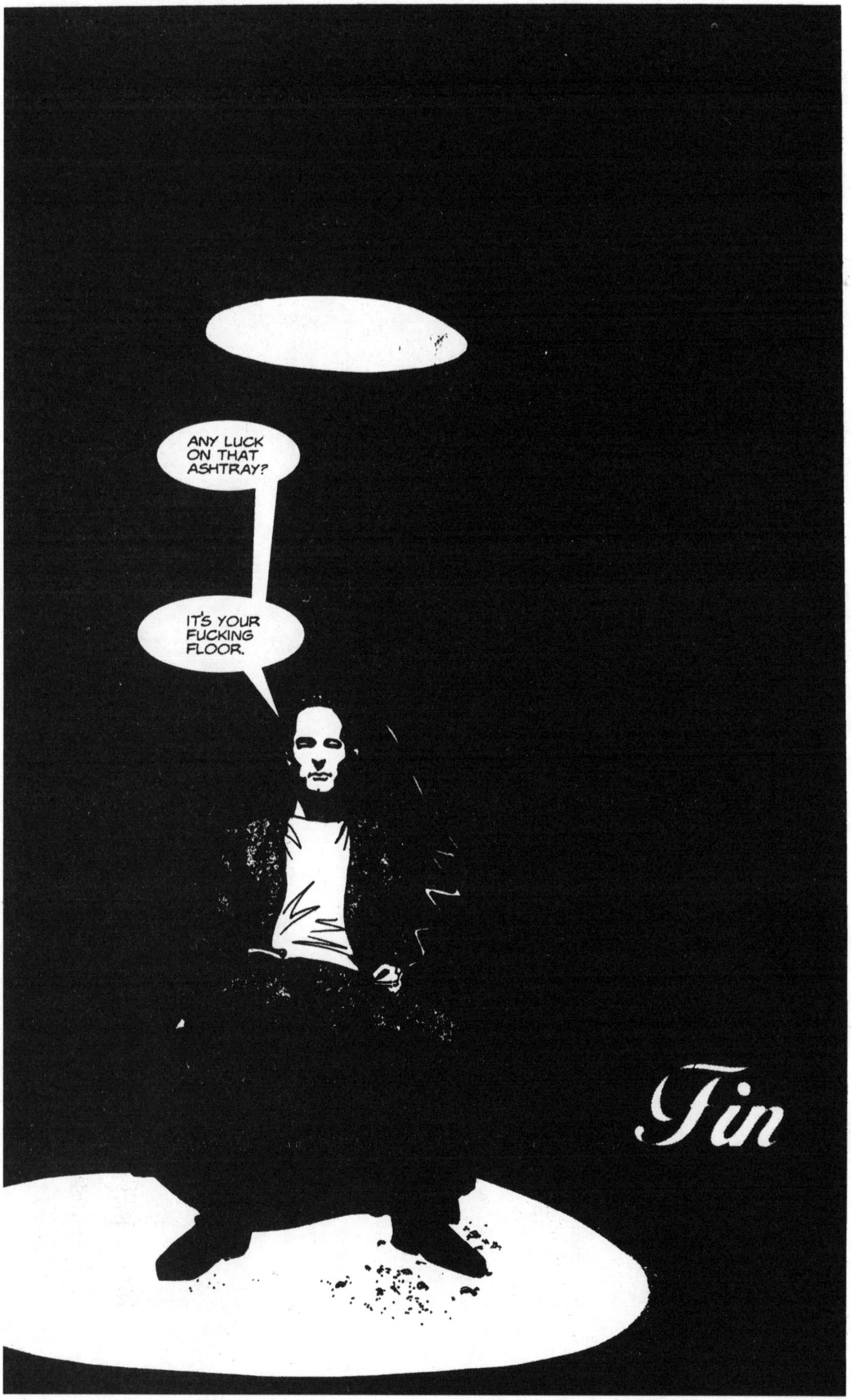
ANY LUCK ON THAT ASHTRAY?
IT'S YOUR FUCKING FLOOR.
Fin

goldfish
special
featurees

In this following section, it is my pleasure to present to you...

The Goldfish sneak preview originally presented in Caliber Spotlight 1.

A one-sheet Goldfish advertisement story.

A Goldfish prose story- based on the sneak preview.

A retrospective look at the development of the book.

A selection of advertisement art.

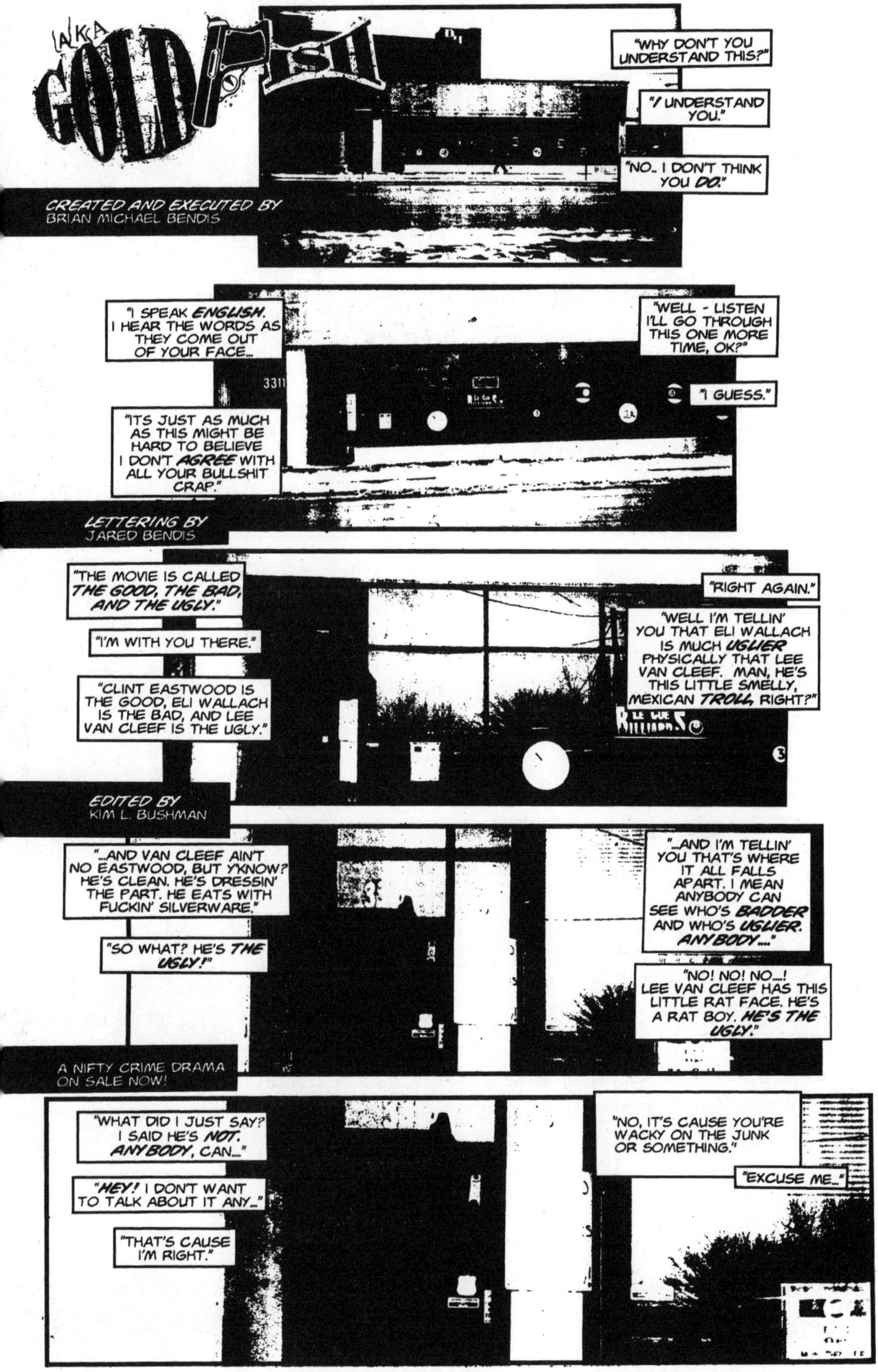

"WHY DON'T YOU UNDERSTAND THIS?"
"I UNDERSTAND YOU."
"NO.. I DON'T THINK YOU DO."
CREATED AND EXECUTED BY
BRIAN MICHAEL BENDIS
"I SPEAK ENGLISH. I HEAR THE WORDS AS THEY COME OUT OF YOUR FACE..
"WELL - LISTEN I'LL GO THROUGH THIS ONE MORE TIME, OK?"
"I GUESS."
"ITS JUST AS MUCH AS THIS MIGHT BE HARD TO BELIEVE I DON'T AGREE WITH ALL YOUR BULLSHIT CRAP."
LETTERING BY
JARED BENDIS
"THE MOVIE IS CALLED THE GOOD, THE BAD, AND THE UGLY."
"RIGHT AGAIN."
"I'M WITH YOU THERE."
"WELL I'M TELLIN' YOU THAT ELI WALLACH IS MUCH UGLIER PHYSICALLY THAT LEE VAN CLEEF. MAN, HE'S THIS LITTLE SMELLY, MEXICAN TROLL, RIGHT?"
"CLINT EASTWOOD IS THE GOOD, ELI WALLACH IS THE BAD, AND LEE VAN CLEEF IS THE UGLY."
EDITED BY
KIM L. BUSHMAN
"...AND VAN CLEEF AIN'T NO EASTWOOD, BUT Y'KNOW? HE'S CLEAN. HE'S DRESSIN' THE PART. HE EATS WITH FUCKIN' SILVERWARE."
"...AND I'M TELLIN' YOU THAT'S WHERE IT ALL FALLS APART. I MEAN ANYBODY CAN SEE WHO'S BADDER AND WHO'S UGLIER. ANYBODY...."
"SO WHAT? HE'S THE UGLY!"
"NO! NO! NO...! LEE VAN CLEEF HAS THIS LITTLE RAT FACE. HE'S A RAT BOY. HE'S THE UGLY."
A NIFTY CRIME DRAMA ON SALE NOW!
"WHAT DID I JUST SAY? I SAID HE'S NOT. ANYBODY, CAN..."
"HEY! I DON'T WANT TO TALK ABOUT IT ANY..."
"THAT'S CAUSE I'M RIGHT."
"NO, IT'S CAUSE YOU'RE WACKY ON THE JUNK OR SOMETHING."
"EXCUSE ME..."

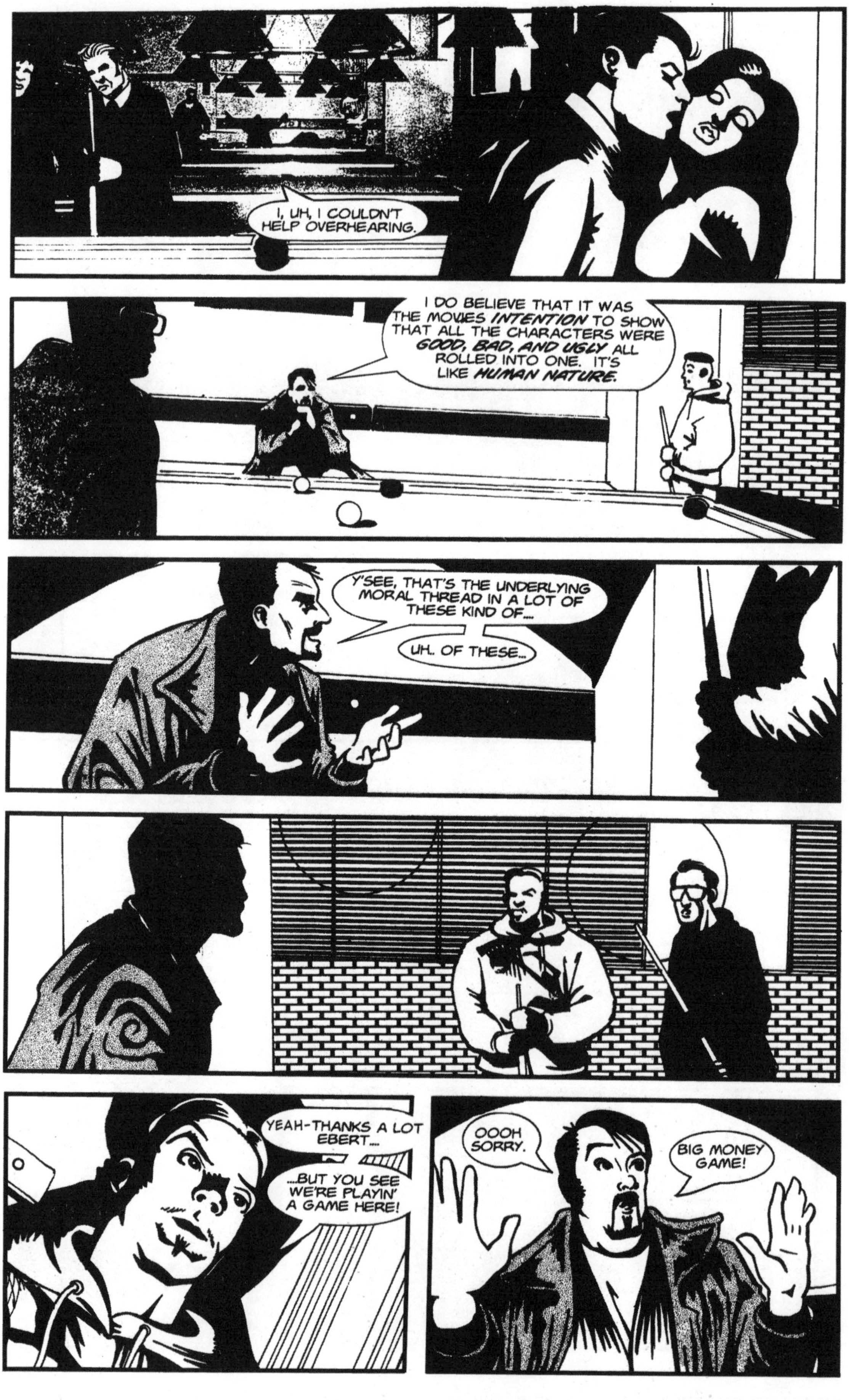
I, UH, I COULDN'T HELP OVERHEARING.
I DO BELIEVE THAT IT WAS THE MOVIES INTENTION TO SHOW THAT ALL THE CHARACTERS WERE GOOD, BAD, AND UGLY ALL ROLLED INTO ONE. IT'S LIKE HUMAN NATURE.
Y'SEE, THAT'S THE UNDERLYING MORAL THREAD IN A LOT OF THESE KIND OF...
UH.. OF THESE...
YEAH-THANKS A LOT EBERT...
...BUT YOU SEE WE'RE PLAYIN' A GAME HERE!
OOOH SORRY.
BIG MONEY GAME!

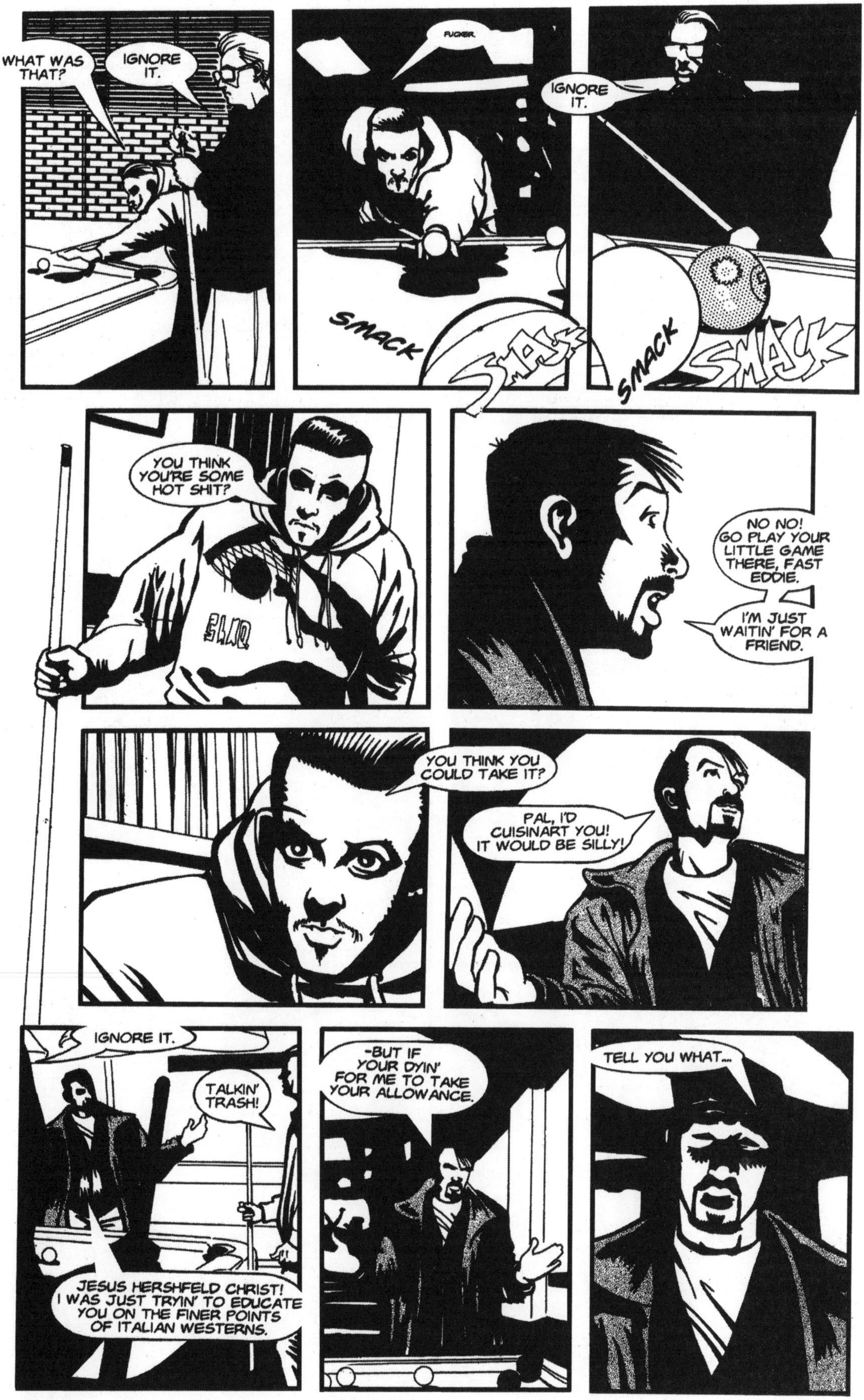
WHAT WAS THAT?
IGNORE IT.
FUCKER.
IGNORE IT.
SMACK
SMACK
SMACK
SMACK
YOU THINK YOU'RE SOME HOT SHIT?
NO NO! GO PLAY YOUR LITTLE GAME THERE, FAST EDDIE.
I'M JUST WAITIN' FOR A FRIEND.
YOU THINK YOU COULD TAKE IT?
PAL, I'D CUISINART YOU! IT WOULD BE SILLY!
IGNORE IT.
TALKIN' TRASH!
JESUS HERSHFELD CHRIST! I WAS JUST TRYIN' TO EDUCATE YOU ON THE FINER POINTS OF ITALIAN WESTERNS.
-BUT IF YOUR DYIN' FOR ME TO TAKE YOUR ALLOWANCE.
TELL YOU WHAT...

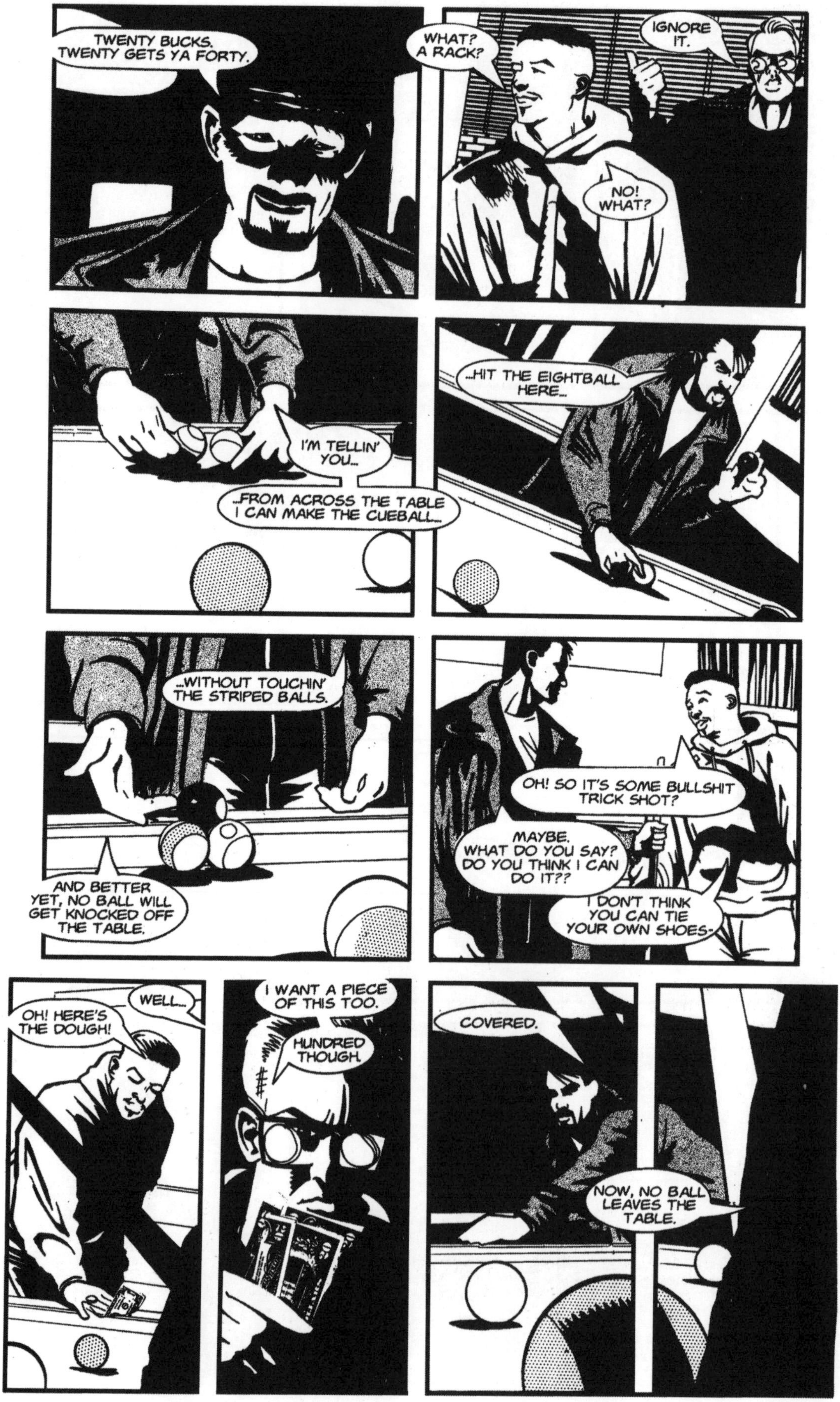
TWENTY BUCKS. TWENTY GETS YA FORTY.
WHAT? A RACK?
IGNORE IT.
NO! WHAT?
I'M TELLIN' YOU...
...FROM ACROSS THE TABLE I CAN MAKE THE CUEBALL...
...HIT THE EIGHTBALL HERE...
...WITHOUT TOUCHIN' THE STRIPED BALLS.
AND BETTER YET, NO BALL WILL GET KNOCKED OFF THE TABLE.
OH! SO IT'S SOME BULLSHIT TRICK SHOT?
MAYBE. WHAT DO YOU SAY? DO YOU THINK I CAN DO IT??
I DON'T THINK YOU CAN TIE YOUR OWN SHOES-
WELL...
OH! HERE'S THE DOUGH!
I WANT A PIECE OF THIS TOO.
HUNDRED THOUGH.
COVERED.
NOW, NO BALL LEAVES THE TABLE.

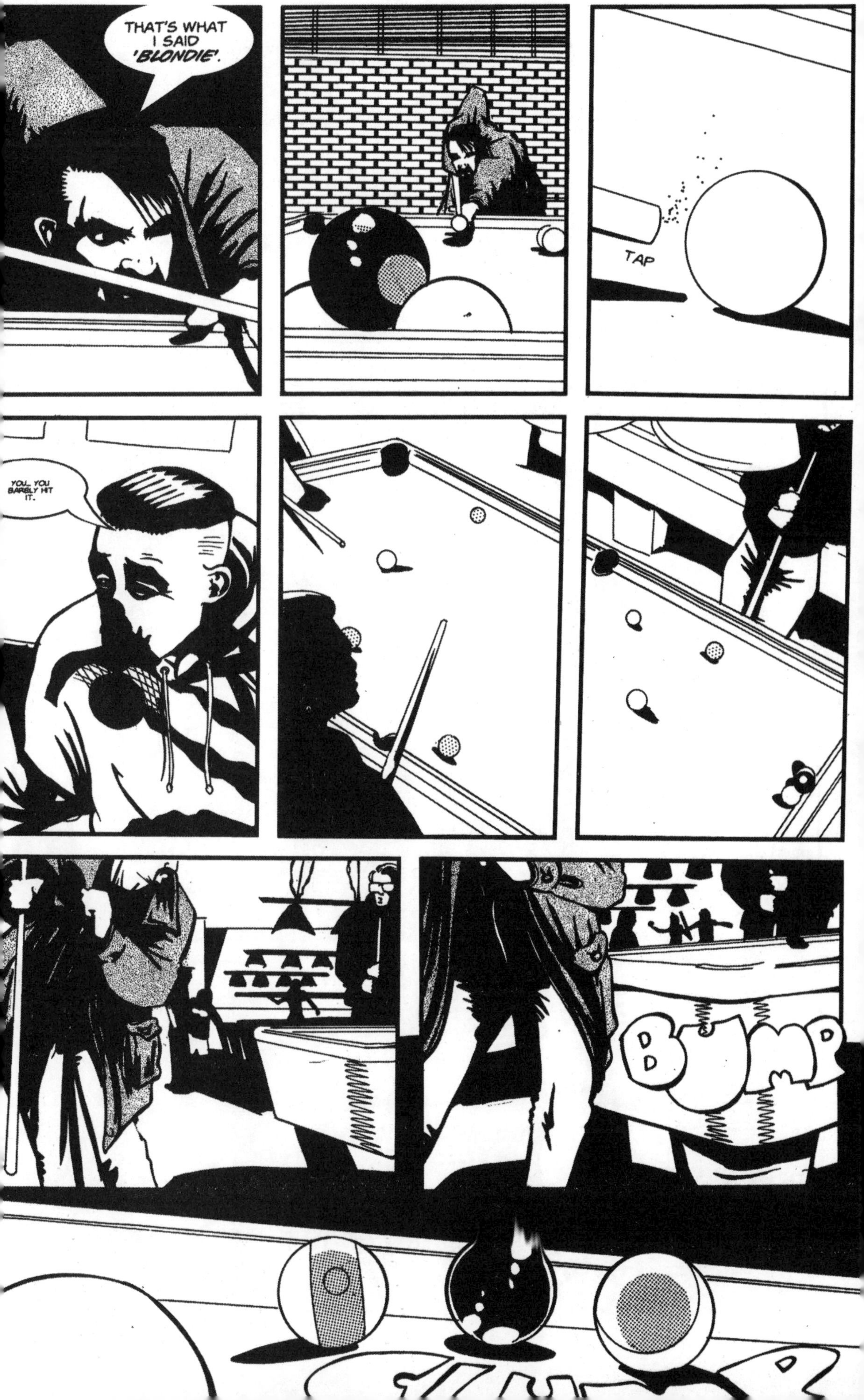
THAT'S WHAT I SAID 'BLONDIE'.
TAP
YOU... YOU BARELY HIT IT.
BUMP

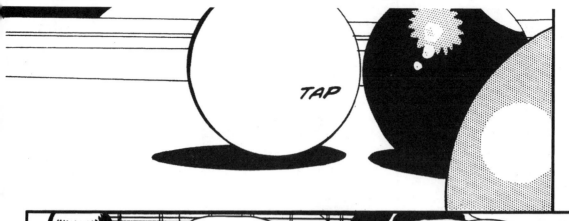

TAP

HEY NOW!

YOU HIT THE TABLE!!

SHOULDA FUCKIN' IGNORED HIM.

SHIT! TOLDJA.

AH AH AH.

I DO BELIEVE THAT'S MINE.

HEY! YOU HIT THE TABLE.

THAT DOESN'T COUNT.

FUCKER! IT DOESN'T COUNT!!

WELL, LIKE I ALWAYS SAYS...

...IT ISN'T WHETHER YOU WIN OR LOSE...

...IT'S WHETHER I WIN OR LOSE.

AKA GOLDFISH: ACE, JACK, QUEEN. ON SALE NOW.

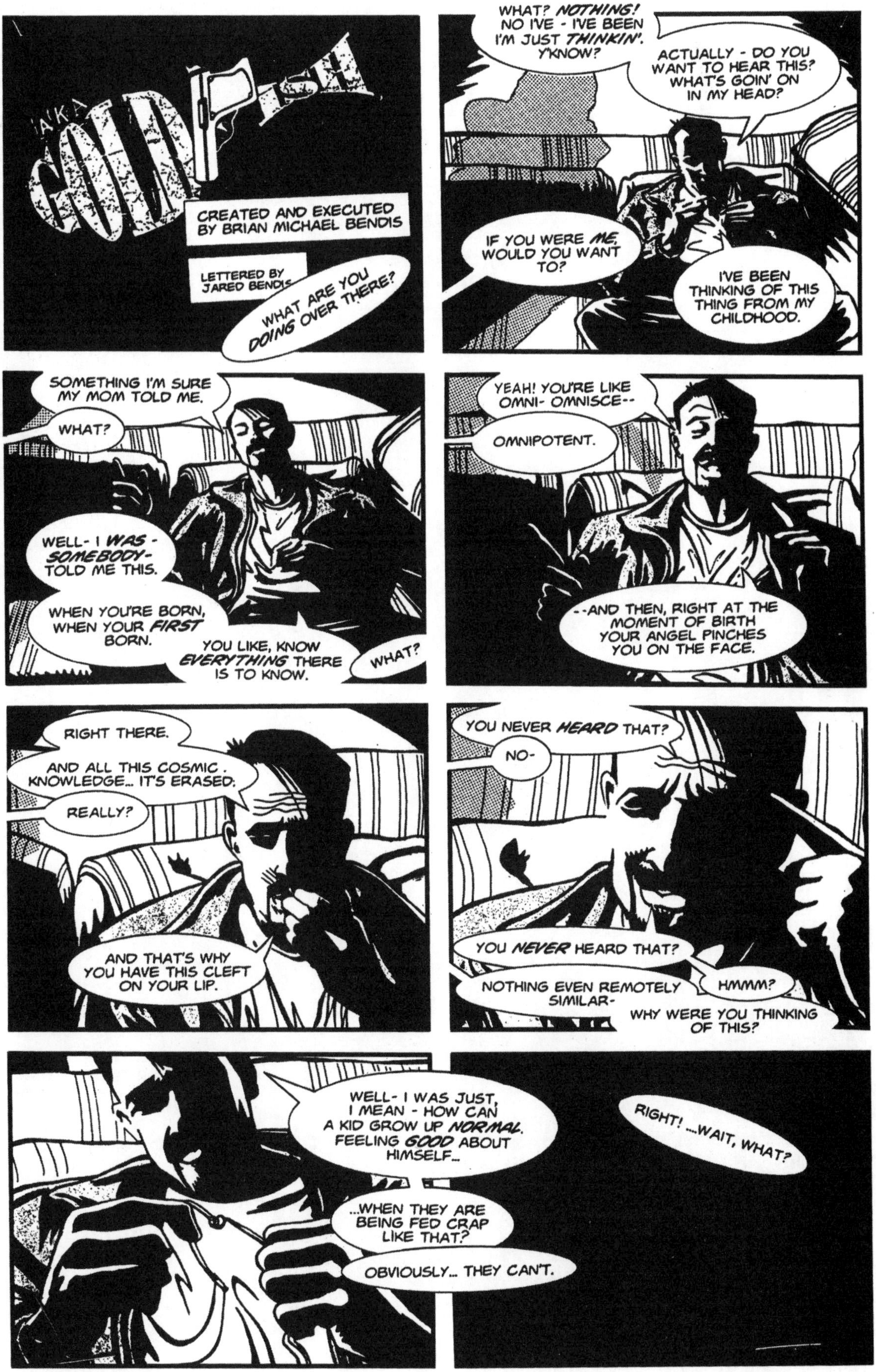
A.K.A. GOLDFISH
CREATED AND EXECUTED BY BRIAN MICHAEL BENDIS
LETTERED BY JARED BENDIS
WHAT ARE YOU DOING OVER THERE?
WHAT? NOTHING! NO I'VE - I'VE BEEN I'M JUST THINKIN'. Y'KNOW?
ACTUALLY - DO YOU WANT TO HEAR THIS? WHAT'S GOIN' ON IN MY HEAD?
IF YOU WERE ME, WOULD YOU WANT TO?
I'VE BEEN THINKING OF THIS THING FROM MY CHILDHOOD.
SOMETHING I'M SURE MY MOM TOLD ME.
WHAT?
WELL- I WAS - SOMEBODY- TOLD ME THIS.
WHEN YOU'RE BORN, WHEN YOUR FIRST BORN.
YOU LIKE, KNOW EVERYTHING THERE IS TO KNOW.
WHAT?
YEAH! YOU'RE LIKE OMNI- OMNISCE--
OMNIPOTENT.
--AND THEN, RIGHT AT THE MOMENT OF BIRTH YOUR ANGEL PINCHES YOU ON THE FACE.
RIGHT THERE.
AND ALL THIS COSMIC . KNOWLEDGE... IT'S ERASED.
REALLY?
AND THAT'S WHY YOU HAVE THIS CLEFT ON YOUR LIP.
YOU NEVER HEARD THAT?
NO-
YOU NEVER HEARD THAT?
NOTHING EVEN REMOTELY SIMILAR-
HMMM?
WHY WERE YOU THINKING OF THIS?
WELL- I WAS JUST, I MEAN - HOW CAN A KID GROW UP NORMAL. FEELING GOOD ABOUT HIMSELF...
...WHEN THEY ARE BEING FED CRAP LIKE THAT?
OBVIOUSLY... THEY CAN'T.
RIGHT! ...WAIT, WHAT?

Goldfish looks around the run-down Cleveland city street perfectly convinced that it has not changed a brick since 1952. Wednesday afternoon and it's a virtual ghost town, so quiet that the buzz and click of the traffic light switching is consuming.

He approaches Rusty's billiard room, decorated with a weather beaten, old-style painted sign and a large neon cue ball that has never been turned on for as long as Goldfish can remember. With his ratty leather coat lightly flapping behind him, he slips inside.

It's exactly as he remembered it. Not almost like, or sort of like, exactly. Seven rows of tables, each with its own row of low track lights; dingy smoke-stained burgundy walls accented by scarce of neon advertisements for beer and cigarettes.

As soon as his already tired eyes adjust from walking into this dungeon from the bright light of outside, as soon as the thick pool hall smell puffs him in the face, he immediately feels more relaxed than he has since he popped back into town. What a Pavlov dog, he thought.

His eyes dart around the room. Evan wasn't here yet. Goldfish shakes his head to the tune of what a high-definition loser the guy is. He wishes he could think of a better word to describe him, but nothing else fits. He then contemplates his own status in life if he's relying on guys like Evan to do his dirty work.

The afternoon "rush" for Rusty's was perfect for Goldfish's purposes today. It was dead. Two would-be/ might-be hustlers brushing up off each other in the corner. A freakishly attractive Hispanic couple in the other corner making out like they're audition-ing for a Zalman King movie and three young guys playing hooky, drinkin' brewkies, and shooting some pool.

Goldfish approaches the counter. There's Rusty, with the same stance, the same shirt, with the same "had it up to here" look on his face he had a decade ago. If Lawrence Tierney and Lawrence Tierney had a baby…it would be Rusty.

Goldfish ordered his Coke and was surprised at his own disappointment Rusty didn't recognize him. But how could he. It was a brick hard 10 years, a different hair color and a goatee ago. But Goldfish didn't broach the subject with Rusty; figuring it didn't matter either way. Small talk sucks for people who are good at it. What kind of disaster would their exchange be?

Goldfish saunters past the romance novel couple on his way over to the three guys, the only ones that look like they might supply some people viewing entertainment while he waits. The couple is definitely cheating on someone. His hand so far up her skirt. Her fists clenched behind his back. Goldfish quickly abandons the pretense of not looking and just takes as much of the sight in as he walks past.

Goldfish plants himself a few feet from the friendly game and swigs the refrigerated can of Coke. A couple drops slip into the jungle of his goatee. Goldfish realizes that this facial hair experiment may not be working out as well as originally planned. He'll give it a couple more days but that's it.

His follicle reverie is broken by the increased volume of the young trio

"Why don't you understand this?" whines the one in the Nike hooded sweatshirt and rose tinted glasses.

"I understand you, I just barely care. Take your turn." mutters his friend, his competitiveness bleeding through every word, and his eyes never leaving the table.

This one is a real character, a pencil thin Fu Man Chu mustache, a bolo tie, and a shaved sides haircut, with the tuft on top secured by a generous helping of men's hair mousse. Goldfish does not recall ever having seen someone go to such grooming lengths to look like such shit.

The third sits 10 feet from Goldfish on the pool-hall length bench. He stares ahead, nursing his second beer and trying to recover from whatever disheartening event brought these three here instead of to work. Goldfish thinks there's nothing like a good old-fashioned dumping to make a couple of pals from the factory take a hooky day to go play some pool with you in the guise of consolation.

"No, I don't think you do," challenges Nike.

"I speak English. Fluently. I hear the words as they come out of your face," his friend retorts, gesturing toward the table. "It's just as hard as this might be for you to believe- I don't care about any of this bullshit crap."

"Then I'll go through it one more time," Nike insists as he lowers his cue.

The bolo tie clicks against itself as its owner slaps his hands against his sides in frustration.

"The movie is called what? The Good, the Bad, and the Ugly," Nike lectures. Immediately Goldfish perks up.

"Well, I'm with you so far," humors bolo.

"Clint Eastwood is the good. Eli- what's his name?- Wallach, is the bad, and the other one, Van Cleef, is the ugly."

"Right."

"Well, I'm telling you that Eli Wallach is so, so much uglier physically than this Lee Van Cleef. Man, he's like this little smelly Mexican troll, right? And Van Cleef ain't no pretty boy like East-wood is, but, y'know, he's dressed. He's clean. He eats with fucking silverware. So how's he 'the Ugly'?"

Bolo doesn't even try to answer, well aware that his hyper friend is only mid stream. He just lazily stares at the peep show in the corner as Nike barrels on.

"And I'm telling you, that's where it all falls the hell apart for me. I mean, anyone can see who's badder and who's uglier. Any-body. When I was a little pisher sittin' in front of the tube on, like, Saturday afternoon and I first saw this movie. It confused the shit out of me 'cause first of all, they have those god-damn ridiculous Spanish subtitles or whatever you call them, and second I'm sitting there going: 'What the fuck? Who's supposed to be the ugly?'" Nike finally runs out of words and air.

Bolo summons the strength to break in. "No, no, no. I am telling you, this Van Cleese guy, he's -he's got like a little rat face. He's a rat boy. He's 'the Ugly!'"

"What did I just say? I said he's not."

"Hey! Don't bite my dick off. I don't even want to talk about this anyhow."

"'Cause I'm so right."

"No, 'cause I'd say you were on crack if I didn't know you were to cheap to invest in a pipe."

"No, see you got it all wrong…" As soon as Goldfish hears these words escape his mouth, he's sorry.

"Excuse me," Sneers Bolo.

Too late now, Goldfish says to himself, commit to it.

"Yeah, I, uh, I do believe that it was the director's intention, Leone, to show that, uh, that all the characters were, y'know, good, bad, and ugly, all rolled up into one, sort of. Human nature."

The audience of three all stare silent.

"Y'see," Goldfish says trying to bring it home, "that's the underlying thread in a lot of these kind of...these kind of...." Goldfish fully realizes there's no way out and no point in continuing.

The trio staring at the intruder. The jukebox's Clapton guitar solo is Goldfish's only friend.

"Yeah, well, thanks a lot, Ebert," snaps Bolo, " but we're playin' a game here.

And that's all it takes. Goldfish feels the churn again. He feels the itch and scratch that used to slowly creep up but now just pours all over him. So fast. So definite. He had just wanted to sit and drink the Coke. But, oh- it's the tie, that pasty skin and purplish hue around the pebbly eyes. It's the shine off the hair sculpture. And it's definitely the 'tude.

Goldfish has to take this guy's money.

"Oh sorry, Fast Eddie." Goldfish holds up his hands as a back-off. "You go play that big money game-show us how it's done there, big time."

Bolo grimaces and leans to set up his shot.

" What was that?" he mutters.

"Ignore it," Nike whispers as he chalks his cue.

Bolo takes his shot. The balls crack together once, twice. They roll but do not tumble.

"Wow! You the man". Goldfish beams.

"Fucker!" Bolo sneers.

"Ignore it!" Nike says in a half command.

"And what are you?" Bolo barks to Goldfish. "You think you're some hot shit? Back on outta here. Get your own game."

"Hey, I'm not lookin' for a game. I'm just waitin' on a friend. Don't mind me."

Bolo tries to ignore Goldfish and calm himself as his friend lines up a shot.

"But this added bonus, that I'll get to watch a master pool player, is just God shining down on lucky me. Please continue..." Goldfish's mockery stabs into Bolo. His grip on his stick tightens.

"You think you got something?" Bolo challenges. "You think you could take it?"

"Are you speaking English?"

"You heard me man. You think you got a better game? Let's see what you got tough guy."

"Oh pal, don't do that. It would be silly." Goldfish sneers as he rolls his eyes and snorts. A more well practiced goading of a male there never was.

"Ignore it!" Nike barks, adjusting his glasses

"Talkin' trash!" Bolo pleads to his friend.

Goldfish slowly gets off his bench, puts down his Coke and flattens his long leather coat.

"Jesus Herchfeld Christ, man. I was just trying to educate you all on the finer points of Italian westerns- spaghetti westerns," Goldfish approaches the table and lets the overhead lighting mask the gleam in his eye. If you're dying for me to take your allowance, tell you what…"

The three just stare at their new adversary, waiting for the bomb to drop.

"What?" Bolo belts.

Goldfish smirks.

The oldest trick in a very old book. The one most anxious is the one that will hand over the money the fastest. He directs all his instructions to Bolo. "Twenty gets you forty, slick."

"Ignore it!" Nike barks again.

"No! What?" Bolo breezes past his friends toward Goldfish. "What choo mean? Twenty gets you forty what?"

"I'm telling you." Goldfish picks up the seven ball and the nine and holds them loose in one hand.

"Hey, there's a game in progress," Nike sneers.

"Yeah, I saw that."

Goldfish holds the balls up and rolls them between his fingers, fully aware that the glare of the overhead light is rolling across them. All three marks stare at the balls, never looking Goldfish straight in the eyes.

He takes the two balls and puts them next to each other in the middle of the far end of the table. They touch each other and the table itself.

"I say that from across the table there, I can hit the cue ball." Goldfish then picks up the eight ball. He displays it to them with the flair of a magician and carefully rests it atop the other two balls creating a mini pyramid.

Goldfish does this all with grace and precision. He thinks about the guy who taught him how when this game made the pyramid fall apart a couple times, the philosophy being that this creates a doubt in the mark's mind of the grifter's steadiness and ability. But Goldfish thinks bigger than that: the stronger the pyramid looks, the harder it will appear that, "...I can hit the eight ball with it, without, now get this, without touching either ball or knocking any ball off the table."

"Some bullshit trick shot," sputters Bolo.

"So, you think I can do it?"

"Dude, I don't think you can tie your own shoes."

"Well then, sounds to me like a wager is in order."

Bolo had already pulled out his wad, throwing no less then 50 on the corner of the table. "Oh I got the money, and an intense desire to watch you fuck up, choke, and just overall stick your own dick in your mouth."

"I want a piece of this too." Nike pulls out two fresh-as-a-morning- trip-to-the-ATM fifties. "But I'm in for a hundred."

"Covered." Goldfish purposefully doesn't look at the pile of green. He saunters to the other end of the table, cue stick and cue ball in hand. He lines the cue ball up rather casually, holds the cue stick firm, bends for the shot.

"No ball leaves the table," clarifies Nike as he tries to weigh the geometrical, gravitational and physiological ramifications of what is being proposed to him through the beer-drenched prism of his noggin.

Goldfish, focused on the task at hand, continues to line up the shot and gives just a vaguely audible: "What I said."

"Cover three bills more?" says a voice. Goldfish turns his head to see the third member of their party finally broken from his melancholy, just to give Goldfish his money.

Goldfish just smirks at him faux-warmly.

"Covered." And with that Goldfish takes his first look at the now attractive pile of cash.

Goldfish returns to lining up his shot. The cue ball is in perfect alignment with the pyramid. "Der Kommisar" pops into the jukebox. The cue stick is perfectly aligned with the center of the cue ball. Goldfish shuts his left eye and examines the shot. He switches eyes and repeats the process. His audience captive, respectfully silent, with no idea of what happens next.

Goldfish pulls the stick back firmly as if he will smack the cue ball with a thunderous slap. But instead comes back down with a confident but dainty tap of the ball. Enough to make it roll, but not a pound of force more.

The cue ball leisurely rolls toward the pyramid, allowing enough time for mark number three to get up and join his mates, and for Goldfish to straighten and again straighten his jacket. The only noise is the almost circular sound of the ball rolling and rolling.

Then as the ball rolls only a quarter of the table away from the pyramid, Goldfish starts to sing along with the juke, "Don't turn around, uh-oh…." rhythmically shaking his hips and on beat thrusts his hip onto the pool table.

The delicate pyramid collapses. The eight ball falls straight down. And the cue ball has just enough steam in it to slide up against the eight ball with the daintiest of taps.

"Der Kommisar's in town, uh-oh!" Goldfish shoots his fists and stick in the air, then falls to one knee tapping the stick on the ground.

"You hit the table!" blurts Bolo, making a dash for the money pile.

With an: "Ah-ah-ah!" Goldfish beats him to the punch and grabs his prize. "I do believe that this here is mine."

"Hey! You hit the fucking table!" Bolo points as his cohorts sternly flank him. "That doesn't count!"

Goldfish coolly adjusts the pile into a more ruly collection. The three marks look at each other then back to Goldfish.

"It doesn't not count." Goldfish consoles with a smile.

"Fucker!" blurts Bolo, holding his pool cue up as a warning.

"Hey, it's like I always say," offers Goldfish wagging the tighter pile to its previous owner, "It's not whether you win or lose it's whether I win or lose."

"Oh, that is fucking it!" Bolo reaches back a swing the cue stick. oldfish, shocked by the public outburst, neither runs no braces himself.

"Hey!" a crackling voice rings out.

All turn to see Rusty, baseball bat in a two-handed grip, wel ocked for a swing himself. His glare is intent, his posture is sure and practiced, and his aim is at no one in particular. "Goldfish, I thought I told you no more hustling in my joint!"

"Rusty, I thought...well...that was 10 years ago, my man." Goldfish can't hold back the warm and curious smile.

"I don't care if it was during the god-damn Civil War, I don't need this kind of headache, you bastard." Rusty readjusts his grip. The gravel of his voice is almost painful to hear. "Rule of the joint: if you make the bet, you pay the bet," he barks at the three.

"Yeah, but this asshole...," pleads Nike.

"...And the other rule is <u>no betting</u>. This is the fucking state of goddamn Ohio, you punks. Now I want all of ya's to vacate the goddamn premises. Don't you three have a goddamn job?"

"But he...," squeaks Bolo.

"What am I, your mammy? Out!" barks Rusty, followed by a wheeze-like, "Bastards."

Hesitantly the three grab their coats and roll out. Goldfish watches in admiration of the focus of Rusty's glare and grip. Rusty never takes his eyes off the trio as they slump out the door with a clang of the hanging doorbell.

Rusty turns his glare to Goldfish but lowers his bat. "Assface." He offers. "Always actin' like a god damn assface."

Goldfish just looks to the floor and snickers. When he looks back up, Rusty's callused hand outstretched in his direction.

"What?" mumbles Goldfish.

"What do you think you good-for-nothing, ungrateful sack of crap? Pony up 'fore I brake somethin'!"

Goldfish shakes his head, peels off a 50, folds it to a crease, and slides it in Rusty's shirt pocket.

"Cheap fucking Jew," Rusty mutters.

"I'm not even Jewish," Goldfish retorts.

"Yes you are!!" Rusty turns back to his counter. "Sit and stay out of trouble, or I crack you like a melon."

"Yes, sir." salutes Goldfish to his back.
"And shave your lip.

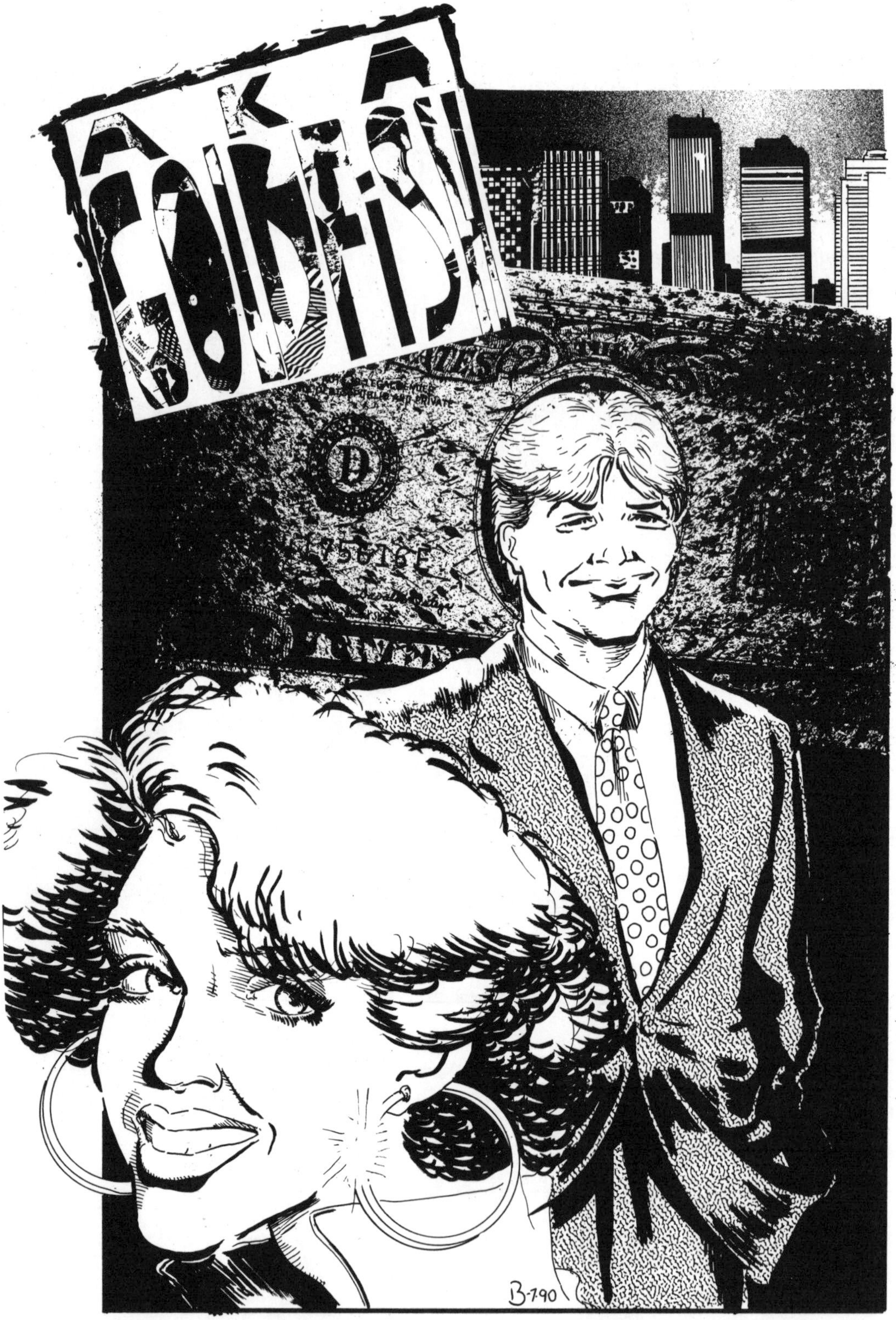
A K A
GOLDFISH
B-7-90

"You've come a long way baby" I've been working on this monkey for longer than I should have been. The following is an evolution. The 12 page short, (that I have mercifully condensed for you) is the first try circa 1988. Ironically I was able to tell the same story in 12 pages here in what it took me 85 in this graphic novel. The following pin-ups are dated for posterity.

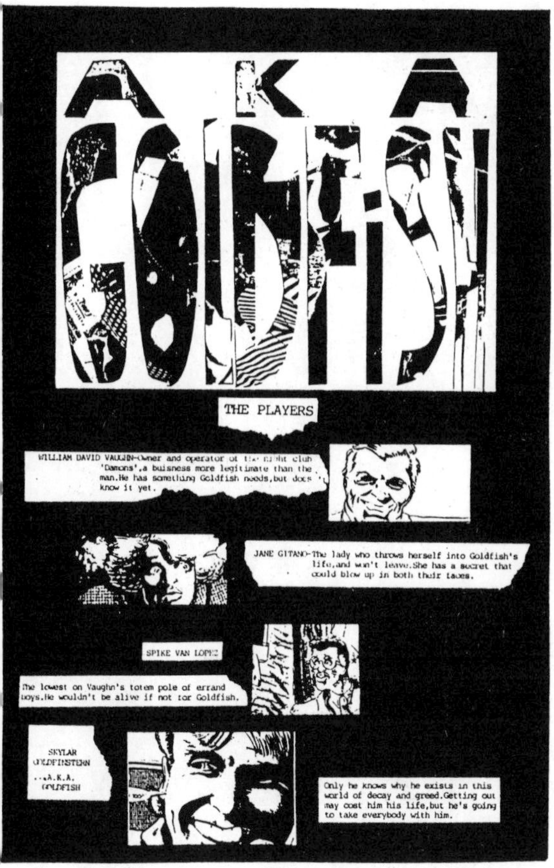
A K A
GOLDFISH
THE PLAYERS
WILLIAM DAVID VAUGHN-Owner and operator of the night club 'Damons',a buisness more legitimate than the man.He has something Goldfish needs,but does know it yet.
JANE GITANO-The lady who throws herself into Goldfish's life,and won't leave.She has a secret that could blow up in both their faces.
SPIKE VAN LOPEZ
The lowest on Vaughn's totem pole of errand boys.He wouldn't be alive if not for Goldfish.
SKYLAR GOLDFINSTERN
...A.K.A. GOLDFISH
Only he knows why he exists in this world of decay and greed.Getting out may cost him his life,but he's going to take everybody with him.

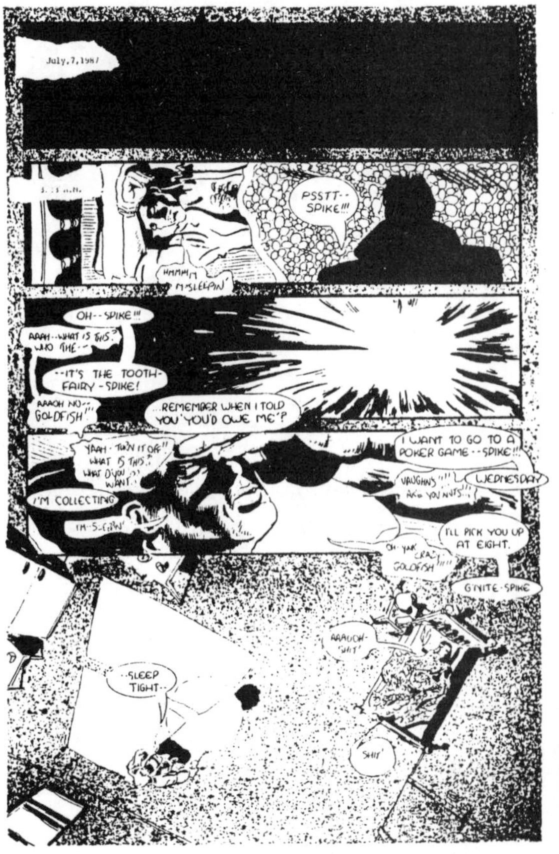
July.7,1987
PSSTT-- SPIKE!!!
OH--SPIKE!!!
AAAH--WHAT IS THIS? WHO THE--
--IT'S THE TOOTH-FAIRY-SPIKE!
AAAOH NO--GOLDFISH!
...REMEMBER WHEN I TOLD YOU YOU'D OWE ME'?
I WANT TO GO TO A POKER GAME--SPIKE!!
WEDNESDAY
I'M COLLECTING
I'LL PICK YOU UP AT EIGHT.
G'NITE-SPIKE
...SLEEP TIGHT--

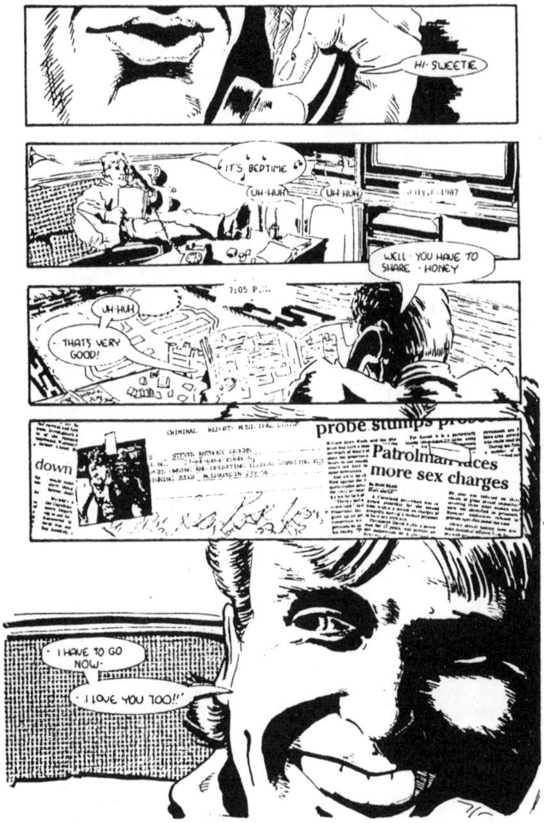
HI-SWEETIE
IT'S BEDTIME
UH-HUH
UH-HUH
July.7.1987
WELL-YOU HAVE TO SHARE - HONEY
7:05 P.M.
UH-HUH
-THAT'S VERY GOOD!
probe stumps pros
Patrolman faces more sex charges
I HAVE TO GO NOW-
-I LOVE YOU TOO!!

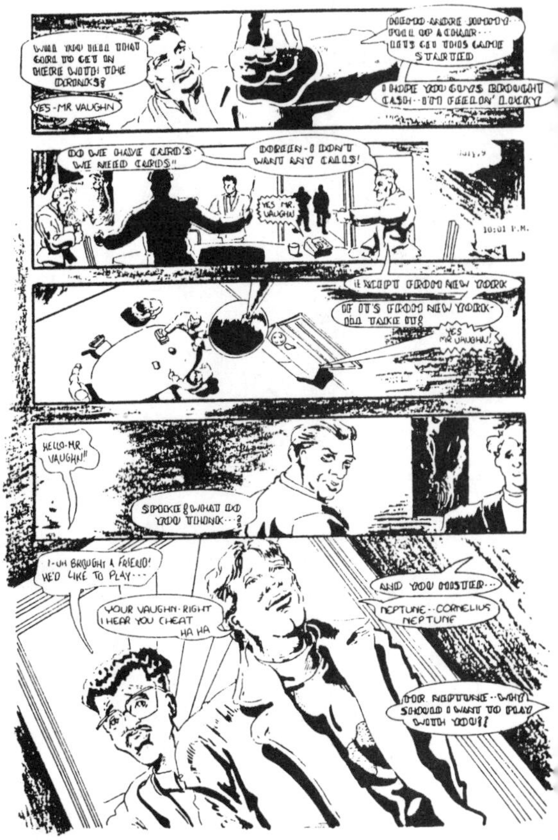
WILL YOU TELL THAT GIRL TO GET IN HERE WITH THE DRINKS?
YES-MR VAUGHN
I HOPE YOU GUYS BROUGHT CASH--I'M FEELIN' LUCKY!
DO WE HAVE CARD'S WE NEED CARDS!!
DOREEN-I DON'T WANT ANY CALLS!
YES MR. VAUGHN
10:01 P.M.
EXCEPT FROM NEW YORK
IF IT'S FROM NEW YORK-I'LL TAKE IT!
YES MR VAUGHN!
HELLO-MR. VAUGHN!!
SPIKE!WHAT DO YOU THINK...?
I-UH BROUGHT A FRIEND! HE'D LIKE TO PLAY...
YOUR VAUGHN-RIGHT I HEAR YOU CHEAT HA HA
AND YOU MISTER...
NEPTUNE--CORNELIUS NEPTUNE
MR NEPTUNE--WHY SHOULD I WANT TO PLAY WITH YOU!!

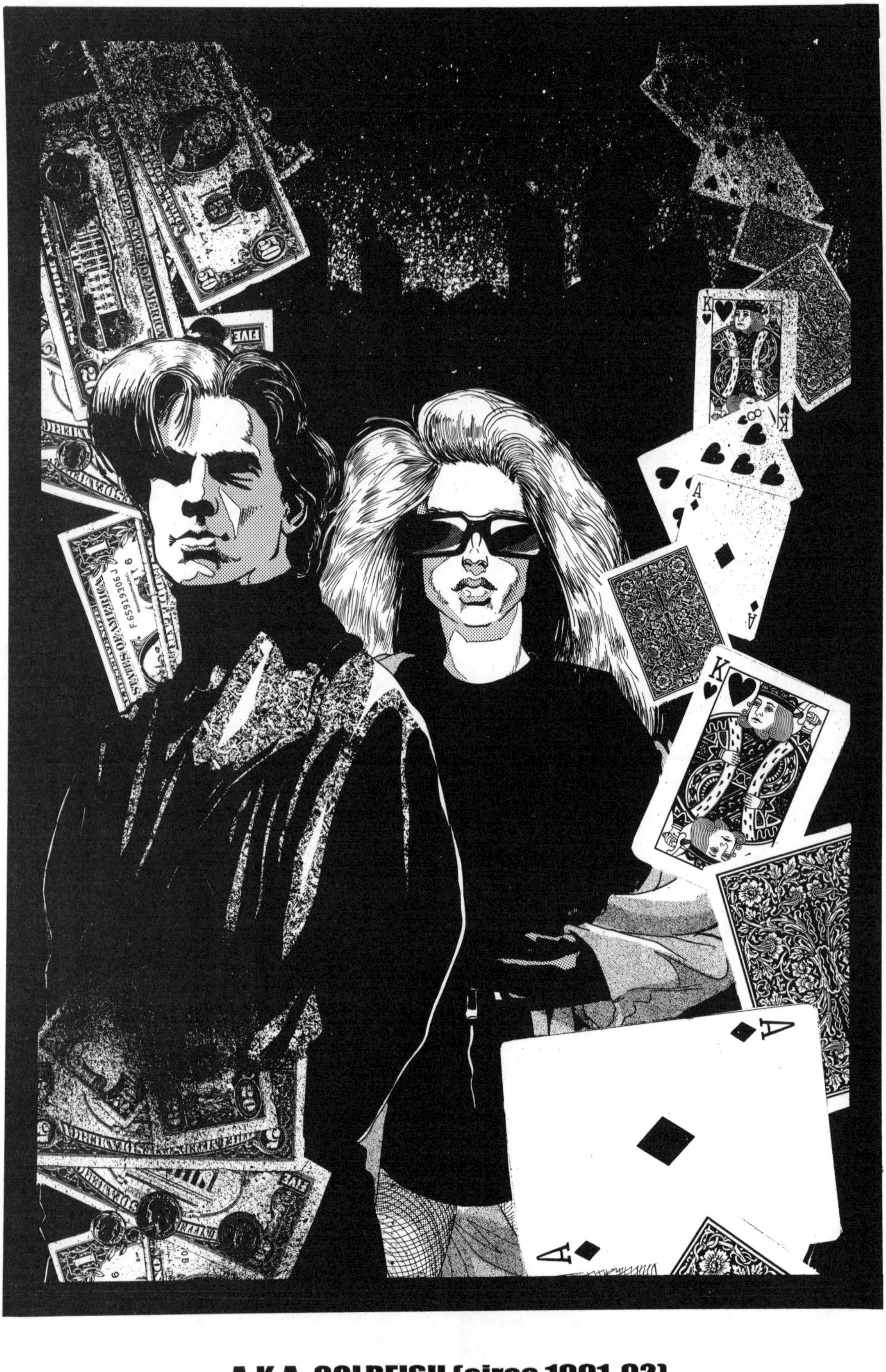

A.K.A. GOLDFISH (circa 1991-92)
GQ, big hair, pouty lips.
(Thank God, I worked this out of my system)

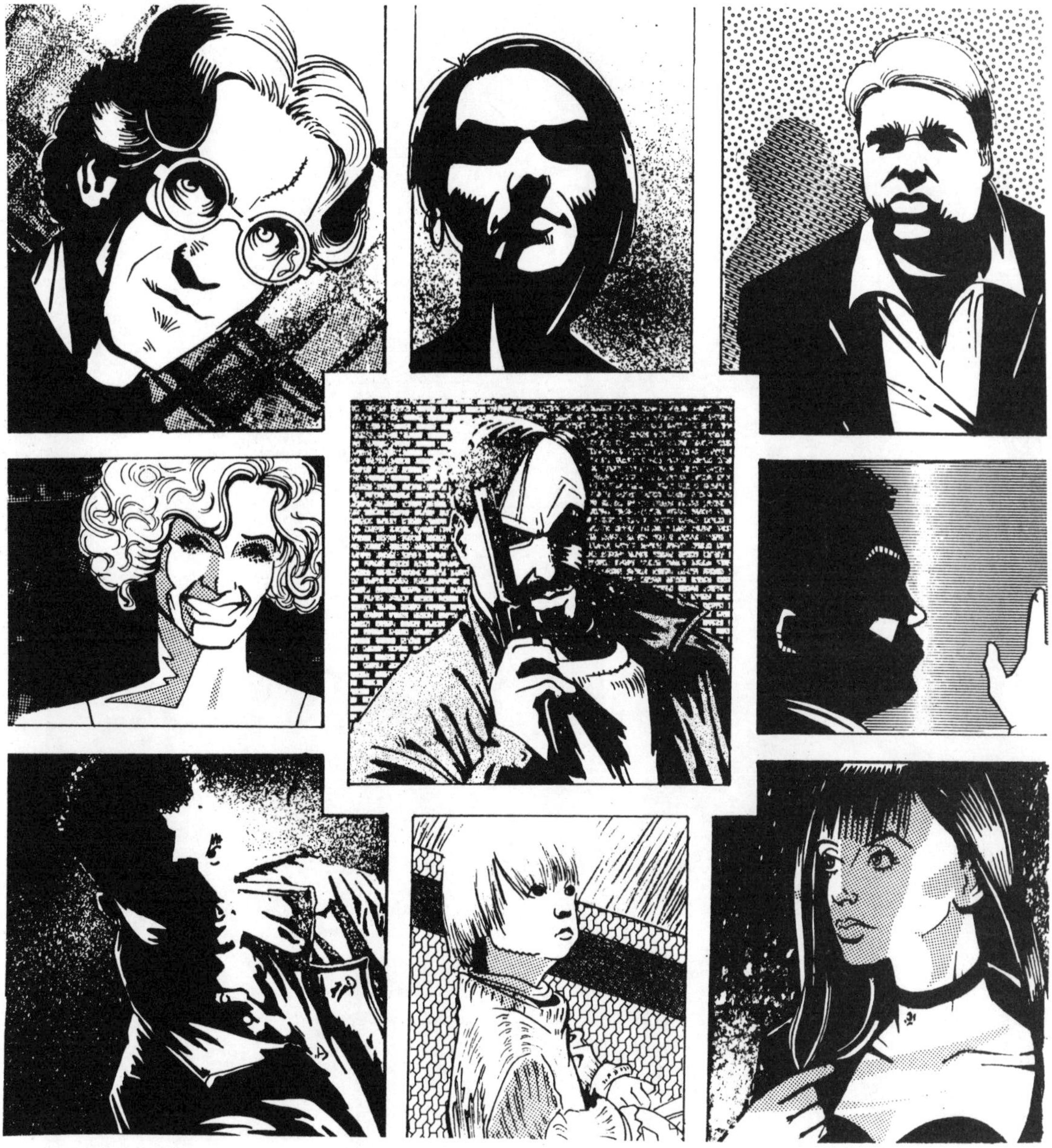

A.K.A. GOLDFISH: PROMO CHARACTER SHEET - (circa 1994)
...and we're off and running.

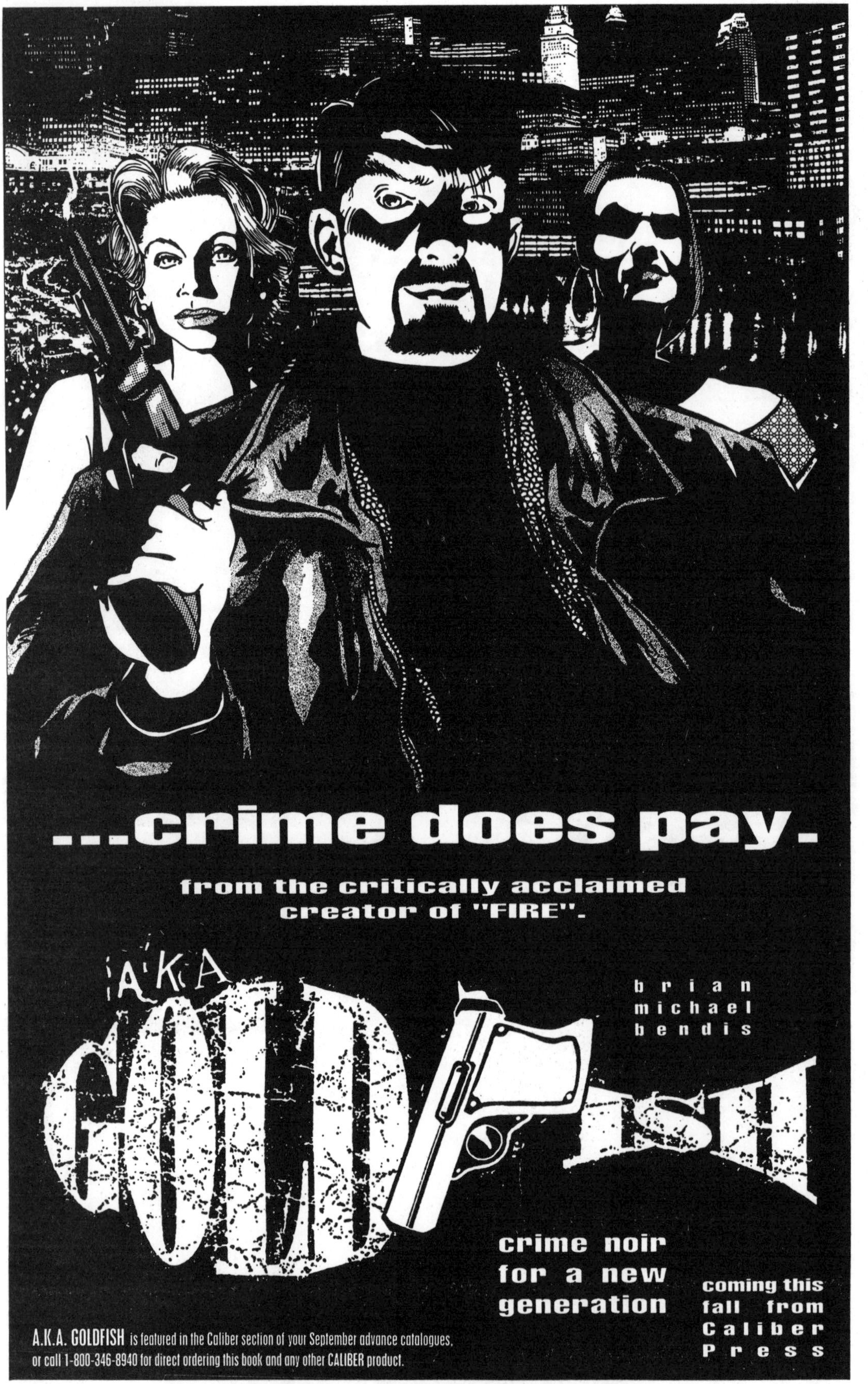
...crime does pay.
from the critically acclaimed creator of "FIRE".
A.K.A.
GOLDFISH
brian michael bendis
crime noir for a new generation
coming this fall from Caliber Press
A.K.A. GOLDFISH is featured in the Caliber section of your September advance catalogues, or call 1-800-346-8940 for direct ordering this book and any other CALIBER product.

A.K.A. GOLDFISH PROMO PIECES
(Used for ads, posters and trading cards)

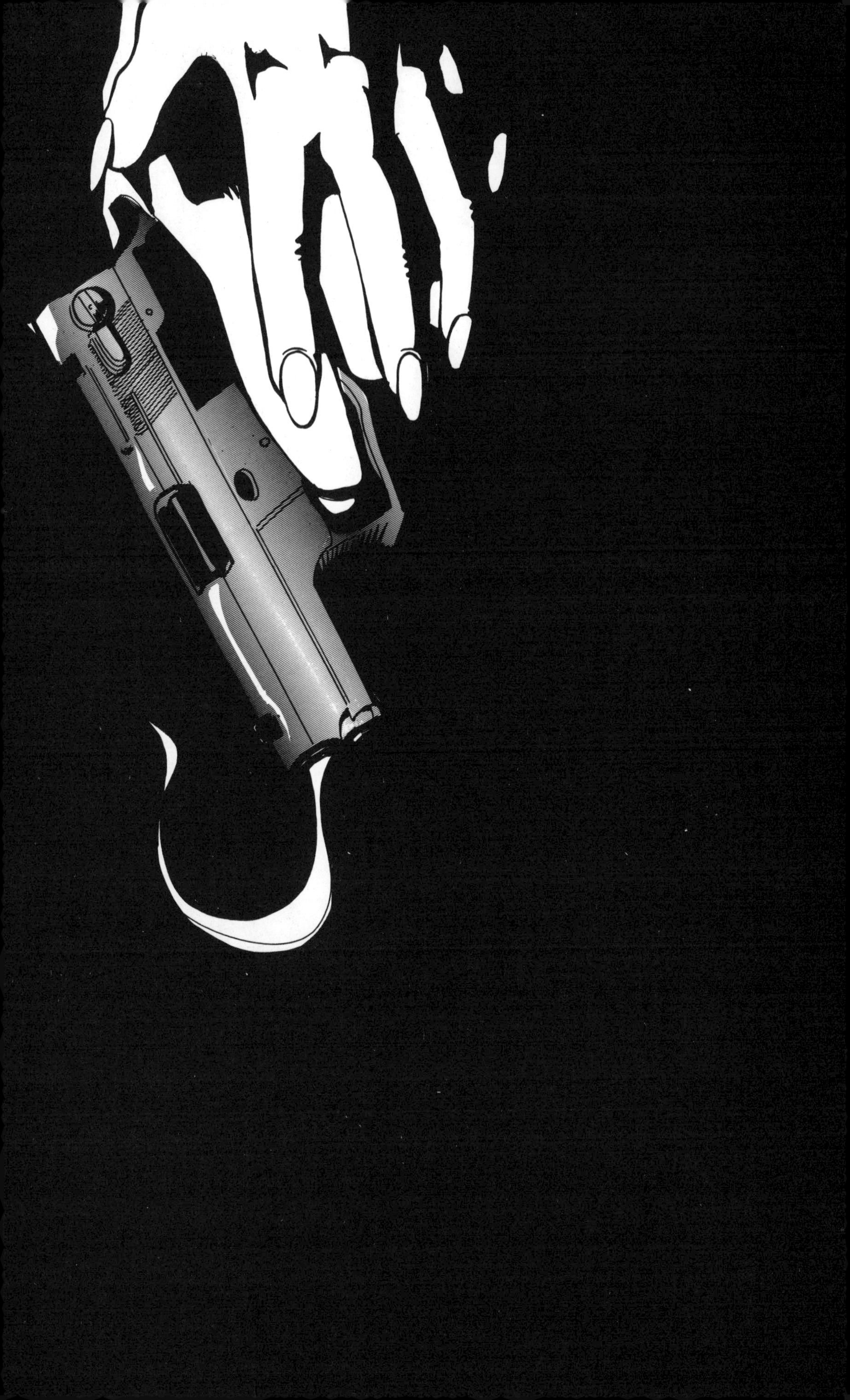

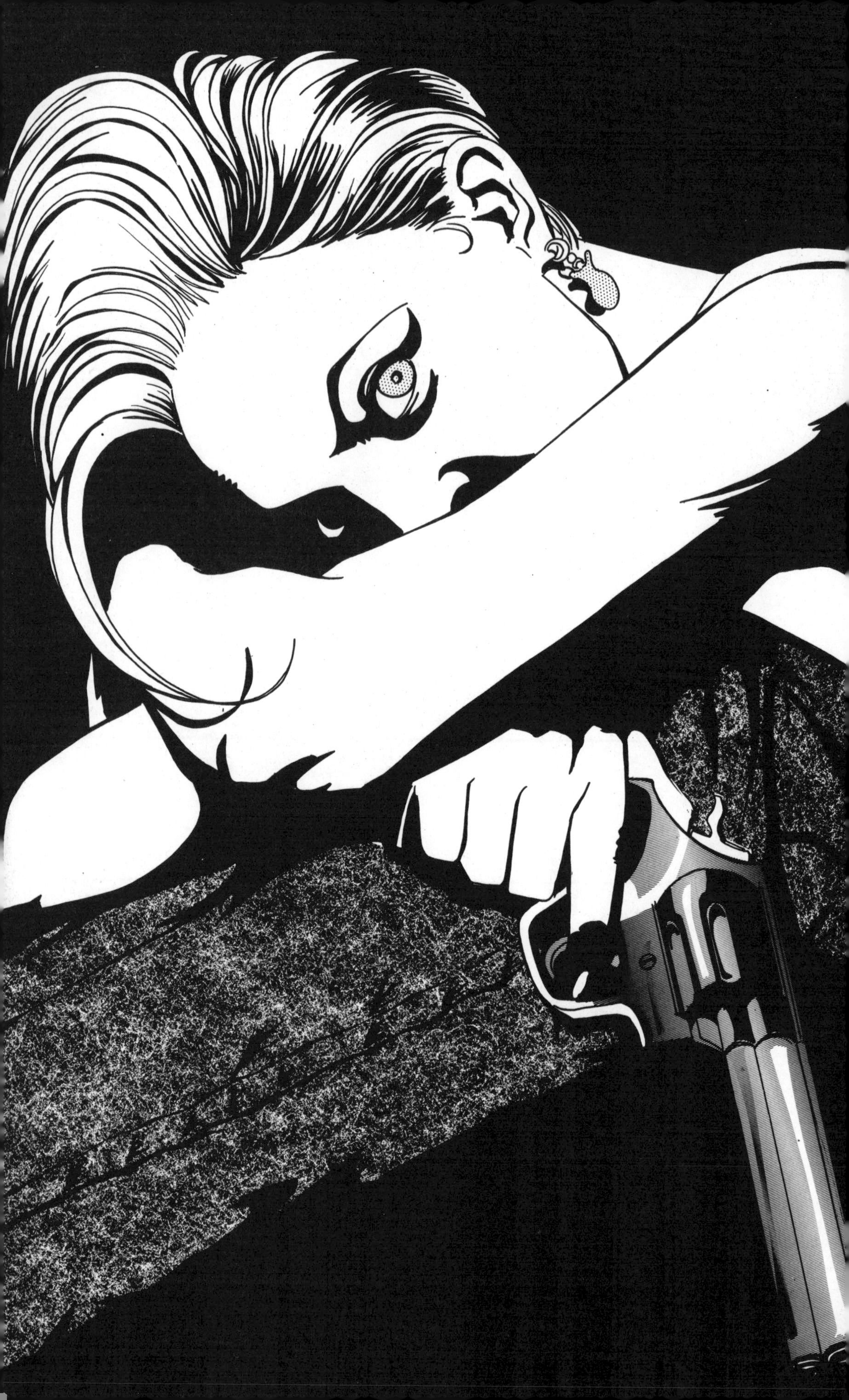

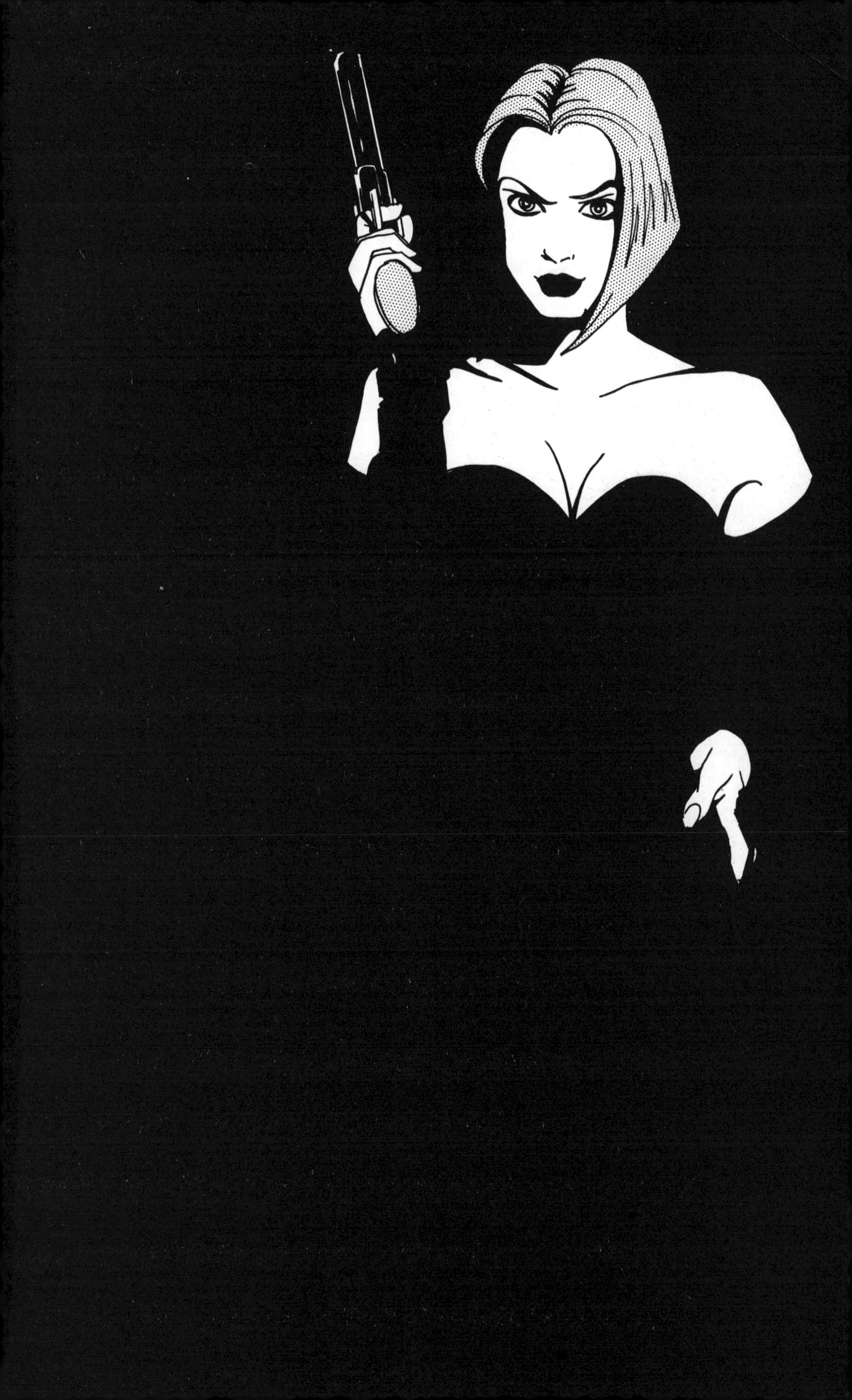

the models

JOHN SKRTIC AS GOLDFISH
KYRA KESTER AS LAUREN
DAVID CRONENBERG AS MAX
ANTOINETTE BILIC AS GENA
MICHAEL HAHN AS BILLY
JULIA R. AS TIFFANY DE LA ST. CROIX
KENNY WILLIAMS AS VISA
JIMMY WILLIAMS AS WEDNESDAY
SHECKY FINKLESTIEN AS ADAM, EVAN, AND SNIPER JOE
AND IZZY SCHACHNER AS HIMSELF

INCREDIBLE THANKS TO:
DAVID MACK, JIM VALENTINO, BOZZI, TRACI, BRENT, MIKE OEMING, MARK RICKETTS, MIKE SANGIACOMO, JARED, DAVID ENGEL, THE RETAIL COMMUNITY, THE MODELS, AND THE JINXWORLD MESSAGEBOARD.

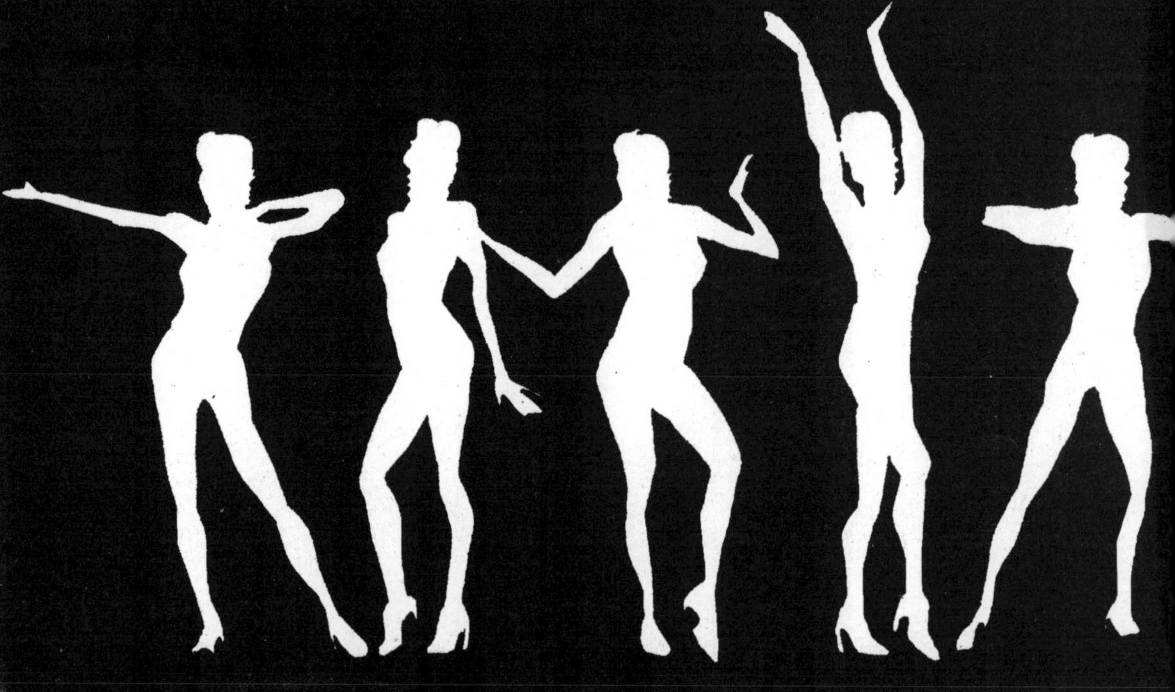